BARRON'S

HOW TO PREPARE FOR THE

Advanced Placement Exam

U.S. GOVERNMENT & POLITICS

4TH EDITION

Curt Lader (Retired)
Northport High School
Northport, New York

All inquiries should be addressed to:
Barron's Educational Series, Inc.
250 Wireless Boulevard
Hauppauge, New York 11788
http://www.barronseduc.com

ISBN-13: 978-0-7641-3302-2
ISBN-10: 0-7641-3302-0
Library of Congress Catalog Card No. 2005058874

Library of Congress Cataloging-in-Publication Data

Lader, Curt.
How to prepare for the advanced placement examination. AP U.S. government and politics / Curt Lader.—4th ed.
p. cm.
At head of title: Barron's.
Includes index.
ISBN-13: 978-0-7641-3302-2 (alk. paper)
ISBN-10: 0-7641-3302-0 (alk. paper)
1. United States—Politics and government—Examinations, questions, etc. I. Title: AP U.S. government and politics. II. Title.

2005058874

PRINTED IN THE UNITED STATES OF AMERICA

9 8 7 6 5 4 3 2 1

Table of Contents

Preface

The Advanced Placement U.S. government and politics course and test, unlike the other Social Studies AP courses and tests, is contemporary in nature. Students taking the course and the test are among the best and brightest and most politically aware.

The update to this book, prepared in late 2004, reflects a six-year cycle of test changes that were first incorporated in the May 1998 exam. It also includes significant political events such as the 2002 mid-term election and the 2004 presidential election. This revision also follows the progress made on the War on Terror and describes the events leading up to the Iraq war and its aftermath, all of which occurred after the publication of the second edition. Additionally, I have included a sample free-response essay along with a sample free-response data-based question at the end of each chapter. These questions are similar in format to those on the actual Advanced Placement exam. Many of the essay responses are "longer" than what students can be expected to write in a 25-minute time period; however, I use the responses for illustrative purposes. Some responses include case studies, while others answer all the choices offered even though students may not be required to address all choices in their essays. I have also made revisions to the multiple-choice questions and model answers after each chapter. I also changed some of the questions and essays.

In preparing the text for this book, I had to juxtapose the events that created the foundation of modern political theory to the daily happenings "inside the beltway." I was fortunate that, with the growth of the information superhighway, many new and exciting avenues were opened up. They provided important statistics, documents, and different perspectives on the political news of the day. Particularly helpful were the many government "sites" on the Internet such as the White House and the Bureau of the Census.

I gave the multiple-choice questions, including the model examination, to my AP government class. Many of the questions were changed, and others were removed. My students wrote many of the essays following each of the chapters and in the model examination, and, with their permission, I edited the best of them. Thus these essays are truly student generated. And many of them take on a contemporary slant as a result of the important political changes that occurred.

Lastly I particularly want to recognize a few individuals. Thanks to my colleagues at Northport High School. I would also like to recognize my editor, Mark Miele, who provided guidance and support especially during the update of this book. Finally I thank my wife, Phyllis, who without a doubt is the best editor I have ever known; my children, Craig and Glenn, who throughout the process kept reminding me to "get a life" when it came to getting political information for this project; and my parents, who have always encouraged me. I could not have completed the book without their support.

Curt Lader

Introduction

Using the Book

Purpose

The Advanced Placement U.S. Government and Politics Examination is offered once a year, in May. More than 100,000 students nationwide took the test in May 2004. This book offers a comprehensive review of the key concepts taught in the AP U.S. government and politics course, with many historical examples cited for illustration. In addition, each chapter contains:

- an overview of the topic,
- thesis statements illustrating the key concepts,
- both historical and contemporary examples,
- multiple-choice questions and answers,
- free-response and data-based essay questions and sample essays.

The last section of the book offers the student the opportunity to take two model examinations including free-response and data-based essay questions with suggested answers. A complete glossary of terms and an index related to government and politics follows the examination.

Suggested Uses for This Book

- If you are taking the course for a full year, use the book as a supplement to your text. Highlight significant areas such as thesis statements and create index cards for glossary terms.
- If you are taking the course in the fall, use the book as a supplement to your text; then go back to it in the spring, highlighting the significant areas such as thesis statements and creating index cards for key terms.
- If you are taking the course in the spring, use the book as a supplement to your text, highlighting key areas such as thesis statements and creating index cards for glossary terms.
- Answer the questions following each chapter. Keep track of the types of questions you answer incorrectly so that you can analyze why you got them wrong.
- Take the model examinations under test conditions.

A Note to the Teacher

Suggest to your students that they use this book along with their text. They can use the overview section of each chapter in conjunction with class assignments, evaluating current trends in each area. They can also use the thesis statements to develop additional free-response and data-based essay questions. The sample multiple-choice questions can be used to develop test-taking skills. Particular emphasis is given to the types of questions posed so that students can better understand the nature of what is being asked.

The book offers you the opportunity to use the material for review. Those of you who are teaching a semester course can appreciate the value of having review material available for study at a more leisurely pace than what sometimes takes place in a semester class. For those of you who are teaching a full-year course, the book and test material can motivate your students to improve their understanding of the material as well as their ability to take the test.

A Note to the Student

Because of the manner in which each chapter is organized, you have the opportunity to pretest your skills in each area related to U.S. government and politics. You can also apply the overview and thesis statements to current issues and use the glossary terms as you study current events in government and politics.

How you use this book depends to a certain extent on how your school offers the course (see Purpose section). Nevertheless, by answering the sample questions at the end of each chapter and by taking the model examinations, you will have an indication of how well you will do on the actual exam.

If you organize your time and systematically review the material in the book and then intensify your studies in March and April, you will have an excellent foundation for the test in May.

A Guide to the Exam

One of the keys to doing well on the AP U.S. Government and Politics Examination is an understanding of the structure of the test as it relates to the course itself. The next section explains how the test is organized and developed. Percentage ranges are given for the multiple-choice section, and a thematic topic breakdown is given for the essay questions. In addition, an analysis of the manner in which the exam is graded will help you create test strategies for success.

The Structure of the Test

Time and Format

The Advanced Placement U.S. Government and Politics Examination is 2 hours and 25 minutes long and consists of

- Section 1—60 multiple-choice questions (45 minutes)
- Section 2—Free-response essay questions (100 minutes)
  Four mandatory essays (25 minutes each)

The free-response section will take 100 minutes. Students are given four mandatory essay questions. They must develop a thesis or opening statement and give concrete examples to support each of the essays. One or more of the free-response essays may be data based (consisting of graphs, charts, cartoons, excerpts of documents, etc.). These essays require that the student specifically respond to the data-based material.

The multiple-choice section of the test is worth 50 percent of the total grade. The free-response essay section is also worth 50 percent of the grade.

Test Outline and Range of Percentages for Each Area (Multiple-Choice Section)

A. The Constitutional Foundations of the United States—5 to 15 percent
- Historical development and adoption of the Constitution
- Separation of powers
- Checks and balances
- Federalism
- Theories of modern government

B. Political Theory and Beliefs and Their Influence on Individuals—10 to 20 percent
- The theories of modern government including elitist, pluralist, and hyperpluralist
- Views that people have about government and their elected officials
- Characteristics and impact of public opinion
- Voting patterns of citizens
- Characteristics of political beliefs and the differences between liberals and conservatives

C. The Development and Philosophies of Political Parties, Interest Groups, and Mass Media—10 to 20 percent
- Characteristics, organization, and history of political parties
- Impact of key elections
- Voting patterns and the effect on the political process
- Laws that affect elections
- Interest groups and political action committees
- Legislation affecting the political process
- The mass media and its effect on politics

D. The Branches of Government, the Bureacracy, and the Development of Public Policy—35 to 45 percent
- Characteristics and power of each institution
- Relationships among each institution
- Linkage between these institutions and the political process, political parties, interest groups, the media, and public opinion
- How public policy is formulated and implemented

E. Public Policy—5 to 15 percent
- The nature of public policy
- The creation of public policy
- The impact of the three branches of government on public policy
- The impact of the bureaucracy on public policy
- The relationship between public policy and linkage institutions

F. Civil Liberties and Civil Rights—5 to 15 percent
- The Bill of Rights and how it evolved
- The incorporation of the Fourteenth Amendment
- Judicial review and key Supreme Court cases
- The fight for minority rights

Skills Needed to Take the Test

Students taking the AP U.S. Government and Politics Examination should be able to demonstrate proficiency and competency in the following areas:

- the institutions of United States government and politics,
- political theories and political processes,
- voting patterns and the manner in which political parties operate,
- the relationship between United States government and politics,
- the impact that governmental institutions and politics have on public policy development and implementation,

Furthermore, they should be able to:

- analyze, interpret, understand, and respond to stimulus-based data including charts, graphs, cartoons, and quotes,
- interpret data, develop a thesis, and support it through written essays.

How the Test Is Scored

The Educational Testing Service sends students their scores in July. Depending upon the student's choice, the scores are also sent to colleges and universities. The scores are reported on the following scale:

	Average College Grade
• 5—Extremely well qualified	A
• 4—Well qualified	B
• 3—Qualified	C
• 2—Possibly qualified	D
• 1—No recommendation	F

Most colleges and universities accept a score of 4 or 5 for credit and placement. Many colleges and universities may accept a score of 3 for credit and/or placement. Scores of 1 or 2 are not accepted by colleges and universities for either credit or placement.

The rule of thumb in determining how well you will probably do on the exam is to look at the number of multiple-choice questions you answer correctly. If you consistently get between 50 and 60 percent correct, you should be able to score a minimum of a 3. If you score consistently between 66 and 75 percent of the multiple-choice questions, you should be able to achieve a 4, and if you score 80 to 100 percent correctly you can get a 5. (This assumes, of course, that you adequately answer the questions in the free-response section.)

The test is scored so that random guessing for multiple-choice questions is taken into consideration. In a statistical breakdown of the multiple-choice section of a sample test, approximately 40 percent of the students taking the test achieved a 1 or 2, 31 percent achieved a 3, 20 percent achieved a 4, and 9 percent of the students received a 5.

Strategies for Studying United States Government and Politics

Unlike courses in American history or European history, U.S. government and politics has a more contemporary approach. Even though you must understand the historical perspective of each topic in the review chapters, more often than not examples are drawn from 1960 to the present.

In a U.S. government and politics course, the structure and goals of government are explained in much greater detail than in the typical civics course. There is an in-depth approach to the organizational components of the institutions of government as well as the application of how government works in relation to achieving public policy goals. Because many students have an inherent bias when it comes to politics, you must be careful to separate your opinions from the study of politics. Even though most students use one major textbook for a U.S. government and politics course, you should be able to see clearly the manner in which the author(s) analyze the subject matter. If you use supplementary books, you should look for any biases and understand that it is important to evaluate different points of view.

Using the Internet, reading a daily newspaper (including columns and editorials) and a weekly newsmagazine, and watching the Sunday morning political discussion television programs is as important as any text or supplementary reading on U.S. government and politics. Through those media you will develop a complete understanding of the nature and function of government and politics in America. Additionally, you can also get involved in the political process by volunteering to work in a local campaign.

How to Develop an Understanding of United States Government and Politics

- *Look at the overview.* Each chapter begins with an overview of the topic. The overview establishes an historical perspective and outlines each area.
- *Read the thesis statements.* Since generalizations are such an integral part of any understanding of government and politics, you should be able to give examples to support the thesis statements found in each chapter.
- *Connect the thesis statements to specific test questions.* After each thesis statement a multiple-choice or free-response question that relates to the

statement appears. You should be able to answer the sample question after reading the text following the thesis.

- *Develop a working vocabulary.* So much of the content related to U.S. government and politics is vocabulary and concepts. Study the list of key terms in each chapter and check their definitions in the glossary. These words appear in many of the multiple-choice questions and answer choices.

Getting the Entire Picture

In studying U.S. government and politics, you should understand the details related to each governmental institution as well as the impact of politics on the success or failure of government. In doing so, you must be familiar with the cast of characters, vocabulary, historical context, and bias of the author. One important way a student of government can master this material is by prereading. Anytime you are unfamiliar with any subject matter, this method will be helpful.

Prereading the Material

Before reading any specific text, supplementary book, document, or article, look at the material as if you were surveying the landscape. In this survey you should

1. look at the table of contents,
2. determine the flow of chapters or specific readings,
3. read the overview,
4. look for thesis statements,
5. underline the cast of characters and key terms,
6. read the author's conclusions,
7. look over any review material at the end of each chapter, and
8. determine if there is any bias.

Through this process, you will be able to cull sufficient material prior to any in-depth reading and notetaking.

Mining the Material

After you preread any material, you should do what any good surveyor does—mine the material. Through a detailed excavation you should use a series of focus statements to direct your attention to the specifics of the material presented.

- What general principles of government and politics are presented?
- What historical examples are given to illustrate these principles?
- Who are the main personalities related to these principles and historical examples?
- Why are these principles, examples, and personalities significant?

As any good prospector, you are looking for the gold ore rather than fool's gold!

Reading the Text

After you have finished prereading and have mined the material, you should be ready to go through the text slowly and systematically. It is highly recommended that you highlight the material if you own the book. If you don't own it, you will have to develop a system of notetaking.

If you highlight the material, be careful not to overhighlight. There is nothing to gain by highlighting paragraph after paragraph of material. In fact, you have more to lose—your valuable review time. Highlight key phrases, key people, key terms, and key statements. Even if you own the text, you may want to go one step further and transfer the highlighted material as notes on index cards. If you use index cards for your notes, you will be forced to conserve space. You can also use the cards as flash cards. For example, one side of the card can have the topic, and the other side of the card can have specific examples from the text. You can create separate cards for vocabulary terms, key court cases, presidential decisions, legislative acts, bureaucratic agencies, and the list goes on.

As an alternative to highlighting and taking notes, some students prefer to outline the material. If you use this technique, you should purchase a notebook and in an organized and consistent manner create an outline going from general topics to specific examples. The advantage of outlining over highlighting is that you get a much more complete picture of the chapter. The drawback is that it is much more difficult to study an outline than individual note cards or highlighted material. The best way to summarize the material is really up to each student.

Sample Reading with Underlining, Notes, and an Outline

Underlined Example

<u>Interest groups</u> and their relatives, <u>political action committees</u>, or <u>PACs</u>, were formed to influence the political and legislative agenda. Utilizing <u>lobbying techniques</u>, individuals representing <u>special interests</u> attempt to gain the favor of elected officials. Some examples of interest groups are the <u>National Rifle Association (NRA)</u>, the <u>National Education Association (NEA)</u>, <u>Pro-Choice</u>, and <u>Pro-Life</u> organizations. Many of these groups also make contributions to the coffers of specific politicians or political parties. Attempts to reform the amount of money PACs can give resulted in the passage of the <u>Federal Election Commission</u>. There are many supporters of interest groups who claim that because of the knowledge of these organizations, legislators acquire a great deal of valuable information regarding proposals. An example of this kind of testimony was when the <u>insurance industry</u> provided statistical evidence during the <u>healthcare</u> debate in 1994.

Notes

Interest Groups
AKA political action committees using lobbying techniques.

Special interest groups such as NRA, NEA, Pro-Choice, Pro-Life try to influence legislation.

Reform—Federal Election Commission.

Outline

Interest Groups

I. Nature of Interest Groups
   A. Political Action Committees
   B. Lobbyists
II. Examples of Interest Groups
   A. National Rifle Association (NRA)
   B. National Education Association (NEA)
   C. Pro-Choice Organizations
   D. Pro-Life Organizations
III. Impact of Interest Groups
   A. On politicians
   B. On legislation

Summary of Reading Techniques

1. Get the entire picture—look at the overview, thesis statements, vocabulary, and test questions.
2. Preread the material—determine the flow of chapters, underline the cast of characters, and look for conclusions.
3. Mine the material—look for principles of government and politics, historical examples, main personalities, and principles.
4. Read the text—highlight, underline, or take notes.

Building Your Government and Politics Vocabulary

Just as you have become familiar with those key words that reappear in an historical context, you will also see a repetition of terms, phrases, and concepts related to U.S. government and politics. The more you use them, the faster you will internalize them. Become familiar with the terminology through readings, your own essay writing, debating topics with your classmates, and answering test-related questions. When you watch the news, listen for the lingo. You will be surprised how fast you start using the same language as politicians and elected officials.

FOR EXAMPLE, you may be talking about the prospects of a presidential veto of a rider to the defense department appropriations bill.

TRANSLATION: The president may not sign a piece of legislation because an amendment he did not agree to was included as part of a revenue bill for the defense department.

Analyzing an Author's Bias

More than any other social science, the study of U.S. government and politics has the potential of being viewed in a biased manner. Even a textbook can have a liberal or conservative slant depending upon the political point of view of the author. When you add to this your own political viewpoint, you may have an extremely difficult time separating your own viewpoint from that of the author. Or you may be so opposed to what the author is suggesting that you totally miss the point. For example, in a discussion of the impact of the *Roe v Wade* Supreme Court decision (which deals with abortion), you will definitely miss the central point of the piece if you hold an extreme point of view on either side. When you are assigned any book of "Readings on Government and Politics," you should be prepared to expect a biased presentation from the outset. For instance, if you are investigating the issue of term limitations, a representative who has been elected for ten terms could certainly have a bias against the issue.

Multiple-Choice Question Strategy

A Quick Review of the Multiple-Choice Section

There are 60 questions and each question has five answer choices. You will be allowed 45 minutes to complete this section, which accounts for 50 percent of the grade. This section covers the following topics:

- 5 to 15 percent Constitutional Foundations of Democracy
- 10 to 20 percent Political Theory and Beliefs and Their Influence on Individuals
- 10 to 20 percent The Development and Philosophies of Political Parties, Interest Groups, and Mass Media
- 35 to 45 percent The Branches of Government, the Bureaucracy, and the Development of Policy
- 5 to 15 percent Civil Liberties and Civil Rights
- 5 to 15 percent Public Policy

As a general rule, you must answer 50 percent of the multiple-choice questions correctly and get an acceptable score on the free-response sections in order to receive a score of 3 (qualified).

Strategies for Answering the Multiple-Choice Questions

- Read the entire question. Underline key words in the question such as: all of the following EXCEPT, which of the following, increases, decreases, are commonly used, is responsible, principles, most accurately compares, is recognized as, best describes, is correct, results, reflects, is most likely, is true, all the following are true, least likely, and which best DEFINES.
- Look for and underline key vocabulary words in the questions and answer choices.
- Read the entire answer. Using process of elimination can usually increase your ability to find the correct answer. In questions where there is an

"All of the above" or more than one correct choice, make sure that you look for multiple answers.

- Be aware of "negative" questions such as "All of the following EXCEPT."
- Don't guess wildly. A one-quarter point penalty is assessed for each incorrect answer. If you can eliminate one or more choices, you should attempt to answer the question. If you are uncertain whether you want to answer a question, circle it and return to it after you finish the rest of the questions. You should be able to answer at least 50 of the 60 questions.
- Go with your first instinct. Usually, your first response is the correct one. Only change answers if you are absolutely certain.
- Be aware of the time limitation. Unlike other AP history tests, you have only 45 minutes, rather than 60 minutes, to answer all the questions. Try to give yourself a breather between the time you complete the section and that last check to determine if you want to answer any of the circled questions.

A Variety of Multiple-Choice Questions

The AP U.S. Government and Politics Examination relies on a variety of multiple-choice questions including identification and analysis. Those kinds of questions can be further identified as generalizations, comparing and contrasting concepts and events, sequencing a series of related ideas or events, cause and effect relationships, definitional, solution to a problem, hypothetical, and chronological. More than 75 percent of the multiple-choice questions fit into these categories.

In addition to identification and analysis questions, there are stimulus-based questions that rely on your interpretation and understanding of maps, graphs, charts and tables, pictures, flowcharts, photographs, political cartoons, short narrative passages, surveys and poll data, quotations that come from primary source documents, Supreme Court decisions, or personalities.

In this exam the trend is to increase the number of these stimulus-based questions in the multiple-choice section of the test.

Examples of Multiple-Choice Questions

IDENTIFICATION AND ANALYSIS QUESTIONS

Definitional

1. Which best reflects the principle of separation of powers in the U.S. system of government?
   (A) political linkage institutions
   (B) the division of power between the federal government and state governments
   (C) qualifications for U.S. senator
   (D) Congress having the ability to make laws that are necessary and proper
   (E) federal regulatory agencies

Cause and Effect Relationships

2. Incumbents would most likely be successful in their reelection campaigns because of which of the following factors?
(A) voter identification
(B) rejection of PAC money
(C) limited services to their constituents
(D) an aggressive campaign by a young opponent
(E) a third-party candidate entering the race

Sequencing a Series of Related Ideas or Events

3. Which of the following statements describe the process of how Congress passes a bill?
I. reports the bill out of the appropriate committee
II. debates the bill on the floor of the respective houses
III. rejects or accepts amendments to the bill
IV. resolves any differences in a conference committee

(A) I only
(B) I and II only
(C) I, III, and IV only
(D) I, II, III, and IV

Generalization

4. In *Miranda v Arizona*, the Supreme Court based its decision on which constitutional principle?
(A) Convicted felons cannot be tried for the same crime twice.
(B) Citizens can exercise free speech except when there is a proven clear and present danger.
(C) People have the right to exercise their religion freely except when that religion is supported by public funds.
(D) The rights of the accused are protected by the due process right of a lawyer being present at the time of interrogation.
(E) A person's house cannot be searched without a warrant.

Solution to a Problem

5. Which of the following individuals would be most likely to register to vote?
(A) a person with a college education
(B) somebody who moves from job to job
(C) a senior citizen living in a nursing home
(D) an unemployed person on welfare
(E) a homeless person

Hypothetical

6. If a candidate is thinking of running for president, the person would do all of the following EXCEPT
(A) begin fund-raising activities at least two years before the election.
(B) make frequent visits to the early primary states.
(C) announce the choice of the running mate when the candidate enters the race.
(D) work with party leaders to develop a national platform.
(E) attempt to get favorable media coverage.

Chronological

7. Which election is an example of a shift of party realignment?
   (A) the election of 1980 and a shift of blue collar Democrats to Reagan
   (B) the election of 1932 and a shift of business executives to Roosevelt
   (C) the election of 1960 and a shift of Catholic voters to Kennedy
   (D) the election of 1976 and a shift of religious conservatives to Carter
   (E) the election of 1952 and a shift of corporate Republicans to Eisenhower

Comparing and Contrasting Concepts and Events

8. Which of the following statements most accurately compares the political, social, and economic philosophy of the participants at the Constitutional Convention regarding the debate over the inclusion of the Bill of Rights into the document?
   (A) Federalists favored the inclusion of a bill of rights.
   (B) Anti-Federalists favored a bill of rights as part of a constitution.
   (C) Wealthy property owners favored the inclusion of a bill of rights.
   (D) Farmers were against the inclusion of a bill of rights.
   (E) Slave owners favored the inclusion of a bill of rights.

Negative Question

9. All of the following are powers of the Supreme Court EXCEPT
   (A) judicial review.
   (B) preside over impeachment trials of the president.
   (C) hear cases on appeal from state courts.
   (D) decide cases deriving from original jurisdiction.
   (E) rewrite congressional legislation that the Court declares unconstitutional.

Multiple Correct Answers

10. Which of the following serve on the President's cabinet?
    I. FBI Director
    II. Secretary of State
    III. Secretary of Defense
    IV. Attorney General
    V. White House Press Secretary

    (A) II and III only
    (B) I, III, and IV only
    (C) III, IV, and V only
    (D) II, III, and IV only
    (E) I, II, III, IV, and V

COMMENTS ON IDENTIFICATION AND ANALYSIS QUESTIONS

Once you identify the specific kind of identification and analysis question, you must then proceed to answer it by process of elimination or through specific knowledge of the concept or information. Unlike stimulus-response questions, where the answer can be found in the data, identification and analysis questions are factually based.

1. **(D)** Question 1 requires an understanding of the definition of separation of powers as well as definitions of political linkage institutions (choice A)

and division of power (choice B). You also must have factual knowledge regarding the role of federal regulatory agencies (choice E) to understand that qualifications for office do not represent a power of a branch of government (choice C). Choice D is correct because the only stated power is the elastic clause giving Congress the power to make laws necessary and proper.

2. **(A)** Question 2 asks what factor (the cause) would result (the effect) in the reelection of incumbents. Choices B and C are completely wrong and can be eliminated right away. Choices D and E are not directly related to the cause and effect nature of the question. Choice A is correct because the only factor that has a direct impact on the success of the incumbent is voter identification.
3. **(D)** Question 3 illustrates the nature of sequencing. For the purposes of making you see the sequence of events, the choices follow the sequence of events that takes place when Congress debates legislation. Usually in sequencing questions, the order of events is mixed up. Also, there may only be one correct answer, rather than the "All of the above" choice in this question. In this question, however, "All of the above" (choice D) is correct.
4. **(D)** Question 4 gives you a specific event and asks you through analysis to identify the general principle that came about as a result of the event. In order to answer it, you must know what the event is all about. In this case you must know something about the *Miranda* decision. You may be able to eliminate two of the choices (B and C) if you know that the decision had to do with a criminal. But, to answer the question, you really had to know that Miranda did not have a lawyer present when he was interrogated (choice D).
5. **(A)** Question 5 presents a problem. Which type of individual would most likely register to vote? You probably could eliminate three choices (B, C, and E) because logically people in these groups would not have an incentive or desire to vote. That leaves you with two choices related to socioeconomic status. Even though it would be to the advantage of an unemployed person on welfare (choice D) to register, it is highly unlikely that a person on welfare would do so, thus you would have to eliminate that choice as well. This leaves choice A as the correct answer.
6. **(C)** Question 6 combines a made-up situation with an exception as the answer. This combination makes the question one of the more difficult. You must approach the question knowing that there are four factually correct choices and one incorrect choice (in this case, choice C), which answers the question. If you read the question too quickly, you may pick one of the factually correct answers. In this situation, you should know from political history that a person seeking the presidency does not pick his vice-presidential running mate until the nomination seems certain.
7. **(A)** Question 7 really combines two forms of identification and analysis questions—the definitional and chronological. You must know the definition of *party realignment* and something about the history of presidential elections. The only election in the choices given that resulted

in a dramatic party shift was choice A, the Reagan election of 1980 where many traditional blue collar Democrats voted Republican. They became known as Reagan Democrats.

8. **(B)** Question 8 compares and contrasts the differences between the participants at the Constitutional Convention in relation to their attitude toward inclusion of the bill of rights. This is an extremely difficult question because you must have factual knowledge about the issues. You must know that in fact certain groups and individuals did not want a bill of rights as part of the original Constitution; you must know the characteristics and names of the groups represented at the convention, and you must know something about the socioeconomic status characteristics of those groups. If you knew the differences between the Federalists and Anti-Federalists, then the question is much easier to answer because choice B gives a straightforward factual response.
9. **(E)** Question 9 presents the problem of determining which of the listed choices are legitimate powers of the Supreme Court. The strategy for answering this question is to look for the factually correct statements. By doing so, you will end up with the one incorrect or negative answer, which is the correct choice. In Question 9, the powers of the Supreme Court are outlined in the Constitution and have developed as a result of judicial practice. Choice A is factually correct because of the decision reached in *Marbury v Madison*. Choices B, C, and D are all listed powers found in Article III of the Constitution. Choice E, the correct choice, is factually incorrect because though the Court can declare congressional legislation unconstitutional, only the Congress can rewrite the law.
10. **(D)** Question 10 is very similar to EXCEPT questions. Instead of looking for the one factually incorrect choice, you should be looking for the factually correct choice or choices presented. For example, if you go down the list of cabinet officials, it is a relatively easy task to identify the Secretary of State and Secretary of Defense as cabinet members. The other correct choice is the Attorney General. Because that position does not start with Secretary of, it may throw you off, especially with the FBI director as a choice.

A word of caution: If you can reasonably attack the question through a process of elimination or if you have factual knowledge regarding the content of the question, then you should attempt to answer it. You may be able to identify the type of question, but if you don't understand the issues involved you are not going to be able to find the correct choice. In that case, skip the question and take the quarter-point penalty.

STIMULUS-BASED MULTIPLE-CHOICE QUESTIONS

Here are a few examples of the more common type of stimulus-based questions found in the multiple-choice section of the test.

Short Narrative Passage

1. Many critics of presidential poll taking point to the manner in which polls are taken and the number of polls released prior to election day. We have Democratic-sponsored polls, Republican-sponsored polls, daily tracking polls, polls that ask registered voters who they are voting for, and polls that ask likely voters who they are voting for. In the final analysis, it is no wonder that a pollster can make a serious mistake in the final days of a campaign.

   An example of a presidential campaign that reflects the point of view of the author is
   (A) the election of 1948—Truman vs Dewey.
   (B) the election of 1952—Eisenhower vs Stevenson.
   (C) the election of 1964—Johnson vs Goldwater.
   (D) the election of 1972—Nixon vs McGovern.
   (E) the election of 1984—Reagan vs Mondale.

Short Quotation

2. "My day is frittered away with the personal seeking of people when it ought to be given to the great problems which concern the whole country. . . ." *President James Garfield*

   Which choice best describes the nature of the reform that took place as a result of the feelings described by President Garfield?
   (A) civil rights reform
   (B) antitrust reform
   (C) civil service reform
   (D) consumer reform
   (E) constitutional reform

Supreme Court Decision

3. "If there is a bedrock principle underlying the First Amendment, it is that the Government may not prohibit the expression of an idea simply because society finds the idea itself offensive or disagreeable. . . . We have not recognized an exception to this principle even where our flag has been involved."

   The *Texas v Johnson* Supreme Court decision quoted above did which of the following?
   (A) made flag desecration legal for nonpolitical reasons
   (B) upheld the Texas statute, which resulted in Johnson's arrest for burning the flag
   (C) made Congress pass a constitutional amendment prohibiting flag burning
   (D) recognized that burning a flag for political reasons is a form of symbolic speech protected by the First Amendment
   (E) expanded the ways government can prohibit freedom of speech because of offensive actions

CARTOON FROM UNITED STATES DEPARTMENT OF AGRICULTURE

Grill our experts with your food safety questions. Call the USDA Hotline.

4. The subject of the cartoon presents what point of view?
   (A) It is the responsibility of the consumer to be aware of potential food hazards.
   (B) The United States Department of Agriculture fought for the passage of the Meat Inspection Act.
   (C) Congress should conduct oversight hearings regarding food safety.
   (D) A major task of the Department of Agriculture is to provide public information related to regulations.
   (E) The president supports the Department of Agriculture's efforts in establishing regulatory reform.

OIL IMPORTS vs DOMESTIC CRUDE PRODUCTION

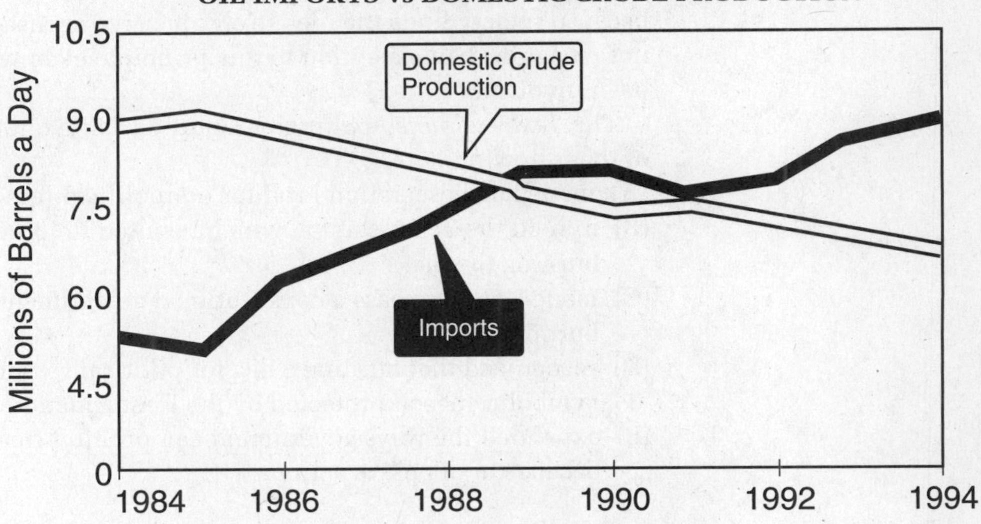

5. According to the information in this chart, which of the following statements is true?
   (A) The amount of domestic crude oil production has increased from 1984 to 1994.
   (B) Overall imports of crude oil have remained constant from 1984 to 1994.

(C) The amount of crude oil produced was equal to the amount of oil imported from 1984 to 1988.
(D) A trade surplus resulted from the overall production of domestic crude oil.
(E) The decrease of domestic oil production has led to an increased reliance on oil imports.

COMMENTS ON STIMULUS-BASED MULTIPLE-CHOICE QUESTIONS

1. **(A)** The question 1 narrative passage makes the point that there is much criticism levied at poll takers. The author supports the point by illustrating the number of different polls released prior to election day. The question asks you to apply the conclusion to an actual presidential election. Even if you missed the central point, by looking at the choices you could easily eliminate choices C and D because they were both landslides predicted by the pollsters. The other choices require that you have some knowledge about the elections. The Truman–Dewey election, choice A, was probably the biggest blunder pollsters have ever made.
2. **(C)** Question 2 requires you to apply the context of Garfield's quote to one of the most significant reforms that took place in his administration. Only because the Pendelton Act, reforming civil service, is a landmark piece of legislation, would the exam even use a quote from Garfield. Thus you would need to know that this act (choice C) was passed during Garfield's administration in order to answer this question. A hint is given in the actual quote when Garfield makes reference to "the personal seeking of people. . . ."
3. **(D)** Question 3 incorporates an excerpt from a recent Supreme Court decision, *Texas v Johnson*, which received a great deal of notoriety. Even if you didn't know the background of the case, the quote gives enough information to lead you to the conclusion that choice D is correct, because flag burning is a symbolic political act protected by the First Amendment to the Constitution. Choice A is a trick answer aimed at catching the student who does not read every choice. In fact the decision made a distinction between political and nonpolitical acts. Choices B and E refer to results that contradict the actual decision.
4. **(D)** Question 4 is a political cartoon that deals with the theme of a federal cabinet providing a service to the consumer. It asks you to determine the *point of view* of the cartoon. This direction sometimes presents a problem because in the choices there could be an accurate statement that does not reflect the cartoon's perspective but that reflects another accurate answer. This was the case in choices A, C, and E, three reasonable responses. However, they do not represent the point of view of the cartoon. Choice D is an obvious answer based on the caption and information pictured in the cartoon.
5. **(E)** Question 5 simply asks the student to interpret information given in a graph dealing with oil imports versus domestic oil production. All the student has to do is cross reference the choices with the information

provided in the chart to determine that choice E is correct. The only knowledge required to answer this question is the ability to accurately interpret the trends presented and not confuse the line representing oil imports with the line representing domestic oil production. The pitfall in this kind of question is when the student superficially looks at the information. In that case, some students would pick choice A as the answer because oil imports have risen consistently over the period.

A Final Word about the Multiple-Choice Section

Throughout the course of study, your instructor should be giving you a variety of sample multiple-choice questions with five possible answers. These questions can come from this review book, other books that have test banks, self-generated tests, or sample questions available from the Educational Testing Service.

You should become sensitive to the kinds of questions you score well on as well as those questions that give you trouble. Without a doubt, the best way to improve your multiple-choice test-taking ability is through practice and repetition. Keep an ongoing list of vocabulary concepts you are not familiar with.

Also be aware that, statistically, the multiple-choice questions when scored provide for a wide range of students correctly answering any given question. The percentage of students answering questions correctly on a sample test ranged from a high of 94 percent to a low of 19 percent depending upon the difficulty of the particular question. Taking the average of the percent correct of all 60 questions on a sample exam, for the students attempting to answer the questions, the percent correct was 65 percent. This does not correlate to the final score of the exam but provides an insight into the range of difficulty of the questions.

As far as the actual scores are concerned, of those students with multiple-choice scores of 49 or higher (corrected for guessing), most earned scores of 4 or 5. Of those with multiple-choice scores of 41–48, the majority received a 4, whereas most others earned a 3 or 5. Of those scoring 29–40, the majority got a 3, whereas most others earned a 2 or 4. Students scoring between 17 and 28 usually earned a 2, whereas most others received a 1 or 3. And of the test-takers with scores of 16 or less, the majority got a score of 1, whereas all others earned a 2 or 3.

Free-Response Essay Question Strategy

A Quick Review of the Free-Response Essay Section

You must answer four mandatory essay questions in 100 minutes (25 minutes per essay). This section is worth 50 percent of your grade.

As a general rule, if a student scores above 50 percent on the multiple-choice section and scores in the middle to upper range of the free-response essay, that student probably will receive an overall score of 3.

There are different approaches that the student can take in answering the four required essay questions. Depending on the specifics of the question you may have to write an essay that is based on:

- a formal thesis (i.e., evaluate the extent)
- an introductory statement that lists the tasks you are going to answer (i.e., give examples that illustrate, discuss the nature of . . .)
- data (graphs, charts, quotes)

The following text provides the general criteria for scoring the free-response essay section:

> Each of the four free-response essays is worth 12.5 percent and, together, the essays total 50 percent of the exam's overall score. In scoring the essay, raters are given a rubric (general scoring criteria) that ranges from 3 to 9 points. These totals are then converted into an overall score for the free-response section.
>
> Students should recognize the major components of the essay. They are relatively easy to pick out. Key words include:
>
> 1. list
> 2. identify
> 3. describe
> 4. explain
> 5. evaluate
>
> Depending on the criteria established for a question, students receive 1 point for each task successfully completed. Full credit is obtained for each part of the essay when, for example, students identify the correct answer and then explain it through the use of examples. Students can also receive partial credit if they fail to answer a question completely.

It is important to remember that when answering an essay the goal is to give a solid introductory statement, whether it is a formal thesis, an explanation of what is asked of you, or references to data. You must then give specific examples to support your introductory statement. Students who answer the questions completely and correctly and provide adequate examples will receive full credit.

The four essays are worth 50 percent of the examination. Each essay must be completed in 25 minutes and each will be weighted equally.

As you can see, the development of a thesis, strong introductory statement or data analysis, and numerous supporting examples are essential to good essay writing.

Examples of Key Terms Used in Free-Response Essays

- Briefly discuss
  SAMPLE: *Briefly discuss* how the presidential nominating system has changed over the past 40 years.
- Explain
  SAMPLE: *Explain* how incorporation of the Bill of Rights has had an impact on the states.
- Evaluate the extent

SAMPLE: *Evaluate the extent* of the relationship between Congress and the executive branch by identifying two pieces of legislation that have been enacted.

- Discuss
  SAMPLE: *Discuss* how demographics influence voter turnout.
- Identify and explain
  SAMPLE: *Identify and explain* how the media plays a role in presidential campaigns.
- Identify and describe
  SAMPLE: *Identify and describe* the role that special interest groups play in policymaking.
- Support your answer
  SAMPLE: *Support your answer* by listing several examples of checks and balances.
- Using the information from the chart
  SAMPLE: *Using the information from the chart*, identify and explain how the creation of the budget impacts public policy.
- List and identify a solution
  SAMPLE: *List* problems associated with the Articles of Confederation *and identify* how the Constitution helped to *solve* those problems.
- Using the map
  SAMPLE: *Using the map*, identify those sections of the country that voted Democratic and those sections that voted Republican.
- Select and provide
  SAMPLE: *Select* examples of campaign finance reform *and provide* information explaining the difficulty in enacting effective legislation.
- Perform the following tasks
  SAMPLE: *Perform the following tasks* in identifying the advantages and disadvantages of congressional incumbency: define the franking privilege, discuss the impact of a political party's endorsement, and explain the role of mid-term elections on a challenger's chances for success.
- Provide an explanation
  SAMPLE: *Provide an explanation* as to why it is difficult for the federal government to pass effective laws.

Notice how the key phrases are very similar and call for the completion of a task. Additional sample and practice free-response essay questions appear in the review chapters and in the model test.

Topics Appearing in the Free-Response Essay Section

Students in Advanced Placement United States government and politics classes who took the test have summarized the topics that they selected as free-response essay questions since 1998. These topics illustrate the nature of the questions and in no way are meant to reflect the exact language of the questions.

- the changing nature of the presidential nominating process
- the extension of the Bill of Rights to the states through Supreme Court

cases such as *Gitlow v New York* (1925), *Wolf v Colorado* (1949), and *Gideon v Wainwright* (1963)

- the balance of power between the executive and legislative branches as exemplified by the War Powers Act and the Budget and Impoundment Control Act
- the reasons for low voter turnout using different demographic features and how laws have made it more difficult to vote
- the contrast between the candidate-oriented and issue-oriented presidential campaigns of the 1990s and how the media and the candidates have contributed to these types of campaigns
- how special interest groups such as the American Association of Retired Persons (AARP), the American Medical Association (AMA), the National Association for the Advancement of Colored People (NAACP), and the National Association of Manufacturers (NAM) target the federal government and how these groups use specific tactics and resources to achieve their goals
- the weaknesses of the Articles of Confederation and how they were remedied by the adoption of the Constitution
- how federalism has been affected by environmental policy, gun control policy, and people with physical disabilities
- how the appointment process of Supreme Court justices has become politicized by looking at the characteristics of nominees and showing how interest groups affect the process
- why it has been so difficult to pass campaign finance legislation by looking at the Supreme Court decision in *Buckley v Valeo* (1976), soft money, and the issue of congressional incumbency
- formal and informal methods of amending the Constitution and why informal methods have been used more often
- why the Fourteenth Amendment to the Constitution is so important by examining two specific provisions and applying the first to a landmark case such as *Brown v Board of Education* (1954), *Baker v Carr* (1962), or *Regents of the University of California v Bakke* (1978) and applying the second provision to another landmark case such as *Mapp v Ohio* (1961), *Gideon v Wainwright* (1963), or *Miranda v Arizona* (1966)
- why it is difficult to create effective public policy as a result of divided government, weak party discipline, and the increase in the number of special interest groups and political action committees (PACs)

Notice how many essays relate to the issue of implementation of public policy.

Strategies for Answering the Free-Response Essay Question

- Read the entire question. Underline key words (listed in a previous section) that will help you understand what the question is looking for.
- Base your decision on your overall familiarity with the subject matter of the questions and the specific areas related to the general question asked.
- Read all of the questions, looking for potential thesis development, appropriate opening statement or references to data, and supporting examples to illustrate your arguments.

- On the exam, jot down a possible thesis, appropriate opening statement or references to data, and specific examples that relate to the question.
- Outline your argument starting with your thesis, appropriate opening statement, or references to data and making sure that you provide a specific example for every statement made. At this point try organizing your essay going from general to specific in your outline.
- Use factual data, both historical and current, to support your answer. If you are not sure of a specific name, date, or term, then don't use it. However, if you can describe an example filling in most of the details, do so.
- Make sure that your supporting evidence and data support your thesis and your opening statement or references to data.
- Start writing your essay beginning with your thesis statement, appropriate opening statement or references to data, and main argument.
- Using your outline, use the specific factual data and examples to support your thesis. Make sure that your answer refers to the key term used in the question.
- If the question gives you specific data areas to comment on, make sure that your examples and answer refer to the areas in the question.
- Your summary should reiterate your thesis statement.
- Reread! Revise! Be aware of the 25-minute time limit, but do not hesitate to cross out, add, or change any part of your essay.

How to Write the Free-Response Essay

Once you follow the strategy advice, actually writing the free-response essay is an easy task. For some inexplicable reason, students have a phobia about writing essays. Try to approach this task as if you were creating a multilevel building using building blocks. The foundation would represent the premise of the question, usually in the form of a thesis statement. The first floor represents the first task, usually asking you to identify an issue, statement, policy, or the like. The second floor explains what you have identified. The third floor represents the second task, and the next floor describes or explains what you have previously identified as part of the second task. Some essays have just one task, whereas other essays can have two or more tasks. Other essays are based on an illustration, and they will be covered later in this chapter.

BUILDING BLOCKS OF A TYPICAL FREE-RESPONSE ESSAY

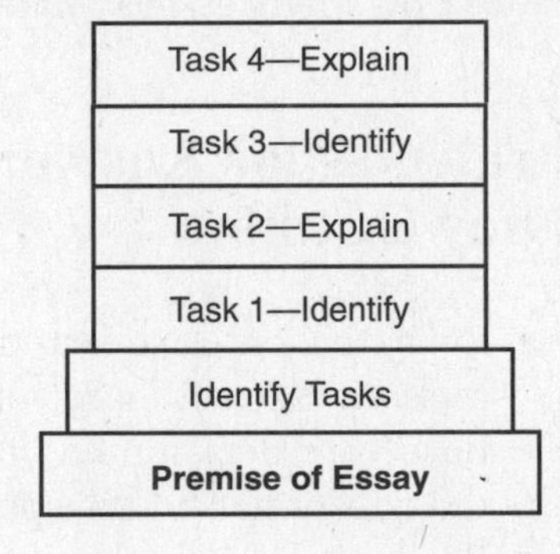

The most important start to your essay is to understand what the question is all about. Typically, the essay will start with a statement related to a topic. Then the essay will ask you to complete a series of tasks. It is advisable to begin your essay with an opening paragraph that restates what you are planning to do. Then proceed to follow the "building block" model discussed earlier and complete each task. These building blocks of information will help demonstrate your knowledge of the subject matter that you have decided to write about. There is no need to include a formal conclusion or summary.

Let the reader know what you are doing every step of the way, and don't be afraid to apply your extensive data bank of information to the questions posed.

A Brief Recap

1. Read all the questions.
2. Look for key terms and any specific information contained in the questions.
3. Write a thesis statement if the question calls for one.
4. Outline your argument using building blocks as a way of organizing your information.

Things to Avoid in Answering the Free-Response Essay

- statements that are implausible, can't be proven, or don't relate to the question
- unsubstantiated generalizations in the body of the essay
- imposing your own opinion—your own thoughts and feelings are not evidence
- incorrect data or irrelevant information
- avoid lengthening your essay with excessive wordiness to make it appear as though you are saying more than you are—you are not fooling anyone. If you use what may be called building slippage (BS), your building blocks will begin to tumble under their own weight, and all you will be left with is a conclusion with no support.

SAMPLE FREE-RESPONSE ESSAY

For illustrative purposes, model essay responses in this book may include more material than the question requires. For example, the question may ask the student to choose two out of three topics, but the model essay will address all three topics to give readers the most thorough information. In addition, many model essays presented may take the average student longer than the 25 minutes allotted. This is done so you can clearly see how building blocks are used. Students should, however, practice writing essays that are complete and that stay within the 25-minute limit.

DIRECTIONS: You have 25 minutes to answer the following question. This question is based on your knowledge of United States government and politics, and it may contain materials from charts, graphs, and tables which you will have to analyze and draw conclusions from. Make sure you provide specific and sufficient information and examples in your essay.

> Some people have made the claim that the Supreme Court's decision to hear controversial cases has the potential of altering public policy. Using one of the following issues:
>
> 1. The legality of Proposition 187
> 2. The constitutionality of state-imposed term limits for members of Congress
>
> Identify both sides of the issue you choose and provide one example of how the Court's opinion impacted public policy.

Sample Student Response

Proposition 187

Proposition 187 was a very controversial and serious issue. The citizens of California claimed that an influx of illegal immigrants had economically drained the state and made conditions unbearable. The proposed legislation, which was approved by 60 percent of the voters on November 8, 1994, sought to stop the draining effects of illegal immigration. This legislation had the potential for denying undocumented aliens education, non-emergency health care, and a host of other public social services. The proposition also addressed the issue of making and selling false documentation, restating the fact that it was a felony. This legislation also sought to investigate the background of each and every student enrolled in California's schools as well as the parents of the students. This included more than ten million people. The proposition allowed for undocumented immigrants to remain in school for 90 days from the time that their legal status was discovered, giving them so-called "ample time" to be relocated to a school in their country of origin. The proposition also required that employers know the legal status of the people working for them, and report all undocumented immigrants to the Immigration and Naturalization Service (INS). The supporters of Proposition 187 felt that its requirements were justified by the economic condition of the state of California and felt that the state had the right to impose such legislation under the reserved power clause of Amendment X.

The opponents to Proposition 187 felt that it was an unjustified, immoral, inhuman way of dealing with societal problems. The opposition claimed that the proposition violated many aspects of the Constitution, most notably the equal protection clause of the Fourteenth Amendment, the due process clause of the Fifth Amendment, and Article I, Section 8, where it states that Congress has the power "To establish a uniform Rule of Naturalization. . . ." The opposition felt that Proposition 187 infringed on the power delegated to the federal government.

The California Supreme Court found that the proposition was unconstitutional declaring that immigration is a power granted to the Congress of the United States. The court also pointed out that the proposition violated the equal protection clause of the Constitution. The United States Supreme Court refused to hear the case on appeal.

State-Imposed Terms Limits

In 1992, residents of the state of Arkansas voted in an initiative on term limits for that state's senators and representatives. This initiative (amendment 73 of the Arkansas Constitution) was challenged in *Thorton v Arkansas*.

The petitioners in this case argued that state-mandated term limits violated the sovereignty of the federal government. Term limits might have restricted a voter's right to choose the best possible candidate for office and state-imposed term limits enacted by only a limited number of states would disrupt the congressional seniority system, and, in turn limit the power of the senators and representatives from those states. Furthermore, the petitioners believed that state-imposed term limits were unconstitutional. The criteria for becoming a member of Congress are clearly written out in the Constitution: age (25 for representatives, 30 for senators), residency in the state and district they represent, and U.S. citizenship for a specified number of years prior to taking office. Nowhere in the Constitution does it say that a member of Congress can only be in office for a given number of years. That qualification isn't mentioned, and state-imposed term limits take away federal powers and are unconstitutional.

The respondents in this case believed that state-imposed term limits were Constitutional under the Tenth Amendment's reserve powers clause (states can regulate who they send to Congress) and Sections 4 and 5 of Article I of the Constitution. Article I, Section 5, says, "each House shall be the judge of the elections, returns and qualifications of its own members." Article I, Section 4, states, "the times, place and manners of holding elections for Senators and Representatives, shall be prescribed in each state by the Legislature thereof. . . ." The respondents believed that these three parts of the Constitution gave the individual states, including Arkansas, the right to impose term limits on its congressmen.

In 1995, the Supreme Court decided by a 5–4 margin that state-mandated term limits were unconstitutional. The impact of the Supreme Court's decision on this case has been mostly political. The current political status quo will remain in Washington, and until a constitutional amendment is passed states will not be able to impose their own limits.

Evaluation of Free-Response Sample Essay

1. Did the essay clearly identify both sides of the issue?
2. Did the writer create sufficient building blocks to explain the answer?

1. This essay had two distinctive parts. The first asks the writer to evaluate the impact of Supreme Court decisions on political, economic, and social policy. The second asks the writer to apply that position to controversial issues that either have come before the Court or are being challenged. Again, for the purposes of illustration, we have included all the events in the body of the essay. For the actual test, be sure to read the instructions carefully and answer only one issue. The writer restates the premise that the Supreme Court has the potential of altering the three major components of public policy. Then the specific manner in which the Court will have an impact on Proposition 187 and term limits is presented. The reader knows immediately what to look for—the clash between federal versus state power in dealing with Proposition 187 and term limits, both having political implications.

2. The building blocks of the essay—the specific explanation of what the two events are all about and what would happen if the Supreme Court ruled that they were unconstitutional—give the reader a clear understanding of each of the events. The writer has clearly laid out the essence of each issue and how it effects political, social, and/or economic public policy. The writer also substantiates generalizations and the strength of this essay is the specific manner in which each event is dissected.

Data-Based Free-Response Essay Question Strategy

A Quick Review of the Data-Based Free-Response Essay

Each chapter will give you examples of essay questions based specifically on data, as well as other essay questions that do not rely on a specific database. Questions that are based specifically on data such as charts and graphs may be historical or contemporary in nature. The student is expected to analyze, evaluate, and interpret material from a variety of sources. The evaluator will look for evidence that the student understands the data, explains the data in relation to the question, and gives specific examples to answer the question as it relates to the data. Examples of data material include, but are not limited to:

- charts
- graphs
- tables
- diagrams of drawings
- political cartoons, both historical and contemporary
- flowcharts
- short narrative passages
- historical documents
- lyrics to songs or poems
- quotes
- primary source documents
- political campaign material such as posters and pamphlets
- survey or poll results

Examples of Use of Key Terms Used in Data-Based Free-Response Essays

The directions are very clear that the student must analyze and integrate an analysis with a general understanding of United States government and politics. Be especially aware of the following phrases:

- using data identify
- explain
- using data describe

- using quotation, identify and explain
- give an argument to support a position
- give an argument to refute a position
- give general similarities and differences
- identify trends
- give point of view of cartoonist

Just as in the multiple-choice section, you should underline the key terms used in the question. You should also highlight significant points within the data itself. If the data is a graph, underline the title of the graph and the graph's statistical parameters.

Topics Appearing in the Data-Based Free-Response Questions

The following topics give the reader a good sample of data topics. Students in Advanced Placement United States government and politics classes who took the test have summarized the topics since 1998. These topics illustrate the nature of the questions and in no way are meant to reflect the exact language of the questions.

- Analyze the nature of discretionary and mandatory spending through pie charts from 1963 through 2003 (projected) and how they create barriers that impact lawmaking.
- Describe voting patterns in the 1992 and 1996 presidential elections using a map and identify geographic regions that voted strongly Democrat and strongly Republican.
- Explain how congressional reelection patterns have created an advantage for incumbents using a pie chart and describe the impact that incumbency has on the political process.

Describe, identify, and explain a chart regarding the distribution of government benefits for children and the elderly from 1965 through 1986.

Identify trends in a graph comparing the number of federal and state employees between 1945 and 2000 and how block grants and federal mandates impacted these trends

Identify the point of view of a political cartoon dealing with Ralph Nader's candidacy in the 2000 presidential election. Explain how the electoral system hurts a third party's chances in winning elections and describe how third parties make a contribution to the political system.

How to Write the Data-Based Free-Response Essay Question

The data-based essays require you to interpret, analyze, and evaluate a base of information and then to make conclusions related to specific questions. In looking for the question you want to respond to, keep in mind that much of the data provided can be used as part of your thesis or introductory statement.

After you have completed reading the data-based question(s), you should methodically follow a series of steps:

1. Highlight or underline the key terms in the question.
2. Write a thesis or introductory statement that incorporates the data into your answer if the question requires one.
3. After you finish your thesis or introductory statement, you should then provide specific examples that illustrate your understanding of the data.

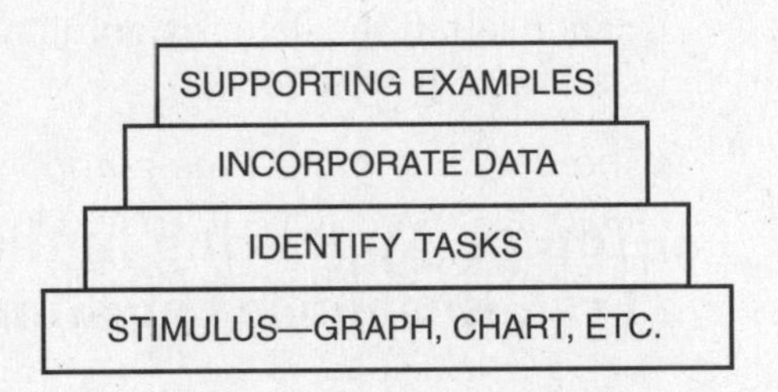

4. As you can see, just like the non–data-based free-response essay, you should identify the tasks, give supporting examples, and then provide a historical or contemporary description which reinforces your thesis or opening statement.

SAMPLE STIMULUS-BASED FREE-RESPONSE ESSAY

DIRECTIONS: Address these tasks using the following data.

- Seventy million viewers watched an average of 12 hours in the first televised presidential party conventions in 1952.
- An average of 85 percent of viewers watched an average of 7 hours of presidential party conventions in 1968.
- An average of 69 percent of viewers watched an average of 2 hours of party conventions in 1988.
- ABC, CBS, and NBC covered the Republicans and Democrats in 1992, 1996, and 2000. They provided between 1 and 2 hours of prime-time coverage from the convention halls in addition to reports on nightly newscasts, current affairs programs, and morning news shows.
- Combined Big 3 prime-time viewership of the four-night Republican convention in 1996 averaged 11.8 million homes per night, down 27 percent from 1988's average of 16.2 million homes, according to Nielsen Media Research.
- The Democrats averaged 13.2 million homes per night in 1996, a 24 percent decrease from 17.4 million in 1988.

Using the data above and your knowledge of United States politics, complete the following two tasks:

1. Identify two significant patterns in the television coverage and viewing of political conventions.

2. Explain how the patterns you chose reflect the role of the media in politics.

Analysis of Question

The data compare the number of viewers watching national nominating conventions, both Democratic and Republican, in 1952, 1968, 1988, 1992, and 1996 and the percentage of television households viewing some of the convention. The first part asks you to look at the patterns of coverage including the number of viewers and the percentage change from previous years. The second part then asks you to draw conclusions about the media's impact on the political system as a result of the trends discussed in the first part.

Sample Student Response

The data summarize the number of viewers tuned into some part of the national conventions televised in 1952, 1968, 1988, 1992, and 1996 and illustrates the dramatic decline in viewership since 1952. It also reflects how the major networks have decreased their coverage of the national nominating conventions since 1988.

It is clear from the statistics provided that there has been a downward trend of viewership from 1952 to 1996. With a decline in viewership, there was also a general downward trend of network coverage of the conventions. It is interesting to note that even though there was a downward trend both in coverage and viewership, a significant percentage of TV households did view some part of each of the conventions listed in the data.

One should also be aware that during conventions such as the 1968 Democratic National Convention, when there was rioting in Chicago, and the 1976 conventions, the first held after the Watergate scandal, the number of hours of viewership as well as the percentage of TV households viewing any part of the convention jumped. Most recently, however, the average number of hours viewed and the total network hours devoted to broadcasting the conventions has reached an all-time low.

The role of the media in influencing United States politics during the entire presidential campaign is extremely important and significant. It reaches a peak during the nominating conventions. Even though the total hours devoted to coverage has declined since 1952, television networks provide the political parties with an opportunity to showcase their candidates. For the challenger, it is the first time that most Americans will get a chance to judge the candidate's vision. For the incumbent, it gives the candidate a great opportunity to reinforce the accomplishments of the past four years.

The media has been very careful to give equal coverage to both political parties, and they have chosen very specific aspects of the convention to cover. In the early days of convention broadcasting, gavel-to-gavel coverage was the norm. However, the networks quickly discovered that there were large gaps of time when very little was going on, and network correspondents were accused of inventing stories. Once this type of coverage was dropped, the networks selected significant parts of the convention to televise. The keynote speech, for example Governor Cuomo's stirring speech in 1980, the nominating speeches (Governor Clinton rambling on for over a half hour in 1988 and then getting the nomination himself in 1992) and the actual acceptance speeches are some of the most widely covered events of the conventions. The media has also been very much aware of the other issues surrounding the convention—the choice of vice-presidential candidates and the demonstrations that take place both inside and outside the convention arena. These include Gregory Lee Johnson's flag burning in 1984 at the Republican National Convention in Texas and, of course, the Chicago riots in 1968.

Through media coverage of the conventions, candidates generally get a "convention kick" in the polls. In 1988 Governor Dukakis of Massachusetts was more than 15 points ahead in the polls after the Democratic convention. Those results were fleeting and soon after President Bush was nominated, he passed the Massachusetts governor in the polls. In 1992, Clinton took advantage of the media coverage and went on a bus tour immediately following the Democratic convention.

The Democratic and Republican conventions in 1996 and 2000 also illustrate the changing role of the media coverage. Both parties attempted to orchestrate the live television coverage. Highlights of the 1996 Republican convention were a speech by retired General Colin Powell and a floor speech by Elizabeth Dole that many analysts compared to an Oprah Winfrey presentation. The Democrats answered in kind in 1996 by preventing any dissenting voices from being heard on live television. To a great degree, they succeeded. However, viewership reached an all-time low, and the major networks continued to cut back significantly in their coverage of the 2000 conventions. The Republicans met in Philadelphia and staged a convention for George W. Bush that was highly orchestrated and put a united and diverse face on the Republican Party. The Democrats met in Los Angeles and had a more difficult task. The media covered Bill Clinton's swan song and focused on Al Gore's passionate kiss as he attempted to separate himself from the outgoing president.

Evaluation of Data-Based Free-Response Sample Essay

1. Does the answer fully identify the significant patterns of television coverage as well as viewer response? Does the writer use statistics to support the answer?
2. Does the writer give specific examples showing the role the media plays in covering political conventions as well as illustrating significant media events at nominating conventions?

1. The data offered by the writer presents a comparison of the number of viewers who watched national nominating conventions, both Democratic and Republican, in 1952, 1968, 1988, 1992, and 1996 and the percentage of television households that viewed some of the conventions. The first part of the question asks you to look at the patterns of coverage, including the number of viewers and the percentage change from previous years. The writer analyzes the statistics and concludes that there is a significant decline in viewership. A specific example, the 1968 Chicago convention, is given to illustrate the exception to this decline.

2. The student gives excellent examples of how the media influences politics during a campaign, reaching a peak at the national nominating conventions. Illustrations such as Mario Cuomo's speech in 1980 and Bill Clinton's speech in 1988 are used to contrast the impact of media events at the conventions. In addition the dual importance of the coverage of a convention—by demonstrators who use the convention as a means to get their message across and by the politicians who gain public support—is also explored.

A Summary of the Free-Response Essay Section

- Four mandatory essays worth 50 percent of the examination.
- Each essay should be written within 25 minutes. Listen for the proctors to signal the end of each writing period.
- Non–data-based essays may require either a formal thesis or introductory statement that relates to the tasks which the student is writing about.
- Data-based essays should have an opening statement that makes references to the data.
- All essays should give supporting evidence in the form of specific historical or contemporary examples.
- Perform all tasks listed in the essay question.
- Questions attack specific issues related to politics and government.
- Students should read questions carefully and understand the topics tested.
- In some questions, the interrelationship between two subjects may be explored.
- Tasks will vary from essay to essay. One essay may ask you to explain, while another part of an essay may ask you to illustrate, describe, discuss, or list.
- If you are asked to list or identify, you should do so and can use incomplete sentences, bulleted statements, or phrases in your response.
- The free-response essay will require you to understand the nature of the question, write a response that demonstrates an understanding of the question using specific examples, and develop a logical, coherent response.
- Write neatly so the rater can easily read your response.
- If you run out of time, **outline** the remainder of the essay you are working on.

PART ONE

CONSTITUTIONAL DEVELOPMENT

CHAPTER 1 The Theory of Modern Government

Chapter Overview

When looking at the interrelationship between government and politics, you need to understand the theoretical nature of both concepts. Government has an impact on our everyday lives in many ways. Our federal form of government has a huge effect on the manner in which we are able to function as part of our society—from the manner in which our recycled garbage is picked up to the speed limit on interstate highways. The political decisions that come into play result in these many policy decisions.

A working definition of government is those institutions that create public policy. Constitutionally defined, the formal institutions of government on the national level are the executive branch headed by the president, the legislative branch consisting of the Congress, and the judicial branch made up of the Supreme Court and lower courts. A similar structure exists on the state and local levels. In addition to the defined institutions of government, modern government is also characterized by those agencies that implement public policy—bureaucracies, including regulatory agencies, independent executive agencies, government corporations, and the cabinet. These institutions, sometimes acting independently, sometimes acting in concert, create and implement public policy.

The noted political scientist Harold Laswell, in a famous description, defined politics as "who gets what, when and how." This definition can be expanded to include why—why politicians are able to succeed or fail in getting elected and why they succeed or fail in the process of creating policy. Politics, unlike government, is not defined constitutionally but evolved from the writings of James Madison, Alexander Hamilton, and John Jay in the Federalist Papers, unwritten traditions and precedents that started with the formation of the first political parties, and the philosophical differences that emerged after candidates were elected to office. Politics is characterized by conflict and resolution, compromise, and the interrelationship of individuals and groups.

KEY TERMS

- Conservative
- Direct democracy
- Elite and class theory
- Government
- Hyperpluralism
- Liberal
- Linkage institution
- Loose construction
- Pluralism
- Policy agenda
- Political parties
- Politics
- Public policy
- Representative Democracy
- Strict constructionists

THE LIBERTY BELL HAS LONG BEEN A SYMBOL OF DEMOCRACY

Government and politics, thus, can be defined by a formula that combines both concepts and results in an end goal: government plus politics equals the creation of public policy. In other words, what government does through politics results in public policy. In evaluating how successful government and politicians are, you must look at the extent that public policy is achieved. This chapter will explore in detail those forces that come into play in the quest to control the policy agenda on both a theoretical and a practical level.

The Basic Function of Government

Government is essential because it has an impact on your everyday life.

If you look at the basic function of government as protection through defense and support of individuals through raising revenue, you will clearly see that government influences everybody. It is also clear that not everybody has the same needs, shares the same ideology, or has the same priorities. If you consider the principles of the Preamble to the Constitution:

- the establishment of a more perfect union
- the establishment of justice
- the insurance of domestic tranquility
- the promotion of the general welfare
- the security of individual liberty

you can see how people will differ on the meaning, interpretation, and implementation of these functions of government. When you look at specific examples of these functions and how they affect us, you will see the scope of government. Such policy areas as universal health care, the nature and size of our armed forces, the welfare system, Social Security and Medicare, and the extent that government should regulate our lives illustrate the expanding role of government and the impact it has on our lives.

The Meaning of Politics

If you define politics as who gets what, when, how, and why, then you have to determine the nature of the process and outcome. Because politics deals with individuals and their needs, values, and attitudes, it stands to reason that

Politics, the means with which individuals and groups get involved, results in the formal election of officials.

people with similar needs, values, and attitudes will band together to form political parties. Once a political party is formed, in order for the needs, values, and attitudes to translate into actual policy, the party must succeed in electing its members to office. Thus individuals running for office must have a base of electoral support, a base of political support (the party), and a base of financial support. Obviously, the issue of incumbency comes into play as those elected officials who are reelected become entrenched in the system and have an advantage over young political mavericks who want to break into the system.

The role of the electorate is also crucial in determining the means with which individuals get involved. How the voters perceive the candidate's positions on issues, the way people feel about the party, the comfort level of the voter in relation to the candidate and the party, as well as the influence the media have on the election all come into play in the eventual success or failure of the candidate. The campaign attempts to convince the voters that the candidate will fulfill the expectations and satisfy the needs of the voters. An excellent example of this was the 1992 presidential election and the emergence of the third-party candidacy of Ross Perot. He established an independent political party, United We Stand, and attempted to mold a campaign based on a populist perspective. Initially, the voters responded to him, but in the end they rejected his candidacy. On the other hand, in the same election, Bill Clinton, using the issue of change, attracted a constituency that responded to his image and perceived a candidate who would solve the economic problems facing this country.

In 1996 Bill Clinton was the incumbent and had the advantage of an electorate that supported his positions regarding education, the environment, Medicare, and Medicaid, unlike Republican candidate Bob Dole who lacked focus in his campaign. Third-party candidate Ross Perot lost the support of a major part of his constituency. However, he again raised a significant issue of campaign finance reform, which after the election became a scandal for both major political parties.

In 2000 the electorate couldn't make up its mind between George W. Bush, who promised to bring "honor and integrity" back to the Oval Office, and the incumbent vice president, Al Gore, who had to separate himself from Bill Clinton's scandals while still identifying himself with the longest period of prosperity in United States history. In the end, Gore won the popular vote but lost the electoral vote in one of the closest and most disputed elections in history.

George W. Bush campaigned for reelection in 2004 emphasizing that he would "build a safer world and a more hopeful America." His Democratic opponent, Senator John F. Kerry, told the voters that he was the "real deal" and that "America deserves better." The voters decided not to change a commander-in-chief during a time of war and gave the incumbent both a popular and electoral vote majority.

The Function of Interest Groups

The United States political system evolved from various interest groups vying to implement a policy agenda.

In looking at the Federalist Papers, you can see how the United States political system was characterized and created from established groups who had differing attitudes toward how best to form a new government. In Federalist No. 44 James Madison writes in 1787 ". . . We are brought to this undeniable conclusion that no part of the power is unnecessary or improper for accomplishing the necessary objects of the Union. The question, therefore, whether this amount of power shall be granted or not resolves itself into another question, whether or not a government commensurate to the exigencies of the union shall be established; or in other words, whether the Union itself shall be preserved." The Anti-Federalist position found in *The Debates on the Constitution in Letters from the Federal Farmer*, written in 1787, responds by stating that "there appears to me to be not only a premature deposit of some important powers in the general government—but many of those deposited there are undefined, and may be used to good or bad purposes as honest or designing men shall prevail." Even the overall fight over the ratification of the proposed constitution was waged on "party lines." Federalists supported ratification. Anti-Federalists opposed ratification. In this case, the policy agenda was the adoption of a new constitution.

Once the Constitution was ratified, two parties evolved. The Federalist Party, headed by Alexander Hamilton and made up of the country's upper class, supported a strong national government and set a policy agenda that would solve the nation's economic problems. In doing so, the party appealed to business interests such as manufacturing and trade. It believed in a loose construction, or a liberal interpretation, of the Constitution. The opposition party, the Democratic-Republicans, led by Thomas Jefferson after his return from France where he was the United States ambassador, was characterized as the party of the "common man." It believed in a more limited role of the central government and was considered to be strict constructionist, which is characterized by a belief in a conservative interpretation of the Constitution. Its constituency was farmers, merchants, and the middle class of American society. The party was afraid of a powerful president and believed that Congress should be the main cog of government.

As you can see, these two parties had divergent views resulting in differing policy objectives. Ultimately, the Democratic-Republicans prevailed. The Federalist Party failed and eventually faded from the scene. (For a full discussion of political parties, turn to Chapter 11.)

Linkage Institutions—The Informal Institutions

Public policy is affected by the linkage institutions of political parties, elections, interest groups, and the media.

By definition, a linkage institution is the means by which individuals can express preferences regarding the development of public policy. Preferences are voiced through the political system, and when specific political issues are resolved, they become the basis for policy. In today's political system, the two major political parties, the Democrats and the Republicans, each have national platforms that outline their position on various public issues. For instance, the Republican Party has stood for less government, whereas today's Democratic Party has supported government programs such as Medicare. In areas of social concern, Republicans have been opposed to abortion on demand, whereas Democrats have been identified as a party favoring choice. In order to implement these policies, Democrats and Republicans have to be elected to public office. Candidates and political parties must assess the nature of the electorate. Are there a significant number of single-issue groups, those special interests who base their vote on a single issue? Or is the candidate's stand on issues broad enough to attract the mainstream of the voting electorate? The media, through daily newspapers and television newscasts, as well as columnists and editorials, attempt to influence the voters, the party, and the candidate's stand on issues. The media have been accused of simplifying the issues by relying on photo opportunities (photo ops) set up by the candidates and 30-second statements on the evening news shows (sound bites). The interaction of linkage institutions results in the formation of a policy agenda by the candidates running for elected office. An example of how linkage institutions work is the 1980 presidential race between Ronald Reagan and President Jimmy Carter. Reagan and the Republican Party painted a picture of a president who was weak in the foreign policy arena as a result of a hostage crisis in Iran and a domestic economy that was out of control as a result of double-digit inflation. The electorate, following the media's coverage of a series of debates, perceived Reagan to be the candidate who would provide strong leadership both at home and abroad.

Policy-Making Institutions

The formal institutions created by the Constitution including the presidency, Congress, and the courts and bureaucracies are the significant and major policy-making institutions.

Even though each branch of government has separate powers, a significant policy-making function is defined by the Constitution. In addition, the development and growth of bureaucracies becomes a fourth branch of government, because it has independent regulatory power and is connected directly and indirectly to the federal government itself.

The president as chief executive proposes to Congress a legislative agenda. Along with this agenda is a budget proposal that defines the extent of government involvement in supporting legislation as well as the size of government. The decision to sign or veto legislation determines the fate of legislation and the resulting public policy. Congress, through its committee system and ultimately its votes, determines the fate of the president's legislative agenda and the proposed budget. Over the past 30 years, the issue of the nation's deficit has been paramount in determining the nature of legislation passed. This changed in 1996 after President Clinton signed a balanced budget. By 2000 the debate shifted away from deficit spending to what the budget surplus should be used for. After September 11, 2001, tax cuts, a recession, and an expanded war on terrorism resulted in the return of large deficits. The Supreme Court in particular has a direct impact on the public policy through its interpretation of the Constitution and how it relates to specific issues brought before the Court. An activist Court will forge new ground and through such decisions as *Roe v Wade* or *Brown v Board of Education* establish precedents that will force legislative action. A Court that shows judicial restraint will maintain the status quo or mirror what the other branches of government have established as current policy. Decisions that established the legitimacy of state restrictions on abortions such as parental approval, and a narrower interpretation of Miranda Rights (those rights guaranteed to people arrested) were characteristic of a more conservative Rehnquist Court in the late 1980s and 1990s.

The size of government has increased since World War II as a result of the bureaucracy, which became an integral part of the government. Even though the size of the government workforce has decreased, the influence of the bureaucratic agencies on public policy has been dramatic. In particular, regulatory agencies such as the Food and Drug Administration (FDA) and the Environmental Protection Agency (EPA) have issued directives as a result of congressional legislation. The Clean Air Act resulted in a number of policy statements by the EPA regarding auto pollution in the individual states. The FDA debated the advisability of approving the abortion pill RU486 and gave the go-ahead for a private group to conduct testing. It was approved in 2000, and consumers were able to purchase the drug.

Evolution of Representative Democracy

The development of our representative democracy evolved from other forms of democracies.

From the roots of our political system in ancient Greece, to the writings of Enlightenment thinkers such as Montesquieu and Locke, to the principles outlined in the Declaration of Independence, our representative democracy has emerged as a distinct republican form of government.

The origins of Athenian democracy come from the premise that governmental rule should be that of the many rather than the few. In its purest form a direct democracy would have every citizen attending a town meeting and voting on every issue with the majority prevailing. Because of the size of the country, this becomes impractical and works only on a limited scale such as the classic New England town meeting where, for instance, a town's budget is approved.

Enlightenment thinkers proposed that a democracy should rely on the consent of the people. They also felt that there were natural rights that could not be taken away by the government, such as life, liberty, and property. In drafting the Declaration of Independence, Thomas Jefferson felt that these principles of unalienable rights should be incorporated. They were also included in the Constitution. The individual became the central focus of government policy. Such concepts as equality, freedom, and order became the driving forces of our democracy.

The measure of democracy became open and free elections. In order for a democracy to succeed, these elections had to be open to all citizens, issues and policy statements of candidates had to be available to the electorate, citizens could form political parties to advocate policies, and elections would be determined by a majority or plurality. Obviously, our constitutional republic in its early days did not meet the criteria. Slaves and women were not given the right to vote. There were property requirements, and the state legislatures determined who would represent the states as senators. Even today, we still have an electoral college, which determines the official outcome of presidential elections based on the vote of electors rather than the direct vote of citizens.

The basic concepts of our democracy today rely on the worth and dignity of the individual, respect for equality, majority rule with minority rights, compromise, and the guarantee of individual freedom.

Today, the test to determine whether our democracy is working still relies on the way the individual determines the final fate of who runs the government and how policy is determined. Through linkage institutions and sovereignty, individuals must have a forum and a vote to determine their elected officials. Guarantees of voting equality through "one man, one vote" representation, the recognition that the size and make-up of congressional districts should be as democratic as possible, has achieved this goal. Amendments to the Constitution creating direct elections of senators; voting rights for freed slaves, women, and 18 year olds; the elimination of poll taxes; and legislation such as the Voting Rights Bill have accomplished this. Participation in government and politics is another indicator. In addition, a free media that informs the electorate creates an atmosphere of increased involvement by citizens. Government itself must become responsive. It must respect minority rights even though its elected officials were chosen by majority rule. Individual freedom must be respected and is guaranteed through the Bill of Rights. Court decisions such as *Tinker v Des Moines* have reinforced the concept that the First Amendment is even applicable to high school students. Finally, government itself must operate on the basis of consensus and compromise. Otherwise public policy, the measure of whether government succeeds or fails, will not be implemented. During the George Herbert Walker Bush administration the cry of "gridlock" was heard because a Republican president had difficulty achieving his legislative agenda because there was a Democratic Congress.

After the Republicans assumed control of Congress in 1994, a divided government again dominated American politics. In 1995, the Republicans tested a weakened president by forcing a government shutdown caused by a budget stalemate. This backfired when public opinion turned against the GOP. A complete turnaround occurred at the conclusion of the 104th Congress prior to the 1996 election when both the president and Congress reached compromises regarding healthcare portability, the minimum wage, and welfare reform. At the start of the 105th Congress a bipartisan agreement on a balanced budget was reached.

The Importance of Control

Modern political theory revolves around who controls the agenda.

If you control the agenda, you will be the one to get the what, when, and how. There are three schools of thought regarding how the agenda is controlled. The first theory, pluralism, involves different groups all vying for control of the policy agenda. No single group emerges, forcing the groups to compromise. A centrist position is achieved, and, although no one group is totally happy, a number of groups, as a result of the bargaining that goes on, agree on mutually acceptable positions. Elite and class theory revolves around an economic strata of society controlling the policy agenda. An upper class, the wealthy of society, is recognized as the elite and controls the linkage institutions of government. The third theory, hyperpluralism, is an extension of pluralism gone amuck. There are so many interest groups vying for control that government cannot operate. It is almost like gridlock without any means of compromise. Any attempt to mediate or placate the many interest groups results in such a watered down policy that the final product does not resemble the original proposal. There is no logical approach to policy formation. It is dictated by which group most successfully influences government officials.

Our democracy has components of each of these political theories. No one theory is ideal. Each has its own advantages and disadvantages. However, most political analysts would agree that a democracy characterized by a pluralist society working in harmony and achieving compromise through centrist positions usually has a good chance of success. Historically, when the Federalists became the first party to control the government, it was controlled by the elite. Today, many critics of our system contend that there are too many special interest groups who, through their political action committees, are able to influence key lawmakers. During George Herbert Walker Bush's administration, he often accused special interest groups in Congress of contributing to gridlock. Those officials who are able to achieve consensus seem to have the most success in achieving public policy goals.

The Importance of Goals

Modern government changes as a result of who can best serve the public interest.

As we conclude this chapter, you should note that, in evaluating the success or failure of government and our political system, we will continually be coming back to an analysis of whether elected officials are achieving their goals, which translate into public policy. Another way of putting it is whether or not officials are meeting the needs of the public they serve. To make a final judgment, you should ask the following questions about government and politics as you continue reading this text:

- What is the public interest?
- Who determines the parameters of what the public wants?
- How much influence should government have on the lives of its citizens?
- How big should government be?
- How much money should government spend?
- What is the best way to raise money for government spending?
- How should government and its elected officials deal with serious ethical issues such as abortion, euthanasia, and birth control?
- Should candidates campaign negatively in order to get elected?
- How should government and politicians restore the public's confidence in their elected officials and government?

Chapter 1 Review

SECTION 1: MULTIPLE-CHOICE QUESTIONS

1. Which of the following is considered a linkage institution?
   (A) the bureaucracy
   (B) the Congress
   (C) the executive department
   (D) the government
   (E) the media

2. All of the following are characteristics of politics EXCEPT
   (A) individuals with similar ideas banding together to form political parties.
   (B) the means through which individuals and groups get involved.
   (C) who gets what, when, how, and why.
   (D) the passing of laws that serve to further minority rights.
   (E) the interrelationship of individuals and groups.

3. Which of the following institutions established in the Constitution make public policy?
   (A) the Senate, the presidency, and political parties
   (B) the Congress, the presidency, and the courts
   (C) the Congress, the courts, and the military
   (D) the Congress, the presidency, and the military
   (E) the Congress, the presidency, and the bureaucracy

4. Which of the following best defines a set of institutions linking government, politics, and public policy?
   (A) an educational system
   (B) a political system
   (C) a social system
   (D) an economic system
   (E) a socioeconomic system

5. Which of the following are considered linkage institutions?
   I. Congress
   II. political parties
   III. the media
   IV. the courts

   (A) I only
   (B) I and II only
   (C) II and III only
   (D) I, II, and III only
   (E) I, II, III, and IV

6. Which of the following principles describes a philosophy of the Federalist Party?
   (A) Federalists believed in a loose construction of the Constitution.
   (B) Federalists believed in a strict interpretation of the Constitution.
   (C) Federalists believed in a conservative interpretation of the Constitution.
   (D) Federalists believed that Congress should be the main cog of government.
   (E) Federalists believed that the interests of the common man should be reflected in government.

7. All the following characteristics reflect the reasons why political parties are formed EXCEPT
   (A) people band together because of similar needs.
   (B) people band together because of similar values.
   (C) people band together because they have similar income.
   (D) people band together because of similar beliefs.
   (E) people band together because they have similar goals.

8. Which of the following groups examines a candidate's record primarily on specific issues?
   (A) single-interest groups
   (B) elite groups
   (C) plurality groups
   (D) Democrats
   (E) Republicans

9. All of the following are basic principles of our democracy today EXCEPT a belief in
   (A) the worth and dignity of the individual.
   (B) the need for political equality.
   (C) universal healthcare.
   (D) the guarantee of individual freedoms.
   (E) the need for a balance between freedom and order.

10. Which of the following institutions is commonly called the fourth branch of government?
    (A) the bureaucracy
    (B) special interest groups
    (C) the executive branch
    (D) the Congress
    (E) the Supreme Court

11. Which of the following principles is most fundamental to democratic theory?
    (A) free elections and universal suffrage
    (B) minority rule
    (C) universal public education
    (D) political parties
    (E) a written constitution

12. All of the following factors contribute to an enlightened understanding of the electorate EXCEPT
    (A) interest groups.
    (B) the media.
    (C) the right to property.
    (D) political parties.
    (E) the Internet.

13. Which of the following groups believes that bargaining and compromise are essential to a democracy?
    (A) elitists
    (B) pluralists
    (C) hyperpluralists
    (D) Democrats
    (E) Republicans

14. Which of the following theories contends that our society is divided along class lines and that a narrow upper-class strata rules regardless of the formal organization of government?
    (A) elite
    (B) pluralist
    (C) hyperpluralist
    (D) socialist
    (E) egalitarian

15. Which of the following theories claims that too many competing groups cripple government's ability to govern?
    (A) hyperpluralist theory
    (B) pluralist theory
    (C) elite theory
    (D) democratic theory
    (E) class-based theory

16. Which of the following theories stress that the public interest is rarely translated into public policy?
    (A) elitist and pluralist
    (B) pluralist and hyperpluralist
    (C) elitist and hyperpluralist
    (D) Democrats and Republicans
    (E) liberals and conservatives

Answers to Multiple-Choice Questions

1. **(E)** Type of Question: Definitional
   The media, along with elections, political parties, and special interest groups, are the linkage institutions. The government represents the formal institutions such as the Congress. The bureaucracy and executive department are institutions created by law.
2. **(D)** Type of Question: Negative
   Choices A, B, C, and E are all characteristics of politics. Choice D is the outcome of the political process.
3. **(B)** Type of Question: Identification and analysis
   The question asks you to identify the formal institutions established by the Constitution that by definition are responsible for creating public policy. The three formal institutions found in the Constitution are the legislative branch represented by the Congress (Article I), the executive branch represented by the president (Article II), and the judicial branch represented by the courts (Article III). Even though the military and bureaucracy may make policies, they are either responsible to a specific branch of government or, as in the case of the bureaucracy, not formally established in the constitution. Political parties are linkage institutions, and even though they make recommendations regarding public policy, they do not have any power to make it.
4. **(B)** Type of Question: Definitional
   A political system by definition is a set of institutions linking government, politics, and public policy. An educational system, social system, economic system, or socioeconomic system may have components of a political system; however, none of them has all the characteristics of a political system.
5. **(C)** Type of Question: Definitional, more than one correct answer
   This is a variation of question 1. You must know the definition of the term "linkage institution" and be able to identify the fact that there is more than one correct choice. Congress and the courts are not linkage institutions.
6. **(A)** Type of Question: Identification and analysis
   Federalists believed in a loose construction of the Constitution, meaning a broad interpretation. Anti-Federalists believed in a strict interpretation, or conservative view, of the Constitution, and they believed that Congress should have more influence than the president. The Anti-Federalists also reflected the interests of the common man.
7. **(C)** Type of Question: Negative
   Even though the Republican Party has been accused of being the party of the rich, and similar income may play some role in determining political preference, it does not apply as much as needs, values, beliefs, and goals as reasons why people join a particular political party.

8. **(A)** Type of Question: Identification and analysis
Even though a Democrat or Republican may have a strong preference for one issue, by definition a single-interest group such as the National Rifle Association uses guns as the sole criterion in the endorsement of candidates.
9. **(C)** Type of Question: Except/Characteristics
Dignity, political equality, the guarantee of individual freedoms, and a belief in the need for a balance between freedom and order are all characteristics of our democracy. Universal healthcare may be a goal, but it is not a principle of a democracy.
10. **(A)** Type of Question: Identification
Because the bureaucracy can create and implement policy, it is known as the fourth branch of government. Special interest groups may like to consider themselves as being as influential as the formal institutions of government, but by definition they are considered linkage institutions. The other choices are the three branches of government as defined by the Constitution.
11. **(A)** Type of Question: Identification of a characteristic
Though universal public education, political parties, and a written constitution can be features of a democracy, they are not necessary for a democracy to succeed. Free elections and universal suffrage are essential for the establishment of democratic rule.
12. **(C)** Type of Question: Identification/cause and effect
Interest groups, the media, political parties, and the Internet all contribute to an enlightened understanding of the electorate. The right to property is guaranteed by the Constitution but does not directly contribute to an enlightened understanding.
13. **(B)** Type of Question: Definitional
Even though Democrats and Republicans may state that they believe in bargaining and compromise, in reality they do not always practice what they preach. Pluralists fit the definition that the question raises.
14. **(A)** Type of Question: Definitional
Upper-class strata is the clue to the answer. The other groups may accuse the government of being dominated by the elite, but they do not fit the definition in the question.
15. **(A)** Type of Question: Definitional
Hyperpluralism refers to competing groups. The other groups do not fit the definition and, in fact, contradict it.
16. **(C)** Type of Question: Generalization
You need to know the characteristics of hyperpluralists and elitists to be able to make the generalization that the public interest is rarely translated into public policy. The other choices at times in practice may fit the statement, but in theory they would never subscribe to it.

SECTION 2: FREE-RESPONSE ESSAY

DIRECTIONS: You have 25 minutes to answer the following question. This question is based on your knowledge of United States government and politics, and it may contain materials from charts, graphs, and tables which you will have to analyze and draw conclusions from. Make sure you provide specific and sufficient information and examples in your essay.

> In policymaking, American liberals and conservatives express different policy preferences. These differences can be attributed to the theoretical and practical ideologies held by each. Identify and explain two ways in which liberals and conservatives differ theoretically. Then select two policies and explain how a liberal and a conservative would approach each issue.

Sample Student Response

Liberals and conservatives often differ in the way that they would shape public policy. Liberals are usually on one end of the political spectrum, and conservatives are on the other.

There are two main differences between liberal and conservative theory. The first difference relates to the importance each group assigns to freedom and order and the extent to which they value one over the other. Liberals do not want to give up personal freedom in the name of preserving order. They do not think it is the place of government to tell them how to live and what they can and cannot do. Conservative ideology, on the other hand, states that it is the government's primary duty to preserve social order even if certain personal freedoms are sacrificed in the process.

The second difference we've seen arise in the twentieth century. It relates to the balance between freedom and economic equality. Liberals feel that the government has the responsibility to promote economic and social equality among the people. They want to ensure equality of opportunity on both a social and economic level. Conservatives, on the other hand, embrace a policy of personal freedom. They want the individual to decide whether or not to redistribute his own wealth. Thus, they want the government to promote a laissez-faire approach toward business.

These theoretical ideas translate into clearly different beliefs with regard to public policy. The first example is New York State's Rockefeller laws and federal legislation that enforce mandatory drug sentences for possession and selling of illegal substances. Liberals believe that these laws go too far, and they would advocate a policy that offers rehabilitation to people who violate drug laws instead of long prison sentences.

A second policy on which conservatives and liberals differ relates to affirmative action. Again, using the theoretical basis of fostering social and economic equality, liberals support affirmative action programs since the purpose of these policies is to level the playing field for minorities. But in the process, according to conservatives, businesses and government institutions, such as state universities, are forced to give up their freedom to decide who is best qualified for a job or who should be admitted to a school. In fact, conservatives promoted an anti–affirmative action program in California called Proposition 209, which the voters passed overwhelmingly and, in effect, abolished government-sponsored affirmative action programs in that state.

Evaluation of Free-Response Sample Essay

1. Did the essay identify two theoretical ways that liberals differ from conservatives?
2. Did the essay provide supporting examples?
3. Did the essay identify and explain specific policy differences between liberals and conservatives?

1. The essay, after restating the question, presented a clear statement illustrating how liberals and conservatives differ by contrasting how the philosophies of both groups value the concepts of freedom, order, and social and economic equality.

2. Appropriate examples of the theoretical differences between liberals and conservatives have been provided to supply the reader with a sufficient understanding of those philosophical differences.

3. The two policies that were used to illustrate the differences between liberals and conservatives were New York's drug laws, known as the Rockefeller laws, and the issue of affirmative action. Obviously there are many other issues that students could discuss such as abortion, gun control, the role of government in providing social services, and so forth.

SECTION 2: DATA-BASED FREE-RESPONSE ESSAY

Answer questions based on the following poll, which was taken by the news media and released to the public. The results follow:

- 91 percent of the people surveyed said they had little or no confidence in Washington to solve problems.
- 64 percent of the people surveyed considered gridlock between Congress and the president a major problem.
- 48 percent of the people polled said congressional Republicans were to blame for gridlock, whereas 32 percent of those surveyed blamed President Clinton, and 12 percent of the people said Clinton and the Republicans were equally at fault.
- 90 percent of the people polled said they wanted a government that promotes change, whereas 6 percent said the government should keep things as they are.
- 7 percent of those polled said they had a great deal of confidence that President Clinton and Congress could deal with the country's problems, whereas 73 percent said they had only a little confidence and 18 percent said they had none.
- 27 percent of those polled said they would vote in the November 1994 election for an independent candidate for Congress if they had the chance, whereas 29 percent said they would support a Democrat, and 23 percent said they would vote Republican. The remainder of those polled said they were undecided or cited a specific third-party affiliation.

Identify and discuss three attitudes of voters that help explain why they have become cynical.

Sample Student Response

Since the Watergate affair, the public has had less and less confidence in the federal government to solve the nation's problems. This poll is an indication that the voter's disgust with government is not lessening. If anything it's increasing. People supported the notion of change in 1992 when they elected President Clinton, but two years later the vast majority of people polled indicated that they had little confidence in the president's ability to achieve his goals. The consequences of hyperpluralism are being felt as two-thirds of those polled believed that gridlock and infighting between Congress and the president results in conflict rather than compromise. The poll results remained consistent during the 1994 midterm elections and the 1996 presidential elections. In 1994, voters reacted to President Clinton's failed healthcare plan by voting for a Republican majority in Congress for the first time in 40 years. The Republicans responded by initiating their Contract with America, a ten-point plan designed to reduce the size of government. However, gridlock became operative, and a government shutdown was precipitated because of a budget stalemate. This caused a tremendous level of distrust by the American public toward the GOP. President Clinton again achieved the upper hand, and it carried through with his victory in the 1996 presidential election. However, the Republicans were able to maintain their majority in both houses after last-minute compromises in the closing days of the 104th Congress.

Allegations of impropriety levied against President Clinton and the manner in which Republicans, special interest groups, and conservative Democrats appear to prevent legislation from passing are examples of why the public has less and less confidence in government. The Whitewater and Paula Jones scandals are part of the reason why those polled expressed little confidence in the president. Just as Watergate hurt Nixon's credibility, the parade of witnesses appearing before Congress hurt Clinton. Even though it has never been proven that Clinton did anything wrong in his Whitewater investment, which took place prior to his presidency, the public still perceived that Clinton had been less than honest. The character issue was raised when allegations were made by Paula Jones that Clinton made sexual advances when he was governor. These incidents certainly lowered the public's confidence in President Clinton's ability to get the job done. Scenes such as Senator Alfonse D'Amato singing a parody of "Old McDonald" on the floor of the Senate in an attempt to ridicule the pork in the Crime Bill also gave rise to why almost 50 percent of those polled blamed the Republicans for gridlock. Scandals continued to plague Clinton's second term. Whitewater investigations by independent prosecutor Kenneth Starr resulted in indictments of Clinton associates. The Supreme Court decided that Paula Jones could sue President Clinton, even as a sitting president. And both the Senate and House of Representatives held hearings on campaign finance abuses that occurred during the 1996 campaign.

Evaluation of Data-Based Free-Response Sample Essay

1. Were conclusions that went beyond the poll results clearly presented?
2. Was there an adequate explanation of the attitudes of voters?

1. The conclusions reached were independent of the poll results. The writer even uses Watergate as a jumping-off point and then supports it by presenting evidence that explains why the public mistrusts the government so much.

2. The writer indicates that hyperpluralism may be central as an explanation of why there is such little confidence in government. The comparison of why people voted for Clinton in 1992 and the poll results in 1994 substantiates the conclusions reached. The writer also makes references to the 1994 and 1996 elections. In addition, scandals that created more distrust were included in the essay.

CHAPTER 2 Constitutional Foundations

Chapter Overview

The Constitution provides the basic framework of government. It is the supreme law of the land. It evolved from a political philosophy which, although democratic in origin, was cynical and had economic interests in mind when the document was finalized. In order to understand the practical manner in which the Constitution describes the relationship of the branches of government to each other, to the states, and to the individual, you first must look at what preceded its ratification—the history of British rule of the colonies, the American Revolution, and the failed first attempt at creating a workable constitution, the Articles of Confederation. These factors all contribute to the creation of what has been called a living document—the Constitution of the United States.

The Declaration of Independence

A powerful heritage created a climate that influenced our forefathers to turn toward a rocky and risky road of revolution.

Thomas Jefferson, John Adams, Benjamin Franklin, Roger Sherman, and Robert Livingston included the political ideas from philosophers such as Locke, Rousseau, and Montesquieu in the Declaration of Independence. Looking at Locke's *Second Treatise of Civil Government*, you can't help but notice the similarities between the language Locke used and the phrases used in the Declaration of Independence. Ideas such as natural rights as they relate to life, liberty, and property; the consent of the governed; and the concept of limited government were all borrowed by the authors of the Declaration of Independence. For instance, Locke describes natural rights as "the state of nature has a law to govern it, which obliges everyone." The Declaration of Independence calls natural law "Laws of Nature and Nature's God." On equality, Locke refers to people as "men being by nature all free, equal and independent," whereas

KEY TERMS

- Anti-Federalists
- Articles of Confederation
- Connecticut Compromise
- Consent of the governed
- Constitution
- Declaration of Independence
- Democratic Republicans
- Federalist Papers
- Federalist Party
- Great Compromise
- Limited government
- Natural rights
- New Jersey Plan
- *Second Treatise of Civil Government*
- Shays' Rebellion
- Three-Fifths Compromise
- Unalienable rights
- Virginia Plan

THE DECLARATION OF INDEPENDENCE LAID THE FOUNDATION FOR REPRESENTATIVE GOVERNMENT

IN CONGRESS, JULY 4, 1776.

The unanimous Declaration of the thirteen united States of America,

the Declaration of Independence announced that "all men are created equal." In addition, the Declaration of Independence used many of the concepts from English Common Law related to the rights of the accused and the institutions such as representative colonial assemblies as the rationale why the colonists wanted to revolt against Great Britain.

Looking at the Declaration of Independence itself, you should be able to summarize the major parts of the document:

- ***The Philosophical Basis***—Using Locke's philosophy, the Declaration of Independence establishes "unalienable rights" as the cornerstone of natural rights. As a consequence of these rights, limited governments are formed receiving their powers from "the consent of the governed."
- ***The Grievances***—In a lawyerlike dissertation, the second part of the Declaration of Independence makes the case against Great Britain. Taxation without representation, unjust trials, quartering of British soldiers, abolition of colonial assemblies, and a policy of mercantilism created a logic for drastic change.

- ***The Statement of Separation***—Announcing to the world that the colonists had no choice but to revolt, Jefferson stated that it is not only the right, but the duty of the colonists to change the government. You should understand how risky the revolution was for the colonists. Like David against Goliath, the outcome of the American Revolution was far from certain. England had superior power, a navy that was supreme, and resources that could support a war effort. The colonists, resorting to guerrilla tactics and a knowledge of their land, had leadership and a desire for freedom.

The American Revolution restored to the colonists the rights they had as British subjects and carried out many of the major promises of the Declaration of Independence.

Called a "conservative revolution," the new leaders tried to create a government based on the idea of the consent of the governed. Individual state governments guaranteed their citizens the rights they had under British rule. Power was not centralized and the new nation made sure that the new constitution, the Articles of Confederation, could not end up as a government with a king.

Even though the Declaration of Independence stated that "all men were created equal," the societal structure did not reflect equality. The unalienable rights of "life, liberty, and the pursuit of happiness" were assumed to apply to male white colonists. The issue of slaves and women having these rights was not addressed. Because the American Revolution was the first attempt at applying these principles, the fact that all segments of society were not initially included was not surprising because those in power did not want a great deal of political and social upheaval. Whether this principle has been realized is still a debatable question. Today, many minority groups would make the argument that they have not been given full equality.

Property as an indicator of wealth and status was also a requirement for political office. The states and individual state legislatures became the dominant force. Economic problems immediately faced the new nation in the form of repayment of war debts to the central government and individuals facing an economic recession caused by the war. Farmers who believed that the new government was not fulfilling the objectives of the Declaration of Independence took up arms. Even though Shays' Rebellion failed, it sent a signal to the newly formed government that it had major problems.

The Articles of Confederation

The Articles of Confederation were doomed to failure from their onset.

Although the Articles of Confederation recognized the need for a central government, it relied on the states to make the decisions that would ultimately determine whether the country would survive. Under the Articles of Confederation, the national government had two levels of government—a weak national government with a one-house congress and dominant state governments. Congress was given limited power to declare war, make peace, and sign treaties. The national government could borrow money, but it had no power to tax the individual states. The Articles of Confederation created a national army and navy, but the government had no power to draft soldiers. There was no chief executive or national court system, and legislation had to be passed by a two-thirds majority.

The states could create economic havoc by imposing tariffs on each other, by creating their own currency in addition to the national currency, by refusing to amend the Articles of Confederation (an amendment needed unanimous approval by the states), and by refusing to recognize treaties made by the national government.

Foreign policy was virtually nonexistent. The Barbary pirates threatened our ships, and our borders were vulnerable to attacks from both English and Spanish interests.

A success of the national government was the Northwest Ordinance, which abolished slavery in the newly acquired Northwest territories.

The most positive aspect of the government was that a new middle class was developing on the state level. Even though the old guard from the colonial era still existed, small farmers began to dominate state politics. This created a broader political base and started the beginning of opposing political parties (Federalists and Anti-Federalists).

By 1787 it was obvious that, at a minimum, the Articles of Confederation had to be revised, and many felt that they should be totally changed to reflect the realities of what a functional government should be.

A diverse delegation, representing varying interests, met in Philadelphia and concluded that a new constitution was needed to replace the Articles of Confederation.

With the exception of Rhode Island, the rest of the states sent 55 delegates to the Constitutional Convention in Philadelphia in 1789. The make-up included merchants, lawyers, farmers, and bankers as well as state government officials. Leaders such as Thomas Jefferson, Thomas Paine, Patrick Henry, John Adams, and John Hancock doubted that abolishing the Articles of Confederation was the answer to the country's problems and did not attend. Those in attendance felt that a revision of the Articles of Confederation would not go far enough. Hamilton, Washington, and Madison led the fight for a new constitution. Benjamin Franklin, at age 81, was one of the oldest delegates attending the convention and the only delegate to have signed both the Declaration of Independence and the Constitution. Philosophically, the delegates were split on how to reconcile basic differences regarding the organization of a new government. They shared a cynical belief that people could not be given power to govern and that political conflict would naturally occur if there were not built-in checks. Because the delegates came from the newly emerging middle class as well as the traditional rich property owners, they quickly saw that factions would exist both in the government and in society. The Federalist Papers, in Federalist No. 10, pointed out that these factions could ultimately paralyze effective government. Self-interest of the delegates resulted in an agreement that the objective of government should be to protect the property owner. Ultimately a series of checks and balances, outlined in Federalist No. 47, and a structure of government that stressed a separation of powers became the fiber of the new Constitution.

The Constitution

The framers of the Constitution believed that inequities of wealth were a principal source of political conflict, but they did not try to eliminate them from the Constitution.

Constitutional historian Charles Beard in his *An Economic Interpretation of the Constitution* (1913) argued that the founding fathers were concerned with protecting the wealth of the property class. He painted a picture of the delegates to the convention as men who were wealthy and who cared about the financial interests of that class.

The compromises reached at the convention included voting, representation, slavery, and trade. Because wealth was such an important consideration, the delegates decided to let the individual states determine the criteria for voting qualifications. Property became the major criterion, and each state was able to determine who was eligible to vote in the national elections for Congress and the president.

Instead, they agreed to a series of compromises.

The thorny issue of how to create a new Congress split the convention between the larger more populous states and the smaller states. The smaller states, led by New Jersey, insisted that each state should have equal representation. The Virginia Plan argued that a legislature based on population would be more equitable. The Connecticut Compromise, also known as the Great Compromise, resulted in the formation of a bicameral (two-house) Congress—one house is represented equally by the states (the Senate) and the other house is represented by population (the House of Representatives).

Once the structure of the new Congress was agreed upon, the divisive issue of slavery had to be resolved. There was never a doubt that Jefferson's original proposition that "All men are created equal" would never see the light of day in the new Constitution. Nevertheless, the issues of slave trade and slave representation had to be resolved. The South agreed to halt the import of slaves in 1808 if the North agreed to return fugitive slaves. More difficult was the issue of representation. If each slave counted as one person, the South could have easily held the balance of power in the House of Representatives. Thus, the Three-Fifths Compromise was agreed on. Every five slaves would count as three people for representation and tax purposes.

The last major compromise dealt with tariffs. The North wanted to tax Southern exports to Europe and wanted to protect their own manufactured goods. The South did not want to tax European goods so that their own exports would not be taxed. They agreed to tax only imports.

The delegates also addressed the weaknesses of the Articles of Confederation. Because a primary concern was protection of the property owner, they dealt with economic issues. Congress was given the power to tax, regulate interstate and foreign commerce, create a viable national currency, and, in what later became known as the elastic clause, make "all laws necessary and proper" to carry out the stated powers of Congress.

States were strictly prohibited from duplicating the powers of the federal government that would have an impact on the nation's economy (i.e., denied the power to coin money, regulate interstate and foreign commerce, and interfere with the federal government's ability to collect debts).

The drafters also saw the need for a chief executive and a court system; however, as we will soon see, the relationship between these two branches of government became the benchmark of the new Constitution.

The Birth of Political Parties

The first political parties were born during the fight to ratify the new Constitution. Because the philosophy of each party reflected an economic base, it became apparent that the issue of individual rights could

The Federalists, in Federalist Paper Number 10, led by Alexander Hamilton, John Jay, and James Madison, argued that a "tyranny of the majority" could threaten the economic fiber of the nation. They believed that the new Constitution, through its checks and balances and the separation of the three branches of government, would ensure the protection of the minorities. Through a series of articles published as the Federalist Papers and signed by the pseudonym Publius, they outlined the necessity of a government that would be forced to compromise as a result of the separate powers of each branch. They also felt that the Constitution had enough safeguards built in for individuals. The Constitution gave each state "full faith and credit" as well as a "republican" form of government. In addition, as the Federalists were quick to point out, the prohibition of the passage of ex post facto laws (laws that were retroactive in *jeopardize the approval of the new Constitution.*

nature) and bills of attainder laws (laws that dictated prison sentences for accused who were not given a trial) and the prohibition of suspending the writ of habeas corpus (a guarantee of individual due process rights) gave individuals protection against a tyrannical federal government. Typically, the Federalists represented the upper class, bankers, and rich large-property owners. Their economic philosophy was clearly expressed throughout the Federalist Papers.

The Anti-Federalists, led by the newly emerging middle class, had George Mason and Richard Henry Lee as their chief spokesmen. In a rival publication to the Federalist Papers, *Pennsylvania Packet,* and *Letters from the Federal Farmer,* and through individual essays penned under the name of Brutus, they argued that the principles of the Declaration of Independence would be eroded by the new Constitution. They felt that the Constitution would firmly establish an economic elite and would create the potential for an abusive federal government, especially in the area of protecting individual rights. The Anti-Federalists insisted that a bill of rights had to be part of the new Constitution. Otherwise, a powerful president supported by the Congress could easily abuse the civil liberties of the individual. Additionally, the sovereignty of the states became a concern even with the guarantees provided. Nowhere was this argument more heated than in New York. The Anti-Federalists prevented the approval of the Constitution until Madison and Hamilton guaranteed that the first Congress would approve a bill of rights. Typically, the Anti-Federalists represented the farmers and the so-called common people. They rejected the elitist base represented by the Federalists.

Chapter 2 Review

SECTION 1: MULTIPLE-CHOICE QUESTIONS

1. Which statement(s) best reflects what the United States Constitution represents?
   I. The Constitution is a basic framework for the government.
   II. The Constitution is an explanation of the way government operates, assigning separate powers to each branch and guaranteeing citizens their rights.
   III. The Constitution is the supreme law of the land.

   (A) I only
   (B) III only
   (C) I and III only
   (D) II and III only
   (E) I, II, and III

2. John Locke's *Second Treatise of Civil Government* advocates
   (A) a divine monarchy.
   (B) rights for the minority.
   (C) majority rights.
   (D) natural rights.
   (E) democratic rule.

3. Which of the following statements best reflects the political philosophy established after the colonists achieved their independence?
   I. The former colonists eliminated property criterion for political office.
   II. The former colonists reocgnized the need for a strong executive.
   III. The former colonists believed that the states should become the dominant political and social force.

   (A) I only
   (B) I and II only
   (C) I, II, and III
   (D) III only
   (E) II and III only

4. When the Articles of Confederation were adopted, the nation's major concern was dominated by
   (A) slavery.
   (B) religious freedom.
   (C) equality for women.
   (D) political dominance by the central government.
   (E) economic issues.

5. Which of the following documents represents the first adopted Constitution for the United States?
   (A) Declaration of Independence
   (B) Bill of Rights
   (C) Articles of Confederation
   (D) Virginia Plan
   (E) Connecticut Plan

6. Which of the following statements best describes the Articles of Confederation?
   I. domination of the government by the states
   II. a national congress with one house and no executive
   III. no national court system
   IV. no ability of the central government to enforce the collection of taxes

   (A) I only
   (B) I and II only
   (C) I, II, and III only
   (D) I and IV only
   (E) I, II, III, and IV

7. Which of the following statements in the Federalist Papers referred to "the most common and durable source of faction"?
   (A) a new and emerging middle class
   (B) the absence of a strong national government
   (C) the unequal distribution of property
   (D) the abuse of minority rights
   (E) the powers given to the president

8. Madison believed that in order to prevent a "tyranny of the majority" the new government should include all the following EXCEPT
   (A) creating political institutions that could function with the consent of a majority.
   (B) limiting the president's term of office.
   (C) creating different branches of government with distinctive and separate powers.
   (D) creating a system of checks and balances.
   (E) limiting the ability of the electorate to vote directly for government officials except members of the House.

9. Complete the following statement:
   Even though the representatives to the Constitutional Convention came from different parts of the country and had differing economic status, they were able to agree to
   I. a series of political compromises.
   II. a Republican government for each state.
   III. the method to count slaves for representation purposes.

   (A) I only
   (B) I and II only
   (C) I, II, and III
   (D) II and III only
   (E) I and III only

10. Which statement reflects James Madison's point of view in the Federalist Papers regarding the consequences of unequal distribution of wealth?
    I. the formation of factions
    II. the probability of minority discontent
    III. the development of political parties

    (A) I only
    (B) II only
    (C) I and III only
    (D) I, II, and III
    (E) II and III only

11. Which of the following documents created a compromise that led to the formation of a bicameral legislature?
    (A) Articles of Confederation
    (B) Connecticut Compromise
    (C) New Jersey Plan
    (D) Virginia Plan
    (E) Three-Fifths Compromise

12. Which of the following statements reflects an action taken by the delegates to the Constitutional Convention?
    I. setting a date for the abolition of slavery in the North
    II. outlawing future importing of slaves
    III. setting a number for counting slaves for representation purposes

    (A) I only
    (B) II only
    (C) I, II, and III
    (D) I and III only
    (E) II and III only

13. The Federalists believed that a nation dominated by factions would lead to
    (A) a tyranny of the majority.
    (B) protection of minority rights.
    (C) a recognition that factions would be in the best interests of the country.
    (D) another revolution.
    (E) favorable economic growth.

Answers to Multiple-Choice Questions

1. **(E)** Type of Question: Definitional
This question, which is deceptively easy, usually creates problems for those students who don't read the entire question. Choice E is correct because the three statements listed all reflect what the Constitution represents.

2. **(D)** Type of Question: Generalization
You must know the content of Locke's *Treatise* to answer this question. The trick parts of the question are the choices that reflect the consequence of the correct answer. If natural rights are the philosophical basis of government, then it follows that minority rights are protected and there would be democratic rule. If you knew that Locke was a classical philosopher, you might get confused between the concept of natural rights and a divine monarchy.

3. **(D)** Type of Question: Sequencing a series of events
This question requires that you understand the sequence of events that took place after the colonists achieved their independence. You must recognize that the former colonists set up specific voting requirements based on property (Statement I). You also must realize that voting was still restrictive. The only correct choice was answer D, Statement III. The Articles of Confederation set up a political system where the states were the focal point of political power.

4. **(E)** Type of Question: Comparing and contrasting concepts and events
Even though slavery and the ineffectiveness of the central government were factors during the critical period, economic issues, specifically a depression facing the country (remember Shays' Rebellion), was the dominant concern. Religious freedom and equality for women were incorrect choices. Slavery and the role of the central government were issues decided by the Constitutional Convention.

5. **(C)** Type of Question: Chronological
Even if you were not sure of the chronology of the documents, only one of the documents is a constitution. The Connecticut Plan, although adopted, was only a part of the Constitution. The Declaration of Independence stated the philosophical basis of government, but its purpose was to outline the colonists' grievances against Great Britain. Even though much of the Declaration of Independence was eventually incorporated into the Constitution and Bill of Rights, it was not a constitution.
6. **(E)** Type of Question: Generalization
Being able to pick out more than one correct answer is a real advantage to answering this question. Even though it may seem highly unlikely that the Articles of Confederation would not incorporate a chief executive, a national court system, or a way for the federal government to collect taxes, these were all weaknesses of the Articles of Confederation. Most students have a general awareness that the Articles of Confederation stressed the domination of the states over the central government, but they do not realize the extent.
7. **(C)** Type of Question: Stimulus-based short quotation
This is an extremely difficult question because factions could be caused by a conflict between classes, the abuse of minority rights, or the absence of a strong national government. You have to understand the substance of the Federalist Papers to choose the unequal distribution of property (also it is an economic factor) as the best answer.
8. **(B)** Type of Question: Definitional
Drawing upon your knowledge of the Federalist Papers, you must choose the one answer that does not support the prevention of a tyranny of the majority. Even though factually, choice B is correct, the president's term was not limited until the Twenty-Second Amendment was ratified in 1952. Choice A refers to the provisions of the Constitution that provide for a two-thirds vote (i.e., overriding a veto, passing a treaty). Choice D is the foundation of the Federalist viewpoint, and choice E reflects the only branch of government that was voted directly at the time of ratification. The president is elected through the electoral college and the direct election of senators did not occur until the passage of the Seventeenth Amendment in 1913.
9. **(C)** Type of Question: Solution to a problem
The key to answering this question is realizing that each of the answers was included in the original Constitution. Statement II refers to each state being guaranteed a republican form of government. The method of counting slaves for representation purposes (Three-Fifths Compromise) is in fact one of the political compromises reached at the Constitutional Convention.
10. **(D)** Type of Question: Generalization
Even though the Federalist Papers talked a lot about factions, they also referred to what would happen as a result of factions. Minority groups and political parties evolved from the factions that existed during the critical period. Because *special interest groups* is a term used today, it may confuse some students. Also be careful when the first choice seems to be the obvious answer.

11. **(B)** Type of Question: Stimulus-based
After eliminating the Articles of Confederation, you are left with four choices that all relate to the drafting of the Constitution at Philadelphia. The Three-Fifths Compromise dealt with the issue of slavery. The New Jersey Plan and Virginia Plan both attempted to create a single house, the former based on equality of states and the latter based on population. The Connecticut Compromise incorporated both ideas into a bicameral legislature.
12. **(E)** Type of Question: Cause and effect relationships
This question tests your knowledge of the slave compromise. Besides having to know about the Three-Fifths Compromise, you also must know that a separate agreement that outlawed slave trade was reached in 1819. Choice I did not happen until the Thirteenth Amendment was passed.
13. **(A)** Type of Question: Cause and effect relationships
If you connected factions to a major aspect of the Federalist Papers and realized that a consequence of factions could well be a tyranny of the majority (again language used in the Federalist Papers), you should be able to eliminate choices B, C, D, and E.

SECTION 2: FREE-RESPONSE ESSAYS

According to the arguments raised in *The Debate on the Constitution*, the Constitutional Convention "charted the course of the bloodless revolution that created the government of the United States and the world's oldest working national charter."

Using the Federalist Papers and your knowledge of United States politics and government:

1. Explain how the authors of the Federalist Papers defined the character of the national government.
2. Illustrate the Federalist position regarding the creation of one of the branches of government.

Sample Student Response

Federalist No. 51 stresses the fact that federal government is stronger than a confederacy. It also suggests the proper game plan for the structure of government: the formation of three branches—executive (president), legislative (House of Representatives and Senate), and finally judiciary (Supreme Court). Madison had the idea that each branch would have separate powers. The branches should rely on each other but be able to check each other's power. The government would depend upon the people for their support as well as their input on how the government should be run. Once the federal constitution was put in place, it had the effect of, in some ways, supplanting the state constitutions, making the states conform to the central document. With all these elements coming together, a new republican government replaced the Articles of Confederation.

In Federalist No. 10, James Madison showed how factions caused the downfall of the government under the Articles of Confederation and discussed how similar factions could have a serious impact on the newly formed republic.

Madison explained that by setting up republican governments in the individual states of the union, factions based on local levels would be kept from taking control of the national government. He refuted the well-known argument that a republic could be extended only over a certain sphere of territory, which began with the writings of Montesquieu. He said that a large republic has two advantages over a small one: a greater number of worthy candidates for office and a larger electorate, which is more likely to select qualified candidates. This document clearly states that the main problem in government is factions: in a republic those who are most fit to rule do so as elected officials. Madison differentiates between a democracy and a republic. Republics regulate power differently; they also are brought together directly because territory and people are greater in a republic.

Perhaps the most prominent concern of the Anti-Federalists was the issue of a federal government becoming absolutely omnipotent. They favored states' rights above all others. By giving the states the jurisdiction to protect the rights of their citizens and the power to enforce legislature that applied specifically to different regions, the threat of the federal government superseding the rights of the states would be lessened.

In studying both the Constitution and the Federalist Papers, you find many topics related to the executive branch. They also relate to modern-day issues that symbolize the ideas that the framers originally had in mind. Presidential power is a very important part of our country's government. As the Federalist Papers pointed out, a weak and feeble executive who cannot lead will result in a bad execution of presidential powers and the government as a whole. If there is a weak president, then Congress is more influential and powerful. The ideas expressed in the Federalist Papers coincide with those found in the Constitution on many issues concerning the presidency. Through the power of the president as commander in chief, you can see the many characteristics in the Constitution that are derived from the Federalist Papers.

An idea that is covered in both the Constitution and the Federalist Papers is that of a civilian commander in chief being the president. The idea of asking Congress to declare war and develop a viable foreign policy is one of the most important duties carried out by the president. In the Constitution the clause reads, "The president shall be commander in chief of the army and navy of the United States, and of the militia of the several states when called into the actual service of the United States." Similarly, as reported in the Federalist Papers, the Continental Congress voted that the president should have the power to declare war and will act as commander in chief; however, in practice he has to gain approval from the Congress. This process limits the executive power but still allows for a large amount of control by the executive, which is what the Federalists wanted.

Evaluation of Free-Response Sample Essay

1. How well does the essay explain the character of the national government as defined by the authors of the Federalist Papers?
2. How does the essay illustrate the Federalist position regarding the creation of one of the branches of government?

1. The essay focuses on Federalist No. 51 and Federalist No. 10. Both Papers explain the character of the national government. Students could have used

any of the Federalist Papers that explained the basic principles of the new government created by the Constitution.

2. The second part of the essay specifically illustrates and explains how the founding fathers viewed the executive branch of government. By using this branch as the example, the student also connects the Papers to modern-day dilemmas faced by a president in relation to the principle of checks and balances.

SECTION 2: DATA-BASED FREE-RESPONSE ESSAY

It is agreed on all sides, that the powers properly belonging to one of the departments (branches of government) ought not to be directly and completely administered by either of the other departments. It is equally evident, that neither of them ought to possess, directly or indirectly, an overruling influence over the others in the administration of their respective powers. It will not be denied, that power is of an encroaching nature, and that it ought to be effectually restrained from passing the limits assigned to it. After discriminating, therefore, in theory, the several classes of power, as they may in their nature be legislative, executive, or judiciary; the next and most difficult task, is to provide some practical security for each, against the invasion of the others. What this security ought to be, is the great problem to be solved.

Federalist No. 47

Using the excerpt and applying the principles of government and politics:

Identify the relationship and meaning of the departments that Madison is referring to. Illustrate how this is still a problem today.

Sample Student Response

James Madison, in Federalist No. 47 refers to the separation of power that exists among the three branches of government—the president, Congress, and judicial. In the Constitution each branch has specific powers assigned to it. For instance the president as chief executive, in Article II, has the specific power of commander in chief. The Congress in Article I, having the legislative power, is specifically assigned the power to tax, coin money, support an armed force, and declare war. The judicial branch, in Article III, has a specific power of adjudicating specified conflicts and has the power of original jurisdiction regarding specified situations. Even though the powers assigned are specific, there is a very direct relationship among the branches through checks and balances. Even though the president is commander in chief, Congress has the power to cut off funds if they feel the president is overstepping his authority. The Supreme Court, through its power of Judicial Review (*Marbury v Madison* established this power) can declare acts of Congress unconstitutional. In Federalist No. 47, Madison urges the drafters of the Constitution to clearly identify and protect the powers of each branch of government.

The problem of the security against invasion of one branch of government by another has been both protected by checks and balances and has come close to creating constitutional crises for the country. One example of protecting the security of a branch of government is the Congress voting to pass the War Powers Act in order to protect its right to declare war. The War Powers Act was passed during the Nixon administration after Nixon secretly expanded the Vietnam War into Cambodia. It created restrictions on the president's ability to unilaterally commit U.S. forces for an extended period of time without the president being accountable to Congress. Because much as this act protected the security of the Congress, the concept came close to creating a constitutional crisis prior to the Gulf War and when Congress threatened to place major restrictions on President Clinton's authority in maintaining a U.S. force in Somalia. A second example of how the branches are protected from each other through their separate powers is the manner in which the Congress has the ultimate authority in approving the federal budget. Through its appropriations committees, Congress reviews the president's budget recommendations and passes a final budget. The Reagan budget proposal of 1981 is a good example of this process. Obviously, if the Congress goes to an extreme, the president through the veto can prevent a budget from being signed into law. In comparison, the budget battle of 1994 illustrated what can happen if compromise is not reached. Anytime that one party is investigating a president of the opposing party it increases the conflict between the branches. Whether it was Iran-Contra during the Reagan presidency or campaign finance abuses during the Clinton presidency, Congress asserted its power through hearings.

Evaluation of Data-Based Free-Response Sample Essay

1. How well did the writer explain the passage from the Federalist Papers and apply it to contemporary issues?

1. This data-based free-response question asks you to identify and explain the key points Madison made regarding the separation of powers of the three branches of government. The writer clearly demonstrates an understanding of what Madison is saying about the relationship of the departments, which in fact are the branches of government. The writer also draws from this passage the fact that Madison was making a strong argument for a clear-cut delineation of power among the three branches. In addition, once the powers have been defined, the author points out that Madison would make the argument that the autonomy of each branch must be protected through the concept of checks and balances. In the second part of the essay, the writer gives both foreign policy and domestic examples that support the ideas presented in the first part of the essay.

CHAPTER 3 The Constitution

Chapter Overview

After the United States Constitution was ratified in 1789, the future success of this young new republic hung in the balance. After struggling with the Articles of Confederation, the United States found in the Constitution a new opportunity to demonstrate that its form of limited government could work. By 1791 an additional ten amendments, the Bill of Rights, were ratified, fulfilling a promise made to the Anti-Federalists at the state ratifying conventions.

This chapter will explore in great detail the Constitution, the supreme law of the land. It will explain how this document is considered the key instrument of government and how it has evolved in its more than 200-year history. It is a practical document as well as a functional document. Each branch of government can lay claim to certain powers unique to their own function. The interrelationship among the branches is also established in the principle of checks and balances. The powers of the national government are defined. State governments are given legitimacy, and the delicate relationship between the states and federal government, known as federalism, is established. The rights of the citizens are clearly outlined in the Bill of Rights as is the ability of the people to exercise the right to vote. Limits are placed on both the federal government and the state governments.

If you look at the Constitution as a road map and drive through its avenues, you will discover that it is laid out in a manner that is clear, concise, and logical. It provides ample opportunity for the driver to take different routes and explore the heart and soul of the basis of government for the United States.

KEY TERMS

- Bicameral legislature
- Checks and balances
- Concurrent power
- Elastic clause
- Electoral college
- Enumerated powers
- Ex post facto laws
- Executive privilege
- Federalism
- Full faith and credit
- Implied power
- Inherent power
- Judicial review
- Preamble
- Privileges and immunities
- Reserved Power Amendment
- Separation of powers
- Supremacy clause
- Unwritten constitution
- Writ of habeas corpus

Longevity

The Constitution has been called an enduring and evolving document because it has stood the test of time.

Looking at the Constitution, you should be able to picture a document that is laid out simply and directly. From the clarity of purpose in the Preamble, to the organization and structure of the three branches of government, to the amending process, the Constitution provides for orderly and effective government.

The Preamble, starting with "We the People," defines the objectives of the Constitution:

- to form a more perfect union,
- to establish justice,
- to insure domestic tranquility,
- to provide for the common defense,
- to promote the general welfare, and
- to secure the blessings of liberty.

The fact that a reference is made to the longevity of the Constitution to future generations (posterity) indicates that the authors were not looking to make major revisions. They certainly hoped that the document would adapt to changing times.

The major factors creating longevity of the Constitution include

- the separation of powers of each branch of government,
- checks and balances including a recognition that a simple majority vote may not be enough of a check,
- a built-in elastic clause as part of Congress's power,
- a reserved power clause giving states power not delegated to the national government,
- rights guaranteed to the citizens,
- precedents and traditions creating an unwritten constitution,
- judicial review growing out of an interpretation of the power of the Supreme Court,
- an amending process, which is flexible enough to allow for change even though it involves more than a majority vote, and
- the inherent powers of the president.

Branches of Government

The organization of the Constitution separates the formal institutions of government.

The first three articles of the Constitution provide the basis of the organization of the government. Article I broadly defines the legislative powers of Congress. It splits the responsibility between a bicameral (two-house) legislature. The House of Representatives is defined first as the body most directly responsible to the people. The Senate, its make-up based on equal representation, joins in a partnership with the House in passing laws. The rules of impeachment of government officials are also outlined in Article I. It is interesting to note that there are subtle differences (which will be discussed later in this chapter) between the two bodies. The public's view of Congress has continued to deteriorate since the 1970s. In a poll conducted in July 2004, 53 percent of the people questioned were critical of the Congress. Yet in a 2003 poll, 65 percent of the people indicated that they would vote for their incumbent. Another related issue dealing with the organization of Congress is term limitations. The Supreme Court in 1995 in the case *Thorton v Arkansas* ruled that state-imposed term limits were unconstitutional, indicating that the only way congressional terms could be altered was through an amendment.

Article II determines the nature of the chief executive, giving responsibility to a president and vice president. Even though powers are not as specifically defined as in the legislative branch, the president's major responsibility is to administer and execute the public policies of the United States. The inherent power of the president, which includes those powers that the president exercises that grow out of the existence of the national government, expands the power of the presidency. By signing congressional legislation into law, the president assumes the responsibility of enforcing the laws of the land. Reference is also made to the president's authority in the area of foreign policy. This article also outlines the mechanics of the electoral college and determines its procedures in the case where a candidate does not receive a majority of the electoral votes. The article refers to executive departments, though it does not specifically mention the president's cabinet or the federal bureaucracy.

Article III outlines the nature of the judicial branch. It is interesting to note that unlike the first two articles, this article is the most vague regarding the qualifications of its members. It refers to one Supreme Court and the manner in which cases get there. But it does not give the Supreme Court the broad authority it has assumed. This authority of judicial review was given to the Court in the landmark case of *Marbury v Madison*. The scope of the court system is set in Article III, and the jurisdiction of the court system is defined. This article also defines treason, and provides for a range of penalties, including death, if a person is convicted of the crime. The only time that has happened was when Ethel and Julius Rosenberg were convicted of giving the Soviet Union information concerning the development of the atom bomb. They were tried and convicted of treason and executed after the Supreme Court denied their appeal.

By separating the three branches of government, it becomes apparent that the drafters of the Constitution were concerned with the delicate balance of power that would exist among the three branches of government. The Constitution neatly lays out the various powers of each branch of government without any reference to which of the branches should be the lead player.

Legislative Powers

Specific powers and qualifications granted to Congress guarantee the legislative process as well as create distinctive differences between the two houses of Congress that make the House more representative than the Senate.

The two houses of Congress created as a result of the Connecticut Compromise resulted in the establishment of a House of Representatives and a Senate. The House of Representatives is made up of 435 members based on the census taken every 10 years. There is approximately one House seat for every 650,000 people in each state. It also includes "shadow" representatives from the District of Columbia and Guam. Each state has a minimum of two senators and one representative. As a result of the Supreme Court decision *Baker v Carr*, the principle of "one man, one vote" was established. This decision created guidelines for drawing up congressional districts and guaranteed a more equitable system of representation to the citizens of each state. The Supreme Court has been asked to review some districts in the South drawn up to ensure racial representation.

In a highly controversial decision, the Court ruled in 1995 that a racially apportioned district in Georgia set up to comply with the Voting Rights Act of 1965 was unconstitutional based on the equal protection clause of the Fourteenth Amendment. In other situations, in order to rectify congressional boundaries, some state legislatures based on political affiliation created districts that favored the political party in power. This action became known as gerrymandering.

The House of Representatives is considered more representative than the Senate because of its size, term of office, and qualifications for office. The term of office for a representative is two years compared to six years for a senator. A person serving in the House has to be at least 25 years old, an American citizen for seven years, and an inhabitant of the state that the congressman represents. A senator, on the other hand, must be at least 30 years old, nine years a citizen of the United States, and a resident of the state that the senator represents. Many states have passed term limitations restricting the number of consecutive terms a representative can serve. In 1995, the Supreme Court ruled that these laws were unconstitutional.

When you look at the specific power of each house, you also can see how the House is "closer to the people." Besides the fact that senators were originally appointed by state legislatures, the House of Representatives is given the responsibility of starting all revenue bills and initiating the process of impeachment. During the impeachment hearings of Richard Nixon and Bill Clinton, the House Judiciary Committee passed impeachment charges. Nixon resigned before the Senate could try him, whereas Clinton was acquitted by the Senate. The Senate must also pass revenue bills and can certainly pass a different version, but it must wait for the House to pass its version of the bill. The Senate tries impeachment cases and, in the only two cases involving a president, after voting on articles of impeachment, failed to convict Andrew Johnson by one vote and acquitted Bill Clinton. The other major difference in the allocation of power between the two bodies is that the Senate has the responsibility of approving presidential appointments and treaties.

The common powers of the Congress are listed in Article I Section 8. These are the enumerated or delegated powers of Congress. They include the power to

- collect taxes, pay debts, and provide for the common defense and general welfare,
- borrow money,
- regulate commerce among the states (interstate commerce) and with foreign countries,
- establish uniform laws dealing with immigration and naturalization and bankruptcies,
- coin money,
- make laws regarding the punishment for counterfeiting,
- establish post offices,
- make copyright laws,
- establish federal courts in addition to the Supreme Court,
- define and punish piracy,
- declare war,
- raise and support armies and a navy, and
- create a national guard.

In this same section, implied powers are defined in the "necessary and proper" clause, which states that Congress has the power to "make all laws necessary and proper for carrying into execution the foregoing powers. . . ." This clause is also known as the elastic clause and is a major and significant power of Congress, granting the Congress the ability to interpret its lawmaking ability in a broad manner. Even though strict interpreters of the Constitution reject the extent of its elasticity, Congress has demonstrated an ability to change with the times. From the creation of the National Bank in the 1800s to the passage of the Brady Bill (establishing a waiting period for handgun purchase), congressional legislation, more often than not, reflects the tenor of the times.

Powers denied to Congress are the denial of the writ of habeas corpus, giving appeal protection to the accused; the passage of bill of attainder laws, which proscribe penalties without due process; and the passage of ex post facto laws, which take effect after the act takes place. In addition, Congress cannot pass export taxes or grant titles of nobility to its citizens.

The issue of how much power the Congress exerts in comparison to the other branches and whether it becomes an imperial Congress is the theme of Chapter 8, The Congress.

Executive Powers

Specific powers and qualifications granted to the executive department guarantee and define the role of the president as a central player in government.

Because of the unique qualities of the presidency, the qualifications for office are the strictest among the three branches. The president must be a natural-born citizen (unlike senators and representatives, who can be naturalized citizens), at least 35 years old, and a resident of the United States for at least 14 years. The source of power of the president comes from the language in Article II Section 1, "The executive power shall be vested in a president of the United States of America." The term of office is four years, limited by constitutional amendment to no more than two terms.

The president becomes a central and unique player in government as a result of the manner in which the definition of chief executive is stated. The only specific powers and duties listed in Article II Sections 2 and 3 include

- the power to act as commander in chief of the armed forces,
- the ability to obtain information from members of the executive branch,
- the power to grant pardons,
- the power to make treaties with the consent of the Senate,
- the power to appoint ambassadors, justices, and other officials with the advice and consent of the Senate,
- the power to sign legislation or veto legislation,
- the duty to give Congress a State of the Union report,
- the power to call special sessions of the Congress, and
- the inherent power of the president.

Even though there are far fewer powers and responsibilities listed for the president than for the Congress, because the president can interpret the role of the executive in a broad manner, the power of the president in modern times has increased more than the other branches. From the administration of Franklin Roosevelt and the implementation of his New Deal to the new world order of George Bush, the power of the president has been on the rise. As head of state, the visibility of the president in ceremonial areas far exceeds that of a congressman. The president is also considered the titular head of the political party in power and thus wields a great deal of power in relation to party appointments. The issue of whether the presidency is turning into an imperial presidency will be taken up in the Chapter 7, The Presidency.

The vice president's responsibility is also listed in Article II. The only stated responsibility of the vice president is to preside over the Senate and be the deciding vote if there is a tie vote. This occurred in President Clinton's first administration when Vice President Al Gore cast the decisive vote to pass the president's budget proposal. It was a key piece of legislation for the new president and set the course of his economic program. The vice president is also next in line to succeed the president in case of death and, as a result of the Twenty-Fifth Amendment, can take over the presidency if the president is disabled.

Article II also outlines the role of the electoral college, even though it does not use that term, in the election of the president. Simply stated, the electoral college consists of presidential electors in each state. The number of electors is based on the state's population. The states with the greatest population have the most electoral votes. When the voter casts a vote for president, in reality the vote goes to one of the presidential electors designated by the candidate in that state. The number of electors for each state equals the number of senators and representatives that state has in Congress. Thus the number can change based on the census. The candidate who receives the most votes receives all the electoral votes in that state. The candidate with a majority of the electoral votes is elected to office. The electors gather in Washington, D.C., in December and cast their ballots based on the results of the November election. If no candidate receives a majority of the electoral votes, the election of president is determined by the House of Representatives. Specific cases of how the electoral college affected presidential elections will be discussed in the Chapter 12, Nominations, Campaigns, and Elections.

More and more attention is paid to the president by the media and the public. Frequent opinion polls track the job approval of the president. The president's personal and public life has been placed under scrutiny. Presidential candidates like Gary Hart and sitting presidents like Richard Nixon, Ronald Reagan, and Bill Clinton have been criticized for personal as well as presidential acts. This microscopic view of the presidency, according to some political scientists, has weakened the institution.

Judicial Powers

Specific powers and responsibilities granted to the judicial department guarantee and define the role of the courts.

Unlike the legislative and executive departments, the judiciary has no specific qualifications for office. The Constitution in Article III states that judges shall "hold their offices during good behavior." The Supreme Court is the only court established by the Constitution. Lower federal courts are established by the Congress. Even the size of the Supreme Court is not defined. It has remained at nine sitting justices in modern times, although the number has been as low as five. Franklin Roosevelt attempted to pack the Court in 1937-after the Court ruled a number of his New Deal acts unconstitutional. Congress rejected the attempt. Terms of office for Supreme Court justices, by extension of the description of service, is life after appointment. Typically, Supreme Court justices

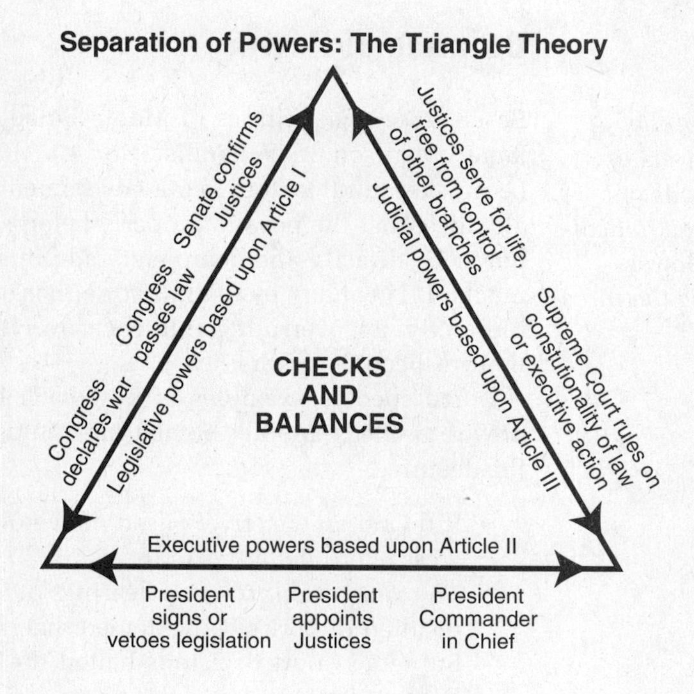

come from other federal judgeships. The appointment process has become more and more difficult as a result of close questioning by the Senate Judiciary Committee. Appointments by Richard Nixon were turned down. One of the most publicized confirmation hearings took place when George Bush sent Clarence Thomas's name to the Senate and he was accused by Oklahoma law professor Anita Hill of sexual harassment. In addition, nominees are also questioned on their attitudes regarding potential issues the Court may have to rule on, such as abortion. Nominees must tread a very thin line during this process and must not be too specific. They must avoid creating a conflict that would arise if they rule on a case they have already spoken about.

The major power given to the judicial branch is defined as "the judicial power (which) shall extend to all cases, in law and equity, arising under this Constitution, the laws of the United States, and treaties made. . . ." The real power, that of judicial review, has grown in importance throughout the history of the Court. Specific cases and the role of the Court in American life will be discussed in Chapter 9, The Judiciary. The Constitution describes cases through original jurisdiction that the Court can hear directly. The vast majority of cases heard in the Supreme Court are brought on appeal from state and federal courts. This is called appellate jurisdiction. Congressional law as well as presidential actions have also been taken up by the Supreme Court.

It is interesting to note that of the three branches of government, the Supreme Court has no direct responsibility or accountability to the voters. Sitting justices, once confirmed, decide on cases based on their own interpretation of the Constitution. The impact of the Supreme Court on policymaking has increased in modern times. Many Court experts point to the landmark decision of *Brown v Board of Education* as a turning point in the history of the Court.

Balance of Power

As a result of the separate powers of the institutions of government, a delicate balance of power exists among the three branches.

Based upon the writings of Montesquieu in *The Spirit of Natural Laws* and James Madison in Federalist No. 47, the concept of checks and balances became a central feature in our government. As Madison stated, "It is agreed on all sides, that the powers properly belonging to one of the departments ought not to be directly and completely administered by either of the other departments. It is equally evident, that neither of them ought to possess, directly or indirectly, an overruling influence over the others in the administration of their respective powers."

Some specific examples of how each branch of government has used its power to check another branch may be useful to illustrate the importance of this feature.

- Bill Clinton effectively used the veto 30 times while the Republican Congress overrode only 2 of them.
- The Senate confirmation hearings of Supreme Court nominee Robert Bork resulted in Bork's being denied that position.
- Supreme Court decisions halted the attempt by Congress to pass a Flag Desecration Act.
- The Senate rejected the 1999 Comprehensive Nuclear Test Ban Treaty.

As of 2004 there have been more than 2500 presidential vetoes of congressional bills. Congress overrode around 100 of them. The Supreme Court has found more than 100 acts of Congress unconstitutional. The Senate has refused to confirm 27 nominees to the Supreme Court and nine cabinet members. Other appointees have withdrawn as a result of sure Senate opposition. There have been several cases of congressional impeachment of federal judges.

The critics of checks and balances point to the potential of a constitutional crisis developing if one branch attempts to challenge the authority of another. For instance if the president as commander in chief deploys troops in a country for an extended period of time and ignores the provisions of the War Powers Act, an act of Congress that limits presidential authority to send armed forces to another country, there is a good possibility that an unresolvable conflict between the executive and legislative branches could occur. Typically, the Supreme Court does not get involved in adjudicating those kinds of conflicts. In fact, Congress has challenged the president's authority in such foreign policy conflicts in Somalia and Bosnia but has stopped short of placing restrictions on his authority.

Probably the most significant feature of checks and balances is that it consistently proves that our government is limited. Even though many political scientists point to the power of the presidency, even our most dominant presidents had to deal with the interests and concerns of the legislature and judiciary. Other features of our government and political system that have an impact on the size and function of the presidency include

- the role of political parties,
- the growth of the federal bureaucracy,
- the development and expansion of the information superhighway and the role of media, which puts a great deal of pressure on elected officials, and

- the emergence of the United States as the last superpower from the cold war, which places a tremendous responsibility on our country's leaders, forcing them to work together to solve major foreign policy problems.

Federalism

The organization of the Constitution defines the relationship between the states and the federal government.

Besides establishing a balance of power among the three branches of government, the Constitution also maps out the relationship between the federal government and the states in two articles and one amendment.

In Article IV, the term "full faith and credit" is used to describe the mutual respect and legality of laws, public records, and judicial decisions made by states. In effect, if Nevada has laws establishing rules for marriage and divorce, New York must recognize those laws as valid. In the case that state laws do conflict with each other, the law within each state is recognized as legal for that state. By extension, Section 2 recognizes that "the citizens of each state shall be entitled to all the privileges and immunities" of citizens in all the states. This provision is significant because it guarantees that the rights of a citizen in one state will be respected by other states. The phrase "privileges and immunities" becomes a significant phrase in the Fourteenth Amendment where states are told they cannot abridge the privileges and immunities of its citizens. States also recognize the legitimate claim to its fugitives through extradition. Finally, in Article IV Section 4, the United States guarantees every state a "Republican form of government." The use of the word *republican* is important. It suggests that every state must establish a limited representative government. It also guarantees that the United States will protect every state from outside attacks or internal strife.

Perhaps the most significant statement that defines the relationship of the federal government to the states is found in Article VI. The supremacy clause states that "the Constitution, and the laws of the United States . . . shall be the supreme law of the land." In effect this clause tells the states that they cannot pass laws or pursue actions that come into conflict with federal actions. It also refers to all state officials pledging their allegiance to the Constitution. The court case *McCulloch v Maryland* in 1819 established this precedent when Maryland was told it could not tax the National Bank.

The concept of federalism, the overall relationship between the federal government and state governments, is defined in the Tenth Amendment of the Constitution. It specifically tells the states that they have reserved powers. Powers not delegated to the government by the Constitution are given to the respective states. The application and interpretation of this relationship will be fully explored in Chapter 4, Federalism.

By including language that gives legitimacy to state governments and establishes a defined relationship among the states and between the federal government and states, a federal system of government is formed.

The principle of limited government is woven in the Constitution.

Throughout the entire document and in the amendments, both the federal government and state governments are told they do not have unlimited power. The three branches are limited through the system of checks and balances. The Congress is told that it cannot deny the writ of habeas corpus, the right of appeal, or pass bills of attainder, predetermined jail sentences imposed before a trial. There are, however, exceptions to some of these limitations. In times of national emergency, the Supreme Court has determined that the federal government can place major restrictions on the civil liberties of its citizens. During the Civil War, Lincoln suspended the writ of habeas corpus in the border states. During World War II, Roosevelt ordered Japanese-American citizens living on the West Coast to internment camps.

In fact the entire rationale for including a Bill of Rights in the Constitution was to reinforce this concept of limited government. From the opening words of the First Amendment, "Congress shall make no law respecting . . . ," to the due process guarantees of the Fifth and Fourteenth Amendments, the government is told that rights of its citizens must be protected. A further examination of this issue will be taken up in Chapter 5, The Bill of Rights and Civil Liberties.

This principle of limited government is the end extension of the philosophy of the Enlightenment thinkers—that government is created by the consent of the governed. If people have natural rights, it must also be assumed that government cannot take these rights away.

Provision for Changes

An enduring document, the Constitution provides for a process in which it can be amended to meet the needs of a changing society.

If you don't count the Bill of Rights and the prohibition amendments, the Constitution has been amended only 15 times. The revisions have been significant and help to strengthen, expand, and explain provisions found in the original document. The amendments can also be classified in five ways:

- creating additional power for the federal government such as the legalization of a progressive income tax (sixteenth),
- limiting power to the state governments such as prohibiting states from making laws that deny equal protection for its citizens (fourteenth),
- adding the right of popular sovereignty to various groups such as former slaves (thirteenth), women (nineteenth), and 18 year olds (twenty-sixth),
- taking away and adding to the power of the voter to elect public officials (seventeenth, direct election of senators; twenty-second, limiting presidential terms),
- changing the structure of government (twenty-fifth, presidential succession and disability).

There are two methods used to amend the Constitution. The one that has been used the most requires a two-thirds vote in both houses of Congress and ratification in three-fourths of the state legislatures. The second method, which has been only used once (prohibition), is when Congress must call for a national constitutional convention after a request is made by two-thirds of the state legislatures; then either three-fourths of the state legislatures must ratify the amendment or three-fourths of ratifying conventions held in the states must approve it. There may also be a time limit placed on the ratification of most amendments passed by Congress. One of the most debated constitutional amendments was the proposed Equal Rights Amendment, which would have guaranteed the equality of rights by the United States and every state based on sex. This amendment was given seven years and then an extension to pass in two-thirds of the state legislatures. It died in 1982, falling short of the necessary votes because of political pressure brought on by groups opposed to public funding of abortion and groups concerned about the effect that affirmative action would have on various labor laws. Other amendments such as the Twenty-Seventh Amendment, which places restrictions on Congress passing pay raises for themselves, took over 200 years to ratify! The vast majority of amendments including the Bill of Rights took less than a year to ratify.

If the Constitution is an enduring document, then one must project that other amendments to the Constitution are a real possibility. Such measures as a balanced budget amendment, a term limits amendment for Congress, the abolition of the electoral college, and a provision for equal rights for women and homosexuals have advocates. However, as was shown after the Supreme Court ruled in *Texas v Johnson* that flag burning is a legal form of political protest, the Congress failed to pass a constitutional amendment supported by President George Bush making it illegal to burn or desecrate the flag.

The Unwritten Constitution

The Constitution's flexibility and adaptability enable the creation of new instruments of government.

The unwritten constitution, as well as the Constitution's elasticity, adds to its viability. Political parties, the president's cabinet, special interest groups, political action committees, and the federal bureaucracy are important examples of traditions, precedent, and practice incorporated into our form of government.

The elastic clause and powers given to the Congress in the Constitution are perhaps the greatest instruments of change that Congress has at its disposal. From the passage of the Judiciary Act of 1789 to the creation of the many executive branch departments, Congress has used its power to expand the size of government. Congress has used the elastic clause to pass civil rights legislation, it has broadly interpreted the meaning of interstate commerce, and has passed a war powers act under its power to declare war.

The president has interpreted the Constitution to allow for executive privilege, the ability of the president to protect personal material. Because the definition of executive privilege is not written, President Nixon in trying to apply this to his Watergate tapes did not succeed in protecting the tapes from a congressional committee investigating potential obstruction of justice charges. The president also has turned into the person responsible for proposing a legislative agenda. It was Bill Clinton who made eliminating the nation's budget deficit a priority in 1992.

Neither the Constitution nor any law provides for the establishment of political parties, nominating conventions, primaries, and most of the political system we are used to. Even though the Federalist Papers warned of the danger of political factions and George Washington echoed that point of view, the influence of political parties has become a dominant feature of government. When the Republican Party can unite and not provide a single vote for the president's budget proposal, one can see the importance of party politics. When a party decides to start a filibuster (continuous debate) in the Senate to block the passage of legislation, this becomes an additional check.

The Supreme Court has also gone beyond the constitutional parameters in establishing precedent. From the *Marbury v Madison* decision establishing judicial review to *Roe v Wade,* which found a way constitutionally to protect the right of a woman to have an abortion, the Court forges new ground based on its interpretation of the Constitution.

Custom and tradition are an integral part of government. After executive departments were established by Congress, Washington announced the formation of cabinet positions. Congress then codified this concept as they approved additional cabinet positions. A two-term president was the accepted tradition until Franklin Roosevelt broke it. After he died, an amendment limiting presidential terms was passed, making the tradition a written component of the Constitution. After John Kennedy was assassinated, the presidential succession amendment was ratified. Little did the country realize that it would be used not as a result of an assassination, but rather because the country's vice president, Spiro Agnew, and, not much later, the president, Richard Nixon, would resign.

This chapter focused on the document that sets the course for American government and politics. An understanding of the Constitution makes your job easier as you look more closely at the specific workings of our government and political system.

Chapter 3 Review

SECTION 1: MULTIPLE-CHOICE QUESTIONS

1. Which of the following illustrates the effects that the system of checks and balances and separation of powers has on the legislative process?
   I. It does not favor the party in power.
   II. It can create gridlock.
   III. It usually makes change easy to come by.
   IV. It can encourage political compromise.

   (A) II only
   (B) I and II only
   (C) II and III only
   (D) I, II, and III only
   (E) II and IV only

2. The Constitution's writers carefully drafted a document that would create
   (A) strong states and a weak central government.
   (B) weakened power in the state and national government.
   (C) the ability to adapt to changing times.
   (D) a dominant national government with no active participation from the states.
   (E) an equal distribution of power between the states and national government.

3. Which of the following governmental bodies is most directly responsible to the electorate?
   (A) the House of Representatives
   (B) the Senate
   (C) the executive branch
   (D) the Supreme Court
   (E) the bureaucracy

4. The question of the constitutionality of a term limit for legislators imposed by a state constitution is based on which of the following arguments?
   (A) the state's ability to set time and manner of elections for state office holders
   (B) the fact that the Constitution sets the qualifications for congressmen
   (C) the ability of people to vote directly for senators and representatives
   (D) the ability of voters to create term limits for state office holders
   (E) the fact that the Congress is scheduled to vote for a term limits amendment to the Constitution

5. The practice of judicial review was first established by which of the following actions?
   (A) The Constitution gives life terms to Supreme Court justices.
   (B) Justices serve as long as they maintain good behavior.
   (C) The Supreme Court exercises judicial precedent.
   (D) The Supreme Court has appellate jurisdiction.
   (E) The Supreme Court can declare a congressional act unconstitutional.

6. Which of the following resulted after the Supreme Court made a ruling in *Baker v Carr*?
   (A) The principle of "one man, one vote" was established.
   (B) Congressional districts became gerrymandered based on political considerations.
   (C) Congressional districts were created as a result of racial considerations.
   (D) Congress modified existing voting districts for state offices.
   (E) Congress was able to modify congressional districts in states where there was not equal representation.

7. All the following are considered enumerated powers of the Congress EXCEPT
   (A) coining United States currency after the Constitution was ratified.
   (B) establishing inferior courts in addition to the Supreme Court.
   (C) setting up the first National Bank of the United States.
   (D) establishing uniform immigration laws.
   (E) regulating commerce among the several states.

8. The implied power clause in the Constitution has been described as the ability of Congress to take which of the following actions?
   (A) pass an assault weapons ban
   (B) withdraw funds allocated to troops in Haiti
   (C) pass a balanced budget amendment to the Constitution
   (D) raise the price of stamps to 34 cents
   (E) pass a law setting quotas for immigrants

9. In addition to the stated constitutional powers of the president, which of the following roles does he take on?
   (A) acting as head of his political party
   (B) granting pardons
   (C) making treaties
   (D) giving a State of the Union address
   (E) signing or vetoing legislation

10. Which of the following is the only stated constitutional responsibility of the vice president?
    (A) attending funerals of foreign dignitaries
    (B) taking on special tasks assigned by the president
    (C) presiding over the Senate
    (D) filling in for the president when he is out of the country
    (E) presiding over the House of Representatives

11. Which of the following represents a major reason why the electoral college was created?
    (A) It would encourage third-party candidates.
    (B) It would enable a select group of electors to cast the final vote for president and vice president.
    (C) It would encourage greater voter turnout.
    (D) It would give more power to the Congress in determining the outcome of presidential elections.
    (E) It would give the voters in smaller states a greater role in selecting the president and vice president.

12. All the following represent examples of limited government EXCEPT
    (A) the application of habeas corpus in criminal appeals.
    (B) the prohibition of passage of bills of attainder laws.
    (C) Congress not being allowed to pass ex post facto laws.
    (D) the inability of the president to grant titles of nobility.
    (E) the Reserved Power Clause of the Tenth Amendment.

13. All the following represent examples of the use of checks and balances EXCEPT
    (A) the 35 successful vetoes made by President George Bush.
    (B) the Senate rejection of the 1999 Comprehensive Nuclear Test Ban Treaty.
    (C) the Supreme Court ruling the Flag Desecration Act unconstitutional.
    (D) Congress passing the Crime Bill after a conference committee made changes.
    (E) Congress invoking the provisions of the War Powers Act.

14. Which of the following actions increases the power of the president?
    (A) a greater reliance on the states to solve problems
    (B) a greater reliance on the federal government to solve problems
    (C) the president having to work with a majority party in Congress different from his own
    (D) an increased investigative role by the media
    (E) the downsizing of the federal bureaucracy

15. The appointment of Supreme Court justices in the 1980s was characterized by
    (A) quick approval by the Senate of nominees.
    (B) rejection of the majority of appointees.
    (C) limited background checks of the nominees.
    (D) limited input from legal associations and special interest groups.
    (E) bitter confirmation battles over personal and philosophical positions of the nominees.

Answers to the Multiple-Choice Questions

1. **(E)** Type of Question: Definitional
Even though the concept of checks and balances and separation of power is basic, because the choices suggest multiple correct answers, students try to find more than one right answer. With the exception of statements II and IV, choice E, each statement about checks and balances is incorrect. Gridlock has become popularized, and it has been characteristic of the relationship between Congress and the president. Compromise also becomes a major tool in achieving change.
2. **(C)** Type of Question: Cause and effect relationships
On the surface, the choices suggest that the correct answer deals with federal-state relationships. Because each of those choices (A, B, D, and E) is factually incorrect and choice C is a correct generalization, you have a broadly defined question with a general statement.
3. **(A)** Type of Question: Comparing and contrasting concepts and events
Based on the responsibility of the Congress to initiate all appropriations bills, the size of the House compared to the Senate and the fact that the people do not directly vote for the president, Supreme Court justices, or appointments to the bureaucracy, the House is considered to be the one governmental body closest to the voter. Every two years, voters have the chance to change representatives, as they did in the 1994 mid-term election.
4. **(B)** Type of Question: Solution to a problem
Term-limits restrictions were argued before the Supreme Court in 1994, and the Court ruled in 1995 that they violated the Constitution.
5. **(E)** Type of Question: Cause and effect relationship
Judicial review was established as a result of the fact that the Court declared the Judiciary Act of 1789 unconstitutional in the case of *Marbury v Madison*.
6. **(A)** Type of Question: Cause and effect relationship
Baker v Carr established the concept of one man, one vote. The intent of the decision was not to create gerrymandered districts or districts created to satisfy racial considerations. The decision directed state legislatures, not the Congress, to draw up new districts and did not have any impact on voting districts for state offices.
7. **(C)** Type of Question: Definitional
You must know what the term *enumerated* means and then be able to apply the definition to a specific example that does not fit the definition. The classic example of an implied power of Congress arose as a result of the *McCulloch v Maryland* decision when the Court said that the creation of the second National Bank was constitutional based on the elastic clause.

8. **(A)** Type of Question: Definitional
Again, you must know the definition of implied power and then be able to apply it to a specific example. In this case, the passing of an assault weapons ban as part of a crime bill was implied as part of the general-welfare-legislating ability of Congress. The other choices are all examples of delegated powers in Article I Section 8.

9. **(A)** Type of Question: Comparing and contrasting concepts and events
Granting pardons, making treaties, giving a State of the Union address, and signing or vetoing legislation are all specific powers and/or responsibilities of the president listed in Article II of the Constitution. Taking on the role as head of a political party is an assumed responsibility that the president has taken on.

10. **(C)** Type of Question: Identification and analysis
The only constitutional function of the vice president is presiding over the Senate and casting tie-breaking votes. Of course, the vice president is also first in the line of succession if the president dies in office. The president can develop other roles for the vice president. For instance, President Clinton gave Vice President Gore the job of coming up with a report on how to reinvent government.

11. **(B)** Type of Question: Cause and effect relationship
The founding fathers doubted that the voters were wise enough to elect the president directly. Instituting an electoral college resulted in presidential electors being given the responsibility of actually voting for the president. These electors were chosen by majority vote, and the number of electors each state had was determined by its population.

12. **(E)** Type of Question: Definitional
In order to answer this question, you must know the definitions of limited government, habeas corpus, bill of attainder laws, ex post facto laws, and titles of nobility. The Reserved Power Clause gives states those powers not delegated to the federal government, thus expanding the power of the states.

13. **(D)** Type of Question: Identification and analysis
After thinking about the definition of checks and balances, you must apply it to the examples given in the question. The only choice that does not involve a direct check is the passage of the Crime Bill after it comes out of conference. The other choices are all excellent examples of checks and balances.

14. **(B)** Type of Question: Cause and effect relationships
Choices A, C, D, and E all limit the power of the president in dealing with solutions to different types of problems. If there is a greater reliance on the federal government to solve problems, you can conclude that a by-product would be an increased role on the part of the president.

15. **(E)** Type of Question: Sequencing a series of events
This question requires that you to know something about the nomination of Supreme Court justices in the 1980s. Even if you just knew about the Clarence Thomas nomination, you would be able to know through process of elimination that these nominations are characterized by bitter confirmation battles.

SECTION 2: FREE-RESPONSE ESSAY

Thomas Jefferson wrote, "The Constitution belongs to the living and not to the dead."

Explain how the Constitution has endured for over 200 years by:

1. Identifying a constitutional provision that supports Jefferson's statement and giving two examples of how the provision had an impact on public policy.
2. Describing the amending process and identifing a constitutional amendment passed since 1960 that illustrates the Constitution's flexibility.

Sample Student Response

The "necessary and proper," or elastic, clause in the Constitution allows the federal government to take action in areas not specifically delegated to it by the Constitution. This clause is most often invoked in justifying the federal government's action regarding issues not originally considered at the Constitutional Convention. A recent example of this clause's impact on public policy is the Brady Bill. The bill mandated a seven-day waiting period prior to the purchase of a gun, during which the purchaser's record would be checked for prior convictions and arrests. Throughout the nation's 200-year history, the "necessary and proper" clause has given the federal government the authority to do many things that it would have been impossible for it to do because the Constitution never specifically granted the government the authority to act with respect to those areas.

Another example of the application of the elastic clause is the healthcare debate, which has often centered on whether or not the federal government has the duty to pay for an individual's medical services. If one believes that, in this day and age, sufficient healthcare is necessary to ensure the welfare of individuals, then there is constitutional precedent stating that the federal government has an obligation and responsibility to fund healthcare.

The aspect of the Constitution that makes it so effective is its flexibility. The document, which is the cornerstone of our government, must be very pliable or else it will crumble under the constantly fluctuating pressure of public opinion.

The most dramatic way of changing the Constitution is through the formal amending process. This process is outlined in Article V of the Constitution. The amendment process has two stages: proposal and ratification. The first stage can be achieved in one of two ways. The first way is for an amendment to be proposed by a two-thirds vote of both houses of Congress. The second way is for an amendment to be proposed by a national constitutional convention requested by the legislatures of two-thirds of the states. The second stage of the amending process, ratification, can also be achieved in two possible ways. The first way is for an amendment to be ratified by the legislatures of three-fourths of the states. The second way for an amendment to be ratified is by a convention called for that purpose by three-fourths of the states.

The Twenty-Fifth Amendment (1967) to the Constitution is a perfect example of the Constitution's flexibility. When the Constitution was first drafted, it did not have any provisions for presidential disability or a vacancy in the office of the vice president. This amendment established a process whereby if the president becomes disabled, the vice president assumes the responsibilities of that office until the president can resume his duties. This provision has never been fully utilized, although when a president undergoes surgery (as Ronald Reagan did when he was shot), the vice president is technically in charge. The second part of this amendment was utilized after Richard Nixon's vice president, Spiro Agnew, resigned and Nixon appointed Gerald Ford. After Nixon resigned, Ford appointed the Governor of New York, Nelson Rockefeller, vice president with the approval of both houses of Congress.

Evaluation of Free-Response Sample Essay

1. Did the essay include an opening statement with appropriate references to Jefferson's statement?
2. Did the essay provide a clear indication of the direction it was going to take?
3. Did the essay provide supporting evidence, data, and facts?

1. After repeating Jefferson's statement, the writer provides a clear explanation of what Jefferson was referring to when he alluded to the fact that the Constitution was a living document. The ability to adapt to social, political, and economic changes becomes the central focus of the essay.

2. The essay uses the terms "flexibility" and "formal and informal changes" as the building blocks for the body of the essay. The reader is quickly able to see where the essay is going, and from the outset, the reader knows that the elastic clause and constitutional amendments are going to be used to answer the question.

3. The main body of the essay contains examples that illustrate how the elastic clause, which is properly defined, gives Congress the flexibility to meet the needs of the country. Such issues as gun control and healthcare are two good examples of the elastic clause in action. The essay's strength lies in the fact that the examples are specific and contemporary. Good examples are provided as the writer discusses the necessary and proper clause and constitutional amendments. There is also an adequate explanation of the process for amending the Constitution, as illustrated by the discussion of the Twenty-Fifth Amendment.

SECTION 2: DATA-BASED FREE-RESPONSE SAMPLE ESSAY

Read the following point of view based on the proposed change of rule voted on in the House of Representatives that would have required a three-fifths vote to enact laws that increase taxes:

When the Constitution departs from its basic commitment to majority rule it does so explicitly: A two-thirds vote of both houses is required to override a presidential veto. Two-thirds majorities are needed when the Senate approves a treaty or impeaches a president. But the Constitution never imposes a supermajority requirement for the passage of routine legislation, and never makes three-fifths, rather than two-thirds, a numerical hurdle of special significance.

Support or refute the validity of the proposal to impose a three-fifths vote to enact laws that increase taxes by giving three examples of how the proposal would impact the legislative process.

Sample Student Response

The passage represents a point of view that is clearly against a proposed rule for the House of Representatives that Speaker of the House Newt Gingrich wanted passed within the first 100 days of the 104th Congress as part of the Republican Party's Contract with America. The rule change would require a three-fifths majority for any measure that would raise taxes. The author points out that no other supermajority, which would have a direct cause-and-effect relationship on a law passed, exists in the House. Any attempt to impose such a rule would be unconstitutional and should be part of a broader constitutional amendment such as a balanced budget amendment. That amendment would require a two-thirds approval of each house and three-fourths of the states.

Examples that support this perspective include FDR's attempt to pack the Supreme Court. Even though the specific number of Supreme Court justices is not specified in the Constitution, when FDR tried to get Congress to increase the size of the Court, his proposal was rejected soundly. The same principle applies in this instance. Speaker of the House Newt Gingrich suggested that since the Constitution is silent about the rules the House can adopt, and since the House has the responsibility to initiate all appropriations measures, it would be legal to implement a three-fifths rule. This rule would also come close to constitutional supermajorities such as impeachment, approval of treaties, and overriding a presidential veto. These rules are all specified by the Constitution. Only rules such as debate and discussion can be changed by the House. The Senate filibuster requiring a three-fifths vote to impose cloture is an example of a legal rule adopted by the Senate.

The clear consequence of the three-fifths rule adoption would be to add an additional requirement to the passage of legislation. Tax hikes, although not popular, may be necessary for programs to continue to exist. A 60 percent majority would add an additional criterion to the lawmaking process and make it virtually impossible to pass legislation that would increase taxes, thus limiting the ability of the Congress to pass other types of legislation that under a balanced budget amendment would not be allowed. Hypothetically, the rule could also limit the ability of the House to lower taxes because any tax cut would also have to be accompanied by other kinds of spending cuts. Thus, the rule would go beyond its intent of applying only to tax hikes. Lastly, if this rule is passed, it is a logical assumption that other kinds of rule changes impacting on other kinds of legislation could also be adopted by either the House or Senate.

The intent of the rule change probably became moot when President Clinton and the Republican majority reached an agreement in 1997 to balance the budget by 2002. Within the context of the agreement, both sides agreed to a $135 billion tax cut over the five-year period. There was also an implicit understanding that any spending programs would have to be offset by other spending cuts, thus making the three-fifths rule unnecessary.

Evaluation of Data-Based Free-Response Sample Essay

1. Was the author's point of view clearly presented and does it go beyond summarizing the article?
2. Were there adequate examples given to support the conclusions?
3. Were there specific examples that gave implications if the rule was adopted?

1. The nature of this data-based free-response question is hypothetical. The author is speculating that a proposal made by Representative Gingrich may be unconstitutional. The writer states that up front and gives a concise explanation of the nature of the proposal. In addition to the underlying solution to the writer's point, the balanced budget amendment is refuted as part of the response.

2. The writer goes back to Franklin Roosevelt's attempt at court packing to give an example that is similar to the Gingrich proposal—using an unspecified part of the Constitution to create constitutional change without going through the amendment process. The writer contrasts the three-fifths proposal to other sections in the Constitution that require a two-thirds majority. The obvious point the writer is making is that if the authors of the Constitution wanted a three-fifths vote to pass tax hikes, it too would have been included in the original Constitution.

3. The logical extension to the passage of the three-fifths rule would be the difficulty of getting tax hikes passed. Additionally, and probably the most important point, other kinds of legislation affecting spending would also be impacted by this rule. A supermajority, be it a filibuster or an override of a veto, makes passing legislation much more difficult. Be careful when you read the stimulus and the questions. It would be very easy to read the question incorrectly and suggest that a three-fifths rule would make it easier rather than more difficult to pass a tax hike. A crucial point is that if other kinds of spending, such as social programs, are going to continue, there may be a need for tax hikes to maintain them. With a three-fifths rule, these programs could also be cut because there would be no way to balance the budget or lower the deficit without a tax hike.

CHAPTER 4 Federalism

Chapter Overview

Federalism, the division of power between the federal government and state governments, has been a central and evolving feature of our system of government. Political scientists also refer to this relationship as one where the federal government is divided among various levels of local government. This chapter will explore the various levels of government, their individual powers, their shared powers, and the historical and constitutional bases of federalism. It will also look at fiscal federalism, the manner in which the federal government offers federal assistance through different kinds of grants to state and local governments.

Advocates of a strong federal system believe that state and local governments do not have the sophistication to deal with the major problems facing the country. They feel that local politicians are provincial in their point of view and would advocate sectional issues that do not take into account the interests of an entire nation. People favoring a strong federal system also point to the inability of state and local governments to support the vast programs without an extensive tax base. They also feel that an elitist group would gain control and ignore the needs of the minority.

Critics of a strong federal system point to the fact that local leaders are most sensitive to the needs of their constituents. They also feel that states have a better ability to develop public policy that can be supported by a broad tax base. And critics point to the many demands made upon local governments by the federal government in order for the states to receive financial aid from the federal government.

Through this debate you can see how important the relationship among levels of government is. It can affect the kind of political participation that exists. It can determine the kind of public policy that is developed and implemented. Such issues as a national drinking age, a national speed limit, and consistent emission standards in every state have emerged in the debate over

KEY TERMS

- Block grants
- Categorical grants
- Commerce clause
- Competitive federalism
- Cooperative federalism
- Creative federalism
- Devolution
- Dual federalism
- Fiscal federalism
- Funded mandates
- Layer cake federalism
- Marble cake federalism
- *McCulloch v Maryland*
- New federalism
- Unfunded mandates

which level of government is best suited to solve the problems facing the country. Additionally, after the Republicans won back control of Congress in 1994, the issue of devolution of federal power, returning the balance of federal-state responsibilities back to the states, emerged in the name of unfunded mandates, those regulations passed by Congress or issued by regulatory agencies to the states without federal funds to support them.

Local Governments

Federalism organizes a country's government, taking into account the needs of local levels of government.

Compared to other means of dividing power, federalism establishes a unique working relationship with the other levels of government and its people. Neither component can abolish or alter the other single-handedly. On the other hand, a unitary system of government centralizes all the power, and a confederation decentralizes all the power. Most parliamentary governments like Great Britain and France are unitary. Power can be taken away from the local unit by the central authority. The former Soviet Union, after its breakup, formed the Russian Confederation. The United States had a confederation, under the Articles of Confederation, that failed after a few short years in existence. The loosest confederation that exists on the international scene is the United Nations. The advantage of the federal system over a unitary system and confederations is that there is a distinctive line drawn between what is in the purview of the central government versus what local governments are concerned with. The central government is concerned with broader issues affecting the entire country such as foreign policy, interstate matters, and immigration. Local governments are concerned with matters that have a direct impact on the daily lives of their citizens such as motor vehicle laws, garbage, education, and public health and welfare. Shared interests involve methods of raising revenues and the creation of a criminal justice system as well as common spending programs. Public policy is developed by both state and federal legislation. Yet, at times, the distinction between which policies are federal and which should be developed by the states becomes cloudy.

Between the operations of the federal government and local governments, our lives are deeply affected by a federal form of government. The sheer number of governments that exist nationwide illustrate the complexity of the federal system. In 1997, based on a census of governments by the United States Department of Commerce, over 83,000 governments including state, county, municipalities, towns, villages, and school districts existed in the United States. Just trace what this means for the average citizen. If you are concerned with the education of your child, you must be aware of the local requirements set up by your town's school board, and you have to support the school district through some kind of tax system. The state government may set up minimum graduation requirements and laws affecting the certification of teachers. The national government may offer states and local districts aid if the districts meet national standards.

In 2001 Congress passed the "No Child Left Behind Act." According to the Department of Education, "The NCLB Act, incorporates increased accountability for states, school districts, and schools; greater choice for parents and students, particularly those attending low-performing schools; more flexibility for states and local educational agencies in the use of federal education dollars; and a stronger emphasis on reading, especially for our youngest children."

History of Federalism

The historical foundation of federalism was established through the writings in the Federalist Papers and early Supreme Court decisions.

Even before the Constitution was ratified, strong arguments were made by Alexander Hamilton, John Jay, and James Madison in the Federalist Papers urging the inclusion of a federal form of government to replace the failed confederation. In Federalist No. 9 Hamilton states, "This form of government is a convention by which several smaller states agree to become members of a larger one, which they intend to form. It is a kind of assemblage of societies that constitutes a new one, capable of increasing, by means of new associations, until they arrive to such a degree of power as to be able to provide for the security of the united body." Those who feared that the federal government would become too strong were assured by Madison in Federalist No. 14 that "in the first place it is to be remembered that the general government is not to be charged with the whole power of making and administering laws. . . . The subordinate governments, which can extend their care to all those other objects which can be separately provided for, will retain their due authority and activity." These excerpts illustrate the fact that a federal form of government was central to the success of the new Constitution. The Anti-Federalists tried to counter these arguments using a strategy suggesting that a central government would be unable to recognize the needs and interests of local governments. According to the writings found in the *Debate on the Constitution,* Brutus writes, "in a Republic the manners, sentiment and interests of the people should be similar. If this be not the case, there will be a constant clashing of opinions; and the representatives of one part will be continually clashing against those of another."

After the Constitution was ratified and the new federal form of government was formed, the new government established lines of authority defining its power structure. By 1819 the first real challenge to the authority of the United States by individual states took place in the case of *McCulloch v Maryland.* The issue revolved around the right of Maryland to tax paper currency needed by a branch of the United States National Bank located in that state. The bank was established by Congress using the elastic clause of the Constitution. In one of a series of landmark decisions, the Supreme Court, under the leadership of John Marshall, ruled unanimously that the "power to tax involves the power to destroy." It reasoned that because the United States had the right to coin and regulate money it also had the right to set up a National Bank to do this under the "necessary and proper" clause. After the bank was created, the laws protecting it were supreme; therefore, Maryland could not tax the federal institution. In another case involving a conflict over a national license versus a state license to operate a steamboat in the waters between New York and New Jersey, the Supreme Court also pointed to the supremacy clause in its ruling. In *Gibbons v Ogden* (1824), the inventor of the steamboat, Robert Livingston, granted a license sanctioned by New York State law giving Ogden the exclusive rights of navigation. Gibbons received his license from the Congress. The Supreme Court, using the interstate commerce clause, ruled that the federal license was valid because there was a flow of commerce between the states. In a third case, *Fletcher v Peck* (1810), the Court ruled unconstitutional a Georgia state law dealing with the sale of land as a result of illegal actions on the part of the Georgia legislature. This case established the principle that the Supreme Court had the right to review state laws. Both the early writings in the

Federalist Papers and the Supreme Court decisions under the Marshall Court set the future course of federalism.

Dual Federalism

The traditional theory of dual federalism evolved from a constitutional basis.

As was established in Chapter 3, the Constitution provides for the rules of the federal system by giving delegated powers to the federal government and reserved powers to the states. This dual federalism became the first type of relationship for the United States. If you picture two intersecting circles, you will be able to get a clear picture what dual federalism represents.

Dual federalism existed historically to 1930. From the outset, when Congress made the determination to admit new states, it offered them a partnership. From the Louisiana Purchase to the pursuit of Manifest Destiny, as our country's borders expanded to the West Coast, every state admitted knew the conditions. However, one key event brought up the issue of what kind of federal government we would have—the Civil War was fought to preserve our federal system of government. Its background was sectionalism, a battle over states' rights, especially dealing with the issues of slavery and tariffs.

DUAL FEDERALISM: THE CIRCLE THEORY

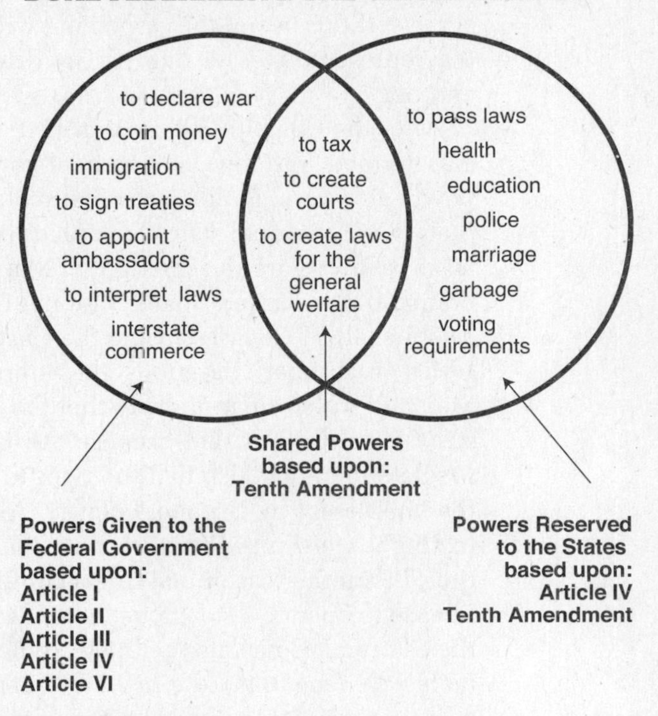

Layer Cake Federalism

An extension of dual federalism developed after the Civil War. It became known, according to political scientist Morton Grodzins, as layer cake federalism. It was a federalism characterized by a national government exercising its power independently from state governments. Following a more traditional approach, layer cake federalism was constitutionally based, and each level of government tried to exercise its own control over its own sphere of influence. After the Civil War, with the passage of the Thirteenth Amendment in 1865, Fourteenth Amendment in 1868, and Fifteenth Amendment in 1870, the federal government attempted to exert more of an influence on state governments. Reconstruction dictated this approach. The Thirteenth Amendment abolished slavery; the Fourteenth Amendment made the slaves citizens, defined the nature of citizenship, guaranteed citizens due process of law, and directed the states to treat its citizens under the "equal protection of law." The Fifteenth Amendment gave the freed slaves the right to vote. However, the eventual incorporation of the Fourteenth Amendment rights did not take place until well into the twentieth century. As late as 1896 the Supreme Court ruled in *Plessy v Ferguson* that Southern states had the right to impose separate but equal facilities on its citizens. Even the federal civil rights acts of the 1870s did little to affect the life of the freed former slaves.

Marble Cake Federalism

While it may sound contradictory, a cooperative federalism developed during the New Deal and lasted until the Great Society, resulting in greater growth of the federal government. Political scientists compare it to a marble cake.

If the federal government's relationship with the state governments could be described as a layer cake in the nineteenth and early twentieth centuries, then with the onset of the New Deal, federalism could be classified as a marble cake. Think of the two circles pictured on page 88 with bits and pieces of marble. The federal government becomes more intrusive in what was typically the domain of state governments.

During the New Deal, President Roosevelt needed drastic action to solve the problems brought on by the Great Depression. Establishing federal relief and recovery programs such as the Agricultural Adjustment Act (AAA) and the National Recovery Act (NRA), and reforming such localized institutions as banks with the Federal Deposit Insurance Corporation (FDIC) resulted in a much greater involvement on the local level by the federal government. Public work programs such as the Civilian Conservation Corps further brought the federal government into cities. Public policy became more of a sharing between the federal and state levels of government. The national government would provide the money; state governments would administer the programs. There were critics of these efforts. New Deal programs such as the AAA were declared unconstitutional by the Supreme Court.

Following the New Deal, cooperative federalism increased further during and after World War II. When the country geared up for a wartime economy, the federal government, through a rationing system, had to direct the citizens regarding essential services. In addition, "Rosie the Riveter" left her traditional home and became part of the massive war effort. Immediately following the war, the federal government responded to the needs of the returning soldiers with the GI Bill of Rights. Especially with the growth of the suburbs and the development of the country's infrastructure, both the state and federal governments began moving toward a cooperative approach to solving common problems.

Creative Federalism

Creative federalism during the Great Society increased the marble cake approach of intergovernmental relations.

The Great Society of Lyndon Johnson provided an even greater reliance on federal programs. Such actions as Medicare, Medicaid, the War on Poverty, and increased civil rights legislation forced the states to rely more heavily on federally funded programs. It also created an era of further cooperation among the many levels of government. The following components describe this creative approach to federalism:

- sharing the costs between the national and state governments for programs that typically would fall under the purview of state control,
- guidelines and rules set down by the federal government in order for the states to reap the benefits of federally funded programs,
- providing for the dual administration of programs such as Medicaid, which has a shared approach financially as well as administratively.

According to a survey conducted by the Advisory Commission on Intergovernmental Relations, titled Significant Features of Fiscal Federalism, in 1977–1978 federal aid contributed an average of 25 percent of the operating budgets of all the state and local governments in the country. In some cities like Louisville, Kentucky, 41 percent of its annual expenditures came from some kind of federal aid program. The major impact of marble cake federalism was that it became extremely difficult to determine where the responsibility of the federal government ended and the role of the state governments began.

Competitive Federalism

Competitive federalism under Nixon in the 1970s and Reagan and Bush in the 1980s reversed the marble cake nature, creating a "new federalism," where the states were given more responsibility.

When Richard Nixon proposed a series of measures aimed at decentralizing many of the Great Society programs of Lyndon Johnson, he dubbed his program "the new federalism." This theme was later picked up by Ronald Reagan in 1980 and became the hallmark of his administration. The aim of competitive federalism was to offer states pieces of the marble cake but to have them accept it with conditions and with a promise to develop programs on their own. Federal orders in the Equal Opportunity Act of 1982 mandated compliance by the states under the threat of criminal or civil penalty. A second example was the placement of restrictions on other federal programs if a state did not meet the criteria of a specific program. Over 60 federal programs ranging from civil rights to the environment have this requirement. A third example is crossover requirements. If a state is going to receive federal money, it must agree to do something in return. For instance, under the Emergency Highway Energy Conservation Act of 1974, states had to agree to limit highway speed limits to 55 mph if they wanted to receive funding for highway repair. Additionally, under this competitive new federalism, states were forced to create their own standards of compliance based on federal legislation. The Clean Air Act of 1970 set national standards for air quality but directed the states to implement the law and enforce it.

During the 1980s the scope of federal programs aiding local interests under this kind of federalism was reduced dramatically. The effect of this reduction has varied from state to state. However, when there is a natural disaster such as Hurricane Andrew in Florida in 1992, the great midwestern floods in 1993, or the Los Angeles earthquake in 1994, the national government responds with massive federal aid to these localities without any strings attached.

Fiscal Federalism

Fiscal federalism, through different grant programs, slices up the marble cake into many different pieces, making it even more difficult to differentiate the functions of the levels of government.

The development of federalism since the New Deal has been fiscal in nature—that is how much funding is appropriated by the federal government to the states, under what conditions, and what the states can do with these funds.

Fiscal federalism can be classified in three major program areas: categorical grants including project and formula grants, block grants, and revenue sharing. They are usually aimed at assisting the states in areas of health, income security, education, employment, and transportation. A categorical grant is defined as federal aid that meets the criteria of a specific category and has specific criteria attached to them. These criteria can range from nondiscriminatory practice to minimum wages. The two types of categorical grants that are given are project grants, which are based on competitive applications by states and individuals, and formula grants, which are based on specific formulas developed by Congress. These grants have an impact on such areas as families with dependent children and nutrition programs. Block grants are a form of federal aid with far fewer strings attached. They go to local communities for specific purposes, and the states decide where and how to spend the money. Along with revenue sharing, which gives money directly to the states with no strings attached, these two forms of fiscal federalism were vastly reduced under Ronald Reagan and George Bush.

An example of the block grant concept implemented during the Clinton administration was welfare reform. After vetoing the Republican-sponsored welfare reform proposal, President Clinton ultimately signed into law a far-reaching welfare reform bill in 1996. This law transferred the responsibility of welfare to the states. The federal government eliminated the entitlement and gave block grants to the states. The states then developed their own programs to move people from welfare to work within a five-year period.

The whole issue of state reliance on federal grant money raises serious questions regarding the amount of independence the states want from the federal government. If a state can achieve a better welfare system or healthcare system than a national healthcare or welfare program, why should the state be burdened by federal mandates? In addition, once a state or locality is used to federal funds, what happens when that particular aid program is cut in the name of reducing deficit spending? And with each set of federal requirements, how much larger will the federal bureaucracy grow? These questions point to an unclear future of federalism based on fiscal arrangements.

Federal mandates force states to bow to the dictates of the federal government in order to get aid.

In answering the questions regarding the use of federal grants, you should have a broad understanding of the overall purposes of the grant and mandate programs. The overall objective is to provide the states and localities with money they normally would not get. This would have the effect of reducing the fiscal burden on the states. In return, the federal government is able to achieve national goals they set in specific areas like education or helping minorities. The federal government through these kinds of grants can direct where this money goes and earmark it to those states with a poorer population. The money could also be used by a target audience with experts controlling the allocation of money received. The end result would be the development of many programs by state and local agencies without creating massive government bureaucracy.

What is not taken into account in these objectives is the politics of grantmanship. Typically the Republican Party in the 1980s and 1990s favored this approach, whereas many "old" Democrats still yearn for the days of the Great Society. "New Democrats" (those Democrats who hold a centrist position, such as President Clinton) were somewhat more realistic, taking a middle of the road approach toward mandates. The other factor is that, to a large extent, the public at large does not directly see the benefits of these programs. They feel that the federal government is intruding on their everyday lives, and many people in surveys taken say that they resent big government.

Future of Federalism

Since 1944 federalism has been moving toward devolution, the return of power to the states.

After the election of 1992, deficit reduction became a primary goal of President Clinton. After his budget proposal was approved by Congress, it became apparent that fiscal federalism and grant programs would be greatly affected by cutbacks in the federal budget. Even so, the trend seemed to support grants based on specific federal requirements. The move toward national educational standards was supported by a number of federal grants to school districts willing to accept the concept.

In addition to budget constraints, the Supreme Court has played a role in defining the extent to which the federal government can dictate the contemporary nature of federalism. In 1976 in *National League of Cities v Usery*, in a 5–4 decision, the Court ruled that the federal minimum wage and maximum hours of the Fair Labor Standards Act could not be extended to state and local government employees. In 1985 the Court reversed itself in *Garcia v San Antonio Metro*. Again in a 5–4 decision, the Court ruled that Congress, not the Court, had the right to determine which actions of the states could be regulated by the federal government, the Tenth Amendment notwithstanding. In 1988 in *South Carolina v Baker*, the Court again affirmed *Garcia v San Antonio Metro* and ruled that federal minimum wage standards could be applied to state employees. Yet, in one of the most controversial areas, abortion, the Court in *Casey v Planned Parenthood* allowed the states to pass laws restricting the unchecked right of women to have abortions. The Rhenquist Court has reflected the changing nature of federalism. It has affirmed the ability of the federal government to pass along programs to the states, yet it has also made it clear that, in areas such as abortion and carrying out the death penalty, states can and should act on their own. In one of the most interesting decisions the Court made, *United States v Lopez* in 1995, the Court, in a 5–4 decision, ruled that the Federal Gun Control Act prohibiting the possession of a gun within 1000 feet of a school was unconstitutional based on a misuse of federal authority. The Court has also limited the power of the federal government to enforce provisions of the Americans with Disabilities Act during the last decade.

The future of federalism seems unclear. After the election of 1994, the Republican Contract with America clearly signaled a return to a more traditional approach now called "devolution." This trend continued as the Republicans maintained their majority in both houses in the 1996 election. Such measures as welfare reform, a balanced budget amendment to the Constitution, and regulatory reform were introduced with the explicit purpose of downsizing government and returning power to the states. Congress passed an Unfunded Mandates Law that placed major restrictions on Congress and the executive branch regarding passing legislation and regulations that had a price tag for the states. In fact states challenged the Motor Voter Act of 1993 as an unfunded mandate placing an unfair fiscal burden on the states. California refused to appropriate the funds necessary to implement it, and the Justice Department brought the state to court. The courts, however, ruled that California must abide by the provisions of the law. Other parts of the contract were passed by one or both of the houses but not signed into law by the president. But the message of the election was clear—federalism was again undergoing a major transformation that will last well into the twenty-first century, and with the election of George W. Bush in 2000, the trend of devolution was high on their agenda.

Chapter 4 Review

SECTION 1: MULTIPLE-CHOICE QUESTIONS

1. Which of the following represents the theoretical definition of federalism?
   (A) a division of power between the federal government and state governments
   (B) a strict separation of power between the federal government and state governments
   (C) a division of power between the federal government and state governments where the power emanates from the states
   (D) a singular relationship that is characterized by control emanating one way from a central government
   (E) an equally shared power relationship among the branches of government

2. Advocates of a strong federal system believe in all the following EXCEPT
   (A) state and local governments do not have many of the resources necessary to deal with the problems facing the country.
   (B) local politicians are provincial in their point of view.
   (C) state and local governments cannot support the vast programs necessary to support citizens.
   (D) local leaders are more suited to solve problems than national leaders.
   (E) factions would be more likely to gain control in a country dominated by local interests.

3. According to the writings of the Federalist Papers, which of the following reflects a major reason for the support of a federal system?
   (A) Local governments are best suited to meet the needs of the majority interests of the country.
   (B) Local governments will maintain their authority and will be able to care for their citizens.
   (C) The central government is best suited to recognize the needs and interests of local governments.
   (D) There will be a constant clashing of opinions between the interests of the local and federal governments.
   (E) Factions would be strengthened by the formation of a federal system of government.

4. All the following Supreme Court cases dealt with the issue of federalism EXCEPT
   (A) *Gibbons v Ogden.*
   (B) *Marbury v Madison.*
   (C) *McCulloch v Maryland.*
   (D) *Barron v Baltimore.*
   (E) *Fletcher v Peck.*

5. The constitutional provision used in the Supreme Court case *McCulloch v Maryland* was:
   I. the "necessary and proper" clause.
   II. the supremacy clause.
   III. the interstate commerce clause.

   (A) I only
   (B) II only
   (C) I and II only
   (D) II and III only
   (E) I, II, and III

6. The constitutional basis of dual federalism can be found in
   (A) the "necessary and proper" clause.
   (B) the Tenth Amendment.
   (C) the elastic clause.
   (D) the implied power provision.
   (E) the enumerated powers.

7. Which general area of policy is generally left up to the states?
   (A) foreign policy
   (B) military policy
   (C) relations among the several states
   (D) health and welfare
   (E) immigration

8. Which general area of policy is generally left up to the central government?
   (A) health
   (B) interstate commerce
   (C) education
   (D) police
   (E) voting requirements

9. Which kind of federalism best describes an autonomous relationship between the states and national government?
   (A) cooperative federalism
   (B) creative federalism
   (C) layer cake federalism
   (D) fiscal federalism
   (E) marble cake federalism

10. All the following are characteristics of marble cake federalism EXCEPT
    (A) there are mingled responsibilities and blurred distinctions between the levels of government.
    (B) the federal government becomes more intrusive in state affairs.
    (C) there is a greater sharing of responsibilities between the federal and state levels.
    (D) the national government exercises its power independently from state governments.
    (E) there is greater cooperation between the federal and state governments.

11. Creative federalism of the Great Society was characterized by
    I. shared costs between the national and state governments.
    II. guidelines and rules set down by the federal government.
    III. singular administration of programs.

    (A) I only
    (B) II only
    (C) I and III only
    (D) I and II only
    (E) I, II, and III

12. Which historical period represents the introduction of competitive federalism?
    (A) the Civil War
    (B) the New Deal
    (C) World War II
    (D) the Great Society
    (E) the 1970s and 1980s

13. Which type of federalism is characterized by a pattern of competitive grants?
    (A) dual federalism
    (B) cooperative federalism
    (C) fiscal federalism
    (D) creative federalism
    (E) marble cake federalism

14. Which of the following best represents the components of fiscal federalism?
    I. the passage of funded mandates
    II. the passage of revenue sharing measures
    III. the passage of categorical grants

    (A) I only
    (B) II only
    (C) III only
    (D) I and III only
    (E) I, II, and III

15. An alternative developed by the federal government that places the primary fiscal responsibility on the states was
    (A) revenue sharing.
    (B) project grants.
    (C) formula grants.
    (D) unfunded mandates.
    (E) reimbursement grants.

16. Which of the following laws was challenged by states because they felt that the federal government imposed an unfair unfunded mandate?
    (A) Family and Medical Leave Act
    (B) Motor Voter Registration Act
    (C) Clean Air Act
    (D) Clean Water Act
    (E) Crime Bill

17. Richard Nixon and Ronald Reagan's vision of a new federalism favored
    (A) an increase in the power and authority of the federal government.
    (B) a cooperative spirit between the federal and state governments.
    (C) an increase in federal mandates.
    (D) the downsizing of the federal government.
    (E) a decrease in the defense budget.

18. Which of the following provisions of the Republican Contract with America addresses the issue of federalism?
    I. term limits constitutional amendment
    II. balanced budget constitutional amendment
    III. Welfare Reform Act

    (A) I only
    (B) II only
    (C) III only
    (D) I and II only
    (E) II and III only

Answers to Multiple-Choice Questions

1. **(A)** Type of Question: Definitional
The key word in this question is *theoretical.* As you have seen, there are many types of explanations and examples of federalism. This question is looking for the student to realize that federalism deals with a division of power. Choice B's use of the phrase "separation of powers" is misleading and choice C, though using "division of power," gives the wrong explanation. Choice D refers to a unitary form of government.

2. **(D)** Type of Question: Comparing and contrasting concepts and events
Looking for the one exception, you must recognize that choices A, C, and E are basic arguments developed for a strong federal system. Because choices B and D are opposites, one of the answers provides the solution to this question. Because an advocate of a strong federal system would not want to concede the fact that local leaders are more capable than national leaders, that answer provides a weak argument for a strong federal system.

3. **(B)** Type of Question: Solution to a problem
The Federalist Papers attempted to provide a rationale not only for the ratification of the Constitution but also for the specific components of the new government including federalism. Even though the Federalist Papers speak of factions and raise the issue of the roles states play, they speak directly to the fact that on the local level governments will still have autonomy regarding local issues.

4. **(B)** Type of Question: Identification and analysis
This question is another in a series of questions that asks the reader to properly identify the significance of key Supreme Court cases. *Marbury v Madison* is the landmark case that established judicial review as a precedent and enabled the Court to make future decisions that had a huge impact on federalism.

5. **(C)** Type of Question: Identification and analysis
This question requires the reader to be able to identify the outcome of *McCulloch v Maryland.* The case dealt with Congress's ability to create the National Bank using the "necessary and proper" clause and prevented Maryland from taxing the federal institution as a result of the supremacy clause. The interstate commerce clause was used in another Court case, *Gibbons v Ogden.*

6. **(B)** Type of Question: Solution to a problem
The Tenth Amendment encompasses both the enumerated powers of the Congress and the reserve powers of the states. The implied power gives Congress the authority to use the "necessary and proper" clause. Thus the Tenth Amendment provides the constitutional basis of dual federalism.
7. **(D)** Type of Question: Comparing and contrasting concepts and events
This question and the following question require a knowledge of the differences among enumerated powers, delegated powers, and reserve powers. Using the process of elimination, you should be able to isolate health and welfare as a reserve power of the states.
8. **(B)** Type of Question: Comparing and contrasting concepts and events
This question asks you to do the opposite from the previous question. Just as in question 7, you should know that choices A, C, D, and E are reserve powers of the state. The interstate commerce clause gives you a clue that it is an enumerated power.
9. **(C)** Type of Question: Definitional
Although it is often easier to come up with the name rather than the definition, in this question you can readily become confused over the different types of federalism. Thus you should use a strategy of eliminating obviously wrong answers. Because cooperative federalism and marble cake federalism are synonymous, you can eliminate them easily. Creative federalism and fiscal federalism both took place during the Johnson and Nixon presidencies. Thus the autonomous relationship was an earlier form of federalism.
10. **(D)** Type of Question: Identification and analysis
Using the definition and visualizing what a marble cake looks like, choice D should jump out as the exception. Choices A, B, C, and E illustrate the mingling of responsibilities between the federal and state governments.
11. **(D)** Type of Question: Chronological
This question gives you a major clue. By identifying the time period as the Great Society, you should be able to think of some Great Society programs that fit the description of creative federalism, two of which are shared costs and federal guidelines. Singular administration of programs is not a characteristic.
12. **(E)** Type of Question: Chronological
The clue in this question is the word *competitive*. If you relate grants as a key component of that kind of federalism, you should be able to identify the correct time period. It is also suggested that you chart out the different descriptions of federalism and relate them to the corresponding time period.
13. **(C)** Type of Question: Identification and analysis
This question is a reversal of the previous question and asks you to relate the predominant feature of competitive federalism—that it is fiscal. Even though there are fiscal components in the other choices, fiscal federalism is directly related to competitive grants.

14. **(E)** Type of Question: Comparing and contrasting concepts and events
Like the other questions, you really need to have a broad understanding not only of the differences between kinds of federalism but also of the characteristics of each of them. Fiscal federalism refers to the differing approaches by the federal government including mandates, grants, and revenue sharing. Thus all three choices are correct.

15. **(D)** Type of Question: Cause and effect relationships
This question is very difficult because you must understand the differences between categorical grants, revenue sharing, formula grants, and unfunded mandates. Only unfunded mandates place on the states the primary responsibility to pay for the service provided by the government.

16. **(B)** Type of Question: Cause and effect relationships
As a result of the Republican victory in 1994 and motivated by the passage of the Unfunded Mandates Law, many states decided to challenge the implementation of the Motor Voter Registration Act based on the cost factor to the states.

17. **(D)** Type of Question: Solution to a problem
Richard Nixon and Ronald Reagan have been credited with creating the concept of new federalism. In general terms, both presidents favored a downsizing of the federal government. The only exception was in the area of the defense where they believed it was necessary to increase the defense budget. This question becomes difficult if you believe that a decrease in the defense budget was a characteristic of the new federalism approach rather than the general downsizing of the federal government.

18. **(E)** Type of Question: Solution to a problem
The Republican Contract with America, initiated during the 1994 congressional campaign and followed through during the 104th Congress, was a comprehensive approach in changing the manner in which government operated. From tort reform to national defense, the Republicans believed that government should be downsized. Two components of the contract that directly accomplish this goal were the Welfare Reform Act and the balanced budget constitutional amendment. Although a major reform, term limits dealt with congressional terms and did not deal directly with the issue of federalism.

SECTION 2: FREE-RESPONSE ESSAY (Both choices are answered for illustrative purposes)

Supporters of the Republican Contract with America claim that it is also a blueprint for the completion of President Reagan's vision of a new federalism for the United States.

Define what is meant by the term *new federalism*. Explain how one of the following provisions of the Contract with America supports your definition.

1. Unfunded Mandates Law
2. Welfare Reform Act

Sample Student Response

This new federalism is the name given to a plan outlined by President Ronald Reagan in his State of the Union message on January 26, 1982. According to his plan, a number of federally administered programs would be turned over to the states. In Reagan's view, the centralization of power in Washington during the twentieth century had diminished the proper constitutional role of the states in the federal system, making government too expensive and removing it from popular control. To remedy this problem, he proposed transferring responsibility for more than 40 health, education, welfare, and transportation programs to the states by 1988. In return, the federal government would assume responsibility for the Medicaid program, distributing $28 billion a year among the states until 1991. Reagan's plan was criticized because it meant that state control would mean reduced benefits for the poor, and the state governments themselves seemed reluctant to take on the burdens it entailed.

Unfunded mandates became popular during the 1980s and 1990s as Congress ran out of money but not enthusiasm for passing regulations. Congress simply told the lower levels of government that they had to pay for the new programs. During the 1980s Congress passed roughly 27 major statutes with new regulatory burdens for state and local governments. Federal bureaucrats also got into the act, issuing thousands of pages of directives to accompany each major piece of regulatory legislation, such as the Endangered Species Act and the Clean Water Act. In all, the Congressional Budget Office estimates that regulations imposed on the local governments between 1983 and 1990 cost up to $12.7 billion.

When state and local governments are forced to use money to work on projects that are not pressing issues, they waste money that could be spent on more important concerns. Mayor Richard Daley estimated that Chicago spent at least $160 million on unfunded mandates in 1991; that money could pay for 3,200 police officers. The passage of the Unfunded Mandates Law clearly relates back to Reagan's new federalism. If the government continues not to fund future mandates, they should expect that the local and state governments will not obey them. The federal government's goal, to "devolve" most social and welfare programs to the states, will not be successful if they continue to follow the new federalism ideas. If Congress were to revert back to cooperative federalism and the state and governments shared the costs, the programs would be much more effective.

The Republicans' Contract with America set the stage for welfare reform. The proposed Welfare Bill under the Contract eliminated the guiding principle of poverty and food programs, which was that anyone who qualifies for these programs automatically gets them. However, President Clinton vetoed the measure because he believed the food stamp provisions, which would replace food stamps and child nutrition programs with a lump-sum payment to each state, were too extreme.

However in the closing days of the 104th Congress and during the 1996 election campaign, the Republican Congress again passed a Welfare Bill, the Personal Responsibility and Work Opportunity Reconciliation Act of 1996, which was signed into law by President Clinton. The key provisions of the law included making welfare a transition to work by requiring welfare recipients to find work after two years on assistance. States would receive block grants in lieu of the former Aid to Dependent Children funds and would help support families during the transition into jobs. A maximum five-year term limit for welfare payments was enacted, with each state creating individualized programs. Other provisions included uniform interstate child support laws and a live at home and stay in school requirement aimed at unmarried minor parents who would be required to live with a responsible adult and participate in educational and training activities in order to receive assistance. The law also guaranteed healthcare for poor children, the disabled, pregnant women, the elderly, and people on welfare. The overriding theme of the law was to have states move people into jobs. One controversial aspect of the law was a denial of welfare benefits to legal immigrants. Opponents of this aspect promised that the new Congress would amend the law to soften this requirement.

Evaluation of Free-Response Sample Essay

1. Does the essay clearly establish the writer's point of view by adequately defining the concepts of new federalism?
2. Does the foundation of the essay give sufficient supporting evidence?
3. Does the writer refer to the themes of new federalism throughout the essay?

1. The strength of the opening paragraph revolves around the extensive definitions and explanation of new federalism. Not only is there a "textbook definition" of the term, but the writer also gives a historical overview, giving examples of how Reagan developed his approach to federalism. The only point missing in the description is the fact that Reagan also advocated an *increase* in the defense budget, which contradicted the philosophy of his new federalism.

2. The building blocks of the essay include both a description of the Unfunded Mandates Law and the proposed Welfare Reform Act and also an analysis of each. This critique illustrates how both laws would impact on the relationship between the federal government and the states as well as on the citizens of the states. This effect is particularly evident in the description of the Welfare Reform Act. Throughout the essay, the writer also makes general references to the Contract with America itself as a document that epitomizes a return to a more traditional federalism.

3. The writer describes the possible implications and significance of the Republican Contract with America on the future of federalism. Overall, the essay clearly establishes how the direction of the country changed in a significant manner as a result of the 1994 mid-term election.

SECTION 2: DATA-BASED FREE-RESPONSE ESSAY

The National Association of Towns and Townships has identified the following programs, which have unfunded mandate costs to the states. The cost of these programs to the states was calculated by the Congressional Budget Office at a total of $44.3 billion in 1998. Specific program costs are as follows:

Asbestos Hazard Emergency Response Act of 1986—$0.7 million
Americans with Disabilities Act—$2.2. billion
Safe Drinking Water Act of 1986—$8.6 billion
Laws dealing with solid waste disposal—$5.5 billion
Clean Water Act of 1986—$29.3 billion

Discuss the application of the Unfunded Mandates Law in terms of one of the examples given and analyze the impact of the Unfunded Mandates Law on the states.

Sample Student Response

With the passage of unfunded mandates, there is a significant cost to the states. Major regulatory legislation that was passed to protect the environment such as the Safe Drinking Water Act has large price tags attached to it that the states must pick up. A conflict arises when people support a devolution of federal power yet still want the benefit of laws, which protect the public interest, passed on to the states. In addition, many of these laws would never be passed by individual states because of the tax burden that would have to be placed on the citizens. Let's take the issue of unfunded mandates related to Aid to Dependent Children. Any constituent who opposes that issue favors the new law. But on the other hand, let's say the constituent favors environmental unfunded mandates. That would cost the state money to enforce. Furthermore, if the priority of the voter is tax decreases, any unfunded mandates passed on to the states or laws adopted by the states would make that priority difficult. Simply stated the formula doesn't add up.

The impact of the Unfunded Mandates Law is that states will no longer have to foot the bill for regulations they do not want to support. However, the flip side of the legislation is that, if the states want to maintain the positive effect of a particular regulation, it must pay for the entire program itself. For example, if there had been an unfunded mandate requiring states to build handicapped-accessible ramps and this was no longer required under the new legislation, the state would have two choices. It could continue the program through its own funding, which could result in a tax increase on its citizens. Or it could abolish the program and consequently a segment of the society that would benefit from it would no longer be able to do so. A specific example of how states have reacted to unfunded mandates is the Motor Voter Registration Act of 1993. This law mandated that states make available voter registration forms in motor vehicle offices and required the states to process the forms through that office keeping tabs on who registers through that procedure and the original procedure of registering at local polling places. States like California claimed that the new procedure would cost millions of dollars to implement. They refused to set up the procedures and potentially thousands of eligible voters did not have easier access to registration. However, when the issue was brought to court, California was directed to implement the motor voter law.

Evaluation of Data-Based Free-Response Sample Essay

1. Does the writer clearly explain the significance of the data and their impact on the issue of unfunded mandates?
2. Are the implications of unfunded mandates described by using specific laws that illustrate its significance?

1. The writer effectively points to the laws that have price tags attached to them and their impact on the states. Concerns of the voter are also discussed as they relate to the difficulty involved in giving citizens tax relief and in having laws that promote health and safety but that cost money. The issue of unfunded mandates also becomes clearer as the writer gives a hypothetical example of how unfunded mandates work.

2. The implications of unfunded mandates is explained by looking at how California reacted to the Motor Voter Registration Act. By describing the fight that many states are taking up, the writer makes it abundantly clear that these mandates are a double-edged sword. On the one hand, they establish through regulations some very important legislation. However, because the states are being forced to pay for them, the writer questions whether it is fair to place the entire burden on the states.

CHAPTER 5 The Bill of Rights and Civil Liberties

Chapter Overview

The Bill of Rights, adopted in 1791 by the states two years after the ratification of the Constitution, established the civil liberties for Americans. Viewing the Bill of Rights you will notice a number of "negative" statements:

- "Congress shall make no law . . ." abridging freedom of religion, speech, press, assembly, petition.
- "The right of people to keep and bear arms shall not be infringed."
- "No soldier shall . . . be quartered."
- "The right of the people . . . shall not be violated . . ." regarding unreasonable searches and seizures.
- "No person shall be held . . ." to be a witness against himself, in double jeopardy, or "deprived of life, liberty, or property without due process of law . . ."
- "Excessive bail shall not be required, nor excessive fines imposed, nor cruel and unusual punishments inflicted."

These excerpts illustrate why the Bill of Rights represents a basic definition of a person's civil liberties—those rights of the people that the government cannot take away. They are guaranteed in the Constitution, in the Bill of Rights, in other amendments passed, as well as through court interpretation. These rights are characterized as substantive, the kind of limits placed on the national government (like the First, Second, and Eighth Amendments) and procedural,

KEY TERMS

Bill of Rights
Civil liberties
Clear and present danger doctrine
Cruel and unusual punishment
Double jeopardy
Establishment clause
Exclusionary rule
Fighting words doctrine
Free exercise clause
Gitlow v New York (1925)
Incorporation of the Fourteenth Amendment
Indictment
Judicial federalism
Libel
Living will
Miranda rights
Prior restraint
Procedural due process
Separation of church and state
Slander
Substantive due process
Symbolic speech
Writ of habeas corpus

outlining how the government is supposed to treat individuals (for instance the Fifth Amendment). Civil liberties differ from civil rights. Civil liberties protect individuals from abuses of the government, whereas civil rights come about as a result of the equal protection under the law. Both civil liberties and civil rights limit the power of government.

This chapter will explore the historical development of the Bill of Rights and give you a breakdown of the nature of the Bill of Rights and how it protects individuals against the tyranny of the government, as well as highlight key Supreme Court decisions. It will also explain how the Bill of Rights through these Court decisions has been extended to the states, creating a form of judicial federalism.

Individual Rights and the Constitution

Historically, the Constitution could not have been ratified without an agreement that a bill of rights would be included.

It became apparent to the founding fathers that, without some kind of compromise regarding a statement of the people's rights, the ratification of the Constitution would be in jeopardy. When the original proposal was made by George Mason, a Virginia delegate, to add a bill of rights to the Constitution in 1787, it was turned down by the Federalist forces controlling the convention. However, when the states began the ratification process, it became obvious that the necessary nine states needed to approve the document would not vote to ratify without an agreement to add a series of amendments that would protect people from the potential abuses by the national government. The Federalists argued initially that a bill of rights was not necessary because the states under a federal system would protect their citizens. The Anti-Federalists insisted that these rights be written and included in the proposed Constitution. States such as Massachusetts, South Carolina, New Hampshire, Virginia, and New York agreed to support a bill of rights immediately after the Constitution was ratified. In the argument over whether or not to include a bill of rights into the original Constitution, James Madison wrote in the Federalist No. 84, "I go further and affirm that bills of rights, in the sense and to the extent in which they are contended for, are not only unnecessary in the proposed Constitution but would even be dangerous." On the other hand, in a *Letter from the Federal Farmer to the Republican* (an Anti-Federalist publication), it was written that "People, and very wisely too, like to be express and explicit about their essential rights, and not to be forced to claim them on the precarious and unascertained tenure of inferences and general principles. . . ." The Anti-Federalist forces prevailed, and the bill of rights was adopted in 1791.

Dual Citizenship

Even after the Bill of Rights was extended to the states as a result of the passage of the Fourteenth Amendment, citizens needed protection

The John Marshall Court of the 1800s was responsible for key decisions that clarified the nature of government. Decisions such as *Marbury v Madison*, *McCulloch v Maryland*, and *Gibbons v Ogden* defined the power of various components of government. And even though the Court ruled that it had the power to rule state laws unconstitutional, it refused to extend the provisions of the Bill of Rights to the states. In *Barron v Baltimore* in 1833, the Court ruled that the Bill of Rights limited only the national government, not the states. In turning down Barron's argument that the city of Baltimore had deprived him of just *against state abuses from the Supreme Court.*

compensation of property under the Fifth Amendment, Marshall wrote that "Each state established a constitution for itself, and in that constitution provided such limitations and restrictions on the powers of its particular government as its judgment dictated . . . the fifth amendment must be understood as restraining the power of the general government, not as applicable to the states." This decision established the nature of judicial federalism regarding the extension of the Bill of Rights to the citizens of the states. It created a concept of dual citizenship, wherein a citizen was under the jurisdiction of the national government as well as state governments. After the Fourteenth Amendment was passed in 1868 with its clear statement that "No state shall abridge the privileges and immunities of its citizens . . . ," the people received the complete protection of the Bill of Rights. Southern states passed Jim Crow laws and segregation became an acceptable practice. Chapter 6 discusses the incorporation of civil rights into the Bill of Rights.

The first time the Supreme Court applied a state case to the Bill of Rights occurred in *Gitlow v New York* in 1925. Gitlow was convicted in New York of advocating the forcible overthrow of the government using violent means. The Court ruled that his actions were in violation of a New York statute because his actions created a "bad tendency," which endangered the public welfare. More important was the statement made by the majority that determined that "freedom of speech and of press—which are protected by the First Amendment from abridgment by Congress—are among the fundamental personal rights and 'liberties' *protected by the due process clause of the 14th Amendment from impairment by the States.*" For the first time, the Supreme Court ruled that there was a direct relationship among the Fourteenth Amendment, actions by the states, and the Bill of Rights. This incorporation reached its peak under the leadership of Earl Warren in the 1950s and 1960s. Each time the Court made a ruling that incorporated an aspect of the Bill of Rights to the states, the concept of judicial federalism was defined more fully.

As we delve into the specific nature of the Bill of Rights and civil liberties, we will also point out which significant cases contributed to the nationalization of the Bill of Rights.

Freedom of Religion

"Congress shall make no law respecting an establishment of Religion, or prohibiting the free exercise thereof . . ."

The First Amendment's guarantee of free exercise of religion is balanced by the separation of church and state.

Called the establishment clause, this component of the First Amendment to the Constitution defines the right of the citizens to practice their religions without governmental interference. It also places a restriction on government, creating a "wall of separation" between church and state. From the settlement of this country by the Pilgrims who sought religious freedom to the belief by the Jehovah's Witnesses that they should not be forced to participate in religious activities in public schools, this clause has been the foundation of religious liberty in this country. However, it is also balanced by what is called governmental accommodation of religion, which is the ability of government to allow certain religious practices possibly including some direct forms of aid to public institutions. The line between government fostering of religious practice in our society and accommodation is the basis of many Supreme Court decisions in this area. Some of the major questions raised in this area follow:

- To what extent does use of the word *God* in public institutions violate the separation of church and state?
- Can states directly support parochial schools with public funds?
- Can states legislate nondenominational prayer, a moment of silence, creationism as a part of the curriculum, and equal access to its facilities to religious groups?
- Can clergy recite a blessing at graduation ceremonies?
- Are seasonal displays at public areas allowable?
- Are vouchers and public monies used for private parochial schools constitutional?

These are just a few of the many questions raised by the establishment clause. The following key Supreme Court decisions have created precedent.

Key Court Cases

***Zorach v Clauson* (1952)**—This decision allows states to provide release time programs for their students because the programs took place away from public places.

***Engle v Vitale* (1962)**—This decision struck down a New York State nondenominational prayer that started with the words "Almighty God, we acknowledge our dependence upon thee . . ."

***Abington School District v Schempp* (1963)**—This decision ruled that a Pennsylvania state law that allowed a Bible passage to be read at the start of the school day was unconstitutional.

***Epperson v Arkansas* (1968)**—This decision struck down an Arkansas law forbidding the teaching of the theory of evolution. This case answered the questions raised in the famous Scopes monkey trial. In 1987 the Supreme Court further defined what can be taught in schools in *Edwards v Aguillard.* This case ruled that Louisiana could not implement a policy that allowed schools to teach creationism as a religious doctrine, even if it was taught *along with* the theory of evolution.

***Lemon v Kurtzman* (1971)**—The Lemon test, which came out of this case, sets the criteria in determining whether the line of governmental interference is crossed. The three-pronged standard indicates that the purpose of the legislation must be secular, not religious, that its primary effect must neither advance nor inhibit religion, and that it must avoid an "excessive entanglement of government with religion." Even though this case struck down a law that provided governmental aid to private schools, it has been used as a barometer to measure other legislative practices of the state.

***Lee v Weisman* (1992)**—This decision directed school officials not to invite clergy to recite prayers at graduation ceremonies.

***Westside School District v Mergens* (1990)**—The Court decided, based on the Equal Access Act, that schools did not violate the establishment clause by allowing Bible study clubs to meet after school using school facilities where public funds were not being used to pay teachers acting as advisors to the club. The club also had to open its membership to students of all faiths.

***Santa Fe Independent School District v Doe* (2000)**—A school policy permitting student-led prayer before the start of a football game was ruled unconstitutional because the school provided the equipment.

***Zelman v Simmons* (2002)**—In a 5–4 ruling, the Court reversed a lower court decision. In its decision, the Supreme Court held that vouchers can be used for private parochial schools as long as the parents have the right to exercise choice in where they send their children.

***Elk Grove Unified School District v Nedow* (2004)**—After a lower court ruled that the phrase "under God" in the Pledge of Allegiance violated the separation of church and state, the Supreme Court decided that the father of the girl, Nedow, lacked legal standing to bring the case to court because he did not have custody of the girl. Three justices disagreed and wrote in their dissent that the phrase was not unconstitutional.

Freedom of Speech and the Press

"Congress shall make no law . . . abridging the freedom of speech, or of the press . . ."

The guarantees of freedom of speech and press are also limited by the interests and well being of the citizens.

The protection of the citizens' right of free expression versus the government's interest of limiting speech and the press for the interests and safety of the country and its citizens is basic to the interpretation of this clause of the First Amendment. From John Peter Zenger's concept of complete freedom of the press on the one hand to Justice Oliver Wendell Holmes' recognition that you cannot yell "Fire" in a darkened movie theater on the other hand, the issue of how much freedom of speech and the press can be allowed has been debated.

Speech can be categorized as symbolic and expressive. It extends to public areas of commercial speech as well as private application. It raises the complex issue of what is acceptable and what is obscene. Government has the role to maintain a balance between order and the ability of its citizens to criticize policy. The issue of what constitutes "fighting words" or a "clear and present danger" goes to the heart of free speech and expression.

Press is characterized by the written word and the ability of a publication to print material without prior review or prior restraint (censorship) by a governmental body. It also raises issues regarding the rights of reporters to pursue a story and what constitutes libel.

Some of the major questions raised in this area follow.

- Can the government limit free speech and press during times of war or other national emergency?
- To what extent can organized "hate groups" such as the Ku Klux Klan and Nazis advocate their views publicly?
- What kinds of actions are considered symbolic speech?
- How do you define speech and expression that is obscene?
- When do libel and slander come into play?

Key Court Cases

***Schenck v United States* (1919)**—Justice Holmes ruled for the majority that Schenck did not have the right to print, speak, and distribute material against United States efforts in World War I because a "clear and present danger" existed.

***Chaplinsky v New Hampshire* (1942)**—In a key incorporation case, a doctrine defining what constitutes "fighting words" was established as a result of spoken words that "by their very utterance inflict injury or tend to incite an immediate breach of peace that governments may constitutionally punish." These words "have a direct tendency to cause acts of violence by the person to whom, individually, the remarks are addressed." However, the Court has also determined that the use of obscenities aimed at governmental policy or worn on clothing as a means of protest do not constitute fighting words in and of themselves.

***Roth v United States* (1957)**—The Court ruled that "obscenity is not within the constitutionally protected speech or press." In 1973 in *Miller v California* the Court set criteria regarding what constitutes obscenity. It determined that if the material appealed to the "purient interests" and if it showed "patently offensive sexual contact," and if it "lacked serious artistic, literary, political or scientific merit" it could be considered obscene. The decision on what is obscene was also left up to community standards.

***New York Times v Sullivan* (1964)**—This decision created a base definition of what constitutes libel—material that is written with malice and a reckless disregard for the truth. Slander criteria are very similar, but much more difficult to prove when charges are made against public officials.

***Tinker v Des Moines* (1969)**—This decision established that students' rights are "not shed at the schoolhouse gates" and defined the students' wearing a black armband in silent protest of the Vietnam War as "a legitimate form of symbolic speech." These rights were later restricted in the student press case *Hazelwood v Kuhlmeier (1988)* when the Court gave school administrators the right to censor a school newspaper.

***New York Times v United States* (1971)**—Known as the Pentagon Papers case, the Supreme Court ruled that the government did not have the right to prevent the *New York Times* from printing information about the history of the country's involvement in the Vietnam War.

***Texas v Johnson* (1988)**—Based on the arrest of Gregory Lee Johnson for burning a flag outside the Republican National Convention in protest of the president's foreign policy, the Supreme Court ruled that this action was a form of symbolic speech protected by the First Amendment. The Supreme Court decisions in this area have tended to tread a thin line.

***R.A.V. v St. Paul* (1992)**—The Court ruled that a city ordinance providing for stricter penalties for "hate crimes" was overly broad and vague, and thus violated the First Amendment to the Constitution.

***Reno v A.C.L.U.* (1997)**—The Court ruled that the provisions of the 1996 Communications Decency Act, which punished Internet providers for making pornographic material available over the Internet, were unconstitutional because they were too vague.

***McConnell v Federal Election Commission* (2003)**—The Supreme Court ruled that the major provisions of the McCain-Feingold campaign finance law were constitutional. Specifically, the justices said that the ban on soft money and the restrictions placed on television advertising did not violate free speech.

***Virginia v Black* (2003)**—Reversing *R.A.V. v St. Paul*, the Court ruled that burning a cross is not protected by the First Amendment because of the long history of hate that cross-burning evokes.

THE CASE *TEXAS v JOHNSON* DETERMINED THAT BURNING A FLAG WAS CONSIDERED SYMBOLIC SPEECH

Freedom of Assembly

"Congress shall make no law respecting . . . the right of the people peaceably to assemble, and to petition the Government for a redress of grievances."

The ability of people to assemble, associate, and petition the government freely may come into conflict with the legitimate interests of the government and individuals.

The rights of people to gather in places they want and express their point of view without government interference, the right of association, and by extension the right to present their point of view to a governmental body are the central themes in the final clause of the First Amendment. These rights must be balanced by restrictions such as the time, manner, and place of assembly. They also must be aware of the protection of the individuals at the scene of assembly. Additionally, the extent to which individuals through their association in political groups can exert pressure on the government must be taken into account.

Some of the major questions raised by the themes of this clause follow.

- What constitutes equitable time, manner, and place restrictions on groups?
- To what extent can these demonstrations take place on public and private property?
- If a group an individual plans to associate with advocates violence, can the government restrict association and the right to petition?

Key Court Cases

***DeJonge v Oregon* (1937)**—In a key incorporation case, the Supreme Court ruled that the Fourteenth Amendment's due process clause applies to freedom of assembly. The Court found that DeJonge had the right to organize a Communist Party and speak at its meetings even though the party advocated "industrial or political change or revolution." However, in the 1950s with the fear of communism on the rise the Court ruled in *Dennis v United States* (1951), that Dennis, who was leader of the Communist Party, violated the Smith Act by advocating the forcible overthrow of the United States government.

***Cox v New Hampshire* (1941)**—The Court approved advance notice and a permit for a demonstration on public property. The right of individuals to petition on private property such as shopping centers has been restricted much more than on public property.

***Coates v Cincinnati* (1971)**—The Court ruled that a Cincinnati ordinance that made it a criminal offense for three or more persons to assemble on a sidewalk and annoy passersby with their conduct was unconstitutional.

***Collins v Smith* (1978)**—This decision is known as the Skokie case. The Supreme Court let a lower court decision stand allowing the Nazi Party to march through the predominantly Jewish section of Skokie, Illinois.

***Chicago v Morales* (1990)**—The Supreme Court ruled that a city of Chicago ordinance that prohibited "loitering" by two or more people who appeared to be engaged in "gang activities" was too broad and violated the right of people to assemble.

***Schenck v Pro-Choice Network of Western New York* (1997)**—The Court ruled that "fixed buffer zones" designed to restrict protesters assembled in front of abortion clinics were legal and did not violate the First Amendment.

The issues revolving around freedom of assembly and petition have continued to challenge restrictions placed on groups. In 1994 an anti-abortion group, Operation Rescue, was restricted in the manner in which they could demonstrate against a clinic performing abortions. The Court said that the group had to picket within a minimum distance from the clinic. Cases such as this illustrate how social issues such as abortion get mixed up with First Amendment issues of assembly.

Right to Keep and Bear Arms

"The right of the people to keep and bear arms, shall not be infringed."

The Second Amendment's provision for the people's right to bear arms has become a rallying call of interest groups as well as a caveat of many segments of society.

Although the historical intent of the Second Amendment was the right of each state to maintain an armed militia, it has been interpreted as the right of individuals to own weapons. The National Rifle Association has become a primary interest group in supporting the gun enthusiast and hunter's right to purchase and use arms. With the issue of crime and violence a significant concern of society, laws have been proposed restricting the availability, use, and kinds of weapons. This clash has resulted in a national debate over the meaning of the Second Amendment as shown in the following questions.

- Should registration and a waiting period be required for a person to own recreational guns?
- Should certain types of arms such as assault weapons be banned?

Key Court Case

The only Second Amendment case to be heard by the Supreme Court is *United States v Miller* (1939). This case determined that a section of the National Firearms Act of 1934, which made it a crime to ship certain kinds of weapons across states lines unless they were registered, was constitutional because it did not have any link to a state militia. Because this was a federal case, the regulation of arms has been a state matter. This was changed as a result of the passage of the Brady Bill in 1993. Named after President Reagan's press secretary who was seriously injured by a handgun in the attempted assassination of the president, it took more than ten years to obtain congressional approval. The law placed restrictions on handgun registration, setting up a minimum waiting period before purchase. Many states had to change their laws based on this legislation. A 1997 Supreme Court decision did, however, strike down the part of the law forcing local officials to perform instant checks. The National Rifle Association lobbied against its passage, insisting that it would not stop criminals from obtaining weapons. They used the same rationale in arguing against the passage of an assault weapons ban that was part of the Crime Bill passed in 1994.

Right of Privacy

Quartering of soldiers "in time of peace" shall be illegal "without the consent of the owner."

"The right of the people to be secure in their persons, houses, papers, and effects, against unreasonable searches and seizures, shall not be violated, and no Warrants shall issue, but upon probable cause . . ."

The Third and Fourth Amendments protect individuals from arbitrary invasion of a person's house or an individual's privacy.

The first of three amendments that deal with the due process rights of individuals, those procedural rights that protect individuals from governmental interference, are the Third and Fourth Amendments. They deal with such issues as search and seizure and the right of privacy. Included in the Bill of Rights because of abuses in this area by Great Britain when it ruled the colonies, these amendments prevent the unrestricted quartering of soldiers, blanket search warrants, and the unlimited invasion of privacy by the government.

By and large, the only time the Third Amendment has been used by the government was during the Civil War when the North quartered troops in Southern mansions. There have been no Supreme Court cases involving the Third Amendment.

The Fourth Amendment has come under the scrutiny of both the federal and state governments in determining how far they can go in obtaining evidence. The key criterion in determining the legitimacy of the search is probable cause. That becomes the first component of the due process rights of individuals, which also applies to the states as a result of a similar clause in the Fourteenth Amendment. An exception to the probable cause component is the "plain view" characteristic. It allows police to obtain evidence that is in sight of the investigators. Situations such as emergencies, investigations requiring wiretapping, and the extent a police official can search a car are also raised by the Fourth Amendment. Some of the major issues related to the Fourth Amendment follow.

- To what extent can police conduct a search without a warrant and obtain evidence found to prosecute an individual?
- What methods can law officials use to obtain evidence?
- Can the right of privacy extend to social issues such as abortion?

Key Court Cases

***Mapp v Ohio* (1961)**—A key state incorporation case, *Mapp v Ohio* established the exclusionary rule for states. The exclusionary rule determined that police may obtain only that evidence available through a legitimate search warrant. Other evidence found at the scene of the crime is not admissible in the trial; it must be excluded. This doctrine has been modified by the plain view doctrine. Many people have been critical of the exclusionary rule, suggesting that it handcuffs the police from obtaining legitimate evidence necessary to prosecute a criminal. Since *Mapp v Ohio*, other cases have created further exceptions. In *Nix v Williams* (1984) the Court allowed "inevitable discovery" of tainted evidence, that is, evidence that would have eventually been discovered with a legal warrant. *United States v Leon* (1984) created a "good faith" doctrine, which stated that if the police obtained essential evidence in good faith and did not violate the spirit and intent of the Fourth Amendment, that evidence would be allowed.

***Griswold v Connecticut* (1965)**—The Court struck down a Connecticut law that prohibited the use of contraceptives. It arose after a doctor was arrested for distributing birth control devices. Using the privacy provision of the Fourth Amendment, the Court stated that individuals had the right to privacy in the area of sexual relations.

***Katz v United States* (1967)**—Reversing the long-standing Olmstead doctrine, which allowed federal wiretapping to obtain evidence, the Supreme Court outlined stricter criteria for wiretapping in the *Katz* decision. Congress set down allowable procedures for wiretapping in a crime bill passed in 1968, which allowed federal and state officials to use the procedure with probable cause. The Court and Congress have even set procedures for wiretapping in the case of domestic subversion.

***Roe v Wade* (1972)**—Using the concept of being "secure in their persons," the Supreme Court ruled that abortions are constitutionally protected. It set up a trimester system allowing unrestricted abortions in the first trimester but regulated abortions during the second trimester and allowed the states to ban abortion during the third trimester unless the mother's or baby's life was endangered. This decision has been most controversial and set the stage for a national debate. We will come back to this issue in the next chapter.

***United States v Leon* (1984)**—In this decision, the Court created a "good faith" exception to the exclusionary rule, allowing the introduction of illegally obtained evidence where police can prove that the evidence was obtained without violating the core principles of *Mapp v Ohio*.

***Planned Parenthood v Casey* (1992)**—The Court upheld a Pennsylvania law requiring minors to wait 24 hours after receiving parental approval before getting an abortion as constitutional. The decision also struck down a provision mandating that women obtain "informed spousal consent" and upheld, in principle, *Roe v Wade*.

***Sternberg v Carhart* (2000)**—The Court ruled that state laws limiting "late term" or "partial birth" abortions were unconstitutional because they violated the principles established by *Roe v Wade.*

The basic tenets of the Fourth Amendment create procedural rights of the accused. The next three amendments further define procedural due process rights of individuals.

***Owasso v Falvo* (2002)**—The Supreme Court ruled that the privacy rights of students under the Family Educational Rights and Privacy Act (FERPA) were not violated if students graded each other's papers in a classroom setting.

***Pottawatomie v Earls* (2002)**—Extending the 1995 random drug testing of student athletes, the Court ruled that schools can use random drug testing for any student participating in extracurricular activities without violating their privacy rights.

Right of Procedural Due Process

"No person shall be held to answer for a capital . . . crime, unless on a presentment or indictment of a Grand Jury . . . nor shall any person be subject for the same offense to be twice put in jeopardy . . . nor shall be compelled . . . to be a witness against himself, nor be deprived of life, liberty, or property without due process of law . . ."

"In all criminal prosecutions, the accused shall enjoy the right to a speedy and public trial . . . and to be informed of the nature and cause of the accusation; to be confronted with the witnesses against him; to have . . . process for obtaining witnesses . . . and to have the Assistance of Counsel for his defense."

". . . the right of trial by jury shall be preserved . . ."

The Fifth, Sixth, and Seventh Amendments, which establish procedural due process for the accused, have been viewed by critics as an overprotection of criminal rights and the placement of an undue burden of proof on the government.

Procedural due process can be viewed as a series of steps established by the Fifth, Sixth, and Seventh Amendments that protect the rights of the accused at every step of the investigation and limit how governmental power may be exercised. The following steps represent the steps taken: the manner in which the evidence is gathered (Fourth Amendment), the charges made by the police upon arrest (habeas corpus), the formal indictment and interrogation (allowance made for obtaining lawyers, witnesses), the trial (speedy and public trial, impartial jury, guarantees against self-incrimination, trial by jury), and the right to confront witnesses. Another kind of due process, substantive, places limits on the government as they relate to the content of legislation and the extent government can use its power to enact unreasonable laws.

Before looking at key cases, you should have a clear understanding of the intent of each of these steps. Habeas corpus, a right that cannot be taken away by government, found in the body of the Constitution in Article I Section 9, has also been called a writ of liberty. It directs the police to show cause why a person may be held for a crime. It has also been used by convicted criminals as a route to appeal their conviction from the state courts to the federal courts based on procedural issues. An indictment is a formal list of charges made by a grand jury. When enough evidence is given to the grand jury, it develops a list of formal charges that is presented to the accused prior to trial. A speedy trial has been defined by law on the federal level as a trial that must take place no more than 100 days after arrest. Each state has laws addressing this issue. A public trial means that it is held in a public courthouse. Depending upon the specific issue, the extent of public viewing and media coverage can be determined by the judge. The right to a jury trial does not necessarily mean that the jurors will be identified by name. In the trial of the World Trade Center bombers, the jury was chosen in this manner. In obtaining an adequate defense, the conditions in which a defendant can obtain a lawyer based on financial considerations and the exact time a lawyer is brought in are not defined. Double jeopardy means that once a verdict is handed down, you cannot be tried twice for the same crime. That does not mean that if you are found innocent of state charges, you cannot be tried for a federal offense dealing with the same issue. That is what happened to the police involved in the beating of Rodney King.

Surveys taken have shown that much of the public is critical of the manner in which courts have interpreted these provisions. Crime and violence have become a national concern. Anticrime legislation and Supreme Court decisions have responded to the public's concern.

Some of the questions raised by these amendments follow.

- Can due process rights be suspended during times of national emergencies?
- Is live media coverage of trials allowable?
- Does a lawyer have to be assigned to a defendant who cannot afford one?
- At what point does the accused have the right to consult a lawyer?
- To what extent do the police have to advise the accused of their rights?

Key Court Cases

***Escobedo v Illinois* (1964)**—Danny Escobedo requested the assistance of a lawyer after he was arrested for the murder of his brother. The police would not grant the request even though there was a lawyer at the police station. Escobedo made a number of incriminating statements without his lawyer present, which were later used against him at the trial. The Supreme Court ruled Escobedo's due process rights of self-incrimination and right to counsel were violated and he was released from prison.

***Gideon v Wainright* (1964)**—This landmark case established that the accused has the right to an attorney even if he or she cannot afford one. Gideon, accused of a felony in Florida, requested the assistance of a lawyer. The Florida criminal justice system allowed free assistance only in cases that were punishable by death. Gideon defended himself and lost. The Supreme Court ruled that his Sixth Amendment due process rights made applicable by the Fourteenth Amendment were denied.

***Miranda v Arizona* (1966)**—In probably one of the most publicized cases of its kind, Ernesto Miranda, mentally retarded, was accused and convicted of rape and kidnapping. He confessed to the crime under intense interrogation without any mention by the police of his right to obtain a lawyer or what consequences the answers to their questions would have on the outcome of the trial. The Supreme Court, in its landmark ruling, established the Miranda rights. Those rights directed the police to inform the accused upon arrest that he has a constitutional right to remain silent, that any thing said can be used in court, that he has a right to consult with a lawyer at any time during the process, and that a lawyer will be provided if the accused can not afford one.

The accused must be asked if he understands these rights and told that he has the right to remain silent and at any time request a lawyer. Since the *Miranda* ruling, the courts have begun to limit some of the rights established by these cases.

***New York v Quarles* (1984)**—The Court created a "public safety" exception to the *Miranda* warnings allowing the police to arrest an accused criminal without reciting the *Miranda* rights where public safety is threatened.

***Dickerson v United States* (2000)**—The Court upheld *Miranda* and struck down a 1968 congressional act that permitted local law enforcement officials to accept voluntary confessions made before the accused was read his *Miranda* rights.

***Rasul v Bush* (2004)**—Enemy combatants held at the Guantanamo Naval Base in Cuba captured during the war in Afghanistan and Iraq may challenge their detention in federal courts.

***Hamdi v Rumsfeld* (2004)**—Enemy combatants held in the United States have due process rights.

"Excessive bail shall not be required, nor excessive fines imposed, nor cruel and unusual punishments inflicted."

The Eighth Amendment completes the due process cycle and raises the issue of the extent a government can impose punishment on convicted criminals.

As part of the procedural due process, an accused has the right to post bail, an amount of money set by the court as a guarantee that the person will return to stand trial. This amount may not be excessive and is imposed based on the nature of the crime and the history of the accused. Critics of the system raise the issue that if the accused cannot afford the bail, even if it is not excessive, then the person is unduly punished prior to the trial.

Excessive fines and cruel and unusual punishment have resulted in some of the most passionate arguments revolving around the nature and extent of government imposed punishment.

Some of the major issues posed by this amendment follow.

- What constitutes excessive bail?
- Is the death penalty cruel and unusual punishment?

Key Court Cases

***Stack v Boyle* (1951)**—Deals with federal cases and establishes clearly that any bail set that goes beyond what is reasonable to guarantee that the accused will appear at a trial is excessive under the Eighth Amendment. States determine their own standards of reasonableness under their own criminal justice statutes.

***Gregg v Georgia* (1976)**—The landmark case, which held that "the punishment of death does not invariably violate the Constitution." However it did affirm standards and criteria set down in *Furman v Georgia (1972),* regarding discretion of judges and make-up of juries. Since *Gregg,* other criteria have been established regarding the kinds of cases that can result in the kinds of executions and the manner in which states impose death penalties. The Court has also ruled that other forms of treatment of criminals while they are in prison can also be cruel and unusual. Such penalties as denial of medical assistance or an interpretation that narcotics addiction is a crime rather than an illness that can be treated violated the Eighth and Fourteenth Amendments.

These issues have resulted in a national debate regarding the best way to create a balance between society's needs of protecting its citizens and the rights of the accused. A federal crime bill that created a "three strikes and you're out" feature passed the Congress in 1994 and has been duplicated in many states. This bill mandates that life imprisonment be given for federal crimes if a criminal is convicted of three felonies.

***Harmelin v Michigan* (1991)**—The Supreme Court upheld a life sentence imposed on the defendant for cocaine possession as a first-time offender, ruling that the state law imposing the sentence was not a violation of the Eighth Amendment.

***Atkins v Virginia* (2002)**—The Supreme Court ruled that mentally retarded individuals sentenced to the death penalty cannot be executed because it violates the Eighth Amendment's cruel and unusual clause.

Undefined Rights

"The enumeration in the Constitution, of certain rights, shall not be construed to deny . . . others retained by the people."

"The powers not delegated to the United States by the Constitution, nor prohibited by it to the States, are reserved to the States respectively, or to the people."

The Ninth and Tenth Amendments to the Constitution further define rights not listed in the Constitution to the people and states.

Called by some the elastic clause of the Bill of Rights, the Ninth Amendment guarantees that those undefined rights not listed anywhere in the Constitution cannot be taken away. Such issues as abortion and the "right to die" have come under the umbrella of this amendment.

The Tenth Amendment, discussed in Chapter 4, extends to the states the right to create laws for the best interests of their people. It is the basis of federalism, and when this amendment comes into conflict with the other amendments of the Bill of Rights and the Fourteenth Amendment, the outcome of the dispute further defines the changing nature of federalism. The more the Supreme Court nationalized the Bill of Rights through the application of the Fourteenth Amendment, the more judicial federalism made the Bill of Rights apply directly to the states.

Some of the questions raised by these amendments follow.

- Does an individual have the right to die?
- How do the courts resolve the conflict between state-developed laws and issues raised by the Bill of Rights?

Key Court Cases

***Cruzan v Missouri Department of Health* (1990)**—The Supreme Court ruled that a "living will" is a legitimate document that can be used to direct a hospital to "pull the plug" of a patient. It did not sanction unrestricted euthanasia procedures. The issue of physician-assisted suicide was decided in 1997. In a 9-0 decision, the Court decided that states have the right to make laws banning physician-assisted suicide (the cases decided were a Washington state case, *Washington v Glucksberg*, and a New York case, *Vacco v Quill*).

***United States v Lopez* (1995)**—The Supreme Court ruled that Congress misused its authority in enacting the Gun-Free School Zone Safety Act, which made the possession of a gun within 1000 yards of a school a federal crime. The Court held that enforcement of such an act comes under the authority of the states.

***Printz, Sheriff/Coroner, Ravalli County, Montana v United States* (1997)**—Challenging the provision of the Brady Law, which mandated local officials to perform background checks on people purchasing handguns, the Supreme Court ruled that that specific part of the law was unconstitutional.

The discussion involving the relationship of the Bill of Rights to the state's right to develop its own laws and procedures goes to the heart of what the future of federalism will be. There is no doubt that the nationalization of the Bill of Rights through the incorporation of the Fourteenth Amendment has had a significant impact on state laws. From the interpretation of the First Amendment freedoms to the rights of the accused, the states increasingly have to be responsive to the principles of the Bill of Rights. However, decisions reached by the Rehnquist Court have tilted some of the power back to the states.

Chapter 5 Review

SECTION 1: MULTIPLE-CHOICE QUESTIONS

1. Which of the following arguments represents the best reason why a bill of rights was added to the Constitution?
   (A) The Federalists felt that the central government would not protect the citizens.
   (B) The Anti-Federalists believed that the masses needed to know what their rights were.
   (C) Ratification of the Constitution including a bill of rights was supported by both the Federalists and Anti-Federalists.
   (D) Key states insisted on a bill of rights prior to approving the Constitution.
   (E) The Anti-Federalists felt that the Constitution alone protected citizens from abuses of the central government.

2. Which of the following decisions made by Chief Justice John Marshall's Court established the principle that the Bill of Rights only applied to the federal government?
   (A) *Marbury v Madison*
   (B) *McCulloch v Maryland*
   (C) *Gibbons v Ogden*
   (D) *Barron v Baltimore*
   (E) *Fletcher v Peck*

3. The Supreme Court decision *Gitlow v New York* established the principle that
   (A) there was no relationship between the Fourteenth Amendment and the Bill of Rights.
   (B) free speech was not protected by the Bill of Rights in state cases.
   (C) incorporation of the Bill of Rights in state cases was allowed.
   (D) there was an indirect relationship between the Fourteenth Amendment and the Bill of Rights.
   (E) judicial review could take place in state cases by the Supreme Court.

4. The establishment clause of the First Amendment speaks of
   (A) an officially sanctioned nonsectarian religion for the United States.
   (B) a wall of separation between church and state.
   (C) government not being able to accommodate religion in public places.
   (D) government agencies creating watchdog committees to prevent religious infringement in the schools.
   (E) the passage of the equal access law.

5. Which of the following Supreme Court cases established the "clear and present danger" doctrine?
   (A) *Schenck v United States*
   (B) *Texas v Johnson*
   (C) *Chaplinsky v New Hampshire*
   (D) *Abrams v New York*
   (E) *Tinker v Des Moines*

6. The terms *prior review* and *prior restraint* refer to which of the following constitutional principles?
   (A) freedom of the press
   (B) freedom of speech
   (C) freedom of assembly
   (D) due process
   (E) freedom to petition one's grievances

7. The Lemon test is used to determine if
   (A) there is unfair government interference regarding free speech.
   (B) the government is acting properly in due process cases.
   (C) there are illegal tactics used by PACs.
   (D) death penalty convictions are fair and reasonable.
   (E) legislation that deals with religion creates illegal government interference.

8. The principle established by the Supreme Court in the case of *Tinker v Des Moines* states that
   (A) schools can act in loco parentis.
   (B) student rights did not stop at the schoolhouse gates.
   (C) principals have the right to censor student publications.
   (D) student symbolic speech may be censored by school officials even if it does not create a disruption.
   (E) principals have the right to suspend students without a hearing.

9. The principle established in the Supreme Court case of *Texas v Johnson* was based on
   (A) religious speech.
   (B) active speech.
   (C) symbolic speech.
   (D) fighting words.
   (E) government accommodation of speech.

10. Critics of the Brady Bill and the 1994 Crime Bill point to which of the following principles?
    (A) the due process guarantees of the Fifth and Fourteenth Amendments
    (B) Congress having broad power to regulate guns
    (C) property rights of the Fifth and Fourteenth Amendments
    (D) the right to bear arms section of the Second Amendment
    (E) the cruel and unusual punishment provision of the Eighth Amendment

11. In the case of *Mapp v Ohio*, the Supreme Court established
    (A) the exclusionary rule of evidence.
    (B) the fighting words doctrine.
    (C) the bad tendency doctrine.
    (D) the prurient interest principle.
    (E) the stop and frisk rule of evidence.

12. Which of the following cases used the Ninth Amendment as a constitutional argument?
    (A) *Griswold v Connecticut*
    (B) *Collins v Smith*
    (C) *Cox v New Hampshire*
    (D) *Engle v Vitale*
    (E) *Roe v Wade*

13. All the following steps are part of procedural due process EXCEPT
    (A) habeas corpus.
    (B) formal indictment.
    (C) speedy trial.
    (D) right to an attorney.
    (E) a jury made up of different ethnic groups.

14. The intent of the decision made in *Miranda v Arizona* was
    (A) the guarantee to accused persons that law enforcement agencies videotape confessions.
    (B) to tie the hands of the police after they arrest a suspect.
    (C) to allow the federal government to tighten its criminal laws.
    (D) to allow state governments to obtain confessions more easily.
    (E) to guarantee due process rights of the accused.

15. The "right to die" is an implicit right found in which part of the Constitution?
    (A) the elastic clause
    (B) the due process clause
    (C) the Fourteenth Amendment
    (D) the Ninth Amendment
    (E) the Fifth Amendment

Answers to Multiple-Choice Questions

1. **(D)** Type of Question: Cause and effect relationships
This is a relatively difficult question because the answer reflects a political, rather than a philosophical, reason why the Bill of Rights was added to the Constitution. New York, in particular, insisted that a bill of rights be included in the Constitution. In fact their delegation to the ratifying convention was heavily Anti-Federalist. Until the Anti-Federalists received a commitment that a bill of rights would be included, they were ready to vote against adoption. Philosophically, the inclusion of a bill of rights was a means to ensure that the rights of individuals would not be usurped by the federal government.

2. **(D)** Type of Question: Identification and analysis
A number of questions in this chapter have similar characteristics. You are asked to either connect a Court case to a principle or a principle to a Court case. The cases selected are significant, either as landmark precedent cases or as cases that illustrate the incorporation of the Bill of Rights. *Barron v Baltimore* established that the Bill of Rights did not apply to the individual states. For a citizen to argue a deprivation of rights, the state had to also have in its constitution a bill of rights. Most states, in fact, did provide protection for their citizens.

3. **(C)** Type of Question: Identification and analysis
Gitlow became a landmark incorporation case that dealt with the incorporation of a free speech issue to the states in the twentieth century. The Fourteenth Amendment gave the Court the opportunity to use the incorporation principle. But it took the Court until the twentieth century to really begin the process. Such decisions as *Plessy v Ferguson*, in 1896, rejected the incorporation of civil rights, and other civil liberties cases were not addressed until *Gitlow* was decided.

4. **(B)** Type of Question: Definitional
The establishment clause has two parts. The first speaks of Congress not being able to pass a law establishing a religion and the second part guarantees the free exercise of religious beliefs. These two concepts sometimes clash when the state gets involved in the guarantee part. Thus the concept of a wall of separation was developed, which on the one hand set down a test to guarantee noninvolvement by the government, yet allowed accommodation and protected individual rights to practice and follow a religion.

5. **(A)** Type of Question: Identification/principle
The *Schenck* case, which was argued during World War I, established that in times of national emergencies, the government has the right to take away an individual's civil liberties if the action of the individual presents a clear and present danger to the country and its citizens. The other choices, all First Amendment speech cases, established other speech principles such as symbolic speech.

6. **(A)** Type of Question: Definitional
Prior review allows an authority to look over the content of a story before it is published. Prior restraint gives that authority the right to prevent the printing of a story or newspaper. The Courts have generally prevented government from acting as a censor except in the extreme case of national security. Yet in the Pentagon Papers case, the Court clearly decided that the government did not have the right to stop publication of the Pentagon Papers during the Vietnam War. The Court has allowed prior review and prior restraint in student publications (*Hazelwood v Kuhlmeir*).
7. **(E)** Type of Question: Cause and effect relationships
The Lemon test, derived from the *Lemon v Kurtzman* case, established a three-pronged test to determine if there is excessive government intrusion in establishing religion. The test included that the purpose of legislation must be secular, not religious; its primary effect must neither advance nor inhibit religion; and it must avoid an "excessive entanglement of government with religion."
8. **(B)** Type of Question: Identification and analysis
The *Tinker* case is the landmark case dealing with Bill of Rights protection for students. It involved symbolic speech, but in the decision the Court expanded the application of the rest of the Bill of Rights to students. Choice A is a correct statement but did not derive from the *Tinker* case. Other cases such as *Goss v Lopez* expanded student due process rights. The other choices all deal with Supreme Court cases that limit student rights and more narrowly apply the *Tinker* decision.
9. **(C)** Type of Question: Identification and analysis
The *Texas v Johnson* case dealt with the right of Johnson to burn an American flag as a symbol of protest against the Reagan administration's foreign policy. The First Amendment clearly addresses the issues of free speech, assembly, and petition, but it does not specifically speak of the concept of symbolic speech. The 5-4 decision stated that Johnson had the right to use the flag as a symbol of political discontent, even if in the process he desecrated it.
10. **(D)** Type of Question: Comparing and contrasting concepts and events
The Brady Bill and 1994 Crime Bill both have clauses that, according to critics like the National Rifle Association, place restrictions on the right to bear arms. The Brady Bill places a waiting period and registration procedure before an individual can purchase a gun and the Crime Bill bans a number of assault weapons.
11. **(A)** Type of Question: Identification and analysis
Mapp v Ohio is the precedent case that established the exclusionary rule of evidence to state cases. The exclusionary rule prevents police from introducing evidence obtained without a proper search warrant and gives Fourth and Fourteenth Amendment protection to the accused in state cases. It previously existed for federal cases. The other choices reflect principles established by other Supreme Court cases.
12. **(E)** Type of Question: Cause and effect relationship
The Ninth Amendment to the Constitution has been rarely used in Supreme Court arguments. The amendment has been referred to as the elastic clause of the Bill of Rights guaranteeing to citizens other rights

that are not listed in the Bill of Rights. When *Roe v Wade* was argued, the petitioner used the strategy of applying the Fourth Amendment's "to be secure in their persons" to a women's right to decide whether or not to have an abortion. The right to make that choice was argued using the Ninth Amendment, and it was accepted by the Court, thereby giving constitutional sanction to the abortion issue.

13. **(E)** Type of Question: Definitional
There are two kinds of due process, procedural and substantive. Procedural deals with the procedures in the Fifth, Sixth, Seventh, and Fourteenth Amendments, which take the accused from arrest to trial. Choices A, B, C, and D are all part of the procedural due process guaranteed by the Constitution. Choice E goes beyond the provision of the Constitution, which guarantees the accused the right to a jury of one's peers. Even though there have been Court decisions that have reversed lower court rulings based on the make-up of juries, it is not a specific part of the procedural due process guarantees.

14. **(E)** Type of Question: Identification and analysis
The common misconception that students have in regards to the *Miranda* decision is that the so-called Miranda rights, which came about because of the decision, were original guarantees provided for by the Fifth Amendment. The other difficult part of this question is that many people feel that *Miranda* had the negative consequence of tying the hands of the police. Even though the more conservative Burger and Rehnquist Courts have narrowed the interpretation of *Miranda*, it is still a key due process guarantee.

15. **(D)** Type of Question: Cause and effect relationships
As in an earlier question, the Ninth Amendment's expansion of rights given to individuals suggests clearly that the rights of individuals are not limited to the rights mentioned in the Bill of Rights. The elastic clause aspect of it is implied. Technically, the elastic clause refers to Article I Section 8 and the ability of Congress to make laws that are necessary and proper.

SECTION 2: FREE-RESPONSE ESSAY (Both choices are answered for illustrative purposes)

The Supreme Court has attempted to balance society's needs of protecting its citizens and the rights of the accused. Choose one of the following cases and evaluate how the decision affected society and the accused:

1. *Mapp v Ohio* (1961)
2. *Gregg v Georgia* (1976)

In your answer make sure that you describe the facts of the case, the constitutional issues involved, and the significance of the decision.

Sample Student Response

The Supreme Court's decisions in *Mapp v Ohio* (1961) and *Gregg v Georgia* (1976), which were rendered under two different Courts, sent a clear signal to the country that the rights of the accused and the interests of society sometimes clash. The *Mapp* decision establishing the exclusionary rule was decided by the activist Warren Court, and the *Gregg* decision, overturning a previous case, *Furman v Georgia*, giving the states the right to impose the death penalty, was decided by the more conservative Burger Court.

The exclusionary rule limited the state's ability to use evidence found in unrestricted searches without warrants. It incorporated the finding in the case of *Weeks v United States* in 1914, which had created the same standard for federal crimes, thus applying the Fourteenth Amendment's due process clause to the states. In the case, police officers suspected that Dolleree Mapp was harboring a dangerous and armed criminal in her house and hiding gambling material. They knocked on her door and insisted that they should be able to search the house for the fugitive. Mrs. Mapp did not let the police enter. Shortly thereafter, the police came back waving a piece of paper they claimed was a warrant and forced their entry into the house. During the search they did not find the criminal. They did, however, discover a chest that contained pornographic magazines. Because Ohio law prohibited the possession of this material, they arrested Mrs. Mapp, and she was convicted of possession of obscene materials and sent to prison.

The constitutional issue in the case was whether or not Mrs. Mapp's Fourth and Fourteenth Amendment rights of privacy were violated because the police entered the house without a legitimate search warrant. The state argued that in *Wolf v Colorado,* the Supreme Court established the precedent that in state cases the exclusionary rule of evidence was permissible. Mrs. Mapp's attorney pointed to the federal case and argued that the police acted illegally by taking evidence that was not covered by a search warrant and using that evidence to convict Mrs. Mapp.

The Warren Court wrote that "the prohibition against unreasonable searches would be meaningless unless evidence gained in such search was excluded." The significance of the case is that it limited law enforcement agencies from using illegally obtained tainted evidence called "fruit from the poisonous vine" in state cases. It sent a clear message that protections guaranteed by the Fourth and Fourteenth Amendments applied to the accused, even if it meant that somebody charged with a crime could potentially get off on a "technicality." This rule has been modified by the Rehnquist Court in three ways. First, the Court said that tainted evidence could be used if that evidence "ultimately or inevitably would have been discovered by lawful means." Second, the Court determined a good faith exception to the rule. This meant that, if the police investigation was conducted using good faith, evidence could be used even if there was not a warrant. Third, the Court gave the police greater flexibility in obtaining evidence if they could demonstrate that in the search there had been an "honest mistake." The *Mapp* case clearly illustrates the complexity of how far law enforcement agencies and the state can go to protect the legitimate interests of society.

In the case of *Gregg v Georgia,* the Court had the difficult problem of applying a standard it set in a case heard a few years before, *Furman v Georgia.* In that case the Court determined the death penalty to be illegal based on the fact that judges used arbitrary discretion in applying the penalty and that juries were biased based on their racial make-up. It begged the issue of the cruel and unusual punishment provision of the Eighth Amendment. Therefore, when another Georgia case emerged in 1976, the Burger Court decided to look at the entire issue.

Troy Gregg and Floyd Allen were arrested, after being stopped by police for driving a stolen car, for the brutal murder of two men who were shot and found in a ditch near a highway rest stop. Gregg was searched, and the police found a gun that was later identified as the murder weapon. Allen cooperated with the police and informed them that Gregg had shot the men to rob them and steal their car. Gregg claimed self-defense. Georgia tried Gregg for murder and armed robbery.

Based on the *Furman* decision, Georgia changed its trial procedure and Gregg first was found guilty by a jury that was considerably more balanced than in the *Furman* case. After the guilty verdict, the judge gave the jury clearly defined instructions that they could either impose the death penalty under specific circumstances or sentence Gregg to life imprisonment. The jury sentenced Gregg to death.

Gregg's attorneys appealed the case based on the Eighth Amendment's "cruel and unusual punishment" provision. They also invoked the privileges and immunities clause and due process/equal protection clauses of the Fourteenth Amendment, suggesting that racial minorities were being discriminated against by Georgia. Finally, they claimed that Georgia was still violating the *Furman* standard by allowing the jury to impose the death penalty in an arbitrary and capricious manner. Georgia claimed that imposition of the death penalty for capital crimes was appropriate and reasonable to the intent of the Eighth Amendment and that the guidelines the judge used came under the *Furman* doctrine.

The Court ruled definitively that "the punishment of death does not invariably violate the Constitution." Since the decision, the Supreme Court has had to expand the criteria used in determining death penalty legality in such areas as mentally incompetent criminals, criminals under the age of 18, and the manner in which the death penalty is imposed. In addition, the Court has severely limited habeas corpus appeals of death row inmates, going as far as not granting a stay even when there was new evidence in hand that clearly showed the innocence of the person who was going to be put to death by the state.

This case and other decisions by the Rehnquist Court swing the pendulum to the interests of society in the manner in which the state can deal with the criminal elements. Surveys have shown that given a choice between the rights of the accused established in such cases as *Mapp v Ohio* and the ability of the state to deal with criminals and impose a death penalty, the majority of the people polled would favor harsher penalties for the criminals and fewer restrictions placed on the police.

Evaluation of Free-Response Sample Essay

1. Did the essay clearly establish the direction it was going?
2. Did the body of the essay give specific examples?

1. The essay asked the writer to analyze the central conflict facing the Supreme Court in the area of civil liberties. The writer had to establish a position regarding the conflict. That position was that, in fact, the rights of the accused and the interests of society sometimes clash. Using the two cases, the writer lays the groundwork for an explanation of how they clash.

2. The heart of the essay uses the facts, constitutional issues, and the outcome of the case to illustrate the premise established in the thesis statement. In the case of *Mapp v Ohio*, the exclusionary rule is used to illustrate how the decision furthered the rights of the accused, while the outcome of the *Gregg v Georgia* decision was used to show how the Court allowed the ultimate form of societal punishment—the death penalty. By tracing the circumstances of each case, the reader understands the dichotomy raised in the question. By providing an explanation of the constitutional issues, the writer built upon the facts of the case and explained why the Court made the decision. It was also significant to note that the decisions in both cases were made by different Courts. The key to answering the question was the explanation of the significance of the cases as they relate to the issue of balancing society's needs versus the rights of the accused.

SECTION 2: DATA-BASED FREE-RESPONSE ESSAY

Using the following headline and your knowledge of United States politics, answer the questions.

Abortion Advocates Call Attacks on *Roe v Wade* the Battle for All Mothers

1. Define the provisions of *Roe v Wade*.
2. Explain the point of view taken in the headline.
3. Apply the case of *Planned Parenthood v Casey* to the issue raised in number 2.

Sample Student Response

The headline entitled "Abortion Advocates Call Attacks on *Roe v Wade* the Battle for All Mothers," a title borrowed from the phrase used by Saddam Hussein during the Gulf War to describe how Iraq would defend itself against the power of the United States, attempts to show how the principles established by the landmark Supreme Court decision, *Roe v Wade,* are under attack by legislation in states such as Louisiana, Pennsylvania, and Utah. The *Roe* decision established the legality of abortion under specific conditions. Specifically, the Court determined that during the first trimester abortions could take place without any state law limitations. During the second trimester restrictions could be set up by the states, and during the last trimester states could outlaw and prevent abortions. *Roe* also established that in the case of rape or incest or if the mother's life was in danger, an abortion could take place anytime during the pregnancy.

The conflict facing the states revolves around the issue of the extent they can pass laws restricting abortions. The laws passed included:

- parental permission by minors who wanted an abortion.
- a 24-hour waiting period before an abortion can take place.
- spousal approval of an abortion.
- consultation with other social agencies and education of the consequences of an abortion before an abortion can take place.

The Supreme Court determined in *Planned Parenthood Association v Ashcroft* (1983) that minors must have either parental or court consent before having an abortion. In *Webster v Reproductive Health Services* (1989) the Court ruled that the state could prohibit the use of public facilities and employees to perform abortions and that the state could lay down a requirement to have physicians conduct tests to determine the viability of fetuses prior to an abortion.

In the case of *Planned Parenthood v Casey,* a Pennsylvania law called the Pennsylvania Abortion Control Act was challenged. The Court in a slim 5–4 margin ruled that the principles of *Roe v Wade* were consistent with the Fourth Amendment's right to privacy. They also, however, declared that the Pennsylvania law that set up a waiting period and parental consent was constitutional. It did strike down the provision of the law requiring a husband's approval of the woman's intent to have an abortion.

The question of abortion has continued to be a volatile issue. There have been violent acts committed by antiabortion activists, including murder of abortion clinic personnel, and the Supreme Court has also had to set rules regarding the right of assembly and protest outside abortion clinics. There continues to be an ongoing "war" between proponents of *Roe* and those who feel that abortion is akin to killing.

Evaluation of Data-Based Free-Response Sample Essay

1. Does the writer give an adequate explanation of the point of view of the headline?
2. Does the writer give specific case law that establishes the trend the Court has taken since *Roe v Wade*?

1. In addition to explaining the point of view of the headline, the writer also gives background information regarding the "Battle of All Mothers" part of the headline. The response also needed an explanation of the *Roe v Wade* decision so that the writer could interpret the data. This interpretation was based on attempts at restricting a woman's right to abortion (thus the explanation regarding the laws passed in Louisiana, Pennsylvania, and Utah). The writer effectively explains the *Roe* decision and compares it with the laws and newer decisions of the Supreme Court, which are found in the second question.

2. The author effectively uses a series of short bulleted explanations of how states have attempted to limit the ability of a woman to obtain an abortion. From parental approval to spousal approval, states have passed laws that if upheld would seriously water down the *Roe* decision. The writer proceeds to illustrate the point by referring to a key Supreme Court decision, the *Casey* decision. Even though the Court ruled in favor of the *Roe* doctrine, the *Casey* decision left the door open for more attacks on the part of the states to dilute the doctrine.

CHAPTER **6**

Civil Rights: Equal Protection Under the Law

Chapter Overview

The history of the civil rights movement parallels the nationalization of the Fourteenth Amendment of the Constitution.

Even though the Civil War solved the problem of slavery and established the legitimacy and dominance of the federal government, the fact remained that many states still passed Jim Crow laws, legislation that legalized segregation even after the adoption of the Fourteenth Amendment. Segregation existed in America, and the Supreme Court in the *Plessy* decision stated "separate but equal" was an acceptable standard. Some inroads were made as civil rights activists pressured the national government to address the issue of racial discrimination. But it took the landmark *Brown v Board of Education* decision for the movement to see results.

Other minority groups such as women, immigrant groups, Native Americans, homosexuals, senior citizens, and the young have faced discrimination. Congressional legislation and Supreme Court decisions have used affirmative action programs as a means of providing equality under the law.

This chapter will explore the constitutional and legislative basis of civil rights for minority groups. It will focus on the issue of affirmative action programs and how government attempts to solve one of the most perplexing problems facing American society.

Equal Protection to All

"No State shall make or enforce any law which shall abridge the privileges or immunities of citizens of the United States; nor shall any State deprive

KEY TERMS

Affirmative action
Americans with Disabilities Act (1991)
Brandeis Brief
Civil rights
De facto segregation
De jure segregation
Declaration of Sentiments and Resolutions
Equal protection under the law
Immigration Act of 1991
Jim Crow laws
Nationalization of the Bill of Rights
Plessy v Ferguson (1896)
Seneca Falls Convention
Separate but equal
Suffrage

any person of life, liberty, or property without due process of law; nor deny to any person within its jurisdiction the equal protection of the laws."

The equal protection clause of the Fourteenth Amendment provides the basis of the civil rights movement.

We previously defined civil rights as the substantive application of equal protection under the law to individuals. Prior to the passage of the Fourteenth Amendment, the Bill of Rights was the only protection citizens had. Even the principles outlined in the Declaration of Independence, natural rights, inalienable rights, and the statement "all men are created equal" suggested that civil rights should be an integral part of our government. But the issue of slavery quickly brought to a stop any fulfillment of these principles. The *Dred Scott* case in 1857 established that slaves were property based on the due process clause of the Fifth Amendment.

The significance of the Fourteenth Amendment is that it aimed to nationalize the meaning of civil rights. On the surface it seemed that states could no longer discriminate against their citizens. Yet one of the first key Court cases after the passage of the amendment had a chilling effect on any thought of nationalization of the Bill of Rights. The slaughterhouse cases, in 1873, involved suits by individuals against states, accusing the states of the denial of property rights under the Fifth and Fourteenth Amendments. The Supreme Court dismissed the suits and ruled that the intent of the Fourteenth Amendment was to protect the freed slaves, not incorporate the Bill of Rights. Yet when the Congress passed in 1875 the first civil rights acts since the Civil War, the Supreme Court did not follow the principle set down in the slaughterhouse cases. When a provision of the civil rights act, which established the legality of access to public accommodations, theaters, hotels, and other public facilities, was challenged, the Supreme Court ruled that aspect of the congressional act unconstitutional. Its logic was that the Fourteenth Amendment applied only to the states "operating under cover of the law." But the definitive action by the Court in *Plessy v Ferguson* in 1896 put the issue to rest. When Homer Plessy challenged the Louisiana state law that created two classes of railroad fares, the Supreme Court, using the fact that the passenger train had only an intrastate route, ruled that separate but equal facilities were constitutional under the equal protection provision of the Fourteenth Amendment.

Even after the Supreme Court case nationalized the Bill of Rights in the *Gitlow* case (described in Chapter 5), it reversed itself in a significant due process case, *Palko v Connecticut.* This case involving the issue of double jeopardy gave Connecticut the right to try an individual a second time. The concept of applying the Fifth and Fourteenth Amendments' due process provisions to citizens who felt their "privileges and immunities" were being violated by the state was rejected. The concept of ordered liberty became the criterion for any incorporation of the Bill of Rights into the Fourteenth Amendment.

Then how did the Fourteenth Amendment finally become the basis of the civil rights movement? It took the Supreme Court over 50 years to finally reverse *Plessy. Brown v Board of Education* signaled the beginning of equal protection under the law for African-Americans. There were, however, other significant First Amendment and due process cases before *Brown*, which started the process of incorporation.

Key Court Cases

- ***Gitlow v New York* (1925)**—freedom of speech
- ***Near v Minnesota* (1931)**—freedom of the press
- ***Powell v Alabama* (1932)**—access to a lawyer in capital cases
- ***De Jonge v Oregon* (1937)**—freedom of assembly
- ***Cantwell v Connecticut* (1940)**—freedom of religion
- ***Wolf v Colorado* (1949)**—unreasonable search and seizure

After the *Brown* decision, an activist Supreme Court used the principle of incorporation in many of their decisions to promote Fourteenth Amendment due process rights and equal protection under the law. The criteria they used were threefold:

- reasonable classification, the distinctions drawn between persons and groups;
- the rational basis test, if the legislative intent of a law is reasonable and legitimate and serves the public good; and
- the strict scrutiny test, which places the burden on the states to prove that laws that discriminate fulfill a "compelling governmental interest."

African-Americans

The civil rights era for African-Americans was ushered in by the Brown decision, other Supreme Court decisions, and congressional legislation.

Supreme Court Justice Stephen Breyer at his confirmation hearings called *Brown v Board of Education* the most significant Supreme Court decision in the history of the Court. In a unanimous decision written by Chief Justice Earl Warren, the Court redefined the meaning of the Fourteenth Amendment. It said that "in the field of public education the doctrine of 'separate but equal' has no place. . . . Segregation is a denial of the equal protection of the laws." It also called upon states to end segregation practices using "all deliberate speed." Yet in a survey taken on the fiftieth anniversary of the *Brown* decision, many school districts still have not fulfilled the *Brown* vision.

Brown put an end to de jure segregation, segregation by law. States and local municipalities have been able to continue the practice through de facto segregation, segregation of schools and other public facilities through circumstance with no law supporting it. Housing patterns, schools, and other public facilities have existed where they set up segregation as a basic practice. The Congress and Supreme Court have attempted to deal with de facto segregation. The landmark Civil Rights Act of 1964 made discrimination in public accommodations such as hotels and restaurants illegal. The law was affirmed by the landmark *Heart of Atlanta Motel v United States* in 1964. This case involved an Atlanta motel on an interstate highway that serviced a majority of travelers. The motel discriminated against African-American patrons. It claimed that the Title II provision of the Civil Rights Act of 1964 was unconstitutional. In a unanimous decision, the Court, using the interstate commerce provision of the Constitution, upheld the legality of the law. The Twenty-Fourth Amendment, passed the same year, made any tax related to the voting process illegal. In 1965 the Voting Rights Act was passed. This law protected the right of African-Americans to vote and made provisions for federal assistance in the registration process. The Civil Rights Act of 1968, called the Open Housing Act, made illegal the practice of selling real estate based on race, color, religion, national origin, or sex. The issue of busing to solve racial discrimination practices was resolved in the *Swann v Charlotte-Mecklenberg County Schools* case in 1971. The Court ruled that busing was a legal means of achieving the "all deliberate speed" component of the *Brown* decision. Even though these actions contributed to the civil rights of African-Americans, civil disobedience, racial riots, and stonewalling attempts on the part of public officials hampered the progress of the civil rights movement.

The modern civil rights movement for African-Americans has been characterized by attempts to achieve gains through affirmative action.

In a split, important decision, the Supreme Court in *California Board of Regents v Bakke* in 1978 established two concepts. A majority ruled that Bakke, a white who was denied admission to the medical school, had been the victim of "reverse discrimination" because the school set up a set of racial quotas that violated Bakke's equal protection. However, in the more important part of the ruling, a 5-4 majority also stated that even though race cannot be used as the sole basis for determining admission, the Constitution and Civil Rights Act of 1964 could be used as a criterion for affirmative action programs. President Johnson, using an executive order, directed all federally supported programs to adopt this criterion.

The *Bakke* case brought the issue of affirmative action into the forefront of civil rights. Both the Supreme Court and Congress have been sensitive to the issue of job discrimination. Legislation and decisions by the Court have dealt with that issue and more often than not have accepted affirmative action as a basis of determining whether job discrimination exists. The public has been very critical of affirmative action as a means of achieving civil rights for African-Americans and other minority groups. We will deal with it in relation to other groups later in this chapter. Insofar as it has had an impact on African-Americans, in 1979 the Court again permitted an affirmative action program favoring African-Americans in private industry if the program corrected past injustices (*Weber v Kaiser Aluminum*). In 1988 Congress passed new civil rights legislation that permitted the federal government to take away federal funds from colleges that discriminate. And in 1991 it passed a Civil Rights Act that placed the burden on the employer to prove that hiring practices are not discriminatory in nature. This 1991 act became a battleground between Congress and President Bush. Bush initially vetoed the piece of legislation calling it a "quota bill." Congress softened the bill to include the hiring provision as well as a provision that placed a responsibility on the employer rather than the worker to determine if any hiring tests were discriminatory. The significance of this act was that Congress, in proposing this legislation, responded to previous Supreme Court decisions that seemed to place the responsibility of initiating antidiscrimination suits on the individual. In addition, it illustrated the heated nature of affirmative action programs.

The nature of affirmative action started evolving in a dramatic form during the Clinton presidency. In a major policy speech, President Clinton indicated that he favored a policy of affirmative action that would "mend it, not end it." However, individual states moved toward ending it. A Texas Federal Appeals Court ruled that the Bakke decision allowing race to be used as a factor for admission did not apply to Texas state colleges. The California State Board of Regents also invalidated race as a factor in admissions in their University system in 1996. California voters also approved in 1996 The California Civil Rights Initiative, also known as Proposition 209. This initiative effectively directed California not to take race or gender into account in government hiring practices. A California appeals court ruled the measure constitutional. The Supreme Court refused to hear the case. Thus, the provisions of the referendum were implemented in California.

Because minority enrollment decreased, California instituted a policy that guaranteed admittance to its university system for the top 10 percent of minority students applying for admission.

In the spring of 2003, a 5-4 Supreme Court ruled in two cases involving the University of Michigan undergraduate school and University of Michigan Law School that the principles laid out in the *Bakke* decision were still valid. Writing for the majority, Justice Sandra Day O'Connor said in the undergraduate case that the school could not use a point system in which race was used as a basis for their admissions system because it was too similar to a quota system. However, in the law school a "critical mass" criteria could be used as a basis for admissions. These cases were significant because they continued the long-standing practice of using race as a basis for admissions.

Even with the significant advances made in the civil rights movement for African-Americans, there still is a perception that two societies exist in the United States. The Kerner Commission first established that point after the 1968 rioting and looting in major cities. In a 1988 *Newsweek* poll, perceptions regarding advances and conditions of African-Americans in America showed that whites believed much more than African-Americans that African-Americans were making gains, being helped by the government, and being treated fairly by the criminal justice system. A 1994 poll in *USA Today* indicated that there were major differences between white and minority attitudes in key areas of civil rights.

Key Court Case

***Richmond v Corson* (1989)**—This case created the impetus for Congress to pass the Civil Rights Act of 1991. It established the following five procedures for evaluating the legitimacy of affirmative action programs.

1. A scrutiny test evaluates programs based on racial classification.
2. Congress has more power than the states through the provisions of the Fourteenth Amendment to enforce equal protection provisions.
3. When the state takes action, it must do so based on evidence that past discriminatory practice existed.
4. Affirmative action remedies must be specific and apply to past injustices.
5. States may develop affirmative action programs "narrowly tailored . . . necessary to break down patterns of deliberate exclusion."

***Gratz v Bollinger; Grutter v Bollinger* (2004)**—The University of Michigan undergraduate school's (*Gratz*) admission practice was unconstitutional because it relied too much on a quota system. The University of Michigan's law school's admission system (*Grutter*) was constitutional because it relied on a broad-based policy of using race as a basis for admissions. Both decisions affirmed the *Bakke* case.

Women

The fight to gain equality for women has been tedious and arduous.

Most political scientists point to the Seneca Falls Convention in 1848 as the beginning of the fight for equality. At this convention Elizabeth Cady Stanton led the fight for political suffrage and supported a doctrine very similar in nature to the Declaration of Independence. The Declaration of Sentiments and Resolutions for women's rights stated in part, "The history of mankind is a history of repeated injuries and usurpations on the part of man toward woman. . . ." It listed a series of abuses such as government failing to allow women to vote, the compelling of women to submit to laws in which they had no voice in passing, and the withholding of rights given to other members of society. It took the passage of the Nineteenth Amendment in 1920 for woman to gain the right to vote.

From that time until the 1960s the women's movement was stagnant. The traditional family dominated. The Brandeis Brief, a friend of the court opinion offered by Louis Brandeis in *Muller v Oregon* (1908), which spoke about inherent differences between men and women in the workplace, was the prevalent viewpoint. Laws protecting women in the workplace were virtually nonexistent. Only during World War II, when women were forced to leave their homes for the war effort in the factories, were they recognized as essential labor. A turning point in the battle for equality was the publication of Betty Friedan's book *The Feminine Mystique* in 1963. The dawn of the age of feminism was born. Groups such as the National Organization for Women (NOW) and the National Women's Political Caucus were formed. They supported a proposed amendment to the Constitution, the Equal Rights Amendment. Previously described in Chapter 4 in the section dealing with the amending process, it attempted to do for women what the Fourteenth Amendment eventually did for African-Americans. It was ironic that one of the arguments used against its passage was that the amendment was not necessary because the equal protection clause of the Fourteenth Amendment already existed. One of the earliest acts passed was the Equal Pay Act of 1963, which required employers to pay men and women the same wages for doing the same jobs. However, the issue of "comparable worth," paying women equally for jobs *similar* to those held by men, has not been resolved by the courts or federal government.

Women's rights became a reality as a result of many of the acts of Congress and Supreme Court decisions that came about initially to give African-Americans their civil rights. The Civil Rights Act of 1964 had an anti-sex discrimination provision. In 1972 those Title VII provisions were extended by the Education Act of 1972. Title IX of that act made sex discrimination in federally funded education programs illegal. Just prior to that legislation, in 1969, a presidential order directed that equal opportunities for women be considered as national policy. It took a key court case, *Reed v Reed* (1971), which made a state law that favored men over women in the selection of an estate's executor unconstitutional, to establish a legal precedent. Two years later in *Frontiero v Richardson* (1973), the Court spoke definitively, stating that "There can be no doubt that our nation has had a long and unfortunate history of sex discrimination. . . ." A "medium scrutiny" standard was established in 1976 in *Craig v Boren* when the Court ruled that if discrimination was apparent, whether it was aimed at men or women, it would be illegal. The courts have also ruled that certain work-related situations constitute job discrimination. In 1977 in *Dothard v Rawlinson*, the Court struck down an Alabama law forbidding women from serving as prison guards in all-male prisons. In 1992 in *UAW v Johnson Controls*, the Court ruled that Johnson Controls could not prevent women from working in a battery factory, even if the work caused infertility in women.

A related issue, sexual harassment in the workplace, has been raised since the confirmation hearings of Supreme Court Justice Clarence Thomas. Since University of Oklahoma law professor Anita Hill raised those charges, the public's awareness of the issue has been on the rise. President Clinton's appointment of Ruth Bader Ginsburg to the Supreme Court in 1994 sent a signal that job discrimination and sexual harassment would not be tolerated.

Advances in political office also became a feature of the quest for women's rights. From the victory of Connecticut Governor Ella Grasso in 1974, to the appointment of Sandra Day O'Connor as the first woman Supreme Court Justice in 1981, to the nomination of Geraldine Ferraro as Walter Mondale's running mate in the 1984 presidential election, women have successfully attained significant public positions. In the 1992 elections more women were elected to Congress than ever before, including the first African-American Senator, Carol Moseley Braun. The trend continued in the 2000 election when more women senators were elected, including Hillary Rodham Clinton, who was elected as a senator from New York. She is the first former first lady elected to public office.

Homosexuals

Gay rights have lagged behind the gains of other minority groups.

Since the realization that AIDS, Acquired Immune Deficiency Syndrome, has been a spreading health problem, homophobia, the fear of homosexuals, has been on the rise. Attempts by gay activists and federal and state legislatures to guarantee equal protection for homosexuals have fallen short. In fact many initiative referendums, including one in Colorado in 1993, not only rejected gay rights proposals but also established legal obstacles for gays. Even the Supreme Court was not sympathetic. *Bowers v Hardwick* in 1986 dealt with the issue of the legality of a Georgia antisodomy law. Because the challenge took place by two homosexuals who violated the law, the case was viewed as a test for gay rights. The Supreme Court upheld the validity of the Georgia state law. In 2003, the Court reversed *Bowers* in *Lawrence v Texas*, ruling that a Texas sodomy law was unconstitutional.

However, in 1992, the people of Colorado adopted a statewide initiative known as Amendment 2. This provision provided that the state could not adopt any laws providing protected status for homosexuals. The referendum was brought to court and reached the Supreme Court in a case entitled *Roemer v Evans*. The Court found Amendment 2 to be unconstitutional based on the fact that "this class of persons was being denied the 'equal protection of the laws' because they were being precluded from seeking protection under the law against discrimination based on their defining characteristic." The decision provided a victory for gay rights supporters.

But in 2000 the Supreme Court, in a narrow 5–4 decision, ruled that a homosexual Boy Scout leader could be barred from that position by the Boy Scouts of America's national organization. The case arose when the Boy Scouts barred New Jersey Scout leader Jim Dale, a homosexual, from his position. The

Scouts claimed that they had a right under the First Amendment's freedom of association to decide whom to exclude from membership in their organization. New Jersey claimed that since the Boy Scouts' meetings took place in a public school, the Scouts violated New Jersey's public accommodation laws. The Court ruled in favor of the Boy Scouts. Fallout from the decision was widespread as many schools throughout the country refused to allow the Boy Scouts to meet if homosexuals were barred from participation.

In 1992 President Bill Clinton, through an executive order, directed the military to follow a "Don't ask, don't tell, don't pursue" policy. It allowed homosexuals to enlist and serve in the military as long as they did not disclose the fact that they were gay. This policy was criticized by many in Congress, and it had a difficult time being accepted by the military establishment. The order was challenged in federal court and the Court declared part of the policy unconstitutional based on the First Amendment free speech provision and the Fifth Amendment due process provision. The policy did not change during the administration of George W. Bush.

Although there have been few concrete victories, gay activist groups have been outspoken in their quest for equal protection under the law. They have insisted on marching alongside mainstream groups in parades, and they have made inroads on college campuses.

However, the biggest victory for gay rights came in the spring of 2004 when the Massachusetts Supreme Court ruled that gay marriages were legal. A firestorm reaction from opponents of the decision resulted in the drafting of an amendment to the United States Constitution that would define marriage as the union of a man and woman and make illegal any attempt to recognize on a national basis the legality of a gay marriage. Even though Congress passed and Bill Clinton signed the Defense of Marriage Act in 1996, a law that allowed states not to recognize gay marriages from other states and made illegal any federal benefits to states that did allow gay marriages, proponents of the amendment and President George W. Bush felt that its passage would be the only way to protect the institution of marriage. The Senate debated the issue and the amendment never came to a vote because of a Democratic filibuster.

Other Minority Groups

Senior citizens, the handicapped, and young people seeking civil rights and equal protection under the law have influenced government, resulting in the creation of public policies.

The minority group pie is being cut up into smaller and smaller pieces. Lobbyists and special interests represent almost every segment of the American society. Senior citizens, also known as gray panthers, have become an activist group, especially since life expectancy has increased tremendously. Society and government have become very sensitive to the needs of the handicapped. And with the realization that young people are the future leaders of the country, Congress has passed civil rights legislation especially in areas affecting educational policy that has an impact on the youth.

Ever since Social Security became an entitlement as part of Franklin Roosevelt's New Deal program, senior citizens have been recognized as a segment of the society that is a responsibility of the government. Today they are one of the fastest growing in numbers. Anytime there is talk of government cutbacks on Social Security or Medicare, groups such as the American Association of Retired Persons (AARP) lobby against the cuts. Senior citizens care about the issue of job discrimination. Even with many seniors retiring voluntarily at age 65, a number of complaints regarding employer discrimination against senior citizens have surfaced. Age discrimination acts were passed by Congress in 1967, and in 1975 civil rights laws made it illegal for any employer to discriminate against people over 40. In 1978 an amendment to the Age Discrimination in Employment Act raised the compulsory retirement age to 70. However, today there is a growing movement to ban any kind of mandatory retirement age. The issue of healthcare has also been a major concern of senior citizens.

Handicapped Americans make up around 20 percent of the population. They include people with physical, mental, and emotional disabilities. Many of them have been denied support services. It is only in the last 20 years that government has recognized the needs of this group. The exception to this was the recognition that veteran groups needed aid when they returned from World War I and World War II. The GI Bill of Rights was a major piece of legislation passed at the conclusion of World War II. In 1975 the Education of All Handicapped Children Act was passed, giving children the right to an education with appropriate services that meet the needs of specific disabilities. The landmark act passed in 1991, the Americans with Disabilities Act (ADA), required employers, schools, and public buildings to reasonably accommodate the physical needs of handicapped individuals by providing such things as ramps, elevators, and other appropriate facilities. This act also extended into the job market, making it illegal for employers to discriminate against the handicapped. The courts have recognized these acts protecting the rights of disabled Americans. Yet there are issues that may not be as definitive. Does the ADA protect individuals with chronic diseases? The Supreme Court has imposed limits. But in a decision reached in 2001, the Court ruled that a professional golfer, Casey Martin, who had a physical handicap would be able to use a golf cart during tournament play.

In subsequent decisions, the Court using the sovereign immunity provision of the Eleventh Amendment limited individual lawsuits against states under the provisions of the Americans with Disabilities Act.

Many of the same problems facing senior citizens or the handicapped also face young people, who have no significant lobby group. How have their civil rights been taken away? Cases like *Hazelwood v Kuhlmeir* (1988), which gives school administrators the right to censor school-sponsored publications and plays; *Bethel School District v Fraser* (1986), which gives school officials the right to discipline students as a result of a speech that was given by a student running for office containing obscenities; and *New Jersey v TLO* (1985), which gives school officials an almost unlimited right to search a student suspected of violating school rules, weaken the *Tinker* doctrine and severely limit the civil rights of young people. In 1995 the Court ruled in *Vernonia v Acton* that random drug testing of student athletes was constitutional. There has been legislation protecting young women and the handicapped. Title IX of the Civil Rights Act prohibited gender discrimination in such areas as sports and the right to enroll in all classes. The Americans with Disabilities Act applied to students attending school and in fact provided for extensive special education opportunities. State laws also protect young people against child abuse and mandate child support to families who have experienced divorce. Youth today have cried out for protection against violence and drugs in the schools and community. They have expressed the need to have employment opportunities after graduation from high school and college. And they received legislation in 1993 that established a National Service Program, making it easier for high school students to obtain government aid so that they can attend college in return for national service. One of the issues affecting young people that has become very controversial is adoption practices. Cases involving child custody point out the necessity for laws that recognize the needs of the child as well as the natural and adoptive families.

Other minority groups such as Native Americans and "new immigrants" continue the struggle for civil rights.

Virtually every segment of American society, including Native Americans and groups who have immigrated to the country and have obtained either citizenship or legal alien status, pursues their right to obtain the "American Dream." In order to accomplish this goal, their quest for civil rights is ongoing and is perhaps even more crucial because these groups have had a very difficult time reaping the benefits of living in this country.

Native Americans have an official government agency established as part of the Department of Interior. The Bureau of Indian Affairs has the responsibility of seeing that all legislative benefits are administered to Native Americans who by law are American citizens and have the right to vote whether or not they live on reservations. Native Americans living on reservations have a separate status and are recognized by treaty as possessing the full characteristics of sovereign nations. They are immune from state and federal laws, and they have the right to govern their reservations as they see fit. Other Native Americans living outside the reservation have faced severe poverty and must seek the assistance of the states they live in. Militant leaders such as Russell Means and related groups have pressured the government for specific aid packages regarding healthcare, educational opportunities, housing, and jobs. One of the significant trends that has boosted the standard of living for Native Americans living on reservations is the establishment of gambling casinos. Even in states that prohibit gambling, Indians by law have the right to build large casinos. The results of these ventures suggest that Native Americans have been able for the first time to develop a prospering economy for their people.

Immigrant groups such as Hispanics and Asians have grown in numbers as problems facing their home countries have increased. Cuban and Haitian immigrants have settled in Miami. Puerto Ricans and Jamaicans have made New York City a second home. Mexicans have fled poor economic conditions and have settled in Texas, Arizona, and California. Asians have fled war in Southeast Asia and have left Korea and Japan. Many have become citizens; others have obtained legal status. Unlike natural-born Americans, they are having an extremely difficult time obtaining civil rights. There is a tremendous resentment on the part of the American people to those groups placing an additional burden on America's welfare system. Even though these groups are increasing in numbers, they have yet to achieve complete political equality. There are an increasing number of Hispanic and Asian representatives in Congress. A Congressional Hispanic Caucus has been formed. Representative Henry Gonzalez, a Democrat from Texas, served as the chairman of the powerful House Banking Committee until the Republican takeover in 1994. Former San Antonio Mayor Henry Cisneros served in President Clinton's cabinet as Secretary of Housing. The courts have recognized the problems facing these groups. In the case of *Lau v Nichols*, in 1974, the Supreme Court ruled that Title VI of the Civil Rights Act of 1964 mandates schools to offer English as a second language to non–English-speaking students. A corollary language problem facing these groups arises when cities pass legislation making English the official language of the municipality. States like California have passed referenda abolishing bilingual education programs.

Just as nativist groups turned against immigrants after the first great influx (1880s–1920), Americans during the 1990s reacted in a strong way against immigrants and illegal aliens. From the efforts of California voters, who passed Proposition 187 in 1994, which attempted to deny illegal aliens social services and education, to the attempts of Republicans to deny welfare for legal immigrants, Americans continued to express concerns about the impact of immigration on the country.

Chapter 6 Review

SECTION 1: MULTIPLE-CHOICE QUESTIONS

1. Which of the following historical events advanced the intent of the Fourteenth Amendment?
   (A) Jim Crow laws
   (B) black codes
   (C) grandfather voting laws
   (D) literacy voting tests
   (E) civil rights acts

2. Which of the following judicial principles reduced the impact of the Fourteenth Amendment?
   (A) separate but equal
   (B) all deliberate speed
   (C) equal protection under the law
   (D) privileges and immunities of people
   (E) habeas corpus

3. Which of the following doctrines made the Bill of Rights applicable to the states?
   (A) incorporation principle
   (B) clear and present danger
   (C) separation of powers
   (D) the reserved power clause
   (E) the elastic clause

4. All the following criteria were used to establish the nationalization of the Fourteenth Amendment EXCEPT
   (A) reasonable classification of race.
   (B) the rational basis test.
   (C) the strict scrutiny test.
   (D) the suspect class test.
   (E) the police power of states.

5. Which of the following represents a legal difference between de facto and de jure segregation?
   (A) De facto segregation has been made illegal.
   (B) De jure segregation is legal.
   (C) De jure segregation is illegal based on Supreme Court decisions.
   (D) De facto segregation is supported by real estate agents.
   (E) De jure segregation was overturned by the *Plessy v Ferguson* decision.

6. Which of the following constitutional provisions has been used to strike down discrimination in public accommodations?
   (A) Tenth Amendment's reserve power clause
   (B) Article I Section 8's commerce clause
   (C) First Amendment's right to assemble
   (D) affirmative action laws
   (E) Fifteenth Amendment's suffrage clause

7. A major impact of the *Bakke* decision was that
   (A) racial quotas were legal.
   (B) racial preferences for minority groups were illegal.
   (C) reverse discrimination based on quotas was illegal.
   (D) affirmative action programs sponsored by the government were illegal.
   (E) affirmative action programs sponsored by the states were illegal.

8. All the following criteria represent procedures used for evaluating the legitimacy of affirmative action programs EXCEPT
   (A) a scrutiny test based on racial classification.
   (B) affirmative action programs based strictly on quotas.
   (C) states taking action based on evidence that past discriminatory practice existed.
   (D) affirmative action remedies must be based on specific remedies.
   (E) affirmative action programs must be based on narrowly tailored principles.

9. "The history of mankind is a history of repeated injuries and usurpations [in the past] of man toward woman."

   Which of the following documents contained this passage?
   (A) Declaration of Sentiments and Resolutions
   (B) Equal Rights Amendment
   (C) Seventeenth Amendment
   (D) *The Feminine Mystique*
   (E) Title VII of the Civil Rights Act

10. Which of the following furthered the cause of civil rights for women?
    I. the Brandeis Brief submitted in the case of *Muller v Oregon*
    II. Title VII of the Civil Rights Act of 1964
    III. decisions of the Court regarding the issue of comparable worth
    IV. medium scrutiny standards established in judicial decisions

    (A) I only
    (B) II only
    (C) II and III only
    (D) I, II, and III only
    (E) II, III, and IV only

11. Which of the following cases helped further civil rights for students?
    (A) *Tinker v Des Moines*
    (B) *Hazelwood v Kuhlmeir*
    (C) *New Jersey v TLO*
    (D) *Bethel v Frasier*
    (E) *Cleveland Board of Education v Lafleur*

12. Discrimination in the workplace has been made illegal by all the following EXCEPT
    (A) Civil Rights Act of 1964
    (B) Supreme Court decision in *Craig v Boren*
    (C) Supreme Court decision in *Dothard v Rawlinson*
    (D) Supreme Court decision in *UAW v Johnson*
    (E) passage of Proposition 187

Answers to Multiple-Choice Questions

1. **(E)** Type of Question: Cause and effect relationships
   Choices A, B, C, and D all weakened the intent of the Fourteenth Amendment. Jim Crow laws and black codes legalized segregation. Grandfather voting laws permitted former Confederate officials to vote even though they were technically not eligible and prevented African-Americans from voting under the Fifteenth Amendment. Literacy tests also made it very difficult for African-Americans to vote. The civil rights acts in the 1880s were the first attempt by Congress to nationalize civil rights. The Supreme Court, however, ruled that the public accommodation sections were unconstitutional.
2. **(A)** Type of Question: Cause and effect relationships
   Like the previous question, choices B, C, and D increased the importance of the Fourteenth Amendment. All deliberate speed was a key part of the *Brown v Board of Education* decision; equal protection under the law and privileges and immunities of people are key provisions of the Fourteenth Amendment. Habeas corpus is a civil liberty guarantee. Choice A, separate but equal, was one of the most significant results of the *Plessy v Ferguson* case and institutionalized segregation.
3. **(A)** Type of Question: Definitional
   The incorporation or nationalization of the Bill of Rights began with civil liberty cases in the early part of the twentieth century. It was not until the *Brown* case that this principle began to apply fully to civil

rights cases. Clear and present danger came from the *Schenk* case. Separation of powers, the reserved power clause, and the elastic clause are all constitutional principles.

4. **(E)** Type of Question: Negative
A compelling interest of the state such as the police power tends to weaken the doctrine of nationalization of the Bill of Rights. A major characteristic of incorporation stems from the phrase "No State shall deprive persons. . . ." Choices A through E are all tests the courts apply to equal protection cases.

5. **(C)** Type of Question: Definitional
By definition, de jure segregation is by law and de facto segregation is by fact or circumstance. After the *Brown* decision, de jure segregation was illegal. Choice D may happen, but if it can be proven, it would be just as illegal as de jure segregation.

6. **(B)** Type of Question: Sequencing a series of events
If you think of the court case *Heart of Atlanta Motel v United States*, you would conclude that the commerce clause was responsible for the decision that made the Civil Rights Act of 1964 apply to public accommodations located on the interstate highway. Even though choices C, D, and E are related to civil rights issues, they did not directly result in the recognition that discrimination in public accommodations is illegal.

7. **(C)** Type of Question: Cause and effect relationships
The *Bakke* decision had two major components. The first answered the question posed by Bakke. Could he be denied admission to Davis Medical School because of a quota? The Court, using the equal protection clause of the Fourteenth Amendment, said that quotas were illegal. However, the Court also ruled that racial preferences could be used as part of an overall plan when it came to schools or work.

8. **(B)** Type of Question: Generalization
The Courts have ruled that strict racial quotas invalidate affirmative action programs. Choices A, C, D, and E are all standards the Court has used in determining whether there is a sufficient cause to rule that an affirmative action remedy is necessary.

9. **(A)** Type of Question: Chronological
By process of elimination you can probably eliminate choices C, D, and E. A constitutional amendment would not have that kind of language. Neither would a legislative act. The *Feminine Mystique* may have dealt with the issue of feminism, but it was not historical in nature. The Equal Rights Amendment never passed, and it would not contain such an emotional statement. However, just like the Declaration of Independence, the Declaration of Sentiments and Resolutions became the first rallying call for women suffrage.

10. **(E)** Type of Question: Solution to a problem
The Brandeis Brief made the argument that there were inherent differences between men and women and convinced the Supreme Court to rule against the owner of a laundromat who wanted a woman employee to be able to work beyond the legal limit set by the state of Oregon. Statements II, III, and IV contribute to civil rights for women. Title VII applies to the workplace. Comparable worth deals with equal pay,

and medium scrutiny is a standard used by the Court to evaluate equal protection issues.

11. **(A)** Type of Question: Identification and analysis
Even though choices B, C, and D all deal with students, the outcome and significance of those cases weakened the doctrine established in *Tinker* that student rights are not shed at the schoolhouse gates. *Hazelwood* dealt with student press censorship. *TLO* enabled a school administrator to search a student without a warrant. Frasier's First Amendment rights were limited by the school as a result of the content of a speech he was making. The *Lafleur* case dealt with the issue of maternity leave.

12. **(E)** Type of Question: Negative
This question requires a knowledge of the decisions made in specific cases as well as the content of the Civil Rights Act and Proposition 187. You can probably figure that the Civil Rights Act of 1964 would prohibit discrimination. Because three Supreme Court cases are given, you could possibly eliminate the three of them as similar answers. Proposition 187, a voter initiative, took away state social services for illegal aliens in California.

SECTION 2: FREE-RESPONSE ESSAY (All choices are answered for illustrative purposes)

The federal government through executive action, congressional legislation, and Supreme Court decisions has pursued an active policy of civil rights for minority groups.

Discuss the validity of this statement by showing how executive orders, congressional acts, or Supreme Court decisions have either helped or hindered the civil rights of one of the following groups

1. African-Americans.
2. women.
3. the handicapped.

Sample Student Response

Over the past several years, the federal government through executive action, congressional legislation, and Supreme Court decision has pursued an active policy of civil rights for minority groups. Civil rights are those personal and property rights recognized by governments and guaranteed by the Fourteenth Amendment, the Constitution, and laws.

The meaning of civil rights has changed greatly over the years. The end of slavery marked a new chapter in the development of civil rights in the United States. After the Civil War a number of constitutional amendments were proposed to protect the newly freed African-American citizens and, less directly, other victims of discrimination. The Thirteenth Amendment abolished slavery and involuntary servitude. The Fourteenth Amendment extended American citizenship to all people born or naturalized in the United States. The Fifteenth Amendment extended the rights of suffrage to African-Americans. The phrase "equal protection of the laws" became crucial in the twentieth century struggle against discrimination. Although the Supreme Court was slow to address the concept, it stands today as the major constitutional means for combating sex and race discrimination in America. In its decision in *Brown v Board of Education* (1954), the Court declared that segregation in public schools was unconstitutional because separate facilities were inherently unequal. Rights have also been expanded through legislation. Since 1957, federal civil rights acts have been passed in an effort to guarantee voting rights, access to housing, and equal opportunity in employment. Affirmative action is also another area of public policy that is affected by the Supreme Court. Affirmative action is any action taken by the federal government to benefit minorities (sort of like reverse discrimination). Affirmative action can be seen in many aspects of society from quotas in college to minority candidates trying to get a broadcast license. The latter point is the foundation of the case *Metro v FCC*. The FCC uses reverse discrimination when giving out broadcasting licenses and favors minorities intentionally when considering broadcast licenses. The Court ruled that affirmative action was constitutional and the FCC won this case decisively. Judicial activism is used in this case to prove that affirmative action is constitutional by the Supreme Court, and the judges have created a new law separate from the legislative branch. Affirmative action is a concept built up by the courts and is a product of judicial activism. School policy, affirmative action, and civil rights are integral areas of public policy that need to be understood and followed through watching the courts. Judicial activism and restraint are very important ideas to understand because they usually help mold the decisions of many cases and play vital roles in our judicial system. These have been accompanied by much state and local civil rights legislation.

The successes of African-American militants encouraged women activists. Even though the struggle for suffrage had achieved voting rights for U.S. women under the Nineteenth Amendment in 1920, women now sought equal treatment in other social relationships such as employment and property rights. The Equal Rights Amendment (ERA), proposed as the Twenty-Seventh Amendment to the U.S. Constitution and intended to outlaw discrimination based on sex, states that "equality of rights under the law shall not be denied or abridged by the United States nor by any State on account of sex." Originally drafted by Alice Paul of the National Woman's Party and introduced in Congress in 1923, the ERA lay dormant until 1970, when great support was generated for it by the National Organization for Women (NOW). The ERA was approved by the House of Representatives in 1971 and by the Senate in 1972. On June 30, 1982, ratification of the ERA fell three states short of the 38 it needed. A Supreme Court case that enhanced civil rights for women is another way public policy has been impacted. Civil rights has a long and powerful historical background and has been shaped in many ways by many cases. One Supreme Court case that involves the conflict of civil rights is *Cleveland Board of Education v Lafleur*. In this case three female schoolteachers were forced to take a mandatory maternity leave without pay for six months before the expected date of birth. This type of law was found to be a violation of the Fourteenth Amendment under the due process and equal protection clauses. The civil rights of pregnant women is a perfect example of judicial restraint being used in a civil rights case. The judges stick to the Fourteenth Amendment in this case and strengthen its meaning, thus backing up something created by Congress. The judges decided that Lafleur was entitled to compensation for the hours of work she missed as well as reinstatement of her job and ruled in favor of Lafleur. Judicial restraint is clearly seen here as the driving force for this decision of this case.

The overriding purpose of the ERA was to give women explicit constitutional protection not afforded by the equal protection clause of the Fourteenth Amendment. The objective was to place sex discrimination within the direct context of violation of constitutional rights, the most serious sanction in the U.S. legal system.

Millions of people around the world have some type of mental, physical, or emotional handicap that severely limits their ability to manage their daily activities. Today, the preferred word for a handicapped person is *disabled.* This change in usage reflects the new attitudes toward the disabled in recent years.

This change has been most evident in the United States, with more than 43 million disabled persons (about 17 percent of the population). The independent living movement began in the early 1970s in Berkeley, California, and then spread throughout the nation. Independent living is based on the concept that disabled people should be given opportunities to work and live independently.

Hundreds of independent living centers provide for or arrange a wide range of services for the disabled, from hiring attendants and finding housing to getting a driver's license and maintaining a checking account. The central idea is to free the disabled from depending on relatives or institutions.

Beginning in the early 1970s, too, advocates of the independent living concept and others fought for and won the passage of scores of federal, state, and local laws making buildings, education, and employment more accessible to the disabled. For the most part, these laws have been aimed at breaking down the societal barriers that have denied disabled persons equal opportunities. They include statutes that mandate the elimination of physical barriers and the adoption of affirmative action programs to hire and advance disabled persons. Passed in 1975 was a federal law that assures all disabled children the right to a free and appropriate education in the least restrictive setting possible. A 1990 law extended comprehensive civil rights protection to the disabled.

Evaluation of Free-Response Sample Essay

1. Does the essay fully develop by definining key terms and establishing the direction the essay will be taking?
2. Does the body of the essay give sufficient and specific examples that illustrate how, through executive action, congressional legislation and/or Supreme Court decision civil rights have been achieved by African-Americans, women, and the handicapped?

1. The writer does an effective job in defining civil rights. Once the definition is established, the writer gives a historical basis of the civil rights constitutional amendments. The point is made that the foundation of the civil rights movement was in place. Using the *Brown* decision as a turning point, the essay proceeds to explore how executive action, congressional legislation, and other Supreme Court decisions have had an impact on the civil rights of African-Americans, women, and the handicapped.

2. The body of the essay reflects these examples. The writer gives specific examples of presidential leadership, laws, and court decisions to illustrate the point. For African-Americans the civil rights acts, Voting Rights Act, constitutional amendments outlawing poll taxes and literacy tests, and court decisions such as *Metro v FCC* are solid examples. For women the Nineteenth Amendment, the attempt to get the ERA passed, and the impact of the *Lafleur* case are excellent examples. For handicapped people the laws requiring equal access to facilities was an excellent choice. Of the three areas, the examples given in the section on the handicapped were the weakest because the writer did not give specific names for the laws referred to.

SECTION 2: DATA-BASED FREE-RESPONSE ESSAY

Look at the following excerpt from a Supreme Court decision:

> We conclude that in the field of public education the doctrine of "separate but equal" has no place. Separate educational facilities are inherently unequal. Therefore, we hold that the plaintiffs . . . [are] deprived of the equal protection of the laws guaranteed by the Fourteenth Amendment.

Explain why the Fourteenth Amendment has been called the guardian of civil rights. Use the Supreme Court decision discussed above to support your answer.

Sample Student Response

The Fourteenth Amendment has been called the guardian of civil rights ever since it truly resulted in the nationalization of the Bill of Rights. When the amendment was finally ratified by the states in 1868, it did not have the immediate impact that was hoped for. Southern states passed Jim Crow laws and black codes, which resulted in the creation of a segregated society. Even after the Congress passed the civil rights acts in the 1880s, the Supreme Court overturned the provisions of the acts that guaranteed integration of public accommodations. The slaughterhouse cases and the *Plessy* doctrine sealed the fate of the incorporation of civil rights provisions of the Bill of Rights until the *Brown* decision. Even though civil liberties cases included Fourteenth Amendment arguments prior to *Brown,* the Court acted very cautiously until *Brown.*

The decision cited in the preceding passage comes from the landmark ruling in *Brown v Board of Education* (1954). The arguments made by NAACP lawyer Thurgood Marshall convinced the Warren Court to overturn the doctrine of "separate but equal" established in the case of *Plessy v Ferguson* in 1896. The Court made it clear that de jure segregation in public schools is unconstitutional based upon the following clauses of the Fourteenth Amendment:

- A state cannot deny its citizens the "privileges and immunities" of the law.
- A person under the jurisdiction of the state cannot be deprived of due process including liberty and property rights.
- A person is guaranteed equal protection under the law.

Because school systems, both in the North and the South, set up what they called separate but equal facilities, they argued that they met the conditions set forth by the *Plessy* decision. They also felt that they lived up to the intent of the Fourteenth Amendment. One of the key factors in the Court's thinking was the evidence provided by sociologist Kenneth Clarke. He conducted an experiment in which he showed groups of African-American students white dolls and black dolls. Clarke asked the children which doll they most closely identified with. In most cases, the African-American children identified with the white doll. Clarke's conclusion, which he offered to the Court, was that these children felt inferior in a white society that pursued a policy of segregation. The Supreme Court pointed out that even if the facilities, curriculum, and expenditures were identical, there still would not be equal education. They therefore called for integration of the school systems with "all deliberate speed." This ruling became the catalyst for the larger civil rights movement, which culminated with the passage of the Civil Rights Act of 1964 and Voting Rights Act of 1965.

Once *Brown* was decided, the activist Warren Court used the equal protection clause of the Fourteenth Amendment to extend civil liberties, rights of the accused, and civil rights to the citizens of the states. For example *Mapp v Ohio* extended the exclusionary rule to the states. *Engle v Vitale* extended the doctrine of separation of church and state, and *Miranda v Arizona* extended due process provisions of the Fifth and Sixth Amendments to the states. But the equal protection clause has been applied in the area of civil rights, resulting in children being bussed to achieve integration and many state laws being declared invalid, which prohibited the inclusion of minorities in the workplace as well as access to public accommodations. The Fourteenth Amendment has also been used by the white majority who claimed that they were being discriminated against in affirmative action cases. The *Bakke* case is a good illustration of this principle. One other factor comes into play. Depending upon the philosophical direction of the Court, the Fourteenth Amendment principles can be either accelerated or slowed down when applied to civil rights cases. But overall, the Court has certainly viewed this amendment as a key player in protecting the rights of citizens.

Evaluation of Data-Based Free-Response Sample Essay

1. How does the writer evaluate the overall impact of the Fourteenth Amendment?
2. To what extent does the writer explain the relationship between the passage and the civil rights movement?

1. In order to answer how the Fourteenth Amendment became the guardian of civil rights, you must understand the concept of nationalization and incorporation of the Bill of Rights. The writer accomplishes this through a discussion of those principles. Specific incorporation cases are also brought into the discussion. The writer effectively demonstrates the far-reaching impact of the amendment on civil rights, civil liberties, and the rights of the accused by giving examples of activist Supreme Court decisions. Concluding, the writer observes that, depending upon the philosophical position of the Court, issues such as affirmative action can also come into play.

2. The writer does an effective job of analyzing the decision. First, the excerpt is identified as the *Brown* decision. Then the writer explains the cast of characters involved in the case. The key to the answer is picking out the constitutional provisions that are reflected in the decision. Because the Fourteenth Amendment is the key to the decision, the writer summarized the sections of the amendment that apply to civil rights. The writer also gives additional evidence from the Kenneth Clarke experiment, which ties in the Fourteenth Amendment to the "inherently unequal" part of the decision. The *Plessy* decision must be brought in to the discussion in order to explain the "separate but equal" part of the decision being overturned. Finally, added information regarding the impact of the decision is also raised by the writer when "all deliberate speed" is brought into the discussion.

PART TWO THE INSTITUTIONS OF GOVERNMENT

CHAPTER 7 The Presidency

Chapter Overview

The first of four institutions to be covered, the presidency has evolved into the focal point of politics and government in America. It is the political plum for those seeking elected office. The institution plays a predominant role in government having formal and informal relationships with the legislative and judicial branches and the bureaucracy. Other roles that make the president involved more than any other individual or institution in politics and government will be evaluated. Potential conflicts and the reasons why the institution has been criticized for having an arrogance of power are important areas to explore.

This chapter will focus on the factors that create a successful presidency. It will illustrate how, historically, the institution has grown in importance. The constitutional basis of power as well as the manner in which the president has used executive agencies such as the cabinet, the executive office, and the White House staff will demonstrate this growth. Additionally, the shared legislative relationship that the president has with the Congress will point to the complex issue of whether the institution has developed into an imperial presidency, a presidency that dominates the political agenda.

Whether or not the president succeeds, to a large extent, depends on the nature of the agenda that is set. The interrelated manner in which the president is able to communicate the agenda with the public, the way the media reports the agenda, and the approval rating of the electorate are factors that define the presidency. As Harry Truman said about the office, "the buck stops here."

KEY TERMS

Appointment power
Bully pulpit
Cabinet
Chief executive
Commander-in-Chief
Council of Economic Advisors
Executive office of the president
Executive order
Executive privilege
Impeachment
Imperial presidency
Line item veto
National Security Council
Office of Management and Budget
Pardon power
Pocket veto
Riders
Senatorial courtesy
State of the Union Address
Trial balloons
Twenty-fifth Amendment
Veto
War Powers Resolution
White House staff

A Quick Constitutional Review

- Basis of constitutional power found in Article II
- Must be 35 years old, a natural-born citizen, and a resident of United States for 14 years
- Chief Executive
- Commander in Chief of the armed forces
- Power to grant pardons
- Power to make treaties
- Power to appoint ambassadors, justices, and other officials
- Power to sign legislation or veto legislation
- Duty to give a State of the Union report
- Election by electoral college
- Definition of term limits, order of succession and procedures to follow during presidential disability through constitutional amendments
- Informal power based on precedent, custom, and tradition in issuing executive orders, interpreting executive privilege, and creating executive agencies

The Electoral Process

The vast majority of presidents have reached the office through prescribed methods, and only eleven have served two or more terms.

The first step in viewing the presidency is looking at the nature of the electoral process. Future chapters will deal with the political process of the primary system and nominating convention. Once nominated, the outcome of the election is generally determined by whoever receives the most electoral votes. The potential for a third-party candidate drawing enough votes to throw the election into the House of Representatives exists. When Ross Perot received almost 20 percent of the popular vote in 1992 and established his own political party, many political scientists predicted that in a future presidential election no candidate would receive a majority of the electoral votes. Two factors contribute to this threat. First, the rules of the electoral college system dictate that the winner takes all the electoral votes of a state even if one candidate wins 51 percent of the vote and the losing candidate gets 49 percent. Second, the allocation of electoral votes does not always reflect true population and voter patterns. California, with 55 electoral votes, has approximately one vote for each 550,000 people, whereas Alaska has three electoral votes for approximately 183,000 people based on the 2000 census.

On four occasions in American history, presidential candidates have lost the election even though they received the most popular votes. In 1824 Andrew Jackson received a plurality of popular votes and electoral votes, over 40 percent of the popular votes to 31 percent of the vote obtained by John Quincy Adams. Yet, Jackson did not receive a majority of the electoral votes; Adams received a majority of the votes from the House and was elected president. In 1876 Republican Rutherford B. Hayes lost the popular vote by a little more than 275,000 votes. Called the "stolen election" by historians, Hayes received an electoral majority after an electoral commission was set up by Congress to investigate electoral irregularities in Florida, Louisiana, South Carolina, and Oregon. The commission voted on party lines, and Hayes was officially elected president. In 1888 Grover Cleveland won the popular vote but lost the electoral majority to Benjamin Harrison. In the 2000 election, Vice President Al Gore received more popular votes than George W. Bush. Bush, however, won the majority of the electoral votes and became our 43rd president. If third-party candidate Ralph Nader had not run, Gore would have won enough electoral votes to have won the election.

Even though this has occurred only four times, there have been extremely close elections, such as the 1960 election between Kennedy and Nixon and the 1976 election between Carter and Ford, where a small shift in one state could have changed the outcome of the election. There is also a potential constitutional problem if a designated presidential elector decides not to vote for the candidate he was committed to support. They are called faithless electors. That happened on nine occasions without having an impact on the outcome. The third anomaly of the system could take place if the House and Senate must determine the outcome of the election. The Twelfth Amendment to the Constitution outlines this procedure, and even though it has happened only once, strong third-party candidates make this a distinct possibility in the future. Elections in 1912 (the Bull Moose candidacy of Theodore Roosevelt), 1968 (the American Independent Party candidacy of George Wallace), and the recent candidacy of Ross Perot all influenced campaign strategy. Two proposed constitutional amendments have been offered to make the system fairer. The first one would create a proportional system so that a candidate gets the proportional number of electoral votes based on the size of the popular vote received in the state. A second plan offered would simply abolish the electoral college and allow the election to be determined by the popular vote with perhaps a 40 percent minimum margin established. Any multiparty race resulting in a victory with less than 40 percent would create a run-off.

Presidential disability and succession are defined by the Twenty-Fifth Amendment. It allows the vice president to become acting president after the president's cabinet confirms that the president is disabled. This happened for a short period when Ronald Reagan was undergoing surgery after an assassination attempt. In 1996, a self-appointed panel of 50 experts, including three White House doctors, issued a report which established the criteria for declaring a president impaired and unable to perform the job of the presidency. The recommendations included: (1) a transfer of power contingency plan implemented prior to the president's inauguration, (2) the use of the president's personal doctor to make recommendations related to the health of the president, (3) a determination of what constitutes impairment be based on a medical evaluation, (4) the determination of when a president cannot serve be made by constitutional officers, and (5) there should be an accurate disclosure of the president's health which should balance his right to privacy. Although this report was advisory, President Clinton endorsed it and indicated that he hoped it would be used as a future guideline. The amendment also outlines the procedures for selecting a new vice president when that office becomes vacant. This happened after Spiro Agnew resigned in 1973. Nine presidents have not completed their term of office. Eight presidents have died in office, and one, Nixon, resigned. After Franklin Roosevelt died, in 1945, a constitutional amendment limiting the term of office to no more than two terms or a maximum of ten years was passed. There has been a growing movement to further limit presidential terms to one six-year term to reduce the amount of time and energy devoted to raising campaign funds and the time it takes to campaign for office.

Presidential Power

The power and influence of the president have evolved and increased as the United States has grown as a world leader.

If you think of the presidents who have been powerful and influential and who have demonstrated leadership, you probably will come up with the names of Washington, Lincoln, Theodore Roosevelt, Woodrow Wilson, Franklin Roosevelt, Kennedy, Johnson, Nixon, Reagan, George H. W. Bush, and George W. Bush. Even though Nixon resigned in disgrace as a result of the Watergate affair and Bush was not reelected, all the presidents listed dominated the national scene because of perceived leadership during times of national emergencies—war and economic hardship or domestic development. These leadership attributes can be categorized as the ability to manage a crisis, the ability to demonstrate leadership as perceived by the public, the ability to appoint quality officials, the ability to set and clarify the national agenda, the ability to achieve a legislative agenda, and the ability to achieve success in the foreign policy arena. These presidential attributes have also been classified by James David Barber in *The Presidential Character* as "Active-Positive," "Active-Negative," "Passive-Positive," and "Passive-Negative."

George Washington established the tenor of the institution. Virtually everything he did set precedent. The appointment of a cabinet, the establishment of a working relationship with Congress, and his warning to stay neutral in world affairs set the tone of the presidency for years. Even though, as a populist president, Andrew Jackson has been recognized as making a positive contribution to the institution, it was not until Lincoln resolved the issue of states' rights that the office really grew in power and influence. Theodore Roosevelt with his "square deal," the trust-busting policies of his administration, and his announced Latin American policy of "walk softly, but carry a big stick" brought the presidency to the forefront. Woodrow Wilson successfully piloted the country through the first World War, but did not succeed in obtaining a lasting peace. His failure to achieve Senate approval of the Versailles Treaty and the League of Nations weakened his overall performance. Without a doubt, the single most influential president during the twentieth century was Franklin Delano Roosevelt. His New Deal policies and the mobilization of the country to fight the Axis powers during World War II created a dynamic presidency, some say the first imperial presidency. Kennedy's New Frontier and the manner in which he stood up to Russia during the Cuban Missile Crisis, as well as a public perception that he was creating change for the country, strengthened the institution. Lyndon Johnson's Great Society programs were compared to many of Roosevelt's New Deal programs. The country became embroiled in the Vietnam War, and Johnson decided not to seek another term. Nixon's foreign policy accomplishments, the eventual ending of the Vietnam War, the détente with the Soviet Union, and the diplomatic recognition of China contributed to his presidency. Reagan and Bush have been credited with being catalysts in ending the cold war. They were in office during the demise of the Soviet Union, and George H. W. Bush's vision of a New World Order put the presidency in the middle of crucial policy-making decisions. President Clinton's legacy includes a balanced budget agreement and the longest period of economic prosperity in United States history. George W. Bush will be remembered as the president who declared war on terrorism that included invading Afghanistan and Iraq.

The Executive Departments

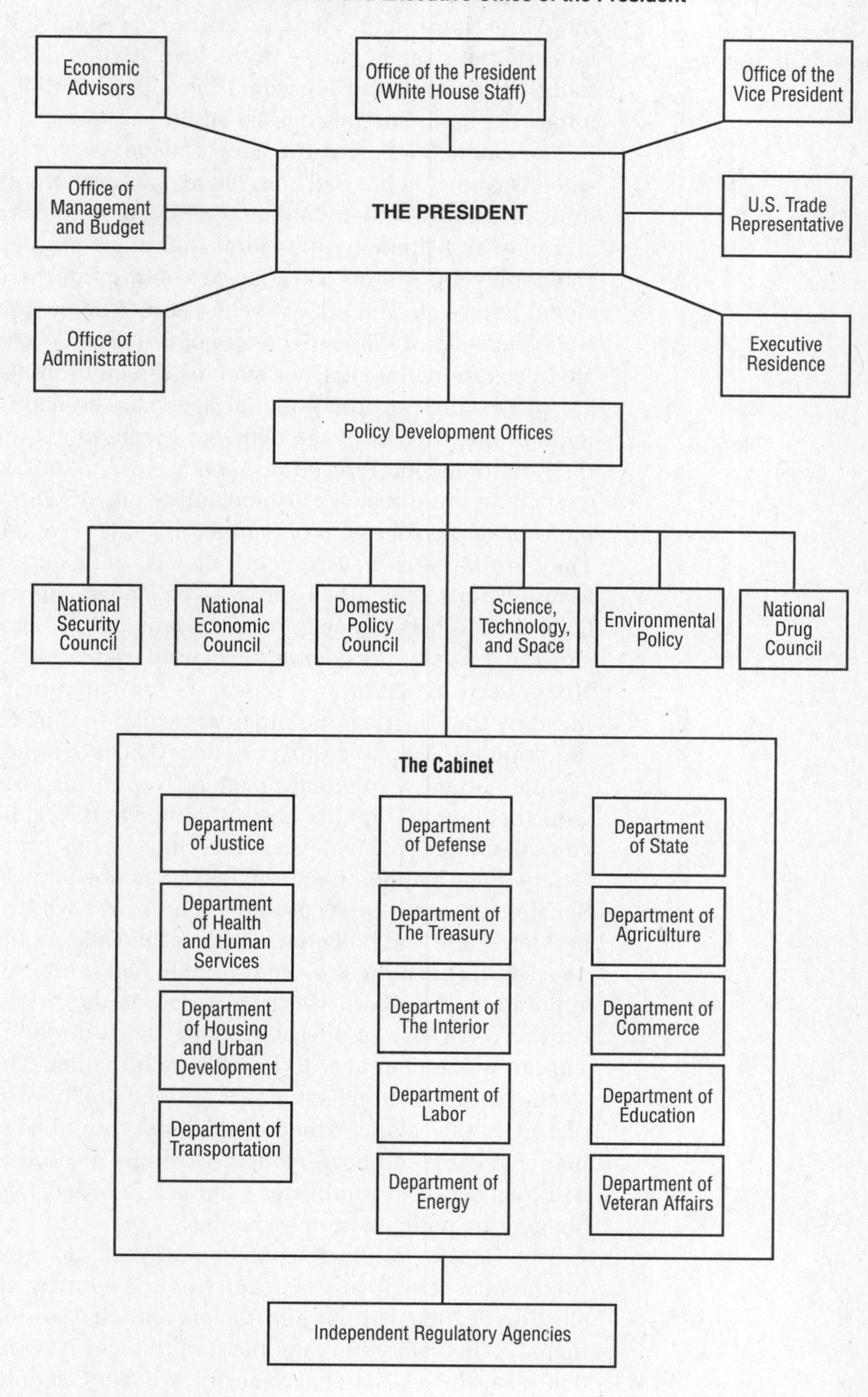

The growth of the executive departments has also contributed to the increase of presidential power.

As the nation's chief executive, the president must "faithfully execute the laws" of the nation. In doing so, the president has developed and organized the executive department into three areas—the cabinet, the executive office, and the White House staff. The administrative responsibilities of these departments increase the size and scope of the executive department as a whole. Through tradition, custom, and precedent these presidential appointments have determined the nature of presidential administrations.

The cabinet was instituted by George Washington. Every administration since Washington has had one. There have been unofficial advisors such as Andrew Jackson's Kitchen Cabinet. Cabinet appointees need Senate confirmation and play an extremely influential role in government. There are currently 18 cabinet-level positions. Creation or abolition of these agencies needs congressional approval. There have been cabinet name changes such as the change from Secretary of War to Secretary of Defense. Cabinet agencies have been created because national issues such as the environment, energy, and education are placed high on the national agenda. The cabinet has been expanded to include the director of the Office of Management and Budget, the director of the Environmental Protection Agency and, in 2002, the cabinet was expanded to include the director of Homeland Security. The vice president is a sitting member of the cabinet too. Cabinet officials have come from all walks of life. They are lawyers, government officials, educators, and business executives. Many cabinet officials are friends and personal associates of the president. Only one, Robert Kennedy, was a relative of the president. That practice was stopped by law. Presidents have used cabinet officials in other capacities. Nixon used his Attorney General as campaign manager. Cabinets are scrutinized by the American public to see whether they represent a cross section of the population. It was only recently that full minority representation in the cabinet became a common practice. To put this issue in perspective, the first woman, Frances Hopkins, was appointed to the cabinet in Franklin Roosevelt's administration. Cabinet nominees have been turned down by the Senate. George Bush's appointment of Texas Senator John Tower was defeated by the Senate as a result of accusations that Tower was a womanizer, had drinking problems, and had potential conflict of interest problems with defense contractors. During his term, President Clinton had trouble gaining approval of cabinet appointees. Zöe Baird was nominated as the first woman Attorney General. However, because of allegations that Baird hired an illegal alien as a nanny, Clinton was forced to withdraw the nomination. The event became known as "Nannygate." Issues facing a president are how much reliance should be placed on the cabinet, whether a cabinet should be permitted to offer differing points of view, and how frequently cabinet meetings should be held. Each cabinet member does administer a bureaucratic agency and is responsible for implementing policy within each area.

The George W. Bush cabinet and staff appointments signaled that the president was serious about unifying the country after the close and divisive election of 2000. Former Joint Chiefs of Staff Chairman Colin Powell was nominated as Secretary of State, the first time an African-American was named to that post. Bush's National Security Advisor Condoleeza Rice, a Stanford University professor, was the first African-American woman appointed to that post. A third African-American, Rod Paige, Superintendent of the Houston Independent School District, was named Secretary of Education. Mel Martinez was appointed Housing Secretary, and another Hispanic, Texas Supreme Court

Justice Alberto Gonzales, was named the White House Counsel. Women were also prominent appointees. New Jersey Governor Christie Whitman was named Director of the Environmental Protection Agency, and former California Agriculture Director Ann Veneman was appointed Secretary of Agriculture. Elaine Chao, former Director of the Peace Corps, was named as Labor Secretary. Bush also relied heavily on personnel from his father's and former President Ford's administrations. The only Democrat named to the Bush cabinet was Transportation Secretary Norman Mineta, who was the first Asian-American to serve as Commerce Secretary in President Clinton's cabinet.

Three controversial appointments ran into opposition. Former Colorado Attorney General Gale Norton was named Secretary of the Interior, even though environmental groups opposed her nomination. Linda Chavez, the former Executive Director of the United States Commission on Civil Rights, was originally nominated as Secretary of Labor but withdrew under pressure, after failing to divulge the fact that she had employed an illegal alien in her home for two years. Former Senator John Ashcroft was nominated as Attorney General and was opposed by civil rights and pro-choice organizations. Ashcroft had to endure a tough confirmation hearing before being confirmed by the Senate.

After the 2004 election, President George W. Bush's cabinet went through a major overhaul. Nine out of the fifteen cabinet members left including Secretary of State Colin Powell, Attorney General John Ashcroft, and Homeland Security Director Tom Ridge. Bush replaced the Secretary of State with his National Security Advisor Condoleeza Rice, his long time close advisor and the first African-American woman to hold the post of Secretary of State. His chief legal counsel, Alberto Gonzalez became the first Hispanic American to be appointed to the post of Attorney General. After appointing Bernard Kerik, a top associate of former New York City Mayor Rudy Guiliani, to the Homeland Security post, Mr. Kerik removed himself from consideration because he had employed an illegal alien as a nanny. Upon further independent investigation, other allegations were levied against Kerik. This raised questions regarding the so called "vetting" process (a process used by officials to check on the background of appointees). The consensus among political scientists was that the Bush nominees reflected diversity and because some came from the White House staff, it was interpreted as an attempt by Bush to promote his inner circle advisors to cabinet level positions. The nine resignations tied President Nixon for the most turnovers for a second term president.

Separate from the cabinet is the executive office of the president. It was created by Franklin Roosevelt in 1939. Today it has four major policy-making bodies: the National Security Council, the Council of Economic Advisors, the Office of Management and Budget, and the Office of National Drug Control Policy. The National Security Council, chaired by the president, is the lead advisory board in the area of national and international security. The other members of the council include the vice president and secretaries of state and defense as well as the director of the Central Intelligence Agency and the chairman of the Joint Chiefs of Staff. The president's national security advisor is the direct liaison. Even though the function of the council is advisory, under President Reagan, it conducted the Iran-Contra operations, which attempted to obtain hostages for arms. It was the mismanagement of this operation that resulted in the accusations that the president violated congressional acts prohibiting aid to the Nicaraguan Contras.

The Council of Economic Advisors consists of individuals who are recognized as leading economists. They are approved by the Senate and help the president prepare the annual Economic Report to Congress. This report outlines the economic state of the nation. The largest agency in the executive office is the Office of Management and Budget (OMB). Its director, appointed with the consent of the Senate, is responsible for the preparation of the massive federal budget, which must be submitted to the Congress in January each year. Besides formulating the budget, the OMB oversees congressional appropriations. It is a key agency because it has tremendous policymaking ability based on its budget recommendations. The department is also the president's direct link to other agencies and helps prepare executive orders and presidential budget policy.

The Office of National Drug Control Policy is a recent addition to the executive office. It is chaired by a director appointed by the president with the consent of the Senate. The head of the agency has been dubbed the nation's drug czar. The responsibility of the agency is to prepare recommendations on how to combat the problem of drug abuse. It also coordinates the policies of other federal agencies in this area. Other departments that exist in the executive office are the Office of Policy Development, the Office of Science and Technology Policy, the Council on Environmental Quality, the Office of Administration, and the Office of the United States Trade Representative. The Office of Homeland Security is the latest addition to the cabinet. Created after the terrorist attacks of September 11, 2001, the Office of Homeland Security is responsible for protecting the United States against future attacks. Each agency is responsible directly to the president and makes policy recommendations appropriate to each area.

In the summer of 2004, the 9/11 presidential commission held hearings and issued a report that recommended the creation of a new National Counterterrorism Center headed by the director of national intelligence. After much political in-fighting in the Republican-controlled House of Representatives, the bill, which was supported by a majority of Democrats, passed both houses in a lame-duck session of Congress. The law signed by President George W. Bush created a new counterterrorism center with a director appointed by the president and confirmed by the Senate. This director was given broad powers and coordinates intelligence among the many existing agencies. This new director and the agency also has the major responsibility of working with the Department of Homeland Security and becoming a link between federal and state agencies. The law expanded a security system for airlines, expanded security technology to other areas not previously covered such as transportation threats, ports, and illegal immigrants. The law also set up a Privacy and Civil Liberties Board, consisting of private citizens appointed by the president, ensuring that the security policies of the federal government do not breach the civil liberties of Americans.

The White House staff, managed by the White House Chief of Staff, directly advises the president on a daily basis. The Chief of Staff, according to some critics, has an inordinate amount of power, often controlling the personal schedule of the president. Nixon's Chief of Staff, H. R. Haldeman, kept a personal diary. It revealed the close relationship between the president and his Chief of Staff as well as the influence the Chief of Staff plays in policy formation. Other staff include the more than 600 people who work at the White House, from the chef to the advance people who make travel arrangements. The key staff departments include the political offices of the Office of Commu-

THE SEAL OF THE OFFICE OF THE PRESIDENT OF THE UNITED STATES

nications, Legislative Affairs, Political Affairs, and Intergovernmental Affairs. It includes the support services of Scheduling, Personnel, and Secret Service and the policy offices of the National Security Affairs, Domestic Policy Affairs, and cabinet secretaries. Each plays an important role in formulating policy and making the White House run smoothly. The first lady has her own office and staff as does the vice president. The role of the nation's first lady has been defined by each of the president's wives. Hillary Rodham Clinton was given the responsibility of chairing the Health Care Reform Task Force and moved from the traditional office in the White House reserved for the first lady to the working wing of the White House where other White House staff members work. After the efforts to get a comprehensive healthcare bill failed, Mrs. Clinton took on a more traditional role as the country's first lady. This role continued during Clinton's second administration. During the Whitewater investigation, Mrs. Clinton testified before a Grand Jury. Charges were not brought against her. Using the theme of her book *It Takes a Village to Raise a Child*, Mrs. Clinton continued to be an advocate for children's causes. Mrs. Clinton also became the only first lady to seek elective office. She was elected to the Senate in 2000 by the voters of New York.

Presidential Powers

The president not only has separate powers and inherent powers but also has shared powers with the other government and political institutions.

Besides the constitutional authority delegated to the president, the nation's chief executive also has indirect roles. These duties such as chief legislator, head of party, chief of state, and chief diplomat truly define the scope of the presidency. Depending upon the skills of the person in office, the power of the presidency will increase or decrease. Each role has a direct relationship with either a political institution or governmental policymaking body. The skills and ability to use these roles result in a shared power relationship.

The president as chief legislator develops legislative skills and a shared relationship with Congress. In developing a legislative agenda, the president sets priorities and works closely with members of Congress. Three contrasting presidents—Johnson, Carter, and Clinton—developed different styles in this area.

Johnson, having the experience as Senate Majority Leader, already had the skills of working with Congress when he assumed the office after Kennedy's assassination. He was able to achieve a great deal of success with his Great Society programs. Carter, coming from the Georgia governorship, was unable to work with congressional leaders and did not implement his agenda. Clinton, although a former governor, used his support staff and developed a working relationship with his own party leaders who held a majority in each house. For the first three years of his presidency, he was able to push through significant legislation including the Family and Medical Leave Act, a National Service Program, Americorp, and the Crime Bill. The fact that Democrats held a majority was a key factor in whether the president's legislative agenda was completed. George Bush, who as a Republican had to work with the Democratic majority, used a veto 45 times successfully.

The veto is a primary tool used by the president to influence Congress to meet his agenda priorities. Historically there have been over 1454 regular vetoes and fewer than 200 have been overridden by Congress. The presidents who have exercised the most vetoes were Franklin Roosevelt (372), Grover Cleveland (304), and Harry Truman (180). Another form of veto a president can use is the pocket veto. This occurs if the president does not sign a bill within ten days and the Congress adjourns within the ten days. This tactic has been used over a thousand times. One of the reasons why the pocket veto is used is that very often there is a rush to pass legislation at the time of planned recesses. One of the issues surrounding the veto is the attempt by some presidents to obtain a line item veto. Many times Congress will attach riders or amendments to bills. These riders, often in the form of appropriations, sometimes have nothing to do with the intent of the bill itself and are often considered to be pork barrel legislation. It becomes a means of forcing the president to accept legislation he would normally veto. In 1994 both houses of Congress passed a line item veto law, which President Clinton signed. Taking effect in 1997, the purpose of the line item veto was to let the president strike individual items from the 13 major appropriations bills submitted by Congress that he considered wasteful spending. The goal of the law was to prevent Congress from increasing appropriations with pork. The law was brought to the Supreme Court and was declared unconstitutional as an illegal expansion of the president's veto power.

As party leader, the president is the only nationally elected official. Other party leaders such as the Speaker of the House and the majority and minority leaders of the Senate and House are elected by their own parties. In this role, the president has much influence in setting his agenda, especially if he is a member of the majority party. Many times the president will make the argument to the congressional party leaders that their support will "make or break" the presidency. This kind of pressure was put on the Democratic Party when Bill Clinton lobbied for the passage of his first budget. Another key action the president can take to send a message to Congress is to impound funds. By this act the president refuses to release appropriated funds to executive agencies. President Nixon used this practice to curb congressional spending. Congress retaliated by passing the 1974 Congressional Budget and Impoundment Act, which set limits on this practice and set up an independent Congressional Budget Office. This act was significant in shifting the checks and balances scale to Congress. Even though he does not directly have the power to appoint congressmen to committees, the president certainly can influence a party member by promising to support pet legislation of the congressman in return for voting in favor of legislation supported by the president.

Another area of potential conflict between the president and Congress is that of national security. As chief diplomat, the president has the delegated constitutional authority of commander in chief of the armed forces, the person who can make treaties with other nations and appoint ambassadors to nations that are recognized. With treaties and appointments, Congress has a built in check—the Senate must approve treaties by a two-thirds margin and approve presidential appointments by a majority vote. Most judicial appointments are made after checking the appointment with the senator of the state the appointee comes from. This kind of "senatorial courtesy" often guarantees the acceptance of an appointment even if there is some minor objection from other senators. Such significant treaties as the 1962 Nuclear Test Ban Treaty and the Strategic Arms Limitation Treaty are good examples of the president working closely with the Congress.

However, it is the war-making power of the president that has caused the most problems. Since the Vietnam War, Congress has become concerned with the president's unilateral commitment of American troops. The Congress responded by passing the War Powers Act in 1973, overriding a Nixon veto. This act states that a president can commit the military only after a declaration of war by the Congress or by specific authorization by Congress, if there is a national emergency or if the use of force is in the national interest of the United States. Once troops are sent, the president is required to keep the Congress informed about the action and must stop the commitment of troops after 60 days. Congress has the leverage of withholding military funding to force the president to comply. This act has been compared to a legislative veto. The proponents of this measure point to such military action as Reagan's invasion of Grenada, Bush's Panama invasion, and Clinton's Somalia and Bosnia policies as examples of why it is necessary for Congress to have authority. Opponents of this measure point to the fact that only the president has the complete knowledge of what foreign policy actions can really have an impact on the national security of the United States. The issue has never been resolved by the courts, and the legislation remains on the books. Other attempts at legislative vetoes of presidential actions have been declared unconstitutional by the Supreme Court. In *INS v Chadha* (1983) the Court ruled that "we have not yet found a better way to preserve freedom than by making the exercise of power subject to the carefully crafted restraints spelled out in the Constitution." Congress does have oversight responsibilities over the intelligence agencies through committee hearings.

The president's influence over the judiciary comes from his power to appoint Supreme Court justices and grant pardons and reprieves. The difference between a pardon and a reprieve is that a reprieve is a postponement of a sentence and a pardon forgives the crime and frees the person from legal culpability. One of the most controversial pardons came in 1974 when Gerald Ford pardoned Richard Nixon, who had been named as an unindicted co-conspirator in the Watergate scandal. An instance when the Court told the president he went too far was the Supreme Court decision in *Nixon v United States* (1974). The Court told Richard Nixon he must turn over the Watergate tapes and rejected his argument of executive privilege. An extension of the pardoning power is the power of amnesty. For instance, in 1977 Jimmy Carter granted a blanket amnesty to Vietnam War draft evaders who fled to Canada.

President Clinton was criticized after announcing over 100 pardons in the last hours of his presidency.

Taken in total, the scope of presidential power raises the issue of whether the office has turned into what historian Arthur M. Schlesinger characterized as the imperial presidency. Looking at the manner in which Johnson and Nixon used presidential power, Schlesinger concluded that "power was so expanded and misused by 1972 that it threatened our Constitutional system." Even if one assumes that a president must use his power, especially in wartime, the question still remains how much power of the president should go unchecked by the other branches of government. It is a question that is still being debated today. In fact, there are proponents of the imperial presidency who feel that the president must exercise both delegated and inferred powers with the cooperation of the other institutions of government for the best interests of the country.

Relationship with the Media

The president's association with the media can be characterized as a love/hate relationship.

From the time John Kennedy instituted televised press conferences, to the challenge by Gary Hart to find some personal indiscretion in his private life, to the limited number of press conferences Ronald Reagan wanted, the role of the press has been a double-edged sword for the president. This issue will be fully explored in the chapter dealing with the media. However, let it suffice to say that modern presidents depend and rely on the media to tell the story of the president's agenda. The president uses his press secretary and the office of communications to deal directly with the press corps. He has a great deal of access to television, making prime time speeches for his State of the Union address. He also makes a weekly radio address talking directly to the public on any issue he wants to raise.

The press feels that they must establish an adversarial relationship with the White House in order for them to maintain their independence and integrity. Ever since the Woodward-Bernstein investigative reporting that helped bring down the Nixon presidency, presidents have tried to control the media.

There has been the often-described "inside the beltway" coverage of presidential politics versus what the rest of the country views on the evening news. The White House attempts to manipulate the media. Presidential appearances are designed to maximize his message. A public relations strategy by the White House of blaming the media for the nation's problems has been countered by the press who claim that they are the messengers. Yet the president needs the media to get his message to the American people. The press secretary holds daily press briefings. Reporters are given special invitations to have exclusive interviews with the president. Whether the press is biased against the White House is debatable. During the 1992 presidential campaign, supporters of President Bush accused the media of favoring Bill Clinton. As soon as Clinton was elected, his administration suggested that the press was portraying only the negative aspects of his administration. The tag *gate* has been attached to presidential politics. Iran-Contragate, Travelgate, Nannygate, Whitewatergate, and Interngate are just a few of the scandals, major and minor, that the press has covered in recent years, sometime described as a "media frenzy." This type of coverage can certainly make or break a president.

In one of the most bitter and partisan political clashes in American history, the House of Representatives passed two articles of impeachment on December 19, 1998. The events leading to the first elected American president's impeachment read like a sordid novel. Special Prosecutor Kenneth Starr had been investigating President Clinton's role in the Whitewater land acquisition and other alleged White House abuses including the dismissal of travel office personnel and illegally obtained FBI tapes. President Clinton had also been fighting other legal battles. Paula Jones, an Arkansas government official, accused the president of sexual misconduct when Clinton was governor of Arkansas. Clinton denied the charges, and Jones sued the president. The Supreme Court ruled unanimously that Jones's civil suit could proceed while Clinton was still in office. Clinton testified and denied the charges as well as charges that he had been involved sexually with a White House intern. When this relationship with Monica Lewinsky was reported over the Internet in January 1998, Starr began investigating the president to determine whether Clinton lied during his testimony in the Jones suit. Clinton publicly denied any sexual misconduct with Lewinsky; Starr's inquiry took seven months to complete.

The investigation culminated with the unprecedented testimony of the president appearing before a grand jury on video. Clinton again denied any legal wrongdoing, but admitted publicly that he misled the American people and, indeed, had a relationship with the young intern. Starr completed his report in August 1998 and concluded that there was "credible" evidence that Clinton may have committed impeachable offenses. The House Judiciary committee voted on four articles of impeachment. The full House rejected two of the articles and submitted to the Senate the final articles accusing the president of high crimes and misdemeanors as a result of grand jury perjury and obstruction of justice.

The Senate convened in January 1999 and, following the same rules that were in place when Andrew Johnson's impeachment trial took place more than a century earlier, met for nearly two months. The Chief Justice of the Supreme Court, William Rehnquist, delivered the final roll call vote on both counts. The Senate voted 55–45 for acquittal on the perjury charges with 10 Republicans joining with all 45 Democrats. On the count of obstruction of justice, the Senators voted 50–50. Neither of the charges received the necessary two-thirds majority required, and President Clinton was acquitted.

Public opinion played an important part in the impeachment of the president. Throughout the entire investigation, Clinton's job approval ratings were over 60 percent, the highest ratings of any second-term president. His personal approval ratings, however, were well under 40 percent. The public was suggesting that the president's private life should be separated from his public duties. One of the consequences resulting from the public's perception of the impeachment inquiry was that the Democrats gained seats in the November mid-term election. This was very unusual since, historically, the party in power usually loses seats. As a result of the election, Speaker of the House Newt Gingrich resigned from the House, forcing the Republican majority to select a new speaker.

As much as the press tries to gain access, the president in the end can control to a certain extent the nature of the coverage. For instance, when the marines landed in Somalia for a humanitarian purpose, the Bush administration gave full disclosure, and there was live coverage of the event. On the other hand, during the Gulf War, the media complained that the administration was preventing the press from doing its job.

Public Approval

The president must obtain public support for his agenda to be completed.

Public approval and mobilizing public support are crucial for the president to achieve his policy agenda. Public opinion polls (to be discussed more fully in Chapter 13) are constant barometers of the public mood. From periodic job approval polls to specific polls on how the public feels about public policy proposals, the president's program is constantly being evaluated. The average approval rating of presidents who have finished their term is only around 50 percent. Job approval, when a president is serving, fluctuates greatly. When the Gulf War ended, George H. W. Bush had an approval rating of close to 90 percent. At the closing days of his presidency, it was under 40 percent. After September 11, 2001, George W. Bush also had a 90 percent approval rating. During the presidential campaign in 2004, his job approval hovered around 50 percent. Public approval is dependent on party affiliation, age, education, and religious affiliation as well as how a specific event influences the public perception of a president's leadership ability. Specific areas such as the economy, foreign policy crisis, scandals, and legislative successes can influence approval ratings.

Every president wants to believe he has a mandate from the American people. Whether an election was won by a slim majority or a landslide, every president coming into office talks about a "mandate for change." Presidents have used their bully pulpits—the ability to use the office of the presidency to promote a particular program—to influence Congress to accept legislative proposals. Such techniques as Roosevelt's fireside chats and Clinton's town meetings have been successful in getting the president's message out to the public. Once support is obtained, the president must use it as a wedge to get Congress to approve his agenda. Such actions as Clinton's bus trip called a "buscapade" for his proposed Health Security Act, even though in the end it did not succeed, and Reagan's media blitz to obtain support for his tax cut are good examples of how the president uses his bully pulpit. Staged events such as bill signings solidify the support so that the next agenda item can be addressed.

Chapter 7 Review

SECTION 1: MULTIPLE-CHOICE QUESTIONS

1. The Constitution stated that the requirements for being president are all the following EXCEPT
   (A) obtaining a majority of the electoral votes.
   (B) having resided in the United States for at least 14 years.
   (C) being a natural-born citizen.
   (D) being at least 35 years old.
   (E) being a member of a political party.

2. Which of the following represents reasons why presidents have trouble getting their legislative agenda passed?
   I. Other policymakers have their own agendas and interests.
   II. Other policymakers have their own sources of power.
   III. Congress is not beholden to the president but to other interests.
   IV. The influence of special interest groups and lobbyists play a significant role.

   (A) I only
   (B) II only
   (C) I and III only
   (D) II and IV only
   (E) I, II, III, and IV

3. Examples of people on the White House staff include all the following EXCEPT
   (A) the Chief of Staff.
   (B) the White House cook.
   (C) the National Security Advisor.
   (D) the vice president.
   (E) the press secretary.

4. After Congress passes an appropriations bill, the president may do all the following EXCEPT
   (A) sign it into law.
   (B) send it directly to the Supreme Court for judicial review.
   (C) veto it, sending it back to Congress with the reasons for rejecting it.
   (D) let it become law after ten working days by not doing anything to it.
   (E) not sign it after Congress adjourns, exercising a pocket veto.

5. When the president needs support, which of the following does he look to?
   I. the federal bureaucracy
   II. the cabinet
   III. the president's party leadership in Congress
   IV. public support

   (A) I only
   (B) II only
   (C) II and III only
   (D) III and IV only
   (E) I, II, III, and IV

6. Using the bully pulpit refers to a president
   (A) using the power and influence of his office to exert pressure.
   (B) calling upon members of his cabinet to influence legislation.
   (C) using his veto power to reject legislation.
   (D) signing a piece of legislation into law.
   (E) taking a trip to a foreign country to sign a treaty.

7. When an international event that is interpreted as an imminent threat to the United States takes place, the immediate effect in the president's approval rating is usually
   (A) a sharp increase.
   (B) a sharp decline.
   (C) a slight increase.
   (D) a slight decline.
   (E) no change at all.

8. Which of the following describes a presidency that has become too powerful?
   (A) an imperial presidency
   (B) a presidency that refuses to react to the threat of foreign policy problems
   (C) a presidency facing a recession
   (D) a president that refuses to compromise with Congress
   (E) a president who vetoes the majority of legislation sent to him

9. All the following help to explain the president's difficulty in controlling the media EXCEPT
   (A) there are too many media outlets.
   (B) the media is protected by the First Amendment.
   (C) the public opposes censorship of the media.
   (D) the president's press secretary encourages media scrutiny.
   (E) the media acts as a linkage group.

10. Which of the following is responsible for the preparation of executive spending proposals submitted to Congress?
    (A) Treasury Department
    (B) Council of Economic Advisors
    (C) Federal Trade Commission
    (D) Department of Commerce
    (E) Office of Management and Budget

11. All the following are formal or informal sources of presidential power EXCEPT
    (A) presidential authority to raise revenue.
    (B) presidential access to the media.
    (C) precedents set during previous administrations.
    (D) public support.
    (E) the Constitution.

12. Which of the following methods is used by a president who wants to persuade reluctant members of Congress to vote for a particular bill? The president
    (A) transfers members who oppose the bill to unpopular committees.
    (B) denies campaign funds to members who oppose the bill.
    (C) threatens to deny renomination to members who oppose the bill.
    (D) threatens to veto a different bill that enjoys bipartisan support in Congress.
    (E) makes a direct appeal to the public.

13. Invocation of the War Powers Act of 1973 would be most important in determining
    (A) the nature of the commitment of United States Marines to a peace-keeping role in Bosnia.
    (B) the amount of financial aid to the Contras of Nicaragua.
    (C) the timing of naval maneuvers off the coast of Libya.
    (D) the appointment of the Joint Chiefs of Staff.
    (E) the legality of extraditing foreign agents responsible for acts of terrorism.

14. The usefulness to the president of having cabinet members as political advisers is undermined by the fact that
    (A) the president has little latitude in choosing cabinet members.
    (B) cabinet members have little political support independent of the president.
    (C) cabinet members are usually drawn from Congress and retain loyalties to Congress.
    (D) the loyalties of cabinet members are often divided between loyalty to the president and loyalty to their own executive departments.
    (E) the cabinet operates as a collective unit and individual members have limited access to the president.

ANSWERS TO MULTIPLE-CHOICE QUESTIONS

1. **(E)** Type of Question: Negative
   At the time of the adoption of the Constitution, the issue of citizenship was very important. The authors of the Constitution created citizenship requirements for elective office. The only elective office that required a person seeking office to be a natural-born citizen was the presidency. Choice E is the correct answer because nowhere in the document is a political party even mentioned. It is part of the unwritten Constitution.
2. **(E)** Type of Question: Sequencing a series of events
   The concept being discussed is what prevents presidents from accomplishing their agenda. The key to the answer is that other policymakers such as Congress and the judiciary sometimes do not have the same goals as the president. In addition, the importance of special interest groups and lobbyists creates obstacles for the president.
3. **(D)** Type of Question: Negative
   The vice president of the United States, although a member of the president's team, is still an elected official. The Chief of Staff, the White House cook, the National Security Advisor, and the president's press secretary are all members of the White House staff.
4. **(A)** Type of Question: Identification/except
   The president has other options as outlined in choices C, D, and E. Choice B is incorrect because only the Supreme Court can decide to hear a case dealing with a bill signed into law.
5. **(E)** Type of Question: Hypothetical
   Depending upon the situation, the president has a number of different avenues to gain support for his position. The bureaucracy, even if there

are some components that are independent, still can be called upon to give information the president can use. The cabinet members are loyal members who understand that if the president needs support, they will respond. The president's party leadership, although they may differ on occasion, more often than not support the president's programs. And public support sometimes can tip the balance.

6. **(A)** Type of Question: Definitional
Even though the president has many different tools at his disposal, the bully pulpit of the office is quite effective in gaining public support or giving a message to the Congress, the media, and the public. Through the proper timing of a speech, the president can clearly indicate whether he will be supporting a particular position.

7. **(A)** Type of Question: Hypothetical
The student who reads too much into this type of question will usually come up with the wrong answer. The clue to the answer is "imminent threat." The public looks to the president for leadership. If an international event takes place and the public believes that it threatens national security, they will look to the president. In doing so his approval rating will take an immediate jump. However, if the president fails to respond or if the results include American soldiers being wounded, then the approval rating will decline.

8. **(A)** Type of Question: Generalization
An imperial presidency can be described as an administration such as Franklin Roosevelt's or Lyndon Johnson's during the time before the Vietnam War escalated. These presidencies dominated the agenda and succeeded in getting legislation passed without interference of the other policymakers. There has been a debate over the last 25 years whether the political scene has been dominated by an imperial Congress or imperial presidency. The other part of the debate is whether or not a clear winner in the argument would be good for the country.

9. **(D)** Type of Question: Negative
The relationship between the president and the media has undergone significant changes. In its coverage of Franklin Roosevelt, the media did not make reference to his disability. Though the media knew about John Kennedy's indiscretions, they did not publicize them. Choice D is the correct answer because the president's press secretary does not encourage media scrutiny. If you think of Bill Clinton's impeachment, this choice becomes even clearer.

10. **(E)** Type of Question: Identification and analysis
This is a factually based question. The major difficulty is discerning whether the Treasury Department, the Council of Economic Advisors, or the OMB has primary responsibility. By law it is the Office of Management and Budget, although there certainly is input from other agencies in this process.

11. **(A)** Type of Question: Negative
This question requires that you have knowledge of both formal and informal sources of presidential authority. All formal powers are listed in the Constitution (choice E). Choices B, C, and D are sources of informal authority. The president's access to the media furthers an agenda. The support of the people can be used as leverage, and precedents are as significant as written law. Raising revenue, choice A, is a power delegated to Congress.

12. **(E)** Type of Question: Sequencing a series of events
The president has limited actual powers in taking action against members of Congress who don't agree with him. He may have some influence regarding committee appointments. He has more influence with the chairman of the national committee, but it does not extend to denying campaign funds or renomination. And threatening to veto a popular bill would not accomplish any positive results. Sometimes a direct appeal to the public or using his bully pulpit can succeed.
13. **(A)** Type of Question: Cause and effect relationships
The passage of the War Powers Act over President Nixon's veto was prompted by the United States' involvement in Vietnam. The act has never been recognized by a sitting president nor has it been declared unconstitutional by the courts. Since its passage, Congress has threatened to use it when forces were committed to Grenada, Panama, and the Persian Gulf. The president was able to justify those actions. Choices B, C, D, and E are all actions within the legal perview of the president. Committing troops to Bosnia over an extended period of time could be challenged.
14. **(D)** Type of Question: Cause and effect relationships
Even though a cabinet member has a primary loyalty to the president, because there is also a huge responsibility to administer a large agency, the secretary also has a loyalty to that department. The president has a wide latitude in choosing cabinet members and many times selects a secretary who was a close political ally. Even if a cabinet member is drawn from Congress, once sworn in, the official's first loyalty is to the president. Cabinet members do have other sources of political support and certainly have more than limited access to the president.

SECTION 2: FREE-RESPONSE ESSAY

Assess the validity of the following statement.

> Presidential greatness is, to a large extent, determined as a result of a president being in the right place at the right time.

Be sure to use three examples from 1960 to 2000 in the essay as well as define the criteria you believe is necessary to characterize a president as great.

Sample Student Response

"Presidential greatness is, to a large extent, determined as a result of a president being in the right place at the right time." This statement is a true reflection on the qualifying of great presidents. When you think of some of the better presidents of all time, Washington, who was the first; Lincoln, who freed the slaves; Roosevelt, who ended the Depression; and Nixon, who ended Vietnam, you not only think of the presidents but also the corresponding events that occurred during their presidencies. Conversely, when you think of bad presidents such as Hoover, who was in office during the start of the Depression, or Polk, who did nothing, you think of their lack of effectiveness because of their inactivity.

When you start to define who is and who isn't a good president, you must first establish some criteria. Leadership, the president's ability to sway public opinion and persuade the Congress to support his ideas, is one criterion. Domestic policy, the president's ability to deal with issues arising at home and his ability to establish policy to anticipate or react to changing times, is another. Foreign policy, the president's ability to establish peaceful relations in some cases and to use force in other cases as well as his ability to use the force effectively, is yet another criterion. Finally, the last criterion is the president's ability to handle national emergencies effectively and at little cost to the American public.

Some of the other criteria that characterize a president as great: the ability to maintain faith in the government during times of crisis; the ability to maintain faith in the American people during times of crisis; the ability to communicate ideas clearly; the ability to lead the American people in positive ways; the ability to enact positive changes; the ability to present a plan and then enact it; and the ability to follow through.

John Kennedy instilled a pride of the nation in the American people. People were proud of being American and wanted to improve their nation. Kennedy's policy of the New Frontier and the way in which he withstood the pressures of the Cuban Missile Crisis established him as a symbol of greatness for the American people. Lyndon Johnson's vision of a Great Society and the beginning of the Vietnam War were the issues that confronted him and his position of leadership.

When the issue of foreign policy is raised, Richard Nixon has to be considered one of the greatest presidents of all time. He was the first president ever to travel to Russia and China, establishing détente with Russia, and recognizing China, making him one of the best foreign policy presidents. The president's ability to deal with a national emergency is a characteristic that encompasses all these other categories.

Both Ronald Reagan and George H. W. Bush had much to do with the eventual ending of the cold war that had plagued world history for years. The issues that faced these presidents put them in crucial positions that affected the policy-making of the entire nation and the direction it was to take. All the aforementioned presidents had significant accomplishments that were made possible by the times and the situations that were present during each of these periods.

Evaluation of Free-Response Sample Essay

1. Does the essay assess the validity of the statement as well as refer to the criteria being used to determine what makes the president great?
2. Are sufficient examples that support the criteria given?

1. The essay specifically establishes a premise that throughout our history presidential greatness has been determined by being at the right place at the right time. Even though the writer does not state definitively whether there is agreement with the statement, the extensive criteria set up gives a clear indication that there are other factors besides circumstance which determine

presidential greatness. The strength of the thesis is the diverse criteria set up including leadership, response to foreign and domestic crisis, the ability of a president to communicate effectively, and the ability of a president to accomplish his agenda.

2. The writer, through a historical survey, highlights the presidents who meet the criteria. Even though there is a great deal of disagreement among historians and political writers regarding who the best and worse presidents were, the writer does an effective job in giving specific examples to support the presidents selected. Even a president who resigned in disgrace, Nixon, is given credit in the area of foreign policy.

SECTION 2: DATA-BASED FREE-RESPONSE ESSAY

Look at the following table based on generally reported press releases:

Event	Approval of President's Actions (%)
Bay of Pigs Invasion	Preevent: 73 Postevent: 83
Cuban Missile Crisis	Preevent: 61 Postevent: 74
Nixon's Trip to China	Preevent: 49 Postevent: 56
Camp David Meeting on the Middle East	Preevent: 42 Postevent: 56
Terrorist Bombing of Marines in Lebanon	Preevent: 48 Postevent: 56
Welfare Reform Legislation Signed	Preevent: 39 Postevent: 58

List three factors that influence public perception regarding how well a president is doing his job. Analyze how the chart above explains the relationship between an event and approval ratings.

Sample Student Response

The major factors influencing public opinion polls based on this chart include:

- pre- and postelection upswings—Most presidents, even those with negative ratings, usually have a jump in the ratings prior to and immediately following elections.
- the ability of a president to handle foreign policy crisis—Such issues as ending wars, getting embroiled in unpopular wars, and responding quickly to foreign crisis has a dramatic impact on public opinion.
- the condition of the economy—Inflation, economic recessions, periods of economic recovery, and taxing polices influence the public's viewpoint.
- leadership shown during a domestic crisis—Moral and ethical issues as well as the way a president responds to national emergencies play a big part in the way the public responds to a president.

- the ability of a president to get his programs through Congress—If a president is viewed as ineffective (Carter's relationship with Congress) or can get his agenda through (like Clinton achieving welfare reform), the public takes notice.

The conclusions that can be reached from this chart are that each president has had a major event during his administration that caused a sharp decline or increase in his approval rating. For example, during Truman's administration, after the dropping of the atomic bomb in 1945, which ended World War II, his approval rating rose sharply. Eisenhower was generally liked throughout his administration, although, when the economy started a downward trend, his approval rating dropped. Another factor influencing the approval rating of a president is foreign policy failures. For instance, after the Bay of Pigs invasion failed, John Kennedy's approval rating dropped to one of the lowest points of his administration. The difference between Johnson's ratings during the successes of his Great Society program versus the ratings he had at the height of the Vietnam War were striking. Scandals such as Watergate and Iran-Contra also have turned public opinion against a sitting president. A period of economic instability such as the high inflation during Carter's presidency in addition to the hostage crisis resulted in a double whammy of public disapproval.

As noted, all the presidents in the chart were involved in major events, foreign and domestic, which they responded to in different ways. Generally, if a president handled the situation well, the public perceived him as a leader and gave him a high approval rating. The converse is also true. Those presidents who were ineffective include Carter, for his response to the Iranian takeover of the United States Embassy and Nixon, for his involvement in Watergate. They received negative response from the American public. Even when the country rallies around a president, such as when Gerald Ford became president after Nixon's resignation, the public turned against him after he pardoned Nixon.

Evaluation of Data-Based Free-Response Sample Essay

1. Does the writer describe the table and give examples that support the conclusions reached?
2. Are criteria developed from the conclusions in the first part which establish why a presidential approval rating goes up or down?

1. The writer does a superb job describing the manner in which the table traces the approval ratings of the presidents from Truman to Bush. Interspersing events with the presidents involved and correlating the approval rating trends leads the reader through different examples that explain why approval ratings increase or decrease. In a question like this, the writer who offers more than one or two concrete examples gets the most credit.

2. The criteria developed stem from the examples used in the first part. Again, the writer uses more than one or two criteria to make the point that the public responds to many different circumstances in determining whether or not to support a president. The writer also demonstrated a close scrutiny of the table by pointing out that there are pre- and post-election swings that usually take place. Another strength of the response was that, in addition to giving criteria, the writer also gave a short explanation of what the criteria meant. Notice that the writer was able to "bullet" a part of the answer.

CHAPTER 8 The Congress

Chapter Overview

The Congress can be viewed as the citizens' direct link to the branch of government that is responsible for forming public policy. It has a number of functions including, but not limited to, representing the interests of constituents, lawmaking through consensus building, oversight of other governmental agencies, policy clarification, and ratification of public policies.

As the focal point of public policy development, the Congress has come under public criticism. Polls have reflected deep voter concern regarding the issues of congressional gridlock, term limits for representatives and senators, and the influence of lobbyists and PACs on representatives. Many newly elected representatives have committed themselves to reforming congressional structure, procedures, and practices.

This chapter will explore these public concerns of the Congress, the advantage of incumbency and the changing face of Congress, the structure of Congress, the lawmaking process, the constituent relationship between the voters and their representatives, the influence of lobbyists, and the attempts at congressional reform. The issue of whether an imperial Congress is threatening our system of government will also be discussed in the sample essay at the end of the chapter.

A Quick Constitutional Review

- Basis of constitutional authority found in Article I.
- A House member must be at least 25 years old, an American citizen for

KEY TERMS

Baker v Carr	Logrolling
Cloture	Majority leader
Conference committees	Minority leader
Congressional oversight	Pork barrel
Constituent	President pro tempore
Filibuster	Reapportionment
Franking	Regulatory policy
Gerrymandering	Select committees
Gridlock	Speaker of the House
Imperial Congress	Standing committees
Incumbents	Whips
Joint committee	

seven years, and an inhabitant of the state the representative represents. Representatives serve two-year terms.

- A senator must be 30 years old, an American citizen for nine years, and a resident of the state the senator represents. Senators serve six-year terms.
- Common powers delegated to Congress, listed in Article I Section 8 include the power to tax, coin money, declare war, and regulate foreign and interstate commerce.
- Implied congressional power comes from the "necessary and proper" clause, which has been referred to as the elastic clause.
- House of Representatives has the power to begin all revenue bills, to select president if there is no electoral college majority, and to initiate impeachment proceedings.
- Senate has the power to approve presidential appointments and treaties and to try impeachment proceedings.
- Congress may overrule a presidential veto by a two-thirds vote of each house.

Reelection

Even though congressional elections have favored incumbency, a new face of Congress has evolved.

The history of Congress reflects long-standing traditions. The first meetings in both houses established the committee system, which still exists today. Even though the Senate was originally selected by state legislatures (corrected by the Seventeenth Amendment in 1913), both houses fulfilled their lawmaking responsibility. The reelection rate of the Congress in its early days was low. In the first ten years, over one-third of the senators resigned before the end of their terms. In the House a large number of representatives served only one or two terms.

As political parties began to develop, the congressional reelection rate began to increase. By the time of the Civil War, many election victories resulted from party affiliation and incumbency. After the Seventeenth Amendment, the entire political structure of the Congress changed. By the time of the modern-day presidents (Kennedy, Johnson, Nixon, Ford, George H. W. Bush, Clinton, and George W. Bush), it became evident that influential senators and representatives could use their office as an entrée to the presidency.

Other factors that changed the nature of congressional elections were the make-up of congressional districts, the primary system for nominating candidates, the importance of party politics, and the resulting election of most incumbents. The Constitution defines the manner in which Congress must reapportion its make-up after each census. However, once the total number of seats was established (435 in 1910), Congress found it difficult to adopt new representation procedures. In fact, the Reapportionment Act of 1929 is still the standing law. It provides for a permanent size of the House and provides for the number of seats, based on the census, each state should have. Currently, each seat represents an average of about 650,000 people. However, it is left to the individual states to determine the make-up of each congressional district based upon census changes. This make-up leads to charges of political gerrymandering, or the drawing up of congressional districts that favor either the political party that controls the state legislature or the incumbent. As a result, many districts were oddly shaped and created unfair representation patterns. Supreme Court cases have defined the manner in which states must create representation patterns. *Wesberry v Sanders* (1964) dictated that population differences in Georgia congressional districts were so unequal that they violated the Constitution. This decision followed the landmark *Baker v Carr* ruling in 1962, which established the one man, one vote doctrine. Both decisions furthered minority representation.

However, this doctrine was modified by the Supreme Court in the 1990s. Decisions that have struck down oddly shaped congressional districts, which guarantee minority representation, suggest that a more conservative interpretation will be taking place. And in 1995 the Court ruled that a district in Georgia, which was apportioned to create representation for African-Americans, was unconstitutional.

Primaries and party politics have resulted in the election of incumbents through the 1980s and 1990s. Even though the success of Senate incumbents lags behind the House, it is obvious that once elected a sitting representative has a distinct advantage. The exception to the rule is if there is a scandal involving a representative or if a sitting president is unpopular at the mid-term, a smaller percentage of incumbents are reelected. When it became known in 1992 that House members were abusing their checking and post office privileges, many incumbents either decided not to seek reelection or were defeated. Mid-term elections in 1994 reflected the public's disapproval of President Clinton's job performance. For the first time in 40 years, the Republicans captured control of both the House and the Senate. In fact, not a single Republican incumbent was defeated in what has been described as an electoral revolution. The Republicans maintained control of Congress after the 1996 presidential election. The 1998 mid-term election maintained Republican control, though the margins were cut in both the House and the Senate.

Though the Republicans held on to the House and Senate after the 2000 election, the Senate majority was only sustained in a 50–50 Senate as a result of the vote of a Republican vice president. This was short-lived as a Republican Senator, Jim Jeffords of Vermont, decided to leave the Republican Party in 2001, thus giving the Democrats majority control of the Senate. After the 2002 mid-term elections, the Republicans regained control of the Senate.

The statistics of incumbency are staggering. Only two members of Congress lost in 1986 and one lost in 1988; on the average fewer than 2 percent are defeated in primary elections and fewer than 7 percent lose general elections. The Senate reelection rate is slightly lower because, unlike House members who represent smaller districts, senators represent the interests of an entire state. Why do incumbents have this advantage? Incumbents are highly visible. The cable network C-SPAN routinely broadcasts proceedings of the House and Senate. Representatives have free franking (sending of mail) privileges, and most pride themselves in establishing close constituent relationships. They also make sure to co-sponsor legislation. Representatives are quick to take credit for obtaining funds through legislation that favors their home districts. This practice is called pork barrel legislation and has been criticized by such political watchdog groups as Common Cause. As a result of campaign fund raising and contributions made by political action committees, incumbents also have a built-in money advantage over their challengers. This advantage results in many weak opponents being nominated. They are compared to cannon fodder and frequently lose by more than 60 percent of the vote.

It is interesting to note the make-up of the 105th Congress (1997–1999). The median age of representatives serving in the House was 51, while the median age for Senate members was 58. House members were 63 percent Protestant, while their counterparts in the Senate were 61 percent Protestant. Eleven percent of House members were female, while only 9 percent of Senate members were female. All members of Congress earned over $50,000 a year. Sixteen percent of House members had assets worth over $1 million, while 33 percent of Senate members had personal wealth exceeding $1 million.

Structure

The organization of the Congress relies on a seniority and party system and the use of a committee system, which facilitates the day-to-day operations.

The bicameral (two-house) structure of the Congress made it a necessity to develop an organization that would result in the ability of both houses to conduct their own business, yet be able to accomplish the main function—the passage of legislation.

Each house has a presiding officer. The influence of the Speaker of the House cannot be underestimated. The speaker is selected by the majority party, and even though a House Majority Leader is also part of the unofficial structure of the House, it is the speaker who is really the leader of the majority. In 1993 Speaker Thomas Foley and House Majority Leader Richard Gephardt worked together to pass much of President Clinton's legislative agenda. After the 1994 mid-term elections, the Republicans chose controversial and conservative Representative Newt Gingrich as the new speaker. Promising to deliver on the Republican Contract with America (a description concludes the review portion of this chapter), he immediately consolidated control. He earned a reputation as one of the most powerful speakers since the days of Joe Cannon. His power was diminished after the 1996 elections. Facing serious ethics charges, Gingrich was forced to loosen his grip on committee chairs and Republican representatives who disagreed with him. After the Republicans lost seats in the House in the 1998 mid-term elections, Gingrich resigned from the House. Representative Dennis Hastert was elected the new speaker. The speaker presides over House meetings and is expected to be impartial in the way meetings are run even though he or she is a member of the majority party. However, in the power to preside and keep order, the speaker wields a great deal of power: recognizing speakers, referring bills to committees, answering procedural questions, and declaring the outcome of votes. The speaker also names members to all select (special) committees and conference committees (a committee that meets with the Senate to resolve differences in legislation). The speaker usually votes only to break a tie and has the power to appoint temporary speakers, called speakers pro tempore, to run meetings. The speaker is also third in line after the vice president to succeed the president.

The presiding officer of the Senate, the president of the Senate, is the vice president of the United States. It is a symbolic office, and more often than not the Senate chooses a temporary presiding officer, the president pro tempore to run the meetings. The only specific power of the vice president in the capacity of Senate presiding officer is to break ties. The president pro tempore does not have the same power or influence as the Speaker of the House. From 1989 to 1994 the president pro tem, as the position is called, has been Senator Robert Byrd of West Virginia. In 1994 the Republicans selected 92-year-old Strom Thurmond as the new pro tem. He served in that capacity until 2001, when

Senator Byrd again became the president pro tempore after the Democrats regained control. Ted Stevens of Alaska took over as president pro tempore after the Republicans took control of the Senate in 2002. Unlike the House, the real power in the Senate lies with the Senate Majority Leader. Kansas Senator Robert Dole was elected as the new Senate Majority Leader after the Republicans took control of the Senate in 1994. After Dole resigned from the Senate to actively run for president in 1996, Senator Trent Lott from Mississippi was elected the new Majority Leader. He retained that position after the 2000 election, only having to give it up to South Dakota Senator Tom Daschle after the Democrats regained control. He again became majority leader in 2003. His tenure was brief as he was forced to relinquish the position to Tennessee Senator Bill Frist after Lott made what were considered racial comments.

Committee chairs, those representatives who chair the standing committees of the House and Senate, wield a great deal of power. In fact, most of the work is done through the committee system. Committee chairs are selected as a result of the seniority system, an unwritten custom that established the election of committee chairs as a result of length of service and of which party holds the majority in each house. Four types of committees exist in both houses. Standing committees deal with proposed bills and are permanent, existing from one Congress to the next. Examples of standing committees are Banking, Foreign Affairs, Energy, Governmental Affairs, and Appropriations. Select committees are specially created and conduct special investigations. The Watergate Committee and Iran-Contra investigators were select Senate committees. The Senate and House Banking Committees held hearings on the Whitewater affair in 1994 and 1995. Joint committees are committees made up of both houses for the purpose of coordinating investigations or special studies and expedite business between the houses. Conference committees resolve legislative differences between the House and Senate. Such bills as the Crime Bill of 1994 and the Welfare Reform Act of 1996 had to go through a conference committee. Many bills, in fact, must be resolved in this manner. Committee makeup is determined by the percentage of party representation in each house. Representatives attempt to get on influential committees such as the House Ways and Means Committee (which is responsible for appropriations measures), the House Rules Committee (which determines the order in which legislation will reach the floor for a vote), and the Senate Judiciary Committee (which makes a recommendation regarding presidential judicial appointments). Most representatives are members of at least one standing committee or two subcommittees (smaller committees that are organized around specific areas). These committees influence legislation by holding hearings and voting on amendments to legislation that has been referred to their committees. After the 1994 elections the Republican majority passed new rules that limited the terms of House committee chairs to no more than six years and reduced the number of committees and their staffs.

Along with the committee system, each house has a party system that organizes and influences the members of Congress regarding policymaking decisions. The majority and minority leaders of both houses organize their members by using whips, or assistant floor leaders, whose job is to check with party members and inform the majority leader of the status and feelings of the membership regarding issues that are going to be voted on. Whips are responsible for keeping party members in line and having an accurate count of who will be voting for or against a particular bill. The party caucus or party conference is a means for each party to develop a strategy or position on a particular issue. The majority and minority party meet privately and determine which bills to support, the type of amendments that would be acceptable, and the official party positions on up-coming business. They also deal with the selection of the party leadership and committee membership.

Policymaking

The avenues taken by Congress to achieve policymaking go beyond the mere passage of legislation.

Besides the legislative power of Congress, it also has nonlegislative responsibilities. Constitutional amendments, election of a president and vice president if there is no electoral college majority, impeachment, approval of executive appointments, and congressional oversight are used by Congress to influence and determine public policy. Congress uses the power of congressional oversight to gather information useful for the formation of legislation, to review the operations and budgets of executive departments and independent regulatory agencies, to conduct investigations through committee hearings, and to bring to the public's attention the need for public policy. An example of a Congressional Oversight Committee was the Whitewater hearings chaired by Senator Alfonse D'Amato of New York, head of the Senate Banking Committee.

By far the most important function of Congress is the legislative responsibility. Before explaining the different approaches to lawmaking, it is important that you understand the way a bill becomes a law.

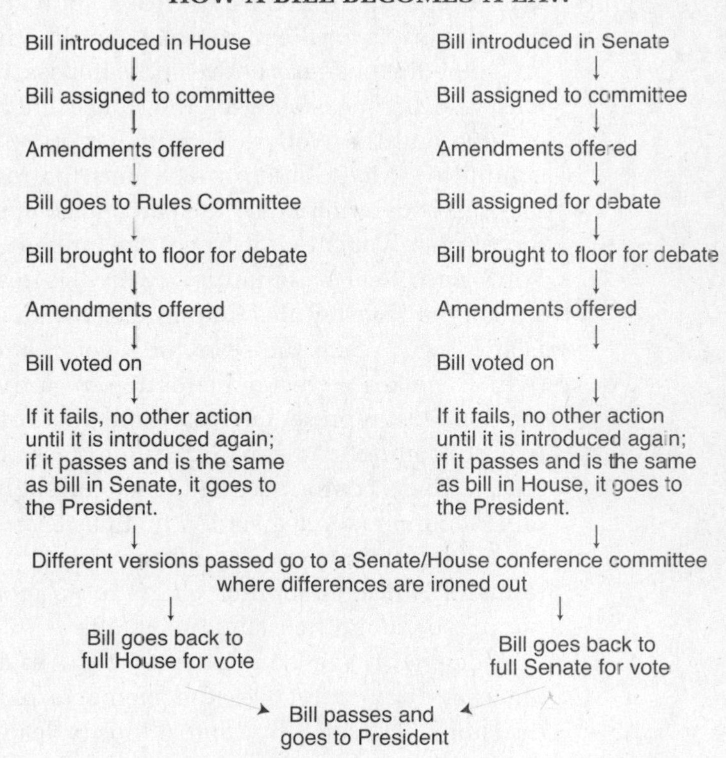

Obviously, this is a simplified version of the process. And if the president vetoes the bill, the Congress must vote separately to determine whether each house has a two-thirds majority to override it.

There are three kinds of legislative actions taken by the Congress. Distributive legislation results in the distribution of goods and/or services to the general population. Such laws affecting highway construction, health research, or defense appropriations come under this umbrella. Redistributive legislation involves taking money from one segment of the population from taxes and giving it back to another through entitlements such as welfare. The recipients must demonstrate a need, and Congress determines the criteria for these programs. Regulatory legislation sets limits on groups and individuals. Through such acts as the Clean Air and Water Act, Congress sets requirements for industry and for states for the purpose of protecting the environment.

It's one thing to introduce legislation, and it's another to get it passed into law. In a typical congressional session, over 10,000 bills are offered, and fewer than 10 percent of them are enacted. Tactics such as the Senate filibuster, an ongoing debate that needs a vote of 60 senators to cut off debate, protect minority interests. In an attempt to increase legislative output, Congress can use several techniques to move legislation along. Logrolling (or "I'll vote for your legislation, if you vote for mine") coalitions, consensus building, and pork barrel deals often result in agreement to pass bills. An excellent example of consensus building was the passage of the North American Free Trade Agreement (NAFTA).

Lobbyists and Interest Groups

Lobbyists and interest groups have grown in importance as a major influence in the passage of legislation.

We will be devoting an entire chapter to this issue. However it is important to note that lobbyists and interest groups play a crucial role, not only in the election of senators and representatives, but also in the passage of legislation. Take, for instance, the healthcare debate. The Federal Election Commission provided the following table, which illustrates the number of Political Action Committees formed between 1980 and 1998.

Political Action Committees— Number, by Committee Type: 1980–1998
[As of December 31]

COMMITTEE TYPE	1980	1985	1990	1991	1992	1993	1994	1995	1997–1998
Total	2,551	3,992	4,172	4,094	4,195	4,210	3,954	4,016	4,599
Corporate	1,206	1,710	1,795	1,738	1,735	1,789	1,660	1,674	1,821
Labor	297	388	346	338	347	337	333	334	353
Trade/membership/health	576	695	774	742	770	761	792	815	921
Nonconnected	374	1,003	1,062	1,083	1,145	1,121	980	1,020	1,326

Source: U.S. Federal Election Commission, press release of June 8, 1999.

This table illustrates how intrusive interest groups have become in the legislative process. Calls for reform (which will be discussed later) have increased in this area. If Congress is supposed to be the people's representative, then the extent of the influence of special interests is a very important question.

Constituency

Constituency relationships provide essential information and services and the foundation for reelection.

If the essence of a senator or representative revolves around the issue of representing one's constituency, then the elected official must define the kind of congressperson he or she will be. Once elected through the formal process of an open and free election, the definition must begin. Demographic representation mirrors the desires of the people being represented. Symbolic representation is defined by the style and message of the representative and the manner in which the people perceive the job he or she is doing. How responsive the legislator is to the constituents' wishes is the last characteristic of representation. The question of whether the representative should reflect the point of view of his or her constituents or vote his or her own opinion after hearing information on any issue is a long-standing problem for elected officials. In a survey given to representatives in 1977, the question of whether they feel they should be looking after the need and interests of their own district or the needs and interests of the nation as a whole was asked. Of those surveyed, 45 percent responded that the interests of the nation should be first; 65 percent said that, if a conflict developed between what they feel is best and what they think the people in their district want, they would follow their own conscience.

Nevertheless, members of Congress must represent their districts, taking into account individual constituents, organized interests, and the district as a whole. For their individual constituents representatives set up mobile offices and respond personally to written letters. They contact with federal agencies, sponsor appointments to service academies, and provide information and services. For organized groups, they introduce legislation, obtain grants and contracts, give speeches, and attend functions. For the district as a whole, representatives obtain federal projects (sometimes from pork barrel legislation), look for ways of getting legislation that will increase employment or tax benefits, and support policies that will directly benefit the geographic area of the district.

Through such public relations practices as sending out a congressional letter highlighting a reference in the Congressional Record of individuals or the achievements of people in their districts, representatives attempt to get close to the people they represent.

Reform

Attempts at reforming Congress aim to clean up abuses of the people's branch of government.

Of the three branches of government, the public has given Congress the lowest approval ratings. Yet every election they send a majority of incumbents back to Congress. There seems to be a love/hate relationship between the people and their representatives and senators. Many suggestions have been made to improve and reform the organization and productivity of Congress. The poll pointed out the following beliefs:

- Gridlock is a problem—Congress is seen as inefficient, and because of the complicated legislative process, most bills never see the light of day. Reforms such as streamlining the committee system, improving the coordination of information better between the House and the Senate, and requiring some kind of action on all bills proposed have been made.
- Congress does not reflect the views of its constituents—As the poll indicated, a majority believe that they should do what is in the national interest rather than what their constituents want. People have suggested that with the information superhighway growing, representatives should interactively get information from their constituents before voting on crucial issues.
- Representatives take advantage of their perks—After the revelations of abuses of the House checking system and House post office, people felt that many House members were unethical. Add to that the number of representatives taking money from PACs and the double standard that exists

THERE HAVE BEEN MANY SUGGESTIONS ON HOW TO REFORM CONGRESS

between the application of many laws for them and the public, and you can see why Congress is not trusted. Ethics bills have been passed, and there is public disclosure required for income and property holdings.

- Representatives are so busy running for office, that they become beholden to special interest groups and PACs—The response has been that some states voted to establish term limits. The Supreme Court decided this issue in 1995 and ruled that it was unconstitutional for states to enact term limits for senators and representatives.
- Congress either delegates too much power to the executive or has tried to take control, becoming an imperial Congress—The overall role of Congress has been debated. Should Congress let the president and the executive agencies make the important decisions for the country? Or should the Congress take an adversarial approach by using threats of legislative vetoes, demanding a balanced budget, rejecting presidential appointments and treaties, overriding vetoes, or challenging the president's authority in the area of foreign policy?

Reforms

The House of Representatives has responded to some of the calls to reform itself through its Contract with America.

As mentioned earlier in the chapter, the new Republican majority in the House of Representatives, elected in 1994, campaigned on a platform called the Contract with America. This contract became a blueprint for legislative action in the first 100 days. It promised the American people that the following items would be brought to the floor for a vote:

"In the first 100 days, we're pledging in writing to bring to a vote:

1. A balanced budget amendment and line item veto;
2. A crime bill that funds police and prisons over social programs;
3. Real welfare reform;

4. Family reinforcement measures that strengthen parental rights in education and child support enforcement;
5. Family tax cuts;
6. Stronger national defense;
7. A rise in the Social Security earnings limit to stop penalizing working seniors;
8. Job creation and regulatory reform policies;
9. Common sense legal reforms to stop frivolous lawsuits; and
10. A first-ever vote on term limits for members of Congress."

In a remarkable demonstration of party discipline, the Republican majority succeeded in bringing to a vote every item in the contract. In fact, on the first day of the 104th Congress, in a marathon session that lasted well into the early morning hours of the next day, the House voted to reform itself, cutting down the number of committees and their staffs, restricting the terms of committee chairs, and changing the rules of the House itself, making it easier to offer amendments. In many cases the Senate stymied the House's attempt to achieve legislative success with a significant number of the provisions of the contract defeated or modified in the Senate. A significant bill signed into law by President Clinton was a measure designed to mandate representatives to follow the same laws that Americans must follow such as civil rights legislation and minimum wage laws. The Contract with America hit a responsive chord with the American people as shown by a survey that suggests the approval rating of Congress increased from previous years. By 1996 the Republican agenda changed and became less extreme. The Democrats and President Clinton reached compromises regarding welfare reform, healthcare, the minimum wage, and balancing of the federal budget. The Contract with America helped create a path for these significant pieces of legislation to become signed into law. However, after the impeachment trial of President Clinton in 1998, relations with Congress deteriorated and the public, once again, was mistrustful of the institution. After George W. Bush was elected in 2000, he was able to get a significant part of his legislative agenda passed working closely with Congress. After the attacks of September 11, the Congress supported Bush's War on Terrorism.

Chapter 8 Review

SECTION 1: MULTIPLE-CHOICE QUESTIONS

1. The qualifications for members of the House of Representatives are found in Article I of the Constitution. All the following are requirements for a House member EXCEPT
   (A) must be 25 years old.
   (B) must be an American citizen for seven years.
   (C) must be a resident from the state represented.
   (D) can be a naturalized citizen.
   (E) cannot serve for more than two consecutive terms.

2. Which of the following political theories would claim that many senators and representatives come from the upper middle class or the upper economic class of American society?
   (A) elite
   (B) pluralist
   (C) hyperpluralist
   (D) centrist
   (E) majoritarian

3. Which of the following factors generates the most significant advantage for a Congressional candidate?
   (A) being wealthier than the opponent
   (B) getting the most press coverage
   (C) being invited to the most town meetings
   (D) being an incumbent
   (E) taking positions on key social issues

4. All the following represent reasons why voters choose congressional candidates EXCEPT
   (A) endorsements by groups who represent different views than the voter.
   (B) political advertisements.
   (C) the positions the candidates take on key issues.
   (D) party affiliation of the voter.
   (E) the candidates positive standing in political polls.

5. Which of the following functions of senators and representatives would be the most important to their constituents?
   (A) attending political fund raisers
   (B) networking with lobbyists
   (C) accepting PAC money
   (D) recommending a high school student to one of the military academies
   (E) making a speech about national defense that is printed in the Congressional Record

6. Senators and representatives are often criticized for making deals with other legislators or the president in order to get programs, projects, and grants moving along the legislative process. What is this legislation called?
   (A) constituent laws
   (B) rider legislation
   (C) logrolling
   (D) pork barrel legislation
   (E) legislative veto

7. All the following happened as a result of the Connecticut Compromise agreed to at the Constitutional Convention in 1789 EXCEPT
   (A) Congress was made into a bicameral institution.
   (B) there had to be a minimum of two congressman for each state.
   (C) each state's representation in the House would be determined by population.
   (D) each state was guaranteed two senators.
   (E) senators would be elected directly by the people.

8. Which of the following represents an indirect consequence of a bicameral legislature?
   I. Gridlock may take place.
   II. Political compromise can take place.
   III. An additional check and balance takes place.
   IV. There is usually a tremendous decrease in proposed laws.

   (A) I only
   (B) II only
   (C) II and III only
   (D) III and IV only
   (E) I, II, and III only

9. Which of the following House committees is responsible for setting the agenda for legislation coming to the floor?
   (A) Rules Committee
   (B) Ways and Means Committee
   (C) Appropriations Committee
   (D) The Policy Committee
   (E) The Armed Services Committee

10. Even though the Congress is primarily responsible for legislation, each house also has specific nonlegislative responsibilities. Which of the following represents a specific Senate responsibility different than the House?
    I. ratifying all treaties
    II. confirming presidential appointments
    III. trying impeached officials
    IV. introducing all appropriation legislation

    (A) I only
    (B) II and III only
    (C) IV only
    (D) I, II, and III only
    (E) I and IV only

11. Which of the following individuals presides over the House of Representatives?
    (A) the House Minority Leader
    (B) the House Pro Tem
    (C) the House Majority Leader
    (D) the Speaker of the House
    (E) the House Majority Whip

12. The Speaker of the House has many responsibilities. All the following reflect roles the speaker plays EXCEPT
    (A) acting as chief presiding officer of the House.
    (B) serving as third in line in presidential succession.
    (C) making committee assignments for both parties.
    (D) playing a key role in appointing committee chairs.
    (E) working hand in hand with the president relating to the legislative agenda if they are both from the same party.

13. All the following contribute to the success of incumbent members of Congress in election campaigns EXCEPT
    (A) incumbents usually raise less campaign funds than do the challengers.
    (B) incumbents tend to understand national issues better than do their challengers.
    (C) incumbents are usually better known to voters than are their challengers.
    (D) incumbents can use staff to perform services for constituents.
    (E) incumbents often sit on committees that permit them to serve district interests.

14. A member of the House of Representatives who wishes to be influential in the House would most likely seek a place on which of the following committees?
    (A) Agriculture
    (B) District of Columbia
    (C) Public Works and Transportation
    (D) Rules
    (E) Veterans Affairs

15. All of the following are examples of congressional oversight committees EXCEPT
    (A) the Banking Committee holding Whitewater hearings.
    (B) the Select Committee on Campaign Activities to investigate campaign abuses.
    (C) the House Judiciary Committee's hearing on the impeachment of President Clinton.
    (D) the Select Senate Watergate Committee.
    (E) the Select Iran-Contra Committee.

16. Which of the following has INCREASED in Congress over the past 20 years?
    I. the chances of members' reelection
    II. the influence of committee chairs
    III. the power of subcommittees
    IV. the cost of congressional elections

    (A) I only
    (B) I and II only
    (C) I, III, and IV only
    (D) I, II, and III only
    (E) I, II, III, and IV

17. Pork barrel legislation helps the reelection chances of a member of Congress because such legislation
    (A) gives the member of Congress national standing and coverage on national television news.
    (B) helps earn the member of Congress a reputation for service to his or her district.
    (C) attracts campaign contributions from ideological political action committees.
    (D) prevents other candidates from claiming that the member of Congress is too liberal for his or her district.
    (E) requires the member of Congress to travel extensively.

Answers to Multiple-Choice Questions

1. **(E)** Type of Question: Negative
   Choices A, B, and C are all listed in Article I as criteria for qualifications for members of the House. Remember that the qualifications for the Senate and the president are different. Only the president cannot be naturalized. A term limit is not mentioned in the Constitution, although over 20 states have imposed this qualification.
2. **(A)** Type of Question: Hypothetical
   The clue in this question is found in the description that senators and representatives come from the upper middle class or upper economic class. From Chapter 1, you should be able to identify that characteristic as elite. A pluralistic approach would suggest that candidates come from a broader spectrum. A hyperpluralistic approach would suggest that so many candidates are able to run. Centrist and majoritarian are positions taken after the election.
3. **(D)** Type of Question: Cause and effect relationships
   Even though choices A, B, C, and E are all factors that can create electoral advantages, by far incumbency plays the most important role in determining an inherent advantage. In fact, sometimes press coverage and taking positions on key social issues can result in negative publicity, and the mere appearance at town meetings does not necessarily translate into votes. Finally, wealth can be countered by PAC donations.
4. **(A)** Type of Question: Comparing and contrasting concepts and events
   Political advertisements, the stand a candidate takes, party affiliations, and the candidate's standing (either positive or negative) in polls all have an impact on voters. Even though endorsements play a role, if the endorsement is by a group or a paper the voter does not agree with, it does not play a role in why a voter would support a particular candidate.
5. **(D)** Type of Question: Solution to a problem
   The problem is to determine which function a senator or representative plays is most important to their constituent. Even though choices A, B, C, and E are all functions of elected officials, the most important role a senator or representative can have is constituent service such as recommending a voter's child to a service academy.
6. **(C)** Type of Question: Sequencing a series of events
   Logrolling is a deal-making process that fits the definition. Pork barrel legislation benefits constituents and can be added as riders to other pieces of legislation.

7. **(E)** Type of Question: Chronological
The direct election of senators took place in 1913 as a result of the Seventeenth Amendment to the Constitution. Prior to that, state legislatures selected the senators.
8. **(E)** Type of Question: Cause and effect relationships
Over the course of the history of government and politics, a bicameral legislature has encouraged compromise and results in an additional check in the legislative process. In the era of modern Congress, gridlock may also occur because the House and Senate often pass different versions of bills that never become law.
9. **(A)** Type of Question: Identification and analysis
By definition the Rules Committee is responsible for determining the order of action on proposed legislation. The Ways and Means Committee reviews bills dealing with appropriations. The Appropriations Committee is a Senate committee. There is no Policy Committee, and the Armed Services Committee deals with the military.
10. **(D)** Type of Question: Definitional
Choice I and II are obvious answers. The House votes on impeachment charges; the Senate tries impeached officials. And the House is responsible for introducing appropriation legislation before the Senate.
11. **(D)** Type of Question: Definitional
By definition, the Speaker of the House presides over meetings of the House of Representatives. There is no House pro tem, only a Senate pro tem. The House Majority Leader and Majority Whip play specific functions dealing with party unity and delivering on the legislative agenda set forth by the majority party.
12. **(C)** Type of Question: Sequencing a series of events
The Speaker of the House has many functions. Even though the speaker has significant input in the committee assignments of members, it is up to each party to select specific committees for their members. The speaker has direct input in the selection of all committee chairs.
13. **(A)** Type of Question: Cause and effect relationships
The understanding of the issue of incumbency in the election of senators and representatives is essential to your understanding of the institution. Incumbents usually have a significant advantage over challengers in every area of the campaign. In fact, studies have indicated that because of the factors mentioned in choices B, C, D, and E, incumbents are more often than not elected. This does not occur in a midterm election where the president's popularity is low.
14. **(D)** Type of Question: Cause and effect relationships
Any representative who gets a position on the Rules Committee has an inherent advantage over representatives who have positions on the other committees listed. The Rules Committee determines the order of all pending legislation and House policy, whereas the other committees only review legislation germane to a particular area.
15. **(C)** Type of Question: Definitional
By definition, an oversight committee is a watchdog committee. It may be a select committee like the Watergate or Iran-Contra Committee. Or it could be a standing committee like the Banking Committee. The House Judiciary Committee had a constitutional responsibility to hear impeachment evidence.

16. **(E)** Type of Question: Sequencing a series of events
Congress as an institution has been characterized as being imperial since Watergate. More members get reelected. Committees and subcommittees bring up legislation, which results in a decrease of influence of the president, and because of its increased power, it has also cost more to get elected.

17. **(B)** Type of Question: Definitional
By definition, pork barrel legislation is done so that a particular district gets the benefit of congressional representation. Voters perceive their representatives and senators as providers for their districts and, therefore, owe a debt of thanks to them. Even though elected representatives and senators can get national coverage and PAC donations and may travel extensively, it is the constituent aspect that helps the reelection chances of a representative or senator who can successfully deliver the pork.

SECTION 2: FREE-RESPONSE ESSAY (Both choices are answered for illustrative purposes)

Discuss why political scientists have described Congress as imperial in its relations with the president in regards to

1. formulation of domestic policy.
2. formulation of foreign policy.

Make sure you give a definition of the term imperial Congress and provide two examples of how Congress has become increasingly imperial since 1976, using either domestic or foreign policy to illustrate your answer.

Sample Student Response

Throughout the nation's history, one of the political battles that has had the most impact on the formulation of public policy has been the struggle for power between the Congress and the president. Even though the issues have changed and the tactics are different now than during the country's infancy, the president and the Congress have never stopped competing for public support of their initiatives. The Constitution established the Congress and the president as natural rivals by giving each a portion of the other's authority. Congress is primarily a legislative body, but it has some executive powers such as approval of executive appointments; the president is primarily the chief executive, but he has some legislative authority such as the veto. Nowhere is this seesaw battle more evident and publicized than on domestic issues. Since 1976, Congress has generally taken the lead and controlled the legislative agenda, and some political scientists have gone so far as to call it an imperial Congress, or one that is dictatorial and takes sole control of the policy agenda. Whether this term can be applied to Congress is debatable, but to a large extent Congress in recent years has attempted to wrench power from the presidency after years of playing second fiddle to dominant presidents.

In the wake of the Watergate scandal, the presidency was tarnished in the eyes of the people, and the country looked to Congress to provide leadership. Congress, resentful of the broad powers accumulated by a string of imperial presidents that ended with the disgrace of Richard Nixon, gladly obliged by making it more difficult for the president to assume powers traditionally left to Congress. Gerald Ford assumed the presidency following Nixon's resignation and became one of the weakest presidents in the nation's history. His most noted accomplishment was the pardoning of former President Nixon for any wrongdoing associated with Watergate, an act many considered to be blatantly political and an outrageous miscarriage of justice. Congress paid him no respect and continued to redefine the roles of the Congress and the president. Ford was mocked by the general public and lost the 1976 election to Jimmy Carter, making him the first president never to have been elected to either the presidency or the vice presidency.

Carter campaigned as a Washington outsider. Although that approach was a popular image out on the campaign trail, it made it difficult for him to get his agenda passed by Congress. During Carter's term, Congress was more imperial for what it did not do than for what it did. It failed to pass any substantial economic measures, as the economy stagnated into recession. It refused to pass any comprehensive social legislation as well, and Carter spent much of his term trying to find a focus.

Ronald Reagan defeated Carter in 1980 by pledging to revolutionize the country with an array of new economic initiatives. Although he has been the most powerful president in the post-Watergate era, he needed to compromise with Congress in some way on almost every vote. Due to the sway of public opinion and a Republican Senate, he was able to pass much of his economic agenda. But when the Iran-Contra scandal broke, it became virtually impossible for Reagan to win support. Congress took the opportunity to use the scandal as a reason for opposing the president's efforts, and Reagan was in many ways a lame duck for the last two years of his presidency.

Since Reagan, Congress has become exceedingly imperial. Under President George Bush, the Democratic Congress successfully played opposition politics to win back the presidency. They failed to support the president's initiatives and passed many measures that the president vetoed, setting up issues with which the Democrats attacked his performance. As a result of persistent needling, Bill Clinton was able to defeat President Bush in the 1992 election.

Even though he started off strong after his spirited inauguration, President Clinton quickly became bogged down in sidetracking issues, such as gays in the military, which he firmly believed in but which were not a main part of his agenda. Congress swarmed to these issues like vultures and turned the tide of public opinion against him. As with President Carter, Congress more effectively battled the president by preventing legislation than by creating their own. Healthcare reform, which Clinton signaled as a top priority by placing First Lady Hillary Rodham Clinton in charge of the plan, was stifled by Congress and helped tag Clinton as a bleeding heart liberal rather than the New Democrat he ran as in 1992. In the 1994 mid-term elections, Republicans won a landslide victory, taking control of both houses of Congress for the first time in four decades. This was due in large part to their scapegoating of President Clinton. Now in office, Congress has taken control of the legislative agenda, and the president can only watch and hope that they are unable to deliver on their promises. Never in the twentieth century has Congress been more firmly in charge of the course of government action than in 1995. After the 1996 presidential election, both President Clinton and the leaders of the House and Senate interpreted the election results as a mandate for bipartisanship. Quick legislative agreement at the start of the

105th Congress seemed to signal a greater balance of power between the executive and legislative branches.

Evaluation of Free-Response Sample Essay

1. Did the essay establish a working definition of the imperial Congress and a foundation statement regarding how imperial the body has been since 1976?
2. How effective was the writer in describing the actions of the Congress in relation to domestic and foreign policy from 1976 to the present?

1. This essay has a built-in thesis. The question sets forth the premise that since 1976 Congress has become increasingly imperial in its assumption of power, both in the areas of domestic and foreign policy. The net result is a weakened presidency. The date 1976 plays a significant part in the reason why an imperial Congress grew in power. That year represented the first presidential election since Watergate and Richard Nixon's resignation. The writer recognized that fact and, after defining what is meant by the phrase "imperial Congress," began to create a case for the increased power of the Congress.

2. The strength of the essay lies in the body. The writer uses historical references to bolster the argument that Presidents Carter, Reagan, Bush, and Clinton were much weaker compared to imperial presidents such as FDR and Lyndon Johnson. Specific examples such as Iran-Contra and the failure of the Clinton administration to get healthcare passed helped illustrate the argument that Congress has taken control of the legislative agenda. A weakness of the essay is that the writer does not clearly delineate how Congress has accomplished its imperial status in the areas of domestic and foreign policy.

SECTION 2: DATA-BASED FREE-RESPONSE ESSAY

Look at the map and answer the following questions:

Discuss the political implications of the apportionment of the House of Representatives in terms of the changes that have occurred from 1990 to 2000.

Sample Student Response

The political implications evident from these changes create a shift in the nature of House representation that causes a shift in the policy agenda. It also creates a different political strategy for presidential candidates. The South, Rocky Mountain states, and especially California took on political significance. Congressional elections saw candidates becoming sensitive to the problems faced by senior citizens. These candidates also had to react to the influx of immigration, both legal and illegal in states such as Florida, Texas, and California. In addition, congressional reapportionment was more clearly defined by such court cases as *Baker v Carr,* which established the one man, one vote doctrine and helped equalize congressional districts. Political gerrymandering also became a factor to take into consideration when a state gained or lost representation as a result of population shifts. One of the best examples of how this population shift had an impact on presidential elections was the 1980 election. The emergence of Reagan

APPORTIONMENT OF MEMBERSHIP IN THE HOUSE OF REPRESENTATIVES BY REGION, 1990 AND 2000

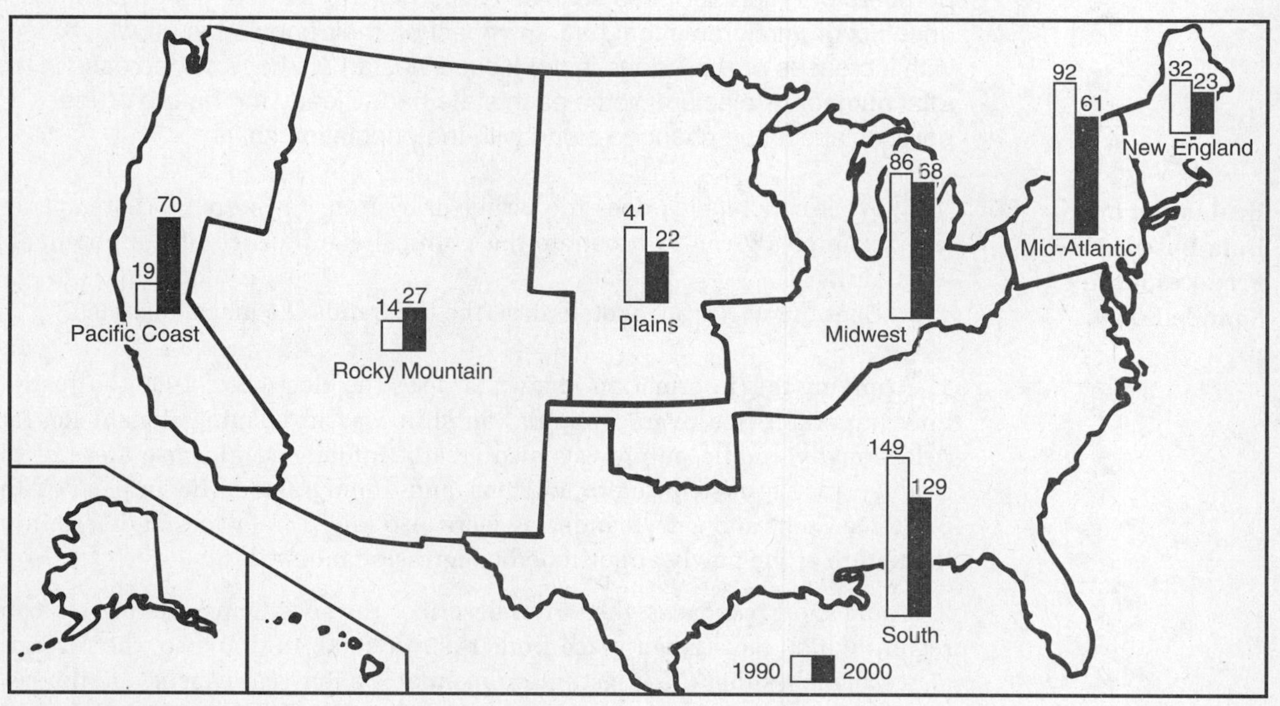

SOURCE: Bureau of the Census

Democrats and the importance of a viable Southern strategy became crucial factors in the election of Ronald Reagan. Even Jimmy Carter's strategy in 1976 drew upon the fact that the South would play a significant role in choosing and electing a candidate. As far as public policy is concerned, representatives from newly created districts had to be aware of such issues as Social Security, Medicare, and welfare. Areas where senior citizens moved turned into bastions of defenders of issues related to that constituency. The Northeast lost the greatest number of people and representatives during this time period and thus became less significant politically. However, candidates still concentrated their efforts on the big industrial states when it came time to campaign for the presidency.

The map titled "Apportionment of Membership in the House of Representatives by Region, 1990 and 2000" clearly shows the population shifts resulting from the census surveys taken every ten years, a constitutional requirement. The net result is a clearly established pattern of population movement:

- a decrease from the Northeast and New England;
- an increase to the Rocky Mountain states and West;
- a decrease from the plains, border states, and Midwest.

As a result of the declines and increases, the regions that lost population also lost congressional apportionment, and the regions that gained population gained in the number of representatives they could send to the

House. It is also clear that the areas that picked up the greatest number of people, commonly known as the sunbelt states, also picked up large numbers of retirees. States such as California, Texas, and Florida also had an influx of immigrants that had an impact on their population growth. Along with increases or reductions in the House was an increase or decrease in the total number of electoral votes each state had. Clearly the nature of the political landscape changed along with the population shifts.

Evaluation of Data-Based Free-Response Sample Essay

1. What conclusions does the writer draw from these trends? Are specific examples given to illustrate the political significance of the population shifts?
2. Does the writer adequately describe the trends the map illustrates?

1. Applying this information, the writer uses the election of 1980 to illustrate how important this overall population shift was in electing Ronald Reagan. Additionally, public policy was also greatly influenced in those areas of the country that attracted senior citizens and immigrants. The impact of the Supreme Court and gerrymandering were also raised as factors in determining the nature of the newly apportioned congressional districts.

2. Using short responses, the writer describes the specific population shifts by region, which have taken place from 1990 to 2000. In doing so, the response also establishes that the Constitution mandates a ten-year census and that as a result the number of representatives in the House and the number of electoral votes states have will be affected. In addition, the writer refers to the specific kind of people migrating from one part of the country to another.

CHAPTER 9 The Judiciary

Chapter Overview

One of the more dramatic changes incorporated into the new Constitution was the creation of the judicial branch of government. Realizing that a separate branch was needed to adjudicate legal issues, the Founding Fathers set up a court system that had at its top a Supreme Court holding the final power of constitutional review. In addition to a federal judiciary, consistent with the federal system, states set up their own court systems.

This chapter will explore the nature of the judicial branch of government. It will look at how the court system is organized, how justices are appointed, and the background of judges. A central issue that will be discussed is the policymaking function of the Supreme Court. How cases get to the Supreme Court and how they are decided directly relates to this issue. By looking at the history of the Court, you will also be able to understand the impact the Court has had on American society. Finally, we will look at the ongoing debate regarding the issue of whether the Court's policymaking function should be activist or whether justices should show judicial restraint.

Unlike the other two constitutionally established institutions of government, the judiciary, to many, is the most distant from the average citizen. There is a lack of understanding regarding the powers and function of the Court, and since federal justices serve for life, they are not directly responsible to the electorate. Yet the judiciary helps to maintain a delicate balance between order and liberty. It has a major impact on the average citizen. If you trace the influence of

KEY TERMS

Amicus curiae
Appellate jurisdiction
Burger court
Cases of equity
Civil law
Common law
Concurring opinion
Constitutional courts
Criminal law
Dissenting opinion
Fletcher v Peck
Gibbon v Ogden
Judicial activism
Judicial restraint
Judiciary committee
Litigation
Majority opinion
Marshall court
McCulloch v Maryland (1819)
Minority opinion
Oral argument
Original jurisdiction
Precedent
Rehnquist court
Senate confirmation
Special courts
Stare decis
Unanimous opinion
Warren court
Writ of certiorari

the Supreme Court from the Marshall Court to the Rehnquist Court, you will see how public policy is affected.

A Quick Constitutional Review

- Basis of constitutional power found in Article III.
- Judges are appointed by the president with the consent of the Senate and serve for life based on good behavior.
- Judicial power extends to issues dealing with common law, equity, civil law, criminal law, and public law.
- Cases are decided through original jurisdiction or appellate jurisdiction.
- Chief Justice of the Supreme Court presides over impeachment trials.
- Congress creates courts "inferior" to the Supreme Court.

Dual Court System

The American judicial system has a duality that is consistent with our federal system of government.

The dual nature of the court system reflects the shared power of the national and state governments. According to the Constitution, the Congress can establish lower federal courts. It also permits the states to develop their own criminal justice system and courts to support it. Although they are independent from the federal courts, the state courts are linked by an appeals process that enables individuals to challenge state statutes in federal court. On the federal level Congress has created two kinds of courts—constitutional courts and special courts. Constitutional courts were formed to carry out the direction in the Constitution for the courts to exercise judicial power. Special courts were created by Congress to deal with cases deriving from the delegated powers of Congress such as military appeals, tax appeals, and veteran appeals.

The jurisdiction of federal and state courts depend upon the nature of the cases. The Constitution specifically assigns federal courts jurisdiction in cases dealing with laws arising from the Constitution, treaties, all cases dealing with ambassadors, cases dealing with admiralty and maritime issues, cases in which the United States is involved with two or more states, or cases between citizens of different states. The Supreme Court has original jurisdiction only in those "cases affecting ambassadors, other public ministers and consuls, and those in which a State shall be a party." Exclusive state court jurisdiction involves those cases deriving from state laws. However, through the appeals process, many of those cases could eventually end up in federal court.

By far, the most common kind of jurisdiction is concurrent jurisdiction, those matters that may be tried in either a federal or state court. These cases fall into the category of "Judge made law":

- Common law—Based on the legal concept of stare decis, or judicial precedent, this law originated in England in the twelfth century when judges settled disputes based on custom and tradition. A large number of modern common law cases involve contracts, property, and divorce. Since there is no federal common law, common law cases that are appealed to the federal courts become cases of equity.
- Cases of equity—Those cases that cannot be resolved under common law precedent become cases of equity. Judges may be asked to issue injunctions or award damages against an individual.

The second category arises from cases brought about by statutory law, laws that come about as a result of legislative action, treaties, and executive orders.

- Civil law—Cases that deal with contract issues and tort cases such as negligence and slander and define the legal rights of individuals.
- Criminal law—Cases that derive from criminal laws passed by the federal and state governments. In some instances a person can be tried for the same type of crime under federal and state statutes. An example of this is the Rodney King case, where the police were tried by California and by the federal government under existing civil rights law.
- Public law—Cases that include constitutional law, involving constitutional issues, and administrative law, involving disputes over the jurisdiction of public or administrative agencies.

Cases that are litigated involve parties called defendants and plaintiffs or, when on appeal, petitioner and respondent. Recently, federal courts have been attempting to slow down the number of appeals from state courts.

Structure

The structure of the federal court system facilitates the judicial process.

The Constitution allows the establishment of "inferior" courts or lower courts. The first major organizational act of Congress occurred in 1789 with the Judiciary Act creating district courts. Congress has also responded by creating specialized or legislative courts and courts of appeal.

District courts, of which there are currently 97, handle 80 percent of the federal cases brought to them. Each state has at least one federal judicial district. The district court is the court of first hearing for cases involving federal crimes, civil suits involving federal laws, bankruptcy proceedings, admiralty and maritime cases, and immigration cases. United States attorneys are appointed by the president and confirmed by the Senate. They are responsible for bringing cases to the district courts.

The courts of appeal were established by Congress in 1891. They were created to set up an intermediate level of appeal before cases got to the Supreme Court. There are 13 courts of appeal and a Supreme Court Justice is assigned to act as liaison. These courts are responsible to review decisions of district courts and special courts. They review and enforce decisions of federal regulatory agencies and review cases on appeal from state supreme courts. The Supreme Court is the last final court of appeals, and it will be looked at as a separate topic later in this chapter.

Selection of Justices

The appointment of federal justices has as much to do with partisanship as ideology and is another example of the relationship

The other two branches of government, the executive and legislative, are linked in the process of selecting federal justices. In addition, special interests such as the American Bar Association give their input. The result is a process that sometimes gets embroiled in political controversy. The president must get the approval of the Senate for all federal judgeships. In addition, the tradition of senatorial courtesy, the prior approval of the senators from the state from which the judge comes, has been part of the appointment process. This cour-

among government branches and institutions.

tesy does not apply to Supreme Court justice nominations. Once nominated, the judicial candidate must appear before the Senate Judiciary Committee and is given a complete background check by the Department of Justice. Usually, lower court justices are not hand picked by the president. They come from recommendations of other officials. Many lower court judgeships are given as a result of prior political support of the president or political party. From the administration of Franklin Roosevelt to the administration of George W. Bush, with the exception of Gerald Ford, every president has appointed over 90 percent of lower federal court judges from his own political party. There have been an increasing number of minority judges appointed, especially women, African-Americans, and Hispanics. When the Senate refuses to move forward on a presidential nominee, the president can make a recess appointment. Such an appointment bypasses Senate confirmation but only lasts for the remainder of the congressional session. Both President Clinton and President George W. Bush used this process to make judicial appointments.

The consideration of judicial ideology has become increasingly important in the selection of Supreme Court justices. When a Supreme Court nominee appears before the Senate Judiciary Committee, issues such as constitutional precedent, judicial activism, legal writings, and past judicial decisions come under scrutiny. Other issues such as feelings of interest groups, public opinion, media opinion, and ethical and moral private actions of the nominee have been part of the selection process. Let's look at four recent nominees to illustrate this point.

When Justice Lewis Powell left the Court in 1987, President Reagan nominated Robert Bork. Bork had been an assistant attorney general in the Justice Department and was part of the "Saturday Night Massacre" when Nixon fired Attorney General Elliot Richardson. Bork was third in line and carried out Nixon's order to fire the special prosecutor, Archibald Cox, who was investigating the Watergate break-in. Bork was a conservative jurist and believed in judicial restraint. Many of his writings were questioned, as well as a number of his views regarding minorities and affirmative action. He was rejected by the Senate.

After his defeat, the term "Borked" was coined. It refers to a presidential appointee who does not get approved by the senate because of ideological reasons.

Douglas Ginsburg was nominated by Reagan after Bork's rejection. He was also considered extremely conservative. Under intense Senate questioning, conflict of interest issues surfaced as well as allegations that Ginsburg had used marijuana when he was a professor in law school. Reagan withdrew his nomination and finally succeeded in getting unanimous Senate approval for the more moderate Anthony Kennedy.

The most heated debate over confirmation occurred when President Bush nominated Clarence Thomas in 1991 to replace the first African-American Justice, Thurgood Marshall. This nomination brought to national attention the actions of the male-dominated Judiciary Committee when it came to questioning both Thomas and Anita Hill. Thomas was narrowly confirmed by a vote of 52–48. The confirmation process brought to the forefront the conflict between the president's constitutional authority to nominate the person he feels is best qualified and the responsibility of the Senate to approve the nominee. The partisanship of the committee as well as the leaks leading to the testimony of Hill added to the controversy.

When Clinton became president, his first two nominees, Ruth Bader Ginsburg and Stephen Breyer, reflected an attempt on his part to depoliticize the process. Both nominees received easy Senate approval.

The second term of George W. Bush brought about a major change in the makeup of the Supreme Court. Sandra Day O'Connor, the Court's first female appointee resigned. President Bush nominated Judge John G. Roberts, Jr. to replace her. Judge Roberts clerked for William Rehnquist in 1980 when Rehnquest was an associate justice. Roberts went on to serve on the U.S. Court of Appeals for the D.C. Circuit in 1992. He had previously argued 39 cases before the Supreme Court. Roberts described himself as a "strict constructionist" who relied heavily on precedent in determining the outcome of cases that came before him.

Before the confirmation process began, Chief Justice William Rehnquist died and President Bush decided to nominate Roberts as Chief Justice leaving O'Connor's replacement vacant until Roberts was confirmed. After the confirmation hearings were completed, the Senate voted to confirm Roberts as the seventeenth Chief Justice of the Supreme Court. Roberts became the youngest Chief Justice since John Marshall.

The death of William Rehnquist ended an era of judicial restraint and conservative activism. Rehnquist's legacy will be far reaching. Decisions in the areas of federalism and the rights of the accused turned the Court to the right. O'Connor's legacy as a swing vote on the Court was also significant.

Limited Number of Cases

Even though the Supreme Court receives thousands of cases to review, it chooses only between 75 and 100 cases each session from state courts, courts of appeals, and district courts. Critics claim that the limited number of cases accepted limits the Court's ability to make public policy.

Based on "the rule of four" (a minimum of four justices agreeing to review a case), the Supreme Court's docket is taken up by a combination of appeals cases ranging from the legality of the death penalty to copyright infringement. The process it takes for a case to reach the Court has been documented by Peter Irons in his book and audiotape research *May It Please the Court*, the traditional salutation given to the justices. Irons interviewed attorneys who argued landmark cases and for the first time released audiotapes of the oral arguments. The controversy surrounding the release of the book and tapes brought to light the question of whether television should be allowed at Supreme Court sessions as they are in the Congress. The Court released audiotapes for the first time in 2000, immediately following the disputed 2000 presidential election and the legal challenges that followed. The tapes were released to the media and were played over the Internet. They continued this practice during subsequent terms whenever there was a case that evoked a large amount of public interest, such as the University of Michigan affirmative action case, the Guantanamo Bay detainee case, and the McCain-Feingold campaign finance law case.

Irons describes the process it takes for a writ of certiorari (Latin for "to be made more certain"). The appeal is heard based on five criteria:

- If a court has made a decision that conflicts with precedent.
- If a court has come up with a new question.
- If one court of appeals has made a decision that conflicts with another.
- If there are other inconsistencies between courts of different states.
- If there is a split decision in the court of appeals.

If a writ is granted, the lower court sends to the Supreme Court the transcript of the case that has been appealed. Lawyers arguing for the petitioner and respondent must submit to the Court written briefs outlining their positions on the case. The briefs must be a specified length, must be on a certain color of paper, and must be sent to the Court within a specified period of time. Additional amicus curiae, "friend of the court," briefs may be sent to support the position of one side or the other. Once the case has been placed on the docket, the lawyers are notified, and they begin preparing for the grueling process of oral arguments before the Court. Attorneys are often grilled by the sitting justices for 30 minutes. Often, the Solicitor General of the United States represents the government in cases brought against it. Although these arguments do not usually change the position of the judges, they offer the public an insight into the legal and constitutional issues of the case. After the case is heard, the nine justices meet in conference. A determination is made whether a majority of the justices have an opinion on the outcome of the appeal. Once a majority is established, sometimes after much jockeying, the Chief Justice assigns a justice to write the majority decision. Opposing justices may write dissenting opinions and if the majority has a different opinion regarding certain components of the majority opinion, they may write concurring opinions. The decision of the case is announced months after it has been reached. Sometimes, when the case is significant, the decision is read by the Chief Justice. At other times a pur curiam decision, a decision without explanation, is handed down. Once a decision is handed down, it becomes public policy. The job of implementing the decision may fall on the executive branch, legislature, or regulatory agencies, or it may require states to change their laws.

Probably one of the most far-reaching cases was *Roe v Wade* (previously discussed), which invalidated a number of state laws. However, a number of cases attempted to redefine the *Roe* doctrine. The fact that the number of cases decided has decreased during the Rehnquist years illustrates the restraint of that Court in tampering with Court precedent. Another route of appeal used by people convicted of a crime has been through the writ of habeas corpus. Claiming that their constitutional rights were violated procedurally, criminals appeal their case to the federal courts. In *Herrerra v Collins* (1993) the Supreme Court rejected the appeal of a Texas man on death row who claimed that he had new evidence that proved his innocence. The Court ruled that the writ was not in their jurisdiction and sent a clear message to other states that they should handle these appeals.

Effect on Public Policy

The history of the Supreme Court illustrates its impact on public policy.

From the landmark *Marbury v Madison* ruling, to the *Miranda* decision, to the controversies surrounding the separation of church and state, the Supreme Court has had a significant impact on public policy. By looking at the history of the Court, you will be able to see how various chief justices have been identified as contributing to the importance of the Court in the public policy arena.

John Marshall has been given credit for setting the course of the young Supreme Court. When the issue of federal judgeships came to him in the *Marbury* case, Marshall had to find legal rationale to rule that the Judiciary Act of 1789 was unconstitutional. The case revolved around the arguments made by William Marbury, who had been appointed to a minor judgeship by outgoing

Federalist President John Adams at the midnight hour of his administration. The incoming Secretary of State, James Madison, refused to deliver the commissions, and Marbury asked the Supreme Court to issue a writ of mandamus directing the executive branch to make the appointments. The argument was made directly to the Supreme Court, using the route of original jurisdiction prescribed by the Judiciary Act. Marshall, who was originally the Secretary of State under Adams responsible for delivering the commissions, was in a real bind. He convinced the rest of the Court that even though Madison was wrong not to deliver the commissions, the Judiciary Act of 1789 was unconstitutional because it did not meet the requirements outlined in the Constitution related to original jurisdiction. The principle of judicial review was established, and the Supreme Court began making crucial policy decisions. Other cases, previously described, such as *Gibbons v Ogden* and *McCulloch v Maryland,* further strengthened the power of the Marshall Court.

The Roger Taney Court (1836–1864) made critical rulings that some feel contributed to the Civil War and then made decisions that gave Lincoln the power to take away the writ of habeas corpus. The *Dred Scott* decision, declaring that slaves were property and invalidating the Missouri Compromise, set the course for the start of the Civil War. Once the war broke out, the issue of trying Southern sympathizers in the border states in a military court was allowed by the Court. The Court also established the right of the president to take away civil liberties guaranteed by the Constitution during a national emergency.

During Reconstruction, under Chief Justice Salmon Chase, the Court overturned some of the statutes passed by the radical Republicans. Congress retaliated by reducing some of the appellate powers of the Court. After Grant was elected, the Court took less of an active role.

During the period of great industrial growth, the progressive era, and the Great Depression, the Court had to deal with highly charged economic issues. Areas such as trust-busting, child labor regulations, and the right of women to work the same hours as men were brought before the Court. The landmark case *Swift v United States* (1905) held that the interstate commerce nature of the Swift meat packing factory came under the provisions of the Sherman Antitrust Act. Called the "nine old men" by Franklin Roosevelt after they decided in *Schechter Poultry Corporation v United States* (1935) that the National Industrial Recovery Act was unconstitutional, Roosevelt attempted to pack the Supreme Court, asking Congress to increase its size. They rejected his plan, but because of retirements, Roosevelt was eventually able to make new appointments.

Perhaps the most activist Court in the history of the Supreme Court, the Warren Court (1953–1969) faced the question of determining the future of the civil rights movement. Appointed by President Eisenhower in 1954, Chief Justice Earl Warren convinced a split court that it was essential to overturn the separate but equal doctrine established by *Plessy v Ferguson*. The Court also expanded the rights of the accused and ordered states to reapportion their legislatures (see Chapters 6 and 7).

When Warren retired in 1969, President Nixon had an opportunity to change the face of the Court. He appointed Warren E. Burger, a conservative jurist. He also filled another vacancy by appointing Harry Blackmun to the Court. The Court, however, continued to make rulings that irked those strict constructionists. Even though more conservative than the Warren Court, it continued to break down segregation by ordering bussing to end segregation patterns. It upheld affirmative action programs, and even though it limited aspects of the

Miranda decision, it continued to recognize the rights of the accused. The Burger Court will be remembered most for the *Roe v Wade* decision. Blackmun also emerged as the Court's liberal spokesperson. Ironically, Burger had to write the majority decision in *United States v Nixon,* which rejected Nixon's claim of executive privilege in not turning over the Watergate tapes.

In 1986 after Republican appointments made by Ford and Reagan, William Rehnquist became the nation's 17th Chief Justice. Along with Sandra Day O'Connor, Anthony Kennedy, and Antonin Scalia, the Court was the most conservative in American history. It began to reverse many of the earlier Warren and Burger rulings. When George Herbert Walker Bush was elected president in 1988, he added to the Court's conservative majority by appointing David Souter and Clarence Thomas. However, Souter has taken more of a middle of the road approach and has emerged as a crucial swing vote in many cases. After Clinton was elected in 1992, he had the opportunity to start the process of reversing the conservatism of the Court by appointing Ruth Ginsburg and Stephen Breyer. The future of the Supreme Court will depend to a large extent on the new coalitions formed and on the outcome of presidential elections. One thing has certainly become evident: a majority may vote on one issue, and on another issue an entirely new majority may emerge.

This scenario occurred during the 1995–1996, 1996–1997, and 1998–2001 terms when a number of landmark cases were decided by a slim majority. In many of these cases, Justice Sandra Day O'Connor and Justice Anthony Kennedy became the important swing votes. The following cases illustrate the turn toward the center that the Rehnquist Court followed during the Clinton presidency:

- *Roemer v Evans* (1995)—States may not prevent local governments from passing laws protecting homosexuals from discrimination. Declared illegal an initiative passed by voters denying homosexuals equal protection under the law.
- *United States v Lopez* (1995)—Federal Gun-Free School Zone Act declared unconstitutional because it violated the commerce clause.
- *Virginia v United States* (1995)—Decided that the Virginia Military Institute must admit females to the all male school, even though a separate school for women existed.
- *Shaw v Hunt* (1995)—The first of many cases which determined that black "majority-minority" gerrymandered districts were unconstitutional.
- *Clinton v Jones* (1996)—The court found unanimously that President Clinton could stand trial while still in office and was not protected by the doctrine of presidential immunity to civil suits.
- *Reno v American Civil Liberties Union* (1996)—In the first case which dealt with the Internet, the Court declared unconstitutional the part of the Communications Decency Act which made sending obscenity over the Internet illegal.
- *Washington v Glucksberg* (1997)—In a unanimous decision, the Court declared that the right to physician-assisted suicide was not protected by the Constitution.
- *Printz v United States* (1997)—The court declared unconstitutional the part of the Brady Law requiring local authorities to perform background checks on people purchasing handguns.
- *Wyoming v Sandra Houghton* (1999)—The Court held that police can search the interior of a car without a warrant, even if the search involves

the personal belongings of a passenger, when the vehicle is lawfully stopped for a traffic violation and police have general probable cause to search the vehicle for controlled substances.

- *Boy Scouts of America v Jim Dale* (2000)—The Court ruled that the Boy Scouts had the constitutional right to bar a homosexual from becoming a Scout leader on the basis that the Scouts are a private organization and have the right to associate with whomever they choose.
- *Bush v Gore* (2000)—In an historic 5–4 decision, the Rehnquist majority ruled that Florida's Supreme Court erred when it ordered a recount to determine the winner of Florida's electoral votes in the 2000 presidential election. The majority cited the guarantee of equal protection, stating that if the ballots were only recounted in selected counties, it would constitute a violation of the due process clause of the Fourteenth Amendment. The decision resulted in the awarding of Florida's electors to George W. Bush, thus giving him a majority of the electoral votes and the presidency.
- *Food and Drug Administration v Brown and Williamson Tobacco Corporation* (2000)—The Supreme Court struck down administrative regulations on the tobacco industry developed by the FDA, including restrictions on advertisements and the right of the FDA to regulate tobacco as a drug.
- *Sternberg v Carhart* (2000)—In a 5–4 decision, the Court struck down a law restricting "partial birth" abortions in Nebraska, stating that the law was an undue burden on women in need of the procedure.
- *United States v Antonio Morrison* (2000)—In another 5–4 decision, the conservatives on the Court struck down provisions of the 1994 Violence Against Women Act, which allowed women who felt they were victims of violence to seek remedy in federal courts. The Court, citing the Eleventh Amendment, held that Congress misused its commerce power authority and that the states where the alleged crime occurred had to provide the remedy.
- *Hunt v Cromartie* (2001)—Basing its decision on an earlier decision in *Shaw v Reno*, the Court ruled that a racially gerrymandered district in North Carolina was constitutional.
- *University of Alabama v Garrett* (2001)—Citing the Eleventh Amendment, the Court ruled that states could not be sued under provisions of the 1990 Americans with Disabilities Act. The issue of federalism was central in the Court's opinion, which gave states more power.
- *Pottawatomie v Earls* (2002)—Extending the 1995 random drug testing of student athletes, the Court ruled that schools can use random drug testing for any student participating in extracurricular activities without violating their privacy rights.
- *McConnell v Federal Election Commission* (2003)—The Supreme Court ruled that the major provisions of the McCain-Feingold campaign finance law were constitutional. Specifically, the justices said that the ban on soft money and the restrictions placed on television advertising did not violate free speech.
- *Gratz v Bollinger; Grutter v Bollinger* (2004)—The University of Michigan undergraduate school's (*Gratz*) admission practice was unconstitutional because it relied too much on a quota system. The University of Michigan's law school's admission system (*Grutter*) was constitutional because it relied on a broad-based policy of using race as a basis for admissions. Both decisions affirmed the *Bakke* case.

- *Rasul v Bush* (2004)—Enemy combatants held at the Guantanamo Naval Base in Cuba captured during the war in Afghanistan and Iraq may challenge their detention in federal courts.
- *Hamdi v Rumsfeld* (2004)—Enemy combatants held in the United States have due process rights.

Some of these decisions have been characterized as a new form of judicial activism "conservative activism." The cases that overturned federal laws sent a signal that the federal government was using too much of its inherent powers to create law.

Judicial Philosophy

The debate on whether the Supreme Court should reflect an activist position or exhibit judicial restraint has not been resolved.

In the early days of the republic, arguments revolving around strict constructionist versus loose constructionist interpretation of the Constitution abounded. Today, we see people arguing whether the Court should be activist or demonstrate judicial restraint. All Supreme Court nominees are asked to describe their judicial philosophy.

The critics of judicial activism make the argument that it is not the Court's responsibility to set policy in areas such as abortion, affirmative action, educational policy, and state criminal law. They feel that the civil liberty decisions have created a society without a moral fiber. The fact that judges are political appointees, are not directly accountable to the electorate, and hold life terms makes an activist court even more unpalatable to some. On the other hand, proponents of an activist court point to the responsibility of the justices to protect the rights of the accused and minority interests. They point to how long it took for the doctrine of separate but equal to be overturned. And they point to how many states attempt to circumvent court decisions and national law through laws of their own. Proponents of judicial activism also make the argument that you need the Supreme Court to be a watchdog and fulfill its constitutional responsibility of maintaining checks and balances. As Alexander Hamilton wrote in Federalist No. 78, "Laws are dead letters without courts to expound and define their true meaning and operation."

The critics of judicial restraint feel that the interests of government are not realized by a court that refuses to make crucial decisions. They suggest that the federal system will be weakened by a court that allows state laws that may conflict with the Constitution to go unchallenged. Proponents of judicial restraint point to the fact that it is the role of the Congress to make policy and the role of the president to carry it out. They feel that the Court should facilitate that process rather than initiate it. They point to the fact that in many cases the Constitution does not justify decisions in areas where there are no references. The right to an assisted suicide, for instance, became an issue that advocates of judicial restraint urged the Court to reject on the grounds that it was not a relevant federal issue to hear on appeal. The Rehnquist Court, in fact, ruled against a group of physicians arguing for the constitutional right to assisted suicide.

One of the ironies in the debate is that those favoring judicial restraint would like to see precedent be the guiding light. However, in declaring congressional laws unconstitutional and creating new precedent, those advocating restraint have themselves become conservative activists.

Chapter 9 Review

SECTION 1: MULTIPLE-CHOICE QUESTIONS

1. Judicial authority extends to issues dealing with all the following areas EXCEPT
   (A) common law.
   (B) equity.
   (C) civil law.
   (D) criminal law.
   (E) pending legislation.

2. Which of the following represents the best example of a case dealing with original jurisdiction?
   (A) a review of New York and New Jersey arguing over property rights related to Ellis Island
   (B) an appeal by a convict on death row
   (C) a review of the constitutionality of a school district allowing prayer at a graduation ceremony
   (D) a review of President Nixon's decision not to turn over the Watergate tapes to Congress
   (E) a review of a federal law mandating affirmative action in industries that have contracts with the government

3. Which of the following principles does common law rely on?
   (A) judicial precedent
   (B) contract issues
   (C) judicial restraint
   (D) habeas corpus
   (E) judicial activism

4. Which of the following actions requires senatorial courtesy?
   (A) A bill introduced by a senator from one state must get agreement from the other senator in that state.
   (B) Members of the same party agree on the order of legislation.
   (C) Senators from the state in which a judicial appointment is being made by the president are informed of who the candidate is prior to the actual appointment.
   (D) The majority leader of the Senate informs the minority leader who he is appointing as committee chairman.
   (E) The president informs the chairman of the Judiciary Committee of a Supreme Court nominee prior to the announcement.

5. Which of the following committees is responsible for reviewing Supreme Court nominees?
   (A) House Judiciary
   (B) Senate Judiciary
   (C) House Rules
   (D) Senate Appropriations
   (E) House Ways and Means

6. Acceptance of a writ of certiorari is based on all the following criteria EXCEPT
   (A) a vote by three Supreme Court justices.
   (B) a court decision that conflicts with precedent.
   (C) a court of appeals decision that conflicts with another court of appeals decision.
   (D) inconsistencies between courts of different states.
   (E) a split decision in the court of appeals.

7. Which represents a major reason for the submission of an amicus curiae brief?
   (A) The Court must rely on precedent cases.
   (B) A friend of the court wishes to provide additional information to the Court.
   (C) Lower courts must provide transcripts of its decisions.
   (D) The Supreme Court requires related interests in the case to submit briefs.
   (E) The brief from the petitioner provides amended information about the case.

8. The Court of which of the following Chief Justices handed down the most activist decisions?
   (A) Salmon Chase
   (B) William Rehnquist
   (C) Earl Warren
   (D) Roger Taney
   (E) Warren Burger

9. An example of a decision that would be classified as activist is
   (A) *San Antonio v Rodriguez.*
   (B) *Dred Scott v Sanford.*
   (C) *Plessy v Ferguson.*
   (D) *Brown v Board of Education.*
   (E) *New Jersey v TLO.*

10. The Court of which of the following Chief Justices is best known for exercising judicial restraint?
    (A) John Marshall
    (B) William Rehnquist
    (C) Roger Taney
    (D) Earl Warren
    (E) Warren Burger

11. Critics of judicial activism would favor a Supreme Court that would
    (A) give greater protection to the accused.
    (B) expand civil rights.
    (C) act as a watchdog over the other branches of government.
    (D) increase the power of the federal government.
    (E) allow the president to influence the opinion of the Court.

12. Critics of judicial restraint would favor a Supreme Court that would
    (A) create new precedent.
    (B) decrease the power of the federal government.
    (C) decrease the power of the state governments.
    (D) only agree to hear a limited number of cases.
    (E) uphold precedent.

Answers to Multiple-Choice Questions

1. **(E)** Type of Question: Negative
   The question calls upon you to know the definition including the limits of judicial authority. Accordingly common law, equity, civil law, and criminal law are all under the umbrella of judicial authority. Another category not listed, constitutional law, is also a major area. Pending legislation cannot be a part of judicial review since it has not been signed into law.
2. **(A)** Type of Question: Cause and effect relationships
   The Constitution defines original jurisdiction as those cases that involve disputes between or among the states. In such instances the case must go directly to the Supreme Court. Most cases get to the Supreme Court on appeal. Thus the only situtation that applies to the definition is choice A. Choices B, C, and E are appeals from the state level, and choice D is an appeal based on the constitutionality of executive privilege.
3. **(A)** Type of Question: Identification and analysis
   The basis of common law is judicial precedent or its Latin equivalent stare decis. Contract law certainly relies on precedent, and advocates of judicial restraint and judicial activism also have specific viewpoints regarding overturning or upholding precedent. Habeas corpus appeals can also call upon precedent. The point is that the principle of precedent is extremely important.
4. **(C)** Type of Question: Sequencing a series of events
   The concept of senatorial courtesy is a tradition that facilitates all judicial appointments to federal courts (not including the Supreme Court). When the president is ready to make the appointment, usually made according to party lines, the president informs and consults with the senators from the state of the appointee. Usually the senators help in the confirmation process.
5. **(B)** Type of Question: Identification and analysis
   According to Article I of the Constitution, the Senate is responsible for "advising and consenting" to presidential appointees to the Supreme Court and other cabinet positions. The specific Senate committee that makes the initial recommendation to the full Senate is the Senate Judiciary Committee. During the Clarence Thomas hearings, this committee came under much criticism.
6. **(A)** Type of Question: Negative
   Choices B, C, D, and E are situations that over the years have become criteria for accepting appeals cases. There is no absolute requirement that states that, if the conditions met in those examples exist, the Court must review the case. However, these examples have become the guiding principles of accepting cases for review. Choice A is incorrect because it is required that four justices agree to hear a case.

7. **(B)** Type of Question: Definitional
If you knew that the definition of amicus curiae is friend of the court, you certainly could pick out the right answer immediately. If you didn't, you could probably proceed to eliminate choice A because, even though it is a truthful statement, it has no relation to the submission of additional briefs. Choice C is also accurate but again does not provide new information. Choice D is a false statement, and briefs do not change information about a case. They make constitutional arguments about the case.
8. **(C)** Type of Question: Chronological
Even though other justices throughout history may have been involved in decisions that have been considered activist, the Chief Justice best known as the leader of an activist court was Earl Warren. Burger's Court continued some of Warren's activism, but it was certainly the intent of Nixon in appointing him to modify the Court's direction.
9. **(D)** Type of Question: Identification and analysis
The classic example of an activist decision is the *Brown* case. The San Antonio case resulted in a decision that affirmed the state's right to fund schools even if it meant that poorer districts did not spend the same amount of money for its students. *Dred Scott* established that slaves were property. *Plessy* affirmed the state's right to allow separate but equal. And New Jersey was able to search TLO without a warrant. These cases are all considered to uphold the principle of judicial restraint.
10. **(B)** Type of Question: Chronological
The justice best known for fostering an attitude that encouraged judicial restraint was Chief Justice William Rehnquist. Marshall's decisions in his time were precedent setting, and Warren personifies an activist justice. Taney and Burger, although making decisions that can be considered by those favoring judicial restraint as such, still did not have an overall record in the area as Rehnquist.
11. **(C)** Type of Question: Cause and effect relationships
Choices A, B, and D are all examples of what proponents of judicial activism would favor. Choice E is the weakest answer since neither activists nor those favoring restraint would want a president to influence Court decisions. Choice C is the correct answer because critics of judicial activism favor a Supreme Court that acts as a watchdog over the other branches of government, ensuring that they do not overstep their authority.
12. **(A)** Type of Question: Cause and effect relationships
If the theory behind judicial activism is that courts should break new ground, then Choice A is the correct answer because creating new precedent allows the Court to test new ground. If you think about the Warren Court, that is what it did in cases such as *Brown v Board of Education, Miranda v Arizona,* and *Mapp v Ohio.* Choices B, C, D, and E are all characteristics of judicial restraint.

SECTION 2: FREE RESPONSE ESSAY (All choices are answered for illustrative purposes)

Depending upon the philosophy of the Supreme Court justices, historically the Court has pursued a policy of judicial activism or judicial restraint.

1. Define the terms judicial activism and judicial restraint.
2. Choose two of the following areas of public policy and describe one case that can be classified as resulting from judicial activism or restraint.
   a. rights of the accused,
   b. affirmative action,
   c. school policy,
   d. civil rights.

Make sure that you refer to specific cases and identify the chief justice presiding over the Court making the decision.

Sample Student Response

Judicial activism and judicial restraint are the two main philosophies that have played major roles in influencing the Supreme Court justices' decisions. Judicial activism is when the judicial branch creates law, almost doing what the legislative branch in fact does. The Supreme Court is considered to be very strong and sets precedents down for future cases. Judicial restraint occurs when the judicial branch defines and strengthens the law that the legislative branch creates. The Supreme Court in these cases simply upholds legislation. These ideas are present among many areas of public policy and can be outlined in specific cases. These areas include rights of the accused, civil rights, school policy, and affirmative action.

The philosophy of the Supreme Court justices has historically had a great impact on whether the Court followed a pattern of judicial activism or judicial restraint. The justices, appointed to their position by presidential nominations, are chosen for specific reasons; the selection of a justice is not an arbitrary and capricious process. The president chooses nominees based on their ideologies, political philosophies, and the likeliness that they will make rulings that will be beneficial to the president and the political party in power.

In the area of the rights of the accused, there has been a pattern of judicial activism. In the matter of *Miranda v Arizona* (1966), the overturned conviction compelled law enforcement officials to carefully inform all suspected persons of their constitutional rights. The Fifth Amendment provides that no person "shall be compelled in any criminal case to be a witness against himself." Miranda was thought to be a prime suspect in the kidnapping/rape of an 18-year-old girl. Miranda was selected by the victim in a police lineup and subsequently questioned for two hours. During the period of his questioning, he was not informed of his constitutional rights against self-incrimination or the right to counsel and proceeded to say enough information that would eventually lead to his conviction. The matter was brought before the Supreme Court and decided in favor of Miranda. This case was also decided under the activist Warren Court as a means of protecting the defendant's rights.

In the less activist Burger Court, the matter of *Nix v Williams* (1984) allowed for the use of illegally obtained evidence when this particular evidence led police to a discovery that eventually would have been made without it. This case established an exception to the exclusionary rule, which was established in 1914 to prevent illegally seized evidence from entering the courtroom. This case illustrates the age of conservatism as the Court was moving away from a policy of activism.

In the case of the *Regents of the University of California v Bakke* (1978), the issues of affirmative action and reverse discrimination were dealt with. Allan Bakke, a 32-year-old white male, had applied to the medical school of the University of California at Davis and been flat-out rejected for two years. In place of his acceptance, students with lesser qualifications and minority backgrounds were being admitted over Bakke. The first decision was in favor of Bakke and ordered UC—Davis to admit Bakke into their freshman class. UC—Davis, losing in the California courts, took the matter to the U.S. Supreme Court. The second decision was in concurrence with the first, although leaving the Court badly divided. The decision was rendered under the Burger Court, with the majority opinion coming from Chief Justice Burger and Justices Powell, Stewart, Rehnquist, and Stevens. The Burger Court did not play a totally activist role because it did not go as far as proponents of affirmative action would have preferred. The Burger Court was more or less settled in a middle ground that enabled it to appease proponents from both sides of the spectrum.

In the arena of civil rights, the Warren Court played a very activist role, overturning such decisions as the *Brown v Board of Education* (1954), and redefining the meaning of the Fourteenth Amendment. In *Brown,* the Court stated that "in the field of public education the doctrine of 'separate but equal' has no place. . . . Segregation is a denial of the equal protection of the laws." *Brown* put an end to segregation by law, even though some states tried to circumvent certain aspects of segregation.

In the matter of the *Heart of Atlanta Motel v the United States* (1964), the Warren Court ruling made discrimination in public accommodations such as hotels and restaurants illegal. The Heart of Atlanta Motel discriminated against African-American patrons, claiming that the Title II provision of the Civil Rights Act of 1964 was unconstitutional. In a unanimous decision, the Court upheld the legality of the law.

As we have seen, the Supreme Court has had a variety of approaches when it comes to pursuing a policy of judicial activism or judicial restraint. After Earl Warren retired, the trend has been to modify the positions and decisions made by that Court. By the late 1980s Ford, Nixon, Reagan, and Bush appointees established a clear new conservative majority. Even with the more liberal appointments made by Clinton, the Supreme Court has pursued a middle ground between the activism of Warren and the restraint of Rehnquist, especially in the areas of rights of the accused, affirmative action, and abortion.

Evaluation of Free-Response Sample Essay

1. Does the essay include a definition of judicial activism and judicial restraint as well as a direction the essay will be taking in relation to the Court's influence on public policy?
2. Does the body of the essay reflect public policy issues related to the rights of the accused, affirmative action, school policy, and civil rights?
3. Does the essay identify specific cases and identify particular courts as advocates of either judicial activism or judicial restraint?

1. The essay does a superb job of evaluating the differences between judicial activism and judicial restraint. The writer includes those definitions in the thesis paragraph. The thesis also assumes that the philosophy of the Court can be changed as a result of presidential appointments. There are exceptions that the writer does not develop. For instance, when Nixon appointed Blackmun he never thought that Blackmun would turn into the epitome of an activist justice.

2. The essay follows the order of the areas presented in the question. Specific cases are used to illustrate how the Court developed public policy through its decisions in the areas of the rights of the accused, affirmative action, school policy, and civil rights. It is important to note that, when a question calls for a comparison, you should alternate examples. In this case the writer discussed cases that reflected judicial activism and judicial restraint for each of the areas. In discussing the cases, it is also necessary to summarize the outcome and significance of the case and show how the case reflects either activism or restraint on the part of the Court.

3. The strength of this essay is that the writer is able to pick out cases from the Warren Court, Burger Court, and Rehnquist Court, which both reflect the philosophy of the Court and have a major impact on public policy. In the conclusion the writer summarizes the overall trends of those Courts and speculates what the future of the Court might be as a result of more moderate Clinton appointees.

SECTION 2: DATA-BASED FREE-RESPONSE ESSAY

Look at the following statement made by President Bush when he announced the appointment of Clarence Thomas to the Supreme Court:

"I believe Thomas will be a great justice. He's a fiercely independent thinker with an excellent legal mind who believes passionately in equal opportunity for all Americans. Judge Thomas' life is a model for all Americans, and he's earned the right to sit on this nation's highest court."

Discuss the role of the president in appointing Supreme Court justices. Using this quote, discuss the impact that Marshall's retirement had on the Supreme Court.

Sample Student Response

The president is suggesting that the civil rights movement would not be hurt by Marshall's decision to leave the Court and that the new justice would take up where Thurgood Marshall left off. The president based his observation on the fact that Marshall, who ironically argued the *Brown* case before the Court in 1954, was known as a justice who was in favor of the Supreme Court's taking on an activist role when it came to civil rights cases. For example in the *Bakke* case, Marshall offered a separate opinion in which he argued for the recognition that African-Americans have had a history of discrimination. Therefore, there should be some manner in which a remedy could be applied so that a more level playing field could be developed. It can be inferred, therefore, that the appointment of another African-American, Clarence Thomas, would make up for the loss of Marshall.

In point of fact, Marshall's replacement has lived up to the expectation by many that civil rights issues would be hurt by his decisions. Clarence Thomas' appointment was controversial from the outset, even though he was the head of the Equal Employment Opportunity Commission. Thomas' background stemmed from conservative roots. He was attracted to government by Indiana Senator John Danforth before becoming EEOC chair. He believed that the civil rights movement was misguided in believing that the government could provide the solution to problems facing African-Americans. Thomas made it clear that he did not feel that Jesse Jackson or the Congressional Black Caucus should be the spokespeople for the movement. Thomas abhorred affirmative action programs claiming that racial preferences only made it easier for African-Americans to become more dependent on a white society. At the EEOC he handled discrimination cases on an individual basis rather than turning them into class action suits. In public speeches he extolled the rulings of Justice Scalia, especially in the areas of affirmative action and abortion. Embroiled in a confirmation battle that included charges by Oklahoma law professor Anita Hill that Thomas harassed her, he barely squeaked through the Senate. Once on the Court, Thomas, known as silent Clarence because he rarely asked questions during oral arguments, often sided with conservative Justices Scalia and Rehnquist and has earned a reputation of believing in judicial restraint even in areas such as civil rights. He has voted against affirmative action programs, has favored restrictions on abortions, has voted to restrict habeas corpus appeals from death row convicts, and has sided with those justices who want to see a smaller separation of church and state.

Evaluation of Data-Based Free-Response Sample Essay

1. Does the writer analyze the content and point of view of Bush?
2. Is Marshall's retirement viewed in the context of evaluating the appointment of Clarence Thomas?

1. Before discussing the retirement of Thurgood Marshall from the Supreme Court, the writer makes observations regarding the quote itself. Bush claims Thomas will be a model Supreme Court justice. The writer speculates that the future of the civil rights movement would be seriously hurt by Marshall's exit from the Court. The writer also comments that Bush's new appointment would not pick up the civil rights mantle. The strength of the analysis lies in the fact that the writer also gives specific examples of why Marshall was regarded as such a strong civil rights leader. Cases that Marshall argued and later decided are given to support the position taken.

2. The second section raises the issue of what the impact of Marshall's retirement would have on both the Court's philosophy and the civil rights movement. The writer answers the question by establishing how the background of Clarence Thomas made it likely that he would not be a civil rights advocate in the same way that Marshall was. Good examples of what Thomas believed in as the Director of the Equal Employment Opportunity Commission are related to actual decisions made by Thomas once he was appointed to the Court. The response is made even more complete by the reference to the confirmation process itself.

CHAPTER 10 The Bureaucracy

Chapter Overview

When you think about bureaucracies, one of the first things that probably comes to mind is the red tape roadblocks you may have to deal with. However, modern bureaucracies play an important linkage role in government. They are primarily responsible for implementing policy of the branches of government. Some bureaucracies also make policy as a result of regulations they issue.

This chapter will focus on four types of governmental bureaucratic agencies—the cabinet, regulatory agencies, government corporations, and independent executive agencies. We will also look at the different theories regarding how bureaucracies function. By tracing the history of civil service, you will be able to understand the role patronage has played in the development of government bureaucracies. You will also see how the permanent government agencies became policy implementers and how they must function in relation with the executive branch, legislative branch, and judicial branch.

There have been 12 attempts to reorganize government to make it more responsive, more efficient, and more effective. The last part of this chapter will focus on the latest efforts to "reinvent" government. Partly a budgetary reform to reduce the deficit and partly an attempt to streamline government, the Clinton administration's efforts in this area have received mixed reviews.

A Quick Constitutional Review

- Constitutional basis found in Article II of the Constitution in the reference to the creation of executive departments.
- Bureaucracies developed as a result of custom, tradition, and precedent.

KEY TERMS

Acquisitive bureaucracies	Iron triangle network
Bureaucracies	Monopolistic bureaucracies
Cabinet-level department	Pendleton Act
Civil service reform	Quasi judicial
Division of labor	Quasi legislative
Government corporation	Red tape
Hatch Act	REGO
Independent executive agency	Regulatory policy
Independent regulatory agencies	Spoils system

Functions of Bureaucracies

The United States has turned to bureaucratic agencies as the best way to organize and operate the federal government.

Bureaucracies are defined as large administrative agencies and have their derivation from the French word *bureau*, which refers to the desk of a government worker, and the suffix *-cracy* representing a form of government. Bureaucracies have similar characteristics. They reflect a hierarchical authority, there is job specialization, and there are rules and regulations that drive them. Within this description are six primary functions of a bureaucracy:

- They have a recognizable division of labor where skilled workers each have a specialized function so that productivity is increased.
- There is an allocation of function where each task is assigned and defined.
- There is an allocation of responsibility where each task is understood by the worker and cannot be changed without approval of the supervisor.
- There is direct and indirect supervision including line authority and staff authority.
- There is control of the full-time employment of the worker so that workers can be held on task.
- Workers make their careers synonymous with the organization because the bureaucracy provides for benefits, and workers perceive that their future success depends on the organization.

Approximately four million government workers make up today's federal bureaucracy. The number is even greater if you consider the number of state and local government workers. A little more than 10 percent of the federal employees actually work in Washington, D.C. The majority work in regional offices throughout the country. For instance, each state has many offices dealing with Social Security. About a third of the federal employees work for the armed forces or defense agencies. The number of workers employed by entitlement agencies is relatively small—only about 15–20 percent. The background of federal employees is a mix of ethnic, gender, and religious groups. They are hired as a result of civil service regulations and through political patronage. Even though many people feel bureaucracies are growing, they are in reality decreasing in size.

Workers in federal bureaucracies have different ways of being held accountable. They must respond to

- the Constitution of the United States,
- federal laws,
- the dictates of the three branches of government,
- their superiors,
- the "public interest," and
- interest groups.

Even with the characteristics described, federal workers are complex individuals who are extremely professional in the jobs they are doing.

The federal government is organized by departments, which are given that title to distinguish them from the cabinet. Agencies and administration refer to governmental bodies that are headed by a single administrator and have a status similar to the cabinet. Commissions are names given to agencies that regulate certain aspects of the private sector. They may be investigative, advisory, or reporting bodies. Corporations are agencies headed by a board of directors and have chairmen as heads.

Executive-Level Departments

The formal organization of the federal bureaucracy has a goal of creating an efficient manner of running the government.

The federal government is organized around the following executive-level departments:

- **The cabinet**—There are 15 cabinet departments headed by a secretary (except for the Justice Department, which is headed by the attorney general). The secretaries are appointed by the president with the consent of the Senate. Each department also has undersecretaries, deputies, and assistants. They manage specific policy areas, and each has its own budget and staff.
- **The regulatory agencies**—Known as independent regulatory agencies because they are quasi legislative (they act in a manner that is legislative when issuing regulations) and quasi judicial (they act in a manner that is judicial when enforcing penalties for violations of their regulations) in nature, they are also known as the alphabet agencies. Some examples are:
  * Interstate Commerce Commission (ICC), 1887—The first created independent agency, the ICC regulates specific areas of interstate relations. Historically, it determined which businesses were in violation of the Sherman Antitrust Act.
  * Federal Trade Commission (FTC), 1914—The FTC regulates fair trade, encourages competition, and is responsible for evaluating unfair or deceptive advertising or products that may be unsafe.
  * Food and Drug Administration (FDA), 1931—The FDA regulates the contents, marketing, and labeling of food and drugs.
  * Federal Communications Commission (FCC), 1934—The FCC regulates the television and radio industry and grants licenses to television and radio stations.
  * Securities and Exchange Commission (SEC), 1934—Established during the New Deal, it regulates the sale of securities and the stock markets, preventing such abuses as insider trading.
  * Environmental Protection Agency (EPA), 1970—Responding to the energy crisis, the EPA implements laws such as the Clean Air Act.
  * Occupational Safety and Health Administration (OSHA), 1972—OSHA sets safety and health standards for the work place.
  * Consumer Product Safety Commission (CPSC), 1972—CPSC tests and reports about products that may injure the public and issues warnings for those products deemed unsafe.
  * Federal Election Commission (FEC), 1975—Created by the Federal Election Campaign Act of 1971, and made even more important as a result of the election abuses uncovered by Watergate, this agency is responsible for monitoring campaign contributions and provides some funding to presidential candidates through matching grants.

- **Government corporations** such as the Tennessee Valley Authority, created during the New Deal, and the Resolution Trust Corporation, created to deal with bankruptcies and the many bank failures of the 1980s—Other corporations are created to take over a failed industry or bail out an essential private industry such as Chrysler.

- **Independent executive agencies** such as the General Services Administration (GSA), which handles government purchasing; the National Science Foundation, which supports scientific research and development; and the National Aeronautics and Space Administration (NASA), which coordinates the country's efforts in outer space.

These agencies each have specific responsibilities that facilitate the day to day operation of the government.

Organization

Bureaucratic theory differs from the reality of management organization.

Bureaucracies exist in virtually every part of our lives. From the religious organizations to which we belong, to the schools that we attend, they each have a distinctive way they operate based on theories of bureaucratic organization.

The father of bureaucratic theory is German sociologist Max Weber. He believed that bureaucracies existed in a "rational" manner, each reflecting

- a hierarchical authority structure—power flows from the top down and responsibility the opposite way;
- task specialization—experts perform prescribed tasks;
- extensive rules—so that the public is treated fairly and uniformly;
- the merit principle—workers get promotion based on merit;
- impersonality—so that no one is favored over anybody else.

Weber's view is that bureaucracies are like well-oiled machines. From this theory, other theories evolved. They stressed that bureaucracies have

- a unity of command—based on hierarchical authority;
- a chain of command—from top down and bottom up;
- line and staff control—staff advises, the hierarchical authority sends down orders;
- span of control—by the hierarchy;
- decentralization of administration—the delegation of decisions.

Modern theorists have modified Weber's theory and include the acquisitive and monopolistic bureaucracy as examples of the way organizations work. Acquisitive bureaucracies become self-perpetuating and demand funding that will result in the continued existence of the agency. A monopolistic bureaucracy suggests that there is no competitive equal that exists in the private sector. If you don't have success dealing with the Social Security Administration, you can't start your own social security department.

In reality, policy administration of federal bureaucracies has been limited by a number of checks such as

- the legislative power of Congress through legislative intent, congressional oversight, and restrictions on appropriations to agencies;
- the Administrative Procedure Act of 1946, which defines administrative policy and directs agencies to publicize their procedures;
- a built-in review process, either internal or through the court system, for appeal of agency decisions;

- the oversight function of agencies such as the Office of Management and Budget and the General Accounting Office;
- political checks such as pressure brought on by interest groups, political parties and the private sector that modify bureaucratic behavior.

History

The history of the civil service parallels the growth of government bureaucracy. As a result of the negative image bureaucracies evoke, it becomes harder to attract people to public service.

The beginning of the civil service awareness can be traced to the election of 1828 when President Andrew Jackson dismissed over 2000 government employees. "To the victor belong the spoils" became the battle cry of elected officials as the spoils system became the practice in that elected officials rewarded their supporters through political patronage. The rationale behind this type of government appointment was that elected officials were best suited to fill jobs that were basically simple. Proponents of the system also believed that through frequent change there would be a rotation of those serving in office; thus preventing corruption in government.

The first major attempt to reform the civil service procedures took place in 1871 when Congress passed the Civil Service Commission. This effort failed due to inadequate funding. When President Garfield was shot in 1881 by a disgruntled office seeker, Congress responded by passing the Pendleton Act, known as the Civil Service Act of 1883. This act set up merit as the criteria for hiring, promoting, and firing federal employees. It set up two kinds of federal employment and gave the president the power to determine how to organize the federal bureaucracy. An independent Civil Service Commission administered tests, and civil servants were prohibited from taking part in partisan politics. The president still had the prerogative of making political appointments, but he had to also follow the provisions of this act. Today over 90 percent of the government workers are classified as civil servants.

The Hatch Act in 1939 placed legal limitations on federal employees. This law places restrictions on the kind of political activity a federal employee may participate in. For instance, civil servants are prohibited from being candidates for office, cannot actively campaign for a candidate, and may not collect funds, organize rallies, or circulate nominating petitions. They may vote, express opinions about candidates, wear political buttons, and privately join a political party. There are certainly times when potential conflicts of interest occur, but on the whole the Hatch Act has depoliticized the federal work force. Even though they may not join formal unions, federal workers are able to form government unions. One such union, the Air Traffic Controllers, felt the consequences of the no-strike provision of federal law in 1981 when President Reagan fired the entire union after they disobeyed a back-to-work order.

The last major civil service reform took place under President Jimmy Carter in 1978. The Civil Service Reform Act was passed. This law replaced the Civil Service Commission with the Office of Personnel Management and the Merit Systems Protection Board. These agencies are responsible for enforcing existing civil service laws, coordinating the testing of applicants, setting up pay scales, and appointing people to federal jobs. In addition the Senior Executive Service, part of the Civil Service Reform Act, was created to attract high-level federal employees.

If there has been an ongoing effort to reform federal civil service, then why has it been so difficult to attract the highest caliber worker to government service? Each time there is a scandal in government, people get more and more disillusioned. The private sector still pays much better than the federal government, and the image of the government worker is still by and large negative. Finally, the most publicized government employees are those who are appointed and confirmed by the Senate.

Relations with Other Government Branches

Bureaucracies are linked, but are not subordinate to the other branches of government. They must also be sensitive to interest groups, the media, and public opinion.

Although having an independent nature, bureaucracies are linked to the president by appointment and direction and to Congress through oversight. Agency operations are highly publicized through the media when they have an impact on the public. Interest groups and public opinion try to influence the actions of the agencies.

Bureaucracies are inherently part of the executive branch. Even though the regulatory agencies are quasi independent, they, too, must be sensitive to the president. The president influences bureaucracies through the appointment process. Knowing that their agency heads are appointed by the president makes them respond to his direction at times. Such agencies as the EPA and Resolution Trust Corporation have come under executive scrutiny in the 1980s and 1990s. Presidents also issue executive orders that agencies must abide by. When President Clinton issued an executive order to start importing the abortion pill RU486, the Food and Drug Administration set up guidelines for testing. The Office of Management and Budget can recommend increases and decreases in proposing new fiscal year budgets. The budgetary process provides the impetus for agency growth. Finally, the president has the power to reorganize federal departments. President Reagan attempted to abolish the Departments of Energy and Education but failed to get the approval of Congress.

Congress uses similar tactics to control federal bureaucracies. Because the Senate must approve both presidential appointments and agency budgets, they become sensitive to the issues on Congress' agenda. Through the process of congressional oversight, agency heads are called before congressional committees to testify about issues related to the workings of the agency. When the Senate and House Banking Committees held hearings regarding potential presidential abuses in the Whitewater land development deal, the head of the Resolution Trust Corporation, Treasury Department officials, and White House staff were all called to testify. A specific congressional committee, the Senate Committee on Government Operations, has been charged with keeping tabs on federal campaign finance abuses. During the summer of 1997, the Committee on Government Operations began extensive hearings. Chaired by Tennessee Senator Fred Thompson, the Committee investigated campaign finance abuses of both parties which occurred during the 1996 elections. Congressional oversight committee hearings have been on the rise since the 1950s. Between 1950 and 1980 the number of oversight hearings has more than doubled. During the 1980s the number declined a bit and during the Clinton years, after the Republicans took control of Congress, oversight again increased. Oversight can also be carried out by individual members of Congress and their staffs. Through the General Accounting Office and the Congressional Budget Office, agency operations can be investigated. Bureaucracies must respond not only to oversight, but they must also be aware of legislative intent.

The best example of the interrelationship among bureaucracies, the government, interest groups, and the public is the iron triangle concept. The iron triangle network is a pattern of relationships between an agency in the executive branch, Congress, and one or more outside clients of that agency. An example of this kind of relationship was the often-criticized military-industrial complex. During the height of the Vietnam War, this relationship between defense-related government agencies and private industry that profited from the war became the antiwar rallying cry of governmental misuse of funds. The close dependence of agencies on interest groups and Congress often results in criticism of that particular agency. If the Environmental Protection Agency has too close a relationship with the industry heads of factories that they are regulating, the potential for abuse certainly exists. If you review the Department of Health and Human Services, you can visualize the iron triangle concept. Their budget is reviewed; legislation that is passed and related to health must be explained to the public; various congressional committees and interest groups such as insurance groups, senior citizen groups, and the medical community review the status of the implementation of law.

Public Policy

Bureaucracies implement policy and act as policy regulators.

The major impact of the federal bureaucracy has been in the area of public policy—its implementation and regulation. The independent regulatory agencies, in particular, have had a significant impact in this area.

The Supreme Court decision of *Munn v Illinois* in 1877 is one of the landmark regulatory cases. The case involved a dispute over whether Illinois had the power to regulate the railroad haulage rates of grain. Illinois passed Grange laws that forced the railroad to abide by state rates. The Court determined that because it was in the public interest, the state had the right to regulate this private industry. This ruling influenced the passage of the Interstate Commerce Act and establishment of the Interstate Commerce Commission in 1887. It is ironic that in 1994 this agency came under fire by Congress and was defended by the same interests who were critical of its creation. The railroad and trucking industry were critical of Congress' budget cutbacks of the first independent agency to be created.

You have to only go as far as tracing your daily routine to see how influential regulatory agencies have become. Some examples are the regulation of

- cable television by the Federal Communications Commission,
- food labeling by the Federal Trade Commission,
- meat inspection by the Food and Drug Administration,
- pollution control by the Environmental Protection Agency,
- airline safety by the National Transportation Safety Board,
- safety and reliability of home appliances by the Consumer Product Safety Commission,
- seat belt mandates by the National Highway Traffic Safety Administration,
- gas mileage standards developed by the Department of Transportation,
- the mediation of labor disputes by the National Labor Relations Board,
- factory inspections for worker safety by the Occupational Safety and Health Administration, and

- the coordination of relief efforts by the Federal Emergency Management Agency.

Each of these examples also has a linkage component described in the last section. They were motivated by presidential direction, acts of Congress, and court decisions. The public, interest groups, and the media have reacted to the regulatory and policymaking process. Even though many of these regulations and policies are in the public interest, critics of regulation point to the fact that the costs far exceed the benefits of the entire regulation process. The fear of an overregulated society is one of the issues that is still being debated.

Reform

Efforts to make the bureaucracy more responsive, more accountable, and less wasteful result in controversial proposals to streamline government.

Efforts to reform the federal government have been attempted 12 times in our nation's history. Past efforts such as the Grace Commission, in 1982, reacted to the cry of "less government." In 1993, when President Clinton and Vice President Gore unveiled their plan to "reinvent government," named "REGO," they said it would make the federal government work better and result in cutting the deficit. Vice President Gore had spent months investigating the working of the federal bureaucracy. He obtained input from the public and government workers and drafted a report titled *From Red Tape to Results: Creating a Government that Works Better and Costs Less.* The plan was presented to the public in what was called one of the greatest photo ops—the president and vice president introducing their plan to a national audience with two forklifts carrying thousands of pounds of bureaucratic regulations in the background.

The plan called for reducing the federal work force by 12 percent, updating information systems, eliminating wasteful programs and procedures, and cutting red tape. The report also evaluated the structure of the federal bureaucracy calling it "top down fostering loyalty only to bloated chains of command and adherence to procedure." It called for the implementation of performance standards that cleared Congress and required federal agencies to use them to measure and account for progress on specific programs. Each agency that spent more than $20 million annually had to submit to the Office of Management and Budget a five-year plan setting out its goals. Accountability became the basis of evaluation.

Other parts of the proposal included

- reducing the number of Agricultural Department field offices,
- eliminating agriculture subsidies for certain products,
- streamlining the Army Corps of Engineers,
- opening government printing jobs to commercial bids, and
- improving the ability of the Social Security Administration to investigate the wrongful issuance of checks to people who are no longer disabled.

The program was wide-ranging and affected virtually every federal department and agency. Many of the components not needing congressional approval were implemented by executive order. Republican critics of the plan called the potential savings exaggerated. They did, however, agree to work with the Democratic majority to streamline government, a traditional Republican theme. After the first year of the program, Vice President Al Gore evaluated the successess and failures and gave it a B+.

The program developed by the vice president and one of the themes of the 1992 campaign was based on a book *Reinventing Government* by David Osborne and Ted Gaebler. It took the vice president over six months to wrap up a National Performance Review. The report concluded that "the federal government seems unable to abandon the obsolete. . . . It knows how to add, but not to subtract."

Chapter 10 Review

SECTION 1: MULTIPLE-CHOICE QUESTIONS

1. An advantage that bureaucrats in federal government have over the president in the policymaking process is that bureaucrats
   (A) control the budgetary process.
   (B) have an independence from the president that is guaranteed by the Constitution.
   (C) find it easier to gather public support than does the president.
   (D) usually have a continuity of service in the executive branch that the president lacks.
   (E) usually have better access to the media than does the president.

2. All of the following influence the Department of Defense's yearly budget EXCEPT
   (A) the desire of the chairman of the Senate Armed Services Committee.
   (B) the budget recommendations of the Joint Chiefs of Staff.
   (C) the rate of increase of the size of the armed forces.
   (D) the number of bases being closed.
   (E) the budget request made by the minority party in the House of Representatives.

3. Cabinet-level agencies are responsible to
   (A) Congress.
   (B) the president.
   (C) the courts.
   (D) the White House staff.
   (E) the executive office of the president.

4. The theoretical bureaucratic structure includes all the following EXCEPT
   (A) a hierarchical authority structure.
   (B) a "spoils" system.
   (C) extensive rules.
   (D) standard operating procedures.
   (E) a division of labor.

5. Many contemporary politicians have come to see bureaucracies as agencies
   (A) that aim to make realistic recommendations that may result in lower budgets than the year before.
   (B) whose main objective is to seek profits.
   (C) whose major goal is to cut back on their powers.
   (D) who strive to maximize their budgets and powers.
   (E) who work more closely with the judiciary.

6. According to some political scientists, which policymaking group is largely responsible for the growth of modern governments?
   (A) bureaucracies
   (B) Congress
   (C) the president
   (D) private business
   (E) the courts

7. All the following are characteristics of the independent regulatory agency EXCEPT that
   (A) it has responsibility for some sector of the economy.
   (B) it makes rules designed to protect the public interest.
   (C) it enforces rules designed to protect the public interest.
   (D) its powers are so great that it is often called the "fourth branch of the government."
   (E) it is exempt from court rulings.

8. All the following are examples of independent regulatory agencies EXCEPT
   (A) the Interstate Commerce Commission (ICC)
   (B) the Federal Communications Commission (FCC)
   (C) the Federal Reserve Board (FRB)
   (D) the Securities and Exchange Commission (SEC)
   (E) the Central Intelligence Agency (CIA)

9. Bureaucratic policy implementation includes all the following elements EXCEPT the ability of the agency to
   (A) abolish a nonfunctioning department in another agency.
   (B) create new operating procedures within its own agency.
   (C) assign new responsibilities within its own agency.
   (D) translate policy goals into operational rules for its own personnel.
   (E) coordinate its own resources and personnel to achieve intended goals.

10. Administrative regulations contain all the following elements EXCEPT
   (A) a grant of power and a set of directions from Congress.
   (B) a set of rules and guidelines by the regulatory agency itself.
   (C) power granted to the Justice Department to enforce heavy sanctions, including abolishing the agency.
   (D) a means of enforcing compliance with congressional goals and agency regulations.
   (E) a set of penalties for noncompliance.

11. When a president tries to control a bureaucratic agency, all the following methods are available to him EXCEPT
    (A) appointing the right people to head the agency.
    (B) reducing the agency's budget.
    (C) issuing executive orders.
    (D) recommending a reduction of the agency's following year's budget.
    (E) using his office to influence agency direction.

12. Which of the following results from an iron triangle relationship?
    (A) each policy being made independently from the others
    (B) policies being made that are contradictory from others
    (C) a lack of an integrated, coherent approach to broad policy problems
    (D) a cooperative relationship among a special interst group, a bureaucratic agency, and Congress
    (E) a hostile relationship among the bureaucratic agencies making policy

13. In recent years presidential policy with respect to the federal bureaucracy has been to
    (A) favor an increase in the number of workers to cope with the complexity of federal programs.
    (B) favor significant budget increases to fund new programs.
    (C) favor a downsizing and reorganization of the work force.
    (D) request the creation of new agencies to regulate the transportation industry.
    (E) request the elimination of the Central Intelligence Agency.

Answers to Multiple-Choice Questions

1. **(D)** Type of Question: Cause and effect relationships
Using process of elimination, you can come up with the answer to this question. Congress controls the budgetary process of bureaucratic agencies. Even though some bureaucratic agencies have an independence from the president (mostly the independent regulatory agencies), this independence stems from laws passed by Congress. Choice C is incorrect because bureaucrats usually distance themselves from the public and do not usually have close contact with the media. Because many bureaucrats are appointed for longer terms than the president or have civil service appointments, they have a continuity of service.

2. **(E)** Type of Question: Negative
The question aims at making the student recognize the many different ways that a department budget can be influenced. Choices A, B, C, and D would all contribute to a potential increase in the Defense Department's budget. Choice E, though having a minimal impact, would not be a significant influence since the mincrity party does not control the agenda.

3. **(B)** Type of Question: Identification and analysis
Because cabinet heads are appointed by the president, you can argue that these agencies are responsible to the person actually making the appointments. Therefore, the agency is ultimately responsible to the president. Congress does have some control through the budgetary process and using congressional oversight.

4. **(B)** Type of Question: Negative
The key word in the question is *theoretical*. Based on theory, choices A, C, D, and E all exist in the formation and operation of bureaucracies. A spoils system stemming from Andrew Jackson's statement of "to the victors belong the spoils" is not part of the theoretical basis, even though it does happen in practice.

5. **(D)** Type of Question: Hypothetical
Because bureaucracies have developed the reputation of wanting to create so-called empires of power, many politicians have become skeptical. In fact, there have been calls to abolish the Departments of Education and Energy. Therefore, choice D represents what many legislators see as a drawback of the modern bureaucracy.

6. **(A)** Type of Question: Cause and effect relationships
Even though Congress and the president have a direct relationship in creating bureaucracies, it is the bureaucracies themselves that have been criticized for being responsible for the growth of government. That is why President Clinton and Vice President Gore came out with REGO, or reinventing government, by downsizing the federal government.

7. **(E)** Type of Question: Negative
Choices A, B, C, and D are all characteristics of an independent regulatory agency. Think of examples of these agencies such as the Food and Drug Administration or Environmental Protection Agency, and you will be able to make the connections. Court rulings can negate regulations from these agencies.

8. **(E)** Type of Question: Negative
The characteristics listed in question 7 all must apply to these agencies. The Central Intelligence Agency may want to act independently at times in the name of national security. However, it is directly responsible to the president. The other agencies in the question all have independent status.

9. **(A)** Type of Question: Negative
The point of this question is that bureaucratic policies are carried out within the department. Choices B, C, D, and E reflect that issue. Choice A goes beyond the parameter suggesting that policy implementation includes the abolition of a nonfunctioning department in another agency. That is not within the authority of a bureaucracy.

10. **(C)** Type of Question: Negative
The enforcement of sanctions and the ability to abolish an agency is given to the executive and legislative branches of government. Choices A, B, D, and E are administrative responsibilities given to bureaucratic agencies themselves.

11. **(B)** Type of Question: Negative
The budgets of bureaucratic agencies are determined by legislative action only. The president can appoint chairs of agencies, can issue an executive order that may negate an agency directive, can recommend a reduction or increase in the budgets of these agencies, and can try to use a bully pulpit to influence the direction of an agency.

12. **(D)** Type of Question: Cause and effect relationships
Thinking of a specific example like the military-industrial complex during the Vietnam War gives you the answer to this question. By definition, an iron triangle relationship exists when a bureaucratic agency, special interest group, and legislative arm work hand in hand to develop policies.

13. **(C)** Type of Question: Generalization
With the implementation of the reinventing government program of the Clinton administration, the trend of both the executive and legislative branches has been to downsize and reorganize the federal work force. This has led to a return of many programs to the states where they too had to deal with the issue of the size of their agencies.

SECTION 2: FREE-RESPONSE ESSAY

The attempt to downsize the federal bureaucracy has been met with both criticism and support. Give two arguments in favor of reducing the size of the government and two arguments against reducing the size of the government. Evaluate how the Clinton administration attempted to reinvent government.

Sample Student Response

The heart of the discussion focuses on whether there is a need for all the agencies because the critics claim there is duplication of services. For instance, proponents of eliminating the Departments of Education and Energy claim that by merging them with other departments, creating new departments such as Health and Human Services for Education and Interior for Energy, will result in a tremendous cost savings as well as eliminate duplication of services. The other part of the debate raises the question of the need for the number of regulations that are issued by independent regulatory agencies such as the Environmental Protection Agency, Food and Drug Administration, and Federal Trade Commission.

On a practical basis there are sound arguments for maintaining the size of the federal bureaucracy. Unless and until the number of federal programs are reduced and/or eliminated, we need these agencies to run and coordinate them. From welfare to Social Security (in fact in 1995, the Social Security Administration became an independent agency), the bureaucracies play an essential role in delivering services for the American people. In addition, there is no doubt that such laws as the Clean Air Act, the Clean Water Act, as well as the scrutiny of harmful products by the Federal Trade Commission and Food and Drug Administration are viewed as important safeguards.

On the other hand, if there is ever going to be a balanced federal budget and real deficit reduction, programs must be eliminated and agencies must be downsized or abolished. A good example of this is the move to abolish the Interstate Commerce Commission. The commission was established in 1887 to monitor the rail and trucking industries. It evolved into a larger bureaucracy, taking on the additional role of overseeing the rates for interstate trucking, railroads, buses, and moving companies. It also ruled on mergers and acquisitions of companies related to interstate commerce. Critics say that another department such as the Department of Transportation can easily take over the functions of the ICC if it was eliminated.

Efforts by the Clinton administration and the Republican Congress in 1995 to move toward reducing the size of the federal government included the Clinton-Gore Reinventing Government program and the Republican Regulatory Reduction Bill, part of its Contract with America. The Clinton-Gore proposal, known as REGO, was first introduced in 1993 as part of a national performance review conducted by the vice president. Pointing out that the federal government has more than 2 million civilian employees and a budget of more than $1.5 trillion, this committee identified the problems and made specific suggestions. These included reviewing presidential executive orders, reducing unnecessary regulations, changing administrative practices, implementing new procedures to enhance services to the American people, and eliminating and reforming wasteful spending.

Within six months of the plan, President Clinton issued an Executive Order on Regulatory Reform. Its aim was to ensure that agencies regulate only when necessary. A working group under the supervision of the Office of Management and Budget met regularly to consider new, creative, and more effective alternatives and approaches to regulating. If this group found that the regulations were necessary, the regulations would be able to move forward in the most cost-effective manner. The goal would be to implement the regulation so as to bring the most benefits to the American people at the lowest possible cost. Built in would be an evaluative measure of the regulation, aiming to see its impact on the economy, the environment, and public health and safety.

If this group decided that existing or proposed regulations were unnecessary, they would be identified, revised, or eliminated. If new legislation was required to accomplish the change, the president would make the appropriate recommendations to Congress. Part of the ongoing review was a recommendation by President Clinton to cut $1.3 billion from four federal agencies. The result would be to reduce or eliminate programs from the Small Business Administration, Interior Department, Federal Emergency Management Agency, and National Aeronautics and Space Administration. Cuts include eliminating some of the smaller field offices of the Small Business Administration, transferring Bureau of Indian Affairs programs at the Department of Interior to the tribes themselves, and restructuring NASA.

Evaluation of Free-Response Sample Essay

1. Does the essay define the pros and cons of reducing the size of government as well as give an explanation regarding the overall proposed solutions?
2. Are there sufficient examples and analysis of how Clinton's reinventing government and the anti-regulatory programs work?

1. The essay statement encompasses the first four paragraphs of the essay. The writer goes from the general to the specific. Giving an explanation of the positive aspects of the federal bureaucracy, the writer develops the premise that if you have regulations that protect the health and safety of the Ameri-

can people, you therefore need agencies to carry them out. On the other hand, the writer recognizes the political realities of the time indicating that there was a broad movement to downsize government.

2. In the heart of the essay, the writer traces the ongoing efforts of President Clinton and Vice President Gore, through their National Performance Review, to "reinvent government." Through a series of recommendations and an executive order, the Clinton administration began the process of downsizing government and developing a process to review regulations in 1993.

SECTION 2: DATA-BASED FREE-RESPONSE ESSAY

The following is an excerpt from the Unfunded Mandates Act of 1994.

Unfunded Mandates Act of 1994

SEC. 2. PURPOSES

The purposes of this Act are—

(1) to strengthen the partnership between the Federal Government and States, local governments, and tribal governments;
(2) to end the imposition, in the absence of full consideration by Congress, of Federal mandates on states, local governments, and tribal governments without adequate Federal funding, in a manner that may displace other essential State, local, and tribal governmental priorities;
(3) to promote informed and deliberate decisions by Congress on the appropriateness of Federal mandates in any particular instance.

Explain the Unfunded Mandates Law of 1994 outlined here. Discuss the development of how Congress acted to address the problem of unfunded mandates by analyzing the impact of the law on the federal government as well as on the states.

Sample Student Response

Unfunded mandates are policies imposed on the states by the federal government. These policies can be in the form of laws or quasi legislative directives from bureaucratic agencies. They are called unfunded mandates because the states are required to implement the policies and also pay for them, regardless of whether the states support the objective of the policy.

One purpose of the law is to change the nature of federal government imposition of policies that the states must pay for. The legislation also requires the federal government to analyze and evaluate every mandate imposed on the states in an attempt to reduce those mandates which would create an undue burden on the states. This is accomplished by a procedure requiring the Congress and federal agencies to "prepare and consider better estimates of the budgetary impact of regulations containing Federal Mandates upon states. . . . " With President Clinton's support, this legislation was one of the first pieces of legislation signed by the 104th Congress.

The impact of this law on the states is potentially far reaching. Some of the legislative regulations that have been previously imposed on the states include social security payroll taxes, wages and hours regulations, clean air requirements as well as implementation of entitlement programs. States have argued that even in the Federalist Papers, the Founding Fathers hinted that the states should be protected from a burdensome federal government. The impact of unfunded mandates on the states ultimately places a burden on the taxpayer because many states simply raise state taxes to pay for these mandates. Let's take a closer look at an unfunded mandate imposed by the EPA. As part of the 1972 Clean Air Act the EPA required states to establish guidelines to control pollutants. The EPA is responsible for developing specific air-quality standards as a way to achieve the goals set forth by the act. It executes the provisions of law by establishing national pollution limitations, such as requiring automobiles to meet emission standards and factories to establish pollutant controls. The EPA also established penalties for violators of the law. It conducted investigations based on complaints and instituted lawsuits to enforce its environmental regulations. An outgrowth of the law is an oversight process established as part of the law. It enables Congress to hold hearings in order to monitor how well the law is working. As a result, other laws, including updated versions of the Clean Air Act, the Clean Water Act, and the establishment of a Superfund were passed. With each new law, the EPA was given more responsibility to implement the law. A specific example of how the EPA created a regulation that impacted on the states was the imposition of centralized emission control stations to replace local service stations doing smog tests in those states which had higher than normal pollution problems. Many of the affected states were not prepared to implement the directive and had to ask for a waiver. Thus, the process of law to regulation sometimes results in the regulation not always being implemented.

Evaluation of Data-Based Free-Response Sample Essay

1. Is there a clear explanation how and why the law was developed by Congress?
2. Are there specific examples of how the law affected the states?

1. Notice how the writer gives the background to the law in the context of the Republican Contract with America. The essay then defines the important terms essential to understanding its purposes—such as unfunded mandates. The law itself is then analyzed using good examples from the data provided. Each example connects to the issues raised in the development of the law itself.

2. The second part of the essay cites specific examples of the impact of the law on the federal government and the states. The writer uses a specific example of the EPA and its mandates on the states. The contrast between the law and its effect on the states gives one a clear picture of why the law was passed—from its development to its purposes and its implementation.

PART THREE THE POLITICAL PROCESS AND POLITICAL BELIEFS

CHAPTER 11 Political Parties and Political Action

Section Overview

This section of the book will explore the four main linkage institutions: political parties, elections, the media, and interest groups. To understand the function of these informal institutions of government fully, you should view them as input agents that result in output from the policymaking institutions we covered in the last section.

Chapter Overview

The first linkage institution, political parties and the manner in which they influence policymaking through political action, will be developed in this chapter. It will cover the major tasks, organization, and components of political parties. We will contrast the party organization with its actual influence on the policymakers in government. Then we will look at the history of the party system in America, evaluating the major party eras. The impact of third parties on the two-party system will also be discussed.

We will also analyze the ideology of the two major parties by looking at their platforms versus the liberal/conservative alliances that have developed. These coalitions may be the first step in the breakdown of the two-party system as we know it.

KEY TERMS

Democratic Party
Divided government
Linkage institution
McGovern-Frasier Commission
National Committee
National nominating conventions
New Democrat
Party dealignment
Party era
Party identification
Party machine
Party platforms
Party realignment
Political participation
Political party
Political socialization
Reagan Democrats
Reform Party
Religious right
Republican Party
Superdelegates
Third political parties
Two-party system

The last part of the chapter will focus on the political participation of the average citizen ranging from conventional means of influencing government to more radical, unconventional tools that have influenced our elected officials.

The Two-Party System

Political parties have various functions and serve as one of the primary linkage institutions to government.

If the definition of politics is "who gets when, what, how, and why," then political parties are the means to achieve that end. The nature of the party system in America can be viewed as competitive. Since the development of our first parties, the Federalists and Democratic-Republicans, different philosophies and different approaches to the development and implementation of public policy have determined which party and which leaders control the government. Our system has been one of the few two-party systems existing in democracies; however, the influence of third-party candidates cannot be underestimated. Parliamentary democracies have multiparty governments.

Because the aim of a political party is to influence public policy, in order to succeed, parties must draw enough of the electorate into their organization and ultimately must get enough votes to elect candidates to public office. You can, therefore, look at a political party in three ways:

- the party as an organization,
- the party's relationship with the electorate, and
- the party's role in government.

In order to achieve their goals, all political parties have common functions:

- nominating candidates who can develop public policy,
- running successful campaigns,
- developing a positive image,
- raising money,
- articulating these issues during the campaign so that the electorate will identify with a particular party or candidate,
- coordinating in the governing process the implementation of the policies they supported, and
- maintaining a watchdog function if they do not succeed in electing their candidates.

The completion of each of these tasks depends on how effective the party's organization is, the extent the party establishes its relationship with the electorate, and how it controls the institutions of government. A complete discussion of these components and functions will take place in other parts of the chapter.

History

The two major political parties have established party eras by forming broad-based coalitions.

If American government is characterized by a pluralistic approach (see Chapter 1), then it stands to reason that political parties must attract a broad consensus in order to win elections. As we look at the history of the party eras, you will see how these coalitions contributed to the success of the parties and candidates.

The first political parties that formed, the Federalists and Democratic-Republicans, went head to head after Thomas Jefferson, the country's first Secretary of State, resigned from Washington's cabinet in 1793. Jefferson's party was first known as the Anti-Federalists, continuing the name of the party opposed to the ratification of the Constitution. They were eventually called Democratic-Republicans, hoping to convince the electorate that they believed in a more democratic approach to the governing of the Republic. The first contested election in which the parties clashed was in 1796 when John Adams defeated Jefferson by only three votes in the electoral college. Attracting James Madison to his camp, Jefferson beat Adams in the election of 1800, also winning control of the Congress. This victory signaled the death knell of the Federalists. By 1828 the Democratic-Republicans split into the Whigs, led by Henry Clay and Daniel Webster (later evolving into the Republican Party), and the Democrats, led by Andrew Jackson.

Party eras after Jefferson's victory can be broken down into four periods. The first one (1828–1860) was characterized by the Democrats dominating the presidency and Congress. The second period (1860–1932) could be viewed as the Republican era. The third era (1932–1968) gave birth to the success of the New Deal and was dominated by the Democrats. The fourth period (1968 to present) has been called the era of divided government. It has been characterized by the election of Republican presidents having to deal with a Democratic Congress. A new party era may have been ushered in, signaled by the Republican takeover of Congress in 1994. The Republican takeover and the reelection of President Clinton suggests that the era of divided government may be long lasting. In the 2000 election, divided government became the theme. First, in the presidential election, Vice President Al Gore received more popular votes than George W. Bush but still lost the electoral vote. Congress initially remained Republican, but was closely divided. Then in 2001, the Democrats gained a majority in the Senate after a Republican senator left the party. After the mid-term election in 2002, the Republicans again solidified their majority, retaking control of the Senate and increasing their majority in the House of Representatives. The 2004 election may have signaled a more permanent return of a Republican majority as George W. Bush was reelected by a popular vote majority for the first time since his father won in 1988 and the Republicans increased their majorities in both the House and Senate. If this trend continues in the next election cycle, political scientists may be looking at the emergence of a new party era. One thing is certain. Republican gains in the once Democratic South suggest a major party realignment in that area of the country.

After the so-called Era of Good Feeling, which ended in the 1820s, Andrew Jackson emerged as the leading Democrat supported by a populist following of small farmers, Westerners, and the "common man." Jacksonian democracy resulted in universal white male suffrage, popular election of presidential electors as a result of the Twelfth Amendment, national nominating conventions, and the institution of the spoils system. The Whig Party was a loose alliance of Eastern bankers, merchants, industrialists, and large plantation owners. The major tenet of their party was high tariffs. Issues such as state's rights, slavery, and the National Bank created major splits in both parties. The Whigs' only successes were the election of two military leaders, William Henry Harrison in 1840 and Zachary Taylor in 1848.

The onset of the Civil War brought the election of the first Republican president, Abraham Lincoln. Called the Grand Old Party (GOP), even though the Democrats were much older, the Republicans had the former Whigs, many antislavery Democrats, and the remnants of a third party, the Know-Nothings, as the nucleus of their membership. The Republicans supported big business interests, the preservation of the Union, and the eventual abolition of slavery. After the Civil War, many radical Republicans turned on Andrew Johnson and attempted to impeach him. The Republicans maintained control on the national scene, drawing support from ex-Union soldiers, Southern plantation owners, Northern Protestants, and old immigrants. The Democrats, weakened by the support of the ex-Confederacy, could win on the local level only. Their dominance in the South was described as "the solid South" for the Democratic Party. The only Democrat who achieved electoral victory during the latter part of the nineteenth century was Grover Cleveland, in 1884 and then again in 1892. Except for the election of Woodrow Wilson in 1912 and 1916, the Republicans, with their opposition to social-welfare programs and their laissez-faire doctrine, were in control of the White House. It was ironic, due to the influence of a third party, the Populist Party, that what has been called the "progressive era" in American history took place after party realignment occurred in the election of 1896. William Jennings Bryan, one of the nation's top orators, became the populist proponent. Even though McKinley won, a new working class became involved in the political process. Theodore Roosevelt's presidency and the influence of the Bull Moose Party contributed to the era of political, social, and economic reform. The reform movement ended with America's involvement in World War I. Harding's "return to normalcy" signaled a more conservative approach during the raucous roaring 1920s.

Party realignment, the shift of party loyalty, occurred in 1932 after the country experienced the Great Depression. Fed up with the trickle-down economic theories of Herbert Hoover, the public turned to the New Deal policies of Franklin Roosevelt. A new coalition of voters supported FDR's New Deal. They included city dwellers, blue collar workers, labor union activists, the poor, Catholics, Jews, the South, and African-Americans where they could vote. An unusual alliance of Northern liberals and Southern conservatives elected Roosevelt to an unprecedented four terms. This coalition, with the exception of Eisenhower's election, held control of the White House and Congress until 1968. A direct comparison can be made among Roosevelt's New Deal, Kennedy's New Frontier, and Johnson's Great Society philosophy and election coalition. The growth of the federal government and the growth of social programs became part of the Democratic platform.

The Vietnam War and the issue of how this country would fight communism brought the Republicans back to power in 1968. Since then, they have won six of eight presidential elections but were unable to control Congress until 1994. That is why this modern period has been called the period of divided government. The Watergate scandal and Nixon's resignation in 1974 saw a weakened GOP and the eventual loss by Gerald Ford to Jimmy Carter in 1976. That election signaled a new Southern strategy, which Ronald Reagan was able to capitalize on in 1980. Pulling what has been labeled as "Reagan Democrats," Reagan attracted a traditional Democratic base of middle-class workers to his candidacy. It became even more divided from 1981 to 1986 when the Republicans were able to control the Senate. Divided government also existed on the state level with a minority of states controlling both the governorship and state legislatures. Besides being divided on party lines, government became divided on ideological lines. Political scientists began referring to the nation as divided into the "blue states" won by the Democrats and the "red states" won by the Republicans after the 2000 election.

With the election of Bill Clinton in 1992 and his reelection in 1996, the emergence of an ideological party era seemed to be on the horizon. Even though Clinton had a Democratic majority in both houses during his first term, much of his legislative agenda was embroiled in an ideological battle among liberals, moderates, and conservatives who did not always vote along party lines. The rise of the so-called religious right, an evangelical conglomeration of ultraconservative political activists joining the Republican Party, has contributed to this rise of an ideological party era. The attempt at bipartisanship has been replaced by temporary coalitions depending upon the issue of the day. When the North American Free Trade Agreement was passed, one coalition emerged; when the Crime Bill was passed, different alliances were formed.

After the 2000 election, coalitions became even more important since the House was so closely divided and the Democrats had a one vote majority in the Senate. A good example of the development of a moderate coalition was the one which formed to pass a major tax reduction package in 2001.

Third Parties

Third parties have had a significant impact on the political process.

Third political parties, also called minor parties, have played a major role in influencing the outcome of elections and the political platforms of the Democrats and Republicans. Even though these smaller parties and their leaders realize that they have virtually no chance to win, they still wage a vocal campaign. These third political parties can be described as ideological, single-issue oriented, economically motivated, and personality driven. They have been called Socialist, Libertarian, Right to Life, Populist, Bull Moose, and United We Stand. But they all have one thing in common—an effort to influence the outcome and direction of an election. Let's look at some of the more successful third-party attempts.

In the 1840s and 1850s the Free Soil Party opposed the spread of slavery, and the Know Nothings opposed Irish immigration to this country. They were both short-lived, and their supporters joined the Republicans and Democrats. The first party that had a major impact on the electorate was the Populist Party (1892–1908). It supported William Jennings Bryan's free silver movement in 1896, and a number of their political reforms such as initiative, referendum, and recall were adopted. Its insistence that government take a greater role in regulating monopolies later resulted in antitrust legislation. The Bull Moose Party in 1912 played a spoiler role in that election. After being denied the Republican nomination, Theodore Roosevelt formed the party and garnered over 25 percent of the vote, winning 88 electoral votes and coming in second to Wilson. In the same election Socialist Eugene V. Debs and Prohibition candidate Eugene Chafin also ran and pulled in over 7 percent of the vote. These parties faded after their presidential candidates were defeated. The same thing happened to Robert LaFollette's Progressive Party of 1924 and Strom Thurmond's Dixiecrat Party of 1948. Colorful candidates like Norman Thomas ran under the Socialist banner six times, and independent candidate Lyndon LaRouche ran for president from a jail cell.

The modern third-party impact has revolved around a political leader who could not get the nomination from his party. George Wallace's American Independent Party of 1968 opposed the integration policies of the Democratic Party, and he received 13 percent of the vote and 46 electoral votes, contributing to Hubert Humphrey's defeat in a very close election. John Anderson's defection from the Republican Party in 1980 and his decision to run as a third-party candidate had a negligible effect on the outcome of that election. The announcement by Texas billionaire H. Ross Perot that he was entering the 1992 presidential race, and using his own money to wage the campaign, changed the nature of that race. He announced his intention to run on CNN's *Larry King Show* and said that if his supporters could get his name on the ballot in all 50 states he would officially enter the race. A political novice, he decided to drop out of the race the day Bill Clinton was nominated. He then reentered the heated contest in October, appeared in the presidential debates, and struck a chord with close to 20 percent of the electorate. His folksy style and call for reducing the nation's deficit played a significant role in the campaign. He did not win a single electoral vote but pledged to continue his campaign through the United We Stand Party he formed. In 1996 the party nominated Perot to be its candidate. This time he received less than 10 percent of the popular vote. In the 2000 election his party became splintered and divided when it nominated conservative and former Republican Pat Buchanan for president. He received less than 1 percent of the popular vote.

Party Dealignment

Democrats and Republicans have been viewed as having few differences between them. Ideology has become more important than party identification.

If party realignment signifies the shifts in the history of party eras, then people gradually moving away from their parties has become more of a trend in today's view of party loyalty. This shift to a more neutral and ideological view of party identification has been called party dealignment. In fact those people who are strong party loyalists are so because they believe that the party matches their ideology. The shift of traditional Southern Democrats to the Republican Party came about because many voters perceived the Republicans as a more conservative party than the Democrats. Women activists, civil rights supporters, and people who believe in abortion make up the Democratic coalition because the Democratic Party has supported these issues in their national platform. Party organization and party support have remained stronger than party identification because of the ability of the parties to raise funds and motivate their workers.

Although considered unimportant by many, party platforms are perhaps a better barometer of party identification than traditional measurements. If you look at the 2004 national party platform of the Democratic and Republican Parties, you can see the effect ideological differences had on voter support. Here are a few examples.

SYMBOL OF DEMOCRATIC PARTY

SYMBOL OF REPUBLICAN PARTY

Issue	Democratic Party	Republican Party
Abortion	Advocates choice, education, counseling, and the right to an abortion.	Supports a human life amendment to the Constitution that would outlaw abortion, without exceptions.
Taxes	Limited targeted tax cuts that would help the middle class and specifically reduce the burden of college costs. Protect entitlement programs from major cuts.	Across-the-board reduction in income tax rates; seeks to change the nature of entitlement programs.
Affirmative Action and Homosexual Rights	Advocates "the mending, not ending" of affirmative action programs; an end to discrimination against gay men and lesbians with the goal of their full inclusion in the life of the nation.	Endorses Propostion 209, the California initiative that would end government-sponsored affirmative action programs; opposes extending anti-discrimination laws to cover homosexuals.
Gun Control and Crime	Supports the provisions of the Brady Law requiring a waiting period for the purchase of handguns; favors the continuation of the provisions of the 1994 Crime Bill.	Calls for adult trials for juveniles who commit adult crimes; pledges to defend the "constitutional right to keep and bear arms"; calls for the repeal of the assault weapons ban.

Even though the party positions differ significantly, it is interesting to note that, when actual legislation is proposed, there is very rarely bloc voting on these issues.

Then how do you determine what constitutes a liberal or conservative ideology? Political labels are deceptive. You may be a social liberal or a civil libertarian but be a conservative when it comes to the role of government in regulating business. If you have a single issue like abortion that is most important, it will make very little difference whether a candidate is a Democrat or Republican. In 1996 a widely reported poll asked people to classify themselves as a liberal, moderate, or conservative. A plurality considered themselves moderate compared to around a third of those polled who consider themselves conservative. In another poll, when asked what it is meant to be labeled a liberal, people responded in terms of

- accepting change,
- supporting programs that increase spending,
- favoring social programs, and
- believing in the rights of all people.

When asked what it is meant to be a conservative they responded with the following descriptions:

- resistant to change,
- thrifty,
- traditional, and
- narrow-minded.

These general areas translate into specific liberal/conservative differences when applied to actual issues. For instance, on foreign policy, liberals favor defense cuts, while maintaining a strong military. Conservatives, on the other hand, favor government spending on defense over social welfare programs. On social issues liberals favor freedom of choice for abortions, whereas conservatives favor the right to life. Liberals are opposed to school prayer of any kind; conservatives favor moments of silent prayer. Liberals generally view the government as a means of dealing with the problems facing society, whereas conservatives favor a more laissez-faire position. Liberals have been more sympathetic to the rights of the accused, and conservatives have been critical of many of the Warren Court decisions. Yet when you apply these standards to specific bills, there is a clouding up of which party is liberal and which party is conservative.

The term *New Democrat* was applied to President Clinton. Whether this was a public relations gimmick to make Clinton and the Democrats appear to be more conservative, or whether the traditional New Deal liberalism of the party was being modified, is still not clear. What is evident are those politicians who are on the extremes of the political spectrum—Democratic liberals such as Tom Harkin and Edward Kennedy and Republican conservatives such as Pennsylvania Senator Rick Santorum and former Speaker of the House Newt Gingrich. Serious differences do exist between the parties. Part of the differences derive from the fact that one party is in power and controls the agenda and that the party out of power must fight to keep their ideas alive. And there are still constituencies that are attracted to the two parties—for instance big business to the Republicans and labor unions to the Democrats.

Organization

The organization of national political parties helps maintain party discipline. However, it's local party organizations and their party machines that have a major influence on the outcome of elections.

Political parties exist on both the national and local levels. Their organization is hierarchical. Grass roots politics on the local level involves door-to-door campaigns to get signatures on petitions, campaigns run through precinct and ward organizations, county committees, and state committees headed by a state chairman. Local party bosses like Boss Tweed or party machines like the Democratic Tammany machine in New York City or the Daley machine in Chicago have lessened in influence. The national political scene is dominated by the outcome of national conventions, which give direction to the national chairperson, the spokesperson of the party, and the person who heads the national committee. The party machine exists on the local level and uses patronage (rewarding loyal party members with jobs) as the means to keep the party members in line.

The nominating process drives the organization of the national political party. This procedure has evolved, and, even though the national nominating convention (more on this in the next chapter) still selects presidential candidates, the role of the party caucus and party primary has grown in importance. The role of the national convention is one of publicizing the party's position. It also adopts party rules and procedures. Sometimes this plays an important part in the restructuring of a political party. After the disastrous 1968 Democratic Convention, with rioting in the streets and calls for party reform, the McGovern-Frasier Commission brought significant representation changes to the party. It made future conventions more democratic. Delegate selection procedures aimed to include more minority representation. In 1982 another commission further reformed the representation of the Democratic convention by establishing 15 percent of the delegates as superdelegates (party leaders and elected party officials). These delegates helped Walter Mondale achieve his nomination in 1984 and enabled Al Gore to defeat Bill Bradley easily in 2000. There has been some criticism that these delegates have reduced the democratic reforms of the McGovern Commission.

On the other hand, the Republicans were more concerned about regenerating party identification after the Watergate debacle. They were not interested in reform as much as making the Republican Party more efficient. Their conventions are well run and highly planned. There was, however, some negative publicity at their 1992 convention, which critics said was dominated by the conservative faction of the party. The lesson was learned. In 1996, 2000, and 2004 both the Republican and Democratic Conventions were so highly scripted that political scientists concluded that it would be virtually impossible to make a similar mistake.

The national committee, made up of a combination of state and national party leaders, is the governing body of the political party. It has limited power and responds to the direction of the national chairperson. The chairperson is selected by the presidential candidates nominated at the convention. In fact, the real party leader of the party in power is the president himself. The chairperson is recognized as the chief strategist and often takes the credit or blame if gains or losses occur in mid-term elections. Some of the primary duties of the national chairperson are fundraising, fostering party unity, recruiting new voters and candidates, and preparing strategy for the next election. Also, congressional campaign committees in both parties work with their respective national committees to win Senate and House seats that are considered up for grabs. Many times the national chairperson is rewarded if the party's candidate wins the presidential election. In 1992 Democratic chairman Ron Brown was named Secretary of Commerce by President Clinton. He died in a tragic airplane accident while on a trade mission to Bosnia in 1995.

Future

The future of political parties depends on the extent of positive political participation of the electorate and the ability to succeed in creating and implementing public policy.

Participation in the political process is the key gauge of how successful political parties are in involving the average citizen. If you develop the actual vote as the key criteria, the future is certainly not bright. Unlike many foreign countries, the American electorate has not turned out in droves in local or national elections. The reasons why people vote depend on a number of factors including family income, age, education, party identification, and race. A full discussion of this subject will take place in Chapter 12. Then what does the future hold for the Democrats and Republicans? To answer this question, you must look at the continuum of political involvement.

There is no doubt that statistically the majority of the electorate participates in the political process in conventional ways. From those areas that the majority of people participate to those areas that a minority participate, the population as a whole generally is involved in one or more of the following:

- discussing politics;
- registering to vote;
- voting in local, state, and national elections;
- joining a specific political party;
- making contact with politicians either by letter or phone;
- attending political meetings;
- contributing to political campaigns;
- working in a campaign;
- soliciting funds;
- running for office.

Yet one of the ironies of conventional political participation is that less than half of those who are eligible actually vote in most elections.

Unconventional participation involves protest and civil disobedience. Activists such as Dr. Martin Luther King, Jr. have influenced the political process through mass meetings such as the March on Washington in 1963. Elected officials responded by passing the Civil Rights Act of 1964.

The future of political parties depends on how closely associated the voters remain with the party. The future is not bright for traditional party politics. There is a sharp decline in party enrollment and an increase in the affiliation of voters calling themselves independents. More and more ticket splitting (where voters cast their ballots not on party lines, but rather based upon each individual candidate running for a particular office) has taken place. The impact of the media on the campaign has weakened the ability of the party to get its message out. Finally, the impact of special-interest groups and PACs has reduced the need for elected officials to use traditional party resources.

Suggestions have been made to strengthen voter identification with the party by presenting

- clearly defined programs on how to govern the nation once their candidates are elected,
- candidates who are committed to the ideology of the party and who are willing to carry out the program once elected, and
- alternative views if it is the party out of power.

The winning party must take on the responsibility of governing the country if elected and accepting the consequences if it fails. This responsible party model would go a long way in redefining the importance of political parties in America. Even though there is a recognized decline in the importance of political parties, it is highly doubtful that our two-party system will change to a multiparty or ideological party system in the future.

Chapter 11 Review

SECTION 1: MULTIPLE-CHOICE QUESTIONS

1. Which of the following defines a team of men (and women) banding together seeking to control the governing apparatus by gaining office in a duly constituted election?
   (A) political party
   (B) political opportunism
   (C) political constituency
   (D) political agenda
   (E) political policy

2. All of the following are characteristics of politics EXCEPT
   (A) individuals with similar ideas banding together to form political parties.
   (B) the means by which individuals and groups get involved.
   (C) who gets what, when, how, and why.
   (D) the passage of laws that serve to further minority rights.
   (E) the interrelationship of individuals and groups.

3. Relationships among which of the following exist in political parties?
   (A) the party and the electorate
   (B) the party and the individual
   (C) the party and the government
   (D) the party and the candidate
   (E) the party and the courts

4. Which of the following translate inputs from the public into outputs from the policymakers?
   (A) linkage institutions
   (B) bureaucratic institutions
   (C) agenda setters
   (D) policy setters
   (E) policy coordinators

5. Which of the following are considered linkage institutions?
   I. Congress
   II. political parties
   III. the media
   IV. the courts

   (A) I only
   (B) I and II only
   (C) II and III only
   (D) I, II, and III only
   (E) I, II, III, and IV

6. Which of the following philosophies is reflected by the majority of the American electorate?
   (A) a middle-of-the-road philosophy
   (B) extremely liberal philosophy
   (C) extremely conservative philosophy
   (D) radical philosophy
   (E) reactionary philosophy

7. In the long history of the American party system, successful parties rarely stray from
   (A) supporting big government.
   (B) a liberal point of view.
   (C) a conservative point of view.
   (D) the midpoint of public opinion.
   (E) a reactionary point of view.

8. Which of the following best describes the history of American political parties?
   (A) America has had a one-party system with two branches.
   (B) America has always responded to a multi-partied system.
   (C) America has had two parties that have consistently dominated the political arena.
   (D) America has always had a three-party system.
   (E) Third political parties have rarely had an impact on the two major parties.

9. Which of the following results after a critical election occurs?
   (A) redistricting
   (B) party realignment
   (C) party dealignment
   (D) gerrymandering
   (E) coalition division

10. Which of the following terms means that people are gradually moving away from both parties?
    (A) dealignment
    (B) realignment
    (C) gerrymandering
    (D) reevaluation
    (E) criticism

11. All the following choices reflect major changes that have occurred to the party system since Roosevelt's New Deal EXCEPT
    I. party loyalty has declined.
    II. those who do belong to a party are more likely to belong to the party that matches their ideology.
    III. party organizations have become more energetic and effective.
    IV. party loyalty has increased.

(A) I only
(B) II and III only
(C) III and IV only
(D) I, II, III, and IV

12. Which characteristic reflects party politics of the 1990s?
    (A) Southern liberals and Southern conservatives alike vote with the Republican Party.
    (B) The Republican Party's base is in the Northeast.
    (C) Conservative Southerners shy away from the Republican label.
    (D) The Democrats' Solid South no longer exists in national elections.
    (E) The religious right favors Democratic candidates.

13. Which of the following molds the values a person develops?
    (A) personal ideology
    (B) party identification
    (C) political socialization
    (D) party dealignment
    (E) party realignment

14. Which of the following determines the party platform?
    (A) the national convention
    (B) the presidential candidate
    (C) the party bosses
    (D) the local party
    (E) the state party

15. Which of the following reforms took place as a result of the McGovern-Frasier Commission?
    (A) the elimination of "pseudo" delegates
    (B) the development of "shadow" delegates
    (C) the creation of special interest delegates
    (D) the use of caucus delegates
    (E) the incorporation of minority delegates

16. Which of the following time periods reflects a change from the dominance of the Republicans as the nation's majority party?
    (A) the Great Depression
    (B) the Roaring Twenties
    (C) World War I
    (D) World War II
    (E) the cold war

17. Which of the following events signaled the beginning of Republican Party ascendancy for more than 60 years?
    (A) Mexican-American War
    (B) Civil War
    (C) Reconstruction
    (D) Prohibition
    (E) Spanish-American War

18. In which of the following institutions have the Republicans consistently been the minority party from 1968 to 1994?
(A) House of Representatives
(B) Senate
(C) elected judgeships
(D) state legislatures
(E) presidency

19. All the following actions represent the conventional manner people usually participate in the political process EXCEPT
(A) registering to vote.
(B) participating in civil disobedience to achieve political goals.
(C) joining a specific political party.
(D) attending political meetings.
(E) voting in elections.

20. Which of the following has been suggested to increase party identification?
I. The party should present clearly defined programs.
II. The party should present candidates who are committed to the party's positions.
III. The party should rely more on special interest groups.
IV. The party should exercise no control over candidates elected to office.

(A) I only
(B) I and II only
(C) III and IV
(D) II and III
(E) I, II, III, and IV

Answers to Multiple-Choice Questions

1. **(A)** Type of Question: Identification/definitional
The statement is a straight definition of a political party. The process includes the manner in which the nomination is obtained. The constituency involves those who support the party. The agenda is what the party supports. A policy is the result of actions taken by legislators.
2. **(D)** Type of Question: Negative
Choices A, B, C, and E are all characteristics of politics. Choice D is the correct answer because one of the outcomes of government is the making of public policy.
3. **(E)** Type of Question: Identification/sequencing a series of events
Choice E, the relationship between the party and the courts, is an external relationship that goes beyond the organizational characteristics of political parties.
4. **(A)** Type of Question: Solution to a problem
Because a political party is one of the linkage institutions, you should be able to apply the function of a political party to the statement describing the general meaning of a linkage institution.

5. **(C)** Type of Question: Cause and effect relationships
Choice C is the correct answer because political parties and the media are considered linkage institutions. Choices A, B, D, and E are incorrect because the courts and Congress are not linkage institutions.
6. **(A)** Type of Question: Identification and analysis
By process of elimination and realizing that a centrist position is the predominant philosophy of the electorate, you should pick middle of the road as the only reasonable answer.
7. **(D)** Type of Question: Identification and analysis/cause and effect relationships
Similar to question 6, you are asked to come up with a conclusion based on the statement that a successful political party usually does not move too far from the center of public opinion.
8. **(C)** Type of Question: Identification and analysis/description
This is a difficult question. Even though many political parties appear on the ballot, the United States has always been dominated by a two-party system. There have been times that a third party has been influential, but this has not been a consistent feature of the American party system. Choice D does not describe the overall nature of the two-party system.
9. **(B)** Type of Question: Cause and effect relationships
You must know the difference between realignment and dealignment to answer this question. The hint in the question is the phrase *critical election*. This should evoke the image of the start of a party era, which occurs with party realignment.
10. **(A)** Type of Question: Cause and effect relationships
Like question 9, you must know the difference between realignment and dealignment. The clue here is that people are moving away from both parties. The other choices may be part of the political process but do not result from the situation described.
11. **(C)** Type of Question: Cause and effect relationships
This is a very difficult question. You must know that the New Deal was a critical election resulting in party realignment. Once you reach that conclusion, you will be able to determine that statement III and IV are the EXCEPT choices.
12. **(D)** Type of Question: Identification and analysis/relationship
Choice A is incorrect because Southern liberals also vote Democratic. Choice B is incorrect because the Democrats' base is in the Northeast. Choice C is wrong because Southern conservatives strongly identify with the Republican Party. Choice E is incorrect because the religious right favors Republican candidates. Choice D is the correct answer because the Republicans dominate Southern politics.
13. **(C)** Type of Question: Identification and analysis/cause and effect relationships
Choice C, political socialization, molds a person's ideology and a person's party identification. Choices D and E have nothing to do with personal values. They are the results of people moving away from the major parties or moving away from one of the major parties to the other.

14. **(A)** Type of Question: Identification and analysis
The presidential candidate has a major influence on the platform. Party bosses molded the platform in the era before national conventions became more democratic. The local and state parties send delegates who become part of the process of determining the platform. The delegates to the national convention are the people who actually vote on the party platform.
15. **(E)** Type of Question: Identification and analysis/cause and effect relationships
To answer this question, you must know the circumstances under which the McGovern-Frasier Commission was created. As described in the chapter, the Commission was formed after the debacle that took place at the 1968 Democratic convention in Chicago where Mayor Daly almost single-handedly prevented minority delegate representation.
16. **(A)** Type of Question: Chronological
The question is asking you to find a critical election period. The Great Depression and Franklin Roosevelt's election represents a change from Republican to Democratic dominance.
17. **(B)** Type of Question: Chronological
Knowledge of critical elections and party eras will give you the correct answer to this question. The major difficulty is that some students may lump the Civil War and Reconstruction together as one time period.
18. **(A)** Type of Question: Chronological/sequencing a series of events
By process of elimination, you should be able to reduce your choices to A and B. If you knew that during the Reagan administration Republicans controlled the Senate, then you would be able to pick A as the correct choice.
19. **(B)** Type of Question: Cause and effect relationships
Although each of the choices are ways in which people participate in the political process, civil disobedience is considered an *un*conventional choice, whereas the others are conventional.
20. **(B)** Type of Question: Identification and analysis/hypothetical
This is a difficult question. You must know the characteristics of party identification and the factors that strengthen and weaken voter identification with a political party. Though a party may support special interests and attempt to exercise tight control over candidates elected from their own party, voter identification is not strengthened by these actions. Voters have indicated that they want parties to present clearly defined programs and for candidates to possess ideologies similar to their own.

SECTION 2: FREE-RESPONSE ESSAY

People have made the claim that the party platforms of the modern-day Republican and Democratic Parties are all show and no substance. In your answer describe three components of the Democratic and Republican platforms. Explain the relationship between their platforms and the voting patterns of members of each party.

Sample Student Response

The party platforms of modern-day American political parties have been criticized by people as being all show and no substance. This is not the case with the Republican and Democratic Parties.

The Republican Party includes a plank that is characterized by economic conservatism. This plank supports tax cuts and also favors less government spending on social programs. Republicans believe in tax cuts because they feel that more money should go back to the people who pay taxes. The Republicans also oppose affirmative action programs that rely on preferences and support the concept of states determining how to run welfare programs. The Republicans also believe that the government should focus on promoting family values and, thus, support the right to life for the unborn. The Republican platform calls for a constitutional amendment that would ban abortions without any exceptions.

Demographic groups that support the Republican platform include business interests and highly educated people. These groups believe that tax cuts return money to the American people and also promote business growth. An example of a Republican Party platform plank that resulted in enactment of public policy is the passage of the Welfare Reform Act of 1996. This act, originally part of the Contract with America, ended the federal "Aid to Dependent Children" program. The act created block grants to the states and ended "welfare as we know it" by forcing people on welfare to get a job within five years.

The Democratic Party platform includes a strong stand on abortion. Democrats believe in the right of women to choose and support the Supreme Court's decision in *Roe v Wade.* Democrats believe that a woman's right of privacy is central in her right to choose whether or not to have an abortion. Other components of the Democratic platform are the encouragement of social programs and support for the principles of affirmative action. The Democrats also believe in the need for a national prescription drug program for all Americans and a patient's bill of rights.

Demographic groups that support the Democratic party platform include women and minorities. Women support the Democrats' position on abortion, while minorities support the Democrats' views on affirmative action programs. An example of a Democratic platform plank that became public policy is the Family and Medical Leave Act. This law enables people to take unpaid time off from work without penalty in the case of a medical emergency or where the worker needs to attend to other specified family matters.

Evaluation of Free-Response Sample Essay

1. Did the essay provide appropriate definitions?
2. Did the thesis provide a clear explanation of the direction of the essay?
3. Did the essay provide supporting evidence, data, and facts?

1. The essay defines political parties and explains the function of parties. It also defines party platform. Then the essay develops a position on the statement that a platform is all show and no substance—that party dealignment may reflect the lack of importance of the actual platform.

2. The essay then lays out the central direction of the essay—that the platform is used to attract voters even though party members may deviate from the positions taken by the party when it comes to actually voting for legislation.

3. The essay's strongest point is the clear manner in which the writer outlined the respective 2000 Democratic and Republican Party platforms. This illustrated the significant differences between the two parties on major issues such as abortion, gun control, and funding of the arts.

SECTION 2: DATA-BASED FREE-RESPONSE ESSAY

This graph was obtained from the United States Bureau of the Census.

POLITICAL PARTY IDENTIFICATION OF THE ADULT POPULATION, 1960–2000

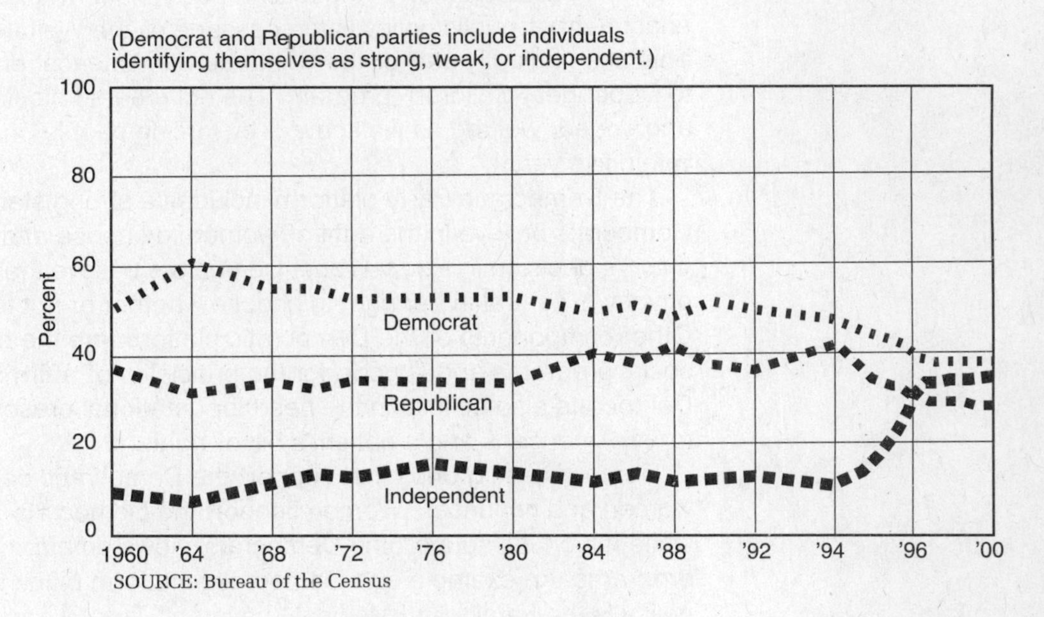

SOURCE: Bureau of the Census

Explain what this graph indicates about the political party identification of the adult population. Based on this graph, indicate three factors that will lead to increased dissatisfaction with the major parties.

Sample Student Response

From this graph it is clear that the Democrats were strongest between 1960 and 2000. This reflected the country's optimism with the election of John Kennedy and the unity the country demonstrated after Kennedy was assassinated. Post-Watergate identification indicates a significant increase in independent identification as a result of the distrust the American people had with both the Democratic and Republican Parties. In fact, you can directly correlate a drop in Republican enrollment and an increase in Independent enrollment after Nixon resigned as president. Republican identification increased again after Reagan was elected and continued to surge after Bush was elected. It is interesting to note that Independent status, although always under 20 percent, still attracts many enrolled Democrats and Republicans.

Assuming that major party dissatisfaction is on the rise, the following criteria would indicate the level:

- Age—As the age increases, the level of dissatisfaction decreases. That is the result of the fact that the so-called younger generation probably has a more liberal point of view on social issues, whereas the older people probably have a more conservative bent. Considering that there has been a Republican Party era since 1968, the age factor may have a lot to do with that trend. Young voters today may be looking for politicians and a new party that will meet their needs.
- Education—As the level of education decreases so does the voter discontent. The more educated people are, the more likely they are to be informed about the political process. Outlets such as C-SPAN and the political talk shows demonstrate the bickering between the parties and the gridlock in government. Statistically, 55–60 percent of those polled who are dissatisfied are either college graduates or have had some college education.
- Party identification—Independent voters want a third party because they are fed up with the other two. However, a significant number of members of the other parties are also calling for a third party. Party members are often splitting tickets trying to find candidates who reflect their viewpoints. Ross Perot struck a chord among the voters when he brought up the deficit as the major issue in his campaign. With the overall approval ratings of political parties being so low, the lack of party identification should be sending a message to the Democrats and Republicans. The likelihood of the emergence of a third major political party seems to be on the horizon.

Evaluation of Data-Based Free-Response Sample Essay

1. Were conclusions that go beyond the poll results clearly presented?
2. Was there an adequate explanation of the conclusions?
3. In the second part, were there specific examples that explained the conclusions reached in the first part?

1. The conclusions reached by the writer specifically use the graph results to show party identification trends. Specific elections are mentioned, and specific events such as Watergate were cited.

2. The writer goes beyond the graph results. The response explains the relationship between the rise and fall of party identification to particular events.

3. In the second part of the question, specific conclusions are reached regarding age, education, and party identification. Each section develops its own minithesis offering the reader specific examples supporting it. Factors such as C-SPAN, the nature of party eras, and the possibility of the formation of a permanent third party are good examples.

CHAPTER 12 Nominations, Campaigns, and Elections

Chapter Overview

"Throwing your hat in the ring" marks the traditional announcement by a political candidate running for office. Today's campaign and election resembles more of a "war room" atmosphere than the old-style "whistle stop" rallies. This chapter traces the characteristics of the nominating process and election campaign. In fact, the nominating process has turned into a campaign itself. Thus many of the strategies used to receive a party's nomination are the same as those used to convince the electorate to vote for a particular candidate.

PRESIDENTIAL CANDIDATES "THROW THEIR HATS IN THE RING" WHEN THEY ANNOUNCE THEIR INTENTIONS TO RUN FOR THE HIGHEST OFFICE IN THE LAND

KEY TERMS

Battleground states	Matching funds
Bell weather states	Nonpreferential primary
Caucus	Party caucus
Coattails	Party regulars
Convention bump	Political action committee
Direct primary	Preferential primary
Dual primary	Presidential primary
Favorite son	Soccer mom
Front loading	Spin doctors
Front-runner	Superdelegate
Gender gap	Super Tuesday
High-tech campaign	Thirty-second spots
Infomercials	Ticket splitting
Invisible primary	Tracking poll
Keynote address	Voter turnout

Specifically, we will focus our attention on the campaign to receive the nomination for president, including the primary route, the party caucus, and the nominating convention. We will trace the process a candidate uses, once given the nod, to organize an election campaign including the money requirements, the fundraising techniques used, the restrictions placed on the candidate by federal election laws, and the different strategies used to reach the voter. We will also explore the role of the media in the high-tech campaign waged to get nominated and elected.

As we play the nomination and election game, we will also point to the various reforms being discussed in relation to the length of campaigns, to the primary system, and to the revision of campaign election laws, especially in the area of contributions by special interest groups.

Election Process

The road to victory is actually a three-round fight involving a dual campaign to get nominated and elected, each involving a complex strategy.

When you calculate the time it takes between a candidate's announcement that he or she is running to the actual convention, it could easily be two years from start to end. Add to that the actual campaign for president, and you can tack on an additional three to four months. A typical time line looks something like this:

ELECTION TIME LINE

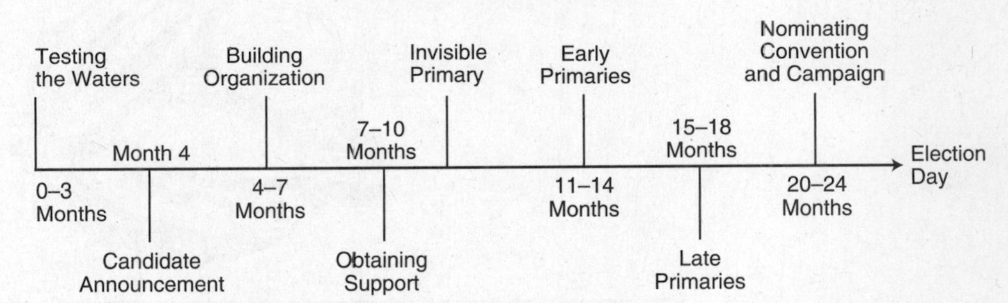

When you consider the number of candidates considering a presidential race and multiply their efforts to get the nomination, you can see how complex and time-consuming the entire process becomes. The first stage is called the invisible primary. In the first three months potential candidates consult with political allies, seek out potential fundraisers, hire pollsters, and let party leaders know that they are thinking of running. In fact, the start-up fee for presidential races has been estimated at around $20 million. The actual announcement is usually self-made and can take a variety of forms. It can be in the halls of Congress as Senator Bobby Kennedy did in 1968 or on the steps of the governor's residence as Bill Clinton did in 1991. For lesser-known candidates and independents, any announcement that they are running for president will undoubtedly be covered by the media. An early visit to Iowa or New Hampshire also is not out of the question. The 1996 campaign started in early 1995 with the announcement by Texas Senator Phil Gramm that he was officially seeking the Republican nomination. Nine other candidates officially announced thereafter with others waiting in the wings. Other candidates, including the front-runner Kansas Senator Robert Dole, former Tennessee Governor Lamar Alexander, multimillionaire publisher Steve Forbes, 1992 presidential candidate Pat Buchanan, California Governor Pete Wilson, California Representative Bob Dornan, Pennsylvania Senator Arlen Spector, self-made industrialist Morey Taylor, and African-American radio talkshow host Alan Keyes quickly jumped into the fray. This guaranteed a rather untypical Republican battle through the early primary season. In addition, former Speaker of the House Newt Gingrich and retired General Colin Powell were watched closely as potential candidates. Neither made the run, however.

Meanwhile, on the Democratic front, President Clinton achieved for the first time what no other Democratic president nominee for reelection had achieved since Franklin Roosevelt—no declared opposition during the primary season. This gave the president a tremendous advantage over Senator Dole, the eventual Republican candidate.

In the 2000 campaign, George W. Bush immediately became the front-runner in a packed Republican field by virtue of having raised over $80 million in campaign funds. During the pre-primary debates, Arizona Senator John McCain emerged as his major opposition. Vice President Al Gore emerged as the favorite to get the Democratic nomination. Former New Jersey Senator Bill Bradley challenged him on the left.

The wild card third-party candidate Ross Perot lurked in the background waiting for the right time to declare his candidacy. As in 1992, he announced it on the *Live with Larry King* show. This time Perot's plan included the creation of a national third party, United We Stand, which would endorse him and make Perot eligible for federal matching funds.

After the announcement is made, the candidate starts building an organization, actively seeking funds and developing an overall strategy to get the nomination. Before the first primary or caucus, the candidate gets endorsements from party leaders and other elected officials and attempts to raise the public's interests through media coverage. The second stage of the campaign is the primary. By the time of the first caucus in Iowa and the first primary in New Hampshire, both in February, the campaign for the party's nomination is well underway—some nine months before election day! By the time these early votes are completed, many candidates will have dropped out of the race. The second-level primaries come in March. In a tactic called "front loading," New York and California have voted to hold their primaries in March. Additionally an increasing number of regional primaries capped by Super Tuesday—a number of primary votes taking place on the same day with a heavy concentration of Southern states voting—were organized. Junior Tuesday, consisting of most of New England and held one week prior to Super Tuesday, became a new primary to analyze. By the time the last primary is over, the nomination is usually wrapped up. The convention sometimes is more like a coronation, and once the business of the party is finished, the candidates get down to serious business.

The election campaign seems like a 100-yard dash compared to the nominating process. Even though there are similarities to the campaign for nomination in terms of organization and strategy, once the candidate has the official party designation, the fall campaign turns into a fight to the finish. In 1960 Richard Nixon decided to be the first candidate to campaign actively in all 50 states, and some analysts believe it cost him the election. In 1992 George Bush decided to take the high road as the incumbent and not begin campaigning actively until he was "officially nominated" and thereby lost valuable time to challenger Bill Clinton. In 1996, President Clinton used the office of the President in what has been described as "the rose garden" strategy to establish the themes of his campaign. In fact, he used primary campaign funds to air political commercials, 16 months before the election, touting his accomplishments. Since there was no incumbent in the 2000 campaign, both the Democratic and Republican nominees began their campaigns after wrapping up the nominations in March.

In 2004, Senator Kerry wrapped up the nomination in early March and both he and President George W. Bush began campaigning against each other.

Primaries

Winning delegate support takes place as a result of a high-tech campaign to convince party regulars that a particular candidate is best suited to run the country.

Today, presidential candidates use the media for every aspect of their campaign. From sound bites to photo ops, and then to the use of pollsters, media moguls play a key role. The candidate knows the make-up of every election district he campaigns in and relies on the media and its tools to market his or her candidacy. Ad campaigns as well as the decision on where to go and who to see are determined by media advisors.

The first step on the road to the White House is the caucus and primary route. Before primaries became the accepted manner in choosing delegates, party regulars met in small groups called the caucus. There they would meet the candidate, ask questions, discuss qualifications, and vote on whether to endorse the candidacy. Party bosses had a great deal of input, and the at-large party membership was locked out of the process. Today states such as Iowa, which have a caucus, involve many more of the party regulars. It is one of the most direct forms of democracy, similar to the town meeting. Because it is the first official indication of the candidate's viability, Iowa has taken on the spotlight of the first test of a candidate's strength. In 1976 Jimmy Carter won the Iowa caucus and received national attention. Bob Dole defeated George H. W. Bush in Iowa in 1988 but could not carry the momentum to the New Hampshire primary. In 1996 the compressed primary schedule resulted in the showing of an inherent weakness in front-runner Bob Dole's ability as a campaigner. Even though Dole won the Iowa caucus, his margin of victory was slim, and a strong showing by Pat Buchanan dashed Dole's hope of early campaign momentum. Dole's campaign continued to falter in New Hampshire and Arizona, where victories by Buchanan and Forbes signaled serious flaws in the Dole candidacy. By the end of the first leg of the primary season, Dole still faced a serious challenge by Buchanan, Forbes, and Alexander. The rest of the Republican field had been weeded out. Dole's victory came in March 1996, a little more that a month after the primary season began, after he won the South Carolina primary. In 2004, after a bitter battle with Arizona Senator John McCain, Texas Governor George W. Bush won his party's nomination for president. In 2004, though Vermont Governor Howard Dean won the "invisible primary," he lost the Iowa Caucus and his candidacy imploded after he gave his concession speech. Senator John Kerry used the momentum of his Iowa victory to carry him through the rest of the primaries to victory.

Without a doubt, the presidential primary has become the decisive way a candidate gains delegate support. It has taken on such importance that key primary states such as New York and California have changed their primary dates so that their primaries take on a much greater importance. Today, 30 states have presidential primaries. The others use caucuses or party conventions. Presidential primaries can be binding or nonbinding. They can ask the voter to express a preference for a presidential candidate or delegates who are pledged to support a candidate at the convention. Primaries are used in many ways:

- proportional representation where delegates are selected based on the percentage of the vote the candidate received in the election.
- winner takes all, where, as in the actual election, the candidate receiving a plurality receives all the delegates. The Republicans use this method in California. Democratic rules have banned the use of this system since 1976.
- nonpreferential primary where voters choose delegates who are not bound to vote for the winning primary candidate.
- a primary vote where all the voters, including cross-over voters from other political parties, can express a preference but do not actually select delegates.
- a dual primary vote where presidential candidates are selected and a separate slate of delegates is also voted on. New Hampshire uses this type of primary.

Primary strategy has changed over the years. For years it was a political axiom that you had to win New Hampshire to win the nomination. Even though Eugene McCarthy came in second to Lyndon Johnson in 1968, because McCarthy received close to 40 percent of the vote, LBJ ultimately decided not to run. In 1992 Bill Clinton came in second to Paul Tsongas. However, the media picked up on Clinton who described himself as "the comeback kid" making it seem like he was the real winner. The overall strategy used by candidates in primaries is to win as many as early as possible in order to gain momentum. Al Gore decided to concentrate on a Southern strategy in 1988 hoping to win on Super Tuesday. He did not campaign actively in Iowa and New Hampshire, and by the time the Southern states held their primaries, his victories were limited, and his candidacy was hurt. In 1996, Dole's Southern strategy became the turning point of his campaign. Focusing on South Carolina, Dole mounted an offensive against Pat Buchanan and Lamar Alexander, which successfully ended their campaigns and ensured Dole's nomination. Candidate debates have also become a feature of the primary season. These debates often draw the attention of voters to image rather than issue. In addition, the media's coverage and analysis of the results of these elections plays an important role in the process.

In the 2000 campaign, the front loading of the primaries gave a tremendous advantage to George W. Bush and Al Gore. Even though Bush lost New Hampshire and Michigan, he defeated John McCain handily in the major primary contests. Gore had a relatively easy time defeating Bill Bradley in both Iowa and New Hampshire. In 2004, after winning the Iowa Caucus, John Kerry used his victory to convince the voters he was the best candidate to defeat George W. Bush. His major primary opponent, first term North Carolina Senator John Edwards, was selected to be Kerry's running mate prior to the party's convention.

The Party Convention

Presidential nominations play an important role in giving the candidate and the party national exposure.

National conventions date back to the 1830s when the first "open" party convention was held by Jacksonian Democrats. Historically, conventions have provided excitement, hoopla, and ultimately the nomination of the party's candidate for president and vice president. The 1924 Democratic Convention took 103 ballots to determine the winner. Backroom deals were cut and strange political bedfellows emerged creating a "truly national ticket." Since 1952 both parties have selected their standard bearers on the first ballot. Even though this has been the case, convention coverage by the media guarantees a national audience. Key convention proceedings such as rules and credentials debates, keynote speeches, platform debates, nomination of the presidential candidates, selection of a running mate, and acceptance speeches pique the interest of the electorate. Even the location of the convention can play a role in affecting the party's choice and creating a positive or negative public impression. In 1952 Governor Adlai Stevenson, Illinois's "favorite son" (the candidate backed by the home state), gave the welcoming address, and many political observers felt that it contributed to his nomination that year. In 1968 the riots in Chicago played to a national audience who came away with the feeling that the Democratic Party was not unified. The close results of the 1968 general election, according to some, would have been different if there had not been riots.

Rule and credential fights have also led to party fights. At the 1952 Republican Convention Senator Robert Taft was given a majority of Southern delegates by the Republican National Committee. Dwight Eisenhower's supporters forced a floor fight and overturned that decision, ensuring Ike's nomination. At the 1972 Democratic Convention the McGovern Commission rules were supposed to create a fairer representation of minorities. Two key votes, one giving McGovern all California's delegation and the other denying Chicago's Mayor Daley representation, helped give McGovern the nomination. In 1976 a rules debate forced by the Reagan supporters attempted to force the apparent nominee, Gerald Ford, to announce his choice for vice president before the balloting began. The convention voted against this rule change, and any chance of Reagan pulling an upset that year disappeared. A Democratic hopeful, Senator Ted Kennedy, also tried to use a rule change to defeat incumbent Jimmy Carter at the 1980 Democratic Convention. The issue revolved around a rule that dictated that delegates pledged to a candidate had to vote for that candidate on the first ballot. Kennedy hoped to change that rule so that some of Carter's supporters would defect to his camp. The convention overwhelmingly defeated the change, and Kennedy knew he had no chance to wrest away Carter's renomination.

Platform fights also have provided interesting public debates. It is ironic that these philosophical arguments could affect the party because party platforms usually fade into the woodwork once the convention is finished. Yet in 1948 at the Democratic Convention, a platform fight over civil rights caused the Southern Dixiecrats to stage a walkout. At the 1964 Republican Convention, Goldwater conservatives were in control of the party's platform and refused to make any concessions to the Rockefeller moderates in the areas of civil rights and dealings with political extremists. In 1968 arguments over a Vietnam peace plank split the convention and hurt Hubert Humphrey's chances against Richard Nixon. The platform has also been used to ameliorate political relations. When Ford knew he had the nomination wrapped up in 1976, he agreed to make concessions to Reagan's views regarding détente. Carter did the same thing in 1980, allowing Kennedy's supporters to add a job program to the platform. And in 1988 Michael Dukakis had to agree to support some of Jesse Jackson's platform modifications in order to get Jackson's support in the campaign. In 1992 columnist Patrick Buchanan hurt the reelection of President George H. W. Bush after attracting a significant vote total in a number of primaries. Even at the 1992 conventions, platform debates concerning abortion caused division in both parties. In 1996 and 2000, both the Republican and Democratic conventions avoided televised platform controversy by reaching consensus over thorny issues prior to the start of the conventions. In 2000, George W. Bush, running as a "compassionate conservative" directed the platform committee of the Republican Party to tone down some of the extreme provisions of earlier Republican platforms. And in 2004 both parties stressed how they would wage a successful war against terrorism and keep the American homeland safe while also maintaining a strong economy.

The balloting for president follows keynote and nomination speeches and is preceded by some tough political wheeling and dealing. One of the most memorable keynote speeches was given by Governor Mario Cuomo of New York at the 1984 Democratic Convention. Tracing his immigrant roots, Cuomo made a case for the fulfillment of the American Dream. The speech immediately thrust Cuomo into a national role, and many political observers felt that he would eventually seek the presidency. Sometimes a nomination speech also brings attention to a candidate. When John Kennedy stepped aside in 1956, clearing the way for his opponent's nomination for vice president, Kennedy's graceful and tactful speech was a factor in many delegates urging him to run in 1960. In 1988 a youthful Bill Clinton, in a long and rambling nomination speech for Massachusetts Governor Michael Dukakis, had delegates cheering when he finally ended. When Clinton announced his own candidacy three years later, he had to refer to that speech and promise to be much briefer in the manner he would speak if nominated. When the Republicans allowed defeated candidates Patrick Buchanan and Pat Robertson to speak in 1992, the result was that many Americans felt that the Republicans were kowtowing to conservatives and the religious right. Both parties learned from past convention mishaps. In 1996, 2000, and 2004, the Democrats and Republicans ran the most tightly controlled political conventions since televised convention proceedings. Each party orchestrated the themes of their respective campaigns. They chose keynote speakers and "prime-time" dignitaries to address both the party faithful and the shrinking television audience. Yet even with the criticism by the media, there was agreement that both parties achieved their purpose of putting their best foot forward and achieving a significant campaign bounce for their candidates. By spotlighting the party's most popular figures including General Colin Powell and dramatic appearances by Hillary Rodham Clinton, who was also running as a candidate for the Senate from New York, both parties tried to convince the electorate that they represented their interests. The 2000 Democratic Convention gave Vice President Al Gore the opportunity to separate himself from President Clinton. Clinton gave his final farewell speech on the first night of the convention.

The actual balloting for president in recent conventions has been a formality. Yet the tactics that are used by the front runner's opponents have put the nomination in doubt. This is counteracted through a tight organization on the floor of the convention and the use of such techniques as verbal and visual demonstrations. In addition, promises are made to delegates who are wavering. A bandwagon effect is achieved. Wheeling and dealing often comes about in the selection of the vice presidential running mate. Since 1940 the political precedent of having the presidential nominees choose their running mates has been established. The philosophy of the presidential nominees in picking a vice presidential candidate has ranged from attempts at "balancing the ticket" to paying off a political debt. The classic choices of Lyndon Johnson as John Kennedy's running mate in 1960, Walter Mondale as Jimmy Carter's selection in 1976, and Lloyd Bentsen's addition to the Dukakis ticket in 1988 illustrate this balancing principle. When George McGovern, in 1972, selected Senator Thomas Eagleton in a rushed decision, he soon regretted the choice. The media uncovered Eagleton's history of mental illness, and he was forced to leave the ticket. When people say that "politics make strange bedfellows," you can look at Reagan's choice of George H. W. Bush and agree with that observation, considering that Bush referred to Reagan's economic plan as "voodoo economics." There sometimes is a sense of history in the elevation of a person to the ticket. Mondale's choice of Geraldine Ferraro of New York was historic, signaling the willingness of the Democratic Party to recognize that a woman had the capability to become president. That the vice president must be qualified to be president in the event of a president dying in office has been a source of controversy when presidential candidates select running mates. George H. W. Bush's selection of Dan Quayle and the questions regarding Quayle's qualifications hurt Bush's campaign. On the other hand, when a politician breaks the rules, it sometimes helps the image of his candidacy. Clinton's choice of fellow southerner Al Gore violated every previous rule. But the strategy worked as this baby boomer ticket caught the fancy of the American public. In 1996, Republican candidate Bob Dole surprised everybody by selecting his former adversary Jack Kemp, a retired Representative and cabinet member during Ronald Reagan's presidency. Vice President Gore surprised the pundits by choosing Connecticut Senator Joseph Lieberman, the first Jewish candidate for vice president. George W. Bush selected former Secretary of Defense Richard Cheney as his running mate. Once the ticket is set, the party attempts to paint a picture of party unity. The acceptance speeches attack the other party and pledge to work for the good of the country. There are some memorable speeches such as Goldwater's "Extremism in the pursuit of liberty is no vice. . . ." Bush also made a pledge, "Read my lips, no new taxes," in 1988 in order to put the Democrats on the defensive.

By the closing night of the convention, there is an attempt to heal wounds and get the party faithful geared up for the general campaign.

The General Campaign

A successful race for president depends on the candidate's ability to develop a strong campaign organization, have a specific strategy, and be able to use the media effectively.

If getting the nomination was round one of the battle for the presidency, then the actual campaign is the final round. The successful candidate must sustain the momentum received at the convention. Bill Clinton was able to do this by taking a campaign bus trip immediately after the 1992 convention. Michael Dukakis decided to go on vacation right after he was nominated and lost the "convention bounce" that he had in the polls. Both Senator Dole and President Clinton achieved poll bounces after their respective conventions in 1996. In 2000 Vice President Al Gore closed the gap after the Democratic convention and even maintained a lead that lasted from Labor Day until the presidential debates. In 2004, for the first time in modern political history, John Kerry did not receive a convention bounce, but maintained a slim lead after his party's convention in July 2004. President George W. Bush got a five point bounce after his party's convention and led the race after Labor Day. He kept this lead until the first debate when Kerry closed the gap.

A candidate usually keeps his campaign staff and has a war chest of funds. Additional funds are solicited by the national committee, and a new strategy must be developed involving the media. Campaign consultants are becoming more and more common. They plan the logistics of the campaign, develop campaign themes, and keep track of daily polls. The role of Clinton advisor Dick Morris illustrates this point. His advice to the president called "triangulation," moving Clinton away from both his own party and the Republicans, helped Clinton maintain his popularity during the campaign. The candidate's press secretary works closely with the candidate and campaign team. Using these factors, the candidate is ready to enter the final leg of his or her journey to the White House.

Specifically, each presidential hopeful must:

- **target the campaign**—plot out the best way to achieve an electoral majority. Some candidates have used a Southern strategy, others look to the largest industrial states. Besides electoral votes, candidates have looked to see how previous candidates have done in states and the potential for victory in a given state. Clinton's electoral strategy in 1996 was simple: maintain and expand his 1992 base of states. This included the industrial Northeast, the industrial Midwest, California, and the same southern states he carried in the 1992 election. Dole attempted to hold the traditional Republican mountain states, Midwest, and the newly emerging Republican south. If both candidates held their states, there would be a battleground in states which had a total of about 100 electoral votes. The 2000 election clearly illustrated how close the electoral contest would be if both candidates held on to their states. In fact, it was one of the closest electoral contests, with Bush winning 271 electoral votes and Gore capturing 267 electoral votes (though a D.C. elector abstained and Gore officially received 266 votes). In 2004, the election came down to Florida and Ohio and Bush won both states and an electoral vote victory of 286–252. The official vote was 286–251 because one "faithless elector" (an elector who decides to vote for somebody other than the official winner) from Minnesota voted for John Edwards.
- **take advantage of political assets**—identifying with one's party is usually done by the Democrats and downplayed by the Republicans because they have a smaller enrollment than the Democrats. If a candidate is the incumbent, he should take advantage of that role. A sitting president will try to use the office of the presidency as much as possible in order to elevate himself above the political fray. Incumbency can also hurt a sitting president if domestic or foreign policy is in disarray. Carter's chances were hurt as a result of the Iran hostage crisis, whereas George H. W. Bush was constantly taken to task over a faltering economy. Incumbent vice presidents have had a much harder time getting elected. Richard Nixon, Hubert Humphrey, and Walter Mondale were defeated even though they had the experience of holding the office of vice president. George H. W. Bush broke this trend in 1988. The major asset that President Clinton had in 1996 was that he was able to position himself as a moderate who was waging a battle against extremists in the Republican Party. Even though Dole chose Kemp as his

running mate, in political commercials you might have thought the highly unpopular Speaker of the House was also on the ticket as Clinton referred to his opponents as "Dole, Kemp, Gingrich." In 2000 Gore portrayed himself as a populist, while George W. Bush ran as a "compassionate conservative." In 2004, George W. Bush used incumbency and the fact that he was the best candidate to wage a war against terrorism to his advantage. He successfully tied the Iraq war with terrorism and the voters responded.

- **develop an image the voter responds to**—This is a double-edged sword. The public seems to respond to personality much more than issues. Knowing this, the media is able to investigate the most intimate details of a candidate's personal life. After revelations about an alleged affair Bill Clinton had, *60 Minutes* gave the candidate and his wife a forum to react to the charges. Candidates also try to portray their opponents negatively through ad campaigns and face-to-face debates. Reagan was portrayed as a forgetful, aging man by Mondale in a 1984 debate, and a Bush ad used ex-convict Willie Horton to portray Michael Dukakis as soft on crime. Bill Clinton successfully portrayed the Republicans as extremists in areas that voters could identify with. From the shutdown of the government over a budget showdown in 1995 and 1996 to attempts by the GOP to lower the increases of entitlements, education, and other government spending programs, the president was able to position himself as a self-proclaimed protector of the middle class. The theme of the 2000 campaign for the Republicans was to "restore honor and dignity" to the White House while portraying Vice President Gore as a candidate who embellished his accomplishments and as a proponent of big government. Gore tried to portray Bush as a candidate without the experience or intellect to be president. He also attacked Bush's tax plan as "risky." In 2004, George W. Bush was able to portray his opponent John Kerry as a "flip flopper" and Kerry was put on the defensive throughout the campaign even though he attempted to make the election a referendum on Bush's economic policies and the Iraq war.
- **attract the support of divergent groups**—Such factors as ethnic, religious, and other minority support are crucial for success in a campaign. Traditionally, the Democrats have attempted to attract votes from labor, minority groups, Jews, and big-city residents. They try to paint a picture that the Republicans are the party of the rich and big business interests. Because Reagan's strategy of attracting traditional Democrats worked, candidates have gone after groups that will translate into a centrist coalition. In 1996 President Clinton attracted a new group—the soccer mom—a group of women voters some of whom are single parents, others who have, besides working, the responsibility of transporting their kids to soccer games. This coalition of women voters voted disproportionately for Clinton, which resulted in a very significant gender gap. In 2000, the gender gap continued to be a factor. However in 2004, according to exit polls, Bush made inroads into traditional Democratic constituencies while expanding his own base. Bush decreased the overall gender gap but a new gap emerged between single women (giving Kerry a majority) and married women, given the name of "security moms" (giving Bush a majority). Bush cut into the African American vote, the Hispanic vote, and for the first time since Ronald Reagan's election, received a majority of the Catholic vote, even though Kerry was a Catholic. But most significantly,

Bush was able to increase by a significant margin the turnout of so called evangelical voters who gave Bush over 70 percent of their vote. The only group that Kerry made inroads with was the youth vote who gave him a 54 percent margin.

- **use issues and events for their own advantage**—There is no doubt that if the Gulf War had occurred during the presidential campaign, Bush would have been elected overwhelmingly for a second term. The lesson to be learned is that a candidate must be aware of the issues facing the country and hope that world events play into his hands. Franklin Roosevelt used the problems of the Great Depression and the hopes of the New Deal to win a landslide victory in 1932. He sustained his popularity during World War II, and the country would have been hard pressed to defeat a sitting president during a national emergency. The fear of communism and Dwight Eisenhower's background as a successful military commander projected him into the Republican standard bearer in 1952. John Kennedy's hopes for a new generation and a new decade helped him against the image of a more conservative Richard Nixon. The war in Vietnam was unpopular in 1968. Richard Nixon promised a plan to end it and was elected. In 1980 Reagan took advantage of the negative image of America abroad and the runaway inflation at home, asking the electorate "Are you better off today than 4 years ago?" Looking at a poll of the top 20 worries of the American electorate in 1996, you can begin to understand why President Clinton struck such a positive chord with the electorate. From his convention theme of "building a bridge to 21st Century" to his constant mantra of protecting education, the environment, Medicare, and Medicaid the voters became convinced the incumbent president deserved reelection. In the 2000 campaign, George W. Bush succeeded in convincing the voters that he was a different kind of Republican, making education reform a top priority. His mantra that he would "leave no child behind" struck a chord with voters. The events of September 11, 2001 dominated the 2004 campaign. Seventy percent of voters polled called this election "the most important election of their lives." Bush's senior political consultant Karl Rove, the architect of Bush's election victories, developed a three-pronged strategy for Bush. He had Bush emphasize his "steady leadership" thus portraying Bush as a Commander in Chief who could best protect the country against another terrorist attack. Bush became the champion of moral values opposing same sex marriage and supporting a constitutional amendment that would define marriage as the union of a man and a woman. Bush also reminded voters that he was a "compassionate conservative" while making the claim his opponent was a "Massachusetts liberal."
- **take advantage of the media as a primary means of communicating with the public**—The high-tech campaign has become a major characteristic of the modern presidential campaign. The use of paid political ads attempts to bring the message to the voters. The 30- and 60-second spots as well as paid infomercials incorporating charts and graphs have all been used in recent campaigns. Ever since the 1960 televised political debates between Kennedy and Nixon, television has played a decisive factor in the campaign. The irony in that debate was that those people who heard the debate on the radio felt that Nixon won, whereas TV viewers thought

that Kennedy won. Reagan became known as "the great communicator" and established a positive presidential image in his debates with Carter. Reagan's "there you go again" comment portrayed him as somebody who could hold his own. Even the vice presidential debates provide a contrast between the candidates. Lloyd Bentsen's response to Dan Quayle that "I knew Jack Kennedy, and you are no Jack Kennedy" temporarily hurt the Bush campaign. "Spin Doctors," those campaign staff members who attempt to influence the media, also became a part of the campaign landscape. There will be more on the role of the media and debates in Chapter 13. More than any factor, the media contrast between President Clinton and Senator Dole in 1996 portrayed two candidates not only years apart in age, but miles apart in utilizing the media. From the contrast of the 1996 State of the Union address and the poorly received response by Senator Dole to the apparent differences perceived by the public in the three debates, President Clinton had a tremendous media advantage over his opponent. In 2000 the three presidential debates were a turning point. Vice President Gore, though "winning" the debates on substance, lost them on style. He came across as overly agressive, and he made statements that later had to be modified because of his exaggeration. Bush played on low expectations and held his own against the more experienced debater. Political advertisements and the presidential debates took on added importance in the 2004 election. The election was the first since the McCain-Feingold campaign finance law outlawed soft money. Even with that restriction, both campaigns raised record amounts of hard money. In addition the creation of "527" independent groups that were exempt from the law as a result of Internal Revenue Service 527 regulations were created. Even though these groups could not legally coordinate their ad campaigns with the presidential candidates, it became apparent that the backers of these groups were sympathetic to the candidates and their campaigns. *Moveon.org* sponsored many anti-Bush ads and the Swift Boat Veterans made a devastating ad that questioned John Kerry's Vietnam service. The parties and candidates themselves sponsored millions of dollars of ads, many of them negative. There were three presidential debates. Polls showed that Kerry won the first one decisively and that he also won the next two. But this became the first election where the so-called winner of the debates did not win the election.

- **use the campaign organization and workers to get the vote out**—The party faithful on the local level are responsible for getting the vote out. Telephone calls, mailings, and posters drive the message. The selection of a campaign staff on both the national and state levels is crucial for success in the campaign. John Kennedy's choice of his brother as campaign manager, Jimmy Carter's choice of Hamilton Jordan, and Bill Clinton's selection of James Carville had a major impact on their respective campaigns. On the other hand, the ineptness of John Mitchell to run the Committee to Re-elect the President (CREEP) eventually led to his downfall and Richard Nixon's resignation as a result of Watergate. A candidate's coattail potential, the ability of the top of the ticket to help other candidates from the same party win, also plays a role on the state level. Knowing that the election of Lyndon Johnson in 1964 was never in doubt played a motivating role for local organizations. Labor has also been a source of major support for the Democrats, and recently the Republicans have benefited from religious groups who have used the pulpit to urge their congregations to vote for Republicans who are against abortion. Because President Clinton held a double-digit lead throughout the 1996 campaign, there was little suspense regarding the outcome. Therefore, he and the Democrats had to combat apathy and had to concentrate on the contest for control of Congress. However, the Republican strategy was successful. In the waning days of the campaign, when it became obvious that Dole was going to be defeated, the GOP changed its strategy and aired television commercials asking voters what would happen if they elected a Democratic president and a Democratic Congress. The ads worked, and even though the president won an easy electoral victory, the Republicans maintained control of Congress. By the eve of the 2000 election it was clear that the election would be one of the closest in United States history. As a result of a concerted "get out the vote" effort in the black community, Vice President Al Gore won the popular vote but lost the electoral vote to George W. Bush after the Supreme Court ruled that Florida's electoral votes should be awarded to Bush. Getting the vote out was the story of the 2004 election. Final vote totals reflected a record turnout of voters, over 120 million (an increase of more than ten million from the 2000 election). There was a significant increase in overall voter turnout from a little over 50 percent in 2000 to over 60 percent in 2004. This number rivaled the voter turnout from the 1960s. And even though the youth vote (18–29) stayed at 7 percent of the electorate in 2000, the actual turnout increased from 44 percent in 2000 to over 54 percent in 2004 with greater numbers in the so-called battleground states. President George W. Bush and Senator Kerry had the support of their bases but the Republicans did a much better job getting out a constituency that did not come out in big numbers in 2000—the evangelical vote—and they also cut into some traditional Democratic constituencies.

Ultimately it is up to the American electorate in the privacy of the voting booth to determine the winner and the also ran. In Chapter 13 we will focus our attention on voter behavior.

Election Reform

Critics of the nominating process point to the cost, length, and manner in which candidates wage their campaigns for delegates as reasons for reform.

At the time that the primary was introduced during the progressive era, the hope was that it would make the process more democratic by taking the power away from party bosses. The system expanded to include primaries for every elective office. Even though it gives the party regulars a greater choice, it forces the candidates to wage three election campaigns. Another by-product of the general primary system is that the more candidates running against the party's official designee, the more likely there will be a split among the party faithful. And if one of the defeated candidates stays on the ballot on an independent line, the likelihood exists that the winner of the primary may be the loser in the general election.

Major criticism has been directed at the process of the presidential primary. Critics point to the media hype of the Iowa caucus and New Hampshire primary as "make or break" contests. The irony is that the voters in Iowa have similar political philosophies but stress different issues than the voters in New Hampshire. The winner of these contests achieves the "big mo" (momentum), whereas losers must scurry to make up lost ground.

If one of the prerequisites of a successful candidacy is the ability to raise funds, the success in the early primaries and caucuses is necessary to sustain the flow of money. Even with federal matching funds available, Paul Tsongas was forced to drop out of the crucial New York primary, even though he had a chance to defeat Clinton, because he lacked the funds to continue his campaign.

A candidate can win a primary with less than 30 percent of the registered voters participating in primaries. In a caucus, with the exception of Iowa, the figure is well under 10 percent. The voters are more educated and wealthier than those in the general election, suggesting that they are less representative of the average voter.

In response to the overblown importance of the Iowa and New Hampshire votes, many Southern states changed their primary day to the same day early in March. Super Tuesday became a key event for presidential hopefuls and gave an advantage to those candidates who were more conservative and had a Southern political base. Media coverage of the Super Tuesday primary certainly provided the winners with a great deal of publicity and momentum. Even though the Republicans thought the front-loaded primary system hurt their presidential candidate, the nature of the primaries in election year 2004 remained the same as 2000.

If the primary and caucus system is flawed, what are the alternatives? Having a national presidential primary certainly would shorten the primary season especially if it were held in the late spring. Proponents of a single primary vote feel that more people would vote, expenses could be cut down, and the nomination would be wrapped up after the votes were counted. Critics of the plan suggest that a national primary would become as expensive and complex as the regular campaign because of its scope. The role of the media would become even more significant, and they could easily be accused of playing a kingmaker role. An alternative to a national primary would be a series of Super Tuesday regional primaries. This strategy would have the advantage of decentralizing the system and keep the attention focused on different regional issues. However, it would not reduce the cost or emphasis of media attention. The advantage would still remain with the candidate who won the first regional primary. Other suggestions include increasing the number of caucus votes. The supporters of this proposal claim that it is the most democratic and possibly would reduce the amount of media intrusion because it is much more decentralized. Another suggestion is substituting a series of state party conventions for any primary or caucus. The potential of party bosses dominating this system makes its adoption less likely. Of all the proposals made, the one that has been talked about the most is a national primary day. However, states like New Hampshire and Iowa, with all the attention presidential hopefuls and the media give them, are hesitant to give up the national spotlight. As a result of the disputed 2000 election, calls for election reforms were widespread. Florida reformed its own procedures, doing away with the controversial "butterfly" ballot and moving toward electronic voting. Congress voted to allocate funds to help states reform and update their ballot procedures.

Financial Reform

Campaign finance reform aims to remove the influence of special interests by limiting the amount and nature of political contributions by political action committees and lobbyists.

Most political observers point to the funding as a key ingredient for the success of congressional and presidential campaigns. Costs escalate because of the use of the media by candidates, the increase in direct mailing, the reliance on polling, and an increase of campaign staff salaries. There is a definite correlation between the amount of money raised and spent and who wins an election. Even though there is federal funding of presidential campaigns, the cost of those elections has skyrocketed. When Eisenhower beat Stevenson in 1952, he spent a little over $5 million. When Bush beat Dukakis in 1988 he spent over $46 million. The total amount of money in federal elections has escalated from $14 million in 1952 to more than $200 million in 2004.

How do candidates raise funds? They do accept small contributions of $5 and $10 but this accounts for the smallest percentage of funds raised. Jerry Brown, acting like a populist, attempted to convince the other candidates to accept contributions only up to $100 and even established an 800 number for these contributions. One of the complaints by the average voter is that in order to run for elective office, you must have a significant financial base. This was brought home when Ross Perot spent his own money during the 1992 campaign. Political action committees donate millions of dollars to congressional candidates. In the 2000 election, groups such as the American Medical Association, National Education Association, Teamsters Union, National Rifle Association, and National Association of Realtors gave millions of dollars to political candidates. Election committees are also set up for candidates, and this becomes another means for groups to channel money into the coffers of political hopefuls. Campaign donations are considered a direct form of political participation, but there have been many questions raised regarding the kind of influence and payback these contributors expect.

Federal law has regulated campaign financing. The 1971 Federal Election Campaign Act (FECA) set up restrictions on the amount of advertising, created disclosure of contributions over $100, and limited the amount of personal contributions candidates and their relatives could make on their own behalf. Following this act, the Revenue Act of 1971 allowed private contributions through tax credits and tax deductions. A $1 tax write-off was allowed on federal income taxes. This allocation had the effect of publicly subsidizing federal elections. The turning point of campaign finance legislation came after revelations in the Watergate hearings that the Committee to Re-elect President Nixon had "laundered" campaign contributions to support political operatives conducting dirty tricks and providing "hush money" to the organizers of the Watergate break-in. The committee also promised favorable treatment by Nixon to those businesses who contributed large amounts of money.

The 1974 Federal Election Campaign Act established a six-person Federal Election Commission whose responsibility it would be to enforce the provisions of the law and establish matching federal funds for presidential candidates in primaries and the general election. In order to receive these funds, a candidate had to raise $5000 in at least 20 states. The candidate would then be eligible for matching funds as long as the candidate agreed to disclose campaign contributions. It also restricted campaign contributions as follows.

- Citizens were limited to contributions of $1000 per candidate in primary and general federal elections, $20,000 to political parties, and $5000 to political action committees. This type of contribution is known as "hard money."
- The total amount of allowable contributions by an individual was limited in any given year.
- Unlimited and unregulated corporate and labor contributions known as "soft money" were used to support the political parties. In 1996 much of this soft money was raised and used illegally.
- Political action committees were limited to a $5000 maximum contribution to any one candidate in any election. It did not, however, restrict contributions for other purposes such as donations to senators and representatives.
- Candidates who did not accept matching federal funds could spend unlimited amounts of personal funds. Ross Perot did this in 1992. Further amendments to this law in 1974 allowed the formation of political action committees by special interest groups and set down specific requirements related to the operation of these groups. By 1990 PAC contributions to presidential candidates rose by over 35 percent. In 1979 a series of amendments to the FECA increased the power of the Federal Election Commission and authorized state party contributions aimed at increasing voter turn-out programs. Each state, by law, has the responsibility of setting up its own campaign finance laws, and many echo the provisions of federal law. George W. Bush raised a record amount of money during the primaries and refused matching funds. He did accept them during the general campaign. John Kerry also refused matching funds during the 2004 primaries. However, both Kerry and George W. Bush received $175 million in the general election campaign.

The public funding of presidential campaigns has had a significant impact on the election process since it was instituted in 1971. Money has been given to candidates during the primary campaign, to the parties to help fund national conventions, and to candidates in the general election campaign. In 1988 candidates received more than $65 million in federal matching funds. The two parties got over $9 million for their 1988 national conventions, and Bush and Dukakis received over $46 million in public funds. By accepting public funding, candidates must pledge that they will not spend more than what was given to them and that they will not accept other kinds of specified donations. There were loopholes including PAC donations and so-called soft money raised by state and local party organizations. One of the central issues raised during the 1996 presidential election was campaign finance abuses. By the end of the campaign it became apparent that soft money was abused, foreign money was laundered, and there was a possibility that China was using illegal contributions to influence local, congressional, and presidential elections. The Democratic Party returned millions of dollars in illegal contributions. Both the president and vice president were under suspicion for using the White House for illegal fundraising. The issue of "presidential coffees" and "sleepovers" in the Lincoln Bedroom in return for contributions haunted the Democrats. Both parties were criticized for using soft money as a way to create political commercials. This broke a law preventing a national party from using soft money to air ads favoring specific candidates. As a result of the scandal, both houses held hearings regarding the fundraising practices of both political parties. The objective of the hearings was to investigate the extent of the illegal use of funds with the end result being the passage of new campaign finance reform laws.

After the escalating cost of the 2000 presidential election, campaign finance reform reemerged as a political issue. Spurred on by the efforts of Arizona Senator John McCain (R), Wisconsin Senator Russ Feingold (D), Connecticut Congressman Chris Shays (R), and Massachusetts Congressman Marty Meehan (D), Congress passed a comprehensive campaign finance reform bill that President George W. Bush signed in 2000. The main features of the bill include a ban on all soft money, increased individual hard money donations, and a ban on special interest political ads paid for by soft money prior to the primary and general election. In 2002, the Supreme Court ruled that the law was constitutional. In the election campaign of 2004, both parties increased the amount of hard money raised. Special Interest groups got around the ban on soft money donations by forming what was called "527" independent groups such as *moveon.org*. These groups raised large amounts of soft money but were protected by the tax code and they were able to run independent advocacy ads.

Beyond the issues raised by campaign finance, the question regarding the effectiveness of the campaign in convincing the electorate to vote for candidate A or candidate B remains. Whether voters are reinforced, motivated, or converted will be the focus of Chapter 13.

Chapter 12 Review

SECTION 1: MULTIPLE-CHOICE QUESTIONS

1. Which of the following terms represents the official designation of a person running for office?
   (A) party nomination
   (B) voter referendum
   (C) plebiscite
   (D) endorsement
   (E) recall

2. The manner in which candidates attempt to effectively use money and media attention in order to achieve the nomination is called campaign
   (A) gambling.
   (B) risk taking.
   (C) apathy.
   (D) manipulation.
   (E) strategy.

3. Political "spin" means
   (A) the attempts of handlers to present a favorable account of events.
   (B) the whirlwind trips that candidates must make during a campaign.
   (C) a candidate's flip-flopping of his opinions.
   (D) the news media's coverage of political events.
   (E) newspaper editorials taking a stand on an issue.

4. The goal of the nominating game is to win a majority of delegates' support at which of the following stages of the campaign?
(A) invisible primary
(B) general election
(C) straw ballot convention
(D) post convention
(E) national party convention

5. Before primaries existed, state parties selected their delegates to the national convention through which of the following processes?
(A) caucus
(B) referendum
(C) roundtable discussion
(D) blanket primary
(E) open primary

6. With the exception of Bill Clinton and George W. Bush, no one has been elected president since 1952 without first having won which presidential primary?
(A) Iowa
(B) New Hampshire
(C) Maine
(D) New York
(E) California

7. Criticisms of the election process include all the following EXCEPT
(A) disproportionate attention goes to the early caucuses.
(B) disproportionate attention goes to the early primaries.
(C) money plays too big a role.
(D) the system allows little room for media involvement.
(E) participation in the primaries is low and not representative of the entire electorate.

8. In order to organize their presidential campaigns effectively, a candidate must do all the following EXCEPT
(A) line up a campaign manager who is skilled.
(B) get a fundraiser that raises significant money.
(C) hire a pollster who knows how to choose focus groups.
(D) announce his or her choice for vice president during the primaries.
(E) get positive media exposure.

9. If presidential candidates accept federal support in the form of matching campaign financing, then they
(A) are no longer required to disclose their contributions.
(B) agree to limit their campaign expenditures to an amount prescribed by federal law.
(C) no longer have any limit to their campaign expenditures.
(D) are no longer required to disclose how they spend their money.
(E) no longer can accept PAC money.

10. Presidential candidates must file periodic reports with the Federal Election Commission, listing who contributed money and how it was spent
    (A) if they receive matching federal funding.
    (B) if they did not receive matching federal funding.
    (C) regardless of whether or not they receive matching federal funding.
    (D) only if their contributions top $1 million.
    (E) if they receive any kind of PAC money.

11. Few developments since the Watergate crisis have generated as much cynicism about government as the
    (A) explosive growth of special interest groups and PACs.
    (B) lack of qualified presidential candidates.
    (C) high turnover rate in the House of Representatives.
    (D) high turnover rate in the Senate.
    (E) difficulty of getting the Senate to approve Supreme Court justices.

12. Which of the following concerns most bothers politicians about the rising costs of campaigning? They
    (A) are forced to accept money from PACs that they may not agree with.
    (B) are involved with fundraising, which takes up much of their time.
    (C) don't feel that they are getting their money's worth from high-priced media consultants.
    (D) don't believe that high-tech campaigns achieve results.
    (E) don't feel that political advertisements achieve results.

13. Which of the following campaign financing reforms has been adopted?
    (A) increasing the amount of PAC contributions a candidate can accept
    (B) abolishing soft money contributions
    (C) decreasing government subsidies to congressional campaigns
    (D) allowing more lobbyist gifts to candidates
    (E) eliminating federal matching funds for presidential campaigns

14. Television news coverage of a candidate generally focuses on all the following EXCEPT
    (A) where the candidates appeared.
    (B) how big the crowds were.
    (C) a candidate's explanation of a complex policy statement.
    (D) sound bites from the candidate's speech.
    (E) photo opportunities staged by the candidates.

15. Four decades of research on political campaigns lead to the following conclusion:
    (A) campaigns typically convert voter preferences.
    (B) campaigns mostly reinforce and activate, only rarely do they convert.
    (C) campaigns have no effect on voter preference.
    (D) money has little or no effect on the outcome of an election.
    (E) the media coverage of a candidate has little to do with the outcome of an election.

16. All the following factors tend to weaken a candidate's chances for election EXCEPT
    (A) challenging an incumbent.
    (B) not using political advertisements.
    (C) recognizing that voters have a remarkable capacity for selective perception.
    (D) recognizing that party identification has a major influence on voting behavior.
    (E) raising large amounts of money.

17. Which of the following provides voters the chance to directly approve or disapprove a legislative proposition?
    (A) a recall petition
    (B) a secondary primary
    (C) a referendum
    (D) a run-off primary
    (E) an indirect primary

18. The first time a candidate attempts to effectively use money and media attention in order to achieve name recognition is the
    (A) invisible primary.
    (B) the general campaign.
    (C) the primary.
    (D) the debates.
    (E) the caucus.

19. Many political scientists concluded that Bill Clinton had won the election of 1996 because
    (A) he decided to bring up the character of his opponent as an issue.
    (B) he closely aligned himself with the liberal wing of his party.
    (C) he refused to debate his opponent.
    (D) he selected Al Gore as his running mate.
    (E) there was unity in the Democratic Party.

20. All the following statements about campaign strategy are true EXCEPT
    (A) the candidate must target the campaign.
    (B) the candidate must take advantage of political assets.
    (C) the candidate must campaign in all 50 states.
    (D) the candidate must use issues and events to his or her advantage.
    (E) the candidate must use the campaign organization.

Answers to Multiple-Choice Questions

1. **(A)** Type of Question: Definitional
   The key words in the question are "official designation." The only other answer that could possibly fit the question is an endorsement. However, an endorsement does not represent the designation of a candidate.
2. **(E)** Type of Question: Definitional
   Again, you need to fill in the definition, looking at the key words "achieve the nomination." There may be gambling, risk taking, or manipulation, but the use of money and media is part of an overall campaign strategy.

3. **(A)** Type of Question: Definitional
Political spin is a term that came into use during the Clinton administration. His political advisers (handlers) were adept at putting the best face on issues with which Clinton was involved. Choices B, C, D, and E are incorrect because they don't apply to the concept of spin.
4. **(E)** Type of Question: Cause and effect relationships
If you win the majority of the delegates at the national party convention, then you get the party's nomination.
5. **(A)** Type of Question: Sequencing a series of events
You must know that the development of the primary system evolved from the caucus system.
6. **(B)** Type of Question: Chronological
Even though you probably do not know the chronology of every primary winner since 1952, because Clinton broke the pattern of having to win the New Hampshire primary and being called "the comeback kid" despite his loss, you should be able to easily identify which primary the question was talking about. Bush lost the primary in 2000 but went on to beat John McCain.
7. **(D)** Type of Question: Solution to a problem
You should be looking for criticism of the election process and then determine the one choice that does not support the premise—there is an increasing role of the media in the election process, from the high-tech campaign to election coverage.
8. **(D)** Type of Question: Hypothetical
Again, look for things candidates must do to organize their campaigns effectively and find the one thing that does not contribute to the effectiveness of a campaign. In this case, you should realize that it is not essential and sometimes can hurt a candidate to announce the choice of the vice president prior to the convention.
9. **(B)** Type of Question: Cause and effect relationships
You must know the components of the Federal Election Campaign Act and understand that the key characteristic is the limitation of campaign expenditures as a result of accepting federal matching funds.
10. **(C)** Type of Question: Cause and effect relationships
Just like question 9, you must know that a requirement of the Federal Election Commission is financial disclosure once a candidate decides to accept matching funds.
11. **(A)** Type of Question: Cause and effect relationships
Watergate is the key to answering this question. What happened after Watergate in the area of cynicism about government? Even though you may feel that there was a lack of qualified presidential candidates and even though there have been Supreme Court justice nominations that have had problems, the proliferation of PACs has been the dominant criticism post-Watergate.
12. **(B)** Type of Question: Generalization
This question requires your understanding of the nature of the political campaign. It is similar to an EXCEPT question because the answer is negative. Even though the other choices are negative, they are not accurate.
13. **(B)** Type of Question: Solution to a problem

The problem is campaign finance reform. The solution is lowering the amount of PAC contributions. Although the other choices are viable, they have not been offered as possible reforms.

14. **(C)** Type of Question: Generalization
Thinking about television coverage of campaigns and the fact that it focuses on superficial coverage should give away the answer that complex policy statements are rarely covered.

15. **(B)** Type of Question: Chronological
We are looking for a generalization that describes the nature of political campaigns. Through the process of elimination, choice B is the best choice. You can eliminate choices D and E because they are false. Choice A is incorrect because most campaigns do not convert voter preferences, whereas choice C is incorrect because voter preference is reinforced.

16. **(E)** Type of Question: Cause and effect relationships
In this question you are looking for a factor that will strengthen a candidate's chance. The only choice that fits that criterion is the raising of large sums of money. Choice C will be chosen by those students who do not understand what selective perception is.

17. **(C)** Type of Question: Identification and analysis
The question describes the characteristics of a referendum. Although recall petitions are also voter initiated, they do not result in the approval of any kind of legislation. Primary votes result in the selection of candidates.

18. **(A)** Type of Question: Sequencing a series of events
Though candidates need to use money effectively and gain media attention throughout the entire campaign, the first time this occurs is during the invisible primary, Choice A. The invisible primary is the period when a candidate, after throwing the proverbial hat into the ring, begins the process of seeking major donations and attempts to gain front-runner status so that the media gives his campaign coverage.

19. **(E)** Type of Question: Solution to a problem
You need to understand the nature of the 1996 election. One of the major reasons why Clinton was reelected was because the Democratic Party was united. Choices A, B, and C are false; choice D may be true but did not have an impact on the campaign.

20. **(C)** Type of Question: Generalization
This question deals with the nature of campaign strategy. Choices A, B, D, and E are all valid characteristics of campaigning. Choice C was a mistake that Richard Nixon made in the 1960 presidential campaign.

SECTION 2: FREE-RESPONSE ESSAY

Politicians have claimed that elections are determined as a result of the fact that "all politics is local." Assess whether the 1994 midterm election supported this statement by giving two examples from that election.

Sample Student Response

Tip O'Neill, former speaker of the House, once said "all politics is local." It is ironic that the mid-term election in 1994 proved how wrong he was. Even though, historically, elections focus on local issues, there are times when elections can become nationalized. Such was the case with the 1994 congressional elections, which resulted in a repudiation of President Clinton and for the first time in over 100 years a loss for the sitting speaker of the House.

The 1994 mid-term elections provided a salient example of this phenomenon. Although typical local issues remain, the electorate expressed its discontent with the Clinton administration. Because much of Clinton's presidential campaign centered on national issues, such as deficit reduction, welfare, and healthcare, and because President Clinton failed to cure the latter two ills, the public once again focused on addressing these federal problems. Therefore, for the most part, local issues have become secondarily important. Realizing such sentiment, Republicans broadened the elections' scope. The GOP, under the leadership of Haley Barbour and Newt Gingrich, attempted to focus the electorate on President Clinton's shortcomings with respect to national issues. By linking Democratic incumbents to President Clinton, Republicans capitalized on Clinton's low approval ratings. New "morphing" technology has even enabled Republican contenders to link physically congressional candidates and President Clinton. A case in point: Representative Rick Santorum, running against incumbent Senator Harris Wofford for the Pennsylvania senatorial seat, centered his campaign on Wofford's role in drafting and supporting the president's defunct and unpopular healthcare legislation. Although healthcare affects people locally, it is not a local issue (as much as perhaps mining legislation would be). Therefore, Santorum has extended the race beyond local politics, and into a realm in which Democrats face obvious disadvantage. Here, such action reflects the assertion that national discontent produces concern for federal issues, and federal solutions. Accordingly, the GOP offered with its Contract with America a panacea for national fiscal problems and successfully convinced the public that the Democrats' controlling the executive branch had produced national political and economic ruin.

The Republicans have adapted using the Contract for what appears to be a singularly brilliant approach to the off-year election. Instead of focusing on local affairs, in which Democratic incumbents have a relative advantage (because the benefits of incumbency would ordinarily favor Democrats), they address national issues, in which Democrats are at decided disadvantage. In response, Democrats have nevertheless attempted to recenter their campaigns. Incumbent senators and representatives stress what they have accomplished for their constituencies and often retract from larger, national concerns.

Massachusetts Senator Ted Kennedy, in an election bid against conservative Republican Mit Romney, talked about the advantage of being reelected so that he would continue to chair the Senate Labor and Human Resources Committee, an especially important issue for a labor-strong state. Kennedy admonished Massachusetts' progressive voters, many of whom were largely concerned with labor matters, not to support a man whose company allegedly denies health insurance to its workers. Therefore, Kennedy emphasized his abilities in relation to an important local issue. Similarly, Senator Pat

Moynihan, who faced Bernadette Castro for the New York senatorial seat, maintained that he, as chair on the enormously powerful Senate Finance Committee, is in position to provide financial benefits to New York State. The Democratic Party leadership, under the control of David Wilhelm, attempted to refute Republican claims that President Clinton's (and by extension Democrats') policies are flawed. Rather, they have actively engaged in campaigns against the Contract, and widened the debate to transcend local issues into the national arena. This had the effect of creating an off-year referendum on Democratic and presidential leadership. As a result, having retreated from local matters, the Democrats suffered the greatest loss in the history of mid-term elections.

Evaluation of Free-Response Sample Essay

1. Did the essay define what is meant by the phrase "all politics is local"?
2. Did the essay provide a clear explanation of the direction the essay was going?
3. Did the essay provide supporting evidence, data, and facts?
4. Did the essay support or refute the statement?

1. The essay, though not defining politics, did attribute the quote to former Speaker of the House Tip O'Neill. The writer offers an observation of the irony of the statement since the mid-term elections held in 1994 were based on national, not local issues.

2. The writer proceeds to use the 1994 mid-term election as evidence that sometimes national issues transcend local politics. This is especially true when the voters perceive the election to be a referendum on the job the president is doing.

3. Supporting evidence is given by looking at how the Republican challengers focused on national public policy issues such as healthcare, welfare, and deficit reduction as well as criticizing President Clinton.

4. In addition to offering examples of national issues, the writer also effectively pointed to the successful campaigns of Democratic senators and representatives who were able to keep their campaigns localized. Two examples of winning incumbents highlighted were Senator Edward Kennedy of Massachusetts and Representative Gary Ackerman of New York.

SECTION 2: DATA-BASED FREE-RESPONSE ESSAY

Look at the following transcript of two political commercials.

"HOW TO SPEAK LIBERAL"

Announcer: How to speak liberal.

CLINTON: I can tell you this, I will not raise taxes on the middle class to pay for these programs.

Announcer: That's liberal for I raise taxes right on the middle class. How to speak more liberal.

CLINTON: People in this room are still mad at me at that budget 'cause you think I raise your taxes too much.

Announcer: That's liberal for I raise taxes even on social security.

CLINTON: It might surprise you to know that I think I raise them too much.

Announcer: That's liberal for I raised your taxes and got caught.

WRONG IN THE PAST

Let's go back in time—to the 1960s.

Bob Dole's in Congress. Votes against creating Medicare. Against creating student loans. Against the Department of Education. Against a higher minimum wage.

Still there. Against creating a Drug Czar. Against the Brady Bill to fight crime. Against family and medical leave. Against vaccines for children. Against medicare__again. Dole-Gingrich tried to cut 270 billion.

Bob Dole: wrong in the past; wrong for our future.

Identify the role that political advertisements play in the modern presidential campaign. Analyze these two ads and then show how they help explain the role that ads play.

Sample Student Response

Political ads play a significant role and, in some cases, can even be the contributing factor in the outcome of an election. Ads are used for local, state, and national elections; from the school board races to the congressional contests and of course to the election of president of the United States. Negative ads have become popular primarily because they work. Even though the electorate speaks out against them, polls have indicated that it is the negative ad which strikes a chord with the voter. Ads have become so deceptive that news organizations have set aside "ad watch" segments. In fact, the Public Broadcast System's Point of View had a special during the 1996 campaign in which they focused on how to dissect an ad. The PBS site has archived the best of the political ads on the internet (www.pbs.org).

The Bob Dole ad is an attack ad using one of the favorite targets—the "L" word—attaching liberal to President Clinton. The ad is even more effective because it uses Clinton's own words to describe his regrets about raising taxes on the very wealthy, another favorite Republican topic. The announcer provides the commentary and sets up the only logical conclusion for Clinton's action: that Bill Clinton is liberal, and a liberal will raise your taxes. The ad is most effective because of its simplicity and direct message. You don't get caught up in statistics. You don't have to search for the message. And if you think liberals raise taxes, then you won't vote for Bill Clinton—especially because he apologizes for doing it!

The Clinton ad is equally effective and uses a traditional Democratic theme—the Republican Party and specifically Bob Dole are out to reverse the legislative gains made by the Democrats and Bill Clinton over the past 30 years. How do you prove the point? By going back in history and tracing the voting record of the former Senate Majority Leader and current presidential candidate. The Clinton ad in rapid fashion makes it clear that Dole voted against some very popular programs— Medicare, student loans, the Department of Education, and a higher minimum wage. It then updates the Senator's voting pattern suggesting that Dole was still voting against such popular measures as the Brady Bill, family and medical leave, and that he is continuing to oppose Medicare. The theme of the ad ends the piece— "Bob Dole: wrong in the past; wrong for our future."

Both ads illustrate how the candidates use the records of their opponents to emphasize to the voter the negative aspects of the opposition. In Dole's case it is how Clinton is a liberal; in Clinton's case it is tying Dole to Gingrich for the purpose of trying to make the public believe very popular programs are in danger if Dole is elected. Are these ads accurate? For the most part they are factually correct. Do they distort the records of the candidates? Probably, since both Dole and Clinton do not have a chance to respond or fully explain their positions. Is there an alternative? Although political ads are part of political campaigns, many people believe these ads should emphasize the positive programs of the candidates rather than attack their opponents.

Evaluation of Data-Based Free-Response Sample Essay

1. Was the message of each commercial clearly presented?
2. Was there an adequate description of the commercials that illustrates the message?
3. In the second part, were there specific conclusions that go beyond the description of the messages of the commercials?

1. The answer focuses on the negativity of each of the ads. The use of specific words used in the commercials by both candidates illustrates the point. In addition, the writer refers to the text of the commercials found in the data and makes the point that these were attack ads. The answer also supports the point that, within the structure of the negative ads, you can also find statements that are technically truthful. The description was balanced. Both candidates' ads were evaluated.

2. The description of the commercials is the heart of the response. First, the kind of words, all negative in nature, were used to illustrate the message. Then, specific aspects of each commercial were highlighted to back up the point that the essence of the political ad was to point out negative characteristics, actions, and accusations made against each of the candidates.

3. The conclusions reached in the second part include the distrust the ads tried to communicate to the electorate, how the public responds to negative ads, and the amount of negativity a 30-second ad contains. The response also went beyond the scope of the question by pointing out the results.

CHAPTER 13 Voting Behavior: The Impact of Public Opinion and the Media

Chapter Overview

Ever since Harry Truman held up the front page of the *Chicago Tribune*, which declared "Dewey defeats Truman," politicians have stopped taking voters for granted. They also view polling and the media with skepticism and rely on their own pollsters and media advisers. If elections prove the legitimacy of a candidate's campaign, the task of the politician is to find the way to influence the citizen to vote for him or her.

This chapter will explore why people vote and why they stay home on election day. By looking at the demographics of America, you will be able to understand voter trends. Even though Americans are notorious in the manner in which they exercise this essential quality of a democracy, recent elections have provided optimism that voter turnout is on the increase. When you view the constitutional basis of voting and its history, you should see how long it has taken for all suffrage to be obtained by every citizen.

In recent elections, public opinion, measured through polls, became a primary barometer of how and why the voter behaved. Political polls were conducted to gauge the feelings and attitudes of the electorate. We will evaluate how polls are conducted, how candidates rely on polls and the media, and the impact of exit polls and the media.

The role of the media, including its historical development and its impact on public opinion and the political agenda, will be the focus in the last section of the chapter. Topics such as the limits placed on the media, the bias in the media, and the future importance of the information superhighway will be discussed.

KEY TERMS

- Civil Rights Act of 1964
- Fairness doctrine
- Information superhighway
- Literacy laws
- Mass media
- Media bias
- Motor Voter Act of 1993
- Party identification
- Photo ops
- Political socialization
- Poll tax
- Public opinion polls
- Sampling error
- Simpson-Marzzoli Act (1987)
- Solid South
- Sound bites
- Suffrage
- Talking heads
- Voting Rights Act of 1965

A Quick Review of the Constitutional and Legal Basis of Suffrage

- Article I Section 2 Clause (1) required each state to allow those qualified to vote for their own legislatures as well as the House of Representatives.
- Article II Section 1 Clause (2) provided for presidential electors to be chosen in each state with the manner determined by state legislatures.
- The Reserve Power clause of the Tenth Amendment gave the states the right to determine voting procedures.
- The Fifteenth Amendment gave freed slaves the right to vote.
- The Seventeenth Amendment changed the meaning of Article I Section 2 to allow eligible voters to elect senators directly.
- The Nineteenth Amendment made it illegal for the states to discriminate against men or women in establishing voting qualifications.
- The Twenty-Fourth Amendment outlawed the poll tax as a requirement for voting.
- The Twenty-Sixth Amendment prohibited the federal government and state governments from denying the right of 18 year olds to vote in both state and federal elections.
- The Voting Rights Acts of 1957, 1960, and 1965 increased the opportunities for minorities to register and allowed the attorney general to prevent state interference in the voting process.
- The Supreme Court decision in *Baker v Carr* (1962) established the one man, one vote principle.
- Supreme Court decisions in the 1990s established that gerrymandering resulting in "majority-minority" districts was unconstitutional.

Voting Patterns

Demographics, the type of election, socioeconomic status, religious background, and extent of party identification are some of the factors that influence voting patterns.

In order to understand why people vote, you first must look at the potential make-up of the American electorate. Demographic patterns are determined every ten years when the census is conducted. Besides establishing representation patterns, the census also provides important information related to the population's

- age
- socioeconomic make-up
- place of residence and shifting population movement
- ethnicity
- gender

Once this demographic study is evaluated, certain things become obvious. The impact of immigrants has been a key factor in the nation's population increase. When you look at immigration patterns, historically, you will see that there have been three distinctive immigrant trends affecting population patterns. The first wave occurred before the Civil War when immigrants came from northwestern Europe and included English, Irish, and Germans. The second period, the greatest influx of immigrants, took place after the Civil War and peaked from 1890 to 1920. Italians, Jews, Asians, Poles, and Russians came to this country looking for the American Dream. Ellis Island became the center of immigrant activity and America was described as a melting pot, denoting a mix of immigrants whose cultures and ideas had an influence on the culture of this country. Immigrants assimilated into the mainstream of the country. The flow stopped with the passage of restrictive immigration quota laws in the 1920s and 1930s. The new immigrant period began after World War II and peaked in the 1980s when immigrants came from Central and Latin America and Asia. In 1987, after the passage of the Simpson-Marzzoli Act, illegal aliens who were living in this country since 1982 were allowed to apply for legal status. Almost two million did so. The most recent immigration act was passed in 1991. This act shifted the quota of immigrants to Europe and aimed to attract immigrants who were trained workers. In 1994 angry California voters passed Proposition 187, which denied social services such as education and welfare to illegal aliens. The law was challenged in federal court and declared unconstitutional. Congress also passed the Welfare Reform Act of 1996, which denied welfare benefits to legal immigrants. Thus you can see an ongoing "nativist" reaction to the issue of modern-day immigration.

Key aspects of the 2000 census reflect an aging America, a population shift to the sunbelt, and a decrease in those who would be classified as earning an income close to or below the poverty level. Immigrant patterns and these factors have public policy consequences and are therefore important to the political process. Political socialization is the factor that determines voting behavior. There is growing interest in how people actually develop their political orientation, thus making it more likely they will vote. Studies have determined that these attitudes are determined by the family, the media, and public schools. Party identification, the voter's evaluation of the candidates, and policy voting, the actual decision to vote for a particular candidate based on these factors, all come into play in evaluating the overall voting process.

What are the factors, then, that make people decide to cast their vote for a particular candidate? They can be classified in two major categories, sociological and psychological. Sociological factors include

- income and occupation,
- education,
- sex and age,
- religious and ethnic background,
- region of the country where you live, and
- family make-up.

Psychological factors include

- party affiliation and identification,
- perception of candidate's policies and/or image, and
- the feeling that your vote will make a statement.

Based on these factors the following statements about who votes, what party those who vote lean toward, and who doesn't vote can be made.

- Voters who are in the lower income brackets and laborers tend to vote Democratic. Those upper-middle to upper income level voters, many of whom are business and professional white-collar workers, tend to vote Republican. Yet when you compare voting rates of both groups, you will see that citizens with higher incomes and greater education vote in greater numbers than those with lower incomes and less education. This is the number one factor in what determines voter turnout. This pattern held true in the 1976–2004 presidential elections.

- Voting patterns do not usually correlate strongly with gender. Analysts suggest there is a gender gap in national politics, a significant deviation between the way men and women vote. In addition, there is no guarantee that even if a woman ran for national office, she would get the women's vote. With Geraldine Ferraro on the 1984 Democratic ticket, more women voted for the Reagan-Bush ticket, proving that women did not vote just because there was a woman running for vice president. However, since 1988 a trend has developed where women vote for Democratic candidates in greater percentages than men vote. This was particularly true in the 1994 mid-term election when polls showed that "angry white" voters heavily supported Republican candidates, whereas women still supported Democratic candidates. Yet in 1996, because for the first time the male vote was split almost 50–50 between Clinton and Dole, women voted for Clinton by more than 10 percent. As stated in the previous chapter, the soccer mom became a new term illustrating why certain women voters favored Clinton so heavily. This trend repeated itself in 2000. In 2004, both campaigns went after the so-called "NASCAR dad." President George W. Bush even opened up a NASCAR event with the traditional "Gentlemen, start your engines." John Kerry went goose hunting hoping to siphon the gun owners' vote. But the most significant change that occurred in 2004 was a new gender gap described in Chapter 12, the gap between single and married women.
- The youth vote is undergoing a major change. Ever since the Twenty-Sixth Amendment was passed, political parties wanted to capture the young voter. Even though they seem to vote more Democratic than Republican (with the exception of youth supporting Reagan and Bush), the fact remains that they have voted in much lower numbers than other groups. From 1976 to 1988, for instance, the turnout among the youngest voters, those 18–20 years old, was less than 40 percent of the eligible voters. In the 1992, 1996, 2000, and 2004 elections, MTV ran a "Choose or Lose" campaign resulting in an increased enrollment and turnout of young voters.

THE YOUTH VOTE HAS BEEN GREATLY INFLUENCED BY MTV'S ROCK THE VOTE CAMPAIGN

- Religious and ethnic background highly influences voter choice and voter turnout. Dating back to the early days of immigration, Catholics and Jews tend to vote Democratic (Republicans traditionally supported anti-immigration legislation), whereas northern Protestants tend to vote Republican. Strongly affiliated religious groups also tend to vote in general elections compared to those people who don't identify themselves as being closely connected to a religion. Minority groups, although voting heavily for Democratic candidates, do not turn out as much as white voters. Jesse Jackson and his Rainbow Coalition, minority groups of "color" rallying around the causes espoused by Jackson, have been attempting to increase minority registration and voter turnout. Minority groups are a fertile field for political parties to pursue. After the 2000 election, a religious gap became evident. Those people who were regular churchgoers tended to vote Republican, while those who did not attend religious services regularly tended to vote Democratic.
- Historically, geography has dictated a voter preference. The South voted solidly Democratic after the Civil War. However, the solid South has become much more conservative. They vote Republican more on the national level, continue to vote Democratic in local elections, but it is sometimes hard to tell the difference because of ideology. Comparing voter turnout, proportionally, Northerners vote in greater numbers than Southerners. This difference is explained by large number of minority voters who are still not registered. New England and sunbelt voters tend to vote Republican, whereas the big industrial states, especially in the big cities, lean to the Democrats but are considered toss-ups in close presidential elections.
- In terms of a specialized group, government workers turn out in large numbers because, for many of them, their jobs depend on and are affected by who is elected.
- Even though party identification plays a key role in determining voter choice and voter turnout, more and more people are registering Independent. There is a greater overall Democratic registration, but voters tend to respond more to the individual candidate and issues, along with the sociological factors, than just party identification alone.

Party Identification

Voting patterns vary from election to election and reached a peak in the 1960s presidential elections.

If we assume party identification is a key factor in determining voter turnout and voter preference, then we would assume the Democrats would have the edge. This was definitely true in Congress where Democrats dominated both houses since World War II. This changed dramatically in 1994 when the Republicans gained control of the House for the first time in 40 years as well as the Senate. When you look at presidential elections, personality and issues rather than party have been a conclusive factor in determining the outcome of the election. In many elections ticket splitting occurred more than straight party line voting. This was especially evident in 1996 when the voters kept in office the Democratic president and Republican Congress.

In order to vote, you must be registered. Historically, this was an important factor explaining why voter turnout was low. In 1992 Jesse Jackson's Rainbow

Coalition increased minority voter registration. To make voter registration easier for all groups, the Motor Voter Act of 1993 was signed into law by President Clinton. This law enabled people to register to vote at motor vehicle departments. In fact, it has not been since the Voting Rights Act of 1965 that so many new voters registered. More than 600,000 voters became eligible to vote. Another interesting point is that even though Republicans were concerned that there would be a Democratic imbalance in the new registrants, it was in fact the Republicans who made significant gains. However, in post-1996 election analysis, most of these new voters did not vote. California, along with four other states, challenged the constitutionality of the law arguing that it was an unfunded mandate. The federal courts have dismissed that contention.

Even though it is easier for people to vote and a greater number of people have registered, there has been a consistent downward trend from 1968–2000. The number of people of voting age has more than doubled since 1932. Yet after reaching a high in 1960, the percentage of eligible voters who voted actually declined (except for a small increase in 1984 and 1992). Because of the increase in young voters and successful efforts to enroll minorities and get them to vote, there was a significant increase in the 1992 election when close to 55 percent of the registered voters turned out. In 1996, because of negative voter reaction to the campaign issues raised by President Clinton and Senator Dole, the voter turnout was again below 50 percent. In 2000 the percentage rose to a little above 50 percent. In 2004, there was a record voter turnout that translated into a 60 percent turnout. Since 1932 the highest presidential turnouts (60 percent or more) were in the three elections that took place in the 1960s. National and international events, as well as new legislation that increased voting opportunities for minorities, were probably responsible for the higher numbers. After Watergate the percentage of voters dropped dramatically. It is interesting to note that in off-year congressional elections, voter turnout is significantly lower. From 1974 to 2002 turnout in mid-term congressional elections averaged around 45 percent.

There is a real inconsistency between voter participation and the amount and type of election coverage provided in the campaigns. Everything from presidential debates to town meetings and an increased use of the mass media should result in an increased voter turnout. But because of a decline in party identification and a distrust of politicians, it seems that many eligible voters would rather sit out elections.

History

The history of suffrage reflects increased opportunities to vote.

The country has seen a tremendous change in the legal right to vote. When the Constitution was ratified, franchise was given to white male property owners only. Today there is a potential for close to 200 million people who are at least 18 years old to vote. It has been a long struggle to obtain suffrage for individuals who were held back by such considerations as property ownership, race, religious background, literacy, ability to pay poll taxes, and sex. In addition, many state restrictions lessened the impact of federal law and constitutional amendments.

THE HISTORY OF SUFFRAGE HAS BEEN CHARACTERIZED BY MINORITY GROUPS FIGHTING FOR THEIR RIGHT TO VOTE

By the 1800s all religious qualifications were eliminated from voting requirements. Property considerations also were legislated out of existence by most states in the middle of the nineteenth century. The aftermath of the Civil War provided a major attempt to franchise the freed race. However the passage of the Fifteenth Amendment was countered by the passage of literacy laws and poll taxes by most Southern states. The progressive era of the early twentieth century saw the passage of two key amendments, the direct election of senators and the granting of voting rights to women. After the *Brown* decision in 1954, Congress began formulating voting rights legislation such as the Voting Rights Act of 1965, and these changes were backed by the passage of the Twenty-Fourth Amendment, eliminating the poll tax (or any other voting tax). The final groups to receive the vote were Washington, D.C., voters, as a result of the Twenty-Third Amendment in 1961 and the 18 year old as a result of the passage of the Twenty-Sixth Amendment in 1971.

Even though these trends resulted in an increase in the potential pool of voters, it was still left up to the individual states to regulate specific voting requirements. Such issues as residency, registration procedures, age, and voting times affect the ability of people to vote. However, federal law and Supreme Court decisions have created more and more consistency in these areas. This was especially apparent in the 2000 election when the Supreme Court intervened in the Florida recount and decided to stop the recount in *Bush v Gore*. For instance, the Supreme Court has ruled that a 30-day period is ample time for residency. The Motor Voter Act does provide for the centralization of voter registration along with local registration regulations. Some states have permitted 17 year olds to vote in some primary elections. Literacy tests have been outlawed in every state as a result of the Voting Rights Act Amendments of 1970 and Supreme Court decisions.

The two significant pieces of modern legislation increasing voting opportunities were the Civil Rights Act of 1964 and the Voting Rights Act of 1965. The Civil Rights Act prohibited the use of any registration requirement that resulted in discrimination and paved the way for the involvement of the federal government to enforce the law. The Voting Rights Act of 1965 finally made the Fifteenth Amendment a reality. It was reinforced by other amendments in 1970, 1975, and 1982. As a result of this act, the poll tax and literacy requirements were addressed. The act gave the attorney general the power to determine which states were in violation of the law and led to the passage of the constitutional amendments after the Supreme Court ruled on the legality of the law. The act also prohibited states from passing their own restrictive voting laws without "preclearance" from the Department of Justice.

There are some cases where restrictions can exist on a person's right to vote. People in mental institutions, the homeless, convicted felons, and dishonorably discharged soldiers have been denied the right to vote in some states.

Public Opinion

Public opinion is molded through a combination of factors at a very early age.

Public opinion can be defined as the attitudes, perceptions, and viewpoints individuals hold about politics and government. Some political scientists view this process as one of political socialization. It is interesting to see the parallels between the factors that influence voting patterns and the factors that mold public opinion and political socialization. They include

- the family,
- the schools,
- the church,
- molders of public opinion, and
- the mass media.

People internalize viewpoints at a very early age and act on them as they grow older. "Family values" has become an overused phrase but, in fact, is the primary source of the formulation of political opinions. When Vice President Dan Quayle made family values an election issue in 1992, he touched a chord that set off a debate. The reality is that children internalize what they hear and see within their family unit. If a child lives with a single parent, that child will certainly have strong attitudes about child support. If parents tend to speak about party identification, most children will tend to register and vote for the same party as their parents. Schools and the church play a secondary role in the formation of political views. There is no doubt that the Catholic Church's position on abortion has had a tremendous impact on Catholics taking a stand for the "right to life." However, the family unit reinforces the viewpoint. Schools and teachers inculcate the meaning of citizenship at very early ages. Children recite the pledge and sing the national anthem. Depending upon how open the educational system is, students will also learn how to question the role of government. People who are in the public spotlight—whether they are politicians, union officials, successful businessmen, spiritual leaders, or your personal doctors, lawyers, or accountants—play an impressive role in molding public opinion. When Lee Iacocca or Donald Trump talk about government, people respond to their perspective. People holding important offices also command respect and use different techniques to influence the public. The mass media (covered in the last part of this chapter) is playing an increasingly important role in the formation of people's political attitudes. TV talk shows, interactive technology, and the print media comment on every aspect of our lives. Surveys have shown that the average household watches television more than seven hours a day.

The translation of public opinion into public policy takes place when policymakers truly understand opinion trends. This is one of the most difficult aspects of policymakers. They rely on such things as polls, letters, and personal input from constituents. The next section will discuss polling techniques.

Opinion Polls

Public opinion polls take the pulse of America regarding many different issues. They also are predictors of the outcome of elections.

In recent years, poll-taking has increased in scope and importance. Pollsters want to determine what the American public is thinking. The results are widely reported in the media, and in a number of cases polls themselves are newsworthy. The qualities that are measured in polls include

- how intense people are in their beliefs and attitudes,
- the real wants and needs of individuals that can be translated into policy,
- whether public opinion on any given issue is constant or changing, and
- the extent the public is polarized or has a consensus on any given issue. Issues such as the Vietnam War and healthcare are two examples of the public displaying polarization and consensus.

Using scientific methodology and computer technology, professional pollsters such as Gallup, CNN, and daily newspapers have mastered the art of measuring public opinion. When looking at political polls, you should consider

- who conducts the poll—There is a real difference between a candidate who reports polling results and a neutral organization that conducts a poll.
- the sample size—Make sure that a random sample was obtained.
- a clear distinction regarding the population sample (i.e., in a presidential preference poll, whether those polled were likely voters)
- when the poll was conducted
- the poll methodology
- the sampling error, which gives the poll statistical validity—A ±3 percent is usually an acceptable standard.
- how clearly the question was worded

During the presidential campaign, CNN and other media outlets took daily tracking polls of both likely voters and those voters who were eligible. The results differed significantly. In 1996, the increased popularity of the Internet contributed to the proliferation of daily tracking polls. On any given day one could find as many as a dozen polls broken down nationally and by state, by registered voter, by likely voter, by electoral vote, by popular vote, and by over a three-day period as well as over a one-day period. The result was conflicting data, which critics of polling blamed as the reason for voter apathy in the election. On the eve of the election, most polls gave Clinton an easy electoral victory and a double-digit popular vote margin. It was only the Reuters Poll that accurately predicted Clinton's 9-point popular vote margin.

Public opinion polls have become so sophisticated that the use of exit polls in carefully selected precincts can accurately predict the outcome of an election minutes after the polls close. In addition, these polls can give valuable information regarding why people voted the way they did. By 4:30 in the afternoon, CNN had exit polls indicating an electoral sweep for Bill Clinton but refrained from reporting it. A serious question has been raised regarding the prediction of elections using exit polls in presidential elections. If the East Coast results are reported right after the polls close, will it influence West Coast voters to stay home? There have even been attempts to legislate restrictions on the use of exit polls. In 1996 the same arguments continued. And, as in 1992, by 9:00 P.M. eastern time, it was obvious that Clinton was assured a large electoral victory.

There have also been historical polling mistakes. The most famous polling error took place in the 1936 election when a magazine mailed out straw ballots to more than 10 million people. It got back more than 2 million of them and predicted that Governor Alfred Landon would defeat incumbent Franklin Roosevelt. Roosevelt won the election by one of the greatest landslides, carrying every state with the exception of Maine and Vermont. Obviously, the poll lacked a valid sample, getting its population from automobile registration lists and telephone numbers. That kind of sample during a depression would obviously favor the Republicans. Another polling disaster occurred in the 1948 election between Truman and Dewey. Pollsters had been accurately calling the election extremely close. In September the Gallup organization ended their polling and predicted a Dewey victory. Pollsters quickly learned they would have to continue polling to the final day of the campaign to gauge subtle shifts in public opinion accurately. Overall, most polls have accurately predicted voter trends and have been responsible in the manner in which they have been taken and reported.

In the 2000 presidential election polling organizations came under fire. The Voter News Service, a conglomerate of the major media organizations pooling their resources to provide exit poll information, gave inaccurate statistics to the networks regarding the results of the Florida vote. This caused the networks to first call the election for Vice President Gore. Then, when additional information was evaluated, the networks pulled back their initial projection and the state remained in the "too close to call" column until the networks again, based on faulty information, gave the state to George W. Bush in the early hours of the next morning. Based on this, Gore called Bush and conceded the election until it became clear that the real results were so close that a recount of Florida's votes was required. Voter News Service took responsibility for the poor methodology used and, along with the networks, promised to implement new procedures for the 2004 election.

The Mass Media

The history of print and broadcast journalism reflects a linkage role of the media to politics and government.

From the coverage of the ratification of the Constitution, to the announcement that the Civil War had begun, to the eyewitness accounts by CNN correspondents of the beginning of the Gulf War, the mass media has been a main source of information.

When we speak about the mass media, we are talking about television, newspapers, radio, and magazines. We also include books, film, and audiotapes as methods of communication. With the growth of the Internet, numerous forms of new media such as computers and cable television are appearing on the scene.

The true linkage of the media to the government can be understood by taking an historical trip describing the development of the mass media. Newspapers dominated the early coverage of political events in American history. Specialized publications such as the Federalist Papers and its counterpart, *The National Gazette*, were forums for arguments for and against the ratification of the Constitution. The invention of the telegraph and the development of the rapid printing press increased the availability and circulation of newspapers. Private publishers took more of an independent stand, and they were not afraid to cover political scandals such as the Credit Mobiler affair which took place in Grant's administration. By the turn of the century, the good, bad, and ugly heads of newspaper coverage appeared on the scene. The yellow journalism of

William Randolph Hearst's *New York Journal American*, instigating United States involvement in a war against Spain, contrasts dramatically with muckrakers calling for social reform in such magazines as *McClure's* and *Collier's*. *The New York Times* with its motto, "All the news that's fit to print," looked upon themselves as the journalistic benchmark.

By the 1920s the advent of radio changed the nature of mass communications. Mayor LaGuardia of New York City used it to read the funnies during a newspaper strike. Franklin Roosevelt kept the American public informed about his administration in his famous fireside chats. He also used the press effectively, holding over 300 press conferences during his administration, a record that still stands today. During the 1950s, television networks experimented with the first broadcasts of a national political convention. But the true impact of television as a medium came when they covered the McCarthy hearings. Televised presidential debates have been a part of national politics since the 1960 debates. Coverage of the assassination of President Kennedy and the events that followed held the nation captive in 1963. Congressional hearings such as Watergate, Iran-Contra, and President Clinton's impeachment trial have had a major impact on the public's perception of presidential behavior. What follows is a list of the highlights of television "firsts," which led to the increased awareness of the importance that the medium plays in keeping the public informed.

- 1939—Television demonstrated at World's Fair in New York City.
- 1947—*Meet the Press* has its first broadcast on NBC.
- 1952—Television covers the political conventions with gavel-to-gavel coverage.
- 1954—The McCarthy hearings are broadcast live on ABC.
- 1960—First televised presidential debates between Kennedy and Nixon.
- 1961—Live televised press conferences given by Kennedy.
- 1963—Live coverage of the aftermath of the Kennedy Assassination, including Oswald's murder and Kennedy's funeral.
- 1968—*60 Minutes* premieres on CBS.
- 1968—Coverage of the Vietnam War intensifies antiwar demonstrations.
- 1973—Watergate hearings dominate all three networks.
- 1979—C-SPAN begins live coverage of the House of Representatives.
- 1980—CNN premieres as first all-news television network.
- 1980—ABC's *Nightline* makes its first broadcast in response to the Iran hostage crisis.
- 1984—Networks drop gavel-to-gavel coverage of national conventions.
- 1991—CNN provides live coverage of the Gulf War.
- 1991—Unsuccessful Soviet coup covered live by CNN and the major networks.
- 1992—Ross Perot announces potential candidacy on *Larry King Live*, and Bill Clinton plays saxophone on *Arsenio Hall Show* and appears on MTV.
- 1992—Operation Restore Hope Somalian invasion covered live on television.
- 1993—The Waco standoff and the decision of Attorney General Reno and FBI to force the Branch Davidians to surrender and the eventual burning of the complex was covered live.

- 1995—The Oklahoma City Bombing and aftermath was covered from the bombing to the trial and to the conviction of Tim McVeigh.
- 1995—The O. J. Simpson murder trial became a national media obsession.
- 1996—The most limited coverage of national political conventions suggested that future political conventions would have even less coverage.
- 1997—The summer Senate Campaign Finance hearings, chaired by Tennessee Senator Fred Thompson, held little public interest and unlike Watergate and Iran-Contra received no continuous coverage by any major media.
- 1997—Funeral of Princess Diana.
- 1998—The media frenzy surrounding an alleged affair between President Clinton and a White House intern.
- 1999—Impeachment trial of President Clinton.
- 1999—The shootings at Columbine High School.
- 2000—The disputed election.
- 2001—Attack on the United States by terrorists.
- 2003—Iraq war.
- 2004—Presidential election.

The Internet

The impact of the information superhighway on the political and public agenda has far-reaching consequences.

As the media continues to quench Americans' thirst for information, different kinds of media conglomerates form, and new kinds of technologies are made available. This has led to the growth of the information superhighway. This "thruway" of information has many different exits. Media conglomerates and the Internet are two of the major characteristics of the information superhighway. The media concentration that exists gives the public access to the highway. The structure can be viewed as a three-tiered structure—an inner, middle, and outer tier. The inner tier consists of the three major networks, cable news channels, the national news magazines (*Time*, *Newsweek*, and *U.S. News and World Report*), and the four national newspapers (*The New York Times*, *Washington Post*, *Wall Street Journal*, and *Los Angeles Times*), as well as the national wire service the Associated Press. The middle tier embraces other national newspapers including *USA Today*, *Chicago Tribune*, the *Christian Science Monitor*, and other news services as well as magazines with a strong political slant (*The New Republic* and *National Review*). The outer tier consists of local newspapers and local television and radio stations. Crossing these tiers is a concentration of power among major media conglomerates such as Gannett and AOL-Time Warner, Disney, and General Electric. The impact of talk radio and such commentators as Rush Limbaugh and G. Gordon Liddy cannot be underestimated and contribute to what has been characterized as a hyperdemocracy, the influence of the masses through the media on government.

The formation of new media pathways to the information superhighway has proliferated in the 1990s. Such new media as computers, satellites, cable television, VCRs, direct broadcast satellite services, laser discs, CD-ROM, and other interactive technologies such as e-mail, videoconferencing, and teleconferencing on-line services, and the tremendous growth of the Internet have created a congested information highway. The net result is a greater impact on the political agenda. In the 1996, 2000, and 2004 elections every major political candidate had a "web site" on the Internet. Candidates also use the Internet for fundraising. In the 2000 election Senator John McCain raised over $1 million using his web site. In 2003, presidential candidate Howard Dean set an Internet fund-raising record. Sites such as *moveon.org* and *meetup.org* have changed the political landscape. Listed on the next page is a chart of the major political Internet sites. As the public has more and more access to information, the media has the potential to influence the way the public thinks. For instance, having the capability to react immediately to an issue raised by using voice mail enables instant polling to take place. The media, by selecting the events that are covered, also influences what the public perceives as being important. This capability also applies to political leaders. Knowing that they are being broadcast live on C-SPAN certainly encourages House and Senate members to play to a sophisticated TV audience. The White House Office of Communications monitors the media on a daily basis. It is interesting to note that during the Gulf War, Iraqi leader Saddam Hussein received much of his information from CNN broadcasts. The media has also been blamed for the decline of party identification and party politics. Why should an individual get involved with a political party when the interactive media makes it easy to not only access information but also influence office holders? Candidates and office holders also use the media to get their message out in their high-tech campaigns. They use selective leaks, known as trial balloons, to test the political waters. They become "talking heads," with the media focusing on the face of politicians during speeches and talk shows often ending up as sound bites. The information superhighway, thus, certainly is growing in importance, but it may be a double-edged sword. The faster it grows, the less direct control policymakers may have on the average citizen.

Media Coverage

The media is both blamed and praised for the type of coverage it provides.

Virtually all candidates and every president feel that the media is unfair in the manner in which they cover a campaign or administration. They attempt to control and manipulate the media, creating media events and photo opportunities. Presidents such as Ronald Reagan have even developed successful strategies to control media access by planning the event, staying on the offensive, controlling the flow of information, limiting access by the media, talking only about the issues the administration wants to talk about, speaking in one voice as an administration, and constantly repeating the same message. This worked for Reagan, but when Clinton attempted to move the White House press out of their briefing room, there was a hostile reaction, forcing the president to back down. The irony of Clinton's lack of success with the media is that during the campaign, many felt that he was their fair-haired boy. However, statistical studies indicated that on balance, the media covered both Bush and Clinton, praising and criticizing them whenever events dictated. During the 1996 election, the media was criticized by both candidates. Senator Dole complained that the media was not pursuing ethical and character issues of the president. President Clinton accused the media of not focusing on his accomplishments in office. A general criticism was raised by "think-tanks" that a media mentality created a winner-loser horse race when covering the election. In fact, a study conducted by the Media

MAJOR POLITICAL SITES ON THE INTERNET

Campaign Commercials	*http://www.ammi.org/livingroomcandidate/*
Center for Political Debates	*http://www.debates.org/*
CNN/Time Inside Politics	*http://www.cnn.com/politics*
Dave Leip's Atlas of U.S. Presidential Elections	*http://uselectionatlas.org/*
Election Maps	*http://www.lib.virginia.edu/gic/elections/index.html*
Elections	*http://www.multied.com/elections/*
Electoral College—Calculator	*http://www.nara.gov/fedreg/elctcoll/naracalc.html*
Find Law: Supreme Court Opinions	*http://www.findlaw.com/casecode/supreme.html*
Government Resources on the Web	*http://www.lib.umich.edu/libhome/Documents.center/govweb.html*
History and Politics Out Loud	*http://www.hpol.org/*
National Political Index	*http://www.politicalindex.com/*
Policy.com— Issues Forum	*http://www.policy.com*
Political Dictionary	*http://www.fast-times.com/political/political.html*
Polling Report.com—Public Opinion Online	*http://www.pollingreport.com/*
POTUS—Presidents of the United States	*http://www.ipl.org/ref/POTUS/*
Statistical Resources on the Web	*http://www.lib.umich.edu/libhome/Documents.center/stats.html*
Television and the Presidency	*http://foxnews.com/politics/presidency/*
THOMAS: Legislative Information on the Internet	*http://thomas.loc.gov/*
The United States Senate	*http://www.senate.gov/*
Vote Smart Web	*http://www.vote-smart.org/*
Web White & Blue	*http://www.webwhiteblue.org/*
The White House	*http://www.whitehouse.gov/*

Studies Center entitled "The Media & Campaign 96 Briefing" indicated that the public was also critical of the media coverage of the campaign. The survey concluded that media coverage "discourages good people from running for president." However, in general, the public thought the media was also doing some positive things. The survey found a public that (1) was pleased with the unbiased nature of the media, (2) was impressed with specialized networks such as CNN and C-SPAN, (3) was viewed as impartially related to favoring one political party over the other, and (4) still gets most of its news about the campaign from the media. After the disputed election of 2000, the major polling organizations surveyed the public regarding the overall coverage of both the election and the recount. By a slight majority, the public was satisfied with the coverage given to the candidates by the media. However, a large majority of people were critical of the way the networks used exit polls.

The key questions raised regarding coverage are: is it fair and balanced and, if there is an editorial stand, does it make a difference? The question of media bias is answered by the media when they point to what they call the canons of good journalism—objectivity and responsible reporting. There has never been any correlation between newspaper endorsements of a political candidate and the candidate winning the election because of it. In addition, legal restraints such as slander and libel as well as legislative direction from the FCC force the media to abide by standards. During the campaign, the FCC sets down equal-time provisions, which give equal time to all candidates who seek the same office. The Fairness Doctrine, scrapped in 1987, provided that the media air opposing opinions of the same issue. The FCC decided that this provision violated the First Amendment and that, with the proliferation of cable television and the number of talk radio programs, there was a diversity of opinions aired. As a result of the mistakes the media made in reporting the results of the 2000 election, the networks and Congress pledged to review alternatives to exit polls. Suggestions such as a standard time to close the polls nationwide have been discussed.

The rise of investigative reporting and adversarial reporting gave rise to complaints that the media was going after politicians and government officials. The rise of TV news magazines such as *60 Minutes*, *20/20*, and *Prime Time Live* added fuel to the fire. As previously indicated, muckrakers such as Upton Sinclair during the country's progressive era helped stimulate political changes such as the passage of the Pure Food and Drug Act and Meat Inspection Act. The Vietnam War television coverage created a hostile relationship between the media and Lyndon Johnson. The president's military leaders would claim that "the corner has been turned," and television would show the return of body bags. A credibility gap existed, and Lyndon Johnson eventually decided to use a television address to announce a new peace initiative and that he would not seek another term of office, stunning the nation. The turning point of investigative journalism came when Bob Woodward and Carl Bernstein of the *Washington Post* "followed the money," which led to the president's reelection committee and ultimately to President Nixon himself. During the 1980s the press pursued the Iran-Contra dealings of Oliver North and took up Gary Hart's challenge when Hart stated that there was no monkey business in his personal life. The press shot pictures of Hart and Donna Rice on a boat called *Monkey Business* and his presidential aspirations ended. During the 1988 campaign President Bush literally told *Nightline* correspondent Ted Koppel that he overstepped his bounds as an impartial moderator. The press also went after the personal indiscretions of cabinet nominee John Tower in 1989 and Supreme Court nominee Clarence Thomas in 1991. Bill Clinton was able to defuse the Gennifer Flowers allegation in a post–Super Bowl broadcast of *60 Minutes*. And, in 1996, the financial scandals of President Clinton's campaign were deflected by the Democrats.

Government has had to open up its records to the public as a result of such laws as the 1974 Freedom of Information Act and a number of other sunshine laws. These acts opened up meetings and made records of the government available to the public and media. In the end, a balance must be reached between the needs of the candidate or the government and the legitimate interests of the media in providing accurate, relevant information to the public.

Media coverage in the future can go in many different directions. Tabloid journalism programs such as *Inside Edition* and the proliferation of more respectable network newsmagazines such as *Dateline* and *48 Hours*, and the competition among the various cable news networks suggest that the media realizes that the public's insatiable appetite for information has yet to be filled.

The Internet has also played a key investigative role. In 1998 Internet gossip columnist Matt Drudge broke the story of Bill Clinton's affair with a White House intern on his web site before any other traditional media outlet.

Chapter 13 Review

SECTION 1: MULTIPLE-CHOICE QUESTIONS

1. Which of the following conclusions can be made about voting behavior?
   (A) Young people turn out more than any other age group.
   (B) Minorities generally support Republican candidates.
   (C) Southerners vote more than Northerners.
   (D) Voting is a class-based activity.
   (E) Women vote more for Republican candidates than men.

2. Which section of the country has the lowest voter turnout?
   (A) the South
   (B) the Northeast
   (C) the Midwest
   (D) the West
   (E) the Southwest

3. Which class of people has the highest percentage of voter turnout?
   (A) middle class
   (B) lower class
   (C) upper class
   (D) upper-middle class
   (E) Voter turnout has no relationship to class.

4. Which of the following definitions reflects the idea that the victorious party should carry out its proposed agenda?
   (A) constituent service by the elected representatives
   (B) the integrity of the political party
   (C) the party's platform
   (D) voter referendums
   (E) the mandate theory of elections

5. Which of the following is a major result of media-centered politics?
   (A) a greater interest in the election
   (B) a greater loyalty to political parties
   (C) an increase in voter turnout
   (D) a decrease in voter turnout
   (E) an increase in the analysis of issues by the media

6. Which of the following represents the most effective way for a president to manage news coverage?
   (A) controlling the flow of information
   (B) staying on the defensive
   (C) having different staff members speak to the press
   (D) explaining a policy issue multiple times
   (E) giving reporters unlimited access to his daily routine

7. All the following are criticisms aimed at the media EXCEPT
   (A) the media defines the campaign agenda rather than the candidate.
   (B) the media accepts too many negative advertisements.
   (C) the media relies too much on polling.
   (D) the media's investigations of politicians usually emphasize serious issues.
   (E) talk radio places an unfair emphasis on conservative issues.

8. Which of the following groups represents the audience the media aims to develop stories for?
   (A) the college-educated
   (B) the upper class
   (C) the masses
   (D) the lower class
   (E) people looking for in-depth analysis of issues

9. All the following reflect the constitutional basis of suffrage EXCEPT
   (A) states determining the time, manner, and place of elections.
   (B) term limits on United States senators and representatives passed by individual states.
   (C) the Fifteenth Amendment to the Constitution.
   (D) the Seventeenth Amendment to the Constitution.
   (E) the Nineteenth Amendment to the Constitution.

10. All of the following statements best explain why people vote EXCEPT
    (A) religious views.
    (B) political socialization.
    (C) gender politics.
    (D) the economic class to which they belong.
    (E) political surveys.

11. Which of the following trends most closely reflects the last 40 years of American electoral history?
    (A) an increase in suffrage opportunities
    (B) a consistent increase in voter turnout
    (C) third-party victories
    (D) campaign finance reform affecting congressional races
    (E) congressional incumbents losing elections

12. All the following conclusions are true about voting behavior EXCEPT
    (A) voting is a class-based activity.
    (B) young people have the highest turnout rate.
    (C) whites vote with greater frequency than members of minority groups.
    (D) Southerners vote in smaller numbers than Northerners.
    (E) Women voters tend to support candidates with views similar to their own regardless of whether the candidate is a man or woman.

13. The Motor Voter Act signed by President Clinton makes it easier than ever to vote. All the following provisions accomplish the goals of the act EXCEPT
    (A) it provides for automatic registration of eligible citizens when they fill out an application for a driver's license.
    (B) it requires that states periodically review their voter lists for accuracy.
    (C) it authorizes $50 million to help cover implementation costs.
    (D) it purges people from voter rolls because they didn't vote in the previous election.
    (E) it provides for automatic registration of eligible voters as a result of license renewal.

14. In a presidential election, if no candidate receives an electoral college majority,
    (A) the winner of the popular election becomes president.
    (B) a run-off election is held with a new slate of electors.
    (C) the election is thrown into the House of Representatives.
    (D) the election is thrown into the full Congress.
    (E) the Supreme Court determines the winner.

15. It has been shown in recent elections that during times of severe economic troubles, the electorate
    (A) do not vote as often as they do during good times.
    (B) tend to vote out incumbents.
    (C) tend to vote incumbents back in.
    (D) are more likely to vote in congressional races than the presidential race.
    (E) register in large numbers.

16. Which of the following has had a positive impact on the youth vote?
    I. large numbers of youth involved with the religious right
    II. Jesse Jackson's Rainbow Coalition efforts
    III. MTV's "Rock the Vote" efforts
    IV. Republican support of the Motor Voter Bill

    (A) I only
    (B) III only
    (C) III and IV only
    (D) I, II, and III only
    (E) II and III only

17. Which of the following statements is true about the effect of ethnic groups on voter choice during the presidential elections of the 1990s?
    (A) Catholics tend to vote Republican.
    (B) Northern Protestants tend to vote Democratic.
    (C) Jews tend to vote Democratic.
    (D) The religious right tends to vote Democratic.
    (E) Hispanics tend to vote Republican.

18. The validity of a poll is best determined by
    (A) a sample that represents more than half of the people in a population polled.
    (B) a large gap between the time the poll is taken and the time the results are released.
    (C) partisan groups taking and reporting the results of the poll.
    (D) complex questions to be answered by the people being polled.
    (E) a sampling error of those polled under 5 percent.

19. Which of the following represents what media watchers would portray as the benchmark of investigative journalism?
    (A) tabloid papers reporting accusations by Gennifer Flowers
    (B) magazine articles using anonymous sources accusing President Clinton of a secret rendezvous with Paula Jones
    (C) the media stalking Gary Hart looking for evidence of indiscretion during his 1984 presidential campaign
    (D) the efforts of Woodward and Bernstein in uncovering the Watergate cover-up
    (E) the press going after personal indiscretions of cabinet nominee John Tower

20. Which of the following represents an effect of the passage of the Freedom of Information Act?
    (A) More meetings were opened to the public.
    (B) It became more difficult to obtain documents from governmental organizations.
    (C) Government operations were held in executive session.
    (D) Stricter regulations governed the shredding of documents.
    (E) The government was forced to open up top secret military documents.

Answers to Multiple-Choice Questions

1. **(D)** Type of Question: Solution to a problem
   The question asks you to identify the characteristics of voting behavior. Through the process of elimination, you should be able to pick choice D as the only factually correct answer. The other choices provide reverse solutions. Young people turn out less than any other age group, Northerners vote more than Southerners, minorities generally support Democrats, and women usually vote for Democrats.
2. **(A)** Type of Question: Identification and analysis
   This is a factually based question that requires you to know something about voting patterns. If you thought of the fact that many African-Americans are still not registered in the South, you would have chosen A as the correct answer.

3. **(C)** Type of Question: Definitional
If you knew the definition of political efficacy, those groups who are most aware who they are voting for and why they are voting, it would stand to reason that the upper class would best represent that group.
4. **(E)** Type of Question: Definitional
If the electorate speaks loudly and clearly for a candidate or a party, the election is interpreted as a mandate or direction for change. The other choices reflect different characteristics of parties, candidates, and voters.
5. **(D)** Type of Question: Cause and effect relationships/definitional
To answer this question, you must know the definition and implications of media-centered politics. Once you determine that the phrase relates to how the media dominates political campaigns through its coverage of the candidates, you should be able to reach the conclusion that the electorate has become disillusioned with the election process and, therefore, there has been a decrease in voter turnout since 1960. Choice A is the opposite of the correct answer. Choices B and C contradict the impact of media-centered politics. Choice E is also incorrect as in-depth analysis of the issues has decreased over time.
6. **(A)** Type of Question: Sequencing a series of events
Using the Ronald Reagan model, the question asks you to identify how a president controls news coverage. Choice A gets to the heart of the solution, whereas the other choices would hurt the management of news by a president.
7. **(D)** Type of Question: Solution to a problem
If you think of specific examples, you will find it easiest to select D as the correct choice. A criticism of the media is that it investigates the personal lives of politicians rather than the serious issues of the campaign. The other choices have been talked about by media critics as being negative characteristics of the media.
8. **(C)** Type of Question: Generalization
If you have ever heard the phrase "mass media" you know the correct answer to this question. College educated, the upper class, and people looking for in-depth analysis are groups that represent a minority audience. Even though the lower class may be large in number, they also represent only a segment of the society.
9. **(B)** Type of Question: Identification and analysis
If you know the provisions of the Fifteenth, Seventeenth, and Nineteenth Amendments, you would know they all deal with suffrage. Choice A is part of the Reserved Power clause of the Tenth Amendment. Choice B was ruled unconstitutional by the Supreme Court.
10. **(E)** Type of Question: Generalization
Gender and class are reasons why people vote, as well as religion and the process of political socialization. Surveys have no direct impact on why people vote.
11. **(A)** Type of Question: Solution to a problem
Choices B, C, D, and E are all incorrect conclusions relating to the electoral history of the past forty years. Voter turnout has been on the decline; third parties have never won significant electoral victories;

campaign finance reform has had an impact on presidential races, and congressional incumbents win the vast majority of the time. Even though there has not been a consistent increase in actual voter turnout, there has been an increase in the opportunity to register and vote.

12. **(B)** Type of Question: Generalization
Young people, even with greater opportunity to register and vote, still lag behind all other age groups. Perhaps one of the reasons is because many young people fail to obtain absentee ballots when they go to college.

13. **(D)** Type of Question: Cause and effect relationships
If you did not know the specific provisions of the Motor Voter Act, you should be able to guess that states can't purge names if people don't vote in just one election. If there is a process, odds are that it would take a number of elections before individuals would have to reregister.

14. **(C)** Type of Question: Cause and effect relationships
You must know the way the electoral college works (if a candidate does not receive a majority of electoral votes, the election is thrown into the House of Representatives) to answer this question. If you know of any historical examples, you could probably eliminate the other choices. It is interesting to note that the other choices may have seemed correct because the electoral college has been criticized.

15. **(B)** Type of Question: Sequencing a series of events
If you think of the Depression or Clinton's victory in 1992, you should be able to reach the conclusion that incumbents are voted out during times of economic hardship.

16. **(E)** Type of Question: Cause and effect relationships
The obvious answer is B. However, Jesse Jackson's efforts also had a significant impact on registering African-American youth in the inner city. There may be youth involvement with the religious right, but there has not been any evidence of increased voter involvement as a result of it.

17. **(C)** Type of Question: Identification and analysis
Traditionally, the one ethnic group most closely identified with a political party has been Jews. Ever since the Great Depression, Democrats could count on Jewish voters for support. Catholics tend to vote Democratic because of the support given to them when they were immigrants. Northern Protestants tend to support Republicans. The religious right have supported the Republican Party. Hispanics, with the exception of those living in Florida, tend to vote Democratic

18. **(E)** Type of Question: Cause and effect relationships
Polling has been used more and more to determine attitudes and trends. If you do not construct a poll with a sampling error of under 5 percent, you risk the opportunity of reaching invalid conclusions.

19. **(D)** Type of Question: Comparing and contrasting concepts and events
You are being asked to compare and contrast and evaluate the nature of investigative journalism. Each of the examples given has some merit to the way the media acted. However, Woodward and Bernstein have been given the credit for cracking Watergate, the mother of investigative journalism. Thus, that choice is the only correct answer. The other choices all focus on the personal lives of the politicians.

20. **(A)** Type of Question: Identification and analysis
In this relatively simple question, you must know the provisions and intent of sunshine laws. The impact has been to open up governmental meetings based on the public. Even though the government has been forced to release documents, top secret national security documents have been protected. Certain government operations are still able to be held in secret session, but there has to be a legal reason for that action to take place.

SECTION 2: FREE-RESPONSE ESSAY (Both choices are answered for illustrative purposes)

Party preference, polls, and the media all have had a significant impact on recent presidential elections. Explain the relationship that issues, party preference, polls, and the media have had on the outcome of one the following presidential elections:

1. The election of 1996.
2. The election of 2000.

Sample Student Response

Voting has been a constitutional right since the ratification of the United States Constitution. Although there have been many limits on these voting privileges in the past, many constitutional amendments have been passed to ensure universal suffrage. In addition, political socialization contributed to the factors that determine the outcome of elections. Voters tend to exhibit patterns that are influenced by demographics, socioeconomic status, party identification, religious background, and of course the media. These patterns vary from election to election. Polls, along with commercials, have influenced public opinion in many elections.

The 1996 presidential election was a battle between incumbent President Bill Clinton and his Republican challenger, the former Senate Majority Leader and veteran of presidential campaigns Bob Dole. Regardless of the outcome, it would be the first time a Democratic president was reelected for a second term since Franklin Roosevelt. It would also be the first time a Senate Majority Leader was elected to the presidency. (Lyndon Johnson was a Democratic Majority Leader when he was selected to run with John Kennedy in 1960).

The race was interesting because the issues were established even before Dole was officially nominated. Because Clinton had no organized opposition within the Democratic Party, he and his key campaign strategist Dick Morris devised a plan to air political commercials even before Clinton officially declared his intention to run again and prior to the outcome of the Republican primaries. This decision coupled with Clinton's positioning himself away from the Republican Party's unpopular stands related to the shutdown of the federal government in 1995 and 1996 and his own party's traditional liberal policies (a policy called triangulation) gave him a lead, which was never relinquished throughout the entire campaign.

Once Dole became the official nominee for the Republicans, the issues became finalized. Clinton developed a theme of "building a bridge to the 21st century" protecting "Medicare, Medicaid, the environment and education." In a constant mantra that I call E-squared, M-squared, Clinton repeated this message in political ads, at rallies, and during the debates. He was focused and stayed on message. Dole, on the other hand, never developed a message that stayed on target. The heart of his campaign was a 15 percent across the board tax cut. However, when the proposal fell flat with the electorate, Dole then switched to attacking Clinton on being soft on drugs and attacked Clinton on character and ethical issues, raising the Whitewater scandal and revelations about campaign finance abuses. The public responded to these issues, but they fell short of giving Senator Dole the momentum to win.

More than any recent presidential election, polls and the media have had a significant impact on the outcome. Both parties hired key political consultants to conduct focus polls to help determine what positions on issues would strike a positive chord with the electorate. Daily tracking polls kept both the candidates and the public aware of the fact that Clinton was maintaining a consistent double-digit lead throughout the campaign. The media played its role of looking for the sound bite or photo op rather than closely scrutinizing the issues. One example of this was when Senator Dole made the statement on the *Today* show that he didn't believe tobacco was addictive. The media replayed the interview countless times, and it then became an issue for Clinton. The debates, another media event, solidified Clinton's position, and the outcome of the election reflected Clinton's traditional strength within his Democratic base and an increased advantage among women, Catholics, Hispanics, and young voters.

The first campaign for the presidency in the new century resulted in an election that was disputed for five weeks. It was resolved by the United States Supreme Court, in a decision that indirectly gave victory to Governor George W. Bush of Texas, the son of a former president. By defeating Vice President Al Gore, Bush became the fourth president in American history to lose the popular vote while winning the electoral vote.

Florida's 25 electoral votes, which would have given Bush an immediate victory, were contested when, on election night, Bush won the state by a margin of just over 1000 votes. After a mandatory recount reduced Bush's margin to 538 votes, Gore waged a legal battle to get a hand recount of disputed ballots. The Florida Supreme Court ordered a recount to get underway, but, on an appeal from Bush, the United States Supreme Court ruled the recount violated the equal protection clause of the United States Constitution by a 5–4 vote and ordered an end to the hand recounts. Gore, who had won the popular vote by over 500,000 votes, conceded the election, but his supporters continued to have lingering doubts about the outcome of the election. After Florida's results were certified, Bush won a razor-thin victory in the electoral college: 271 votes for Bush and 268 votes for Gore. Third-party candidate, consumer advocate Ralph Nader, running on the Green Party ticket, took away enough Democratic votes from Gore to ultimately cost Gore the electoral votes of several states. Bush's running mate, former Secretary of Defense Richard Cheney became the new vice president. Gore's vice presidential hopeful, Joseph Lieberman, the first Jewish candidate for that office, returned to the United States Senate after his defeat.

The race for president reflected the fact that the country had enjoyed eight years of relative peace and unprecedented prosperity. According to a study by Harvard University, entitled "The Vanishing Voter," the electorate was turned off to the campaign until the closing days. Just over 50 percent of all eligible voters cast ballots on election day, a slightly higher percentage than that of the 1996 election. Both candidates agreed on the broad issues facing the country—education, healthcare, Social Security reform, tax cuts, and a strong national defense—but they differed in their approach to handling these matters. Polls forecasted a tight race, with most showing Bush with a very narrow lead in the final days. Nobody however, predicted that Bush would lose the popular vote while winning the electoral vote. The media was criticized on election night for announcing exit poll results before the polls in Florida were closed. And three times, based on inaccurate exit poll data, the networks had to change their predicted results of the vote in Florida. Critics suggested that these mistakes could have influenced the final outcome of the election, and the media pledged to use exit polling differently in the next election. During the confusion following the election, "the Battle for the White House" dominated the news. Ironically, the country paid closer attention to this phase of the election than to the campaign itself. Bush characterized himself throughout the campaign as "a uniter, not a divider." The results made this slogan a real challenge for the newly elected president.

Evaluation of Free-Response Sample Essay

1. Did the essay have an opening statement with appropriate definitions?
2. Did the thesis statement provide a clear explanation of the direction the essay was going?
3. Did the essay provide supporting evidence, data, and facts?

1. The thesis statement established the parameters of the essay. The writer began with a short discussion of the basis of suffrage—a factor that influences elections. Then other factors relating to political socialization and demographics were added to the issues the essay raised—policy, party identification, and the role of the media.

2. The reader had a clear idea that each of the elections would stress some aspect of the thesis. The election of 1996 stressed party identification, negative campaigning, and the role of the media. The election of 2000 stressed the role of the media.

3. Each of the elections focused on specific examples to support the thesis. Themes of the 1996 and 2000 campaigns, the use of negative advertising, and the significance of the results completed the supporting evidence of the essay. The essay reinforced the thesis and echoed the themes raised in the two elections. Issues such as party dealignment, ticket splitting, and the impact of the media supported the thesis and the examples given in the body of the essay.

SECTION 2: DATA-BASED FREE-RESPONSE ESSAY

Using the illustration and your knowledge of United States politics and government, answer the following question:

1994 REPUBLICAN AD

Discuss the political implications of the illustration shown above by giving four examples of how voter preference, issues, parties, and candidates influenced the 1994 mid-term election.

Sample Student Response

The picture is pointing out the consequences of the fact that voters in 1994 were unhappy with the performance of Democratic members of Congress. They wanted change. That is why the headline "Under New Management" is superimposed over the Capitol. Because Congress had a Democratic majority in both houses, the sign represents the fact that Democrats were no longer in power. The picture also suggests that the vote reflects a revolution of sorts. The Republican takeover has revolutionary consequences, especially if the Contract with America that the Republicans supported is carried out. The voters' discontent is aimed particularly at the Democratic incumbent. Implicit in the headline is the fact that the new Republican majority will also change the way government operates by implementing the provisions of the Contract with America.

Characteristics that describe the 1994 voter preference include:

- Voters are sick of government and want change. The Republicans represent the party that will reduce the size and function of the federal government.
- The voters feel that the Democrats are not getting the job done. Even though there were legislative victories, the fight over health reform and the crime bill convinced the electorate that the Democrats could not carry out their '92 promises.
- Therefore, the voters rejected only Democratic incumbents and, in a majority of open seats, elected Republicans, which resulted in a turnover in both houses of Congress.
- The Republicans used their Contract with America as the focal point of the campaign. Even though many voters were not aware of the specifics,

they felt that the Republicans would do better in such areas as taxes, crime, welfare, and healthcare. Even though the economy had been improving under the Clinton administration, for the most part many voters believed that the Republicans would in the end do a better job. The Contract was a set of specific proposals which gave the American people an agenda of items that would be voted on during the first 100 days of the new Congress. The strategy was simple: nationalize the election and make it a referendum on Clinton. The following provisions from the Contract with America are provided to give additional information related to the 1994 mid-term election. Here is a summary of the Contract with America and an analysis of whether the Republicans succeeded in getting these proposals signed into law:

1. THE FISCAL RESPONSIBILITY ACT
   Included a balanced budget amendment to the Constitution and a line item veto power for the president. By 1997, both parties agreed in principle to a balanced budget by the year 2002 and a line item veto was passed into law.
2. THE TAKING BACK OUR STREETS ACT
   A series of laws including stronger sentencing procedures, exclusionary rule exemptions, more effective death penalty provisions, and cuts in social spending from the Democrats' crime bill. It never was passed as a comprehensive bill, although certain provisions became law as riders to other laws.
3. THE PERSONAL RESPONSIBILITY ACT
   As one of the major provisions of the Contract, it became known as the Welfare Reform Act of 1996 and incorporated many of the original parts of the Contract—block grants to the states and a workfare provision.
4. THE FAMILY REINFORCEMENT ACT
   Several laws attempting to strengthen the morals of the American family including antipornography laws, education vouchers, and tax incentives for adoption—never enacted into law.
5. THE AMERICAN DREAM RESTORATION ACT
   A $500 per child tax credit and other middle class tax relief. This became part of the 1997 budget deal.
6. THE NATIONAL SECURITY RESTORATION ACT
   No United States troops under UN command—never enacted into law.
7. THE SENIOR CITIZENS FAIRNESS ACT
   Raise the Social Security earnings limit and repeal the 1993 social security tax hikes. The earnings limit was repealed.
8. THE JOB CREATION AND WAGE ENHANCEMENT ACT
   Lowering the capital gains tax and providing other business incentives. A lower capital gains tax was part of the 1997 budget deal.
9. THE COMMON SENSE LEGAL REFORM ACT
   "Loser pays" laws, reasonable limits on punitive damages, and reform of product liability laws. Passed by both houses, but vetoed by President Clinton.
10. THE CITIZEN LEGISLATURE ACT
    A self-imposed term limits vote limiting the number of terms that a representative can serve. Never passed the House as a constitutional amendment.

Evaluation of Stimulus-Based Free-Response Sample Essay

1. Was the point of the illustration clearly presented, giving an adequate description of the picture that illustrates its message?
2. In the second part, were there specific examples given that go beyond the description of the illustration?

1. The major points raised by the illustration—that of voter anger, bordering on revolution—were discussed by the writer. The key hint, the headline "Under New Management" also suggested a path that may lead to a new American Revolution. The writer also indicated that voter anger was aimed specifically at the Democratic candidates and made the comparison that the Contract with America was the result of the announcement of a management change.

2. Notice how, in the second part, the writer lists the response to the question. Using this technique makes sure you cover each of the areas—voter preference, issues, parties, and candidates. Thus the writer focuses the answer on characteristics of voter preference, the nature of party identification with the possibility of this election marking the beginning of political realignment, especially in the South, and how the election was a repudiation of the Democrats.

CHAPTER **14** Special Interest Groups—Lobbyists and PACs

Chapter Overview

Special interest groups including their lobbyists and political action committees have been one of the most criticized components of the political process. This chapter will explore the reasons why special interest groups exist, how they developed, and the roles they play in the political process.

We will also apply the group theory that we introduced in Chapter 1 illustrating how special interests operate in the context of a pluralist, hyperpluralist, and elite society. These interest groups all reflect specialized characteristics and can be classified by categories such as economic, occupational, environmental, and minority. The main role of these groups is to influence public policy and the policymakers through lobbying efforts, the formation of political action committees, and legal action.

We will look at the successes and failures of these groups through case studies. When you look at the money spent in the efforts to get senators and representatives to vote for a particular bill and the perks given to them as well as the contributions made to reelection committees, you will understand why citizen groups are calling for major legislative reforms. We will conclude the chapter by taking a look at these reform efforts and evaluating future trends.

Characteristics of Special Interest Groups

Interest groups have common traits and functions and have the common goal of attracting a membership that is interested in affecting public policymaking.

For the purposes of establishing a common understanding, the definition of an interest group is a linkage group that is a public or private organization, affiliation, or committee that has as its goal the dissemination of its membership's viewpoint. The result will be persuading public policymakers to respond to the group's perspective. The interest groups' goals are carried out by special interests in the form of lobbyists and political action committees. They can take on an affiliation based on specialized memberships such as unions, associations, leagues, and committees. The chart on the next page illustrates how special interest groups are formed.

KEY TERMS

- Campaign finance reform
- Elite and class theory
- Faction
- Freedom of Information Act
- Hard money
- Hyperpluralism
- Interest group
- Lobbyists
- Political action committees (PACs)
- Soft money

THE FORMATION OF SPECIAL INTEREST GROUPS

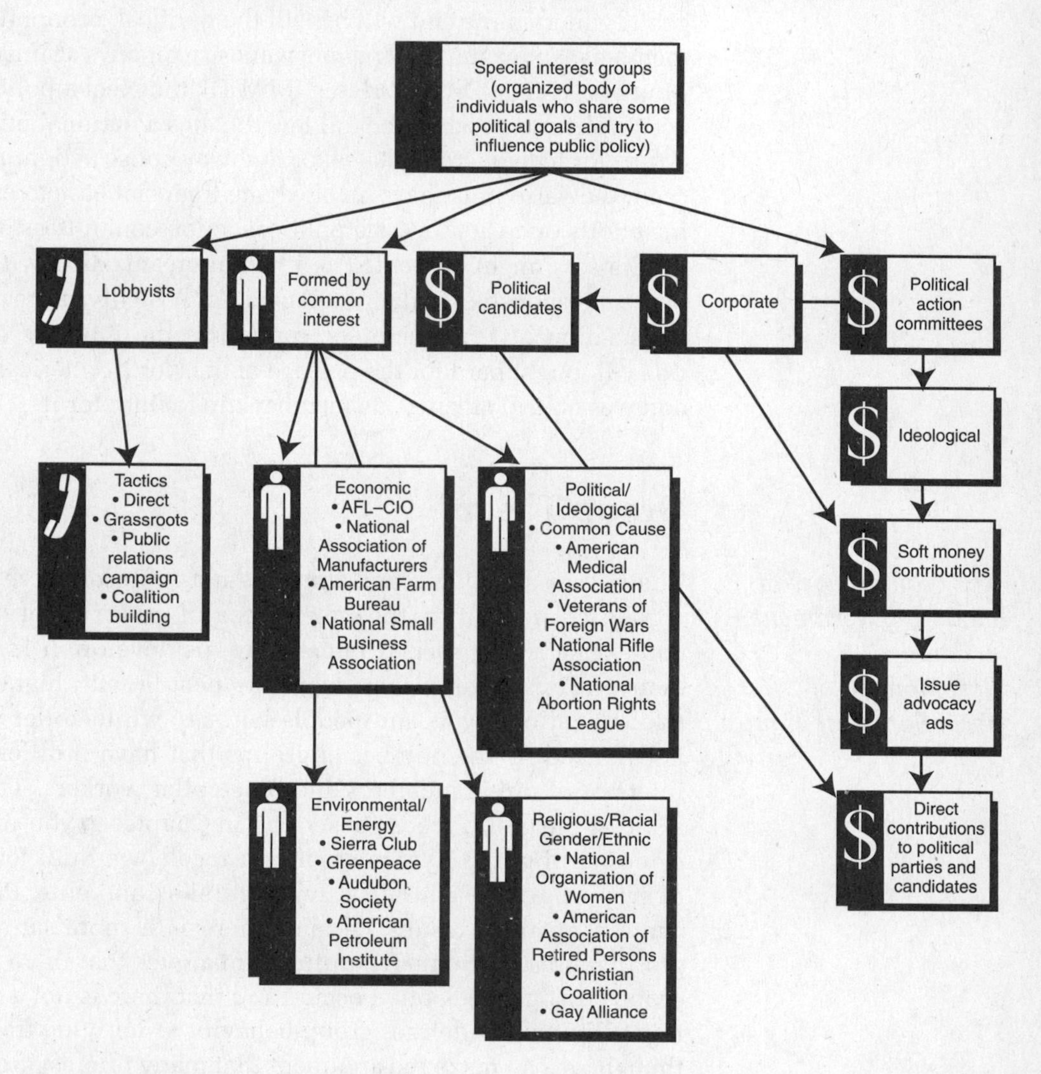

Interest groups and political parties are both characterized by group identification and group affiliation. However, they differ in the fact that interest groups do not nominate candidates for political office. Their function is to influence officeholders rather than end up as elected officials, and they are responsible only to a very narrow constituency. Interest groups can also make up their own by-laws, which govern the manner in which they run their organizations. Because the major function of these groups is the advocacy or opposition of specific public policies, they can attract members from a large geographic area. The only criterion is that the person joining the group has the same interests and attitudes toward the goals of the organization. We should add that in trying to persuade elected officials to a group's position, these groups also provide a great deal of specialized information to legislators. Group advocates also claim they provide an additional check and balance to the legislative system. Critics of the growth of specialized groups claim they are partly responsible for gridlock in government. In addition, critics point to the manner in which groups gain access to elected officials as a tradeoff for political contributions.

Once a specialized group is formed, it also has internal functions such as attracting and keeping a viable membership. Groups accomplish this by making promises to their membership that they will be able to succeed in their political goals, which in the end will benefit the political, economic, or social needs of the members. For example, if people want stricter laws against drunk driving and join Mothers Against Drunk Driving (MADD), they feel a political and social sense of accomplishment when federal law dictates a national minimum drinking age in return for federal aid to states for highway construction. For these groups to succeed, they also must have an adequate financial base to establish effective lobbying efforts or create separate political action committees. Dues may be charged or fundraisers might be held. The internal organization will certainly have elected officers responsible to their membership. A highly successful group, the National Association of Manufacturers, represents the interests of over 13,000 corporations. It fought hard for the passage of the North American Free Trade Agreement and was able to organize its membership to fight for it.

Group Theory

The group theory of modern government encourages the development of special interest groups.

The nature of group membership is not representative of the population as a whole; consequently, the importance of group theory will help explain the context in which special interest groups develop. It is interesting to note that many groups have as their members people with higher than average income and education levels and people who are white-collar workers. However, this is balanced by the number of groups that have proliferated and represent the interests of union members and blue-collar workers. Therefore, when we look again at the group theory described in Chapter 1, you will have a better understanding of group dynamics. If you recall, we outlined three potential kinds of group activity—pluralist, hyperpluralist, and elite. Pluralism suggests that a centrist position results because there is a more far-reaching and balancing group representation. Hyperpluralism argues that there are so many competing groups that gridlock often occurs and that there is not a clear government direction. Elite theory defines group behavior as deriving from an upper class. Even though we can make the argument that many interest groups are elitist in nature because of the socioeconomic characteristics of their membership and that there are so many competing groups that can cause gridlock in government, these groups often compete with each other in a manner consistent with pluralism.

Let's support this assertion by briefly describing the characteristics of each of these theories as they relate to special interest groups. Pluralists maintain that

- competing groups are healthy because they provide a political connection to government, offering government officials a choice;
- the competition often clarifies information and prevents any one group from dominating government; and
- competing groups have each developed political strategies to achieve their goals and that eventually the resources of one group will independently affect governmental policy.

Critics of hyperpluralist group theory feel that

- competing groups become so powerful that government tries to assuage each of them;

- The more groups that exist, the greater potential for each group to find a government agency that will respond to them (this results in the formation of numerous iron triangle arrangements, which was discussed in Chapter 10, The Bureaucracy); and
- The process results in governmental gridlock.

Finally, critics of elitist group theory maintain that

- power is concentrated by the largest and richest organizations;
- the unequal nature of the power of groups negates the fact that groups are proliferating; and
- ultimately money talks, and these large groups will have the most influence.

History

The fear and deep suspicion of special interest groups goes back to the early days of the republic.

As James Madison wrote in Federalist No. 10, "By a faction, I understand a number of citizens, whether amounting to a majority or minority of the whole, who are united . . . by some common . . . interest, adverse to the rights of other citizens, or to the permanent and aggregate interests of the community." He even went as far as saying that "the regulation of these various and interfering interests forms of the principal task of modern Legislation. . . ." Madison's view was that the development of factions was an inevitable feature of society. Even though he was fearful of their potential, he did not make the argument that they should be abolished. He felt that the separation of powers of the three branches of government and the division of government between the national and local governments would, in the end, provide enough government protection and regulation of these interests. In addition the formation of political parties became an additional balance to the formation of private interest groups, many of which were economically based during the early stages of our country's existence.

One of the first examples of why Madison felt factions could be potentially dangerous was Shays' Rebellion. Daniel Shays organized a group of unhappy farmers attempting to help them forestall foreclosure of their land. Frustrated in their attempts to get government relief, they took up arms. Shays was arrested, and the revolt failed.

Once the Constitution was ratified and the Bill of Rights was added, the First Amendment seemed to give legitimacy to the formation of special interest groups. Their right of free assembly, free speech, and free press and the right to petition seemed to create a validity for group formation. Taken together, groups felt they could associate with each other, free from government interference, disseminate the issues that they believe in to their membership and to government officials, and attempt to influence the course of public policy.

Even French philosopher Alexis de Tocqueville saw how factions existed in American society. He wrote in his book *Democracy in America*, "In no country in the world has the principle of association been more successfully used . . . than in America." Historically, interest groups such as suffragettes, prohibitionists, and labor unions had a profound impact on influencing governmental policies. The right to vote for women came after many decades of political pressure applied by Susan B. Anthony. The Women's Christian Temperance Union as well as other prohibition groups spurred Congress into passing the Eighteenth Amendment outlawing alcohol. The formation of the AFL and CIO and their eventual merger stimulated such measures as child labor laws, minimum wage legislation, and health insurance. Civil rights remained on the political agenda as a result of the efforts of the National Association for the Advancement of Colored People (NAACP). Its call for a march on Washington in 1963 helped the passage of civil rights legislation in 1964.

Mode of Operation

Interest groups are categorized according to their function. They all have one common goal—to make their viewpoints part of the political agenda.

As interest groups have grown in number and size, they have also become specialized, representing various concerns. The following represents a cross section of the different kinds of interest groups that have organizations:

- Economic and occupational including business and labor groups, trade associations, agricultural groups and professional associations
  - National Association of Manufacturers—14,000 members
  - Airline Pilots Association—40,000 members
  - AFL-CIO—13.2 million members
  - American Farm Bureau—2.5 million members
  - United States Chamber of Commerce—200,000 members
  - National Small Business Association—600,000 members
- Energy and environmental
  - American Petroleum Institute—52,000 members
  - Sierra Club—550,000 members
- Religious, racial, gender, and ethnic
  - National Organization for Women—266,000 members
  - National Association for the Advancement of Colored People—500,000 members
  - National Urban League—50,000 members
- Political, professional, and ideological
  - Common Cause—225,000 members
  - American Medical Association—270,000 members
  - Veterans of Foreign Wars—2.1 million members
  - National Rifle Association—2.8 million members

The majority of these groups have headquarters in Washington, D.C., and they all have operating budgets and staffs. Most have hired lobbyists who make contacts with senators and representatives as well as the executive branch. Many have separate political action committees with well-financed budgets. They place their views on the political agenda through the following techniques:

- testifying at congressional hearings,
- contacting government officials directly,
- providing officials with research information,
- sending letters to their own membership,
- trying to influence the press to present their point of view,
- suggesting and supporting legislation,
- hiring lobbyists,

- giving senators and representatives feedback from their constituents,
- making contributions through PACs to campaign committees,
- taking congressmen on trips or to dinner,
- endorsing candidates, and
- working on the campaigns.

All these groups and techniques have the potential of helping the legislative process because they do help inform office holders. They also provide elected officials with a viable strategy and a base of support. These groups also have the expertise to give elected officials an additional slant to a problem. Unlike other constituents who have hidden agendas, special interest groups place their goals on the table, up front.

Lobbyists

Lobbyists provide interest groups with specialists to advance their causes and influence policymaking.

Lobbyists are the primary instruments for fostering a special interest group's goals to the policymakers. The term comes from people who literally wait in the lobbies of legislative bodies for senators and representatives to go to and from the floor of the legislatures. Manuals have been published for lobbyists outlining the best ways for a lobbyist to be successful. Some of the techniques include

- knowing as much as you can about the political situation and the people involved,
- understanding the goals of the group and determining who you want to see,
- being truthful in the way you deal with people,
- working closely with the interest group that hired you,
- keeping the people you are trying to convince in your corner by telling them of the support they will receive if they agree to the position of the group, and
- following up on all meetings, making sure the results you want do not change.

Recently, the image of lobbyists has taken a blow because they have attracted negative publicity. Former government officials who become lobbyists have been criticized because they can take unfair advantage of contacts they developed when they were in office. An additional accusation has been made against government appointees who were former lobbyists but still maintain a relationship with the special interest group they worked for before getting the position.

On the other hand, lobbyists also play a positive role as specialists. When tax reform was being considered in the 1980s and 1990s, lobbyists provided an expertise to congressional committees considering the bills. Sometimes lobby coalitions are formed when extremely important and far-reaching legislation, such as healthcare reform, is under consideration. Lobbyists may also take legal action on behalf of the interest group. They file friend of the court (amicus curiae) briefs or may be part of a class action suit. Cases such as *Brown v Board of Education*, *Roe v Wade*, and *Regents of California v Bakke* attracted a great deal of attention and numerous third-party briefs. Lobbyists may also provide ratings of officials. Groups such as Americans for Democratic Action and the American Conservative Union give annual ratings based on their political ideologies.

Lobbyists and special interest groups also use the media to push their viewpoint. During the energy crisis, lobbyists for Mobil ran ads that resembled columns, explaining its point of view.

Political Action Committees (PACs)

Political action committees (PACs) raise money from special interest constituents and donate hard and soft money to political parties and candidates.

When an interest group gets involved directly in the political process, it forms separate political action committees. These PACs raise money from the special interest group's constituents and make contributions to political campaigns on behalf of the special interest. The amount of money contributed over the last few elections has been staggering. PACs such as the National Rifle Association (NRA), labor's "Vote Cope," American Bankers Association (BANKPAC), PAC of the National Automobile Dealers Association, Black Political Action Committees (BlackPAC), and Council for a Strong National Defense have made major contributions to political campaigns and have had a tremendous impact on local and national elections. According to the Federal Election Commission, from January 1, 1993, to June 30, 1994, the top PAC contributors were the American Federation of State, County, & Municipal Employees with $1.55 million.

The next five largest contributors were the corporate United Parcel Service PAC at $1.4 million, the Teamsters' Democratic Republican Independent Voter Education (DRIVE) Committee at $1.2 million, the Machinists Non-Partisan Political League at $1.2 million, and PACs for two trade organizations, the Association of Trial Lawyers of America at $1.2 million, and the American Medical Association at $1.1 million.

The remaining four PACs included more labor PACs, each giving about $1 million: the International Brotherhood of Electrical Workers Committee on Political Education, Carpenters Legislative Improvement Committee, United Brotherhood of Carpenters & Joiners, the United Auto Workers Voluntary Community Action Program, and the National Education Association PAC.

The amount of contributions to congressional campaigns by PACs has skyrocketed from 1981 to 1994. From 1981 to 1982 $83.7 million was contributed to candidates for the House and Senate as compared to $179.6 million contributed to candidates running for the House and Senate in 1993–94. What is more astonishing is that, even when senators and representatives were not facing any opposition, they received hundreds of thousands of dollars. For example, Representative Charles Rangel of New York was given more than $300,000 from PACs for an election campaign in 1988 when nobody was running against him. In 1996 the FBI investigated the accusation that foreign money was involved in political donations. Their investigation revealed that China tried to influence local, congressional, and presidential elections.

According to the Federal Election Commission, as of June 30, 2000, the top PAC contributors to candidates were:

1. The Association of Trial Lawyers of America Political Action Committee—$2,271,500
2. The International Brotherhood of Electrical Workers Committee on Political Education—$1,963,605

3. The American Federation of State County and Municipal Employees—$1,904,794
4. The Democrat Republican Independent Voter Education—$1,816,450
5. The Realtors Political Action Committee—$1,612,628
6. The Machinists Non-Partisan Political League—$1,563,863
7. The Dealers Election Action Committee of the National Automobile Dealers Association—$1,473,450
8. The Build Political Action Committee of the National Association of Home Builders—$1,358,599
9. The United Auto Workers (UAW)— $1,348,800
10. The United Parcel Service Political Action Committee—$1,276,420

Congressional candidates raised millions of dollars in the 1996 and 1998 mid-term elections. However, a study conducted by the Federal Election Commission indicates that there has been a recent downward trend in campaign fundraising and spending. For example, in 1997–98, candidates for House seats raised $494 million and spent $452 million, down from the $505 million raised and $478 million spent in 1995–96. Funds raised and spent by Senate candidates reflected a similar trend. Senate candidates raised over $285 million during the 1997–98 cycle and spent $287 million, spending almost the same amount in the previous election.

Reform

Calls for campaign finance reform and regulation of interest groups stem from the money and perks they give legislators and candidates for elective office.

Special interest public interest groups such as Common Cause and the Center for Independence in Politics have been in the forefront of calling for reform and regulation of interest groups, lobbyists, and PACs. They maintain that these groups are dominated by the rich and ignore the needs of the poor. They accuse big business interests of dominating special interests and give examples of the excessive amounts of money donated and the questionable trips and other perks given to officials. These complaints must be balanced by the legitimate right of special interest groups to exist and do their business. They are constitutionally protected, and as long as they don't break the law, they have the right to pursue their interests. The vast majority of recognized groups do not cross the line, and there are relatively few documented cases of outright corruption.

Federal law in this area goes back to the progressive era when Congress passed legislation regulating contributions to campaigns. In 1925 the Federal Corrupt Practices Act, requiring financial disclosure of political contributions to federal elections, was passed. The Federal Regulation of Lobbying Act in 1946 provided for the registration of lobbyists and information regarding their background, salaries, and expenses. It also directed lobbyists to provide Congress with written reports about their activities. Special interest groups challenged the law. The Supreme Court ruled that the act applied only to those lobbyists who directly contacted elected officials. Indirect lobbying, therefore, was not covered. The net result was that only a small percentage of lobbyists registered. Individual states passed their own laws regulating contributions to state elections. The biggest changes to occur took place in 1971 and 1974 when the Federal Election Campaign Acts were passed. They were covered in Chapter 12, but to refresh your memory, they placed limitations on the extent of contributions to presidential campaigns. The act legitimized and increased the number of interest groups because the law authorized open participation by these groups allowing them to set up "separated segregated funds." To further complicate matters the Supreme Court ruled in 1976 in *Buckley v Valeo* that it was unconstitutional to place limitations on individuals making donations in presidential elections because matching public financing was involved. It extended this ruling to PACs in 1985, thus giving these committees much greater latitude. President Clinton made congressional campaign spending and PAC gifts a major campaign issue in 1992. The House passed its version of an act providing for some public financing of congressional campaigns, whereas the Senate version induced limits on campaign spending by taxing candidates who failed to do so. Both versions overhauled disclosure requirements for lobbyists, and both sought to impose stricter rules on gifts, meals, entertainment, travel, and other benefits provided to senators and representatives. A conference committee worked out differences, but because of a Republican filibuster in the Senate, it failed to pass. After an historic campaign-type meeting in the summer of 1995 between President Clinton and Speaker of the House Newt Gingrich before a senior citizen group in New Hampshire, both men publicly shook hands and agreed to make campaign reform a priority. However, because of presidential politics, the issue was never followed through. And, ironically, one of the overriding characteristics of the 1996 campaign was the number of campaign finance abuses previously discussed. The issue of campaign finance reform was prominent in the 2000 campaign. Both Vice President Gore and Texas Governor George W. Bush pledged to support campaign finance reform. As a result of the McCain-Feingold Campaign Finance Law and the subsequent Supreme Court decision, special interest group political action committees (PACs) were prohibited from donating soft money to the national political parties and individual presidential candidates.

Public Awareness and Effectiveness

The success and failure of interest groups, lobbyists, and PACs to achieve their goals depends, to a large extent, on their public image and their ultimate ability to influence the outcome of public policy.

In order for an interest group to succeed, not only must a public awareness of the group's position take place but legislators must also accept the bill of sale presented to them. There is no doubt that the National Rifle Association's membership consists of a small percentage of the American public. Yet because of its image, for example, the "We are the NRA" commercials and its advocacy of the constitutional right to bear arms, the public is certainly aware of its stand, and polls indicate that many people support its position. Even with the issue of crime high on the national agenda, the NRA was still able to be part of a coalition that slowed down the passage of the Omnibus Crime Prevention Bill of 1994.

ONE OF THE AIMS OF THE NATIONAL RIFLE ASSOCIATION IS TO SUPPORT THE RIGHT TO BEAR ARMS

Let's use this bill as an example of how special interest groups attempt to use their influence. The National Rifle Association was founded in 1871, and it claims a membership of more than three million people. The association has a staff of more than 300 people and a budget well over $5 million, which is used to hire lobbyists, keep its membership informed of current activities through mailings, and establish an effective political action committee. It has a constituency that includes gun collectors, hunters, and the millions of people who feel guns are an acceptable hobby. Presidents Reagan, Bush, and Clinton all accepted the premise that hunting is a sport. To drive that point home, President Clinton even took a hunting trip in the middle of a debate over the Brady Bill. This law, which we spoke about earlier, had the support of James Brady and the formation of a new antigun lobby group, Handgun Control, but was opposed by the membership of the NRA. After numerous attempts over the years to pass it, public opinion prevailed, and the NRA took a major setback. Even before the final vote, the NRA was experiencing difficulty. Their membership dropped, gun-related violence was on the increase, and public support increased for gun control. There was even a new billboard constructed in Times Square in New York City that chronicled the number of gun deaths in the United States.

When the Omnibus Crime Prevention Bill of 1994 passed both houses of Congress, it included a ban on assault weapons. A Senate-House conference committee kept this provision in the compromise conference bill. The NRA opposed the ban and decided it would heavily lobby those senators and representatives who were given PAC financial support and those legislators who came from districts where guns were used for sport. Even though the NRA did not have enough votes to keep the provision out of the new bill, when it was reported to both houses, the NRA waged a successful campaign to initially prevent the House from being able to vote on it. As Representative Barbara Kennelly of Connecticut said after the procedural vote, which succeeded in tying up the bill, "The NRA did it, and don't tell me it wasn't about guns." A bipartisan group of legislators met after the vote and agreed on new provisions, keeping the gun ban in and strengthening the crime prevention aspects of the bill. The full House voted for the new bill and sent it to the Senate.

The Senate Republicans tried a similar tactic, offering a "point of order" that would have had the effect of killing the conference bill, because new amendments could have been added if the point passed. Because it was a special procedural vote, it needed 60 votes to defeat the motion. The Democrats, who had 54 votes, were able to convince six moderate Republicans to vote against the procedural rule. The $33.3 billion bill was finally passed. The new law provided for crime prevention programs such as midnight basketball, an increase of 100,000 policemen, programs for battered women, and a series of block grants enabling the states to use federal money to fight crime. The anticrime provisions of the new law included the ban on 19 different assault weapons, an extension of the death penalty to more than 50 federal offenses, new prison construction, the registration with law enforcement agencies of convicted sex offenders for federal offenses, and a three strikes you're out provision that would allow lifetime imprisonment for three-time violent and drug felons for federal crimes. The new Republican majority attempted to reverse some of the legislation early in 1995 but failed to get the president's support. In the fall of 2004, the assault weapons ban expired and, because of the presidential campaign, it was not renewed.

There are very few consistent winners or losers in the attempts by special interests to control the policy agenda. What is clear is that, when the system works, compromise and bipartisanship take place. What is also evident is that when the system breaks down, gridlock occurs, and special interests are called to task. Whether Madison was right in his concern about factions is debatable. They are an important part of the political process. They have major constituencies who rely on them as much as they rely on elected officials.

Chapter 14 Review

SECTION 1: MULTIPLE-CHOICE QUESTIONS

1. An interest group is most likely to have influence in Congress with which of the following situations?
(A) an issue that is narrow in scope and low in public visibility
(B) an issue that is part of the president's legislative package
(C) an issue that has been highly dramatized by the media
(D) an issue that engages legislators' deeply held convictions
(E) an issue that divides legislators along party lines

2. All the following statements concerning interest groups are true EXCEPT that they
(A) are policy experts.
(B) attempt to appeal to a broad spectrum of political interests.
(C) often run their own candidates for public office.
(D) lobby different levels of government.
(E) have specific policy goals.

3. Special interest groups do all of the following EXCEPT
(A) testify at congressional hearings.
(B) donate money to federal judges.
(C) endorse candidates for political office.
(D) try to influence the media.
(E) work on the campaigns of candidates.

4. All the following arguments are essential to the special interest theory of politics EXCEPT
   (A) interest groups compete with each other.
   (B) interest groups provide linkage between people and government.
   (C) one or two interest groups may dominate the debate over legislation.
   (D) interest groups encourage membership from diverse groups that may disagree with their goals.
   (E) interest groups have been protected by Supreme Court decisions.

5. Which of the following represents a major reason for the proliferation of special interests and lobby groups?
   (A) the reactive nature of interest groups and lobbyists to new issues
   (B) the increase in donations received by interest groups from their membership
   (C) the trust citizens have in the legislative process
   (D) the ability of lobbyists and special interest groups to get members from their own group to run for political office
   (E) the increasing demand for campaign reform

6. Which of the following officials do lobbyists most succeed with?
   (A) officials who have a basic philosophical affinity with the lobbyist
   (B) officials who have a basic philosophical difference with the lobbyist
   (C) officials who are neutral with the lobbyist's position
   (D) officials who have strong convictions
   (E) officials who are very conservative

7. A significant amount of PAC money most likely goes to
   (A) candidates challenging Republican seats.
   (B) candidates challenging Democratic seats.
   (C) candidates who are new to the political scene.
   (D) candidates who have wide philosophical differences with the PAC.
   (E) candidates who hold incumbent status.

8. Which of the following techniques would a lobbyist be likely to use to influence legislation in Congress?
   I. organize a demonstration in Washington just before a key House vote
   II. ensure that the corporation's political action committee makes donations to the campaigns of members of key committees
   III. meet informally with Senate aides over lunch or cocktails
   IV. bring influential constituents to Washington to discuss important policy matters with their representatives

   (A) I only
   (B) II only
   (C) II, III, and IV only
   (D) I, II, and III only
   (E) I, II, III, and IV

9. Which of the following statements represents the main function of special interest groups? They
   (A) eventually want to end up as political office holders.
   (B) nominate candidates for political office.
   (C) have the primary function of funding political campaigns.
   (D) want to influence officeholders and achieve legislative goals.
   (E) attempt to recruit an elite membership in order to become influential.

10. Which of the following situations represents a legislative victory for a special interest group?
    I. the NRA's repeal of the assault weapon ban
    II. MADD's successful lobbying for a national drinking age
    III. the Veterans of Foreign Wars' successful fight for the Americans with Disabilities Act
    IV. the NAACP successfully lobbying for the Civil Rights Act of 1964
    (A) I only
    (B) II only
    (C) II, III, and IV only
    (D) I, II, III, and IV only
    (E) I and IV only

11. All the following are techniques used by lobbyists EXCEPT
    (A) testifying at congressional hearings.
    (B) providing officials with research information.
    (C) appearing on the floor of Congress as staff assistants to senators and representatives.
    (D) taking senators and representative to conferences sponsored by a special interest group.
    (E) giving senators and representatives feedback from their constituents.

12. Which of the following statements represents a potential conflict of interest? Lobbyists
    (A) work closely with the interest groups that hired them.
    (B) are former government officials who have close ties with current legislators.
    (C) are persistent in making sure that the results they get do not change before a vote.
    (D) know as much and sometimes even more than legislators about pending legislation.
    (E) attempt to convince senators and representatives that if they support their position they will receive the support of their constituency.

13. The major impact of the Federal Election Campaign Act of 1974 was that it
    (A) eliminated lobbyist gifts and vacations for legislators.
    (B) set strict contribution limitations for congressional campaigns.
    (C) created matching funds for congressional campaigns.
    (D) legitimized and increased the number of interest groups.
    (E) created strict registration procedures for lobbyists.

Answers to Multiple-Choice Questions

1. **(A)** Type of Question: Hypothetical
Even though interest groups are involved with all the situations that are described, because of the nature of special interest groups, a narrowly scoped issue with low visibility has the greatest chance of lobbying success. For instance, the NRA may fail to stop the Congress from passing an assault weapons ban, but it could prevent other related legislation from passing.
2. **(C)** Type of Question: Negative
Even though interest groups support candidates for political office through their political action committees, it is highly unlikely that they will actually run their own candidates for elective office. One of the problems that arises is a clear conflict of interest. Another problem is that, because a special interest group usually is interested in a specific issue, running a candidate would attract only a small segment of the electorate.
3. **(B)** Type of Question: Negative
Just as in the previous question, the role of special interest groups is analyzed. It should be obvious that special interest groups cannot donate money to federal judges. Therefore, choice B is the correct answer.
4. **(D)** Type of Question: Negative
By definition, a special interest group is formed over a very specific issue. Whether it is abortion, guns, or a general category of supporting labor or business interests, these groups still recruit membership from the sphere they are trying to influence. Therefore, to say that interest groups attempt to attract a diverse membership is contradictory. Choice E may throw some students because there have been Supreme Court decisions protecting interest groups.
5. **(A)** Type of Question: Cause and effect relationships
For most issues brought up before Congress, you will be able to find some interest group that exists and hopes to influence the legislative process. Even though some interest groups are getting increased donations from their members, that is the exception rather than the rule. And even if there is an increased demand for campaign reform, it does not follow that more interest groups would form. Choice C is clearly not the perception of the public, and interest groups do not run their own members for political office.
6. **(A)** Type of Question: Hypothetical
The problem with this kind of question is that in some situations lobbyists may be able to accomplish their task with all the officials described in the question. But the best chance for success comes with the elected official who, going into the situation, basically agrees with the position of the special interest group or has a constituency who has strong feelings about the issue being discussed.
7. **(E)** Type of Question: Hypothetical
Although millions of dollars are pumped into the political coffers of both political parties and even candidates who are new to the political scene, most PAC money goes to incumbents. It is rare for money to be invested in candidates who most likely will vote against the position the PAC is taking.

8. **(E)** Type of Question: Sequencing a series of events
Because a lobbyist has a link to special interest groups who also have links to their political action committees, a lobbyist can and does act as a catalyst before a major vote takes place. Therefore, each of the situations described can and does take place as a result of lobbyists' efforts, though the lobbyists themselves may not be directly involved in each of the situations.

9. **(D)** Type of Question: Generalization
By definition, a special interest group attracts membership as a result of an identification process. People who believe that every woman has the right to have an abortion will look for pro-choice groups; gun advocates will look for a group like the NRA. Choices A and B are incorrect because these groups' major function is to endorse candidates. Choice C is wrong because funding is not their primary function. And choice E is incorrect since most likely a special interest group only can attract a narrowly based membership.

10. **(C)** Type of Question: Identification and analysis
Historically, special interest groups have succeeded in achieving their legislative aims. However, even though the NRA is one of the most influential and successful groups, they did not succeed in convincing Congress to appeal the ban on assault weapons (80 percent of the American people supported the ban). MADD, the Veterans of Foreign Wars, and the NAACP all were successful in achieving their legislative goals.

11. **(C)** Type of Question: Solution to a problem
According to political history the term lobbyist came about because special interest groups hired individuals to "hang out" in the lobby of Congress so that, when senators and representatives entered or left the floor the lobbyist could approach the representative without an appointment. There are strict rules regarding who actually can be on the floor of Congress—lobbyists are not permitted.

12. **(B)** Type of Question: Generalization
Although the other choices are all factually correct, the only answer that represents a conflict of interest is that many lobbyists are former senators, representatives, or executive staffers who may have retired, resigned, or been defeated. In some cases these individuals have abused the system and have been accused of ethical misconduct.

13. **(D)** Type of Question: Cause and effect relationships
This question is extremely difficult. You must not only know the major provisions of the FEC of 1974 but also not get confused over proposed legislation that almost passed the Congress in 1994. In addition, even though the law had a registration provision, in reality it opened up the opportunity for the formation of an increased number of interest groups. The act created matching funds for presidential, not congressional, campaigns and was silent regarding gifts, vacations, and campaign contributions for congressional campaigns.

SECTION 2: FREE-RESPONSE ESSAY

There are distinct differences in the roles that special interest groups, lobbyists, and political action committees play. Define each of those terms and give one example of the tactics used by each group to accomplish its goals.

Sample Student Response

The classic definition of an interest group is an organization, affiliation, or committee whose prime incentive is to publicize its member's viewpoint. Lobbyists and PACs are usually formed through a common interest that unites a group as it gains strength. These types of interest groups usually try to advance their goals through political means. Lobbyists are defined as instruments used to enhance a special interest group's goals through government officials, while PACs raise money from the group's constituents through committees that become directly involved in the political process. All three groups are interconnected, yet they each have different goals and duties. These groups utilize a variety of tactics to accomplish their individual goals; because of these tactics, the public views them in negative ways.

Special interest groups have a common goal of persuading public policymakers to act according to the group's perspective. The actual carrying out of these interest groups' goals are reserved to the lobbyists and PACs. Special interest groups are formed out of a common interest that unites its members through group identification and group affiliation. They try to influence elected officials; because they only concentrate on one issue, they have a very focused constituency. For the same reason, however, special interest groups can attract a great number of people from large sections of the United States. Internal functions, such as promises of succession, benefit the social, economic, and political needs of their members and help to attract membership. Mothers Against Drunk Driving (MADD) is an example of a special interest group that has benefited socially and politically from its accomplishments, which include a federal law that created a national minimum drinking age. Special interest groups by themselves offer a base to which lobbyists and PACs can add to, creating a more powerful group that can have a great impact on public policy.

Lobbyists are the next step in forming a more powerful special interest group. Lobbyists are the people, in the eyes of legislators, who actually write letters to United States congressmen and voice support for or opposition to a particular issue. Lobbyists use a variety of techniques to achieve success in obtaining their goals. Some of these techniques include knowing as much as they can about the political situation and the people involved, being truthful to the people they deal with, and understanding the goals of the group and determining who they want to see. For example, the National Rifle Association (NRA) is so powerful that it literally threatened a Florida senator's seat when the Crime Bill came up for a vote. The success of lobbyists, like PACs and special interest groups, depends upon their public image and their ability to influence public policy.

PACs are the committees that raise money and make contributions to political campaigns. Labor unions began forming PACs during the 1940s, but corporations were barred from doing so until passage of the Federal Campaign Act of 1971 (FECA). By lifting the prohibition against using corporate money to set up PACs, FECA and its 1974 and 1976 amendments legalized a new and much larger role for trade associations and corporations in politics. Thus, FECA brought about a dramatic change in the way political money is raised and fostered an enormous growth in the numbers of PACs involved in active politics. The amount of money raised over the last few elections has been exorbitant. Individual political campaigns have received over $5 million from PACs and other sources. In 2000, about 4200 PACs distributed $284 million to congressional candidates, most of them incumbents.

Evaluation of Free-Response Sample Essay

1. Does the essay define special interest groups, lobbyists, and PACs as well as establish the differences among the three groups?
2. Is a foundation built containing examples of how each group operates and citing specific examples of the successes and failures of each of them?

1. This essay gives the student an opportunity to draw upon basic information, elaborate on characteristics, and give concrete examples of tactics used by special interest groups, lobbyists, and political action committees. One of the fallacies in the study of special interests is the lumping together of these three groups, rather than defining the specific role each plays in the formation of public policy. The thesis statement is really three statements that incorporate textbook-type definitions. An essay receiving full credit must go beyond just defining the function of each group. It must also compare and contrast functions, tactics, and successes and failures. This essay accomplishes those tasks. It even gives a historical perspective that illustrates the underlying legitimacy of the role special interests play in government and politics.

2. The foundation of the essay relies on examples of legislative successes and operational methods of each group. The writer uses Mothers Against Drunk Drivers (MADD) to point out the fact they were able to change public policy in the area of a minimum drinking age.

SECTION 2: DATA-BASED FREE-RESPONSE ESSAY

Study the chart obtained from the Federal Election Commission and answer the question that follows:

TOP TWENTY PACs IN OVERALL SPENDING AND IN CONTRIBUTIONS TO FEDERAL CANDIDATES, 2000

PAC	Overall spending
1. Association of Trial Lawyers of America	$2.27 million
2. International Brotherhood of Electrical Workers	$1.96 million
3. American Federation of State, County, and Municipal Employees	$1.90 million
4. Democrat Republican Independent Voter Education	$1.81 million
5. Realtors Political Action Committee	$1.61 million
6. Machinists Non-Partisan Political League	$1.56 million
7. Dealers Election Committee of the National Automobile Dealers Association	$1.47 million
8. Build Political Action Committee of the National Association of Home Builders	$1.35 million
9. United Auto Workers Voluntary Community Action Program	$1.34 million
10. United Parcel Service Political Action Committee	$1.27 million
11. National Beer Wholesalers' Association Political Action Committee	$1.23 million
12. Service Employees International Union Political Action Committee	$1.17 million
13. Carpenters Legislative Improvement Committee	$1.16 million
14. United Transportation Union Political Education League	$1.10 million
15. United Food and Commercial Workers Active Ballot Club	$1.09 million
16. Laborers' Political League—Laborers' International Union of North America	$1.08 million
17. American Federation of Teachers Committee on Political Education	$1.04 million
18. Ironworkers Political Action League	$.97 million
19. National Rifle Association Political Victory Fund	$.97 million
20. CWA—Cope Political Contributions Committee	$.96 million

Identify the role that PACs play and explain how special interest groups try to block lobby reform.

Sample Student Response

One can conclude the following based on the information provided by the chart listing the top 20 PACs:

- Because Congress had done very little in the area of campaign reform, there were a wide variety of political action committees giving money to federal candidates in 2000.
- As a result of the money given, PACs can influence senators and representatives to vote against any reforms aimed at lobbyists and special interest groups.
- The temptation of campaign contributions as well as other "gifts" offered by lobbyists is hard to resist.
- PACs feel that they can "influence federal candidates based on the fact they are contributing large amounts of money to the campaign coffers."

Because PACs have contributed millions of dollars to the campaign coffers of senators and representatives, most attempts at reforming the system have failed. Just to illustrate the point, in 2000 the top PAC, the Association of Trial Lawyers, gave over $2 million to political candidates.

Ever since the Lobby Registration Act of 1947, which in itself had many loopholes (fewer than half of all lobbyists are registered), there has been public pressure for Congress to clean up its act. Such incidents as Watergate and the House checking and post office scandals have increased the call for ethics and campaign and lobby reform. In response to Watergate the Federal Elections Commission was set up, and stricter spending limits were imposed on presidential candidates in return for matching federal funds. The same standard never was applied to Congress. In the closing days of the 103rd Congress in 1994, a Democratic majority with the support of President Clinton passed an extensive package of reforms banning most gifts to representatives and senators and establishing strict new lobbyist reporting standards. The bill required that all professional lobbyists register and disclose who they are working for and how much they are getting paid. It called for reporting the kinds of issues they are lobbying. The legislation also affected so-called grassroots lobbyists—those professional lobbyists who contact senators and representatives from places outside of Washington, D.C. The most controversial part of the bill banned almost every gift to members of Congress and place strict limits on trips, vacations, and other outings sponsored by lobbyists. Only those expenses related to a legislator's legitimate speaking engagements would be allowed. Even though the bill passed both houses and even a conference committee, the Republicans in a last-minute change of mind filibustered the bill because they felt that it would have an unfair impact on the grassroots lobbyists. The Republicans won the 1994 mid-term election and lobby reform was not part of their Contract with America. Nevertheless, lobby reform passed both houses of Congress in the fall of 1995, mandating the registration of lobbyists and dramatically reducing the kind of gifts a lobbyist could give to an elected official. Further demands for campaign finance reform followed the 1996 elections. In particular, a demand for a ban on "soft money," which is money given to political parties by corporations that is not regulated, was discussed as part of the McCain-Feingold bill.

Evaluation of Data-Based Free-Response Sample Essay

1. Does the writer give a complete explanation of the conclusions reached?
2. Do the examples illustrate the abuses of the system as well as attempts to reform the system?

1. Using a bullet approach, the writer gives four solid interpretative statements that help explain the point the chart is making. Using this kind of approach in a data-based free-response question is an effective way of giving information that can be used in the second part of the question. In this case the writer is commenting on both the amount of money being given to candidates and the attitudes of the candidates accepting the money. The writer reinforces the point by raising the issue that the top political action committee gave over $2 million to political candidates in 2000.

2. The strength of the response is in the solid examples of lobby and campaign reform given by the writer. From the Lobby Registration Act of 1947, to the Federal Election Campaign Act of 1974, to the attempts at campaign reform made in 1994, the writer shows how the system can easily lead to unethical relationships between representatives and lobbyists. The writer also comments about the future status of campaign reform. Looking at the four bulleted statements in the first part of the question and the illustrations given in the second part, you should be able to see how the response flows.

PART FOUR PUBLIC POLICY ISSUES

CHAPTER 15 The Economy

Section Overview

The final section of the review part of this book concerns the definitive measure of whether the institutions of government and the components of our political system succeed—the implementation of public policy. We have selected the following areas as yardsticks to gauge the successes and failures of public policy:

- the economy
- the federal budget
- social welfare and entitlements
- the environment and energy
- foreign policy and the national defense

Each topic will apply the criteria of successful public policy—defined as the final action(s) taken by government in promotional, regulatory, or distributive form. These policies are backed by laws, executive orders, judicial decisions, or other directive measures and are highly influenced by the political linkage institutions. They are developed using the following steps:

- recognition of problems resulting in the development of an agenda,
- formation of policy alternatives,
- enactment of public policy,
- implementation of the policy,
- evaluation of the policy, and
- consideration of any revision of the policy.

KEY TERMS

Consumer Price Index
Discount rates
Distributive policy
Federal Reserve System
Fiscal policy
Gross Domestic Product
Gross National Product
Laissez-faire
Monetary policy
Norris-La Guardia Act (1932)
Open market
Price supports
Redistributive policy
Regulatory policy
Wagner Act

Chapter Overview

The first chapter of this section deals with economic policy. When Clinton campaign manager James Carville, sitting in his Little Rock headquarters called the war room, pasted the message "It's the economy, stupid," as a reminder to Clinton that he should make the economy the focus of the 1992 campaign, the candidate took Carville's advice. In fact, based on exit polls, the economy was the number one factor why voters elected Clinton.

We will explore the direct link the economy has to the political process and to the outcome of elections. We will also look at the government's attempt to regulate economic policy. By evaluating the monetary policies of the Federal Reserve System and the fiscal policies of the government, you will be able to see how specific public policy is developed and how it affects the major areas of American life—agricultural, business, labor, and consumer. Viewing the history of government regulation, we will conclude the chapter by looking at recent attempts at deregulation and focus on the economy's future.

Economic Differences

Economic policy has a direct relationship to politics, political parties, elections, and government.

Basic differences between Republicans and Democrats and ideological differences between conservatives and liberals are great when economic issues are raised. Traditionally, Republicans have been identified as the party favoring the rich and big business, whereas the Democrats have been viewed as being sympathetic to labor and the poor. Democrats have accused Republican presidents of having unsuccessful "trickle-down, supply-side" economic policies, resulting in a recessionary trend and higher unemployment. Republicans accuse Democratic presidents of following a "tax and spend, regulatory" program, causing runaway inflation. The conservative congressional coalition sides with policies aimed at dramatically reducing the deficit, whereas liberals believe government-sponsored economic stimulus programs result in a strong economy.

These differences translate into major political themes in presidential campaigns. From the classic arguments of William Jennings Bryan favoring a free silver base, to the laissez-faire arguments of Herbert Hoover, to Ronald Reagan's and George W. Bush's dramatic tax reform proposals, campaigns have focused on the economic problems facing the nation. Surveys have indicated that voters point to the economy as the primary reason for choosing one candidate over another. When Ronald Reagan ran against Jimmy Carter in 1980, he asked voters whether they were better off then or before Jimmy Carter had become president. Because runaway inflation was rampant at that time, Carter was hard-pressed to counter Reagan's argument. Thus voter selection is determined by one's personal situation. If your family is unemployed during a Republican administration, you will probably vote Democratic. If your business is expanding and making profits when a Republican is president, you're more apt to keep that president in office.

Government plays a dual role in being linked to the nation's economy. It measures the economic status of the nation and attempts to develop effective measures to keep the economy on the right track. The Department of Labor (Bureau of Labor Statistics), the Congressional Budget Office, and the Executive Office of the Council of Economic Advisers all report to the country vital economic statistics such as the

- unemployment rate (adjusted index of people obtaining jobs)
- Consumer Price Index (CPI)—According to the U.S. Census Bureau, "the CPI is a measure of the average change in prices over time in a fixed 'market basket' of goods and services purchased either by urban wage earners and clerical workers or by all urban consumers." It is also a primary measure of inflation when the index rises over a defined period of time.
- Gross National Product (GNP)—The Census Bureau defines GNP as "the total output of goods and services produced by labor and property located in the United States, valued at market prices."
- Gross Domestic Product (GDP)—Lately the GDP has become the key economic measure analyzing an upward or downward economic trend, on a quarterly basis, of the monetary value of all the goods and services produced within the nation. Other factors such as consumer confidence, the actual inflation rate, and the stock market give a complete picture of the economy.

The government's primary policy role, therefore, is to develop a healthy economic policy. Programs such as the New Deal's three Rs—Relief, Recovery, and Reform—set in motion policies that have succeeded in preventing the country from experiencing a depression of the magnitude of the one that occurred in the 1930s. Many of Roosevelt's programs such as Social Security (relief), the Securities Exchange Commission (reform), and jobs program prototypes (recovery) are still part of the economic fabric of the country today.

History

The history of economic policy revolves around the role government should play in regulating it.

The development of economic strategies revolves around three kinds of policies:

- Regulatory—results in government control over individuals and businesses. Examples of regulatory policy include protection of the environment and consumer protection. These policies are administered by the federal bureaucracy.
- Distributive—results in the government giving benefits directly to people, groups, farmers, and businesses. Typical policies include subsidies, research and development funds for corporations, and direct government aid for highway construction and education.
- Redistributive—results in the government taking money from one segment of the society through taxes and giving it back to groups in need. They include such policies as welfare, tax credits for business expenses or business investment, and highway construction made possible through a gasoline tax.

James Madison wrote as Marcus in the *Daily Advertiser* in 1787, "in what then does *real* power consist? The answer is short and plain—in property. . . . Let the people have property, and they *will* have the power. . . ." Much of his defense of the Constitution involved economics—taxes, property, tariffs, and commerce. He expressed a major concern that economic conflict could result from the disparity of the distribution of wealth. Once the Constitution was ratified, property became an essential component of the due process clause of the Fifth Amendment. "Life, liberty and property" became the three ingredients that government could not take away without due process of law.

Economic policy of the United States in the nineteenth century centered on the issues of slavery, tariffs, and the rise of industrialization. Slaves were defined as property in the *Dred Scott* decision, and fugitive slave acts as well as legislation enabling states to determine whether slavery would be legal were passed. Supreme Court decisions further defined economic policies. *Dartmouth College v Woodward* established the validity of contracts, *Gibbons v Ogden* defined interstate commerce as a stream of commerce, and *McCulloch v Maryland* upheld the right of Congress to create a National Bank. Sectional differences related to slavery and tariff disputes ultimately resulted in the Civil War.

Post-Civil War economic issues were directly related to the rise of industrialization in the United States. The growth of railroads opening up markets to the West, and the formation of trusts and monopolies raised the issue of the extent government could regulate the economy. Granger laws were passed by states regulating railroad rates and haulage fees. The populist movement in the 1880s called for the government to further regulate monopolies. The Interstate Commerce Act was passed in 1887 and in 1890 the Sherman Antitrust Act, prohibiting the existence of a monopoly if it restrained trade, was passed. The election of 1896, pitting William Jennings Bryan against William McKinley, became a key test to determine which direction the nation would take. After Grover Cleveland was elected in 1892, the country had experienced an economic panic. The stock market crashed, businesses failed, and unemployment increased. Cleveland's laissez-faire policies came under attack by the nation's premiere orator, William Jennings Bryan. After Bryan gave his famous speech in which he said, "you shall not crucify mankind upon a cross of gold," the campaign was focused on the gold standard and the direction of the economy. But because the Democrats were also blamed for the hard times and there was real doubt about changing over to a silver standard, Bryan lost to McKinley.

The beginning of the twentieth century saw a progressive era with reforms such as the Pure Food and Drug Act, the Sixteenth Amendment (providing for a progressive income tax), and the creation of the Federal Reserve System. The Supreme Court ruled in *Swift v United States* that the Sherman Antitrust Act could be used to break up trusts. The country geared up for a wartime economy during World War I, and it artificially stimulated the economy. Harding's "return to normalcy" and the decade of the 1920s was characterized by a roller coaster economy—periods of unchecked prosperity balanced by periods of recession. The turning point and start of the modern economic role of government came in 1929 with the stock market crash and the beginning of the Great Depression. Although Hoover is often blamed for pursuing a laissez-faire policy of trickle-down economics, he did attempt to use the government by signing the Glass-Steagall Act, which enlarged the role of the Federal Reserve, and he pushed for the creation of the Reconstruction Finance Corporation, a massive effort to loan money to businesses. The New Deal taught the country that the government must take more control of the management of the economy.

Realizing that unemployment had a spiraling effect on the economy, Congress passed the Employment Act of 1946. This law had as its goal to maintain full employment using the efforts of industry, agriculture, labor, and state and local governments. Through these efforts a public policy that promoted maximum employment, production, and purchasing power was enacted. In addition, this law set up the mechanism for measurement including the Council of Economic Advisers, the Joint Economic Committee, and a mandated economic report given annually by the president to Congress. The goal of full employment has been one that every administration strives for. Each president adopts a specific fiscal policy, and the Federal Reserve as the watchdog creates its own monetary policy.

The Federal Reserve

The Federal Reserve System plays a large role in regulating monetary policy. It has been applauded by its supporters as a key watchdog agency and criticized by its critics as too powerful.

Monetary policy is defined as the control of the money supply and the cost of credit. Many leading economists feel that there is a direct relationship between the country's money supply and the rate of economic growth. The Federal Reserve System, or as it is called "the Fed," was established in 1913. It consists of a seven-member board of governors serving by appointment of the president for staggered 14-year terms. Its chairman, appointed by the president and confirmed by the Senate, is a powerful spokesperson of the Fed and serves for four-year renewable terms. The Federal Reserve Board is an independent agency, free of presidential or congressional control. Its chairman during the 1990s, Allen Greenspan, was very effective and influential in setting monetary policy. There are more than 6000 member banks that are affected by Fed policy and then influence monetary policies of other banks, ultimately having an impact on the interest rates consumers pay.

The Federal Reserve System regulates the money supply through:

- Open-market operations—buying and selling of government securities, which affects the money supply and cost of money.
- Reserve requirements—establishing the legal limitations on money reserves that banks must keep against the amount of money they have deposited in Federal Reserve Banks (which give the banks interest). These limits affect the ability of banks to loan money to consumers because actions in this area can increase the availability of money for credit.
- Discount rates—determining the rate at which banks can borrow money from the Federal Reserve System. If rates are raised, interest rates for consumers also rise. The Federal Reserve System uses this tactic to keep inflation in check. This is probably the most publicized action taken by the Fed.

A good example of how the Federal Reserve's monetary policy is used in conjunction with a president's fiscal policy was in 1981 after Ronald Reagan was inaugurated. The country's number one economic problem was double-digit inflation. The Federal Reserve forced a recession by raising the discount rate. The action had the immediate impact of reducing inflation. However, unemployment continued to be a problem. Reagan's fiscal policies (which we will discuss fully in the next section), although eventually creating a long period of prosperity, also saw the greatest increase in the deficit in the nation's history. In 1999, after President Clinton's deficit reduction economic package succeeded in reversing some of the nation's deficit and increased employment, the Fed was forced to raise discount rates as a precautionary measure. It feared that, because the economy was again improving, inflation would tend to increase. The question of having an independent agency be the sole arbiter in these very important functions upsets many economists. On the other hand, the board must be immune from political pressure and pressure from special interests who would benefit if they had the inside track or could influence the monetary policy of the Fed. Most economists give the Federal Reserve high praise for the way it monitored the economy during the 1990s.

Fiscal Policy

Fiscal policy of different administrations is characterized by an active or passive government economic policy.

Fiscal policy is primarily determined by an economic philosophy that determines how the economy is managed as a result of government spending and borrowing and the amount of money collected from taxes. The two contrasting philosophies related to fiscal policy are Keynesian economics, developed by English economist John Maynard Keynes, and supply-side economics, developed by Ronald Reagan's economic team. Keynes advocated an increase in national income so that consumers could spend more money either through investments or purchases of goods and services. He also felt that the best strategy to counter an economic recession was an increase in government spending. A corollary to this viewpoint would be that government would also adopt regulatory, distributive, and redistributive policies as tools to ensure consumer enterprise.

When President Reagan saw the problems the nation was facing, he and his economic advisers, led by David Stockman, decided that the best approach would be to cut both taxes and government spending. As classic supply-side proponents, they contended that large tax cuts would result in increased consumer spending and investment, which would offset any loss of federal revenues because there would be an increase in taxes received from businesses benefiting from these increased purchases. In addition, business investments would increase, businesses would expand their operations, and this expansion would result in an increase in job opportunities. In 1986 Congress passed the largest tax cut in the nation's history. As a result, there was a sense of prosperity, and individuals were able to invest great amounts of money. Unfortunately, the size of the federal budget did not decrease (the defense budget, in fact, increased), and the additional revenues supply-siders hoped would be received, never were. The deficit rose, the country faced severe economic problems, and in 1987 the stock market had its worse crash since 1929. This was completely turned around during the 1990s when the stock market had one of the greatest periods of a "Bull Market" in its entire history. The economy reflected this prosperity with a prolonged period of low inflation and increased economic growth.

The differing philosophies to a large extent can be traced to the laissez-faire philosophy of Hoover versus the regulatory philosophy of Roosevelt. Both fiscal policies attempted to handle the country when it was facing an economic downturn or when the country was facing too much growth. The key to success is to find the best way to balance the tools available to the government. Should it raise or lower taxes? Should it increase or decrease spending levels? How much regulation is really necessary? These are the issues that have perplexed economists and presidents since the Great Depression.

Government's Role

Government-created economic policy has an impact on the major areas of American life—agricultural, business, labor, and consumer.

Remember that government economic policy is categorized as regulatory, distributive, and redistributive. Depending upon the needs of the group and the economic conditions facing the country, the specific measures adopted vary from group to group.

The farm industry's problems were dramatically brought to the forefront as a result of the dust bowl disaster of the 1930s. The Agricultural Adjustment Act of 1933 created the farm subsidy program, which to a great extent still exists today. The heart of this program was price supports—the government guaranteed the prices of certain farm goods by subsidizing farmers not to grow certain crops, and by buying food directly and storing it, rather than letting the oversupply in the market bring the prices down. The philosophy behind these measures is to protect the nation's farmers by artificially keeping prices up in the short term, thus keeping the farmers in business, which will help the rest of the economy. Nearly $22 billion was spent by the government in subsidies and support in 1989. Even though this program, which is administered by the Agriculture Department, is criticized, the plight of the farmer is desperate. Between 1960 and 1990 a majority of American farmers were forced out of business because they had to borrow heavily. As farm industry debts increased, exports decreased, and this further accelerated the bankruptcies.

An essential area of economic life is big business. Megamergers and corporations making huge assets are the leading indicators of the importance of big business in the success of the economy. Government economic policies affecting big business include the balance of trade (tariff rates and trade agreements), the amount of business regulation (antitrust policies), plus the support government has given to failing businesses in the form of bailouts. In 1971, for the first time in more than a century, the country faced a trade deficit, where the United States imported more goods than they exported, creating a trade imbalance. By 2000 we had a trade deficit of more than $29 billion. Competition with Japan and Germany in the car market was fierce. Because there was a strong dollar in the 1980s, Americans bought more foreign goods. By the decade's end, as a result, American business suffered. Business leaders called for higher tariffs, and a protectionist mentality set in. Presidents Bush and Clinton felt that free trade agreements would be a better solution. Such treaties as the North American Free Trade Agreement (NAFTA) and periodic meetings with the economic world leaders are aimed at reducing the nation's trade deficit.

The government is very leery of huge conglomerates and monitors potential monopolies that will hurt consumers. In fact, as a result of government action, AT&T was forced to decentralize its holdings, enabling competing phone companies to come onto the scene. An example of a government bailout of business was the Chrysler bailout, a loan made by the federal government to the Chrysler Corporation that enabled the car manufacturer to stay in business. The net effect of the policy was to save thousands of jobs, which helped the overall economy.

Consumer policy is determined through the efforts of independent regulatory agencies such as the Food and Drug Administration, the Consumer Product Safety Commission, and the Federal Trade Commission. Consumer lobbyists such as Ralph Nader urged the government to make it mandatory for automobile manufacturers to install seat belts. The Federal Trade Commission administers the Consumer Credit Protection Act, which makes it mandatory for a credit card company to accurately inform the consumer about the status of any credit card transactions.

Labor economic policy started in earnest during the Great Depression. In 1932 the Norris-La Guardia Act was passed. It prohibited employers from punishing workers who joined unions and gave labor the right to form unions. Other acts protecting labor include

- The Walsh-Healy Act of 1936—regulated wages and hours of public employees
- The Fair Labor Standards Act of 1936—set a maximum work week for employers engaged in interstate commerce. It also set the first minimum wage provisions
- The Federal Labor Standards Act of 1947—protects children from excessive hours and hazardous conditions and sets minimum age requirements
- The Occupational Safety and Health Act of 1970—created the Occupational Safety and Health Administration (OSHA), which sets safety and health standards for workers in companies involved in interstate commerce

LABOR POLICIES HAVE HAD A GREAT IMPACT ON THE AFL-CIO

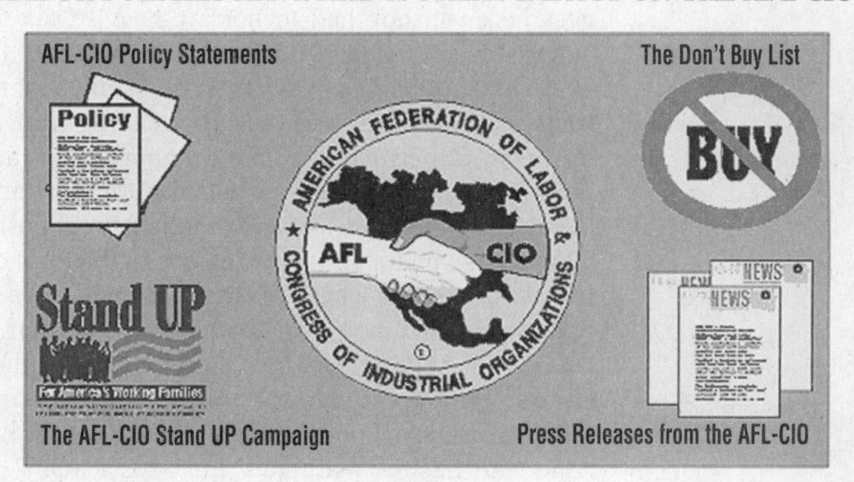

Two acts that regulated labor unions were passed. The Wagner Act, also called the National Labor Relations Act of 1935, gave workers involved in interstate commerce the right to organize labor unions and to engage in collective bargaining and prevented employers from discriminating against labor leaders and taking action against union leaders. A National Labor Relations Board, an independent regulatory commission, was set up. Because there was criticism of this act by business, Congress passed the Taft-Hartley Act in 1947, which struck a balance between labor and employer relations. The act outlawed the closed union shop, outlawed certain kinds of strikes, permitted employers to sue unions for violations of contracts, allowed the use of injunctions to stop union activities, and allowed states to adopt right-to-work laws, giving employers more rights regarding the establishment of union shops. It also created an 80-day cooling off period before labor unions crucial to the economy of the United States could strike. Finally, the act gave the president the right to step in and prevent a strike by an entire industry, such as the steel or auto industry, if such an action would threaten the nation's health and safety. It also prohibited strikes by public employees. When the airline air traffic controllers (government employees) walked out in a dispute with the government in 1981, President Reagan set a deadline and, when it was not met, fired the entire union.

Deregulation

Deregulation of the economy has been favored by both liberals and conservatives in the hope that it would encourage more competition and decrease government involvement in key areas of American life.

As much as we have seen the government involved in regulations, during the 1970s and 1980s there has also been significant government deregulation of the airline industry, trucking and railroads, and the banking industry.

The transportation industry has been a key player in the deregulation movement. The Civil Aeronautics Board (CAB), an independent regulatory agency, was established in 1938. Its task was to protect airlines from unfair competition. It did so by regulating airline rates and determining the nature of competition in the industry. Critics felt that consumers suffered by having to pay higher fares and not having the scheduling advantages that would occur in a more competitive market. In 1978 Congress passed the Airline Deregulation Act. This law phased out CAB, relaxed fare and route restrictions, and authorized a federal bailout to certain airlines in order to keep them in service in unprofitable markets. There have been both positive and negative effects from this act. The consumer has benefited with lower fares but has had fewer choices regarding scheduling. Many new airlines came on the scene, only to go under after a short period of time. In addition, many of the established airlines such as Eastern and Pan Am went out of business, whereas others such as Continental had to restructure their businesses. Consumers have also claimed price fixing by airlines. On balance, though, consumers do get the benefits of choice and lower fares under this reform.

Deregulation of the trucking and railroad industry took place in 1980 when Congress passed the Staggers Rail Act and Motor Carrier Act. Both laws opened up the trucking and rail industries to greater self-regulation and greater competition within the industries.

When the banking industry was deregulated in the 1980s, it caused one of the most far-reaching scandals in banking history. The savings and loan (S&L) problems included consumers losing money that was not protected under the Federal Savings and Loan Insurance Corporation, banks closing, and heads of S&Ls under investigation for improprieties. The federal government under President Bush was forced to bail out the industry, resulting in an increase in the already inflated federal deficit. His administration was highly criticized for allowing the banks to mismanage their affairs, and after congressional oversight hearings took place, there was no doubt that the federal government would have to again regulate that industry.

As a result of the Republican takeover of Congress in 1994, a push toward further deregulation took place, and both houses of Congress passed a regulatory reform bill (see the free-response essay in Chapter 10).

Chapter 15 Review

SECTION 1: MULTIPLE-CHOICE QUESTIONS

1. Traditionally, the Republican Party has been viewed as favoring which of the following groups?
   (A) big business
   (B) the poor
   (C) the middle class
   (D) African-Americans
   (E) Hispanics

2. Traditionally, the Democratic Party has been known as
   (A) supporters of a tax-and-spend philosophy.
   (B) supply-siders.
   (C) believers of trickle-down economics.
   (D) advocates of antiregulation of the economy.
   (E) proponents of repeal of capital gains taxes.

3. All the following items are measures of the nation's economy EXCEPT
   (A) the nation's unemployment rate.
   (B) the rise or fall of the Consumer Price Index.
   (C) the amount of growth or decline in the Gross National Product.
   (D) the amount of taxes corporations pay to the federal government.
   (E) the rise or fall of the Gross Domestic Product.

4. Which of the following economic policies reflects imposed government economic mandates?
   (A) distributive economic policy
   (B) regulatory economic policy
   (C) redistributive economic policy
   (D) supply-side economic policy
   (E) stimulus programs passed by Congress

5. Which of the following strategies results in government giving benefits directly to the people?
   (A) distributive economic policy
   (B) regulatory economic policy
   (C) redistributive economic policy
   (D) increased government regulations
   (E) increasing the personal income tax

6. Which of the following strategies results in government taking money from one segment of the society and giving it back to a group in need?
   (A) distributive economic policy
   (B) regulatory economic policy
   (C) redistributive economic policy
   (D) increasing research and development opportunities for business
   (E) increasing price supports

7. A primary way that the Federal Reserve regulates the money supply is when it
   (A) votes to increase taxes.
   (B) votes to decrease taxes.
   (C) adjusts the discount rate.
   (D) adjusts the rate of inflation.
   (E) votes to increase price supports.

8. Supply-side economists urge
   (A) government stimulation of the economy.
   (B) increased government spending for social programs.
   (C) increased government borrowing of money.
   (D) large tax cuts by the government.
   (E) an increase of the management of the economy by the government.

9. Which of the following presidents pursued a laissez-faire economic policy?
   (A) Theodore Roosevelt
   (B) Herbert Hoover
   (C) Franklin Roosevelt
   (D) Lyndon Johnson
   (E) Bill Clinton

10. Which of the following laws was invoked in response to the air traffic controller strike in 1981?
   (A) Fair Labor Standards Act
   (B) Federal Labor Standards Act
   (C) Wagner Act
   (D) Norris-La Guardia Act
   (E) Taft-Hartley Act

11. Which of the following industries had major economic problems as a result of government deregulation?
   (A) the airline industry
   (B) the telephone company
   (C) the savings and loans
   (D) the railroad industry
   (E) the cable television industry

Answers to Multiple-Choice Questions

1. **(A)** Type of Question: Cause and effect relationships
   Choices B, C, D, and E are all groups that the Democrats like to claim as their constituency. Big business has not only been supported by the Republican Party, but it has also been a big contributor to the Republicans. This question is particularly important in the unit dealing with the economy because Republican control of the legislative agenda can mean that big business gets a tax break.
2. **(A)** Type of Question: Generalization
   Choices B and C are economic issues raised by the Democrats against Republicans; choices D and E are traditional Republican causes. Choice A is an accusation made against the Democrats, but disputed by them.

3. **(D)** Type of Question: Negative
The amount of taxes corporations pay may have an impact on the nation's budget, but it is not a direct measure of how well the economy is doing. The Bureau of Labor Statistics keeps tabs on the unemployment rate and the changes in the Consumer Price Index (a measure of inflation), Gross National Product (a measure of the total growth of the country), and Gross Domestic Product (a measure of the domestic growth of the country).
4. **(B)** Type of Question: Comparing and contrasting concepts and events
Regulatory economic policy takes place as a result of mandates imposed on individuals or businesses by government. The net effect is more restrictions. Distributive policies include subsidies. Redistributive policies include policies such as welfare. Supply-side economic policy is characterized by a minimum of government control, and stimulus programs encourage people and businesses to invest in the economy.
5. **(A)** Type of Question: Comparing and contrasting concepts and events
As in question 4, regulatory policies create controls through mandates. Redistributive policies result in the government taking money from one segment of the society and providing aid to another. Increased government regulations is similar to regulatory policy, and even though increasing the income tax may provide redistributive funds, it is only one part of the process.
6. **(C)** Type of Question: Comparing and contrasting concepts and events
Similar to the previous two questions, examples of a redistributive economic policy include Aid to Families with Dependent Children, tax credits for business or individuals, and other direct government benefits made possible through the collection of taxes. Regulatory policy creates specific things people and business must do. Research and development opportunities do not have to come from government-supported aid programs, and increasing price supports could come directly through budgeted funds not related to taxes.
7. **(C)** Type of Question: Solution to a problem
The Federal Reserve's major function is to keep tabs on the economy. One of the most effective ways the Fed tries to influence it is through the raising or lowering of the discount rate. If the economy is sluggish, the Fed will lower the interest rates. If the economy hints that inflation may set in, the Fed will raise the interest rates. The Federal Reserve Board does not have the power to increase or decrease taxes or price supports. Through the raising and lowering of the discount rate, it hopes to influence inflation. There are no guarantees that inflation will cooperate.
8. **(D)** Type of Question: Cause and effect relationships
The term supply-side was made popular during the Reagan administration by his director of the Office of Management and Budget, David Stockman. The term refers to an economic policy that aims to keep the economy stimulated by the private sector through tax decreases such as a capital gains tax decrease or a reduction in the personal income tax. Choices A, B, C, and E are policies supply-siders would not endorse.

9. **(B)** Type of Question: Chronological
Theodore Roosevelt was known as a "trust buster" and a president who believed in using government to further economic policy. Franklin Roosevelt developed the New Deal. Lyndon Johnson was the father of the Great Society, and Bill Clinton believed that the government should be able to stimulate the economy. Herbert Hoover was a firm believer that the private sector could extricate the country from the Depression.

10. **(E)** Type of Question: Cause and effect relationships
The Fair Labor Standards Act set a maximum work week for employers engaged in interstate commerce. The Federal Labor Standards Act protected children from abuses in the workplace; the Wagner Act gave workers involved in interstate commerce the right to organize labor unions. The Norris-La Guardia Act prohibited employers from punishing workers who joined unions. The Taft-Hartley Act in addition to prohibiting federal employees the right to strike also outlawed the closed union shop and allowed states to adopt right-to-work laws.

11. **(C)** Type of Question: Identification and analysis
The airline industry saw a tremendous growth of passengers, even though airlines did go out of business. The telephone company still prospered after deregulation. The railroad industry did not prosper as much as the airline industry, and cable television still had tremendous growth and major control of the market even with laws deregulating aspects of the industry. The savings and loans took advantage of government deregulation and paid for it in the 1980s with many of them shutting down and needing a government bailout.

SECTION 2: FREE-RESPONSE ESSAY (Both choices are answered for illustrative purposes)

Clinton campaign strategist James Carville is credited with identifying the key theme of the 1992 election when he advised candidate Clinton that "It's the economy, stupid."

Identify and explain the policies of Ronald Reagan or Bill Clinton as they relate to economic philosophy and implementation. Analyze how the president you chose applied economic philosophy to create an economic policy.

Sample Student Response

As James Carville pointed out, the theme of the 1992 presidential election was the failure of a politico-economic system. Just as in the early 1980s Arthur Laffer, David Stockman, and Jack Kemp developed an economic theory initially known as supply-side economics, Bill Clinton maintained that it was the policies of "trickle-down economics" that caused the economic problems of the 1990s.

Supply-siders held that an abundance of efficiently produced goods could actually stimulate demand enough to raise the entire GNP. During the 1979 campaign Reagan construed such a theory as the solution to the lingering problem of stagflation, which apparently had rendered impotent the fiscal tools of the New Deal. If the government was unable to stimulate demand through its social welfare, labor, and taxation systems and deal with runaway inflation of the 1970s, then Reagan maintained government should diminish its economic influence. According to Reaganomics, the federal government should grant American firms enough fiscal latitude to improve their productivity because the government evidently could not. In doing so, a more cost-efficient, supply-side economic policy might well encourage consumption. Reagan's assertions attracted the traditional element of the Democratic Party, the organized labor of the rust belt, which had felt more of the burden of soaring inflation than any other sector of the economy. His theories had consequently attracted a national mandate, and his policies were systematically implemented throughout the mid and early 1980s.

Yet after his election, supply-side economics did not manifest itself in a significant reduction in government expenditures, nor even an increase in federal revenues. Reagan did lessen federal regulation and turned much of the previous administration's social policy to the states. In doing this he reduced programs designed to stimulate demand. In other areas such as defense the federal government expanded its fiscal outlays. The Reagan administration successfully instituted a regressive income tax and lowered the capital gains tax, resulting in an expansion of the upper-income tax bracket. But an examination of the fluctuations in GNP indicated that the economy expanded decidedly unevenly, encouraging a widening distribution of personal income comparable to that of the 1920s. Reagan's policies had indeed provided American firms the capital necessary to invest and develop more efficient and cost-effective goods and services. Yet unlike Japanese businesses, American firms invested little of such assets, so that the proportion of the GNP dedicated to research and development never increased.

This trend may explain precisely why a boost in the incomes of the business class—either from Reagan's capital gains reduction or indirectly from the consumption of other wealthy members of this class—never increased supply and in turn failed to stimulate demand, or produce any massive national wealth. Firms and the wealthy used increased revenue to consume rather than to save. Productivity gradually declined, much technological innovation never hit the factory floor, and, quite simply, businesses consequently did not need to hire more workers and could not afford to increase wages proportional to the amount of revenues businesses were receiving.

The decline in productivity increased the deficit and increased the wealth of the smallest portion of the economy. This wouldn't have been quite so harmful had if not been for one other component of Reagan's policy. Integral to Reagan's economic policy was the systematic reduction of the government's mechanisms of demand. But because this reduction was not offset by an increase in demand, the middle class lost vital programs resulting in a loss of wages and greater employment opportunities.

The decline in the prosperity of the heart of American society precipitated an electoral crisis in confidence. The middle class gradually identified the U.S. deficit as symbolic of the manner in which government had trapped them. Not only did eight years of regressive taxation inhibit them, but they faced the prospect of having to pay back the debt at increasing levels of interest.

In 1992 Bill Clinton successfully defined the agenda of the 1992 election. His campaign staff, including James Carville, identified the principal issue. "It's the economy, stupid." Although Reagan's fiscal policies were largely more liberal than those of Bush, Bush's legislative inaction compounded the middle class' anger. By the beginning of the 1990s the negative effects of Reagan's policies manifested themselves in economic recession, and, particularly, massive unemployment. Yet Bush's philosophy precluded him from directly addressing such a recession. Although Bush's 1988 budget tried to address the issue, his no-tax pledge resulted in continued deficits. The Clinton campaign made this the primary campaign issue. They claimed the recession was a blow to the middle class and an example of an anachronistic application of a failing economic philosophy—trickle-down economics.

The Clinton camp articulated a platform that embodied a large increase in governmental spending. His proposals attempted to attract the middle class, particularly labor, to the Democratic Party; he proposed an increase in educational spending, a middle class tax cut (which would undoubtedly have stimulated demand but was not fiscally plausible, and was never enacted), a reduction of corporate welfare, and a general stimulus package, which the Senate never passed. Such a platform theoretically would have reduced the burden of the middle class, simply because the middle class would not have to rely on the trickle-down generosity of the wealthy business class. And since businesses failed to invest the money that Reagan had provided them, Clinton sought to stimulate innovation and productivity through labor and educational spending. Clinton promised to encourage innovation by reducing the intricate system of corporate welfare, which diminished the incentive for corporations to increase their own productivity.

Although Clinton's fiscal policies, alongside a turn in the business cycle, succeeded in ending the recession and stimulating a new period of growth, other problems ultimately resulted in the Republican mid-term victory. But after Clinton's victory in 1996, the economy remained on solid ground. The deficit was reduced by more than half of what it was when Clinton assumed the presidency. Millions of jobs were created. A balanced budget was passed by Congress. And the first tax cut since President Reagan's tax cuts was approved. So, Carville's 1992 prophecy became an economic reality in 1996.

Evaluation of Free-Response Essay

1. Does the opening paragraph use Carville's statement as a starting point? Does the writer clearly identify contrasting philosophies along with providing background information regarding the different policies created?
2. Does the writer offer analysis of how the philosophy chosen became a policy?

1. The thesis statement uses a comparison of the economic philosophies of Arthur Laffer, Jack Kemp, and David Stockman to the policies of Bill Clinton. The writer then defines supply-siders and offers background information regarding how this theory was put into practice in order to fight what the writer describes as stagflation. The thesis evolves into a discussion of the Reagan philosophy and his implementation of supply-side economics.

2. After explaining the Reagan policies, the writer offers a critical analysis of the impact of those policies that led to the eventual election of Bill Clinton. The writer also makes a fleeting reference to the problems facing Bush after he made his infamous no-tax pledge. The heart of the essay is a critical analysis of how Clinton recognized what the economic problems facing the nation were and how he tried to stimulate the economy while reducing the deficit. The reader is a bit unclear of specific positions taken by the writer; however, in the analysis the writer through incisive criticism makes it obvious whether there is support for the philosophies and policies described.

SECTION 2: DATA-BASED FREE-RESPONSE ESSAY

Answer the following questions based on the graph.

ANNUAL PERCENT CHANGE IN CONSUMER AND PRODUCER PRICE INDEXES, 1970–1996

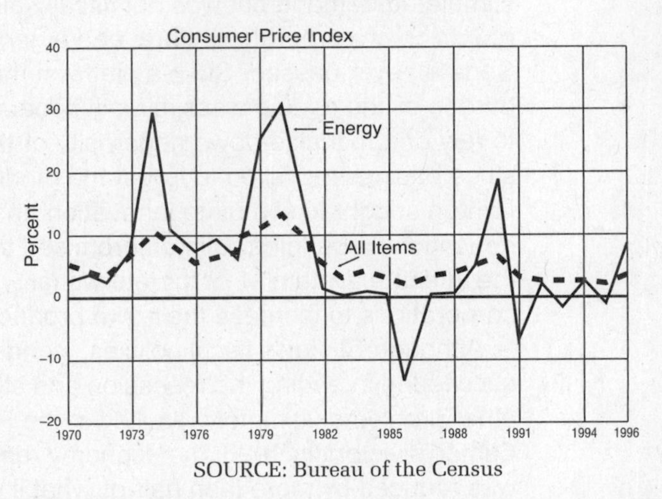

SOURCE: Bureau of the Census

Define the Consumer Price Index by using this chart. Analyze four historical reasons for the trends and give two examples of actions taken by the Federal Reserve.

Sample Student Response

The Consumer Price Index (CPI) is defined as the percentage increase or decrease of goods and services compared to the base year prices of those goods. Specifically, the Bureau of the Census prepares the data based on reports it receives from the Department of Labor. These reports include the market basket list of goods and services indexed to either a base year (for long-range projections) or the beginning of the calendar year (for yearly projections). Some examples of these goods include the price of automobiles, houses, clothing, food, gas, and oil and such services as the price of movies, shows, getting a haircut, etc. If the Consumer Price Index goes up, it has an inflationary impact on the economy, and if it shows a significant decrease, it reflects the fact that there is a decline in the amount of goods and services bought, usually reflected by a nationwide recession. The graph illustrates the following:

- In the period 1970–1996 energy-related goods and services fluctuated much more dramatically than other market basket items.
- The rise and fall of all items calculated reflected periods of inflation, economic stability, and economic recessions.
- Energy fluctuations took place as a result of foreign policy circumstances.

The historical trends impacting on the rise and fall of the Consumer Price Index include the following events:

- During the last years of the Nixon presidency (1970–1974) we were still involved in the Vietnam War and the economy was still prospering. After 1973 OPEC began raising prices on oil, and energy costs skyrocketed. When Ford became president, one of the themes of his administration was put on a button—The WIN (Whip Inflation NOW) button made a proactive statement about the increase of energy costs as well as the percent increase in all items measured by the CPI.
- During the Carter administration relations with the Arab nations worsened, even though the Camp David Accords signaled the beginning of an easing of tensions with Israel. Gas lines became commonplace as the oil cartel limited exports.
- During the Reagan administration the country prospered after Reagan's budget was approved. This budget included one of the biggest tax cuts in the history of the country. However, as reflected by a decrease in the CPI and a significant drop in energy-related goods, the country also experienced a major recession during the Reagan years.
- During the Clinton administration, the CPI reflected low inflation and stable energy costs.

Today, the Federal Reserve Board uses a series of actions in order to try to counter inflationary and recessionary trends signaled by a rise or fall in the Consumer Price Index. If the economy seems to be heading toward higher inflation, the Federal Reserve will raise the discount and interest rates in an attempt to curb spending. If, on the other hand, the economy is sluggish and unemployment is rising along with a reduction of goods, the Fed will lower interest and discount rates to encourage spending. The Board can also borrow more money from member banks in order to stimulate the economy. A good example of the Fed in action was when Allen Greenspan, chair of the board, advocated an aggressive policy of raising interest rates during the first term of the Clinton administration. Even though the economy was on the rebound from a recession and was showing healthy growth, the Fed was afraid that inflation would occur. During the greatest period of economic prosperity (1994–97), the Federal Reserve closely monitored the growing economy. It, along with Greenspan, were given much of the credit for the country's prolonged economic growth. Anytime there was any hint of inflation, the Federal Reserve would raise discount rates. In fact, some economists point to the actions of the "Fed" as one of the most important reasons why the economy sustained itself for such a long period.

Evaluation of the Data-Based Free-Response Sample Essay

1. Does the definition clearly explain what the Consumer Price Index is and how it relates to the graph?
2. Are sufficient and accurate historical examples offered?
3. Does the writer explain the role of the Federal Reserve Board in relation to the trends described in the graph?

1. The writer gives an excellent definition of the Consumer Price Index and links it to the information provided in the graph. The writer also gives an explanation of how the CPI is determined, who reports it, and what impact it has on the economy. Finally, the writer gives three specific results of the graph by referring to time periods and the impact the price of certain goods had on the economy. The writer also offers conclusions regarding why these trends took place. Notice how the writer summarized these results.

2. Four historical examples are offered in response to the trends analyzed in question 1. The writer effectively evaluates events in the Nixon presidency, Carter and Reagan administrations, and Clinton presidency pointing out what the impact of the CPI was on the overall economy.

3. The writer offers a detailed explanation of the role of the Federal Reserve Board and the options the Fed can use in trying to influence the Consumer Price Index. A solid example of what direction the board took under the direction of Allen Greenspan was given to illustrate the points.

CHAPTER 16 The Federal Budget

Chapter Overview

Perhaps the most definitive indicator of the overall public policy direction the government is taking is the development of the federal budget. It involves key players, a proscribed process, and inherent problems. This chapter will focus on who is involved in determining what the multibillion dollar federal budget looks like. We will also explain the players' roles and what happens each step of the way. The problems caused by the growing budget, resulting from a rise in expenditures and a large deficit, and how this area is a primary concern of the public and the players will be one of the themes of this chapter.

In looking at the federal budget, we also will trace the history of key legislation affecting the players and the process. Then we will analyze the components of the budget, including where the government gets its income and how it is allocated. Finally, we will discuss some of the reforms that have been proposed to keep the budget in check.

A Quick Constitutional Review: The Basis of the Federal Government's Budgetary Power

- In Article I Section 8 Clause 1, the Congress is given the power to "lay and collect taxes, to pay the debts, and provide for the common defense and general welfare of the United States."
- Article I also gives the House of Representatives the power to initiate the process of passing all appropriations.
- Article I establishes the power of Congress to impose excise taxes in the form of tariffs.
- However, Article I Section 9 prohibits export taxes.
- Article I directs Congress to impose taxes that are equally apportioned.
- Thus, as a result of the ratification of the Sixteenth Amendment, the income tax is the only direct tax levied.

KEY TERMS

Balanced budget
Congressional Budget Office (CBO)
Continuing resolution
Deficit spending
Direct tax
Entitlements
Indirect tax
Mandatory spending
Office of Management and Budget (OMB)

- Any indirect taxes, such as gasoline, tobacco, and liquor, must be uniform.
- The Supreme Court's decision in *McCulloch v Maryland* (1819) established the principle that states could not tax the federal government.
- Congress is also given the power to "borrow money on the credit of the United States" in Article I.
- Congress can appropriate only money that is budgeted.

Budget Approval

The process of budget development and passage of it involves the key players in the political game.

Even though Congress is given the constitutional power of the purse, the players involved in the process include

- the president,
- executive staff and agencies,
- special interest groups,
- the media, and
- the public.

The president by law must submit a budget proposal to Congress the first Monday after January 3rd. Prior to that date, each federal agency submits detailed proposals outlining the expenses for each department over the next fiscal year. This spending plan is submitted to the Office of Management and Budget, responsible for putting the budget requests together. Following a budget review and analysis, the OMB revises many of the recommendations and prepares a budget for the president to submit to Congress. By the middle of February, the Congressional Budget Office (CBO) evaluates the president's budget and submits a report to the House and Senate Budget Committees. It is interesting to note that the CBO is a staff agency of the Congress, whereas the OMB is a staff agency of the president. Therefore, the results of budgetary analysis by each group may differ. Once the appropriations committees of each house receive the budget, they review it and submit budget resolutions to their respective chambers. These resolutions include estimates of expenditures and recommendations for revenues. By April 15th a common budget direction must be passed. This provides the basis for the actual passage of the following year's budget. The fiscal year begins each October 1st, and both houses must pass a budget that includes 13 major appropriations bills by that date. If any of these bills are not passed, Congress must then pass emergency spending legislation, called a continuing resolution, to avoid the shutdown of any department that did not receive funding from legislation passed. Shutdowns have occurred during the Reagan, Bush, and Clinton administrations. The battle over the 1995–1996 budget was particularly significant. It caused not only the most prolonged government shutdown, but also created unique political consequences. After the Republicans assumed control of Congress in 1994, led by conservative freshmen and spurred on by what was called the "Gingrich Revolution," the GOP believed they could force President Clinton to capitulate when the Congress passed a balanced budget.

By September 30, 1995, the end of the fiscal year, it became apparent that the Republicans' balanced budget which included major social program reductions and an overall objective of reducing the size and scope of the federal government would be vetoed by President Clinton. After Clinton's veto, the budget battle began. Republicans refused to pass continuing resolutions—a stopgap measure to keep the government operating—unless the president agreed in principle to their budgetary demands. President Clinton, using his bully pulpit in a most effective manner, refused and in fact went on the offensive by suggesting that the Republicans were holding the American people hostage. When the media focused their attention on how the shutdown was affecting government workers, and showing dramatic pictures of signs posted outside government agencies and national parks, the Republicans were forced to pass continuing resolutions and reformulate their own budget proposal.

In addition to losing public opinion, the budget battle (the temporary funding of the government) also had a longer lasting impact on presidential politics. It reestablished President Clinton's image after the devastating midterm election defeat in Congress. It also created an election issue that would carry through the entire 1996 campaign.

During this entire process, special interest groups, heads of bureaucratic agencies, the media, and the public are also involved in trying to influence the nature of the budget. Private sector lobbyists argue for increased funding for programs such as entitlements and federal aid, whereas bureaucratic chiefs attend congressional hearings to fight for their departments. The media publicizes the process through objective news reports and editorials. The public through its contacts with legislators (letter writing and phone calls) also gives its viewpoint regarding such issues as a tax increase.

Final passage of the budget is often dramatic, as was the case for President Clinton's first budget. He proposed a tax increase for the wealthiest individuals in the country as well as significant deficit cuts. The final budget passed by a slim margin in the House and by one vote in the Senate, a tie breaker by Vice President Gore.

Deficit Spending

Serious problems, such as how to reduce the nation's deficit while maintaining social programs, face the key players.

What exactly is deficit spending? Ross Perot, during the 1992 campaign, suggested that the problem was so serious that his grandchildren would potentially face the problem of a nation going broke. Very simply put, deficit spending is when expeditures exceed revenues. Beginning with the Revolutionary War, the United States has been forced to be a nation in debt. The debt usually increased after the United States had to react to either a domestic or foreign policy crisis. For instance, during the Depression the country faced one of the largest deficits in its history as a result of the implementation of Roosevelt's New Deal programs. However, the extent of the deficit became unmanageable beginning in the 1980s because of its size and the interest on the debt.

To place the figures in some perspective, during World War I we borrowed $23 billion; during the Depression, another $13 billion, and during World War II, $200 billion. By 1991 the deficit was up to over $3 trillion. The federal government is the only level of government able to borrow more money than it receives. State budgets must be balanced by law. To make matters worse, the interest on the deficit increases the size of the debt to over $170 billion a year. So, even if the government can reduce the size of the debt over a number of years, it still must repay the interest. Who does the federal government borrow money from? It borrows from

- trust funds such as Social Security,
- foreign investors,
- Federal Reserve banks,
- commercial banks,
- state and local governments,
- individuals who own savings bonds,
- money market funds in the form of treasury bonds,
- insurance companies,
- corporations, and
- other areas such as pension funds, brokers, and other groups.

Because the Constitution does not place limits on the extent or method of borrowing, Congress sets limits on the debt. However, the limit has been inching upward and until the passage of the 1993 budget had not decreased since the last time the country showed a surplus, in 1969. By 1997, the deficit was reduced by more than half of what it was when President Clinton assumed the presidency in 1992. As a result of the Balanced Budget Agreement in 1996, and an economy which showed high economic growth, the 1998 proposed budget eliminated the deficit and actually reflected a budget surplus. This surplus was projected to increase throughout the first decades of the new century.

The deficit increased so rapidly in the 1980s due partly to a massive tax decrease proposed by Reagan and passed by Congress without a corresponding cut in expenses. In fact, the defense budget showed a dramatic increase, while the cost of entitlement programs continued to escalate. Bush made campaign promises to reduce the deficit but became frustrated with the Democratic-controlled Congress, which refused to cut social programs. George Bush was forced to renege on his "read my lips, no new taxes" pledge made during the campaign in order to get a budget passed. The consequences of this debt and runaway deficit for the country was a recession that retarded the rate of economic growth and caused an increase in unemployment and failed businesses. Add to the deficit a huge trade imbalance, and you can understand why Congress has attempted to find ways of setting budgetary limits.

Budget Reforms

The history of budget reform measures has resulted in congressional efforts to create an equitable tax structure and reasonable limits on expenditures.

Efforts to control the budget started with reforms of the actual process. Prior to 1974 Congress budgeted in a haphazard manner. The process was decentralized with subcommittees of each house reviewing every request on an agency-by-agency basis. Until the bottom line was totaled, there was never any certainty what the total budget would be.

The Congressional Budget and Impoundment Control Act of 1974 was passed to streamline the process. A secondary objective of the measure was to place controls on the president's ability to determine allocations without appropriate congressional checks. Before the law was passed, President Nixon used his authority to cut off funds for programs he felt would increase the deficit. Congress responded by passing this law, which placed an additional check on the president. It prevented the president from impounding previously passed allocations without congressional approval. The law also provided for

- a budget calendar with a series of built-in procedures,
- the creation of a budget committee in each house whose responsibility it was to recommend to the Congress a total budget by April 1st, and
- the creation of the Congressional Budget Office, which acted as a check on the OMB.

The law established a time line of procedural steps the Congress had to take in order to pass the budget. These included the passage of budget resolutions, budget reconciliation aimed at achieving savings from taxes, other revenue adjustments and authorization bills that established discretionary government programs, and finally appropriations bills that covered the budget year and gave final authorization for spending. Even though the deficit and debt continued to rise after passage of the law, its supporters pointed to the fact that Congress was able to view the entire process from start to finish and therefore was able to understand fully where revenue was coming from and where money was being allocated.

In response to the increased deficit spending, Congress passed the Gramm-Rudman-Hollings Balanced Budget and Emergency Deficit Control Act of 1985. This law was named after its cosponsors Senators Phil Gramm of Texas, Warren Rudman of New Hampshire, and Ernest Hollings of South Carolina. The law set goals to meet the deficit. If these goals were not met, automatic across-the-board spending cuts must be ordered by the president. Programs such as Social Security and interest on the national debt were exempt. In 1989 cuts were made until a budget was approved by Congress. The law also gave direction that the 1993 budget would have to be balanced. Because these were goals and a balanced budget requirement would need a constitutional amendment, Congress has used this law as a guide for overall reductions.

Attempting to find a way of helping the economy and closing tax loopholes, President Reagan asked Congress to pass the most far-reaching tax reform measure since the income tax was instituted. Supported by liberal Democratic Senator Bill Bradley of New Jersey, this law called for tax code changes that would result in a restructuring of tax brackets and eliminating many tax deductions. The law, supported by both Democrats and Republicans, passed in 1986 and succeeded in these two objectives. The result was that many Americans received a tax cut. And because many loopholes were addressed, it was hoped that additional income would offset the loss of revenue from the tax cut received by the middle class. The law reduced the number of brackets from 15 to three, it slightly increased deductions for individuals and families, and eliminated many other deductions. Even though the law succeeded in its objectives, because the expense side of the budget was not kept in check, the deficit still increased dramatically. From 1981 to 1992 the overall deficit quadrupled. However, Clinton's deficit reduction programs eliminated the deficit during his administration. By the year 1998, the budget was balanced, along with an anticipated budget surplus. The political argument then arose as to what should be done with any surplus. Some of the suggested uses for the surplus included reducing the national debt, saving Social Security, decreasing tax rates for all Americans, and increasing spending for government programs.

Political Compromise

The outcome of the budgetary process is often a result of wrangling between Democrats and Republicans. Democrats accuse Republicans of pushing through a budget that would result in "trickle-down economics." Republicans point to Democrats as "taxers and spenders."

Let's look at some characteristics of recent budgets adopted by Congress.

Money comes from

- federal income taxes—49 percent
- Social Security and payroll taxes—33 percent
- corporate taxes—10 percent
- excise taxes such as taxes on liquor, gasoline, and luxury items—3 percent
- customs and duties collected and other sources—4 percent

Money is expended for

- entitlements (Social Security, Medicare, Medicaid)—48 percent
- national defense—16 percent
- interest on the debt—10 percent
- non-defense discretionary spending—19 percent
- other mandatory spending—7 percent

By 2001 the total budget had risen to over $1 trillion.

WHERE MONEY COMES FROM

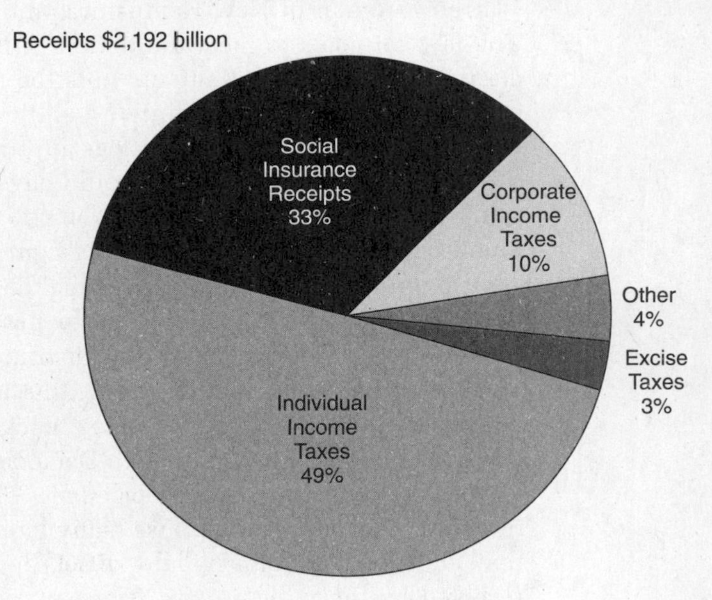

Source: Office of Management and Budget

Even though the defense budget was a distant second to entitlements in expenditures, if you add the components of budgets from other areas, the gap is much smaller. A second issue was why social programs have increased so dramatically. Part of the answer came about from the philosophy of the Democrats to maintain programs passed as part of FDR's New Deal and Johnson's Great Society. When Reagan became president, he made a concerted attempt and succeeded in reducing some of these programs. However, they are still the single largest area of the budget. Economists and political scientists felt that the

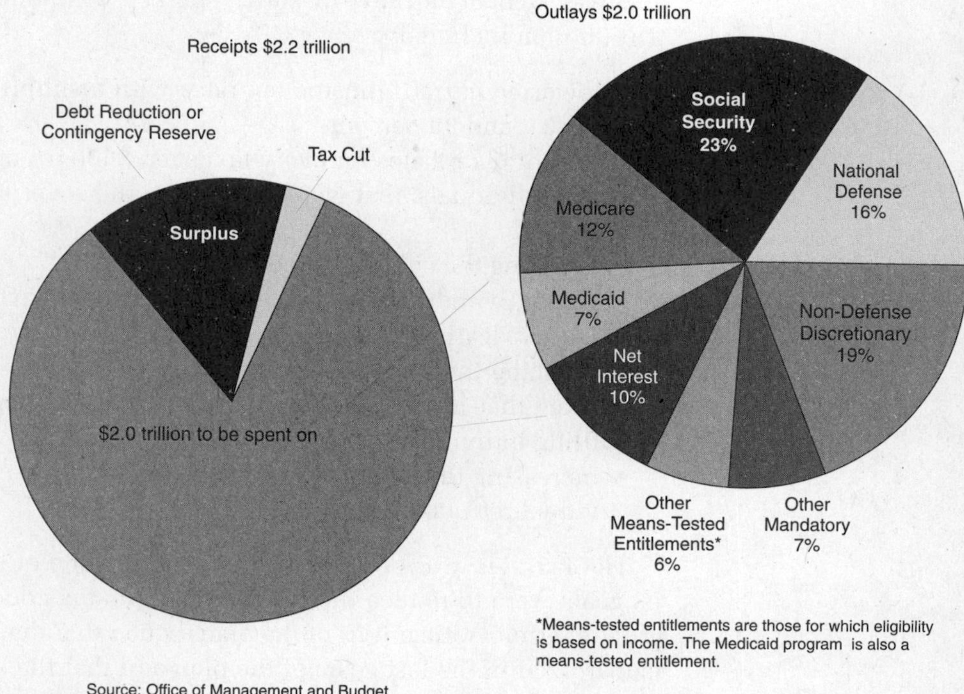

process itself encouraged the increase in this area. They pointed to the incremental manner in which budgets are developed, where the previous year's budget is looked upon as a base and therefore the new budget must increase because of inflation and other factors. Even with attempts at what is called zero-based budgeting, where budget lines start at a ground-floor foundation so that programs can be reviewed, Congress still operated using an incremental approach. Another reason why costs have escalated is that, because entitlement programs are mandated by law, they are already built into the budget and increase as a result of the nature of the particular entitlement. For instance, the cost of Social Security has increased dramatically from $33 billion in 1970 to $265 billion in 1991. In 2001, the cost of Social Security topped $400 billion. In addition to the increase, Congress borrowed from the Social Security trust fund, and projections indicate that by the second decade of the twenty-first century the system will go broke. Congress in 1994 approved the formation of a separate Social Security Administrative agency. By 1997, both Congress and the president recognized the need for major reforms for Social Security, Medicare, and Medicaid. President George W. Bush appointed a bipartisan commission to make recommendations regarding Social Security.

Controversial Budget Reforms

Present-day budget reform efforts attempt to deal with problems created by the deficit.

Three controversial budget reforms were a key part of George W. Bush's campaign for the presidency: the passage of an across-the-board tax cut, the creation of individual retirement accounts that would partially privatize Social Security, and an increase in federal spending on education.

President Bush's tax cut was the first major policy initiative to pass Congress and was signed into law in 2001. The key components of the ten-year $1.4 trillion plan included:

- lowering current income tax rates with a simplified rate structure of 10, 15, 25, and 33 percent
- instant tax rebates for every taxpayer, $600 for married couples and $300 for individuals, that were sent out by the government during the summer of 2001
- doubling the child tax credit
- gradually reducing and eventually eliminating the estate tax, also known as the "death tax"
- reducing the so-called marriage penalty by lowering the amount of extra taxes that a married couple pays above the amount they would pay if filing individually
- increasing the amount of money a wage earner can contribute to an individual retirement account

The tax plan was described as the cornerstone of the Bush presidency and its goals were to reduce the inequities in the tax code and to foster economic growth. Democratic critics of the plan argued that the federal surplus would be jeopardized in the last years of the plan and that the country would again face budget deficits.

The second controversial proposal put forth by President George W. Bush was to modernize and reform Social Security. Arguing that, in the long run, Social Security payments by the government would have to increase dramatically in order to keep up with the aging population and that the return on Social Security benefits would be much higher, Bush proposed the creation of personal retirement accounts. These accounts would be voluntary and would enable individuals to increase their retirement benefits by allowing the investment of a portion of these accounts in what was described as "a balanced portfolio of stocks and bonds." Proponents of this plan predicted that returns on such investments could be as high as 5.5 percent, almost double what an individual collects from Social Security. Critics of the program pointed out that in an economy with a volatile stock market, an individual could lose a significant portion of any investment made. President Bush appointed a commission of Democrats and Republicans to study the proposal and to make recommendations.

The third controversial budget reform was a spending proposal, including a dramatic increase in the federal government's commitment to aid to education. Following up on George Bush's theme of "no child being left behind," George W. Bush submitted to Congress a $44 billion education plan that

- encouraged states to raise standards by mandating tests in English and mathematics in grades 4 through 8;
- maintained local control and empowered parents with educational choices for their children beginning in preschool through college and beyond;
- included a "Reading First" program aimed at early intervention to build strong reading skills in preschool children;

- reformed Head Start by making school readiness the top priority and moving the program under the authority of the Department of Education;
- provided awards to states and schools that improved student performance but promised to withdraw funds from schools that failed to improve performance after three years;
- expanded school choice to include tuition tax credits that would enable parents to send their children to private or parochial schools;
- increased and expanded education savings accounts that helped pay for educational expenses from kindergarten through college;
- increased funds for the "Troops-to-Teachers" recruitment program; and
- required states to measure and improve school safety

Both Democrats and Republicans supported many of these proposals, and by the summer of 2001 a bill incorporating many of the components of this plan passed both houses of Congress. However, one of the key components, tuition tax credits used to send children to private and parochial schools, did not survive even though the Supreme Court ruled that tax credits used for parochial schools were legal.

Chapter 16 Review

SECTION 1: MULTIPLE-CHOICE QUESTIONS

1. Which of the following institutions is given specific constitutional power of the purse?
(A) Office of Management and Budget
(B) president
(C) Congress
(D) special interest groups
(E) executive agencies

2. If Congress does not pass a budget by the beginning of the fiscal year, then which of the following takes place?
(A) The president can impose a budget to keep the government running.
(B) The Courts can step in and create a temporary budget.
(C) The Congress must pass a continuing resolution.
(D) Government offices are automatically shut down.
(E) A contingency budget goes into effect.

3. The federal government may borrow money from all the following EXCEPT
(A) trust funds.
(B) foreign investors.
(C) commercial banks.
(D) money market funds.
(E) the United States Treasury.

4. As a result of President Nixon's practice of cutting off funds for programs he felt would increase the budget,
   (A) Congress passed the line item veto.
   (B) Congress passed the Congressional Budget and Impoundment Control Act.
   (C) the Supreme Court ruled the practice unconstitutional.
   (D) a balanced budget amendment was passed.
   (E) the Gramm-Rudman-Hollings Emergency Deficit Control Act was passed.

5. Which of the following components was part of President Reagan's 1981 tax bill?
   (A) a significant increase in the number of tax deductions allowed
   (B) a decrease in the number of tax brackets
   (C) a decrease in the deficit
   (D) a larger tax cut for the lower class than the upper class
   (E) an increase in the capital gains tax

6. Over the past 20 years which of the following areas has shown the greatest increase in budgetary spending?
   (A) the defense budget
   (B) federal operations
   (C) federal grants
   (D) discretionary spending
   (E) entitlements

7. Which of the following areas gives the federal government the greatest amount of income?
   (A) income taxes
   (B) Social Security and payroll taxes
   (C) corporate taxes
   (D) luxury taxes
   (E) money collected from tariffs

8. All the following are attempts at lowering the nation's deficit EXCEPT
   (A) the attempt to pass a balanced budget constitutional amendment.
   (B) a change in the welfare system forcing people to work.
   (C) the proposal to institute means testing in order to get Social Security.
   (D) the proposal to institute means testing for Medicare.
   (E) the creation of the National Service Program.

9. Proponents of the plan to privatize Social Security argue that
   (A) investments in Social Security would increase.
   (B) the stock market's volatility increases the investment return.
   (C) there is a shrinking number of baby boomers in need of Social Security benefits.
   (D) the government has a surplus in the Social Security trust fund that will last through the twenty-first century.
   (E) senior citizens favor this reform.

10. According to many pollsters, a defining event that voters remembered during the 1992 presidential campaign was
    (A) President Bush's no new tax pledge.
    (B) President Bush's handling of the Gulf War.
    (C) President Bush's success in vetoing Democratic spending proposals.
    (D) President Bush's proclamation that the cold war was over.
    (E) President Bush's agreements with Russia to destroy nuclear arsenals.

Answers to Multiple-Choice Questions

1. **(C)** Type of Question: Identification and analysis
   The Congress is given the specific constitutional power of appropriation, taxing, and borrowing in Article I and Article I Section 8. The president can veto proposed appropriations bills. The Office of Management and Budget prepares a preliminary budget and oversees the passed budget. Special interest groups attempt to influence spending packages, and executive agencies have defined spending limitations based on congressional approval of their budgets.
2. **(C)** Type of Question: Hypothetical
   A continuing resolution prevents the federal government from shutting down if final passage of specific budget items are not approved by October 1st. Neither the president nor the Courts can intercede in this situation. Government offices remain operational when a continuing resolution is passed. A contingency budget suggests that approval is automatic and may differ from the existing budget. That is not the case when a continuing resolution is passed.
3. **(E)** Type of Question: Solution to a problem
   The United States Treasury is responsible for printing currency and is the executive department responsible for dealing with many budgetary matters. It cannot print more or less money to counter economic conditions. The federal government can borrow money from trust funds such as the Social Security system, as well as foreign investors, money market funds, and commercial banks.
4. **(B)** Type of Question: Cause and effect relationships
   The Congressional Budget and Impoundment Control Act was passed in 1974 in order to stop the president from doing away with approved programs in the name of deficit reduction. The law also streamlined the entire budgetary process. The line item veto was approved by both houses of Congress in 1995 but stalled in conference. The Supreme Court never ruled on the legality of Nixon's actions. A balanced budget amendment never passed Congress, even though a direction to balance the budget was passed by Congress in 1995. The Gramm-Rudman-Hollings Act set spending limits.
5. **(B)** Type of Question: Identification and analysis
   Reagan's historic tax plan resulted in a decrease of the number of tax brackets. It increased the deficit significantly. It also gave the upper class a disproportionate tax savings compared to the lower class. The plan did not increase the capital gains tax. Even though it resulted in minor increases in tax deductions, its major impact was the elimination of many tax deductions.

6. **(E)** Type of Question: Identification and analysis
Social Security, Medicare, Medicaid, and welfare account for more than 40 percent of the federal budget. The national defense amounts to 25 percent of the budget. Federal operations, federal grants, and discretionary spending account for the rest of the expenditures along with interest on the debt.
7. **(A)** Type of Question: Identification and analysis
Income taxes account for more than 40 percent of the income. Social Security and payroll taxes account for a little over 33 percent. Corporate taxes account for a little over 10 percent, and luxury taxes and tariffs, under 10 percent.
8. **(E)** Type of Question: Cause and effect relationships
Battling the nation's deficit became a significant issue in the 1990s. Congress attempted to pass a constitutional amendment in 1995, and after it failed a budget that would reduce the deficit to zero by the year 2002 was developed. The National Service Program aimed at giving college students a means to get low-interest loans cost the federal government money.
9. **(A)** Type of Question: Sequencing a series of events
The plan to privatize Social Security would allow individual wage earners to open private retirement accounts that would be used to invest funds in the stock market. These private retirement accounts would provide a higher rate of return on investments than what is currently made on employee contributions to Social Security. Thus, people favoring the plan feel that investments in Social Security would increase, choice A. Choice B is incorrect because the more volatile the stock market, the greater the likelihood that investments would decline. Choice C is wrong because there are an increasing number of baby boomers. Choices D and E are wrong because the Social Security trust fund will run out of money in the twenty-first century and senior citizens oppose this plan.
10. **(A)** Type of Question: Chronological
Even though all the events took place during Bush's administration, the one event that had the most impact on the election was when President Bush, in his 1988 acceptance speech, made a pledge to the nation "Read my lips, no new taxes," and then reneged on it. This opened the door for Clinton to use the statement as evidence that Bush would break other promises.

SECTION 2: FREE-RESPONSE ESSAY

In 1994 and 1995 the Congress failed to pass a balanced budget amendment to the Constitution by one vote in the Senate.

1. Give one argument for and one argument against the passage of the amendment.
2. Describe one public policy initiative aimed at controlling spending that has been passed.
3. Describe the impact that a balanced budget has on the federal budget.

Sample Student Response

The debate over the balanced budget amendment was fiery in Congress. The public, according to polls, indicated that they favored the measure by four to one. Republicans vehemently declared that lowering the deficit was the first priority of the new Congress and that it must be done at all costs. When they were asked to announce the way in which they would lower spending, Republicans refused. They did say, however, that Social Security would not be cut in order to balance the budget. While acknowledging that it will take at least seven years to balance the budget, Republicans believed that it was critical to do so as soon as possible in order to ensure the nation's economic security. Many Democrats also saw the need to balance the budget, but they felt that the Republicans' plan was rash and that it would hurt the middle class. President Clinton had lowered the deficit in each of his first two years in the office, and many people argued that we should stay on the path that he had started down.

Long before a passage of a balanced budget amendment was possible, Congress attempted to decrease the actual size of the deficit. Congress' first step toward balancing the budget was with the passage of the Congressional Budget and Impoundment Control Act of 1974. Before the passage of this bill, President Nixon was able to stop the allocation of funds to programs that he felt would increase the size of the deficit. This circumvented Congress' control of the budget. The bill forced the president to get congressional approval before removing funds from programs to which the funds had already been allocated. The bill also helped to streamline the budget process, expediting the process and allowing for full congressional participation in the budget process. The budget process was sped up to a degree by a budget calendar that was set up with a built-in series of procedures; the law also set up committees in each house whose responsibility it was to propose a total budget by April 1. The law was not successful in decreasing the deficit, but it did streamline the budget process and make the budget more accessible to everyone in Congress, while checking presidential power.

As a result of the 1996 Balanced Budget Act, signed into law by President Clinton, the nation finally had a balanced budget. The act mandated spending caps and resulted in a balanced budget, creating a federal budget surplus in 1998 that was expected to continue into the twenty-first century. As a result of this law and the resulting surplus, the debate began regarding how to best use the federal surplus. Three arguments were put forth—use the money to save Social Security, pay down the national debt, or spend it on needed programs. The balanced budget and new surplus put increased pressure on Congress and the president to achieve policy goals that would maintain the prosperity of the 1990s.

Evaluation of Free-Response Essay

1. Does the essay describe the major reasons why a balanced budget amendment was debated?
2. Is one economic policy fully discussed in the foundation of the essay?
3. Does the writer describe the effects of a balanced budget on the federal budget?

1. The writer does an effective job giving the historical perspective relating to the arguments for and against a balanced budget amendment. The thesis paragraph establishes the economic conditions in 1992 that led to Clinton's election

and eventually the Republican takeover of Congress in 1994. The writer also shows evidence that the deficit was reduced by Clinton even without a balanced budget amendment and establishes some of the criticism in the form of social programs that would have to be eliminated if an amendment were passed.

2. The foundation of the essay describes historically one major attempt to keep the budget in check. Using the Congressional Budget and Impoundment Control Act of 1974, the writer suggests that both Democrats and Republicans were concerned about the direction the budget was taking and the negative consequences of a growing deficit.

3. The last part of the essay evaluates the consequences of a balanced budget on the lives of the American people. Historic social programs such as Social Security, Medicare, and welfare could be drastically changed and the traditional safety net concept be altered dramatically.

SECTION 2: DATA-BASED FREE-RESPONSE ESSAY

Answer the following questions based on the graph.

SURPLUS/DEFICIT IN BILLIONS OF DOLLARS

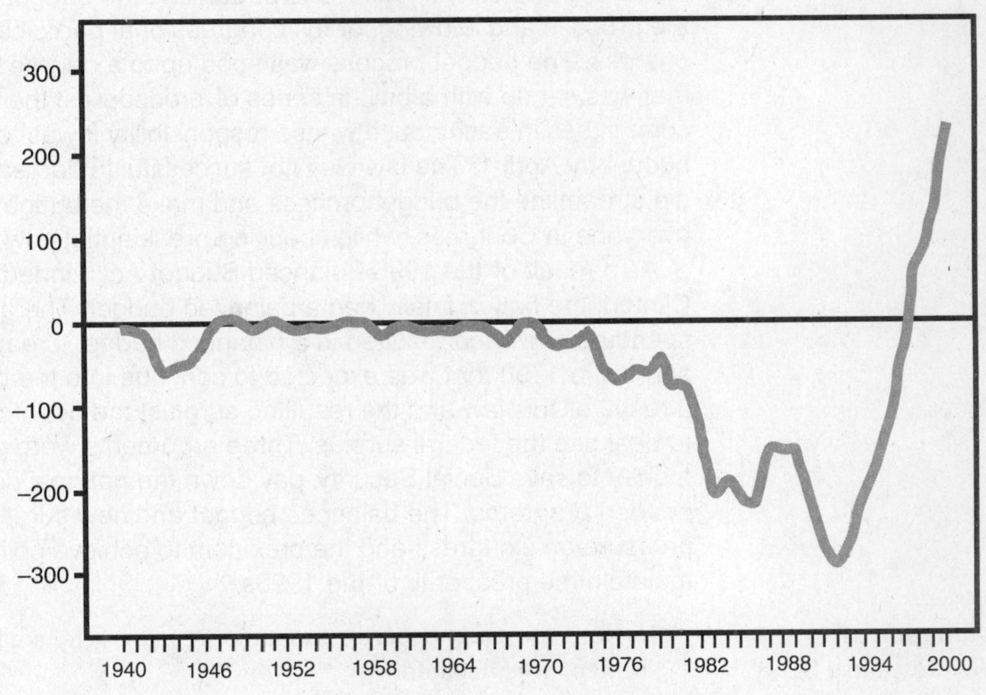

Source: Office of Management and Budget

1. Identify and explain two budget trends from 1976 to 2000 as indicated by the graph.
2. Identify and explain two policy choices that lawmakers had as a result of the trend reflected by the graph from 1998 to 2000.

Sample Student Response

The graph reflects the history of the federal budget deficit and surplus from 1940 through 2000. Two trends indicated by the graph from 1976 to 2000 are an increase in the budget deficit beginning in 1976, which reached its highest deficit level of $300 billion in 1992, and a reduction in the deficit beginning in 1993, eventually resulting in a surplus in 1998, which continued through 2000.

The reason for the growth of the budget deficit during the 1980s was that President Ronald Reagan instituted an economic stimulus plan that included a major tax reduction. As a result, government revenues decreased while spending levels continued to rise, especially in the area of national defense. A Democratic Congress also maintained most of the Great Society programs passed during the administration of President Johnson. This deficit continued during the administration of George Bush and reached its highest level because an economic recession occurred in the last year of the Bush administration.

The reason that the budget deficit began to decrease in 1992 was that the newly elected president, William Clinton, initiated a budget deficit plan that was passed without a single Republican vote. By 1994, when the Republicans took control of the Congress, one of their goals was to implement a balanced budget. Though a constitutional amendment requiring a balanced budget failed by one vote in the Senate, Congress passed and the president signed into law a balanced budget act in 1996. This act set the framework for a balanced federal budget that eventually resulted in a budget surplus in 1998.

Two policy decisions that lawmakers had to struggle with as a result of the new surplus included whether to use the surplus to save Social Security or whether to pay down the national debt. Since the average retiree is expected to collect Social Security benefits for more than 20 years after retirement, experts predict that the Social Security trust fund would run out of money by 2075. President George W. Bush created a commission in 2001 to explore different options. A second policy decision that lawmakers debated was whether to provide tax relief. Republicans favored a ten-year tax reduction program and passed the law in 2001 that reduced tax rates across the board. Concern was expressed that this would again lead the nation to new deficits, especially if a lagging economy did not improve.

Evaluation of Data-Based Free-Response Sample Essay

1. Does the writer identify and explain two trends presented in the graph?
2. Does the essay identify and explain two policy choices resulting from the budget surplus as indicated by the graph?

1. The graph illustrates the history of federal budget deficits and surpluses in the United States from 1940 to 2000. After looking at the graph, students should be able to recognize periods when there have been balanced budgets, budget deficits, and budget surpluses. Between 1976 and 1992, there were clearly budget deficits. From 1993 to 2000, the graph indicates that the deficits began to shrink, and eventually resulted in budget surpluses. The writer identifies these periods and explains how Presidents Reagan and Clinton had an impact on the federal budgets during these time periods.

2. After identifying two trends, the writer discusses the budget surplus. The student is asked to identify and explain two ways the surplus could be used. The writer chooses to discuss Social Security and tax cuts. Other available choices include paying down the national debt and using the money to expand and/or create federal programs. The essay then describes the components of the Social Security plan and the recent tax cuts.

CHAPTER 17 Social Welfare and Entitlements

Chapter Overview

Public policy differences related to social welfare issues have resulted in different approaches by elected office holders. Some call these programs handouts. Others point to the philosophical doctrine of the Declaration of Independence, which proclaimed "all men are created equal . . . ," as a rationale for the creation of such programs. The question of the extent to which government should provide social welfare exists for all levels of government—federal, state, and local.

There is no doubt that we are living in a class-based society. Because that policy emanates from a pluralistic approach to problem solving, the fact remains that there is a tremendous disparity between rich and poor. This chapter will explore the consequences of the unequal distribution of income and wealth as it relates to public policy issues. The government establishes a poverty line that references the point at which an individual is considered living in what has been called a culture of poverty.

Picking up from the previous chapter's discussion regarding taxation, we will look at the specific types of taxes that exist, how they have an impact on people who have different levels of income and wealth, and the types of distributive and redistributive programs, which come under the names entitlement and social welfare, that have been created by government.

Specifically, we will evaluate the history, successes, failures, and future of these programs—Social Security, Medicare, Medicaid, food stamps, aid to the disabled and homeless, and welfare. The pros and cons of social welfare and the impact that these programs have on the nation's deficit will conclude the chapter.

KEY TERMS

- Block grant
- Culture of poverty
- Entitlements
- Flat tax
- Food stamp program
- Income distribution
- Medicaid
- Medicare
- Poverty line
- Progressive tax
- Regressive tax
- Safety net
- Social welfare
- Workfare

Characteristics of Class-Based Society

A class-based society in America is characterized by a disparity in the distribution of income and wealth. In the past 15 years the percentage of people living below the poverty line has decreased.

First we must define some basic terms. Income distribution refers to the portion of national income that individuals and groups earn. Even though there has not been a significant comparative change in income distribution between the lowest and highest fifth of the American population from 1953 to 2000, since then there has developed over that period of time a wider disparity in levels of income for those groups. Specifically, from 1980 to 2000, the incomes of the wealthiest Americans rose at a much greater level than those of the poorest fifth. The median income in 1999 for white non-Hispanics was $44,400 compared to $15,569 for a family living below the poverty level.

Income is defined as the specific level of money earned over a specific period of time, whereas wealth is what is actually owned such as stocks, bonds, property, bank accounts, and cars. Wealth, unlike levels of income, has been even more disproportionate, with the top 1 percent of the country's rich having about 25 percent of the wealth.

Taking into account this disparity of the distribution of income and wealth, the United States Bureau of the Census created a poverty line. This line measures what a typical family would need to spend for what the bureau called an "austere" standard of living. According to the bureau, the poverty rate dropped from 12.7 percent in 1998 to 11.8 percent in 1999, the lowest rate since 1979. The poverty rate and the number of poor declined for every racial and ethnic group.

Which groups become part of this culture of poverty? People who are poor because they cannot find work, have broken families, lack adequate housing, and face a hostile environment. The Bureau of the Census views families as being above or below the poverty level using a poverty index developed by the Social Security Administration. According to the bureau, "the index is based solely on money income and does not reflect the fact that many low-income persons receive noncash benefits such as food stamps, Medicaid, and public housing." People living below the poverty level include a disproportionate number of minorities living in cities when compared to the percentage of all poor people within each group. Liberals make the argument that it is the government's responsibility to come up with solutions for this problem, which they claim is caused by long-term abuses of society including legal restrictions, a lack of educational opportunity, exposure to drugs and crime, and discrimination. Conservatives feel that local programs, privately sponsored, that provide job opportunities while keeping people off welfare rolls are the solution to the problem. What is apparent is that regardless of the point of view you take, there have been education, health, housing, and drug policies that have been created by the public and private sectors and that attempt to break the culture of poverty. These programs will be fully discussed later in this chapter.

Taxes

Taxes impact the level and distribution of individuals' income because of the relative burden they place on people to pay them.

As we stated in Chapters 15 and 16, taxes are the major source of income for federal, state, and local governments. Taxes have been the brunt of comedians' jokes ("the only things certain in life are death and taxes"), but they are recognized as an essential ingredient in the ability of government to provide services to the population. The three types of personal taxes that exist are progressive taxes, regressive taxes, and proportional taxes. They each affect groups in different ways. A progressive tax such as the current federal income tax collects more money from the rich than the poor on a sliding scale. If the government takes an equal share from everybody regardless of income, it is a proportional tax. Also called a flat tax, former California Governor Jerry Brown suggested this approach during the 1992 presidential campaign. Many Republicans suggested this as an alternative to the present tax structure after the 1994 election. A regressive tax such as a sales tax has the poor paying a greater share than the rich. After the 1996 election, some Republicans even demanded the abolition of the Internal Revenue Service as well as for the implementation of a flat tax structure.

Yet, governments have few alternatives other than collection of taxes to pay for the services they provide, especially in the area of social welfare programs. The foundation for these programs stems from the grandparent of entitlement, Social Security. It mandates contributory payments in the form of payroll taxes made by the employer and employee. Part of the payments also go to a Medicare program established as part of the Great Society. Because this program is predicated on forced savings, it differs from other programs such as public assistance programs, which are based on a noncontributory approach.

Finally, if government has these programs, are they making a difference in income distribution? Studies have concluded that despite all the efforts made on the part of federal, state, and local governments the problem of income inequality still exists.

History

The history of social welfare programs reflects a trend of increased government contributory and non-contributory policies.

If we view the general welfare, as stated in the Preamble to the Constitution, in terms of government-sponsored programs in the areas of social legislation, education, and health and housing, the growth and development of "welfarism" can be split into three eras—the state-sponsored era, the federal era, and the safety net era. A return to the state-sponsored era with the support of block grants was advocated by the Republicans in 1995.

The state-sponsored era lasted from 1789 to 1932 and included the following social welfare programs:

- state child labor laws
- state unemployment and workman's compensation measures
- state-mandated pensions

State-sponsored education programs derived from

- the Northwest Ordinance of 1787
- the growth of state universities and public schools
- the federal Morill Act of 1862 for land grant colleges

State-sponsored health and housing programs derived from

- public health ordinances
- the Homestead Act of 1864

The federal era began with New Deal relief measures under the Social Security Act. It was the most far-reaching piece of legislation ever passed. Its primary aim was to help one segment of the society—senior citizens. Previously described, the act established the principle that it was the government's responsibility to aid retirees, even if the aid came from the forced savings of the workforce. Other aspects of the bill provided for unemployment insurance, and today the act has been expanded to include

- Old-Age Survivors Disability Insurance (OASDI)—covers 93 percent of the work force through FICA contributions and provides monthly payments to retired and disabled workers, spouses, and their children.
- Social Security Disability Insurance (SSDI)—monthly checks to disabled workers between the ages of 50 and 64.
- Supplemental Security Income (SSI)—gives money to the needy, aged, blind, or disabled through a formula that equalizes benefits.
- Aid to Families with Dependent Children (AFDC)—establishes federal grants to state governments that will provide money to low-income families with dependent children. This program is the largest welfare program. It was changed dramatically in 1996 when President Clinton signed a major welfare reform act. This law, which will be discussed at the end of the chapter, in the free-response essay, gave block grants to the states. The burden of overseeing welfare was shifted from the federal government to the states.

Other New Deal acts providing federal assistance for health included the creation of the National Institute of Health in 1935. In the area of housing, Congress passed the Wagner-Steagall National Housing Act providing for public housing in 1937. Other welfare acts of the New Deal included a Fair Labor Standards Act in 1938, setting a minimum wage, 40-hour work week, and the prohibition of child labor under 16. The Works Progress Administration (WPA) and the Civilian Conservation Corps (CCC) were also forms of welfare passed to stimulate the economy and help end the Depression.

After World War II the GI Bill of Rights for educational and vocational training was passed in 1944. It was followed by the National School Lunch Act of 1946 and the Housing Act of 1949, providing for subsidized private housing by the federal government. In the 1950s President Eisenhower signed the National Defense Education Act in 1958 in response to the Soviet Union's successful launch of the Sputnik satellite. This act gave substantial federal aid to education especially in the area of science.

The turning point in the federal era occurred as part of Lyndon Johnson's Great Society programs. Much legislation was passed in part as a response to the civil rights movement and also because there was a significant Democratic majority in both houses who agreed with Johnson that the government's role should be to develop programs including

- Medicare—covering hospital and medical costs of people 65 years of age and older as well as disabled individuals receiving Social Security.

- The war on poverty extending benefits to the poor.
- Food stamp program—giving food coupons to people determined to be eligible based on income and family size.
- Medicaid (a shared program between the federal and local governments)—covering hospital, doctor, prescription-drug, and nursing-home costs of low-income people.

In addition, Johnson pushed through Congress civil rights legislation that had the intent of increasing educational and job opportunities for minorities.

During the Nixon, Carter, and Ford years, the Great Society programs were sustained and, in some cases, expanded. In 1972 the Equal Opportunity Act provided for legal recourse as a result of job discrimination. In 1972 cost of living indexing was attached to Social Security and other welfare programs, and in 1973 a job training act, Comprehensive Employment Training Administration (CETA), was passed. The first hint that there were problems with Social Security also occurred in 1973 when the Board of Trustees of the Social Security System reported that the system was running a large deficit.

The "Reagan revolution" of the 1980s, with his assurance that there would always be a "safety net" for those people receiving the benefits of the many programs previously described, attempted to cut back the scope of the Great Society programs. He received the cooperation of the Democrats and cut the rate of increase to OASDI and Medicare. He also succeeded in reducing some of the need assistance programs. However, after 1984 these programs again began to increase. In addition, special interest groups such as the American Association of Retired Persons (AARP) lobbied effectively against cuts in Social Security and Medicare. During the 1995 congressional term, the Republicans passed a series of bills that would substantially cut Medicare and Medicaid in an effort to prevent their collapse and with the goal of moving toward a balanced budget. President Clinton vetoed these measures. A broader agreement was reached in 1997, however. It also became apparent that eventually there would be means testing and increased costs for senior citizens.

Searching for Solutions

Social welfare programs today emphasize the need to provide solutions for homelessness, healthcare coverage, and the scourge of drug abuse.

As homelessness became part of the American city panorama in the 1980s, the Bush administration and big city mayors attempted to develop mutually beneficial programs to improve the plight of the homeless. The president's Housing and Urban Development Secretary, Jack Kemp, urged the passage of a $25 billion authorization for housing programs, and it was included in the 1991 budget. This increase came after Reagan succeeded in cutting back on housing programs. In 1992 it was estimated that there could be close to three million homeless people across the country.

Universal healthcare became the battle cry of the Clinton administration. However, the issue had been originally placed on the public agenda by Presidents Truman and Nixon. One would expect that the United States would be a healthcare world leader. In fact other countries such as Canada and Great Britain have had universal healthcare for years. Critics of America's system pointed to the fact that the United States has a lower life expectancy and higher infant mortality rate than countries providing universal coverage. There are those who pointed out that, even without a universal system, America still spends 14 percent of its Gross National Product on health. But because of such factors as medical malpractice suits, skyrocketing insurance, and health costs, as well as the loss of coverage for many workers who changed or lost jobs, the cry for reform was taken up. In addition, it became evident that access to health insurance was closely tied to race and income with whites, who have higher incomes on average than African-Americans, more likely to have coverage.

Even with Medicare and Medicaid, the country still lagged behind in dealing with health-related coverage. The Family Medical Leave Act of 1993 gave unpaid emergency medical leave for employees with a guarantee that their job would not be taken away in the interim. But what President Clinton hoped would be the benchmark of his administration was the adoption of a national health security plan as extensive as the original Social Security Act. Standing before Congress in 1993, Clinton held up a Health Security Card and threatened to veto any bill passed that did not include universal healthcare as its foundation. The bill itself was well over a thousand pages, and spearheading the drive was the nation's First Lady, Hillary Rodham Clinton. During the summer of 1994 both houses introduced watered-down versions of Clinton's bill. However, the legislation remained tied up as a massive lobbying effort took place. The issues of employer mandates, timing, and the extent of the coverage provided kept Congress from acting on the measure. As a result of the Republican electoral victory in the mid-term elections, the issue of healthcare was placed on the back burner. However, in 1996, a health reform law guaranteeing the portability of health insurance if a worker left a job was signed into law.

Welfare reform has also been high on the political agendas of state governors as well as the federal government. Workfare became an alternative to welfare, and many states have successfully instituted work programs aimed at removing welfare recipients from the rolls. President Clinton as well as the Republicans finally reached agreement on a far-reaching Welfare Reform Act. (See the free-response essay on page 370 for further description of this new law.)

Although the problem of drug abuse extends into the area of criminal laws, the government has also developed social programs aimed at stemming the increase of drug use by the young. On the state level, the DARE program brings a policeman into the classroom. First Lady Nancy Reagan urged American youth to "Say no to drugs." President Reagan appointed William Bennett as the nation's first drug czar—a title denoting one person who is in charge of developing a strategy to fight the drug problem and keep the nation informed. President Bush came up with a plan aimed both at diminishing the supply of drugs and at curbing their use. He even went as far as invading Panama, arresting Panamanian leader Manuel Noriega and successfully prosecuting him in the United States on drug charges.

The Future

The future of social welfare programs depends on whether they remain a public policy priority. An essential component of this debate will be the ability of government to continue to foot the bill.

To illustrate the point, you have to go only as far as looking at the Social Security System. After its board informed the public of the program's deficit, Congress began looking at ways of saving the system. The National Commission on Social Security Reform was created in 1983 by President Reagan. Among the commission's suggestions adopted by Congress were

- a six-month delay in the cost of living index adjustment in July 1983;
- a rescheduling of previously approved increases in Social Security payroll taxes, which would have the effect of kicking in scheduled increases at a slower rate;
- a gradual increase in the age when an individual could first receive Social Security benefits (as a result of an increase in life expectancy, it was felt that people could also work longer);
- having federal employees contribute to the Social Security System; and
- a portion of Social Security benefits being subject to federal taxes for those people with incomes over $20,000.

These reforms resulted in a surplus in the system. The government began borrowing from the reserve, and as a result the system is again in trouble. Projections indicate that by the second decade of the twenty-first century, the Social Security System will not be able to pay everybody who is eligible. A new bipartisan commission was appointed by President George W. Bush in 2001. Its mission was to investigate alternatives and enhancements to Social Security such as partial privatization. The report suggested that the Social Security System would need to be reformed through means testing and studied the feasibility of creating privatized Social Security accounts. Congress did not adopt these reforms. One reason that they refused to pass any legislation dealing with the recommendations was that Social Security was traditionally considered to be "the third rail" of American politics. After President George W. Bush was re-elected in 2004, he made Social Security reform his number one legislative priority. He proposed the creation of Personal Retirement Accounts for anybody who was born prior to 1950. His critics called it privatization.

LIKE SOCIAL SECURITY, MEDICARE IS IN DANGER OF GOING BROKE ACCORDING TO THIS REPUBLICAN AD.

So, if the Social Security System is in jeopardy and the costs of the other entitlement and social welfare programs are continuing to skyrocket, what has the government done to reduce costs and make programs more effective?

- Adopt a workfare program.
- Substitute social workers for social welfare. Develop a system where expert caseworkers assist those in need. The drawback is that these experts do not have all the resources necessary to succeed in assisting those who have problems.
- Give the poor political clout. The poor would succeed by electing officials who are sympathetic to their cause. Also local officials who are elected can create programs to assist the poor through community-based programs, and a program announced by President George W. Bush, entitled "faith-based programs," whereby religious organizations would receive federal funds to help the poor.
- Provide additional income. Government should give enough money so that the culture of poverty is broken. Suggestions such as a guaranteed annual income and family allowance programs may achieve this end.
- Stimulate the private sector to take over many of the government-sponsored social welfare programs. In return, the government would reward the business through tax credits.

The bottom line in all these proposals is that, on the one hand, government recognizes its responsibility to the poor. The programs that exist, although escalating in cost, have a proven track record. Medicare has the support today of many legislators who voted against it in 1964. On the other hand, because these programs are self-perpetuating and are the largest part of the federal budget, there is an ongoing effort to find ways of reducing their costs without reducing their effectiveness. In 1995 the 103rd Congress started the process by offering major legislative initiatives reforming the welfare system, Medicare, and Medicaid. Significant reductions in these programs as well as a move to give the states block grants became a major part of the Republican agenda and were eventually approved by Congress and the president. The public supported many of these programs. Most observers anticipate that a major overhaul of the entitlement programs would be a major objective. One thing is certain: much of the New Deal and Great Society programs have been changed in a dramatic manner.

Chapter 17 Review

SECTION 1: MULTIPLE-CHOICE QUESTIONS

1. Which of the following is true about a class-based society?
   (A) disparity in the distribution of income and wealth
   (B) narrowing of the gap between the wealthy class and the middle class
   (C) increase in what the government determines to be an austere standard of living
   (D) reduction of the culture of poverty in the United States
   (E) move toward workfare rather than welfare

2. Liberals claim that a culture of poverty is caused by
   (A) government attempts to find solutions to the problem.
   (B) the value system of the poor.
   (C) long-term abuses of society.
   (D) the poor taking advantage of government programs.
   (E) the success of minority assimilation into the work force.

3. Which of the following represents the main difference between a progressive income tax and a proportional income tax?
   (A) A progressive tax collects less money from the rich than the poor, whereas a proportional tax collects more from the rich.
   (B) A progressive tax collects more money from the rich than the poor, whereas a proportional tax is regressive.
   (C) A progressive tax collects more money from the rich than the poor, whereas a proportional tax collects the same.
   (D) A progressive tax collects the same amount of money from both the rich and the poor, whereas a proportional tax collects more from the rich.
   (E) A progressive tax has different brackets for different income earners, whereas a proportional tax has a greater number of brackets.

4. Which of the following is an example of a contributory entitlement program?
   (A) Supplemental Security Income
   (B) Aid to Families with Dependent Children
   (C) Social Security
   (D) welfare
   (E) food stamps

5. Listed below are the different eras that describe the history of social policy in America:
   I. safety net era
   II. state-sponsored era
   III. block grant era
   IV. federal era

   Which is the correct chronological order?
   (A) I, II, III, IV
   (B) II, III, I, IV
   (C) IV, III, II, I
   (D) II, IV, I, III
   (E) III, II, I, IV

6. The programs of the New Deal are examples of
   (A) devolution
   (B) the state-sponsored era
   (C) the federal era
   (D) grant blocks to states
   (E) the New Federalism

7. Which of the following philosophies was behind the attempt to create a safety net for individuals?
   (A) Federal government would be the exclusive agent to aid citizens.
   (B) State governments would only use block grants to help citizens.
   (C) The federal and state governments would share the costs equally.
   (D) Private businesses would provide benefits.
   (E) Even with federal government cutbacks, there would still be an assurance that people in need would receive benefits.

8. Which of the following represents legislation that guarantees unpaid emergency medical assistance for workers?
   (A) Medicare
   (B) Social Security
   (C) Family Medical Leave Act
   (D) Medicaid
   (E) Disability Insurance Act

9. All the following were recommendations of the 1983 National Commission on Social Security Reform EXCEPT
   (A) rescheduling previously approved increases in Social Security payroll taxes.
   (B) a means test for senior citizens over the age of 65 to determine their eligibility to receive benefits.
   (C) gradually increasing the age when an individual could first receive Social Security benefits.
   (D) requiring federal employees to contribute to the Social Security System.
   (E) taxing a portion of the Social Security benefits for those people with incomes over $20,000.

10. Which of the following welfare proposals were passed into law in 1996?
    I. workfare
    II. additional income benefits
    III. the denial of welfare to legal immigrants
    IV. increased block grants to the states

    (A) I only
    (B) I and III only
    (C) II and IV only
    (D) I, II, and III
    (E) I, III, and IV

Answers to Multiple-Choice Questions

1. **(A)** Type of Question: Definitional
   By definition a class-based society is characterized by a wide gap between the rich and the poor in the areas of income and wealth. If there is a narrowing of the gap, then the society is moving away from being class based. If the government determines that the base considered to be a modest standard of living increases, then there is also a lessening of the gap. If the society moves toward workfare, it may result in a lessening of a class-based society.

2. **(C)** Type of Question: Comparing and contrasting concepts and events
Traditionally liberal philosophy claims that the abuses of a society cause harm to segments of the society—whether it is the African-American who was discriminated against or the poor who have not been given the same opportunities as the rest of society. Contrasting philosophies suggest that government should not be responsible to find the solutions to the problems. They question the value system of the disadvantaged, and some claim that the poor are taking advantage of government social welfare programs. Minority assimilation would lessen the culture of poverty.
3. **(C)** Type of Question: Definitional
By definition a progressive tax is based on the premise that the more you earn the more you pay in taxes. A proportional tax, also known as a flat tax, is based on the premise that everybody should pay the same percentage of taxes. A regressive tax is based on the premise that everybody has to pay a tax on essential goods. An example of a regressive tax is a sales tax.
4. **(C)** Type of Question: Identification and analysis
Social Security and Medicare are examples of programs that people contribute to through payroll taxes. Supplemental Security Income, Aid to Families with Dependent Children, welfare, and food stamps are all examples of programs that are redistributive in nature based on the premise that the government uses tax money and redistributes it to other groups.
5. **(D)** Type of Question: Chronological
The state era lasted from 1789 to 1932 and was characterized by most social welfare programs being run by the states. The federal era lasted from 1932 to 1980 and was characterized by the New Deal and Great Society programs. The safety net era began with the election of Ronald Reagan and was characterized by a move toward maintaining social welfare programs by using them as a safety net for those who needed them. The block grant era was ushered in by the Republicans after they gained control of Congress in 1994 and was characterized by a move toward eliminating social welfare programs by providing block grants to the states.
6. **(C)** Type of Question: Chronological
A variation of question 5, this question asks you to connect a specific time period to the era. Choice E would be part of the safety net era.
7. **(E)** Type of Question: Hypothetical
Choice A would be the philosophy of the federal era. Choice B would be the philosophy of the block grant era. Choice C has never been accepted as a practical philosophy. Choice D has been talked about, but in practice private business does not have the resources to provide enough money to create a safety net for those in need.
8. **(C)** Type of Question: Identification and analysis
Passed in 1992 after being vetoed by President Bush, the Family Medical Leave Act provides medical assistance and medical leave for workers without the threat of loss of job. Medicare provides healthcare benefits for senior citizens, Social Security provides money for those who contributed to the system and have reached the age set by law, and

Medicaid provides for medical assistance for those who cannot afford to pay for it. Disability insurance provides for money if a person is hurt on the job and cannot return for an extended period of time.

9. **(B)** Type of Question: Negative
The National Commission on Social Security formed in 1983 made a series of suggestions as a result of the fact that the government recognized that the future of the Social Security System was in critical shape. They recommended choices A, C, D, and E. Choice B has been recommended by other commissions and may in fact be part of future Social Security reform.

10. **(E)** Type of Question: Identification and analysis
As part of the Republican Contract with America, the House Republicans passed a sweeping welfare reform bill in 1995. The Senate passed a different version, and President Clinton had differences with both. The House version was the most drastic and included the concept of workfare, the denial of welfare to legal immigrants, and block grants to the states. Ultimately, the president signed a modified version of the original bill.

SECTION 2: FREE-RESPONSE ESSAY

The United States government has created what it calls a poverty line. This concept establishes the point at which an individual is considered living in what has been called a culture of poverty.

1. Identify the contrasting positions taken by the Republicans and Democrats to solve this problem.
2. Discuss three of the components of the 1996 Welfare Reform Act.

Sample Student Response

Social welfare programs and entitlements have greatly aided the lives of Americans and have been implemented in all levels of government—federal, state, and local. Today we are living in a class-based society, which has resulted in an unequal distribution of wealth between the rich and the poor. Most recently, statistics have shown that the wealthiest 1 percent of U.S. households (net worth at least $2.3 million each) own almost 40 percent of the nation's wealth. When contrasted with other countries such as England, the disparity of wealth is much less (1 percent own 18 percent of the nation's wealth). This is a major driving force behind the recent push for the reformation of social programs. In 1994, more than 38 million people were living in poverty, and many people believe this number is too high. The Republicans have tried to answer the public's request by reforming welfare and other social programs under the Republican Contract with America; however, social welfare is a highly controversial and debatable topic that has controlled public policy in the past and the present. New social reform aims to lessen the problem of poverty and the unequal distributions of wealth in the future. The general welfare clause is outlined in the Preamble of the Constitution, which says that the general welfare is a government responsibility.

One of the largest entitlement programs in the federal budget is welfare. In 1995 the Republican Contract with America promised an overhaul of the welfare system. The Democrats responded with a plan of their own sponsored by New York Senator Daniel Patrick Moynihan. The entitlement under the law guaranteed cash assistance to families who met eligibility requirements. The Republicans proposed to substitute the federal government's direct aid payments with block grants to the states. The Democrats opposed this concept. In addition, the Republicans urged a limitation of five years to families on federal welfare. States would be able to set lower limits. The Democrats opposed creating time limits. Under the 1995 existing law there were no restrictions on teen-age mothers receiving welfare benefits. The Republican proposal prohibited any use of federal funds to provide welfare benefits to unwed women under 18 years of age. The Democrats countered by advocating a requirement that most teenage recipients under 18 live at home with their parents in order to continue to receive aid. The heart of the reform measure dealt with the concept of "workfare." Existing law mandated that 20 percent of eligible recipients in states were supposed to enroll in work or training programs. However, because of loopholes many were exempt. The Republicans favored 50 percent of adults on welfare to work with virtually no exceptions. The Democratic plan would raise the requirement to 50 percent but would also provide more federal money for job training. State governors have also had welfare reform on their political agenda. Many states also created workfare as an alternative to welfare; they instituted work programs to remove welfare recipients from the rolls. The 1996 Personal Responsibility and Work Opportunity Reconciliation Act of 1996, commonly called the Welfare Reform Act, consolidated several of the aforementioned components of the different plans into one plan. The final law signed by the president with reservations contained the following provisions:

- Recipients of welfare must work after two years, with only a few exceptions to this provision.
- Child care funding was increased to help more mothers move into jobs.
- Continued healthcare was guaranteed for mothers who move off welfare to work.
- States would receive block grants instead of federal mandated subsidies. These grants would be used to develop state-sponsored workfare programs.
- Families receiving assistance for five cumulative years would be ineligible for cash aid under the new law.
- Legal immigrants would be denied welfare benefits.
- Child support enforcement procedures were strengthened.
- Guaranteed medical coverage for children living in poverty, the disabled, pregnant women, and the elderly.
- Nutrition programs in the form of food stamps would continue.
- Day care health and safety provisions remain intact.
- Unmarried minor parents would be required to live with a responsible adult and participate in educational training in order to receive benefits.
- Funds would be set aside for teen pregnancy prevention.

The new law initiated the biggest change for the welfare system since its inception, with the states assuming primary responsibility in dealing with the problem.

Evaluation of the Free-Response Sample Essay

1. Does the writer explain the concept of culture of poverty?
2. Are the solutions to the problem fully explained by citing specific programs?
3. Is the reform of welfare explored by giving arguments made by the Democrats and Republicans?

1. In the thesis part of the essay, the writer explains and defines what is meant by the culture of poverty. In doing so, the current figures concerning the distribution of wealth are given. This information provides dramatic evidence that a culture of poverty continues to exist.

2. After giving the background to the development of the social welfare system that existed in the country, the writer focuses on the problems created by what is referred to as "welfarism." The writer also discusses Clinton's proposed universal health plan as an alternative to some of the problems evident as a result of the culture of poverty.

3. The heart of the essay focuses on the welfare reform debate. The writer does an effective job comparing and contrasting the Republican plan, which was part of the Contract with America, and the Democratic plan advocated by Senator Moynihan. The key concept of providing block grants to the states was also emphasized as an in-depth look at the new law.

SECTION 2: DATA-BASED FREE-RESPONSE ESSAY

Answer the following questions based on the graph.

POVERTY RATES BY RACE AND HISPANIC ORIGIN: 1959 TO 1999

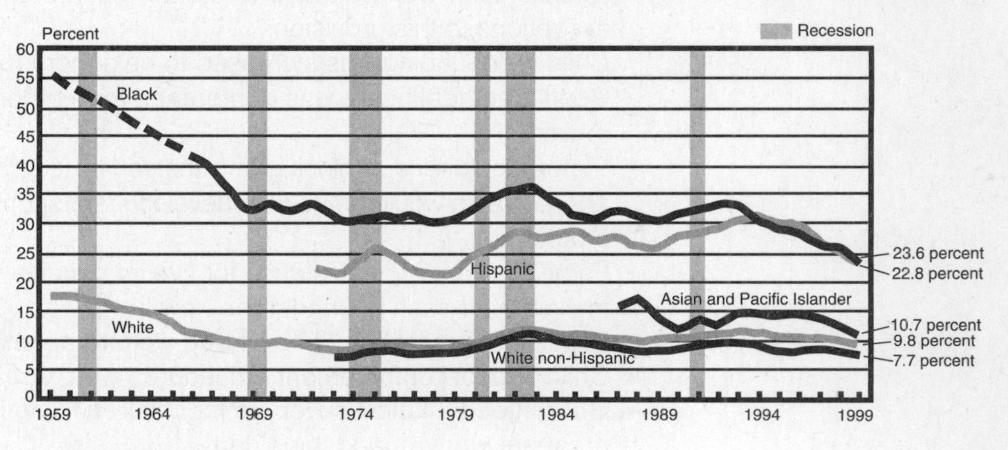

Source: U.S. Census Bureau

Discuss the public policy implications of the poverty level by analyzing the data listed above by

1. Defining what is meant by the poverty level.
2. Giving two reasons for the trends indicated by the graph.
3. Giving one public policy initiative that addressed the problem.

Sample Student Response

By definition the poverty line, which is established by the government, is the point at which an individual is considered living in what has been called a culture of poverty. This line differentiates the following criteria among the ethnic groups living in the United States:

- income,
- adjusted family income based on household size,
- wealth,
- income distribution among the top one percent, and
- the time period measured.

The graph entitled "Poverty Rates by Race and Hispanic Origin: 1959 to 1999" takes into account the time period measured as well as differences among African-Americans, Hispanics, whites, and all races. Implicit in the trends, however, are assumptions dealing with income, adjusted family income, wealth, and income distribution. Clearly the graph shows a decline in the percentage of African-Americans living below the poverty level between 1988 and 1999. It also shows a slight decrease in the number of Hispanics and whites living below the poverty line during the same period. It is interesting to note that, when you evaluate the chart, there was still a wide discrepancy between whites, Hispanics, and African-Americans. As far as public policy is concerned, government-sponsored social welfare programs of the Great Society such as Aid to Families with Dependent Children, Head Start, VISTA, Medicaid, and food stamps lowered the percentage of African-Americans living below the poverty level. However, these programs did little to narrow the gap.

The reasons for the increase in the gap between whites and other races are implicit in the levels of income, wealth, and income distribution among the top 1 percent of the rich. If you continued to plot the graph from 1988 through the 1999 census period, you would find a more dramatic gap between blacks and Hispanics living in poverty compared to whites. As far as income is concerned, regardless of whether government programs and tax structures are taken into account, the income gap between rich and poor has also widened. Household size, due to the increased number of single wage earners and the increased number of women in the workplace has also had an effect on the measurement. The middle class has gained, whereas the share of national income has dropped slightly for the rich and poor. As far as the trends portrayed in the graph are concerned, there is no doubt that the implementation of government programs had a major impact on lowering the percentage of people living below the poverty line but had only a negligible impact on the gap between whites and other races.

The debate that raged in Congress after the 1994 mid-term elections when the Republicans took control of the Congress centered around the efforts to reform welfare and determine the nature of an income tax reduction. The Republicans offered a welfare reform measure that, to a large extent, would create block grants for the states and give them more of a responsibility to deal with the problem. Republican-sponsored tax cuts would, if enacted, increase the gap between the rich and poor as the cuts proposed give wage earners over $100,000 a significant break. President Clinton countered by stressing the importance of his National Service Program, continued government support of the lowest income earners, and a middle class tax cut. The other key variable in this complex question is creating an educational system that will succeed in enabling the nation's poor to attend college.

Evaluation of Data-Based Free-Response Sample Essay

1. Is there an appropriate and accurate definition of poverty level and are the implications of the trends on public policy explained?
2. Are there sufficient examples to explain the implications of the trends?
3. Has the writer explored what Congress and the president have attempted to do to reverse the trends?

1. The response does an effective job of giving a definition of both the poverty line and the culture of poverty. The writer then offers five criteria that reflect the impact on different ethnic groups. By using these examples, the writer analyzes the relationship between the statistics offered in the graph and the status of blacks, Hispanics, and whites. Public policy programs such as those passed during the Great Society were offered as examples.

2. The writer gives excellent statistics that help to explain why there is such a dramatic gap between the rich and poor. Going beyond the data presented, the writer analyzes the differences between the lowest fifth of income earners and those who are among the top 1 percent of families with incomes over $350,000. Using these statistics, the conclusion reached is that government programs, although they had a dramatic impact on lessening the gap in the earlier years, have not yet solved the problem.

3. Good examples such as welfare reform, the National Service Program, and the impact of tax cuts were given in response to the question of how the trend could be reversed.

CHAPTER 18 The Environment and Energy

Chapter Overview

The environment and concerns about energy have hardly ever been a high priority on the public policy agenda, even though Earth Day is celebrated each year and special interest groups such as Greenpeace rally Americans to take action relating to such problems as

- air, water, and land pollution related to
  - global warming
  - acid rain
  - toxic waste
  - auto emissions
  - pesticides
- preservation of wildlife

The federal government has taken an interest in this area, establishing the Environmental Protection Agency in 1970 as its chief watchdog agency. There has even been a suggestion that a new cabinet position, the Environment Department, be created. State and local governments are charged with finding solutions to these problems. Congress has held hearings to determine if there is a relationship between the use of pesticides and the increase of breast cancer rates. Legislation such as the Clean Air Act and Water Pollution Control Act have been passed, and there is an ongoing debate regarding the direction environmental policy should take.

The American people may never forget the energy crisis and gas lines of the 1970s, but they still buy gas-guzzling automobiles. Federal, state, and local governments recognize the problems related to energy and deal with energy policy issues such as

- renewable vs. nonrenewable resources,
- the use of nuclear and coal energy as alternatives,
- the conservation of resources,

KEY TERMS

Clean Air Act
Clean Water Act
Endangered species
Energy dependent
Environmental Protection Agency (EPA)
National energy policy
National Environmental Policy Act (NEPA)
Nonrenewable resources
Nuclear Regulatory Commission
Renewable resources
Superfund

- how to deal with technological advances that have energy requirements,
- how to handle energy mishaps such as oil spills, and
- the extent to which we will be held hostage by energy cartels like OPEC.

On the federal level, the Department of Energy is charged with developing and implementing energy policies.

These issues will be explored fully in this chapter, and we will take an historical overview of these areas as they relate to public policy.

Environmental Concerns

The development of environmental policies involves federal, state, and local levels of government. They coordinate efforts to solve major environmental problems.

Even though the public rates the quality of the environment at the top of a list of problem areas that they expect to worsen in the future, only one percent of the voters polled in 2002 selected the environment as the issue that was most important in determining who they voted for. It has become the job of special interest environmental groups to wage the fight for government action. These groups include

- The Audubon Society—spent $38 million for wildlife protection
- The Wilderness Society—spent $9 million for a federal system of designated wilderness areas
- The National Wildlife Foundation—has a $63 million budget for the preservation of wildlife
- Greenpeace—spent $22 million for issues such as education and antipollution legislation advocacy
- Sierra Club—spent $19 million for environment-related issues

All these groups raise funds via corporate donations as well as individual contributions.

These groups attempt to raise public concerns about the environment. Specifically, they want the public to support governmental policy reform such as

- sponsoring town meetings throughout the nation related to preservation of forestry,
- restoring natural wetland areas,
- protecting rivers and fisheries,
- regulating pesticide use,
- conserving and protecting water resources,
- researching the effects of carbon dioxide emissions, setting new standards, and initiating new taxes, if required,
- establishing wildlife preserves,
- increasing penalties for violations of environmental statutes,
- making the issue of global warming a national priority and exploring the possibility of entering into a treaty with other nations aimed at dealing with the problem,
- regulating ocean dumping and disposal of toxic waste,
- investigating lead contamination of water and establishing acceptable overall safety levels for drinking water, and
- encouraging local municipalities to develop solid waste disposal alternatives and recycling policies.

As far as state and local governments are concerned, many environmental policies derive from regulations issued by the Environmental Protection Agency. These policies will be covered more fully in the next section. As far as traditional actions taken by state and local governments are concerned, each state and local municipality under our federal system is given much latitude in developing policies of their own. Some duplicate federal programs, but many are expanded and improved upon. Unique and original programs such as recycling originally came from local governments.

Early Government Regulations

The federal environmental agenda prior to 1969 was slow in developing a consistent and effective policy.

The environment only became a governmental priority starting in the 1970s. The cold war of the 1950s and 1960s and the concern for civil rights placed environmental concerns on the back burner. Other than public land management, aimed at preserving national parks, forests, and wildlife refuges, which grew out of the conservation movement that began at the turn of the twentieth century, little attention was paid to potentially serious problems facing the environment.

One of the earliest attempts by the government to address the issue of water pollution was the passage of the Refuse Act of 1899, requiring individuals who wanted to dump garbage into waters to obtain permission from the federal government. The Water Pollution Control Act of 1948 created a local assistance program in building sewage treatment plants.

Two authors, Rachel Carson and Paul Ehrlich, raised America's consciousness in the 1960s when they released their books, *The Silent Spring* and *The Population Bomb.* Carson's book traced the impact of pesticides on wildlife, and Ehrlich warned of the impact of population growth on natural resources.

Government regulation of the environment began in earnest with the passage of the National Environmental Policy Act (NEPA) in 1969. This legislation required government agencies, whenever they proposed policies that could negatively affect the environment, to file environmental impact statements with the Environmental Protection Agency. The first Earth Day was celebrated in 1970. The same year the Clean Air Act was passed. This law established national standards for states, strict auto emissions guidelines, and regulations that set air pollution standards for private industry. The critics of the act, business and private industry, were concerned that the costs involved in meeting the standards would raise production costs. The public and environmental interest groups supported the law because they felt it would have a positive impact in improving air pollution.

Water pollution was addressed by Congress in 1972 when it passed the Water Pollution Control Act. This law responded to the serious water pollution problems of the Great Lakes. The EPA issued strict standards to protect bodies of water that cross state lines. As a result, pollution in the Great Lakes decreased significantly. One of the most important actions taken by the federal government was the passage of the Comprehensive Environmental Response, Compensation, and Liability Act in 1976. This law, which had as its centerpiece a $1.6 billion Superfund to clean up abandoned toxic waste dumps, also authorized premarket testing of chemical substances; allowed the EPA to ban or regulate the manufacture, sale, or use of any chemicals that could present an "unreasonable risk of injury to health or environment"; and outlawed certain chemicals such as PCBs. The impetus for this law came from investigations of toxic waste dumping in the Love Canal in New York during the 1950s. Residents of the area contracted serious health problems, but because the chemical company responsible had long since gone out of business, the people had no recourse. The Superfund created was funded through a tax on chemical products. When a similar occurrence in Times Beach, Missouri, took place, the EPA purchased the entire town and evacuated the residents of that community while a cleanup took place.

Recent Government Regulations

Government regulation of the environment in the 1980s and 1990s had the goal of forcing private industry and state government to take action in critical areas.

Numerous government agencies and congressional committees have environmental responsibility including

- agriculture committees—deal with soil conservation, forestry, and pesticide policy
- appropriation committees—fund all federal programs
- energy and commerce committees—oversee Clean Air Act, nuclear waste policy, safe drinking water, hazardous waste, and toxic substances
- interior affairs committees—oversee public lands, wilderness, and mining
- public works and transportation committees—control water pollution, oil pollution, and emissions policy
- science, space, and technology committees—monitor nuclear waste and environmental research and development
- Council of Environmental Quality (executive office)—coordinate all environmental programs and oversee the National Environmental Policy Act
- Office of Management and Budget (executive office)—review budget and coordinate agency
- Department of Justice—litigate environmental abuses
- Department of Defense—control pollution from defense facilities
- Department of Housing and Urban Development—develop housing and urban planning
- Department of Health and Human Services—assess environment's impact on health-related issues
- Environmental Protection Agency—regulate air and water pollution, pesticides, radiation, solid waste, and toxic substances (the main environmental regulatory agency)

When Ronald Reagan took office, a new course was set into motion for environmental policy. Reagan's new federalism doctrine aimed at reducing the influence of the national government in areas such as environmental regulations. He felt that the states should take the initiative in this area. He also set up cost-benefit criteria to determine the value of environmental regulations. Reagan's appointments to environmental agencies reflected this point of view. Anne Burford was appointed as the Director of the EPA and James Watt was named Secretary of the Interior. Both initiated major cuts in their budgets related to environmental matters, promoting plans such as off-shore drilling and exploration of the national wilderness for mineral resources. They ran into major conflict with the Democrats and were criticized by the media and environmental groups. Burford was cited in contempt of Congress for failing to turn over documents dealing with alleged secret deals made with polluting industries. Watt made insensitive comments about the racial makeup of a commission he appointed. They were both forced to resign in 1983.

A DEPARTMENT OF JUSTICE STUDY REPRESENTING THE AMOUNT OF MONEY SPENT ON VARIOUS ENVIRONMENTAL PROGRAMS.

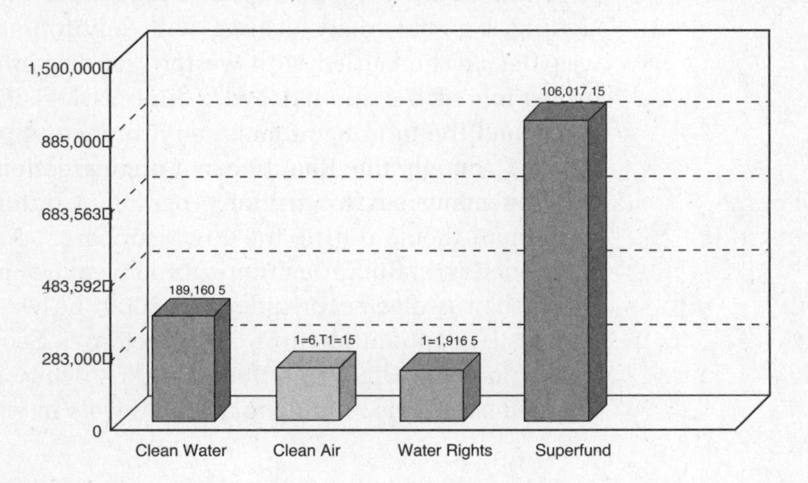

Even with the president opposed to further environmental legislation, Congress in the 1980s strengthened the Resource Conservation and Recovery Act in 1984 and continued the Superfund tax support in 1986. It continued in 1986 the policies created by the Safe Drinking Water Act and in 1987 approved the Clean Water Act. Other laws passed by Congress during Reagan's two terms included the Food Security Act of 1985, establishing a conservation reserve program; the Global Climate Protection Act of 1987, authorizing the State Department to develop a policy related to the problems of global climate change; and the Ocean Dumping Act of 1983, establishing regulations for ocean dumping.

Environmentalists were not pleased when the Bush–Quayle ticket was elected in 1988. Both candidates had very low ratings from environmental groups when they were in Congress. However, during the campaign Bush promised to address concerns about acid rain, promising to reduce sulfur-dioxide emissions, end ocean dumping of garbage, prosecute illegal disposal of medical waste, and promote recycling and the protection of wetlands.

After his election, George H. W. Bush was faced with an environmental crisis—the worst oil leak in United States history, caused when the *Exxon Valdez* ran aground off Alaska in 1989. Bush agreed to allow Exxon to clean up the spill, and, when it failed to act expeditiously, the Coast Guard was finally sent in to complete the job. Like Reagan, Bush developed an environmental policy based on the power of the marketplace, the encouragement of local initiatives, the emphasis on prevention in addition to cleanup with strict enforcement of violators, and the fostering of international cooperation. The centerpiece of his legislative achievement was the passage of the Clean Air Act of 1990. This law set overall sulfur-dioxide standards and attempted to deal with acid rain problems by cutting down nitrogen emissions. In addition, cities would have to regulate factories so as to reduce emissions that would deteriorate the ozone layer. Oil companies were required to develop cleaner-burning fuels. Tighter emission standards were also issued.

During the 1992 campaign, Bush and Clinton locked horns over environmental policy. Clinton's running mate, Al Gore, wrote *Earth in the Balance*, detailing measures Gore supported such as a move to electric cars. Although not part of the Democratic platform, Gore's views were criticized by the Republicans. Clinton supported the traditional Democratic viewpoint that government should take a greater regulatory role. He criticized Bush for not signing a global treaty dealing with environmental concerns. After Clinton was elected, he battled with western mining interests when he supported the protection of the spotted owl. Clinton's legislative agenda by his mid-term continued the funding of major environmental programs of previous administrations though the Republican Congress attempted to deregulate and cut back on many environmental programs. Clinton used the environment as a prominent theme during the 1996 campaign. After he was reelected, Clinton succeeded in maintaining funds for key environmental programs. After George W. Bush was elected president in 2000, he was criticized by environmental groups. His appointment of Gale Norton as Secretary of the Interior was not a popular one. President Bush was also hurt politically when he opposed lowered standards relating to arsenic levels in water.

Misuse of Energy Sources

Energy sources can be classified as renewable and nonrenewable. The trend has been to use nonrenewable sources and become energy dependent.

Energy policy is closely related to environmental policy. Conservation of natural resources and the impact energy sources have on the environment result in a unified approach to policy development. Before we address that issue, you should understand the nature of our energy sources.

As our society became highly industrialized and technologically advanced, we became an energy-dependent country. Because only a small percentage of our energy sources are renewable (such as wind, water, and solar energy), the country has had to turn to nonrenewable sources of energy, which include oil, gas, coal, and nuclear.

The problem with nonrenewable forms of energy is that the primary form we use, oil, is found in the Middle East. Even though states like Texas, Oklahoma, Louisiana, and Alaska produce significant amounts of oil, it is not enough to meet the needs of the United States. In 1990 over 50 percent of our oil was imported. Historically, this dependence on oil has created serious national policy problems. During the 1970s the oil cartel OPEC decided to reduce its export of oil as a result of our decision to support Israel in the war against their Arab neighbors. Long gas lines were the order of the day, and gas prices skyrocketed from 30 cents to well over a dollar a gallon, never to return to their original levels. In 1991 when Iraq invaded Kuwait and threatened Saudi Arabia, one of the underlying reasons the United States eventually invaded Iraq was the ramifications Iraq's action would have had on our ability to import oil. In 2001 the nation again faced an energy crisis. California experienced "rolling" electrical blackouts and the price of gasoline peaked at over $2.00 per gallon in the spring of 2001. By the end of the summer of 2001, the situation began to improve. Prices continued to decline through the end of that year, but reached all time record highs again in the spring and summer of 2004.

Coal is America's most abundant fuel. Estimates place 90 percent of the nation's energy resources in coal deposits. Yet, coal is used by only 20 percent of the American public because of the health problems faced by coal miners digging for it and the pollution it causes when it is burned.

Nuclear energy seemed to be a viable alternative in the 1970s. In fact, many nuclear plants were built as a way of delivering power effectively and for less cost than other sources. But after the Three Mile Island disaster in 1979 the popularity and desirability of this alternative lessened considerably. The Shoreham nuclear plant on Long Island was dismantled in the 1980s as a result of public pressure. The problem of nuclear waste disposal also was a major factor against the future development of nuclear energy.

To illustrate the problems that arise from our dependence on nonrenewable energy sources, look at how we produce electricity. The United States produces over 40 percent of its electricity by burning coal and 30 percent from natural gas or oil, whereas nuclear energy accounts for 14 percent and hydroelectric sources account for 13 percent of its production.

Energy Policy

Energy policy revolves around conservation, conversion, research, and control of resources.

In viewing the development of a public policy toward energy use and abuse, public officials are looking toward a consensus approach that will result in conservation of resources, conversion of abundant sources of energy into usable resources, research into alternative energy sources, and regulation of energy abusers. Specifically, advocates of this approach look at solar energy as an alternative because it is abundant and will not harm the environment. New technologies such as solar-powered electric cars could result from federal research and development. Private industry could be given tax incentives and other rewards for energy conservation measures taken.

Federal law would try to deal with overconsumption through taxes. It would also set energy standards and impose penalties for using energy sources that are environmentally harmful. Specific proposals that have been made include

- the Department of Energy adopting a national energy policy that allows all energy investments to compete on a fair economic basis. Proposals include removing unfair and costly tax subsidies from the fossil fuel and nuclear industries. This would allow energy-efficient and renewable energy resources to compete with conventional resources on an equal basis.
- the Department of Energy giving aid to the states that develop conservation techniques.
- the Department of Energy establishing research centers for energy-intensive industries, thus promoting energy efficiency.
- exploration of the Arctic National Preserve for new sources of oil.

As you can see, the Department of Energy, established in 1977, is the primary agency responsible for development and implementation of the country's energy policies. Since its creation, it has succeeded in improving energy efficiency through a series of recommendations. Republicans have called for the abolition of the department because they believe that other cabinet agencies could handle the responsibilities of the Energy Department. Many of the environmental laws previously described have had energy components that improve the environmental impact as well as create a more effective energy use. The Clean Air Act of 1990 incorporated these principles, too.

A key piece of energy legislation was passed in 1974. The Energy Reorganization Act created the Energy Research and Development Administration and the Nuclear Regulatory Commission. The Nuclear Regulatory Commission was given jurisdiction to license and regulate commercial use of nuclear technologies and monitor waste storage and transportation of materials arising from its use. The agency licensed nuclear reactors and was the key bureau investigating the Three Mile Island incident.

Congress also established the Federal Energy Regulatory Commission, which is directly responsible to the Department of Energy. It is responsible for interstate regulation of electric utility activities, natural gas pipelines and rates, and hydroelectric power operation. It has independent regulatory status. In 1987 it set up guidelines for the implementation of the National Environmental Policy Act.

An agency born out of the New Deal, the Tennessee Valley Authority (TVA), still exists today with the responsibility of acting as the primary electric utility for the area it serves. It is an agency in crisis, and there have been suggestions that it should be abolished. It owes more than $16 billion to nuclear plants that are not producing power. Its conservation and resource management goals are in disarray. Its original goal, when it was created in 1933, was to provide navigation, flood control, electricity, and economic development to an area home to 6 million people in Tennessee, Mississippi, Alabama, and Kentucky. Today close to 100 percent of its budget goes to power consumption.

What's in store for energy policy in the future? Much depends on technological advances. Every time there has been a major technological improvement, there has also been a corresponding energy need to drive it. From the invention of the automobile to the launching of spacecraft, energy sources have been used, resulting in a depletion of nonrenewable resources. Foreign policy problems related to energy are also on the horizon. As long as this country remains energy dependent, OPEC can hold America hostage.

Chapter 18 Review

SECTION 1: MULTIPLE-CHOICE QUESTIONS

1. All the following are special interest environmental groups EXCEPT
   (A) Audubon Society.
   (B) National Association of Manufacturers.
   (C) Greenpeace.
   (D) Sierra Club.
   (E) Wilderness Society.

2. The main purpose of the National Environmental Policy Act was to
   (A) require government agencies to issue environmental impact statements if their policies would have a negative impact on the environment.
   (B) require the Environmental Protection Agency to monitor clean air standards.
   (C) establish clean water standards.
   (D) establish a superfund to clean up environmental abuses.
   (E) require the Department of the Interior to establish criteria for ocean dumping.

3. The Superfund was originally enacted in response to which of the following events?
   (A) the oil spill caused by the grounding of the *Exxon Valdez*
   (B) the nuclear meltdown at the Three Mile Island nuclear plant
   (C) toxic and chemical dumping at the Love Canal
   (D) the nuclear catastrophe at Chernobyl
   (E) the dismantling of the Shoreham nuclear plant

4. All the following choices represent features of the Clean Air Act of 1990 EXCEPT
   (A) it established standards to protect the ozone layer.
   (B) it set overall carbon dioxide standards.
   (C) it established standards to attack the acid rain problem.
   (D) it directed factories to reduce emissions.
   (E) it directed auto manufacturers to sell electric cars.

5. Which of the following choices was a major consequence of United States reliance on nonrenewable resources during Middle East tensions?
   (A) It made the United States less dependent on the Middle East.
   (B) Texas, Oklahoma, and Louisiana were able to meet the demand for energy.
   (C) OPEC decided to reduce exports.
   (D) The United States decided to turn to nuclear energy as a primary energy source.
   (E) The United States' use of hydroelectric sources increased.

6. Which of the following was created as a result of the Energy Reorganization Act?
   (A) Nuclear Regulatory Commission
   (B) Federal Energy Regulatory Commission
   (C) Department of Energy
   (D) a superfund for energy
   (E) the continued operation of the Tennessee Valley Authority

7. Which of the following congressional actions took place the same year as the first Earth Day in 1970?
   (A) the creation of the Department of Health and Human Services
   (B) the passage of the Clean Air Act
   (C) the passage of the Clean Water Act
   (D) the creation of the Superfund
   (E) the passage of the Safe Drinking Water Act

8. Which of the following is considered the main environmental regulatory agency?
   (A) Energy Department
   (B) Council of Environmental Quality
   (C) Commerce Department
   (D) Environmental Protection Agency
   (E) Interior Department

9. In 1994 the Supreme Court considered the constitutionality of the Endangered Species Act. Which of the following issues did environmentalists support?
   I. property rights of land developers
   II. potential harm to animals
   III. potential harm to water
   IV. potential harm to the air

   (A) I only
   (B) II only
   (C) II and III only
   (D) III and IV only
   (E) II, III, and IV only

10. Which of the following proposals that have an impact on the environment was made by the Republicans after they won a majority in the House of Representatives in 1994?
   (A) the passage of antiregulatory legislation
   (B) the institution of increased federal funds for the environment
   (C) the passage of a global treaty protecting the tropical rain forest
   (D) the passage of legislation that would increase federal mandates
   (E) the abolition of the Environmental Protection Agency

Answers to Multiple-Choice Questions

1. **(B)** Type of Question: Identification and analysis
   The National Association of Manufacturers is a special interest group that often opposes environmental measures. The Audubon Society and Wilderness Society are special interest groups that advocate the protection of endangered species. Greenpeace and the Sierra Club are activist environmental groups and often fight for environmental regulations.
2. **(A)** Type of Question: Cause and effect relationships
   This is a very difficult question because all the choices deal with environmental measures. The act, passed in 1969, dealt strictly with the issuance of environmental impact statements of governmental policies. Choice B, although correct substantively, does not come about as a result of the act in question. Choice C takes place as a result of the Clean Water Act. Choice D occurs as a result of the Comprehensive Environmental Response, Compensation, and Liability Act, and choice E is also a correct statement but has no direct relationship to the Environmental Policy Act.
3. **(C)** Type of Question: Cause and effect relationships
   Because there was a tremendous amount of publicity surrounding the toxic and chemical dumping around the Love Canal in New York State,

Congress passed the Comprehensive Environmental Response, Compensation, and Liability Act in 1976. The act authorized $1.6 billion to clean up abandoned toxic waste dumps and authorized the EPA to sue factories that contributed to dumping of hazardous waste. Choices A, B, D, and E all had an environmental impact but did not result in the passage of the act.

4. **(E)** Type of Question: Negative
Even though the EPA has conducted extensive research into the benefits of alternative means of transportation and the impact on the environment, the agency never directed auto manufacturers to sell electric cars. The Clean Air Act came under attack in 1995 by those who believe that there are too many government regulations and a revised version of the act attempted to reduce the number of regulations.

5. **(C)** Type of Question: Chronological
Choice A is wrong because, if anything, the United States became even more dependent on the Middle East but had less oil available because of export cutbacks. Even though Texas, Oklahoma, and Louisiana produce oil, they do not provide enough for the United States to become oil independent. Though the United States used nuclear energy and hydroelectric energy, oil was still the number one source of energy. Throughout the 1970s and even today, the United States is at the mercy of OPEC, an oil cartel, for the primary importing of oil.

6. **(A)** Type of Question: Identification and analysis
This question requires the specific knowledge of the provisions of the act. You probably can eliminate choices D and E because you should be familiar with the derivation of the Tennessee Valley Authority and you should be able to recognize that the Superfund deals with the cleanup of hazardous waste. The Federal Energy Regulatory Commission is responsible to the Department of Energy. The correct choice, A, was created to deal with such related issues as the Three Mile Island meltdown.

7. **(B)** Type of Question: Chronological
In 1995, the twenty-fifth anniversary of the first Earth Day was celebrated. The same year the Clean Water Act came under attack by the new Republican majority in Congress. Earth Day motivated the passage of numerous environmental acts. The Clean Air Act was the first, followed by the Clean Water Act, the establishment of the Superfund (which also came under attack in 1995), and the Safe Drinking Water Act.

8. **(D)** Type of Question: Comparing and contrasting concepts
Though the Energy Department, Commerce Department, Council of Environmental Quality, and the Interior Department all issue regulations that have an impact on the environment, the key regulatory agency that has had the greatest impact on environmental oversight is the Environmental Protection Agency.

9. **(E)** Type of Question: Solution to a problem
Even if you are not familiar with the Endangered Species Act and the case in question, you should be able to figure out that environmental groups would not support the property rights of land developers if they came into conflict with endangered species. The act prohibited the development of land if in the process animals classified as endangered

species could be harmed. If in the process of developing the land, environmentalists argued, water and air were also impacted, then conceivably the species that relied on the water and air could also be harmed.

10. **(A)** Type of Question: Sequencing a series of events
One of the components of the Republican Contract with America was the Unfunded Mandates Bill. This act and other acts aimed to reduce the number of regulations, many of which had an impact on the environment, by the federal government on the states. Thus the Republicans would advocate the passage of antiregulatory legislation. And in fact President Clinton did sign the Unfunded Mandates Bill in 1995. Because there was a move toward a balanced budget, there was never any move to increase funding for the environment. Some lobbyists argued that the Environmental Protection Agency was overstepping its authority, but there was never any serious attempt to abolish it. A global treaty protecting the tropical rain forest was signed by a number of nations.

SECTION 2: FREE-RESPONSE ESSAY

In 1995, the nation celebrated the twenty-fifth anniversary of Earth Day. Over the 25-year period there has been an ongoing movement by people and organizations who believe one of the primary roles of government should be the protection of the environment.

Describe the progress environmental groups have made in getting government to pass laws related to environment and energy problems facing the country by giving three examples of public policy and two examples of groups that lobbied for these policies.

Sample Student Response

The Environmental Protection Agency (EPA) was established in 1970 as an independent agency in the executive branch of the U.S. government "to permit coordinated and effective government action on behalf of the environment." The EPA consolidates in a single body the administration of all federal environmental legislation, ranging from the Refuse Control Act of 1989 to the most recent statutes concerning environmental pollution. The agency monitors environmental quality and seeks to control the pollution caused by solid wastes, pesticides, toxic substances, noise, and radiation. It has established special programs in air and water pollution, hazardous wastes, and toxic chemicals and sponsors research in the technologies of pollution control.

An environmental impact statement is a report on the probable environmental effects of proposed projects, such as highways, large-scale residential or commercial construction, power plants, or dams that might significantly alter the environment. The National Environmental Policy Act, which became effective in 1970, requires every U.S. government agency to issue a statement on any project it plans to undertake, regulate, or fund. The EPA then reviews all federal environmental impact statements to ensure that they comply with the law. The use of environmental impact statements spread to many state and local governments.

Intended to make environmental quality a serious factor in federal planning, the environmental impact statement has been attacked by some as a hindrance to economic growth and by others as too vague to provide a strict standard for environmental control. Litigation may result if environmental considerations conflict with existing zoning or planning laws or with economic interests, or if conservationists seek to block a proposed development. The Endangered Species Act, which is designed to protect rare animal and plant life, has been used to block several projects that might destroy wildlife habitats.

National organizations such as the Sierra Club, the Audubon Society, the National Wildlife Federation, and the Wilderness Society brought litigation and lobbied for stricter laws dealing with almost every aspect of the environment. These laws included the National Environmental Policy Act of 1969, the Clean Water Act of 1972, the National Forest Management Act of 1976, the Clean Air Act amendments of 1977, and the National Acid Precipitation Act of 1980, as well as the creation (1970) of the Environmental Protection Agency and the first annual celebration of Earth Day.

The movement languished temporarily during the late 1970s and early 1980s because of poor economic conditions in the United States. From 1983 on, however, public interest was aroused and further strengthened by a number of events such as the acid rain controversy, the Chernobyl nuclear catastrophe, the *Exxon Valdez* oil spill, tropical deforestation, and the discovery of possible global warming. In Europe, environmentalist sentiment took political form with the formation of a green party in Germany, and of "green" movements throughout the continent.

The organizations participating in the environmental movement are as diverse as the problems they undertake to solve. Some concentrate on specific areas (Save the Redwood League); some do restorative work (Adopt-a-Stream Foundation); some gather and disperse information (Worldwatch Institution); some lobby or bring suit; and a few (Earth First! and Greenpeace) take direct, sometimes confrontational, action. For example, Greenpeace spent $22 million for issues such as education and antipollution legislation, and the Sierra Club spent $19 million for environmental-related issues. All these groups work together to make the residents of the Earth more aware of the problems it is facing.

Greenpeace is an environmental organization founded in 1969 by a group of Canadian environmentalists. It advocates direct, nonviolent action to halt threats to the environment, and its confrontational tactics have earned the group widespread publicity for its causes. The causes include ending commercial whaling and the slaughter of baby seals, halting the dumping of toxic wastes, and creating a nuclear-free world. On July 10, 1985, the Greenpeace ship *Rainbow Warrior*, en route to protest nuclear testing in French Polynesia, was sunk by French agents in the harbor at Auckland, New Zealand, creating an international incident.

Another major problem facing the world today is to provide protection for a nucleus of animals that have become significantly reduced in number and to improve the habitat sufficiently so that the animals will breed and grow in number. The Fish and Wildlife Act of 1956 gave further impetus to the federal refuge program by authorizing the U.S. Fish and Wildlife Service to acquire land for refuge purposes for all kinds of wildlife. The Endangered Species Preservation Act of 1966 provided protection for endangered wildlife and also gave the official designation of National Wildlife Refuge System, which now encompasses 34 million acres within about 420 refuges.

Evaluation of Free-Response Sample Essay

1. Does the essay establish a point of view that is adequately explained?
2. Are there sufficient examples of legislation and the actions of environmental groups to illustrate the point that these groups have been in the forefront in urging government to act?

1. The essay establishes and affirms the impact of environmental groups on the passage of legislation. The writer explains in detail how these groups fought for the creation of the Environmental Protection Agency and passage of the Refuse Control Act. These acts illustrate how government regulations help to improve the environment and how environmental lobby groups support the efforts of government to monitor environmental abuses of private industry.

2. The writer does an effective job of explaining the role of environmental special interest groups such as the Sierra Club, Audubon Society, National Wildlife Federation, and Wilderness Society. Laws such as the National Environmental Policy Act, the Clean Water Act, and National Forest Management Act were all supported by lobbyists for these groups. The writer also differentiates the direction these special interest groups take when it comes to arguing for specific legislative acts.

SECTION 2: DATA-BASED FREE-RESPONSE ESSAY

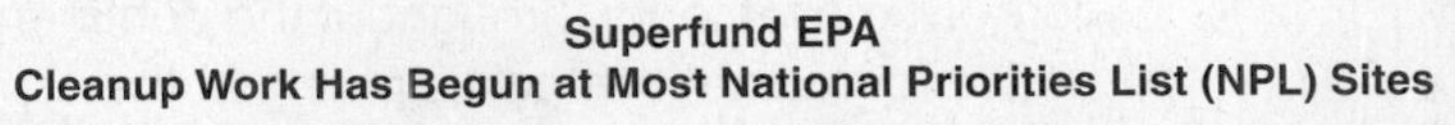

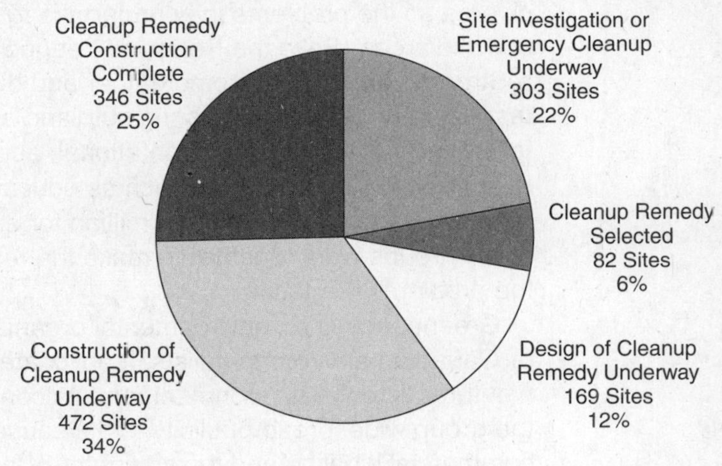

Discuss the environmental and public policy impact of these data. Analyze the importance of the Superfund Law in relation to the data.

Sample Student Response

The key environmental policy question that is raised by the pie chart is what will be the future of the Superfund Law? The law was originally intended to cover a ten-year period and cost less than $10 billion. But because of the large number of industrial abuses, the fund actually could cost over $100 billion if every site were to be taken care of. Another question that was unanswered as of 1997 was whether the law would be renewed. The problem of renewal was significant because by 1995 it was apparent that, because of the limits of technology and the cost factors involved, it would be almost impossible to deal with all the potential sites identified. There have been some real success stories. More than 350 sites have been cleaned up, and more than 3000 sites have had dangerous chemicals removed. A local example of how Superfund worked was on Long Island where 3 out of 24 Superfund sites have been completely taken care of. Another factor that contributed to the success or failure of cleanup programs was the amount of state contributions to the program. Again, using a local example, New York had almost 600 state sites compared to close to 100 federal sites. President Clinton in 1994 proposed changes to the law, which included increased community involvement, a more flexible system in which there would be a reduction of the standards for factories compared to public housing and a substitution of mediation for litigation. These proposals had to be dropped because there was a lack of bipartisan support. After the Republicans took control of the Congress in 1994, the Superfund Law was not renewed.

The pie chart reflects Superfund cleanup related to more than 1,000 sites designated by the National Priorities List. The listings are a result of the passage of the Superfund Law. The original program was initiated as a result of the tragic toxic dumping discovered at "Love Canal" in New York. Since the passage of the Comprehensive Environmental Response, Compensation, and Liability Act in 1976 and its amendments in 1986 and 1990, the federal government has had to deal with more than 30,000 potentially dangerous sites. The Superfund agency in charge of designating sites has developed a priority order for cleaning up the most hazardous sites. One can surmise from the pie chart that more than 82 percent of the sites on the final Superfund National Priorities List are either undergoing cleanup construction or are completed. There are 472 sites where construction of a cleanup remedy is underway, 346 sites where cleanup remedy construction is complete, 303 sites where there is an investigation or emergency cleanup underway, 82 sites where there is a cleanup remedy selected, and 169 sites where there has been a design of a cleanup remedy. The bottom line is that the Superfund Law has worked successfully. Responsible parties perform more than 75 percent of the long-term cleanup commitments, which saves taxpayers more than 12 billion dollars. Since its inception, the Environmental Protection Agency and Superfund enforcement program has reached settlements in more than 10,000 cases. Yet a significant problem still remains. As a result of the Republican majority in Congress, there has yet to be a resolution to adopt the new Superfund amendment. Consequently, the entire program was not reauthorized. In 1996 Republicans and Democrats proposed extending the Superfund, but the bills got bottled up because of the issue of liability. At the start of the 105th Congress, Senate Majority Leader Trent Lott made the extension of the Superfund program a priority.

Evaluation of Data-Based Free-Response Sample Essay

1. Are specific public policy examples given to illustrate the impact of the data presented in the chart?
2. Does the writer use examples from the pie chart to describe the status of cleanup work?

1. The writer focuses on the impact of the Superfund to illustrate how the problem of hazardous waste is addressed. Some important information regarding the success of the Superfund since its establishment supports the premise that this chart had a direct relationship to an important public policy—the use of the Superfund to address the issue. The irony of the issue was that the Republicans successfully prevented the renewal of the Superfund in 1995. This fact is not lost on the writer. It is certainly relevant information if you are dealing with the issue of public policy.

2. The writer does an effective job of giving specific information regarding the number and status of cleanup operations based on a national priorities list. The pie chart illustrated the different levels of cleanup and suggests that the Superfund Law, though not reauthorized as of 1997, has still been very successful in dealing with serious violations of the law. The writer also discusses the fact that the Superfund Law dictates different stages of cleanup procedures. The writer goes beyond the chart and gives statistics related to the overall accomplishments of the EPA and Superfund. Finally, the writer updates the status of the Superfund legislation.

CHAPTER 19 Foreign Policy and the National Defense

Chapter Overview

Trying to identify America's vital national interests creates major problems for the public and the policymakers. Throughout the history of the United States an ongoing debate has raged regarding what constitutes a threat to our security and what our foreign policy goals should be. Answers range from

- defending the United States against attacks from other nations,
- supporting humanitarian interests,
- protecting weaker nations against foreign aggression,
- supporting democracy in other nations,
- protecting jobs of American workers,
- securing a favorable balance of trade,
- defending our allies and participating in mutual defense alliances,
- getting involved with the United Nations peacekeeping activities,
- achieving worldwide arms control,
- giving aid to foreign countries, and
- protecting the United States against terrorist attacks.

Before the cold war ended, a primary goal of the United States was to contain communism and maintain a strong nuclear deterrence. When President George H. W. Bush announced that this country was pursuing a "new world order,"

KEY TERMS

Antiballistic Missile Treaty (1972)
Brinkmanship
Cold war
Collective security
Containment
Détente
Domino theory
Eisenhower Doctrine
Favorable balance of trade
General Agreement on Tariffs and Trade (GATT)
Global interdependence
Good neighbor policy
Intermediate Range Nuclear Forces Treaty (1987)
International Monetary Fund
Isolationism
Manifest Destiny
Marshall Plan
New world order
North American Free Trade Agreement (NAFTA)
Nuclear Test Ban Treaty (1963)
Partnership for peace
Return to normalcy
Strategic Arms Limitation Talks (SALT)
Truman Doctrine
War Powers Act

critics raised the issue whether that meant the United States would become the policeman of the world.

And what about public support of the nation's foreign policy and its national defense goals? Every president, even with the support of Congress and the advice of his national security experts, must achieve public approval in order to successfully pursue and achieve a foreign policy initiative. When that does not occur, the nation becomes split, as it was during the Vietnam War and Iraq War, and the administration's hands become tied not only on the foreign front but domestically as well.

This chapter will deal with who makes foreign policy, how the nation's goals are established, the role of public opinion, the history of the major foreign policy eras, the status of the national defense establishment, and the movement toward a new global interdependence. By looking at these areas, you will see a country that has taken on the role of the last great superpower. What we will do with that title and how we act in the world arena has yet to be fully determined.

Formulation of Foreign Policy

Players in the formulation of foreign policy provide for civilian control over the military. The system does encourage competing interests and strategies among the public and participants.

Depending upon circumstances, the United States has a wide range of options available in formulating its foreign policy. The following continuum represents the various types of strategies.

FOREIGN POLICY CONTINUUM

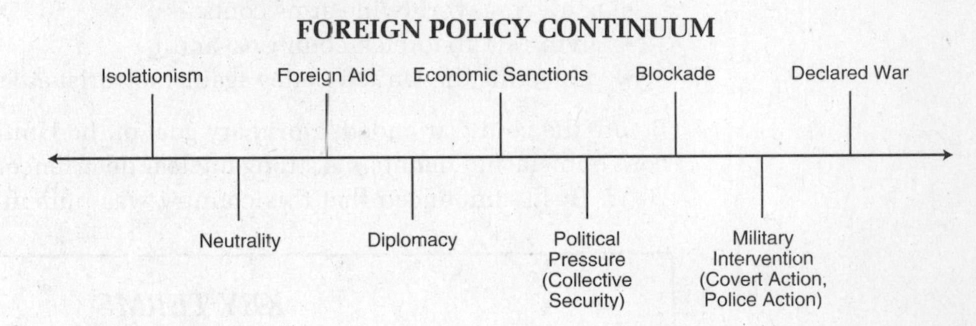

Who are the players and participants in this aspect of public policy? Constitutionally we have already established that the key players responsible are

- President—in Article II, as commander in chief of the armed forces and chief diplomat, having the power to appoint ambassadors and negotiate treaties.
- Congress—in Article I, having the power to declare war, support and maintain an armed force through appropriations, as well as approve foreign aid allocations; the Senate has the power to approve appointments and must ratify treaties.

Through the bureaucratic agencies of the executive department and the oversight responsibilities of Congress, specific policy is made. The president relies on two key cabinet departments for advice—the State Department and the Defense Department, both of which are run by civilians. He also relies on the National Security Advisor, a staff position, the Directors of the CIA, FBI, and Homeland Security. The secretary of defense, formerly called the secretary of war, is second to the president in directing military affairs. The agency is directly in charge of the massive defense budget and the four branches of the military. Direct military command is under the leadership of the joint chiefs of staff. It is made up of representatives of each of the military services and chaired by a presidential appointee, also a member of the military. During the Gulf War, General Colin Powell was the head of the joint chiefs and was a visible and key player giving valuable advice to President George H. W. Bush and Secretary of Defense Dick Cheney. In 1995, after his autobiography, *My American Journey*, was published, he was urged to run for president as a result of his leadership during the Gulf War.

The secretary of state heads the diplomatic arm of the executive branch and supervises a department with well over 24,000 people including 8000 foreign service officers. There are area specialists such as Middle East affairs, and the department includes the many ambassadors who are the country's chief spokesmen abroad. Presidents appoint to the position of secretary of state someone on whom they can closely rely and who can map out a successful foreign policy. Some like John Foster Dulles, Eisenhower's secretary of state, have played a major role. Dulles endorsed the policy of brinkmanship—going close to the edge of an all-out war in order to contain communism. President Clinton appointed the first woman Secretary of State, Madeline Albright, at the start of his second term.

The National Security Act of 1947 established the National Security Council as an executive-level department. It created as its head the national security advisor. One of the most notable people to head the agency was Henry Kissinger, who served under Presidents Nixon and Ford. Kissinger laid the foundation of Nixon's policy to end the Vietnam War and handled the delicate negotiations that led to Nixon's historic visit to China. Condoleeza Rice became a key national security advisor to George W. Bush during his administration. She was appointed and the Senate confirmed her as the first African American woman to serve as Secretary of State in Bush's second term.

Other agencies that are an integral part of the foreign policy arena include:

- The Immigration and Naturalization Service—deals with those people trying to seek residence in the United States from other countries. It is the agency charged with enforcing immigration policy. At times, it becomes embroiled in controversial issues such as when Vietnam, Haiti, and Cuba, at different times allowed their residents to set out to the United States on boats. The agency, along with the military, was directed to intercept the exodus of these "boat people" on the high seas.
- The Central Intelligence Agency—was created by Congress in 1947 and works under the direction of the National Security Council. Its director has the responsibility of
    * coordinating the gathering of information related to foreign affairs and national defense for the other federal agencies,
    * analyzing and evaluating this information, and
    * reporting to the president and National Security Council.

  Besides information reporting, the agency has also conducted covert activities abroad and at times has been criticized for some of its actions. When the Iran-Contra affair was investigated by Congress, it became apparent that the CIA helped coordinate the illegal arms for hostages negotiations.
- The United States Information Agency—acts as the propaganda arm of the United States. It uses the Voice of America shortwave radio station to inform foreign countries of United States policy abroad.

- The United States Arms Control and Disarmament Agency—maintains responsibility for negotiations, participation, and implementation of treaties dealing with disarmament. It has focused its attention on monitoring the Nuclear Test Ban treaties, Strategic Arms Reduction Treaty (START), and the Strategic Arms Limitation Talks (SALT), which resulted in the Intermediate Range Nuclear Force (INF) Treaty in 1988. It also has oversight function regarding the Chemical Weapons Treaty ratified by the Senate in 1997. These treaties are discussed in more detail later in the chapter.
- The Selective Service System—maintains responsibility for coordinating and raising an army. Even though the draft has been used since the Civil War, the first national draft occurred in 1917 as a result of the Selective Service Act and was renewed again in 1940, prior to the United States' entry into World War II. During the Vietnam War it was a source of controversy. Its critics maintained that draft policy favored those who could gain a deferment by attending college, resulting in many lower- and middle-class young men being sent to Vietnam. Since President Nixon established an all-volunteer army, the Selective Service has existed on a standby basis, administering a registration requirement that takes place when young men reach the age of 18.

As you can see, the heart of the foreign policy establishment is led by civilians. When President Truman ran head-on against his military commander in Korea, Douglas MacArthur, there was never a doubt that after MacArthur publicly criticized Truman's decision not to expand the war into China, MacArthur would be fired. In the next sections of the chapter we will explore major foreign policy eras and illustrate further how the public and the players get into the act.

1800–1868

America's foreign policy was characterized by traditions and precedents. Domestic policy became intermingled with foreign policy goals.

George Washington in his farewell address said, "The great rule of conduct for us in regard to foreign nations is, in extending our commercial relations to have with them as little political connection as possible . . . steer clear of permanent alliances with any portion of the foreign world." This Proclamation of Neutrality became the country's prevailing foreign policy doctrine throughout most of the nineteenth century.

Historical Headline Highlights

- 1803—The Louisiana Purchase, masterminded by Thomas Jefferson, doubles the size of the country.
- 1812—The United States engages Great Britain in the War of 1812 over boundary disputes and naval engagements. Washington attacked. No clear-cut victor.
- 1823—James Monroe announces his doctrine, which aims to keep Europe from colonizing the Western Hemisphere.
- 1848—The Mexican War is fought, resulting in America acquiring Texas. Through the Mexican Cession, we also get Arizona, New Mexico, and California.
- 1861—During the Civil War the United States succeeds in preventing foreign countries from intervening on the side of the Confederacy.

Besides pursuing a policy of isolationism and nonalignment during this time period, the United States also adopted a policy of Manifest Destiny—the quest to expand the nation's border from coast to coast, as a driving force. It is a good example of how domestic policy becomes intermingled with foreign policy. The Louisiana Purchase, Monroe Doctrine, and Mexican War are examples of how foreign and domestic policy merged into achieving one goal. Feeling that it was God's will to expand also gave legitimacy to the war with Native Americans. The invention of the steamboat and the building of the transcontinental railroad and the quest for higher tariffs also were good examples of this merged policy.

1870–1917

Late nineteenth-century and early twentieth-century policy reflects interests driven by imperialism and a greater global involvement.

By the 1870s America fulfilled its dream of westward expansion. As a result of industrialization, the country had the need to expand its markets even more. And by the turn of the century, imperialism was a primary factor in our decision to go to war against Spain.

Historical Headline Highlights

- 1872—America acquires Samoan Islands.
- 1875—America signs treaty with Hawaii, which opens up a new market for trade.
- 1898—Spanish-American War results in the United States getting Puerto Rico, Guam, and the Philippines. Cuba receives its independence.
- 1899—The Open Door Policy is jointly announced by China and the United States.
- 1901—United States gets rights to build Panama Canal.
- 1904—Roosevelt Corollary to Monroe Doctrine announced allowing greater intervention in Latin American affairs by the United States.
- 1907—President Roosevelt calls for second Hague Conference aimed at establishing the International Court of Justice to settle world disputes.

If the nineteenth century was characterized by isolationism and manifest destiny, in the early part of the twentieth century the United States became a full-fledged participant in the world community. At first trade was the motivating factor. But by the turn of the century, the country was stirred up by the yellow journalism of William Randolph Hearst's publications. The public demanded action when the headline "Remember the Maine" accused Spain of sinking our battleship. Certainly, imperialistic motives were part of the reason why we were so anxious to declare war against the weaker Spain. After the war ended, Theodore Roosevelt's policy, "speak softly, but carry a big stick," extended into a corollary to the Monroe Doctrine. Our influence in Latin American affairs increased our involvement overall in foreign affairs. We received the rights to build the Panama Canal, and that treaty expired in the year 1999.

1917–1945

Our attempts to remain neutral failed when Europe became embroiled in two world wars.

Although Woodrow Wilson won the election of 1916 with a campaign theme of "he kept us out of war," he was not able to sustain neutrality. Fighting "the war to end all wars," Wilson attempted to ensure that another war would not take place when he helped negotiate the Versailles Treaty. When the Senate rejected the treaty and our involvement in the League of Nations, the handwriting was on the wall—ultimately a new and more devastating war would take place, especially when Harding pledged to "return to normalcy" in the 1920s.

Historical Headline Highlights

- 1917—The United States enters World War I attempting to "make the world safe for democracy." Wilson announces 14 points, which include the formation of a League of Nations and an appeal for nations to be able to achieve political self-determination.
- 1919–1933—Harding's election and the failure of the Senate to approve the Versailles Treaty signal a return to an isolationist policy. The start of the Great Depression pulls the country back even further.
- 1927—Kellogg-Briand Treaty aims at outlawing war.
- 1933—Franklin Roosevelt announces the Good Neighbor Policy with Latin America.
- 1939–1941—After signing a series of Neutrality Acts, the United States also agrees to a lend–lease policy with the Allies. Unrestricted submarine warfare by Germany intensifies the debate.
- 1941—After announcing a trade embargo against Japan, Pearl Harbor is attacked, and we enter the war against Germany, Japan, and Italy.
- 1945—The birth of the Atomic Age is ushered in by the dramatic bombing of Hiroshima and Nagasaki, which ends World War II.

The failure of the United States to participate in the League of Nations sent a signal to the rest of the world that we were once again withdrawing from the world scene. The event was a good example of how politics and public opinion dominated foreign policy decision making. Wilson lost a majority of both houses of Congress during the mid-term 1918 elections. Then he refused to bring any Republican advisors with him to the Paris Peace Conference. He realized that any treaty with the potential of further United States involvement in world affairs would need public support. Wilson went on a whistle-stop-style campaign to get the American people behind the Treaty of Versailles. Members of the Republican majority, led by Henry Cabot Lodge, were determined to defeat the treaty. Many Americans suffered disillusionment from the war itself and felt that the United States should withdraw completely from European affairs. Two groups called the "irreconcilables" joined forces to revise the treaty so much that Wilson could not support it.

After Harding was elected, he did preside over the Washington Conference, which met to deal with naval disarmament and relations with the Pacific powers. After Harding died, Coolidge signed the Kellogg-Briand Treaty.

The Great Depression further intensified our isolationist policies. However, Franklin Roosevelt announced the "good neighbor policy" at his first inauguration. This policy stated that no nation had the right to intervene in the affairs of any Latin American nation. The determination of the United States to remain neutral was evident in the passage of a series of neutrality acts starting in 1936. However, after the war in Europe broke out, America agreed to lend, lease, and transfer military goods and other aid to Great Britain. Roosevelt and Churchill also announced a generalized statement of policy, the Atlantic Charter, in August 1941, which emphasized that both countries urged international cooperation rather than war as an overall goal.

1945–1962

Containment of communism was the primary goal of the cold war. The threat of a nuclear nightmare took the world to the edge of destruction.

Many historians point to the agreements reached at the Yalta Conference in January 1945 as the unofficial start of the cold war. Even though the Allied powers agreed on the destruction of Nazi Germany and her disarmament, there was a sense that Russia was given an implicit go-ahead to establish a sphere of influence in Eastern Europe in return for Soviet cooperation in helping the United States defeat Japan. Ironically, we did not need their help because Japan surrendered after America dropped two atomic bombs on Hiroshima and Nagasaki. Once the war ended, it became obvious that there would be mutual distrust between the Soviet Union and the West.

Historical Headline Highlights

- 1947—Truman Doctrine, which supported the people of Greece and Turkey in resisting communism, announced.
- 1947—The Marshall Plan for economic recovery of Europe implemented.
- 1948—Russian blockade of Berlin thwarted by United States airlift.
- 1949—The North Atlantic Treaty Organization (NATO), a collective security agreement, signed. The Soviet Union counters with the Warsaw Pact, a mutual security treaty of communist countries.
- 1949—The Soviet Union explodes its first atomic bomb.
- 1950—China becomes communist and the Korean War begins.
- 1954—Southeast Asia Treaty Organization (SEATO) signed after North Vietnam establishes communist government.
- 1956—Soviet Union crushed Hungarian uprising.
- 1957—Eisenhower Doctrine, which states readiness to use armed forces to aid Middle Eastern countries threatened by communist aggression, announced.
- 1960—Castro takes over Cuba and establishes communist government.
- 1961—Bay of Pigs invasion fails in Cuba. Berlin Wall built.
- 1962—Cuban missile crisis brings world to the brink of nuclear war.

When Harry Truman succeeded Roosevelt as president, his first major foreign policy decision was whether to drop a nuclear bomb on Japan. There was no doubt in his mind that using the bomb would save hundreds of thousands of American lives.

After the war ended, the cold war lines were drawn in Europe. Eastern European countries became satellite nations of the Soviet Union. Germany was carved up and armies of Russia and the Allies occupied the defeated nation. Support of Truman's containment policies was both popular and bipartisan. The Senate voted 84–12 to approve the NATO Treaty and a majority of the public approved of the Truman Doctrine. Republicans, however, did accuse Truman of failing to win a victory in the Korean War, and his popularity declined after he fired MacArthur.

Eisenhower furthered a policy of containment and there was a growing feeling that a domino theory—if one country fell to communism, others would fall like dominoes—was becoming a reality. The communist leader, Nikita Khruschev, became a thorn and a symbol to Americans. Brinkmanship became a doctrine that caused nightmares of nuclear destruction. The policy was supported by an arms race between the Soviet Union and the United States.

The Cuban Missile Crisis, precipitated by Russia's decision to build nuclear launching pads in Cuba, brought the world to the brink of war. The United States instituted a blockade and finally the Soviet Union backed down and agreed to remove all nuclear weapons from the island. In return, we agreed to remove missiles from Turkey.

1962–1978

The quest for détente was sidetracked by the war in Vietnam.

The longest event of the cold war was prompted by President Johnson's decision to escalate United States involvement in Vietnam. The war brought down his presidency, resurrected the political life of Richard Nixon, and, once it ended, enabled the United States to begin a policy of détente with the Soviet Union.

Historical Headline Highlights

- 1962—American troops are sent to Vietnam as advisors.
- 1963—Nuclear Test Ban Treaty outlawing atmospheric testing signed.
- 1964—Gulf of Tonkin Resolution passes.
- 1968—Antiwar demonstrations reach a peak after the Tet offensive.
- 1968—Nuclear Nonproliferation Treaty agreed to.
- 1969—Nixon announces Vietnamization policy.
- 1970—Secret bombing of Cambodia revealed; students shot at Kent State.
- 1971—United States sends troops to Laos in order to cut off Viet Cong supply lines.
- 1972—Nixon visits China, and a period of détente emerges between the Soviet Union and the United States resulting in the negotiation of an arms control treaty.
- 1973—The United States signs peace treaty with North Vietnam. War Powers Act is passed by Congress.
- 1976—Nuclear Test Pact limiting underground tests is signed.

Any consensus and united support of policy during the cold war collapsed during the Vietnam War. Congress gave President Johnson the green light to increase troop commitment by passing the Gulf of Tonkin Resolution in 1964. As a result of this action, the longest undeclared war in American history began. More than 500,000 troops were deployed and over 50,000 deaths were claimed. The antiwar movement supported by "doves" and "peaceniks" was countered by "hawks," who felt that we had our hands tied behind our backs. In 1968 demonstrations reached a peak and as we have previously discussed, Johnson decided not to seek a second term as president.

The presidency of Richard Nixon was predicated by his hope of "Vietnamizing" the war—that is turning over the fighting to Vietnam's armed forces while withdrawing American troops. Although this policy was actively pursued, the war dragged on and even escalated when Nixon decided to invade Cambodia. Peace discussions got bogged down by hours of debate over the shape of the conference table. Popular support of the war was below 50 percent in polls. The war ended in 1973 when the United States signed the peace treaty with North Vietnam. That same year Congress passed the War Powers Act, which established greater authority by both houses if the president decides to commit American troops in a prolonged armed action abroad.

Although an avowed anticommunist throughout his political career, Richard Nixon was also a pragmatist. He and his national security advisor, Henry Kissinger, understood that a softening of hostility between the Soviet Union and the United States would further the goal of world peace. Thus, Strategic Arms Limitation Talks with Russia began at the tail end of the Vietnam War. The SALT Treaty was signed by Nixon in 1972 and resulted in the first arms reductions since the nuclear age began. After Nixon completed his breakthrough visit to China, Russia became convinced that it would be in their interests to cooperate with the United States. Détente ended in 1979 after the Soviet Union invaded Afghanistan and the Senate refused to approve the SALT II treaty.

1978–1987

The Reagan Doctrine signals a return to cold war rhetoric and policies. However, moves on the part of USSR Premier Gorbachev aimed at perestroika, a move toward domestic reform in the Soviet Union, and glasnost, the move toward easing the cold war, led to the beginning of the end of communism.

The Carter administration experienced triumph and tragedy in the Middle East. The president succeeded in bringing Israel and Egypt together, achieving the Camp David Accords, but failed in stemming the terrorism of Iran when they captured our embassy and took American citizens as hostages. The hostage situation and runaway inflation helped Ronald Reagan defeat Carter for president in 1980. Reagan's victory also ushered in a new era of United States foreign policy.

Historical Headline Highlights

- 1978—Camp David Accords bring peace between Egypt and Israel.
- 1979—American embassy personnel held hostage by Iranians.
- 1983—United States invades Grenada.
- 1983—Terrorist attack on United States Marines in Beirut.
- 1985—Summit meeting held between Reagan and Gorbachev.
- 1986—Iran-Contra affair uncovered; Congress holds hearings.
- 1987—Nuclear Arms Treaty is signed.

The Reagan foreign policy doctrine was a pragmatic mix of anti-Soviet rhetoric and cynicism toward new efforts for détente balanced by a readiness to negotiate with Gorbachev and respond to his overtures. During the 1980 campaign Ronald Reagan described the Soviet Union as "the evil empire." He was against the SALT agreements and felt that the Soviet Union failed to live up to its end of the treaty.

After meeting with Gorbachev at the first summit, Reagan got the impression that the Soviets were willing to negotiate in good faith. Yet he continued to push for a strong nuclear deterrence, calling for an increase of B-1 bombers, the deployment of additional MX land-based missiles, and a new defense strategy, the Strategic Defense Initiative (called Star Wars). Even though the initiative never went beyond the planning stages and cost millions in research, Reagan was able to successfully use it as a ploy in negotiating with Gorbachev. In 1988, after a series of summits, the Intermediate Nuclear Force Treaty was signed. This agreement called for the destruction of a large part of the most dangerous nuclear warheads—the intermediate-range missiles.

The other aspect of Reagan's foreign policy doctrine was a philosophy to aid national liberation movements such as the Contras in Nicaragua, to support an armed military invasion of Grenada, and to put pressure on governments that were antagonistic toward the United States, such as the Philippines, Chile, and South Africa. It was illegal aid to the Contras and an arms for hostages agreement with Iran, though, that discredited Reagan's presidency. It was discovered that Reagan's national security advisors and the CIA approved this plan, counter to congressional direction. Congress held the Iran-Contra hearings and concluded that even though there was no evidence directly linking Reagan to the plan, he was ultimately accountable.

The other dominating factor capturing Reagan's attention was terrorism against United States peacekeeping forces in the Middle East. From the moment Ronald Reagan was inaugurated, he had to deal with this problem. Terrorism reached a dramatic and tragic peak when the United States Marines barracks was bombed in Beirut by terrorists, killing 241 marines and naval personnel.

In the end, Ronald Reagan laid the foundation for George H. W. Bush to develop his new world order.

1987–Present

The new world order is fraught with danger and uncertainty as the United States enters the twenty-first century as the last great superpower.

After successfully defeating Iraq in the so-called 100-hour Gulf War and asserting that appeasement in the area of foreign policy was unacceptable, President George H. W. Bush proclaimed the cold war over and stated that the United States should take the lead in establishing a new world order. As he outlined this policy, it became clear that Bush's vision for world peace centered around the United States taking the lead to ensure that aggression be dealt with by a mutual agreement of the United Nations, NATO, and other countries acting in concert. Combined with the fact that the Soviet Union no longer existed and the cold war was over, the new world order seemed to be a logical and positive step. However, events demonstrated that world events did not always lead to a successful application of this doctrine.

Historical Headline Highlights

- 1989—The Berlin Wall falls and communism ends in Germany, Poland, and Hungary.
- 1990—Communism ends in the Soviet Union; East and West Germany united.
- 1991—United States easily defeats Iraq in Persian Gulf War.
- 1991—Unsuccessful coup fails to oust Gorbachev; Yeltsin emerges as new leader of Russia as Soviet Republics gain independence.
- 1992—Events in Somalia and Serbia challenge principles of new world order.
- 1994—United States ends trade embargo with North Vietnam.
- 1994—United States troops occupy Haiti in order to restore democratic government.
- 1995—Peace accord between Bosnia, Serbia, and Croatia results in deployment of 40,000 NATO and 20,000 United States troops to Bosnia.
- 1997—Expansion of NATO approved, results in admittance of Poland, Hungary, the Czech Republic, and Slovakia.
- 1998—Showdown with Iraq over the issue of UN inspection of chemical weapons sites. The United States and Great Britain launch air strikes.
- 1998—Two American embassies destroyed by terrorist bombs. The United States retaliates with air strikes against terrorist sites in Afghanistan and Sudan.
- 1999—NATO declares war against Kosovo using air strikes to attain victory.
- 1999—Comprehensive Nuclear Test Ban Treaty defeated in the Senate.
- 2000—Fragile peace in the Middle East broken between Israel and Palestine.
- 2001—Serbian leader Milosevic brought to trial in The Hague for war crimes.
- 2001—United States attacked by terrorists.
- 2001—United States invades Afghanistan in response to the terrorist attacks and removes the Taliban from power.
- 2003—United States invades Iraq and removes Sadaam Hussein from power.
- 2004—United States gives sovereignty to Iraq but keeps a large peace-keeping force in place.

Events moved swiftly after George H. W. Bush was elected president in 1988. Gorbachev's call for glasnost and perestroika ended up as a precursor to the end of communism. As the Eastern European countries renounced their governments, Russia too turned away from communism. South Africa abolished the doctrine of apartheid and in 1994 held the first elections where blacks could vote. Nelson Mandela was chosen as the country's first freely elected president. George Bush was the beneficiary of the end of the cold war. Public support soared, and Bush's approval rating after the Gulf War was at a whopping 90 percent. His new world order doctrine seemed to fit the bill in a world void of a communist threat.

Both Bush and Clinton discovered that, even though the United States held the balance of power, it could not provide unilateral answers to the internal troubles facing nations in the former Yugoslavia and in Somalia and Rwanda. The public was quite skeptical of the global role we should take. In a survey taken in 1993, 63 percent of the people polled agreed with the statement that we should not think so much in international terms but concentrate more on our own national problems.

In 1997, trouble spots kept the United States vigilant. Events such as the assassination of Israel's Prime Minister Rabin in 1996 and the turnover of Hong Kong to China in 1997 created new foreign policy hot spots for the United States.

The Clinton Doctrine and the election of George W. Bush left United States foreign policy in a state of evolution. Bush promised that he would be very hesitant to use "nation building" as a rationale for United States foreign policy. The U.S. war on terrorism has changed this policy.

Defense Policy

The defense policy of the United States is caught between the past practice of developing a powerful nuclear deterrence and an uncertain future of budgetary reductions. And yet providing for the common defense is a primary goal for the government.

In Chapters 15 and 16 we discussed how the size of the defense budget had a tremendous impact on the economy of the United States. Many times in our history Congress has debated "guns vs. butter." And now that the cold war is over and the country is facing such a large deficit, the pressure to reduce the size of the military establishment is even greater. The proponents of a scaled-down defense point to the fact that we don't need to deploy as many forces throughout the world as we did in the past. They claim that retraining military personnel could be accomplished and that many industries that are defense-oriented could redirect their resources to other areas. Critics argue that, because the United States is the last remaining superpower, we must maintain a strong defense posture. They also doubt that defense industries can easily move away from defense if contracts are cut. This, they argue, would increase the unemployment rate.

Defense policies are closely tied to the foreign policy goals of the nation. Thus national security and vital national interests are two of the overriding objectives in developing a defense budget and operation. As the country saw during the Gulf War, weaponry is an important part of the defense strategy. Both conventional and nuclear weapons for offensive and deterrent purposes play a significant part in the overall defense budget. In the past 25 years, it has also become obvious that as we develop and maintain weapons, we have also entered into agreements to destroy a good part of our nuclear arsenal. These treaties include

- Nuclear Test Ban Treaty of 1963—banned atmospheric testing
- Nuclear Nonproliferation Treaty of 1968—stopped and monitored the spread of nuclear weapons to countries that did not have the bomb
- Antiballistic Missile Treaty of 1972—America and the Soviet Union limited in antiballistic missile sites and interceptor missiles
- Strategic Arms Limitation Treaty of 1972 (known as SALT II)—never passed the Senate as a result of Russia's invasion of Afghanastan (in 1986 many of the reductions were carried out by both sides)
- Intermediate Range Nuclear Forces Treaty of 1987—provided for the dismantling of all Soviet and American medium- and short-range missiles and established a site inspection procedure
- Strategic Arms Reductions Treaty of 1991—provided for major reductions in United States and Russian nuclear arsenals (the reductions were expanded further in 1992 after Boris Yeltsin became Russia's president)

- Chemical Weapons Ban Treaty of 1997—banned the possession, production, or transfer of chemical weapons for those nations participating
- Comprehensive Nuclear Test Ban Treaty of 1999—the Senate refused to ratify this treaty that bans all nuclear explosions. It marked the first time since the Treaty of Versailles that the Senate refused to ratify a major treaty.

The expiration of the nonproliferation treaty was resolved in 1995 after a meeting sponsored by the United Nations resulted in a decision to renew it indefinitely and unconditionally. The important question of who should be allowed to join the nuclear club still had to be addressed even with the treaty's extension. The issue became a major part of our foreign policy as North Korea and Iraq threatened to become the club's newest members. The new Nuclear Nonproliferation Treaty prohibited any expansion of the nuclear club. The United States obtained concessions from other signees that there would be no new expansion of nations. However, inspection questions and agreement by nations that already have the technology left open the question of how effective the treaty would be to prevent other nations from developing nuclear technology. As a result, the Senate refused to ratify the treaty even though President Clinton urged its passage.

The question of how much is enough has always been part of the policy agenda debate. The so-called military-industrial complex has argued that a strong defense will ensure the future security of the United States. On the other hand, the pressure to adjust to a non-cold-war world has resulted in a serious effort to reduce the scope of the defense budget.

Global Interdependence

Global interdependence provides the opportunity for mutual political and economic support and cooperation.

By definition, global interdependence refers to the degree of linkage among the community of nations. This connection can be economic or political in nature and may have as its basis a formal organization or treaty binding and defining its membership.

The concept of global cooperation goes back to the formation of the League of Nations after World War I. Because the United States was not a participant and the league was not allowed to take military action, it was doomed to fail. When Stalin, Churchill, and Franklin Roosevelt met at Potsdam in 1945, the parties agreed to join and participate in a new international organization to be formed after the war was over. The United Nations was chartered in 1945. The Senate approved United States membership by a lopsided 89–2 vote, and the first meeting of the General Assembly was held in London in 1946. The organization consists of a General Assembly made up of all the member nations. It elects ten nonpermanent members of the Security Council. This council is made up of the ten nonpermanent members and five permanent members including the United States, Britain, France, Russia, and China. The Security Council has the power to place military and/or economic sanctions in order to carry out its primary responsibility of maintaining international peace. It has used this power throughout its history, even though any permanent member can veto any action. Areas where the United Nations has taken such action include

- Korea—allowing a multinational force to fight North Korea, which resulted in the Korean War
- Middle East—maintaining a peace force in Lebanon; forcing Israel and her warring neighbors to stop fighting
- Iraq—allowing economic sanctions; participating in a multilateral force against Iraq, which resulted in the Gulf War
- Haiti—supporting an embargo against the military dictatorship that ousted the democratically elected president
- Somalia—providing a peacekeeping force to settle the nation's civil war and aid the starving population
- Bosnia-Herzegovina—providing a peacekeeping force to protect so-called safe enclaves, allowing NATO to conduct air strikes against Serbian forces when these havens came under attack. (In 1995, the UN arms embargo aimed at preventing Bosnia from obtaining arms came under attack by the United States Congress as both houses passed a resolution directing President Clinton to lift the arms embargo.) Clinton vetoed the measure and NATO resumed air attacks, which forced both sides to the peace table, resulting in the Dayton Peace Accords. In 1997, the combination of NATO and United States troops had established an atmosphere to help ensure lasting peace.
- Kosovo—The greatest threat to peace since the Gulf War took place in this Serbian province after its leader, Slobodan Milosevic, initiated a policy of ethnic cleansing aimed at ethnic Albanians living in Kosovo. Although Milosevic claimed that he was suppressing an armed revolt, the net effect of his actions was the forced removal of hundreds of thousands of Kosovars. The United States and Great Britain demanded that Milosevic stop, and NATO began a massive air attack on the Serbian capital after the United States issued an ultimatum. Great Britain supported the efforts of the United States and from March until June, NATO forces intensified their air campaign against strategic facilities. In one of the strikes, United States aircraft bombed the Chinese embassy in the Serbian capital by mistake. In June, after driving close to one million ethnic Albanians out of Kosovo, Milosevic finally allowed NATO forces to occupy the country and let the refugees return. Milosevic was indicted by the United Nations as a war criminal, but he refused to surrender. After being deposed by an armed revolt, Milosevic was extradited to The Hague, where he is standing trial. The success of NATO forces in this conflict represents the first time in military history that an air campaign alone has led to a victory in a war.

THE UNITED NATIONS CELEBRATED ITS FIFTIETH ANNIVERSARY IN 1995.

The United Nation's secretary general is the organization's spokesperson and often acts as a negotiator. Other bodies of the United Nations fostering economic and political aid are the Economic and Social Council, the Trusteeship Council, and the International Court of Justice.

Regional collective defense organizations such as NATO, SEATO, and the Organization of American States (OAS) have been previously discussed. With the downfall of communist governments in Eastern Europe, the Warsaw Pact was dissolved. This led to the unprecedented request on the part of Russia and other former communist governments to become member nations of NATO. At a NATO summit held in 1993, President Clinton announced a "partnership for peace," which allowed for the gradual recognition of new member nations and the assignment of associate status to Russia. In 1997, Russia agreed to this status and the formal entry of the former Warsaw Pact nations of Poland, Hungary, the Czech Republic, and Slovakia was approved. In Europe, the primary cooperative economic regional organization is the European Economic Community (EEC), also called the Common Market. It has long been felt that the EEC would lead to a unification of the monetary and political systems in a European confederation. At the present time, the organization coordinates monetary, trade, labor policies, and immigration of its member nations.

Global economic interdependence has yet to be achieved. The United States has been an active participant in the move toward free trade. This policy has been controversial because America is still facing a huge trade deficit and because labor has serious reservations. The United States has granted China "most favored nation" status, even though there are serious concerns regarding China's human rights policies. Japan and the United States have reached a series of voluntary trade agreements that have opened up markets for both countries. The General Agreement on Tariffs and Trade (GATT) is the primary mechanism for the negotiation of trade policies including nondiscrimination by member nations. The GATT says that establishment of new trade barriers should be avoided and existing tariffs should be eliminated, and protective tariffs should be used only for emergency situations. There have been periodic meetings of the world's superindustrialized nations, called the G-7, who are also part of GATT. They have pledged continuing aid to Russia and are actively pursuing the reduction of trade barriers.

The United States, Canada, and Mexico signed the North American Free Trade Agreement during the administration of George H. W. Bush. The policy was debated by Congress after Clinton was elected. The agreement called for dramatic reductions of tariffs among the three countries. Stiff opposition to the treaty came from labor unions who were concerned that many businesses would flee the United States and use cheap Mexican labor. President Clinton was able to push the agreement through both houses as a result of significant Republican and public support. In 1997, the first report of NAFTA's status was released by the Clinton administration. It reflected "moderate success" in opening up new trade markets with Canada and Mexico. However, major opposition to NAFTA still existed.

Two monetary organizations that increase economic interdependence are the International Monetary Fund (IMF) and the World Bank. The IMF acts as a clearinghouse for member nations to discuss monetary issues and develops international plans and policies to deal with monetary issues. Regulating monetary exchange rates is the primary task of the IMF. The World Bank, also called the

International Bank for Reconstruction and Development, provides monetary assistance to nations that develop industries and aims to stimulate economic growth of third-world nations. A goal of this assistance program is the hope that these countries will become more politically stable. Countries contribute to the bank, and the bank loans money to nations in need. The United States has been a contributor to the bank. However, there has been crititicism of America's role because some countries have not paid back their loans.

The era of international global cooperation and interdependence has been firmly established. American multinational coroporations have a vested interest in a world economy that is flourishing. Historically, when a worldwide economic depression spread during the period between the two world wars, it gave rise to Germany's acceptance of Hitler. America can benefit as it moves toward becoming an equal partner with its hemispheric neighbors and international community.

The War Against Terrorism

In what President George W. Bush called "the first war of the twenty-first century," Islamic terrorists connected to the *Al Qaeda* organization, led by Osama bin Laden, attacked the United States on September 11, 2001. Nearly 3,000 people from over 80 nations were killed when two hijacked planes crashed into the Twin Towers of the World Trade Center in New York City. The commercial airliners were used as guided missiles, causing the Twin Towers to collapse within an hour and a half after the planes hit the skyscrapers. Among the dead were more than 300 New York City firemen and policemen who had arrived on the scene to aid victims after the two jets struck the buildings.

Just outside Washington, D.C., another hijacked plane crashed into the Pentagon, killing 180 military and civilian personnel along with everyone aboard the hijacked plane. President Bush, who was scheduled to speak at a school in Florida, left in Air Force One but could not return to Washington until it was certain that the nation's capital was safe.

A fourth hijacked jet, purportedly heading toward the White House, crashed into a wooded area of southern Pennsylvania after the passengers on board the flight decided to fight the hijackers rather than allow the plane to be used against another American target. Vice President Dick Cheney and the House and Senate leadership were brought to secure locations during the attack.

Speaking to a joint session of Congress on September 20, 2001, President Bush outlined the objectives of the United States' war against terrorism, which he named "Operation Enduring Freedom."

1. The United States, along with a coalition of nations including the member nations of NATO, Russia, Pakistan, and other Middle Eastern countries, would pursue the terrorists responsible for the attack of September 11. Afghanistan's ruling Taliban government was put on notice that if they did not turn bin Laden over to the United States they would also be held responsible. Other countries that harbored terrorists were informed that they too would be held accountable for harboring, supporting, aiding, or sponsoring terrorists within their borders.
2. A new cabinet-level position, the Office of Homeland Security, was created and Pennsylvania Governor Tom Ridge was named as its head.

3. President Bush committed the full resources of the U.S. government to the massive cleanup in New York City. Recognizing New York City Mayor Rudolph Giuliani and New York Governor George Pataki, the president and Congress paid tribute to the men for their leadership during the crisis.
4. President Bush also announced that the assets of recognized terrorists would be frozen.
5. The United States would also provide massive humanitarian aid to the people of Afghanistan, many of whom are refugees as a result of that country's civil war.

The United States and Great Britain began a sustained attack on military and terrorist targets in Afghanistan on October 7, 2001. The U.S. military also dropped thousands of food packages as part of the humanitarian effort.

On the home front, the FBI issued a warning to the public advising them that other attacks within the United States were possible. There was also an anthrax scare as individuals connected to media interests and state and national governments were exposed to the germ by unknown sources. Congress passed antiterrorism legislation making it easier for law enforcement officials to wiretap and detain suspected terrorists. It also approved an airline industry bailout package and enacted an airline security law.

President Bush and his national security team, including Vice President Dick Cheney, Secretary of State Colin Powell, Secretary of Defense Donald Rumsfeld, Homeland Security Director Tom Ridge, and National Security Advisor Condoleeza Rice, indicated that the war on terrorism would not end until every terrorist was brought to justice. The prospects for a ground war in Afghanistan and an expansion of the war to other countries harboring terrorists supported that view. As President Bush stated in his address to Congress, "We will direct every resource at our command, every means of diplomacy, every tool of intelligence, every instrument of law enforcement, every financial influence, and every necessary weapon of war to the disruption and to the defeat of the global terror network. . . . Freedom and fear are at war. . . . We will not tire, we will not falter, and we will not fail." By the end of 2001, the Taliban had been defeated and an interim government had been established in Afghanistan. Though the war in Afghanistan was hailed as a success, terrorist leader Osama Bin Laden was not captured and escaped to Pakistan. His Al Quaeda organization was disrupted when key members were captured and interrogated. The Department of Homeland Security monitored the terrorist threat in the United States through a color-coded system. Terrorist threats were ongoing and terrorists successfully carried out attacks in foreign nations.

During the 2002 State of the Union address, President George W. Bush suggested that there was an "axis of evil" that included North Korea, Iran, and Iraq. Following his speech, the administration embarked on a policy that attempted to neutralize these countries terrorist policies. The first country the United States dealt with was Iraq. By January 2003, in his State of the Union speech, President Bush informed the country that there was evidence Saddam Hussein had weapons of mass destruction and that the United States would deal with the threat even if it meant a preemptive invasion.

In September 2003, Bush addressed the United Nations and Secretary of State Colin Powell followed up with a detailed report that accused Iraq of being part of the terrorist threat and hiding weapons of mass destruction. The Bush administration sought and obtained a U.N. resolution that gave Hussein a deadline to reveal and turn over all weapons of mass destruction. Iraq issued a detailed report denying that there were any weapons. Congress passed a resolution giving the president whatever authority he needed to make Saddam Hussein comply with the U.N. resolution. The United States rejected the report and, in March of 2003, invaded Iraq in what was called "Operation Iraqi Freedom." Though the international community led by France, Germany, and Russia were against an invasion, the U.S. gained the support of Great Britain and other allies. The United States-led invasion successfully crushed the Ba'athist government and in a three-week period marched into Baghdad where allied forces symbolically toppled a statue of the Iraqi leader. United States casualties were limited at this point and on May 1, 2003 President Bush landed on the aircraft carrier *USS Abraham Lincoln* proclaiming the end of major combat in the war in front of a backdrop sign stating "Mission Accomplished."

However, between spring 2003 and 2005, peacekeeping efforts were met with resistance. Over 2,100 American forces were killed and opposition to the war increased when it became evident that there were no weapons of mass destruction. President Bush maintained that the war was justified because Saddam Hussein posed a threat to the United States and even though there were no weapons, Bush insisted that Hussein had the capability of developing weapons and had connections to terrorists. In June 2004, the United States turned over sovereignty to a provincial Iraqi government. Over 130,000 U.S. troops remained in Iraq facing daily hostile forces. The conduct of the war became a central issue in the 2004 presidential campaign. After Bush was reelected, he pledged to keep American forces in Iraq until a stable government was formed and Iraqi troops could be trained to replace existing American soldiers. In January 2005, free elections were held in Iraq and an interim parliament was formed.

Chapter 19 Review

SECTION 1: MULTIPLE-CHOICE QUESTIONS

1. Since the end of the cold war, which of the following foreign policy goals do conservatives generally support the most?
   (A) addressing threats to United States national security through nation building
   (B) giving aid to foreign countries
   (C) securing a favorable balance of trade through international trade agreements
   (D) getting involved in UN peacekeeping missions
   (E) achieving worldwide arms reductions

2. Who made the following statement?
"the great rule of conduct for us in regard to foreign nations is, in extending our commercial relations to have with them as little political connection as possible . . . steer clear of permanent alliances with any portion of the foreign world."
(A) George Washington in his farewell address
(B) Abraham Lincoln in his Gettysburg Address
(C) Theodore Roosevelt as a rough rider
(D) Franklin Roosevelt in an address to Congress prior to World War II
(E) John Kennedy in his 1961 inaugural speech

3. The late nineteenth and early twentieth centuries were characterized by
(A) isolationism.
(B) neutrality.
(C) containment.
(D) imperialism.
(E) confrontationalism.

4. Which of the following foreign policy treaties was rejected by the Senate?
(A) League of Nations
(B) United Nations
(C) Kellogg-Briand Treaty
(D) Nuclear Nonproliferation Treaty
(E) NATO alliance

5. Which of the following were a corollary to the policy of containment?
I. domino theory
II. brinkmanship
III. détente
IV. neutrality

(A) I only
(B) II only
(C) I and II only
(D) III and IV only
(E) I, II, and III only

6. All the following foreign policy events took place during Nixon's administration EXCEPT
(A) a visit to mainland China.
(B) negotiating an end to the war in Vietnam.
(C) the signing the War Powers Act.
(D) the signing of the SALT Treaty.
(E) following a policy of détente with the Soviet Union.

7. Which of the following Reagan foreign policy programs came about in response to his characterization of the Soviet Union as "the evil empire"?
(A) Star Wars Initiative
(B) Intermediate Nuclear Force Treaty
(C) SALT II Treaty
(D) aid to the Contras
(E) U.S. invasion of Grenada

8. Which of the following best describes the principles of the new world order?
   I. isolationism
   II. internationalism
   III. mutual defense treaties
   IV. humanitarianism

   (A) I only
   (B) II only
   (C) II and III only
   (D) III and IV only
   (E) II, III, and IV only

9. In the debate of "guns vs. butter," those people arguing for guns point to
   (A) the increase in the size of the deficit.
   (B) the need to maintain United States priorities as the last superpower.
   (C) the easy transition of defense industries to other industries.
   (D) the increasing involvement of the United Nations in peacekeeping activities.
   (E) the increased role of NATO in world affairs.

10. Which of the following represents the central feature of Clinton's partnership for peace?
   (A) the abolition of NATO
   (B) the invitation to the former Warsaw Pact countries to join NATO
   (C) the merger of NATO and the European Economic Community
   (D) the invitation to Russia to join NATO as a full member
   (E) the merger of NATO, SEATO, and OAS

11. Which of the following is a major aim of GATT and NAFTA?
   (A) to break down international trade barriers
   (B) to regulate the international monetary exchange rate
   (C) to provide monetary assistance to third-world countries
   (D) to create a common currency among member nations
   (E) to coordinate labor and immigration policies among member nations

Answers to Multiple-Choice Questions

1. **(C)** Type of Question: Cause and effect relationships
Since the cold war ended, conservatives have been concerned about the direction of United States foreign policy. Though they supported the concept of President Bush's new world order, conservatives wanted presidents to address how decisions to become involved in other nations' affairs would impact our national interests. Examples such as Bosnia, Somalia, and Haiti support this premise. Choices A, B, D, and E are positions many liberals would support.

2. **(A)** Type of Question: Stimulus-based quotation/chronological
George Washington crafted a policy of neutrality in his farewell address. This policy was adhered to by most nineteenth century presidents, even though we fought a war in 1812 and pursued a policy of Manifest Destiny. Many twentieth-century politicians pointed to Washington's policy as a rationale for the United States to follow.

3. **(D)** Type of Question: Chronological/definitional
With the rise of industrialization and the desire for new markets, the United States opened up trade markets in Asia in the late 1880s creating

an Open Door Policy with Japan. By the turn of the century we provoked a war with Spain purely imperialistic in nature and character. Neutrality was a policy the United States pursued before World War I and World War II. Containment was a policy the United States adopted to meet the challenge of communism. Confontationalism was a policy the Soviet Union pursued.

4. **(A)** Type of Question: Identification and analysis
After World War I, President Wilson helped negotiate the Treaty of Versailles, which contained a provision to create a League of Nations. Wilson made a political miscalculation by not including Republicans in the process. Senator Henry Cabot Lodge, the opposition, and ultimately the Senate rejected the treaty. The decision to join the United Nations, the approval of the Kellogg-Briand Treaty (a 1927 treaty outlawing all war), the Nuclear Nonproliferation Treaty, and the NATO alliance were all supported by the Senate.

5. **(C)** Type of Question: Definitional
The policy of containment aimed to deal with the treatment of communism during the cold war. The domino theory suggested that, if one country fell to the communists, others would also fall like a row of dominoes tipped over. Brinkmanship was coined by Secretary of State John Foster Dulles during President Eisenhower's administration and suggested that during the cold war the United States and the Soviet Union would confront each other resulting in being on the brink of a nuclear war. This prophecy almost came true during the Cuban Missile Crisis. Détente was a policy pursued by Richard Nixon after he visited mainland China. Neutrality was a policy the United States attempted to pursue before each of the world wars.

6. **(C)** Type of Question: Chronological
This is a very tricky and difficult question because all the events took place during Nixon's term of office. The War Powers Act was passed by Congress during Nixon's administration. The act, creating limitations on the ability of the president to commit American troops abroad, was opposed by President Nixon but passed despite his opposition. Every president since Nixon has claimed that the act is unconstitutional, but the courts have never ruled on it.

7. **(A)** Type of Question: Cause and effect relationships
After Reagan was elected president in 1980, he continued to characterize the Soviet Union as "the evil empire." With a change of leadership and the attempt by Gorbachev to relax relations through his policy of glasnost, Reagan eventually was able to negotiate a Strategic Arms Limitation Treaty. Prior to these events Reagan initiated a strategy to detect incoming nuclear missiles called Star Wars. This policy, even though it never got off the ground, played a key role in the United States relationship with the Soviet Union and was consistent with Reagan's earlier negative beliefs about the Soviet Union.

8. **(E)** Type of Question: Definitional
The new world order, a policy developed by President Bush, was guided by the principle that after the collapse of communism and the Soviet Union, the United States would be the last remaining superpower. As such it would be our responsibility in conjunction with the United

Nations, NATO, and other allies to stop aggression and terrorism. Therefore, internationalism, mutual defense treaties, and humanitarianism became three of the guiding principles of this policy.

9. **(B)** Type of Question: Comparing and contrasting concepts and events
Since the end of World War II, the debate between guns and butter has taken place regarding the amount of money dedicated to the defense industry versus the amount of money budgeted for social welfare programs. Even after the cold war ended, proponents of guns maintained that decreasing the defense budget would be dangerous. Choice A would not be a good argument because increasing the defense budget without decreasing other areas would increase the deficit. One of the difficulties moving away from defense was the loss of jobs; choice D suggests an easy transition. If the United Nations and NATO became the primary vehicles for peacekeeping activities, it would mean less of a burden for the United States.

10. **(B)** Type of Question: Identification
A proposal made by President Clinton early in his administration, the Partnership for Peace attempted to create the circumstances for the inclusion of the former Warsaw Pact countries in NATO. Russia was not happy at this prospect, and its president, Boris Yeltsin, objected to this plan. To counter Russian resistance, Clinton offered Russia eventual associate status, which was accepted in principle by Yeltsin. Choice D is incorrect because the invitation to Russia did not include full membership status.

11. **(A)** Type of Question: Identification and analysis
GATT and NAFTA both dealt with a reduction of tariffs between the United States and other nations. The United States supported this approach because of the tremendous trade imbalance it was facing. The other choices are all components of such organizations as the International Monetary Fund (B, C) and the European Common Market (D, E).

SECTION 2: FREE-RESPONSE ESSAY

Former Defense Secretary Robert McNamara in his book *In Retrospect* described the Vietnam War as "a mistake, a terrible mistake." Critics of the book claim McNamara should have spoken out while he was secretary of defense. McNamara feels that the book should serve as a lesson for the United States in future foreign policy debates.

1. Discuss the public policy issues surrounding the issue of whether the war was a mistake.
2. Give two examples of foreign policy initiatives since Vietnam that have either benefited from the lessons of Vietnam or ignored them.
3. Describe how successful the United States and other nations have been in their attempt to guarantee international peace as part of the new world order.

Sample Student Response

Before the cold war ended, a primary goal of the United States was to contain communism and maintain a strong nuclear deterrence—essentially becoming "policeman of the world." This goal came under attack by members of Congress as well as other segments of the public. Every president, even with support of Congress and the advice of his national security experts, must achieve public approval in order to successfully achieve foreign policy initiatives. When that does not take place, the nation becomes split, and the administration's hands become tied, not only on the foreign front but also domestically.

This is how it was during the Vietnam conflict. Like that war, Robert McNamara's book *In Retrospect,* has come under much criticism. The book has incited many controversies regarding Mr. McNamara's now infamous confession that the war in Vietnam was "a mistake, a terrible mistake." A statement of this kind is paradoxical because he is the man who continued the war efforts for so many years. So, if it was a mistake, can we learn and grow from that mistake?

Today's world confronts the United States with nothing remotely like Vietnam. There is no global struggle with communism to drag the United States into every brushfire conflict. Presidents now have the freedom to pick their wars and fight them as they choose. The United States can also decide to pull forces without worrying about losing credibility or toppling dominoes. The difficulty now is determining whether America's vital interest is at stake. Such conflicts as Somalia, Bosnia, and Haiti in the 1990s are indicative of this point. During the cold war the question was posed whether there was any reason we shouldn't intervene. Now the question is, why should we?

Since Vietnam, the United States has gotten involved in several foreign policy situations. Some cases show that we benefited from lessons learned by the Vietnam conflict, whereas others show that we have ignored them. Some lessons learned from Vietnam include being wary of the dangers of underestimating nationalism, of faulty evaluations, and of asking the military to achieve more than weapons can deliver. Examples of ignoring these lessons include our interventions in Somalia, Beirut, and Bosnia. In each of these cases, we were guilty of poor analysis. We also asked the military to achieve more that the weapons could deliver. Lastly, we underestimated the reaction of the public—whether they supported or opposed our intervention in each situation. Ever since Vietnam, the public has been much more critical of involving ourselves in civil wars in other countries. With each action Vietnam comes to mind. Somalia, Beirut, and Bosnia came across as sloppily done and half-finished. When the Somalian warlords captured an American soldier and dragged him through the streets, the public was enraged and Congress demanded an early withdrawal. Because they were generally considered unsuccessful, Congress reevaluated our reasons for even being there in the first place, much as with Vietnam. In fact, attempts were made by the Republican majority to pass the National Security Act as part of their Contract with America aimed at limiting American use of troops under UN command. Involvement, which seems to consider experiences learned from Vietnam, included our more successful interventions in Kuwait and Haiti. In these instances the situations were well-evaluated and our forces dealt with the problems in an adequate fashion. Both actions were taken care of relatively quickly and without the expenditure of numerous American lives.

Although some people didn't agree with the reasons for our involvement in Haiti, the operation was well-planned and generally considered successful because we accomplished what we went there to do. Lessons have been learned from Vietnam, but whether we will make new mistakes in the future remains anybody's guess.

The United States and other nations have attempted to guarantee international peace as part of the new world order. The new world order was Bush's policy that gave the United States the responsibility of being the "policeman of the world" in conjunction with other peacekeeping forces. This effort has been met with mixed results. The United States successfully liberated Kuwait and a large portion of the world's oil supply in the Persian Gulf War. It was also successful in reinstating President Aristide in Haiti. Both of the conflicts were overcome with minimal loss of American lives. In 1991 there was also the Strategic Arms Reduction Treaty where the United States and Russia agreed to major reductions in nuclear arms. However, despite these successful policies, many Middle Eastern and third-world nations have had a multitude of violent confrontations—Somalia, Sudan, Liberia, Zaire, and Rwanda to name a few. The United States and the UN peacekeeping efforts, especially in Rwanda and Bosnia, have been largely unsuccessful. Future actions in these and other areas will ultimately determine the legacy of McNamara's book.

Evaluation of Free-Response Sample Essay

1. Does the essay establish a point of view regarding McNamara's book and does the writer develop a direction for the essay?
2. Are sufficient examples with adequate description given to support both the foreign policy lessons learned and lessons ignored?
3. Does the essay connect the new world order to the issues raised by the book?

1. The writer immediately outlines the issues raised in McNamara's controversial book. They include the fact that McNamara decided not to speak out while he was secretary of defense under President Johnson and thus the containment policy led to a further escalation of the war in Vietnam. Keeping this in mind, the writer then raises the issues regarding American policy today.

2. Specifically, the writer makes the observation that today's world does not resemble the world during the Vietnam conflict. Because of that, a different policy must be pursued by the United States—a policy dubbed the new world order. However, the possibility that another Vietnam could occur in a place such as Bosnia is raised. It is even suggested that the legacy of Vietnam could have been a decisive factor in the overall direction of our foreign policy toward Bosnia, Somalia, and Haiti. Evidence is given by the writer in viewing the attempts by the Republicans to pass the National Security Act, a proposal that would create restrictions for the United States as peacekeepers.

3. It seems as if McNamara's overall perspective, although highly criticized, was a valid one. The country was growing more weary of playing policeman of the world. One of the 1996 presidential candidates, Patrick Buchanan, even had an "America First" theme to his campaign. The essay does an excellent job of linking current policies to the themes raised by McNamara's book.

SECTION 2: DATA-BASED FREE-RESPONSE ESSAY

Answer the following questions based on this table.

Current members of the nuclear club	
The United States	15,000 warheads
Russia	30,000 warheads
Britain	700 warheads
France	600 warheads
China	500 warheads

Countries that have the bomb, but won't admit it	
Israel	around 100 warheads
India	30 warheads
Pakistan	10 warheads

Countries doing research so that they can get the bomb	
North Korea	Syria
Iran	Libya
	Algeria

Countries that have reduced their arsenal	
South Africa	from 6 to 0
Belarus	from 81 to 54 (the difference going to Russia)
Kazakhstan	from 1410 to 1400 (the difference going to Russia)
Ukraine	from 1650 to 1200 (the difference going to Russia)

Based of these data, discuss the foreign policy implications for the United States regarding

1. The passage of a nuclear nonproliferation treaty.
2. The role the United States should play in this area.

Sample Student Response

The table clearly illustrates the fact that, even though there is a signed nuclear nonproliferation treaty among the five major nations (the United States, Russia, Britain, France, and China), there is the potential for a nuclear catastrophe, there is certainly the potential for other nations to develop nuclear technology, and there is some mystery regarding who actually has nuclear capability. Although it is assumed that Israel, India, and Pakistan have nuclear weapons, because they do not allow inspection, it is impossible to know for sure what their capability is. With the split up of the Soviet Union, though three of its republics have reduced their arsenal, the possibility still exists that they could sell the technology to a nation who wants it or under a worst-case scenario use existing weapons if a crisis in Russia takes place. The movie *Crimson Tide*, released in 1995, suggests such a premise. The prospect of a nuclear nightmare resulting from international tensions, caused by yet another nuclear player, although more remote than during the cold war, still lingers as a possibility. Consider what would happen if Iraq or Syria obtained nuclear weapons and got into a conflict with Israel, a nation that, according to the table, has around 100 warheads.

United States foreign policy must respond to the fact that nuclear warheads are still a fact of life. The first direction the United States pursued was the successful extension of the Nuclear Nonproliferation Treaty. The

United States convinced 177 countries to sign the treaty indefinitely extending the 1970 treaty. A provision of the agreement, which weakens its intent, was a future call for disarmament and leaves the issues of further nuclear testing and inspections up in the air. India, Pakistan, and Israel, countries that did not sign the original agreement, refused to sign the new extension. In 1999 the Senate refused to ratify the treaty, striking a major blow against a ban on all nuclear testing. Another area United States policy will be considering is how to deal with terrorist groups obtaining nuclear weapons and what to do if Russia or its independent republics decide to sell the technology to countries such as North Korea or Iran. After the election of 2000, President George W. Bush urged the passage of a missile defense system similar to the Star Wars initiative proposed by Ronald Reagan. A defined policy that Russia understands would have an impact on the foreign aid given to them has been discussed by the Clinton administration and Congress. Another area that the United States must resolve is the role it will give the United Nations in resolving international crises that have the potential of involving use of nuclear weapons. Lastly, the issue of what will be included in the defense budget will have a significant impact on United States policy in this area. Does the United States develop new nuclear deterrents such as Star Wars? Or do we continue to downsize our current nuclear arsenal? These crucial questions will be central as the new world order gets defined and refined by future presidents.

Evaluation of Data-Based Free-Response Sample Essay

1. Are valid conclusions reached regarding the information presented in the table?
2. Does the writer give adequate options available to the United States regarding public policy in this area?

1. The writer offers the observations that the table presents the possibility of a nuclear nightmare even though there is a Nuclear Nonproliferation Treaty. To illustrate the point, the writer mentions the countries that are not signees but that have nuclear capability. A movie, *Crimson Tide*, is used effectively to illustrate what could happen if a country has nuclear weapons that are taken over by a terrorist group.

2. The central point of this stimulus-based question is what effect the Nuclear Nonproliferation Treaty will have on the future of the spread of nuclear weapons. The writer effectively summarizes the status of the treaty. Then the writer addresses specific policies such as how the United States will have to deal with those countries who don't abide by the spirit and intent of the treaty as well as terrorists who gain control of nuclear technology. The issue of what the United States should do if other countries decided to sell nuclear technology is also discussed. Finally, the writer speculates about the option of developing new nuclear deterrents as a result of threats from other nations.

PART FIVE

MODEL ADVANCED PLACEMENT UNITED STATES GOVERNMENT AND POLITICS EXAMINATIONS

Model Examination I

SECTION 1: MULTIPLE-CHOICE QUESTIONS

TIME: 45 MINUTES
60 QUESTIONS
Section 1 is worth 50 percent of the test

Directions: Each of the following questions has five choices. Choose the best response and record your answer on the answer sheet in the back of the test.

1. A provision in the Constitution that has been used to expand federal power over the states is
   (A) the police power.
   (B) the reserved power clause.
   (C) the due process clause of the Fourteenth Amendment.
   (D) establishment of republican governments by the states.
   (E) separation of powers.

2. Which of the following statements best describes the consequences of hyperpluralism?
   (A) It encourages the formation of third political parties.
   (B) Competing special interests can unduly influence the legislative process.
   (C) A centrist philosophy would emerge resulting in gridlock.
   (D) The elite in society would play a dominant role in the political process.
   (E) The elite would clash with the middle class resulting in class warfare.

3. The exclusionary rule established by the Supreme Court supported the position that
   (A) policemen must knock before they enter a house with a search warrant.
   (B) stop and frisk actions by police could be used only if there was probable cause.
   (C) witnesses to a crime may testify for a trial on videotape rather than in person.
   (D) evidence obtained that goes beyond the stated purpose of a search warrant may not be used in court.
   (E) a suspect may withhold information from the police when a lawyer is not present during interrogation.

4. The Federal Election Campaign Act of 1974 established all the following rules for candidates seeking office EXCEPT
   (A) the option of taxpayers to contribute a dollar to presidential campaigns on their income tax forms.
   (B) the restriction of citizen contributions per candidate.
   (C) the regulation of PAC contributions to candidates.
   (D) the restriction of spending amounts by candidates who decided not to accept matching funds.
   (E) the creation of the Federal Election Commission.

5. A major area that is affected by congressional oversight hearings is the
   (A) structure of congressional committees.
   (B) ability of the president to recommend legislation to Congress.
   (C) reduction of the number of cases heard by the Supreme Court.
   (D) creation of new special interest groups.
   (E) review of the budgets of independent regulatory agencies.

6. The primary function of a lobbyist is to
   (A) find political candidates for special interest groups.
   (B) provide information to members of Congress that is favorable to a position taken by a special interest group.
   (C) poll the public to help determine a position that a special interest group should take.
   (D) raise money for political action committees.
   (E) increase the awareness of special interest groups to the electorate.

7. In viewing the relationship between the president and Congress in the area of foreign policy, which action on the part of Congress attempted to reduce presidential authority?
   (A) Congressional Impoundment Act
   (B) War Powers Act
   (C) Gulf of Tonkin Resolution
   (D) approval of the SALT agreement
   (E) approval of NAFTA

8. One way Congress can respond to a Supreme Court ruling that declares a law unconstitutional is to
   (A) appoint new justices.
   (B) draft a referendum that the voters would approve.
   (C) pass new legislation that addresses the issues raised by the Court.
   (D) pass a law limiting the terms of the justices.
   (E) reargue the case in a state court.

9. In attempting to gain public support for his agenda, the president uses all the following techniques EXCEPT
   (A) using the bully pulpit.
   (B) giving the media a photo op.
   (C) providing sound bites.
   (D) holding a press conference.
   (E) holding a private meeting with the joint chiefs of staff.

10. A Supreme Court that creates precedent is described as one that relies on
    (A) unanimous court decisions.
    (B) judicial federalism.
    (C) judicial restraint.
    (D) judicial activism.
    (E) stare decisis.

Questions 11 and 12 should be answered based upon your knowledge of the Constitution and the United States government.

The powers not delegated to the United States by the Constitution, nor prohibited by it to the states, are reserved to the states respectively, or the people.

11. After the 1994 mid-term election, which of the following laws was passed by the Republican Congress to achieve the objective of this amendment?
   (A) block grants
   (B) funded mandates
   (C) judicial authority to appoint federal judges
   (D) power to reject regulatory agency directives
   (E) the go-ahead to make individual treaties with foreign countries

12. Which principle of government is derived from this amendment?
   (A) separation of powers
   (B) checks and balances
   (C) federalism
   (D) pluralism
   (E) republicanism

13. Whips have which of the following functions? They
   (A) act as direct liaisons to the White House.
   (B) work closely with the minority party in the name of bipartisanship.
   (C) make appointments to the various House and Senate committees.
   (D) are responsible for keeping party members in line when a vote occurs.
   (E) preside over the House when the speaker is absent.

14. Which of the following is a major cause of congressional gridlock?
   (A) the number of bills proposed by the president
   (B) lobbyists influencing Congress
   (C) divided party control of the Congress
   (D) the increased number of southern Republicans elected to Congress
   (E) the change in the party identification of voters

15. Sunshine laws were passed in order to give
   (A) Congress greater flexibility in determining meeting times.
   (B) C-SPAN the ability to televise congressional sessions.
   (C) citizens the ability to get information from law enforcement agencies.
   (D) citizens the ability to attend meetings that previously were held in secret session.
   (E) the press the right to get information from citizens.

16. Which of the following is a characteristic of the electoral college? It
    (A) mandates presidential electors to vote for the candidate they are pledged to.
    (B) establishes a power base for third-party candidates.
    (C) has resulted in frequent occasions when a president wins the electoral vote but not the popular vote.
    (D) became part of the Constitution to give more power to the voters.
    (E) gives the House of Representatives the power to determine who will be president if no candidate gets a majority of the electoral votes.

17. Standing House committees such as the Ways and Means Committee are important because they
    (A) do not engage in partisan behavior.
    (B) mark up bills before they go to the entire House for debate.
    (C) can act independently from established House rules.
    (D) receive conference committee reports.
    (E) are equally divided in membership between Democrats and Republicans.

18. The Constitution provides that one-third of the Senate's membership is up for election every two years so that
    (A) House members may decide whether to run for the Senate.
    (B) committee assignments can be alternated between Democrats and Republicans.
    (C) voters have less of a chance to change control of the Senate from one party to another.
    (D) the entire House and entire Senate are not voted on in the same year.
    (E) congressional apportionment can alter the size of House districts.

19. Which of the following groups voted most heavily Republican during the 1990s?
    (A) Jews
    (B) Evangelical Christians
    (C) African-Americans
    (D) Asian-Americans
    (E) labor union members

20. Proponents of the Second Amendment were most upset when Congress passed
    (A) the Civil Rights Act of 1990.
    (B) the Family and Medical Leave Act.
    (C) the Unfunded Mandates Act.
    (D) the line item veto.
    (E) the Brady Bill.

21. Procedural due process can best be found in
    (A) the First Amendment.
    (B) the Second Amendment.
    (C) the Fifth Amendment.
    (D) plea bargaining agreements.
    (E) the use of cameras in the courtroom.

Answer <u>Question 22</u> based on the following headline.

Reform Party Candidate Jesse Ventura Elected Governor of Minnesota

Some people say we should have a third major political party in the country in addition to the Democrats and Republicans.

22. Which of the following reflects the best explanation for the headline?
    (A) The Democratic and Republican parties have outlasted their effectiveness.
    (B) The media's coverage of the parties has soured the voters.
    (C) Voters don't seem to detect major differences between the Democrats and Republicans.
    (D) Third political parties will have a better chance to elect their candidates.
    (E) Voter registration has been on the decline.

23. What is the result of a continuing resolution agreed upon by both houses of Congress? It
    (A) authorizes the president to borrow money in advance of an approved budget.
    (B) allows a president to send troops abroad on a temporary basis.
    (C) prevents the shutdown of any governmental operation if a new budget is not enacted.
    (D) directs the Congress to meet until a budget is voted on.
    (E) creates a new legislative agenda.

24. The trend of states joining in regional presidential primaries suggests that the states want to
    (A) lessen the cost of the presidential campaigns.
    (B) have greater influence in the outcome of the nominating process.
    (C) lessen the importance of the New Hampshire primary.
    (D) decrease the electorate's influence on the outcome.
    (E) diminish the coverage by the media.

25. Which of the following reflects how the news media covers campaigns?
    (A) The media covers the candidates' positions in an in-depth manner.
    (B) The media is obligated to give equal coverage to all candidates running for office.
    (C) The media's main objective is to change public opinion through its coverage.
    (D) The media's coverage is characterized by candidates' sound bites and photo ops.
    (E) The media has shied away from looking at the personal lives of the candidates running for office.

26. In choosing members of the cabinet, the president usually seeks out people who
    (A) exclusively come from his own political party.
    (B) are primarily from the business community.
    (C) will remain loyal to the president.
    (D) are current government officials.
    (E) are former government officials.

27. Which of the following is true about senatorial courtesy? Senators
    (A) have final say regarding presidential judicial appointments.
    (B) of the state from which the candidate comes are consulted by the president prior to the candidate's appointment as a federal judge.
    (C) rely on the expertise of their fellow senators before approving judicial appointments.
    (D) consult with the American Bar Association before voting on judicial appointments.
    (E) poll their constituents before deciding on whether to accept a presidential appointment.

28. All the following are considered delegated constitutional jobs of the president EXCEPT
    (A) commander in chief of the armed forces.
    (B) chief of state.
    (C) making appointments of ambassadors.
    (D) titular head of their political party.
    (E) signing treaties with foreign countries.

MEDIAN HOUSEHOLD INCOME BY RACE AND HISPANIC ORIGIN: 1967 TO 1999

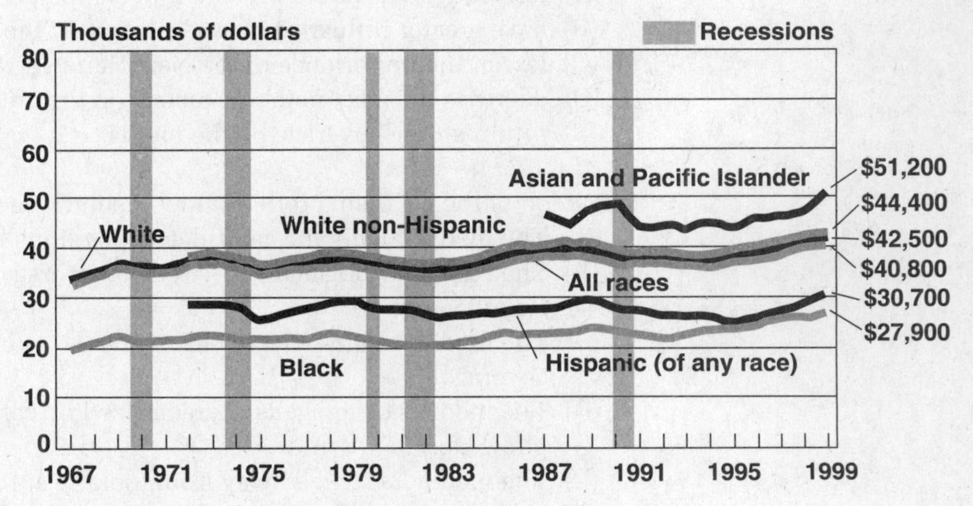

Source: U.S. Census Bureau

29. The graph supports which of the following conclusions?
    (A) Income levels increased for all groups.
    (B) White non-Hispanics earned less than all races.
    (C) Blacks earned more than Hispanics of any race.
    (D) Income levels increased for all groups except Asians.
    (E) There is no correlation between income and recessions.

30. The Founding Fathers relied on which principle developed by Enlightenment thinkers?
    (A) habeas corpus
    (B) guarantees of life, liberty, and property
    (C) one man, one vote
    (D) the right to bear arms
    (E) a single-house legislature

31. Which of the following conclusions did Madison reach in Federalist No. 39 regarding the issue of state sovereignty in the Federal system?
    (A) The government should be a confederacy of sovereign states.
    (B) The federal government should rely on the wisdom of the states more than the states should depend on the federal government.
    (C) The states should not be able to be taxed by the federal government.
    (D) A government should be developed where states retain important governing abilities but are subordinate to the federal government in other areas.
    (E) The states should have delegated powers reserved to them.

32. Which of the following is an example of the Supreme Court accepting a case based on original jurisdiction?
    (A) an appeal by a state regarding the decision of a lower court to overturn the state's restrictive abortion law
    (B) a habeas corpus petition from a convict who is on death row
    (C) a suit on the part of a citizen who believes his First Amendment rights are being violated
    (D) a dispute between environmentalists and land developers regarding the constitutionality of the Endangered Species Act
    (E) a dispute between New York and New Jersey over the plans of New York to build a hotel on Ellis Island

33. A major difference between the Iowa caucus vote and the New Hampshire primary is
    (A) greater turnout of voters in the Iowa caucus.
    (B) more loyal party regulars vote in New Hampshire.
    (C) exit polls are more accurate in caucus votes.
    (D) the fact that candidates must spend more money on caucus votes.
    (E) the fact that New Hampshire encourages crossover participation from people who are registered with other political parties.

34. Which of the following was a major reason the Supreme Court ruled that state-approved term limits for Congress were unconstitutional?
    (A) State laws restricting terms varied from state to state.
    (B) The age, residency, and citizenship requirements in the Constitution could be altered only by a constitutional amendment.
    (C) Congress could pass their own laws changing term limits.
    (D) Most people in the country voiced strong opposition to state-imposed term limit requirements.
    (E) If states passed term limit laws for congressmen, it would also enable them to pass term limit laws for other elected officials.

35. Which of the following is the best indicator that realignment took place in the 1990s?
    (A) Reagan Democrats returned to the Democratic Party and voted for Clinton in 1992.
    (B) There were fewer vetoes during Clinton's first term than Bush had in his.
    (C) The Republicans gained control of Congress in 1994.
    (D) More third-party candidates emerged during the 1990s than in previous decades.
    (E) Democratic Party enrollment declined in the 1990s.

36. Which of the following statements is true about the nature of modern party organizations?
    (A) Local politics generates a grassroots support by party regulars.
    (B) The control of the party machinery is greatest at the national level.
    (C) The party's national committee has the major fundraising responsibility for local candidates.
    (D) They are run by party bosses in a democratic manner.
    (E) The party's chairman is selected by its congressional membership.

Base your answers to questions 37 and 38 on the following excerpt from a Supreme Court decision:

On the other hand, the allowance of the privilege to withhold evidence that is demonstrably relevant in a criminal trial would cut deeply into the guarantee of due process of law and gravely impair the basic function of the courts. A president's acknowledged need for confidentiality in the communication of his office is general in nature. . . .

37. Which event took place as a result of this ruling?
    (A) the impeachment of Richard Nixon by the House of Representatives
    (B) the immediate resignation of Richard Nixon as president
    (C) an order requiring Nixon to turn over private documents
    (D) the release of the Watergate tapes to the Senate Watergate Committee
    (E) the erasure of 18 minutes of a critical tape by Nixon's secretary

38. The principle of executive privilege relates to which constitutional doctrine?
(A) division of powers
(B) reserved powers
(C) separation of powers
(D) judicial review
(E) federalism

39. The major impact third political parties have on presidential elections has been to
(A) recruit leaders from the Democrats and Republicans to run for president.
(B) draw enough votes from the major parties to throw the election into the House of Representatives.
(C) generate increased party identification among the electorate.
(D) develop issues that are later adopted by the major political parties.
(E) encourage a larger voter turnout.

40. A special interest group would probably have the greatest success dealing with a legislator regarding public policy issues that
(A) were favored by the public as reflected by polls.
(B) the president also supported.
(C) were controversial in nature.
(D) the legislator needed specific information about, which the group could provide.
(E) had previously been voted on by Congress but defeated.

41. Which of the following statements best describes congressional incumbency?
(A) Incumbents are usually able to win reelection even when a party realignment occurs during presidential elections.
(B) Incumbents have had fundraising limits imposed on them by the Federal Election Commission.
(C) Incumbents have been able to raise less money than their opponents.
(D) Incumbents are able to use franking privileges to their advantage.
(E) Incumbents look to have numerous debates with their opponents.

42. Compared to marble cake federalism, Reagan's new federalism aimed to
(A) increase the size of the federal government.
(B) reduce the number of block grants given to the states.
(C) downsize the federal government and turn more authority over to the states.
(D) increase the amount of federal taxes to reduce the deficit.
(E) reduce the size of the Defense Department and give the savings back to the states.

43. What is the prescribed basis to increase the size of the Supreme Court?
(A) the voters
(B) the president
(C) Congress
(D) a constitutional amendment
(E) a vote by the Senate Judiciary Committee

44. Which statement is true about the War Powers Act?
(A) It overturned the Gulf of Tonkin Resolution.
(B) It gave Congress the power to appoint the head of the joint chiefs of staff.
(C) It gave the president the authority to declare war.
(D) It established procedures when United States troops were under the command of the UN during peacekeeping missions.
(E) It directed the president to be accountable to the Congress if he sent troops to foreign countries.

45. The guiding principle that governs legislative apportionment is
(A) political gerrymandering.
(B) the establishment of majority-minority districts.
(C) one man, one vote.
(D) judicial authority to create congressional districts.
(E) districts determined by the governors of each state.

46. All the following demographic criteria have had an impact on voting EXCEPT
(A) the number of young people registered.
(B) the socioeconomic makeup of the electorate.
(C) the shift of the population to sunbelt states.
(D) the ethnic make-up of the electorate.
(E) an increase in illegal aliens.

47. What conclusion can you reach from the fact that informal congressional caucus groups such as the black caucus and caucus for women's issues have been formed?
(A) Caucus groups have had little impact on the legislative process.
(B) Democratic caucus groups were more powerful than Republican groups.
(C) There is an indirect relationship between these groups and special interest groups.
(D) Caucus groups were organized to better serve voter constituents.
(E) Republican groups were more numerous than Democratic groups.

48. Which of the following represents the attitudes of citizens with respect to the issue of separation of church and state?
(A) A majority of the population is against a constitutional amendment authorizing silent prayer in the schools.
(B) Liberals tend to oppose Supreme Court decisions such as *Engle v Vitale*.
(C) Conservatives feel that more people should attend churches and synagogues on a more regular basis.
(D) A majority of the population understands the establishment clause but feel students should be able to pray in school.
(E) Citizens in a pluralist society reject the need to recognize the rights of minority religious groups.

49. The commerce clause of the Constitution has been viewed as a way for
 (A) Congress to exercise greater authority over state matters.
 (B) the president to exercise greater authority to commit troops abroad.
 (C) the states to exercise their reserved powers.
 (D) the Senate to increase its authority to advise and consent the president's appointments.
 (E) Congress to exercise greater authority over the Supreme Court.

50. In the 1990s the manner in which legislation passed each house of Congress suggests that
 (A) bipartisanship has been the rule of thumb.
 (B) Congress has passed a greater number of bills than in previous decades.
 (C) there has been an increasing tendency for the president to veto legislation.
 (D) even though the House may pass its legislative agenda, it is often slowed down by the Senate.
 (E) Senate-House conference committees have exercised greater influence than congressional leaders in the formulation of legislation.

51. All the following reflect devolution of federal power EXCEPT
 (A) the approval of block grants to the states.
 (B) the limitations placed on the federal government to pass on unfunded mandates to the states.
 (C) the Supreme Court decisions that allow death row inmates to file petitions for review in federal court.
 (D) the executive orders resulting in the downsizing of the bureaucracy.
 (E) the congressional legislation resulting in the elimination of regulations established by regulatory agencies.

52. Since 1960, which of the following is the most significant factor in determining which candidate receives the party's nomination for president?
 (A) the economic condition facing the country
 (B) the belief that programs favored by the candidate would benefit the country
 (C) the ability of the candidate to win a majority of the primaries
 (D) the support given to the candidate by party leaders
 (E) the polls indicating that the candidate has name recognition

53. All the following are reasons for lower voter turnout in congressional elections compared to presidential elections EXCEPT
 (A) political advertisements use more smear tactics in presidential elections.
 (B) voters are more aware of national issues than local issues.
 (C) there is more media coverage of presidential elections.
 (D) voters believe that presidential elections have a greater impact on the country's future.
 (E) candidates spend more money on presidential elections.

54. The Speaker of the House of Representatives has the primary role of
    (A) breaking tie votes in the House.
    (B) presiding over the House during routine business.
    (C) setting the legislative agenda for the House.
    (D) settling disputes in his own party.
    (E) acting as a liaison with the opposition party.

55. All of the following choices are accurate statements about the nature of bureaucracies EXCEPT
    (A) there are built-in review processes for appeal of agency decisions.
    (B) there are bureaucratic agencies that oversee other agencies.
    (C) the size and scope of the federal bureaucracy has increased in the 1990s.
    (D) there are political checks on agencies.
    (E) legislative power can restrict agency appropriations.

56. Which statement is most true of the media's coverage of presidential campaigns?
    (A) Presidential endorsements by newspapers change the minds of many voters.
    (B) Sunday talk shows pay for their guests to appear.
    (C) There is an increased interest in covering the national conventions gavel to gavel by the major networks.
    (D) Networks like C-SPAN and CNN have played an increasingly important role in reporting the issues of the campaign.
    (E) The fairness doctrine has lessened the accusation that there is bias in the media toward one candidate.

57. Which of the following statements describe voting trends in recent presidential elections?
    I. The gender gap has been a factor.
    II. The youth vote is on the rise.
    III. The religious right is becoming less of a factor.
    IV. More people are enrolling as independents.

    (A) I only
    (B) II and III only
    (C) I, II, and IV only
    (D) III and IV only
    (E) I, II, III, and IV

58. Which of the following statements is a major reason for the increased use of public opinion polls by the media?
    (A) The government assesses the validity of the polls.
    (B) Candidate-sponsored polls compete for the public's attention.
    (C) A smaller random sample can now be used to get accurate results.
    (D) Polls are aimed exclusively at minority groups.
    (E) Elected officials pay attention to poll results.

59. The Federal Reserve Board has grown in importance because it
    (A) influences the trade policy of the United States.
    (B) has printed more money in order to reduce the deficit.
    (C) attempts to control inflation by raising or lowering interest rates.
    (D) can shut down trading on the stock market when the market drops below a certain point.
    (E) can create new branches of the National Bank.

60. All the following choices are characteristics of the high-tech presidential campaign EXCEPT
    (A) 60-second spots on national news shows.
    (B) political debates that include minor party candidates.
    (C) paid infomercials by candidates using graphs and charts.
    (D) sophisticated polling techniques done by paid consultants.
    (E) candidates acting like talking heads.

STOP

This is the end of Section 1.

Do not go on to Section 2 until you are told to do so.

SECTION 2: FREE-RESPONSE ESSAYS

TIME: 100 MINUTES (suggested time: 25 minutes per essay)
Section 2 is worth 50 percent of the test

Directions: Answer ***all four*** of the following questions in 100 minutes. Each essay should take you 25 minutes, so plan your time accordingly. The questions are based on your knowledge of United States government and politics, and questions may contain materials from charts, graphs, and tables, which you will have to analyze and draw conclusions from. Make sure that you give specific and sufficient information and examples in your essays. Please number them clearly on your answer sheet.

1. Special interest groups are often criticized for being divisive as well as for hindering the legislative process.
   (a) Define the term *special interest group.*
   (b) Give one example that supports this statement and one example that refutes it.
   (c) Explain how special interest groups have influenced the development of public policy by discussing specific laws that have been shaped by special interest groups.
2. Party realignment and party dealignment have influenced presidential, congressional, and state elections since 1980.
   (a) Define the terms *party realignment* and *party dealignment.*
   (b) Give one example of how realignment or dealignment has had an impact on two of the following elections:
   - The presidential election of 1980
   - The congressional election of 1994
   - The Minnesota gubernatorial election of 1998
3. The data in the following table show demographic election trends in recent presidential elections. From this information and your knowledge of United States politics, perform the following tasks:
   (a) Identify three demographic characteristics that have played a role in presidential elections.
   (b) Explain how these features contributed to the election of those United States presidents elected during the time periods detailed in the chart.
   (c) Discuss the importance of demographics on presidential politics.
4. The Constitution gives the Senate the power to advise and consent presidential appointments.
   (a) Describe how this procedure works.
   (b) Give two examples of controversial presidential appointments.
   (c) Evaluate the Senate's response to those appointments and explain why the Senate has been criticized in its use of this power.

VOTER TURNOUT IN PRESIDENTIAL ELECTIONS

Characteristic	1992	1996	2000
Percentage of men voting for			
Democratic candidate	41	43	42
Republican candidate	38	44	53
Third-party candidate	21	10	3
Percentage of women voting for			
Democratic candidate	45	54	54
Republican candidate	37	38	43
Third-party candidate	17	7	2
Percentage of whites voting for			
Democratic candidate	39	43	42
Republican candidate	40	46	54
Third-party candidate	20	9	3
Percentage of blacks voting for			
Democratic candidate	83	84	90
Republican candidate	10	12	8
Third-party candidate	7	4	1
Percentage of Hispanics voting for			
Democratic candidate	61	72	67
Republican candidate	25	21	31
Third-party candidate	14	6	2
Percentage of Asians voting for			
Democratic candidate	31	43	54
Republican candidate	55	48	41
Third-party candidate	15	8	4
Percentage of 18–29-year-olds voting for			
Democratic candidate	43	53	48
Republican candidate	34	34	46
Third-party candidate	22	10	5
Percentage of 30–44-year-olds voting for			
Democratic candidate	41	48	48
Republican candidate	38	41	49
Third-party candidate	21	9	2
Percentage of 45–59-year-olds voting for			
Democratic candidate	41	48	48
Republican candidate	40	41	49
Third-party candidate	19	9	2
Percentage of persons 60 and older voting for			
Democratic candidate	50	48	51
Republican candidate	38	44	47
Third-party candidate	12	7	2

Characteristic	1992	1996	2000
Percentage of whites Protestants for			
Democratic candidate	33	36	34
Republican candidate	47	53	63
Third-party candidate	21	10	2
Percentage of Catholics voting for			
Democratic candidate	44	53	49
Republican candidate	35	37	47
Third-party candidate	20	9	2
Percentage of Jews voting for			
Democratic candidate	80	78	79
Republican candidate	11	16	19
Third-party candidate	9	3	1
Percentage of households with incomes under $15,000 voting for			
Democratic candidate	58	59	57
Republican candidate	23	28	37
Third-party candidate	19	11	4
Percentage of households with incomes of $15,000–29,999 voting for			
Democratic candidate	45	53	54
Republican candidate	35	36	41
Third-party candidate	20	9	3
Percentage of households with incomes of $30,000–49,999 voting for			
Democratic candidate	41	48	49
Republican candidate	38	40	48
Third-party candidate	21	10	2
Percentage of households with incomes over $50,000 voting for			
Democratic candidate	39	44	45
Republican candidate	44	48	52
Third-party candidate	17	7	2

Answer Sheet for the Model Advanced Placement Examination

Name ______________________________

Date ______________________________

Grade ______________________________

FOR SECTION 1: MULTIPLE-CHOICE

Sample: 1. Bill Clinton was elected to the United States presidency in
(A) 1986
(B) 1988
(C) 1990
(D) 1992
(E) 1994

1. Ⓐ Ⓑ Ⓒ ● Ⓔ

Box D is filled in because the correct answer for the sample question 1 is D.

1. Ⓐ Ⓑ Ⓒ Ⓓ Ⓔ	**21.** Ⓐ Ⓑ Ⓒ Ⓓ Ⓔ	**41.** Ⓐ Ⓑ Ⓒ Ⓓ Ⓔ
2. Ⓐ Ⓑ Ⓒ Ⓓ Ⓔ	**22.** Ⓐ Ⓑ Ⓒ Ⓓ Ⓔ	**42.** Ⓐ Ⓑ Ⓒ Ⓓ Ⓔ
3. Ⓐ Ⓑ Ⓒ Ⓓ Ⓔ	**23.** Ⓐ Ⓑ Ⓒ Ⓓ Ⓔ	**43.** Ⓐ Ⓑ Ⓒ Ⓓ Ⓔ
4. Ⓐ Ⓑ Ⓒ Ⓓ Ⓔ	**24.** Ⓐ Ⓑ Ⓒ Ⓓ Ⓔ	**44.** Ⓐ Ⓑ Ⓒ Ⓓ Ⓔ
5. Ⓐ Ⓑ Ⓒ Ⓓ Ⓔ	**25.** Ⓐ Ⓑ Ⓒ Ⓓ Ⓔ	**45.** Ⓐ Ⓑ Ⓒ Ⓓ Ⓔ
6. Ⓐ Ⓑ Ⓒ Ⓓ Ⓔ	**26.** Ⓐ Ⓑ Ⓒ Ⓓ Ⓔ	**46.** Ⓐ Ⓑ Ⓒ Ⓓ Ⓔ
7. Ⓐ Ⓑ Ⓒ Ⓓ Ⓔ	**27.** Ⓐ Ⓑ Ⓒ Ⓓ Ⓔ	**47.** Ⓐ Ⓑ Ⓒ Ⓓ Ⓔ
8. Ⓐ Ⓑ Ⓒ Ⓓ Ⓔ	**28.** Ⓐ Ⓑ Ⓒ Ⓓ Ⓔ	**48.** Ⓐ Ⓑ Ⓒ Ⓓ Ⓔ
9. Ⓐ Ⓑ Ⓒ Ⓓ Ⓔ	**29.** Ⓐ Ⓑ Ⓒ Ⓓ Ⓔ	**49.** Ⓐ Ⓑ Ⓒ Ⓓ Ⓔ
10. Ⓐ Ⓑ Ⓒ Ⓓ Ⓔ	**30.** Ⓐ Ⓑ Ⓒ Ⓓ Ⓔ	**50.** Ⓐ Ⓑ Ⓒ Ⓓ Ⓔ
11. Ⓐ Ⓑ Ⓒ Ⓓ Ⓔ	**31.** Ⓐ Ⓑ Ⓒ Ⓓ Ⓔ	**51.** Ⓐ Ⓑ Ⓒ Ⓓ Ⓔ
12. Ⓐ Ⓑ Ⓒ Ⓓ Ⓔ	**32.** Ⓐ Ⓑ Ⓒ Ⓓ Ⓔ	**52.** Ⓐ Ⓑ Ⓒ Ⓓ Ⓔ
13. Ⓐ Ⓑ Ⓒ Ⓓ Ⓔ	**33.** Ⓐ Ⓑ Ⓒ Ⓓ Ⓔ	**53.** Ⓐ Ⓑ Ⓒ Ⓓ Ⓔ
14. Ⓐ Ⓑ Ⓒ Ⓓ Ⓔ	**34.** Ⓐ Ⓑ Ⓒ Ⓓ Ⓔ	**54.** Ⓐ Ⓑ Ⓒ Ⓓ Ⓔ
15. Ⓐ Ⓑ Ⓒ Ⓓ Ⓔ	**35.** Ⓐ Ⓑ Ⓒ Ⓓ Ⓔ	**55.** Ⓐ Ⓑ Ⓒ Ⓓ Ⓔ
16. Ⓐ Ⓑ Ⓒ Ⓓ Ⓔ	**36.** Ⓐ Ⓑ Ⓒ Ⓓ Ⓔ	**56.** Ⓐ Ⓑ Ⓒ Ⓓ Ⓔ
17. Ⓐ Ⓑ Ⓒ Ⓓ Ⓔ	**37.** Ⓐ Ⓑ Ⓒ Ⓓ Ⓔ	**57.** Ⓐ Ⓑ Ⓒ Ⓓ Ⓔ
18. Ⓐ Ⓑ Ⓒ Ⓓ Ⓔ	**38.** Ⓐ Ⓑ Ⓒ Ⓓ Ⓔ	**58.** Ⓐ Ⓑ Ⓒ Ⓓ Ⓔ
19. Ⓐ Ⓑ Ⓒ Ⓓ Ⓔ	**39.** Ⓐ Ⓑ Ⓒ Ⓓ Ⓔ	**59.** Ⓐ Ⓑ Ⓒ Ⓓ Ⓔ
20. Ⓐ Ⓑ Ⓒ Ⓓ Ⓔ	**40.** Ⓐ Ⓑ Ⓒ Ⓓ Ⓔ	**60.** Ⓐ Ⓑ Ⓒ Ⓓ Ⓔ

Answer Key to Model Examination I

SECTION 1: MULTIPLE-CHOICE QUESTIONS

1. C	11. A	21. C	31. D	41. A	51. C
2. B	12. C	22. C	32. E	42. C	52. C
3. D	13. D	23. C	33. E	43. C	53. A
4. D	14. C	24. B	34. B	44. E	54. C
5. E	15. D	25. D	35. C	45. C	55. C
6. B	16. E	26. C	36. A	46. E	56. D
7. B	17. B	27. B	37. D	47. D	57. C
8. C	18. D	28. D	38. C	48. D	58. E
9. E	19. B	29. A	39. D	49. A	59. C
10. D	20. E	30. B	40. D	50. D	60. B

Analysis of Multiple-Choice Questions

1. **(C)** Type of Question: Identification and analysis
Choice A refers to a reserved power of the states. Choice B refers to the Tenth Amendment and gives states powers such as education, health, and safety. Choice C, the correct answer, established that the states could not make laws that violate the rights of individuals living in those states. It also incorporated the Bill of Rights into the states. Choice D establishes state governments. Choice E refers to checks and balances.

2. **(B)** Type of Question: Definitional
Choice B, the correct answer, extends the definition of hyperpluralism, the competing interests of groups, to a logical conclusion—that these groups can have an impact on the lawmaking process. Choice A has very little to do with hyperpluralism. Choice C refers to pluralism and then gives an incorrect consequence of it, choice D refers to the elite theory, and choice E gives an incorrect consequence of the elite theory.

3. **(D)** Type of Question: Definitional
Choice D, the correct answer, is the definition of exclusionary rule. Choices A and B echo Supreme Court rulings. Choice C is factually correct, but has nothing to do with the exclusionary rule, and choice E is an incorrect statement as a result of the *Miranda* ruling.

4. **(D)** Type of Question: Negative
Choice D, the correct exception, is not a component of the Federal Election Campaign Act. In fact, a presidential candidate who does not want to accept federal matching funds can spend as much as he wants. A good example was Ross Perot in 1992. Choices A, B, C, and E are all part of Federal Election Campaign Acts.

5. **(E)** Type of Question: Cause and effect relationships
Choice E, the correct answer, is one function of congressional oversight. Another one is to review aspects of laws passed by Congress related to specific governmental agencies or departments. Choice A is wrong because the majority party has the power to review the structure of congressional committees. Choice B is incorrect because the president

can recommend legislation independently of congressional oversight. Choices C and D are incorrect statements related to the question raised.

6. **(B)** Type of Question: Definitional
Choice B is the correct answer. Special interest groups hire lobbyists for the purpose of influencing legislation favorable to that group. For instance, the National Rifle Association (NRA) will hire lobbyists to provide information to congressmen that will encourage them to vote against gun control legislation. Choice A is incorrect because political parties, not lobbyists, find candidates to run for office. Choice C is incorrect because special interest groups hire pollsters to determine public opinion. Choice D is incorrect because special interest groups contribute money to political action committees or have those of their own. Choice E is incorrect because lobbyists work behind the scenes and do not attempt to influence the electorate at large.

7. **(B)** Type of Question: Cause and effect relationships
Choice B, the correct answer, was a direct result of the president's escalation of the Vietnam War. Choice C was the action by Congress that gave President Johnson the green light to send more troops to Vietnam. Choice A refers to a budgetary action and domestic policy and does decrease presidential authority in that area. Choice D refers to Strategic Arms Limitation Talks, and choice E refers to the North American Free Trade Agreement, both treaties the Senate had to approve.

8. **(C)** Type of Question: Cause and effect relationships
Choice C, the correct answer, is the only manner, other than a constitutional amendment, Congress can act on a ruling by the Supreme Court that declares a law unconstitutional. Choice A is wrong because the Senate approves new justices only when there is an opening on the Court. Choice B is an incorrect statement. Choice D requires a constitutional amendment. Choice E is an incorrect statement.

9. **(E)** Type of Question: Negative
Choice E is the only incorrect choice because a meeting of the joint chiefs of staff, the heads of the military, is usually behind closed doors and would have a negligible impact on influencing public support compared to the other choices.

10. **(D)** Type of Question: Definitional
Choice D, the correct answer, requires that you understand the definition of judicial activism. The other choices are incorrect because by definition they refer to aspects of the Supreme Court that do not support what the question is asking. (Refer to glossary for definitions of each of the terms.)

11 and 12. **(A), (C)** Type of Question: Stimulus-based short quotation
In both questions you must recognize that the quote is from the Tenth Amendment to the Constitution—commonly referred to as the reserved power clause. The clause defines federalism and explains where states get their powers. Once you have determined this, you can see that in question 11, choice A would be the correct choice because block grants give funds for the states to spend without federal strings attached. In question 12, choice C, the correct answer, relates to the principle of federalism, the division of powers between the federal government and state governments.

13. **(D)** Type of Question: Definitional
Choice D, the correct answer, is one of the jobs whips have. Choices A, B, C, and E are incorrect statements. A whip may sometimes preside over a House session, but it is not a function of the job.
14. **(C)** Type of Question: Cause and effect relationships
Choice C, the correct answer, is a primary reason for congressional gridlock. More bills are vetoed and more often than not the country perceives that government is ineffective in solving the nation's problems. Even though lobbyists may influence legislation (choice B) in a negative way, they are not singularly responsible for gridlock. The other choices are incorrect in relation to the question.
15. **(D)** Type of Question: Definitional
Choice D, the correct answer, is an application of the definition of sunshine laws. These laws were passed to stop the practice of legislative bodies meeting in secret executive sessions late at night. Along with the Freedom of Information Act, both laws gave citizens more rights in obtaining information from the government.
16. **(E)** Type of Question: Identification and analysis
Choice E, the correct answer, gives the circumstances when the House of Representatives is mandated by the Constitution to select a president if a majority is not reached in the electoral college. Choice A is incorrect because presidential electors are only morally obligated to vote for the candidate the elector supported. Choices B, C, and D are incorrect statements about the nature of the electoral college.
17. **(B)** Type of Question: Definitional
Choice B, the correct answer, explains a function of a standing committee in the House of Representatives. The question is made even easier because it gives an example of a standing committee. Choices A and C are easy to eliminate as incorrect answers. Choice D may be true in rare instances, but it does not describe the primary importance of standing committees. Choice E is incorrect because standing committees are divided proportionally between Democrats and Republicans based on the majority/minority split in the House.
18. **(D)** Type of Question: Cause and effect relationships
Choice D, the correct answer, is the most obvious reason that the entire Senate is not elected in six-year cycles. A direct result could be a dramatic upheaval of both houses under certain circumstances. Choices A, B, and C are incorrect statements based on fact or circumstance. Choice E is incorrect because apportionment does not relate to the Senate.
19. **(B)** Type of Question: Chronological
Choice B, the correct answer, is an important Republican constituency. The other choices are all traditional Democratic constituents.
20. **(E)** Type of Question: Cause and effect relationships
Choice E, the correct answer, is the only law that deals with the right to bear arms. The Brady Bill mandated a waiting period before an individual could purchase a gun. The NRA and other gun proponents were against the bill.

21. **(C)** Type of Question: Definitional
Choice C, the correct answer, is a constitutional example of procedural due process. The Fifth Amendment provides a road map for due process, including the right to life, liberty, and property. Plea bargaining, choice D, is incorrect because it is not a guaranteed right. The other choices do not have direct procedural guarantees even though through application or court challenge due process questions may arise.

22. **(C)** Type of Question: Stimulus-based short narrative passage
Choice C, the correct answer, reflects voter discontent with the major political parties. Choice A is incorrect because there is still a viable two-party system. Choice B may be true but does not directly relate to the poll results. Choice D is an inaccurate conclusion, and choice E is wrong as a result of the Motor Voter Act.

23. **(C)** Type of Question: Definitional
Choice C, the correct answer, is the basic result of what happens when a continuing resolution is adopted. Choice A represents an illegal action on the part of the president. Choices B, D, and E are factually incorrect.

24. **(B)** Type of Question: Sequencing a series of events
Choice B, the correct answer, reflects the impact of regional primaries such as Super Tuesday. A new regional primary started in 1994, when New England states joined together in what became known as Junior Tuesday, in order to have more of an impact on the process.

25. **(D)** Type of Question: Generalization
Choice D, the correct answer, requires that you understand the definitions of sound bites and photo ops. Choices A, B, and E are factually incorrect. And choice C is deceptive because, although public opinion may change through the media's coverage, that answer does not reflect the purpose of the news media's coverage of campaigns.

26. **(C)** Type of Question: Generalization
Choice C, the correct answer, has become the main criterion related to how and why cabinet appointments are made. Choice A is incorrect because of the use of the word *exclusively*. Choices B and E are incorrect because, although the statements have a degree of factual accuracy, they do not reflect the main criterion. Choice D is factually incorrect because most cabinet members come from the upper levels of the socioeconomic life.

27. **(B)** Type of Question: Definitional
Choice B, the correct answer, is the primary result of senatorial courtesy. Even though choices A, C, D, and E are factually correct, they do not relate to the concept of senatorial courtesy.

28. **(D)** Type of Question: Negative
Choice D is the incorrect answer because it is an assumed duty that is not part of the written Constitution. Choices A, B, C, and E are all constitutionally delegated powers or jobs of the president.

29. **(A)** Type of Question: Stimulus-based
The graph shows median income levels for selected racial groups from 1967 to 1999. It is clear by looking at the graph that median income levels increased for all groups, choice A. The graph also clearly shows that income levels were highest for Asians and that there is a negative correlation between income and recessions.

30. **(B)** Type of Question: Sequencing a series of events
Choice B, the correct answer, comes directly from John Locke's writings and was changed in the Declaration of Independence to "life, liberty and the pursuit of happiness." The other choices are all part of our constitutional foundations but do not derive from the Enlightenment thinkers.

31. **(D)** Type of Question: Sequencing a series of events/generalization
Choice D, the correct answer, is a basic principle of the Federalist Papers. Choices A, B, and C reflect Anti-Federalist thinking. Choice E is factually incorrect.

32. **(E)** Type of Question: Definitional
Choice E, the correct answer, is an example of how original jurisdiction, which is defined constitutionally, works. Choices A–D are all examples of appellate jurisdiction.

33. **(E)** Type of Question: Definitional/sequencing a series of events
Choice E is the correct answer bacause the New Hampshire primary is an open primary that allows crossover participation. The Iowa caucus is a closed vote. Only registered party members can vote in the Iowa caucus.

34. **(B)** Type of Question: Cause and effect relationships
Choice B, the correct answer, comes straight from the Supreme Court ruling *Thorton v Arkansas* decided in 1995. Choice A, although true, was not a primary reason for the decision. Choice C is incorrect because the decision made it clear that the only way to accomplish term limits would be through a constitutional amendment. Choice D is factually incorrect, and choice E is a legal action states can act upon.

35. **(C)** Type of Question: Hypothesis
Choice C, the correct answer, is a good example of realignment. Choice A is incorrect because that event is an example of dealignment. Choices B, D, and E are factually correct but have nothing to do with realignment.

36. **(A)** Type of Question: Generalization/definitional
Choice A, the correct answer, is a political axiom. Choices B, C, D, and E are factually incorrect. Control of party machinery is greatest at the local level. Major fundraising for local candidates is done by the local candidates and on the grassroots level. Party bosses play much less of a role in party organizations than in the days of Boss Tweed, and even those local parties dominated by a party boss are not run in a democratic manner. And the party's chair is selected by the National Committee.

37 and 38. **(D), (C)** Type of Question: Stimulus-based
The quote comes from the Supreme Court case *Nixon v United States*, also known as the Watergate tapes case. In question 37, you first had to identify the passage as a Watergate-related quote. Then you had to sequence the event and know that the result of the ruling was that Nixon had to turn over the Watergate tapes (choice D). In question 38 you had to know the definition of executive privilege and apply the case to the principle of separation of powers (choice C).

39. **(D)** Type of Question: Generalization
Choice D, the correct answer, is derived from the fact that throughout political history many third-party platforms are eventually incorporated into the platforms of the major parties. Examples are the populist reforms

and the issue of deficit spending raised by Ross Perot in 1992. The other choices are not factually correct.

40. **(D)** Type of Question: Sequencing a series of events
Choice D, the correct answer, is true because the actions of lobbyists are measured by whether the lobbyist can convince the legislator to vote for a particular bill. Besides using other means, when a lobbyist is armed with facts and figures, legislators are more likely to respond to the position taken by the lobbyist. Choices A, B, C, and E are all possible but do not relate directly to the issue the question is raising.

41. **(A)** Type of Question: Cause and effect relationships
Choice A, the correct answer, reflects the importance of incumbency under specific circumstances. During national presidential elections, most incumbents have an advantage going into the election. Choice B is factually correct. Choice D, although true, does not get to the heart of the issue of incumbency—the ability to win reelection. Choice E is a false statement.

42. **(C)** Type of Question: Definitional
Choice C, the correct answer, requires a working knowledge of the characteristics of both marble cake federalism and Reagan's new federalism. Choices A, B, and E are factually incorrect. Choice D, although factually correct, does not reflect a practice of Reagan's policies.

43. **(C)** Type of Question: Sequencing a series of events
Choice C, the correct answer, is the prescribed constitutional way the size of the Court can be changed. Historically, when Franklin Roosevelt was unhappy with the decisions made by the Court, he attempted to "pack the court" and Congress rejected the proposal. Even though a constitutional amendment could be an alternative, it is not the answer because it has never been proposed.

44. **(E)** Type of Question: Generalization
Choice E, the correct answer, is a component of the War Powers Act. Choices A, B, C, and D are factually incorrect.

45. **(C)** Type of Question: Identification and analysis
Choice C, the correct answer, derives from the Supreme Court ruling *Baker v Carr* and mandates state legislatures to take into account the make-up and size of congressional districts when redistricting based on population changes. Although political gerrymandering (choice A) or majority-minority districts may be the result, they are not the guiding principles in creating legislative apportionment. Choices D and E are factually incorrect.

46. **(E)** Type of Question: Negative
Choice E, the correct answer, though impacting on an election issue, does not affect voting because illegal aliens cannot vote. Choice D is a different issue since ethnic make-up refers to heritage.

47. **(D)** Type of Question: Cause and effect relationships
Choice D, the correct answer, reflects the fact that most congressional caucuses have as their purpose a constituent base. Choices A, C, and E are factually incorrect. Choice B is incorrect because there is little relationship between power and the existence of a caucus group.

48. **(D)** Type of Question: Generalization
Choice D, the correct answer, is based on numerous poll results. Choices A, B, and E are incorrect factually. Choice C is factually accurate but has nothing to do with the issue of separation of church and state.

49. **(A)** Type of Question: Identification and analysis
Choice A, the correct answer, requires you to know that the commerce clause has been used to pass legislation such as the Civil Rights Act of 1964. Even though choices B, C, and D can take place, they have nothing to do with the commerce clause. Choice E is incorrect because congressional authority relates to the size of the Court.

50. **(D)** Type of Question: Hypothetical
Choice D, the correct answer, is true especially if you consider what happened in the first year the Republicans gained control of Congress in 1994. Although the House passed almost every component of the Republican Contract with America, the Senate took much longer to pass the bills it received from the House. Choice A is incorrect because traditionally there has been bickering between the parties. Choices B, C, and E are incorrect factually.

51. **(C)** Type of Question: Negative
Choice C, the correct answer, has nothing to do with the aim of giving back power to the states. The other choices all have components that reflect the states gaining authority and the federal government giving up its control over the states.

52. **(C)** Type of Question: Solution to a problem
Choice C, the correct answer, is the practical reason why a candidate receives the nomination. Winning a majority of the primaries is crucial to receiving the party's nomination. Although choices A, B, D, and E are all factors, if the candidate does not win primaries, those issues all become irrelevant.

53. **(A)** Type of Question: Negative
Choice A, the correct answer, does not take into account that even in congressional elections candidates use smear tactics. The other choices are all valid reasons why there is lower voter turnout in off-year elections.

54. **(C)** Type of Question: Identification and analysis
Choice C, the correct answer, is a major function of the speaker. Even though the speaker has other roles described (choices A, B, D, and E), the primary role is to establish a legislative agenda. A good example of this responsibility was when Newt Gingrich pushed through the House the Republican Contract in 1994.

55. **(C)** Type of Question: Negative
Choice C, the correct answer, is not true because of President Clinton's efforts to downsize the federal government through his REGO (reinventing government) programs. The other choices are all correct.

56. **(D)** Type of Question: Generalization
Choice D, the correct answer, is a relatively new characteristic of the importance of the media in covering the political scene. Choices A, C, and E are factually inaccurate. Choice B is an exaggeration.

57. **(C)** Type of Question: Identification and analysis
Choice C, the correct answer, illustrates how voting patterns, the youth

vote and how people enroll are influencing voting trends. Statement III is inaccurate, and in fact the opposite is true.

58. **(E)** Type of Question: Cause and effect relationships
Choice E, the correct answer, is an obvious reason and may cause some confusion because it answers the question so simplistically. Choices A, B, C, and D are factually incorrect.

59. **(C)** Type of Question: Identification/definitional
Choice C, the correct answer, is a major function of the Federal Reserve Board and was used frequently in the 1990s in an attempt to head off a period of inflation. Choices A, B, D, and E are factually incorrect.

60. **(B)** Type of Question: Negative
Choice B, the correct answer, does not accurately describe the high-tech campaign. Even though a political debate may be a characteristic of high-tech campaigning, the inclusion of minor party candidates is secondary in importance and does not relate to the point of the question.

SECTION 2: FREE-RESPONSE ESSAYS

Sample Student Response to 1

In present-day politics, special interest groups are often criticized for being divisive as well as for hindering the legislative process. Interest groups are linkage institutions that, along with political parties and the media, serve as a means through which issues and the public's policy preferences get on the government's policymaking agenda. They are the policy specialists and interact with the political parties, which are recognized as the policy generalists. They provide a wealth of information that elected officials need to make accurate and important decisions. However, it is greatly disputed whether interest groups actually aid the policymaking process.

By looking at the Federalist Papers, you can see why special interest groups have been criticized. As early as 1787, James Madison warned about the "mischief of factions," his term for such groups. The United States Congress has periodically investigated alleged corruption and scandals in interest group activities throughout the nineteenth and twentieth centuries.

An example refuting the public's negative view of special interest groups is the fact that they have also been seen as an integral and beneficial part of the American political process, legitimized in the United States Constitution by the First Amendment, which guarantees freedom of speech and the right to "petition the Government for a redress of grievances." Lobbyists and interest groups have important and specific jobs to do. They are responsible for providing Congress with crucial information, often with assurances of financial aid in the next campaign. Although special interest groups are known to hold up legislation in Congress, they also speed up the process by saving congressmen the time needed to research particular issues. Additionally, political observers generally acknowledge that instances of outright corruption and bribery involving special groups are rare.

It can also be argued that special interest groups serve a purpose by helping to develop substantive public policy issues. By examining specific examples, it can be seen how special interest groups can hinder the legislative process while helping to introduce new legislation, useful to many Americans, at the same time.

A good example of how special interest groups have been divisive and slowed down the legislative process is the Brady Bill. The Brady Bill was proposed shortly after James Brady was shot in 1981, during the attempted assassination of President Reagan. The bill required a waiting period before a handgun could be purchased, during which time a criminal background check of the intended buyer would be made. This waiting period would thus help to further regulate the people who could buy handguns. The National Rifle Association (NRA), one of the largest special interest groups in the country, with nearly four million members, opposed the bill. Because of the NRA's interaction with Congress, they were able to delay passage of the bill for more than ten years through a flurry of debates and arguments. It was eventually passed in a watered-down form. This is a clear example of how special interest groups can hinder the legislative process by delaying votes on a particular bill by long drawn-out congressional debates made at their request.

It can also be argued, however, that special interest groups have helped shape our nation's legislative process. Special interest groups have helped to express the views and opinions of large segments of America's population that cannot be represented by one congressional district. Good examples of this are women's rights groups, which have helped women gain treatment more equal to that of men. These groups helped to pass legislation such as the Equal Rights Act of 1966, which gave women in government jobs equal pay for the same positions held by men. Special interest groups representing handicapped Americans helped to get the Americans with Disabilities Act passed in 1991, which gives equal employment opportunities to disabled people and enables them to experience the same American dream as nondisabled Americans. Special interest groups have also been a forum for new ideas in the legislative process, helping to make our representative democracy more representative.

Evaluation of Free-Response Sample Essay 1

1. Does the essay properly define terms?
2. Is a foundation built using appropriate examples that refute and support the introductory statement? Does the essay provide examples illustrating how special interest groups have helped shape public policy?

1. The introductory statement establishes the role of special interest groups by properly defining the term and advancing the hypothesis that they both hinder and help the legislative process. Excellent background information is offered using a quote by James Madison and explaining the constitutional basis of special interest groups.

2. The heart of the essay deals with the specific roles of special interest groups in the legislative process. The writer offers examples of how the NRA opposed the Brady Bill and how other special interest groups fought for legislation in support of their positions. The writer also uses the fight by women's rights groups for passage of the Equal Rights Act of 1966 and by disabled Americans for passage of the Americans with Disabilities Act, to support the thesis statement.

Sample Student Response to 2

The issues of party realignment and party dealignment have become more and more prevalent in America's political arena since the election of Ronald Reagan in 1980. Party realignment is defined as the displacement of the majority party by the minority party during a critical election period. Party dealignment is defined as the gradual disengagement of people and politicians from the major political parties. One cause of party dealignment is decreased party identification. Party realignment and party dealignment have grown more prevalent in the years since Reagan was elected.

In 1980, Ronald Reagan defeated Jimmy Carter, the Republicans took control of the Senate, and "Reagan Democrats" were born. These Democrats, who had become disillusioned with the economic policies of Carter and were upset over the hostage situation in Iran, represented a traditional base of the Democratic Party. Many of them were "blue collar" workers who had suffered the most under the economic policies of Jimmy Carter. Another indicator of the realignment taking place was that even in the South, Jimmy Carter's base, a majority of the electorate voted for Reagan.

In the 1994 mid-term elections, the Republicans took control of the Senate for the first time since 1986. They also took control of the House of Representatives for the first time in 40 years. Using the "Contract With America" as a campaign slogan and successfully drawing national attention to the election, voters defeated more incumbents that year than in any other previous election. This event once more reflected the party realignment of the 1992 "Solid South," as it again switched allegiance and voted Republican. Traditional Democratic voters had left their party and elected Republican majorities in both houses of Congress.

However, the American public has also become disenchanted with the two major political parties. They feel that the parties are too similar on the issues and that the political bickering between the two major parties results in governmental gridlock. No doubt this distaste and distrust in government can be traced back to the era of Richard Nixon and the Watergate scandal. Because of that event, voters have developed a greater distrust of government as a whole and of the party system in particular. This distrust was illustrated in a 1998 state election for governor. With President Clinton's impeachment vote pending, voters in Minnesota rejected both the Democratic and Republican candidate for governor and elected wrestling superstar Jesse Ventura. Exit polls reflected the fact that voters saw no major differences in the platforms of either of the major parties' candidates. Minnesota voters believed that Ventura offered an alternative to the traditional two-party system. His election illustrates how dealignment resulted in a major shake-up of the political scene in Minnesota.

Evaluation of Free-Response Sample Essay 2

1. Does the essay properly define the terms *political realignment* and *political dealignment*?
2. Is a foundation built giving appropriate examples from two of the elections offered?

1. The writer immediately gets to the purpose of the essay in the opening sentence by making a strong statement that both party realignment and party dealignment have played a significant role in the American political scene

since 1980. The terms are properly defined, and the writer clearly proves the thesis by tracing the history of presidential politics.

2. The foundation of the essay compares and contrasts the results of presidential and state elections with the concepts of realignment and dealignment. The writer selects two elections and connects them with key events that have resulted in party realignment and dealignment. The writer also recognizes that Watergate was a benchmark event in the history of party dealignment.

Sample Student Response to 3

Three demographic characteristics that have played significant roles in recent presidential elections include: gender, race, and religion. These three demographic features contribute to the election of a president in different ways.

Gender is perhaps the most intriguing demographic feature since it has made a difference in the outcomes of the last three elections. The concept of a gender gap, the differences in the way men and women form opinions about and eventually select a candidate, helped to create victories for Bill Clinton in the 1992 and 1996 elections. According to the chart, 45 percent of women voted for Clinton in 1992 while only 37 percent voted for George Bush. Although Clinton received more votes from men than Bush, the margin of victory for the male vote was much closer. In 1996, the gender gap was much wider, with Clinton getting 54 percent of the female vote compared to only 38 percent for Bob Dole. In 2000, the gender gap was even more extreme, with George W. Bush receiving a majority of the male votes while Al Gore got a majority of women votes.

A second demographic feature is race. In the last three presidential elections, there have been major differences in the way whites, blacks, Hispanics, and Asians have voted. Among these groups, blacks traditionally have voted Democratic in very large numbers. In 2000 a remarkable 90 percent of African-Americans voted for Al Gore. Bill Clinton also received a large majority of black votes. In 1992, a majority of white voters voted for Bill Clinton, but in the elections of 1996 and 2000 they switched to the Republican candidate. Hispanic voters consistently voted for the Democratic candidate even though George W. Bush had hoped to attract that block of voters. Asian voters voted for the Republican candidate in 1992 and 1996, but voted for Gore in 2000.

A third demographic influence on presidential elections is religion. The influence of the so-called religious right (mainly evangelical Protestants) is as important to the Republicans as the influence of minority groups, such as Jews, is to the Democrats. In all three recent elections, white Protestants voted for the Republican candidate by more than 50 percent. The Catholic vote went to Clinton in 1992 and 1996, but George W. Bush closed the gap in 2000. The Catholic vote now seems to be up for grabs. The Jewish vote has been a traditional Democratic base. This was reflected in the last three elections as the Democratic candidate received more than 70 percent of the Jewish vote.

The importance of demographics on presidential politics cannot be underestimated. By examining the chart, it is clear that demographic trends are consistent, and, where they vary, it can be speculated that political realignment may be underway. Parties and candidates target groups that have traditionally supported them. That's why the Democrats have gone after the African-American and Jewish vote while the Republicans seek the votes of white Protestants and people at the upper income levels. Once the traditional base of voters is locked up, the candidates must go after the so-called swing voter, the voter who can be convinced to change his vote. Swing voters include people in the middle class and those who live in the suburbs. It is these voters who will ultimately determine the winner of an election. Thus, demographics play an extremely important role in presidential politics.

Evaluation of Data-Based Free-Response Sample Essay 3

1. Did the writer identify three demographic characteristics from the chart?
2. Did the writer explain how these features contributed to the election of a president in recent elections?
3. Did the writer discuss the importance of demographics on presidential politics?

1. The essay clearly identifies three demographic features: gender, race, and religion. Other demographic features the writer could have selected include age and income.

2. The essay provides an excellent explanation of the impact that these three features have had on the elections of 1992, 1996, and 2000. Notice how the writer referred to the statistics provided in the chart to help support his answer. The writer also discusses such terms as *gender gap* and *swing voter* to further develop his answer.

3. The analysis of the importance that demographics play on presidential politics was aided by further examples from the chart. The writer also discusses the fact that parties target certain demographic groups. This explanation illustrates the writer's clear understanding of the question.

Sample Student Response to 4

Though the Senate confirmation process is as old as the Constitution itself, the controversy surrounding presidential appointments did not really reach a peak until the hearings were first televised in the late 1960s.

The founding fathers clearly established the notion of checks and balances as a firm prerequisite before agreeing to adopt the new Constitution. Very simply, in the area of presidential appointments, the Constitution ensures that the president does not have the ability to make unchecked political appointments. The Constitution specifically gives the president the power to appoint ambassadors, cabinet level officials, and federal judges. After a hearing is held in the appropriate Senate committee, the Senate must approve the presidential appointment by a majority vote.

In the modern-day politics of the confirmation process, a president, typically, must make hundreds of lower-level appointments, mostly in the form of federal judges. Higher-level appointments include cabinet members, executive level positions, ambassadors, and Supreme Court justices. Senate confirmation of appointments in these categories generated what many political scientists have described as a perversion of the system. The controversy reached a peak during the presidency of George Bush, when Clarence Thomas was nominated as a member of the Supreme Court. The

Democratic-dominated Senate Judiciary Committee heard Anita Hill testify that Thomas sexually harassed her when she worked for him. More controversy resulted with another appointment at the cabinet level when the Democrats scrutinized the personal life of John Tower, who had been nominated for the post of Secretary of Defense. The Senate committee overseeing the confirmation went as far as asking for confidential FBI files.

One of the most illustrative cases of Republican opposition to a Clinton appointment was the attempted nomination of Dr. Henry Foster as the new Surgeon General. Opposition increased when information surfaced that Foster had performed legal abortions. In fact, the Foster nomination was indicative of the highly charged atmosphere that is sometimes created by the system of checks and balances involved in the Senate confirmation process. Background checks by Senate staffers uncovered personal information and policy beliefs that created highly controversial hearings. Ultimately, the Senate never voted on the Foster nomination as a result of a Republican-led filibuster that the Democrats failed to break. However, it was clear that the full Senate would have confirmed Foster had the committee overseeing his appointment approved of his nomination and let it go for a vote.

Although, historically, most presidential appointments go unnoticed by the public and easily pass Senate scrutiny, throughout the 1980s and 1990s the Senate has used its constitutionally delegated power to approve presidential appointments as a means of airing debate regarding public policy issues. The irony is that many believe that the founding fathers never intended the confirmation process as a means of impeding a president's ability to appoint the people he thinks are best qualified. Whether it is the nomination of a Surgeon General, Defense Secretary, or Supreme Court justice, the Constitution sets up the potential for dramatic public hearings. Only when the public perceives that the Senate is abusing its power does the process hurt the democratic process.

Evaluation of Data-Based Free-Response Sample Essay 4

1. Does the writer describe how the confirmation process works?
2. Does the writer provide two examples of presidential appointments and an analysis of the Senate's response to those appointments?
3. Does the writer provide an analysis of the criticism that the Senate has received as a result of their role in the confirmation process?

1. The writer gives a constitutional explanation of the confirmation process and illustrates this process further by explaining the types of presidential appointments that come before the Senate.

2. After discussing the confirmation process, the essay then proceeds to examine how the confirmation process has evolved, especially since the proceedings became televised. The politicization of confirmation hearings is the heart of the writer's response. The writer provides, in great detail, examples of how a Democratic Senate created problems for George Bush and how a Senate controlled by Republicans gave President Clinton problems. The strength of this

essay lies in its flow—a clear description, a short historical perspective, and an analysis of some recent confirmation flaps.

3. The last paragraph reflects on the way the public perceives the Senate after heated confirmation hearings and discusses the criticism leveled at the Senate for their actions during recent confirmation hearings.

Model Examination II

SECTION 1: MULTIPLE-CHOICE QUESTIONS

TIME: 45 MINUTES
60 QUESTIONS
Section 1 is worth 50 percent of the test

Directions: Each of the following questions has five choices. Choose the best response and record your answer on the answer sheet in the back of the test.

1. Which of the following statements is true?
   (A) People have a high degree of trust in their politicians and elected officials.
   (B) Divided government has been endorsed by the electorate in numerous presidential elections.
   (C) Democrats have regained status as the majority party in the South.
   (D) Realignment has created a viable third party.
   (E) People identify themselves more as liberals than conservatives.

2. Which of the following principles of government was articulated in the Federalist Papers?
   (A) checks and balances
   (B) a weak judicial branch
   (C) a weak executive branch
   (D) a strong House and a weak Senate
   (E) a unitary form of government

3. An example of political socialization includes which of the following statements?
   (A) parents who vote Democratic influencing their children to vote Democratic
   (B) children being taught about politics in school
   (C) college graduates deciding to attend law school in order to run for office
   (D) political parties influencing voters through political ads
   (E) a newspaper running an editorial that suggests that a politician should resign

4. Executive privilege has
   (A) protected the president from standing trial while in office.
   (B) protected the first lady from handing over personal materials to special prosecutors.
   (C) resulted in Supreme Court decisions ordering the president to give sensitive materials to investigators.
   (D) created the need for new laws defining what executive privilege means.
   (E) rallied public opinion to support the president using this power.

5. Which of the following reforms has been recommended to change the electoral college?
   (A) Close polls throughout the country the same time on election day.
   (B) Ban exit polling by the networks.
   (C) Eliminate the winner-take-all provision of the system.
   (D) Move up the date that electors vote.
   (E) Expand the concept of choosing electors to congressional races.

6. Supreme Court cases mainly derive from
   (A) plea bargains that fail.
   (B) congressional legislation that is vetoed.
   (C) state legislation that goes unchallenged.
   (D) original jurisdiction cases.
   (E) appellate jurisdiction cases.

Answer Question 7 based on this table:

CONGRESSIONAL BILLS VETOED: 1961–1999

Period	President	Total vetoes	Regular vetoes	Pocket vetoes	Vetoes sustained	Bills passed over veto
1961–1963	Kennedy	21	12	9	21	0
1963–1969	Johnson	30	16	14	30	0
1969–1974	Nixon	43	26	17	36	7
1974–1977	Ford	66	48	18	54	12
1977–1981	Carter	31	13	18	29	2
1981–1989	Reagan	78	39	39	69	9
1989–1993	Bush	44	29	15	43	1
1993–1999	Clinton	30	30	0	28	2

Source: U.S. Congress, Senate Library. *Presidential Vetoes...1789–1999;* U.S. Congress. *Calendars of the U.S. House of Representatives and History of Legislation,* annual.

7. Which of the following conclusions about presidential vetoes is supported by the table?
   (A) More vetoes have been overridden than sustained by Congress.
   (B) Pocket vetoes are routinely rejected by Congress.
   (C) President Reagan had the greatest success in having his vetoes sustained by Congress.
   (D) President Ford had more bills passed over his veto than any other president listed.
   (E) Pocket vetoes were used by every president on the list.

8. The provisions of the Fifth Amendment have all of the following components EXCEPT
   (A) prohibition of double jeopardy.
   (B) the right to a speedy trial.
   (C) the protection against self-incrimination.
   (D) the right of eminent domain.
   (E) protection of life, liberty, and property.

9. The significance of the Great Compromise was that it
   (A) guaranteed equal protection for all citizens.
   (B) created a judicial branch of government.
   (C) counted slaves for representation purposes.
   (D) set up a bicameral legislature.
   (E) prohibited import taxes.

10. Which of the following ideas advocated by Republicans during the 1994 congressional elections best describes the concept of devolution? They
(A) encouraged a return of power to the state governments.
(B) promoted a strong executive branch.
(C) called for an evolutionary approach to checks and balances.
(D) advocated a better relationship between the voter and elected representatives.
(E) insisted on passage of a balanced budget amendment.

11. Which of the following House committees has the most influence in determining the fate of legislation?
(A) Agricultural Committee
(B) Ways and Means Committee
(C) Post Office Committee
(D) Education Committee
(E) Foreign Affairs Committee

12. Which of the following are considered to be leadership positions in the Senate?
I. Judiciary Committee Chairman
II. Majority Whip
III. Minority Leader
IV. Majority Leader
(A) II only
(B) I and II only
(C) I, III, and IV only
(D) I, II, III, and IV only
(E) II, III, and IV only

13. Elite class theory differs from pluralism in that groups from the elite believe that
(A) consensus is essential to political compromise.
(B) representation of many interest groups foster good government.
(C) they are best suited to run government based on their economic status.
(D) sharing wealth and power are foundations of representative government.
(E) gaining access to elected representatives can best be achieved through special interests.

14. Libel and slander most closely come into conflict with the constitutional guarantee of
(A) due process.
(B) free speech.
(C) equal protection under the law.
(D) a fair trial.
(E) the right to an attorney.

15. In the *Gibbons v Ogden* case, the Supreme Court decided for the first time that
    (A) judicial review was a power of the court.
    (B) state contracts took precedence over federal law.
    (C) Congress had the exclusive right to regulate interstate commerce.
    (D) intrastate commerce was a legitimate federal function.
    (E) states could not tax the federal government.

16. A constituent approach to representation reflects a
    (A) congressman who consistently votes his conscience.
    (B) legislator who usually follows the party line.
    (C) lawmaker who introduces a bill which increases defense spending.
    (D) desire on the part of an elected official to represent the view of those who voted for him.
    (E) consistent approach by the representative who challenges the president's programs.

17. What is a major difference between the manner in which both houses of Congress operate?
    (A) The House allows unlimited debate on bills, whereas the Senate has strict time limitations.
    (B) The Senate permits more amendments to bills than does the House.
    (C) The rules of both houses are the same.
    (D) Committee chairman terms are limited in the Senate, but not in the House.
    (E) The Senate Committees always have equal numbers of Democrats and Republicans serving on them.

18. The media play what kind of role related to public policy? It
    (A) raises money to support candidates running for office.
    (B) has the major function of linking the electorate to the formal institutions of government.
    (C) investigates the personal ethics of elected officials.
    (D) competes for the attention of the electorate.
    (E) influences politicians by offering them lower advertising rates.

19. What advantage did the line item veto have over a regular veto? The line item veto allowed the president to
    (A) strike any provision of the 13 major appropriation bills.
    (B) eliminate riders attached to spending bills.
    (C) line out appropriation bills started in the Senate.
    (D) veto legislation designated as essential.
    (E) ignore a continuing resolution.

20. Which step in the development of public policy occurs first?
    (A) enactment of the policy
    (B) formation of policy alternatives
    (C) evaluation of the policy
    (D) recognition of the problem
    (E) revision of the policy

21. Which of the following is a part of the 1974 Federal Election Commission's regulations?
    (A) a ban on all soft money
    (B) public financing of congressional campaigns
    (C) equal time provisions for candidates appearing on television networks during a presidential campaign
    (D) matching funds made available to presidential candidates who raise money within the limits set by the commission
    (E) a ban of all PAC money

22. The aim of the exclusionary rule as defined in the *Mapp v Ohio* Supreme Court case is to
    (A) encourage police to knock before entering a suspected crime scene.
    (B) prevent law enforcement officials from stopping and frisking suspects.
    (C) deny the media access to places where police are conducting an investigation.
    (D) force police to get search warrants for evidence in plain view.
    (E) not allow illegally obtained evidence to be admitted into a court proceeding.

23. The main criticism levied against the Articles of Confederation was that it
    (A) gave too much power to the central government.
    (B) failed to give the national government the authority to lay and collect taxes.
    (C) did not allow the federal government to govern new territories.
    (D) created a powerful judicial branch.
    (E) had a term limit provision for the president.

24. As a result of the Motor Voter Law, there was
    (A) a decrease in registration because states challenged the law's constitutionality.
    (B) an increase in registration, but a decrease in turnout.
    (C) a decrease in registration and a decrease in turnout.
    (D) an increase in registration and an increase in turnout.
    (E) the greatest increase in registration of senior citizens.

25. Which of the following presidential appointments needs to be confirmed by the Senate?
    I. Secretary of the Treasury
    II. White House cook
    III. Ambassador to Mexico
    IV. Supreme Court Justice

    (A) IV only
    (B) I and II only
    (C) I and III only
    (D) I, III, and IV only
    (E) III and IV only

26. The Supreme Court has the constitutional authority to check Congress by
    (A) vetoing legislation signed by the president.
    (B) settling disputes among states.
    (C) applying original jurisdiction to cases brought before them on appeal.
    (D) declaring parts of legislation unconstitutional.
    (E) assigning the Chief Justice to preside over the impeachment trial of the president.

27. An alternate manner in which a president can implement policy without congressional approval is by
    (A) appointing a member of the opposing political party to the cabinet.
    (B) issuing an executive order.
    (C) sending controversial legislation to the electorate for a referendum.
    (D) making a speech in front of a group that opposes him.
    (E) holding a press conference.

COMPOSITION OF CONGRESS, BY POLITICAL PARTY: 1971–2001

Year	Party and President	Congress	House			Senate		
			Majority party	Minority party	Other	Majority party	Minority party	Other
1971[1]	R (Nixon)	92nd	D-254	R-180	0	D-54	R-44	2
1973[1]	R (Nixon)	93rd	D-239	R-192	0	D-56	R-42	2
1975[3]	R (Ford)	94th	D-291	R-144	0	D-60	R-37	2
1977[4]	D (Carter)	95th	D-292	R-143	0	D-61	R-38	1
1979[4]	D (Carter)	96th	D-276	R-157	0	D-58	R-41	1
1981[4]	R (Reagan)	97th	D-243	R-192	0	R-53	D-46	1
1983	R (Reagan)	98th	D-269	R-165	0	R-54	D-46	0
1985	R (Reagan)	99th	D-252	R-182	0	R-53	D-47	0
1987	R (Reagan)	100th	D-258	R-177	0	D-55	R-45	0
1989	R (Bush)	101st	D-259	R-174	0	D-55	R-45	0
1991[5]	R (Bush)	102nd	D-267	R-167	1	D-56	R-44	0
1993[5]	D (Clinton)	103rd	D-258	R-176	1	D-57	R-43	0
1995[5]	D (Clinton)	104th	R-230	D-204	1	R-52	D-48	0
1996[5,6]	D (Clinton)	104th	R-236	D-197	1	R-53	D-46	0
1997[5,6]	D (Clinton)	105th	R-227	D-207	1	R-55	D-45	0
1998[5,6]	D (Clinton)	105th	R-227	D-207	1	R-55	D-45	0
1999[5,6]	D (Clinton)	106th	R-223	D-211	1	R-55	D-45	0
2000[5,6]	D (Clinton)	106th	R-223	D-211	1	R-55	D-45	0
2001[6,7,8]	R (Bush)	107th	R-221	D-212	2	R-51	D-49	1

[1]Senate had one Independent and one Conservative-Republican. [2]House had one Independent-Democrat.
[3]Senate had one Independent, one Conservative-Republican, and one undecided (New Hampshire).
[4]Senate had one Independent. [5]House had one Independent-Socialist. [6]As of beginning of second session.
[7]Senate had one Independent. [8]House had two Independents.
D = Democratic; R = Republican. Data for begining of first session of each Congress (as of January 3),

Source: U.S. Congress, Joint Committee on Printing. *Congressional Directory*. annual: beginning 1977, biennial.

28. The table shown above illustrates what trend regarding the relationship between the party that controlled the presidency and the party that controlled Congress?
(A) The Republicans controlled both houses of Congress in more terms than they controlled the presidency.
(B) The Democrats and Republicans alternated control of Congress in the 1980s.
(C) The party that controlled Congress usually controls the presidency.
(D) Independents are playing a greater role in the House.
(E) Divided government was a dominant feature.

29. The trend of affirmative action programs in the 1990s was to
(A) require a quota system for college admissions.
(B) eliminate requirements for federally funded affirmative action programs.
(C) take race as a factor only in the private sector.
(D) have Congress increase the number of programs.
(E) face challenges on the legality of existing laws.

30. The "fighting words" doctrine outlined in Supreme Court decisions deals with
(A) freedom of the press.
(B) separation of church and state.
(C) freedom of speech.
(D) freedom of assembly.
(E) freedom to petition.

31. A major characteristic of independent regulatory agencies is that they are
(A) quasi-legislative and quasi-judicial in function.
(B) highly influenced by special interest groups.
(C) sensitive to the needs of the electorate.
(D) decreasing in size, scope, and influence.
(E) minimally influential in determining public policy.

32. Which of the following events occurred in the 2000 presidential election?
(A) The Democrats regained control of the House but not the Senate.
(B) The Presidential Commission on Debates ruled that third-party candidates could participate in the three debates.
(C) Women determined the outcome of the election.
(D) There was a higher percentage of voter turnout than in 1992.
(E) The Supreme Court determined the outcome of the election.

33. A trend toward dealignment occurred in the 1990s because
(A) voters had strong party identification.
(B) the Motor Voter Law has increased registration for the Democrats and Republicans.
(C) there was a general mistrust of elected officials.
(D) the Republicans gained control of Congress in 1994.
(E) the Freedom of Information act revealed campaign irregularities by the major parties.

34. A presidential power that has been challenged by Congress since 1960 is the power to
    (A) commit troops to foreign countries.
    (B) give the State of the Union address.
    (C) appoint cabinet members.
    (D) sign treaties.
    (E) receive ambassadors.

35. In 1994, a major difference between a freshman member and a five-term member of the House of Representatives was that the
    (A) freshman was allowed to get top committee assignments.
    (B) five-term representative could not run for reelection because of term limits.
    (C) freshman representative could not offer amendments to proposed bills.
    (D) five-term representative had fewer opportunities to receive PAC money.
    (E) freshman representative had strong convictions and was less likely to compromise.

36. The concept of one man, one vote as outlined in the *Baker v Carr* Supreme Court decision applies to elections for
    (A) United States senator.
    (B) president.
    (C) federal judges.
    (D) state legislatures.
    (E) governors.

37. The original intent of the Fourteenth Amendment to the United States Constitution as interpreted by the Supreme Court was to
    (A) force the states to follow the Bill of Rights.
    (B) provide equal protection under the law for freed slaves.
    (C) expand voting for women.
    (D) give states the right to pass laws that guaranteed separate but equal status to their citizens.
    (E) enable Congress to pass affirmative action legislation.

38. Historically, the approval rating of the president usually
    (A) remains around 50 percent during his entire term.
    (B) fluctuates depending on his response to national and international problems.
    (C) is lowest during times of war.
    (D) is highest toward the end of his presidency.
    (E) depends on the kind of media coverage he gets.

39. All of the following steps are characteristic of the lawmaking process EXCEPT
    (A) revenue bills must start in the Senate.
    (B) conference committees resolve differences between bills.
    (C) filibusters in the Senate are used to stop bills from coming to a vote.
    (D) each House has standing committees that mark up legislation.
    (E) a roll call vote indicates the positions taken by congressmen.

40. The use of racial quotas was made illegal in the United States as a direct result of the
    (A) Supreme Court decision in *University of California v Bakke.*
    (B) Supreme Court decision in *Brown v Board of Education of Topeka.*
    (C) Proposition 209—The California Civil Rights Initiative.
    (D) Civil Rights Act of 1964.
    (E) affirmative action programs created by individual states.

41. A primary election in which voters from one political party can cross over to express their choice for a candidate from another party is called
    (A) a closed primary.
    (B) an open caucus.
    (C) a nonbinding primary.
    (D) an open primary.
    (E) a dual primary.

42. Which of the following resulted from the 2000 election?
    (A) The Democrats made electoral inroads in the South.
    (B) The Republicans maintained their majority in the House.
    (C) The angry white male vote was not a factor.
    (D) Third-party candidates disappeared from the political scene.
    (E) The Democrats assumed control of a majority of state governorships.

43. Congressional oversight committees have the main purpose of
    (A) reviewing governmental operations.
    (B) drafting appropriation bills.
    (C) holding impeachment hearings.
    (D) establishing time limits for debates.
    (E) writing constitutional amendments.

44. A criticism of the United States census is that it
    (A) favors large cities over suburban areas.
    (B) costs the taxpayer too much money.
    (C) is held too frequently.
    (D) is biased toward the party who controls Congress.
    (E) does not take into account the homeless.

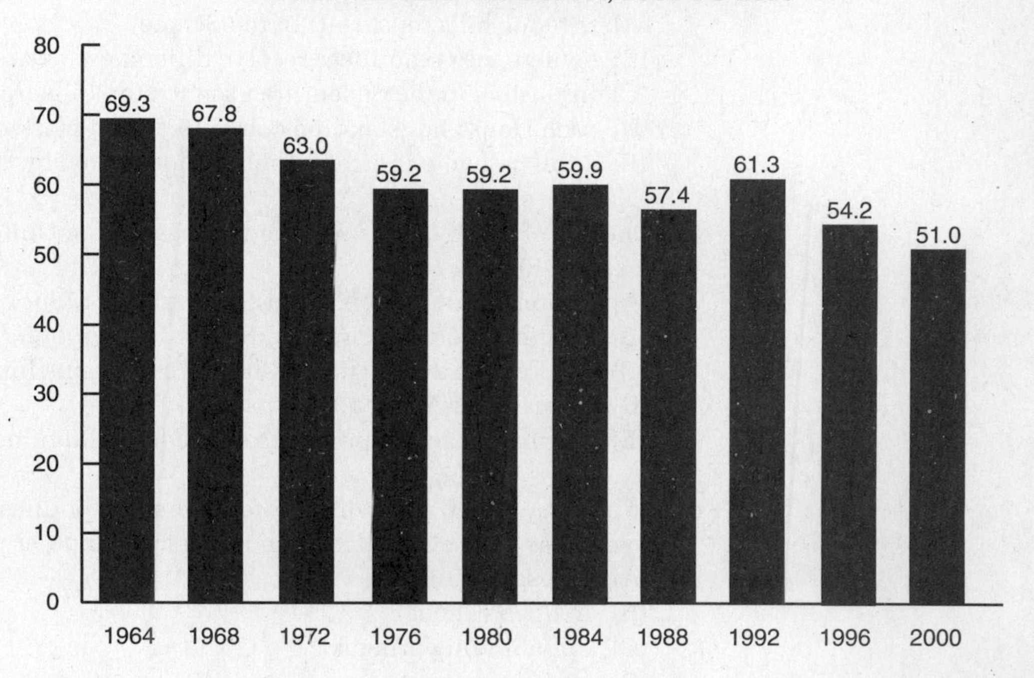

45. According to the graph, which statement is true about voter turnout in presidential elections? Turnout is
   (A) greatest when the country is at peace.
   (B) lowest in elections where there is a landslide.
   (C) determined by the number of candidates running for president.
   (D) lower after presidential scandals.
   (E) increased when a president wins a second term.

46. The president and Congress have all of the following powers in dealing with proposed legislation EXCEPT
   (A) the president may exercise a line item veto on appropriation bills.
   (B) the House and Senate may not send different versions of the same bill to the president for consideration.
   (C) the president has the authority to hold on to legislation after Congress adjourns without signing it.
   (D) the president may issue a veto after receiving legislation passed by both houses of Congress.
   (E) Congress may override a presidential veto by a two-thirds vote of each house.

47. Campaign finance reform advocacy groups such as Common Cause favor
   (A) a ban on soft money.
   (B) the elimination of any free television time for candidates.
   (C) an increase in the amount of money that labor unions can give to both parties.
   (D) special interest groups financing congressional campaigns.
   (E) greater use of personal funds by presidential candidates.

48. Supreme Court decisions in the 1990s related to the separation of church and state reflect the Court's approval of
(A) greater government support for the accommodation of religion in public schools.
(B) the use of school vouchers for tax deductions.
(C) the limited right to have silent prayer in public schools.
(D) a complete ban at time of Christmas on religious symbols in schools.
(E) the right to have clergy speak at school graduation.

49. When apportionment becomes a political football, it is called
(A) census taking.
(B) gerrymandering.
(C) equal representation under the law.
(D) single district representation.
(E) multidistrict representation.

50. What kind of political action committee would most likely support Democratic candidates?
(A) tobacco corporations
(B) labor unions
(C) gun advocacy groups
(D) business corporations
(E) the Chamber of Commerce

51. All of the following powers are granted to Congress by the Constitution EXCEPT the power to
(A) collect taxes.
(B) declare war.
(C) appoint judges.
(D) regulate interstate commerce.
(E) create inferior courts.

52. Which of the following provisions of the Republican Contract With America had the goal of reforming the Congress?
(A) the balanced budget amendment to the Constitution
(B) the Welfare Reform Act
(C) term limit amendment to the Constitution
(D) regulatory reform
(E) legal reform

53. Which of the following is a provision of the Congressional Budget and Impoundment Act?
(A) A time line of procedural steps the Congress had to take to pass the budget.
(B) Authority given to the Congressional Budget Office to delete items from the proposed budget.
(C) A balanced budget by the year 2002.
(D) The power given to Congress to stop mandatory spending after the budget is signed into law.
(E) The ability of the president to have a line item veto.

54. Which of the following events occurs first during the impeachment of a president?
    (A) A media frenzy forces the House to vote to impeach the president.
    (B) The House Judiciary Committee votes on articles of impeachment.
    (C) A special prosecutor issues a report to Congress.
    (D) The Senate Judiciary Committee votes on articles of impeachment.
    (E) The Supreme Court rules on the guilt or innocence of the president.

55. Southern states that created "majority-minority" congressional districts did so because they were
    (A) directed to do so by the Supreme Court.
    (B) attempting to abide by the provisions of the Voting Rights Act of 1965.
    (C) hopeful that African-Americans would vote Republican.
    (D) confident that white candidates would be given an advantage over African-Americans.
    (E) responding to an executive order of the president.

56. Liberal activists would probably support which of the following rulings made by the Supreme Court?
    (A) an abortion case that ruled there should be a 24-hour waiting period before a women could get an abortion
    (B) a search and seizure case limiting the *Miranda* restrictions placed on the police
    (C) a death penalty habeas corpus appeal to the federal courts which was turned down
    (D) a free speech case where a provision of a congressional act restricting access to obscene sites on the Internet was declared unconstitutional
    (E) a free press case giving school officials greater latitude in censoring school newspapers

57. A strong federal system of government has which of the following components?
    (A) a central government dominated by the states
    (B) different levels of government unified by a central government
    (C) three branches of government each having separate powers
    (D) a parliament with a prime minister as head of the government
    (E) a loosely bound union of states

58. According to the Twenty-Fifth Amendment to the Constitution, what happens if a president is disabled when serving in office?
    (A) The House and Senate must vote to allow the vice president to assume power.
    (B) The first lady is given temporary power to govern.
    (C) The Supreme Court decides when the vice president can take over the office.
    (D) After the cabinet makes a declaration of the president's incapacity to govern, the vice president becomes president.
    (E) There is a special election held to determine who will be the next president.

59. The Supreme Court has determined that racial gerrymandering is unconstitutional because it
    (A) violates the reserve power clause of the Constitution.
    (B) deprives elected representatives of their property right.
    (C) ignores the one man, one vote principle of a previous Supreme Court ruling.
    (D) violates the equal protection clause of the Fourteenth Amendment.
    (E) extends affirmative action to a point which goes beyond the intent of the Voting Rights Act of 1965.

60. Which of the following is a significant presidential foreign policy action taken during the 1990s?
    (A) the isolation of China from the rest of the world community
    (B) Senate ratification of the Kyoto treaty on global warming
    (C) United States participation in trade agreements like NAFTA
    (D) Senate ratification of a comprehensive chemical weapons treaty
    (E) forcing NATO to provide peacekeeping troops in Bosnia

STOP

This is the end of Section 1.

Do not go on to Section 2 until you are told to do so.

SECTION 2: FREE-RESPONSE ESSAYS

TIME: 100 MINUTES (Suggested time: 25 minutes per essay
Section 2 is worth 50 percent of the test

Directions: Answer ***all four*** of the following questions in 100 minutes. Each essay should take you 25 minutes, so plan your time accordingly. The questions are based on your knowledge of United States government and politics, and questions may contain materials from charts, graphs, and tables, which you will have to analyze and draw conclusions from. Make sure that you give specific and sufficient information and examples in your essays. Please number them clearly on your answer sheet.

1. Public opinion has strongly favored campaign finance reform. Yet there has not been significant reform since 1974, even in light of the serious abuses brought out during the 1996 presidential election.
   (a) Identify the major provisions of the Federal Election Campaign Act of 1974.
   (b) Describe the abuses that occurred during the 1996 presidential campaign.
   (c) List three components of the McCain-Feingold Bill.

2. The United States has a representative form of government. Yet in many states, people vote directly on legislative proposals through a process of initiative and referendum.
   (a) Define how the process of initiative and referendum works.
   (b) Apply this definition to Proposition 209—The California Civil Rights Initiative and describe its legislative history.
   (c) Discuss a constitutional question that the proposition raised in the courts and describe the proposition's impact.

3. The electoral college has come under much criticism following the disputed 2000 presidential election.
   (a) Identify and explain the process used by the electoral college in choosing a president.
   (b) Describe two problems with the electoral process resulting from the 2000 presidential election.
   (c) Discuss one reform that has been suggested to overhaul the electoral college.

MEMBERS OF CONGRESS—SELECTED CHARACTERISTICS: 1981 TO 1999

[As of beginning of first session of each Congress, (January 3). Figures for Representatives exclude vacancies]

Members of congress and year	Male	Female	Black [1]	API [2]	Hispanic [3]	Age [4] (in years): Under 40	40 to 49	50 to 59	60 to 69	70 and over	Seniority [5]: Less than 2 yrs.	2 to 9 yrs.	10 to 19 yrs.	20 to 29 yrs.	30 yrs. or more
REPRESENTATIVES															
97th Cong., 1981	416	19	[6]17	3	6	94	142	132	54	13	77	231	96	23	8
98th Cong., 1983	413	21	[6]21	3	8	86	145	132	57	14	83	224	88	28	11
99th Cong., 1985	412	22	[7]20	3	10	71	154	131	59	19	49	237	104	34	10
100th Cong., 1987	412	23	[7]23	4	11	63	153	137	56	26	51	221	114	37	12
101st Cong., 1989	408	25	[7]24	5	10	41	163	133	74	22	39	207	139	35	13
102d Cong., 1991	407	28	[7]26	3	11	39	152	134	86	24	55	178	147	44	11
103d Cong., 1993 [8]	388	47	[7]38	4	17	47	151	128	89	15	118	141	132	32	12
104th Cong., 1995	388	47	[9]40	4	17	53	155	135	79	13	92	188	110	36	9
106th Cong., 1999	379	56	[9]39	(NA)	(NA)	23	116	173	87	35	41	236	104	46	7
SENATORS															
97th Cong., 1981	98	2	-	3	-	9	35	36	14	6	19	51	17	11	2
98th Cong., 1983	98	2	-	2	-	7	28	39	20	6	5	61	21	10	3
99th Cong., 1985	98	2	-	2	-	4	27	38	25	6	8	56	27	7	2
100th Cong., 1987	98	2	-	2	-	5	30	36	22	7	4	41	36	7	2
101st Cong., 1989	98	2	-	2	-	-	30	40	22	8	23	22	43	10	2
102d Cong., 1991	98	2	-	2	-	-	23	46	21	7	5	31	47	10	4
103d Cong., 1993 [8]	93	7	1	2	-	1	16	48	22	12	15	30	39	11	5
104th Cong., 1995	92	8	1	2	-	1	14	41	27	17	12	38	30	15	5
106th Cong., 1999	91	9	-	(NA)	(NA)	-	14	38	35	13	8	39	33	14	6

- Represents zero. NA Not available. [1] Source: Joint Center for Political and Economic Studies, Washington, DC, *Black Elected Officials: Statistical Summary,* annual (copyright). [2] Asians and Pacific Islanders. Source: Library of Congress. Congressional Research Service, "Asian Pacific Americans in the United States Congress," Report 94-767GOV. [3] Source: National Association of Latino Elected and Appointed Officials, Washington, DC, *National Roster of Hispanic Elected Officials, annual.* [4] Some members do not provide date of birth. [5] Represents consecutive years of service. [6] Does not include District of Columbia or Virgin Islands delegate. [7] Includes District of Columbia Delegate but not Virgin Islands delegate. [8] Includes members elected to fill vacant seats through June 14, 1993. [9] Includes District of Columbia and Virgin Islands delegate.

Source: Except as noted, compiled by U.S. Census Bureau from data published in *Congressional Directory,* biennial.

4. This table shows selected characteristics of the members of Congress from 1981 to 1989. From this information and your knowledge of United States politics:
   (a) identify three characteristics indicated in the table.
   (b) for each characteristic chosen, discuss the changes in the make-up of Congress during the time period indicated.
   (c) analyze the impact that these characteristics have had on Congress.

Answer Sheet for the Model Advanced Placement Examination

Name ____________________

Date ____________________

Grade ____________________

FOR SECTION 1: MULTIPLE-CHOICE

Sample: 1. Bill Clinton was elected to the United States presidency in

(A) 1986
(B) 1988
(C) 1990
(D) 1992
(E) 1994

1. Ⓐ Ⓑ Ⓒ ● Ⓔ

Box D is filled in because the correct answer for the sample question 1 is D.

---

1. Ⓐ Ⓑ Ⓒ Ⓓ Ⓔ	**21.** Ⓐ Ⓑ Ⓒ Ⓓ Ⓔ	**41.** Ⓐ Ⓑ Ⓒ Ⓓ Ⓔ
2. Ⓐ Ⓑ Ⓒ Ⓓ Ⓔ	**22.** Ⓐ Ⓑ Ⓒ Ⓓ Ⓔ	**42.** Ⓐ Ⓑ Ⓒ Ⓓ Ⓔ
3. Ⓐ Ⓑ Ⓒ Ⓓ Ⓔ	**23.** Ⓐ Ⓑ Ⓒ Ⓓ Ⓔ	**43.** Ⓐ Ⓑ Ⓒ Ⓓ Ⓔ
4. Ⓐ Ⓑ Ⓒ Ⓓ Ⓔ	**24.** Ⓐ Ⓑ Ⓒ Ⓓ Ⓔ	**44.** Ⓐ Ⓑ Ⓒ Ⓓ Ⓔ
5. Ⓐ Ⓑ Ⓒ Ⓓ Ⓔ	**25.** Ⓐ Ⓑ Ⓒ Ⓓ Ⓔ	**45.** Ⓐ Ⓑ Ⓒ Ⓓ Ⓔ
6. Ⓐ Ⓑ Ⓒ Ⓓ Ⓔ	**26.** Ⓐ Ⓑ Ⓒ Ⓓ Ⓔ	**46.** Ⓐ Ⓑ Ⓒ Ⓓ Ⓔ
7. Ⓐ Ⓑ Ⓒ Ⓓ Ⓔ	**27.** Ⓐ Ⓑ Ⓒ Ⓓ Ⓔ	**47.** Ⓐ Ⓑ Ⓒ Ⓓ Ⓔ
8. Ⓐ Ⓑ Ⓒ Ⓓ Ⓔ	**28.** Ⓐ Ⓑ Ⓒ Ⓓ Ⓔ	**48.** Ⓐ Ⓑ Ⓒ Ⓓ Ⓔ
9. Ⓐ Ⓑ Ⓒ Ⓓ Ⓔ	**29.** Ⓐ Ⓑ Ⓒ Ⓓ Ⓔ	**49.** Ⓐ Ⓑ Ⓒ Ⓓ Ⓔ
10. Ⓐ Ⓑ Ⓒ Ⓓ Ⓔ	**30.** Ⓐ Ⓑ Ⓒ Ⓓ Ⓔ	**50.** Ⓐ Ⓑ Ⓒ Ⓓ Ⓔ
11. Ⓐ Ⓑ Ⓒ Ⓓ Ⓔ	**31.** Ⓐ Ⓑ Ⓒ Ⓓ Ⓔ	**51.** Ⓐ Ⓑ Ⓒ Ⓓ Ⓔ
12. Ⓐ Ⓑ Ⓒ Ⓓ Ⓔ	**32.** Ⓐ Ⓑ Ⓒ Ⓓ Ⓔ	**52.** Ⓐ Ⓑ Ⓒ Ⓓ Ⓔ
13. Ⓐ Ⓑ Ⓒ Ⓓ Ⓔ	**33.** Ⓐ Ⓑ Ⓒ Ⓓ Ⓔ	**53.** Ⓐ Ⓑ Ⓒ Ⓓ Ⓔ
14. Ⓐ Ⓑ Ⓒ Ⓓ Ⓔ	**34.** Ⓐ Ⓑ Ⓒ Ⓓ Ⓔ	**54.** Ⓐ Ⓑ Ⓒ Ⓓ Ⓔ
15. Ⓐ Ⓑ Ⓒ Ⓓ Ⓔ	**35.** Ⓐ Ⓑ Ⓒ Ⓓ Ⓔ	**55.** Ⓐ Ⓑ Ⓒ Ⓓ Ⓔ
16. Ⓐ Ⓑ Ⓒ Ⓓ Ⓔ	**36.** Ⓐ Ⓑ Ⓒ Ⓓ Ⓔ	**56.** Ⓐ Ⓑ Ⓒ Ⓓ Ⓔ
17. Ⓐ Ⓑ Ⓒ Ⓓ Ⓔ	**37.** Ⓐ Ⓑ Ⓒ Ⓓ Ⓔ	**57.** Ⓐ Ⓑ Ⓒ Ⓓ Ⓔ
18. Ⓐ Ⓑ Ⓒ Ⓓ Ⓔ	**38.** Ⓐ Ⓑ Ⓒ Ⓓ Ⓔ	**58.** Ⓐ Ⓑ Ⓒ Ⓓ Ⓔ
19. Ⓐ Ⓑ Ⓒ Ⓓ Ⓔ	**39.** Ⓐ Ⓑ Ⓒ Ⓓ Ⓔ	**59.** Ⓐ Ⓑ Ⓒ Ⓓ Ⓔ
20. Ⓐ Ⓑ Ⓒ Ⓓ Ⓔ	**40.** Ⓐ Ⓑ Ⓒ Ⓓ Ⓔ	**60.** Ⓐ Ⓑ Ⓒ Ⓓ Ⓔ

Answer Key to Model Examination II

SECTION 1: MULTIPLE-CHOICE QUESTIONS

1. **B**	11. **B**	21. **D**	31. **A**	41. **D**	51. **C**
2. **A**	12. **D**	22. **E**	32. **E**	42. **B**	52. **C**
3. **A**	13. **C**	23. **B**	33. **C**	43. **A**	53. **A**
4. **C**	14. **B**	24. **B**	34. **A**	44. **E**	54. **B**
5. **C**	15. **C**	25. **D**	35. **E**	45. **D**	55. **B**
6. **E**	16. **D**	26. **D**	36. **D**	46. **A**	56. **D**
7. **D**	17. **B**	27. **B**	37. **B**	47. **A**	57. **B**
8. **B**	18. **B**	28. **E**	38. **B**	48. **A**	58. **D**
9. **D**	19. **A**	29. **E**	39. **A**	49. **B**	59. **E**
10. **A**	20. **D**	30. **C**	40. **A**	50. **B**	60. **C**

Analysis of Multiple-Choice Questions

1. **(B)** Type of Question: Identification and analysis
Choice B, the correct answer, refers to the fact that since 1968 there has been a consistent pattern reflected in the election of a president from one party and the election of a majority of members of the opposite party to Congress. Choice A is the opposite of what people believe. Choices, C, D, and E are factually incorrect.

2. **(A)** Type of Question: Identification and analysis
Choice A, the correct answer, is a central concept of the Federalist papers. The Federalists adopted Montesquieu's principle of checks and balances as the foundation of the separation of powers in the federal government. Choices B and C were weaknesses in the Articles of Confederation. Choice D was never discussed, and Choice E deals with a different form of government.

3. **(A)** Type of Question: Definitional
Choice A is the correct answer because, by definition, political socialization is the process whereby people obtain their political values. These values, such as party identification, views on abortion, and attitudes toward affirmative action, can come from a variety of sources—primarily from parents, but also schools and churches. Choices B, C, D, and E are incorrect because they do not fit within this definition.

4. **(C)** Type of Question: Cause and effect
Choice C, the correct answer, applies the definition of executive privilege to a specific situation. The Supreme Court ruled in the *United States v Nixon* and in a case where Hillary Rodham Clinton tried to use executive privilege in order to withhold Whitewater documents that in both cases the materials had to be handed over. Choices A and B are factually incorrect. Choices D and E were never part of the controversy.

5. **(C)** Type of Question: Solution to a problem
Choice C, the correct answer, deals with the part of the electoral college system that awards a candidate the total electoral votes of a state regardless of the margin of victory. There have been suggestions to reform the system by creating a proportional allocation of electoral votes. Choices

A and B are reforms suggested dealing with the coverage of national elections by the networks. Choices D and E have never been suggested.

6. **(E)** Type of Question: Identification and analysis
Choice E, the correct answer, is the most common manner in which cases get to the Supreme Court. In order to answer the question correctly, you must know the definitions and application of original jurisdiction and appellate jurisdiction. The other choices are incorrect.

7. **(D)** Type of Question: Stimulus-based
The table identifies the nature and number of presidential vetoes used by presidents, beginning with Kennedy and ending with Clinton. The table also defines the type of veto each president used; regular, which can be voted on by Congress, or pocket, which a president makes when Congress has completed its session or is in recess for ten days. Choice D is the correct answer because, clearly, Ford had more vetoes rejected by Congress than the other president listed. Choice A is wrong because more vetoes have been sustained than overridden. Choice B is incorrect because Congress does not vote on pocket vetoes. Choice C is incorrect because even though Reagan had the highest number of vetoes sustained, on a percentage basis, Bill Clinton was more successful. Choice E is wrong because Clinton never used a pocket veto.

8. **(B)** Type of Question: Negative
Choice B, the correct answer, is the only answer that refers to a right not found in the Fifth Amendment. It is a Seventh Amendment right. The other choices are all part of the Fifth Amendment.

9. **(D)** Type of Question: Chronological/definitional
Choice D is the only wrong answer because the Great Compromise referred to an agreement reached after the New Jersey and Virginia plans for representation were rejected. In order to answer this question correctly, you need to know the historical references to Great Compromise and the definition of bicameral (two house). Choice C is misleading because the answer deals with representation and another compromise, the three-fifths compromise.

10. **(A)** Type of Question: Identification and analysis
Choice A, the correct answer, requires that you know the definition of devolution and then be able to apply it to an actual event. In this case, the Republicans wanted more power to be turned over to the states. Choice B is the opposite of devolution. Choices C and D have nothing to do with devolution, and Choice E, though having consequences for the states, does not answer the question as directly as Choice A.

11. **(B)** Type of Question: Identification and analysis
Choice B, the correct answer, is one of the most influential House committees. The other committees may be important in certain situations, but the question asked you to identify specifically a committee that can influence legislation. The Rules Committee determines which bills reach the floor.

12. **(D)** Type of Question: Identification and analysis
Choice D, the correct answer, includes those positions in the Senate that are leadership in nature even if it is a minority position (minority leader).

13. **(C)** Type of Question: Comparing and contrasting concepts
Choice C, the correct answer, is a good definition and application of the elite class theory. Choice A is a good application of pluralism. Choice B is an application of hyperpluralism. Choices D and E may have some truth in their applications, but do not answer the question.

14. **(B)** Type of Question: Sequencing a series of ideas
Choice B, the correct answer, is an application of the definition of libel and slander. If you know those definitions, then you will be able to connect them with an inherent conflict of the free speech provision of the First Amendment. Choice A may apply if a trial occurs over a libel or slander suit. Choice C is a general constitutional guarantee. Choices D and E are components needed in any trial.

15. **(C)** Type of Question: Chronological
Choice C, the correct answer, is the central result of one of the landmark cases the Marshall Court ruled on. The question is difficult because Choices A and E were results of other landmark Marshall cases—*Marbury v Madison* and *McCulloch v Maryland.* Choices B and D are false statements.

16. **(D)** Type of Question: Definitional
Choice D, the correct answer, defines the idea behind the idea of a congressman following a constituent's view when voting on legislation. In order to answer the question, you must know the definition of constituent, and you should be able to recognize the fact that there are other legitimate approaches a representative can take (Choices A, B, and E) that do not answer the question.

17. **(B)** Type of Question: Comparing and contrasting ideas
Choice B, the correct answer, is the only answer which establishes a major difference between the House and Senate. Choices A, C, and E are obviously incorrect. Choice D is tricky because the House has term limits for committee chairmen.

18. **(B)** Type of Question: Cause and effect relationship
Choice B, the correct answer, is a definition of the media as a linkage institution to government. Choice C may be a function of the media, but it does not apply to public policy. Choice D may be true, but it also does not have anything to do with what the question is asking.

19. **(A)** Type of Question: Identification and analysis
Choice A, the correct answer, was the only provision of the line item veto that applied to legislation before it was declared unconstitutional. The line item veto permitted the president to exercise veto power on any part of the 13 appropriation bills that fund the government and make up the discretionary spending portion of the federal budget. Choice B is wrong because it only refers to amendments attached to appropriation bills. Choice C is incorrect because it only refers to action taken in the Senate. Choice D is wrong because there are many bills that can be characterized as essential. Choice E is incorrect because the president can veto a continuing resolution.

20. **(D)** Type of Question: Sequencing a series of events
Choice D, the correct answer, is the first step in the development of public policy. There is a logic behind this procedure, because one would want to identify a problem before enacting, forming, evaluating, or revising the policy.

21. **(D)** Type of Question: Identification and analysis
Choice D is the correct answer because it is the only answer that has an accurate provision of the law. Choices A, B, C, and E are all reforms that groups have recommended to be part of new campaign reform legislation.

22. **(E)** Type of Question: Identification and analysis
Choice E, the correct answer, reflects the definition and application of the exclusionary rule. Choice A refers to the no-knock ruling. Choice B refers to the stop and frisk principle. Choice C can be true in certain situations but has nothing to do with the exclusionary rule. Choice D is a false statement, and in fact police do not need warrants to get evidence in plain view.

23. **(B)** Type of Question: Chronological
Choice B, the correct answer, reflects the major criticism and weakness of the Articles of Confederation. The reason why the Articles were so ineffective, besides giving too much authority to the states, was that the new central government could not pay off Revolutionary War debts by collecting taxes. The other choices are all incorrect because they do not apply to the Articles.

24. **(B)** Type of Question: Cause and effect
Choice B, the correct answer, requires that you understand the nature and provisions of the Motor Voter Law passed by Congress in 1993. If you knew that the law's intent was to make it easier to register, then you could eliminate Choices A and C. Choice D is partially correct, but it is wrong because there was a decrease in actual turnout. Choice E is wrong because senior citizens were already registered and did not have to take advantage of the new law.

25. **(D)** Type of Question: Sequencing a series of events
Choice D, the correct answer, contains those officials who have to be confirmed by the Senate after a presidential appointment. The Constitution is very clear about ambassadors and justices. The appointment of cabinet officials also needs approval. The White House cook and other White House staff do not need senatorial approval.

26. **(D)** Type of Question: Solution to a problem
Choice D, the correct answer, is the primary manner in which the Supreme Court applies judicial review to congressional actions. Choice A is not a power of the Court. Choices B, C, and E are all powers of the Supreme Court, but they do not have anything to do with its ability to check congressional power.

27. **(B)** Type of Question: Identification and analysis
Choice B is the correct answer because an executive order defines the manner in which a president can create public policy without signing legislation. Choices A, D, and E are all legitimate tools a president can use, but they do not necessarily result in public policy. Choice C is not a power of the president.

28. **(E)** Type of Question: Stimulus-based table
Choice E, the correct answer, makes you apply the data in the table to the trend of divided government which was a dominant feature of the modern political scene. The other choices are all factually incorrect.

29. (E) Type of Question: Generalization
Choice E, the correct answer, comes directly from a series of court cases challenging existing affirmative action programs. Choice A is factually incorrect. Choice B would be true if it suggested a reduction of federal programs, rather than a complete elimination. Choices C and D are factually incorrect.

30. (C) Type of Question: Definitional
Choice C, the correct answer, is the only area in the Bill of Rights where the fighting words doctrine applies. It originally came from the Supreme Court case *Chaplinsky v New Hampshire* and it was one of the few decisions that placed limitations on freedom of speech.

31. (A) Type of Question: Generalization
Choice A, the correct answer, is the only answer that gives a major characteristic of many bureaucratic agencies such as the Environmental Protection Agency (EPA), the Food and Drug Administration, and Federal Trade Commission (FTC). They are called quasi-legislative and quasi-judicial because they can issue regulation and then act as judges to see that the regulations are being followed.

32. (E) Type of Question: Sequencing a series of events
Choice E, the correct answer, requires an understanding of the Supreme Court's ruling in *Bush v Gore*, which ordered the recount in Florida to stop and determined the outcome of the electoral vote that gave Bush the presidency. Choice A is wrong because the Republicans remained in control of the House. Choice B is incorrect because minor party candidates such as Ralph Nader did not take part in the debates. Choice C is wrong because even though there was a gender gap, Bush lost the female vote but still won the election. Choice D is wrong because voter turnout was lower than in 1992.

33. (C) Type of Question: Definitional/cause and effect
Choice C, the correct answer, requires that you understand the definition of dealignment. Once you recognize that the term means a moving away from both major political parties, the question becomes relatively easy. Choice A is the opposite meaning. Choice B may be true but does not answer the question. Choices D and E may be factually correct, but they do not provide the correct answer to the question posed.

34. (A) Type of Question: Identification
Choice A, the correct answer, is the one area in which the Congress and the president have disagreed. After the Vietnam War, Congress became very hesitant anytime the president committed American troops to a foreign nation. Situations like Haiti and Bosnia are recent examples. The other choices all contain presidential powers that have not been challenged to any great extent by Congress.

35. (E) Type of Question: Comparing and contrasting ideas
Choice E, the correct answer, is a characteristic of a newly elected ideological representative. You only have to go back to the freshman class of 1994 to see how they came into Congress ready to change the rules of the game. They succeeded to a certain extent. However, they also learned that the art of compromise was essential to the implementation of public policy. The other choices are all false statements.

36. **(D)** Type of Question: Definitional
Choice D, the correct answer, is the only answer that applies the one man, one vote ruling to an election that guarantees equal representation. The original case, in fact, dealt with a state legislature in Tennessee that had major voting representation inequalities. The other choices all deal with elected offices that do not require equal representation. There are two senators in each state. Every citizen within a state has equal weight in voting for a president or governor, and people do not vote for federal judges.

37. **(B)** Type of Question: Chronological
Choice B, the correct answer, is derived from the fact that the Fourteenth Amendment was introduced and ratified after the Civil War to deal with the injustices that the freed slaves had to face. The amendment was later used to incorporate the Bill of Rights into state action (Choice A). Choice C was accomplished through another constitutional amendment. Choice D was the manner in which the Supreme Court interpreted the equal protection clause in the *Plessy v Ferguson* case. Choice E is factually correct, but not the original intent of the amendment.

38. **(B)** Type of Question: Generalization
Choice B, the correct answer, is true because public opinion is quite fickle and usually responds to very visible national and international problems. Choices A and B are factually incorrect. Choices D and E may have some elements of truth, but they do not provide a complete answer to the question asked.

39. **(A)** Type of Question: Negative
Choice A, the incorrect statement, reflects the fact that revenue bills must start in the House. The other choices all reflect important characteristics of the lawmaking process.

40. **(A)** Type of Question: Cause and effect
Choice A is the correct answer because the *Bakke* decision allowed states to take race into consideration when developing affirmative action programs. However, the Court also ruled that a quota system violated the equal protection clause of the Fourteenth Amendment. Choice B is wrong because the *Brown* decision only dealt with the issue of school integration and was silent about quotas. Choice C is incorrect because Proposition 209 eliminated all government-sponsored affirmative action programs in California. Choice D is incorrect because the Civil Rights Act of 1964 banned discrimination in public accommodations. Choice E is an accurate statement of fact but does not answer the question.

41. **(D)** Type of Question: Sequencing an event
Choice D, the correct answer, is the prescribed manner in which an open primary is held. You must know the definitions of the different kinds of primaries to be able to answer this question. Closed primary is limited by party affiliation. Nonbinding primary does not lock delegates to the winner. Dual primary is one in which a presidential preference and a separate slate is voted on. An open caucus does not exist.

42. **(B)** Type of Question: Cause and effect
Choice B, the correct answer, is a direct result of the election. The Republicans maintained control of the House of Representatives for

four consecutive elections. Choices A, C, D, and E are all factually incorrect.

43. **(A)** Type of Question: Identification
Choice A, the correct answer, is the major function of congressional oversight committees. Once the oversight function is completed, appropriate legislation may be drafted to deal with the problem that was investigated. Or a criminal proceeding may result if evidence is brought out in the hearings. Two examples of oversight hearings are the campaign finance irregularities and the Whitewater hearings. The other choices, though functions of congressional committees, do not apply directly to oversight.

44. **(E)** Type of Question: Cause and effect
Choice E, the correct answer, is an aspect of the census that has only become a problem because the homeless do not reside in a specific residence. It is important, especially to the large urban areas, because it could easily impact on the number of representatives from a state that has a large homeless population. The other choices are factually incorrect.

45. **(D)** Type of Question: Stimulus-based graph
The graph shows the percent of eligible voters who actually voted in presidential elections from 1964 through 2000. To answer the question, you must know some presidential history. Choice D is the correct answer. Voter turnout decreased in the elections following the Watergate scandal in 1974 and President Clinton's impeachment in 1999. Choice A is incorrect because the graph indicates that turnout was greatest when the country was at war—look at the rates during the Vietnam War. Choice B is incorrect because turnout was higher in 1964 and 1980, elections years where there were "landslide" victories. Choice E is wrong because turnout decreased in the years when Reagan and Clinton were reelected to second terms.

46. **(A)** Type of Question: Negative
Choices B, C, D, and E are factually correct and illustrate the powers that the president and Congress have in dealing with legislation. Choice A, the line item veto, is the correct answer because it was ruled unconstitutional by the Supreme Court and, therefore, is no longer an option available to the president or Congress.

47. **(A)** Type of Question: Identification
Choice A, the correct answer, requires that you know that advocacy groups such as Common Cause believe that soft money (the money that is unregulated and can go to political parties in large sums) should be banned. The other choices are incorrect because they are not areas that advocacy groups believe would reform campaign finances.

48. **(A)** Type of Question: Cause and effect
Choice A, the correct answer, is true because the Court has drawn a fine line between accommodation and practice of religion, especially in public schools. The other choices all reflect areas the Supreme Court has declared illegal.

49. **(B)** Type of Question: Hypothetical
Choice B, the correct answer, requires that you know the definition of gerrymandering (the redrawing of legislative districts after a census

based on purely political factors). Though Choices C and D are characteristics of congressional districts, they do not answer the question.

50. **(B)** Type of Question: Identification
Choice B, the correct answer, is a classic supporter of the Democratic Party. In fact, labor unions are the target of both Republicans and some advocacy groups because of the manner in which the unions are able to funnel contributions to the Democratic Party. The other choices reflect PACs that traditionally support the Republican Party.

51. **(C)** Type of Question: Negative
Choice C, the correct answer, may provide some difficulty because the Senate must approve the appointment of federal judges. The other choices are specific delegated powers of Congress.

52. **(C)** Type of Question: Identification
Choice C, the correct answer, is a provision of the Contract With America that would have limited the terms of Representatives and Senators, if enacted. It was proposed as a constitutional amendment and defeated twice by the House. The other choices, though all provisions of the Contract, did not impact on the Congress itself.

53. **(A)** Type of Question: Identification
Choice A, the correct answer, is a characteristic of the act and sets in motion the manner in which the budget cycle moves in Congress. It was passed during the Nixon administration in response to Nixon's impounding funds that were budgeted. The other choices, though all aspects of budget development, are not characteristic of the Impoundment Act.

54. **(B)** Type of Question: Sequencing a series of events
Choice B is the correct answer because the Constitution requires the House of Representatives to initiate impeachment charges against the president. In order for the initiation of charges to occur, the House Judiciary Committee must first vote on articles of impeachment. If you only think back to the Clinton impeachment, you may get confused and select another choice based on the events surrounding that episode, such as the media frenzy or the use of a special prosecutor's report. Although those events were associated with the impeachment of Bill Clinton, they are not part of the formal impeachment process.

55. **(B)** Type of Question: Definitional
Choice B, the correct answer, illustrates how states had to abide by the provisions of congressional law to create equality in the voting process. In order to answer the question correctly, you have to understand the nature of majority-minority districts and the historical background. It is a difficult question because the Supreme Court declared many of these districts unconstitutional.

56. **(D)** Type of Question: Hypothetical
Choice D, the correct answer, is an application of the definition of judicial activism (those court decisions which overturn precedent or existing law). The choices are all based on actual decisions. Choices A, B, C, and D are all cases that are judicial restraint in nature.

57. **(B)** Type of Question: Identification/definitional
Choice B, the correct answer, is a major characteristic of a federal form of government. Choices A and E are more typical of a confederation.

Choice C can be a part of a federal system but only if there are state governments that are part of the system. Choice D is a parliamentary form of government.

58. **(D)** Type of Question: Identification
Choice D, the correct answer, is the only choice that is a provision of the constitutional amendment that outlines what happens when a president is disabled. The other choices are all factually incorrect.

59. **(E)** Type of Question: Sequencing a series of events
Choice E, the correct answer, requires that you know the definition of racial gerrymandering and the historical reasons why it existed. Choice D would be correct if the Court ruled that these districts were constitutional. The other choices are factually incorrect.

60. **(C)** Type of Question: Identification
The correct answer, choice C, reflects the fact that both President George Bush and President Bill Clinton favored United States involvement in the North American Free Trade Agreement (NAFTA). Choices B and D relate to treaties that were favored by a president but not ratified by Congress. Choices A and E are factually incorrect.

SECTION 2: FREE-RESPONSE ESSAYS

Sample Student Response to 1

Even though the public has been outraged about the campaign finance abuses of both the Democratic and Republican Parties, there has been little success in achieving meaningful campaign finance reform. This is because those who would be legislating the reforms are most affected by them.

The last time any meaningful reform occurred was after the Watergate scandal. Congress passed and President Gerald Ford signed into law the Federal Election Campaign Act of 1974. Then in 1978, President Jimmy Carter signed into law the Ethics in Government Act of 1978. Since then, vested special interest groups and many entrenched representatives have blocked any further legislation. Although there was a minor bill passed in 1993 that dealt with lobbyist registration, it took massive campaign abuses and two oversight congressional hearings to bring the issue of campaign reform to the forefront.

The early attempts to deal with the problem, after President Nixon resigned from office in 1974, dealt with a limitation of individual contributions to candidates for federal office to $1000 for each primary and general election. Contributions from political action committees to candidates were limited to $5000. However, the bulk of corporate contributions to political parties, known as soft money, remained legal. As part of this 1974 law, candidates, political parties, and others who spend money on campaigns were required to disclose where money was being collected and spent. A Federal Election Commission, whose membership was equally divided between Democrats and Republicans, would oversee the system and administer penalties when they occurred. The law created federal matching funds for presidential campaigns if the candidates chose to abide by the restrictions, but left untouched any reform of congressional campaigns.

By the end of the 1996 presidential campaign, as a result of investigative reporting by the *Washington Post* and other news organizations, it became very obvious that there were serious abuses in the manner in which the Democratic National Committee raised funds for the campaign. Though the Republicans also abused the system, most of the criticism was levied against the Democrats and particularly against President Clinton. Accusations were made that the president raised funds in return for access to meet with him—access which was obtained by being invited to White House coffees and by getting an invitation to sleep over in the Lincoln Bedroom. As a result of subpoenas of documents obtained by the House and Senate oversight investigating committees, it was proved that the Clinton campaign starting as early as 1995 used soft money to craft a series of television commercials favorable to the president's position on Medicare, Medicaid, education, and the environment. Realizing that it would take continued funds to finance an extensive media campaign, both the president and vice president became personally involved in raising large sums of money, some of which was solicited in the White House, a possible campaign violation. However, more serious than these abuses were the accusations raised that much of the campaign funds were from foreign contributions. Clinton operatives such as John Huang raised hundreds of thousands of dollars from Asian sources. Much of that money had to be returned. In the summer of 1997, Senator Fred Thompson chaired the Governmental Affairs oversight committee in the Senate, and in the fall Representative Dan Burton did the same on the House side. Both committees concluded that there were serious questions related to the role that China played in trying to gain access and influence in the 1996 elections. The Democrats on the committee countered by suggesting that the Republicans were doing the same thing.

This brings us to campaign finance reform. If there are abuses, and the voters support change, then what kind of legislation has been proposed? The centerpiece of campaign finance reform legislation has been introduced by Republican Senator John McCain of Arizona and Democratic Senator Russell Feingold of Wisconsin. Known as the McCain-Feingold Campaign Finance Reform Act of 1997, it was also supported by many advocacy groups such as Common Cause. The provisions of the bill are simple:

- Ban soft money,
- Ban special interest PAC contributions,
- Establish spending limits for House and Senate candidates who accept campaign benefits,
- Establish a system of voluntary spending limits, set according to the population of the state,
- Provide campaign resources to qualified candidates,
- Restrict out-of-state contributions,
- Tighten the rules for independent expenditures and issue advocacy, and
- Close campaign loopholes and strengthen enforcement.

The fate of this legislation is still in doubt at the time of the writing of this essay. Even though a similar version passed the Senate in 2000, the House did not vote on the legislation.

Evaluation of Free-Response Sample Essay 1

1. Does the essay establish the direction the essay is taking by properly defining terms and giving background information?
2. Is the foundation built using appropriate examples?
3. Does the essay reflect an application of basic principles of United States government and politics?

1. The essay establishes a contrast between strong public support of campaign finance reform and the fact that there has been little success in obtaining it. The essay gives an overview of the history of campaign finance reform, current abuses of the system, and attempts to reform it.

2. The foundation of the essay is its strength. The writer effectively traces the history of campaign finance reform from 1974 to the present. The essay emphasizes the long period of time that has passed since reforms after the Watergate scandal. The middle part of the essay focuses on abuses that occurred during the 1996 election. The writer was careful to place in perspective both Democratic and Republican abuses, though the stress was placed on Democratic abuses. Even the confusing link to China was connected in a clear and concise manner to the general theme. The essay concludes with a close look at the McCain-Feingold bill, a bill that attempts to fix the system. The writer speculates that the chances of this bill becoming law are very slim even though the public seems to support it.

3. Major principles of American government and politics are brought out in this essay. They include the legislative process, the electoral process, the role of oversight committees, and the role public opinion and the media play in the development of public policy.

Sample Student Response to 2

Though the United States government is based on a representative model, 24 states have made the initiative and referendum process a part of their electoral system.

By definition, a referendum is used in two different contexts. The first occurs when the state wants voters to consider a legislative proposal that, if passed, would either amend the state's constitution or become a law. The second instance in which a referendum is used occurs when a proposal is made to give voters the opportunity to overrule an action taken by the state legislature. This usually happens when a state legislature has passed a law viewed by most voters as unpopular.

The initiative differs from the referendum because it is a process that involves voters organizing themselves around a single issue, gathering signatures on a petition, and then having that issue voted on in the form of a proposition. If the proposition passes, it automatically becomes a law in that state. Sometimes these initiatives are controversial in nature. They include areas such as physician-assisted suicide, affirmative action, homosexual rights, the legalization of marijuana for medicinal purposes, and restrictions on late-term or partial-birth abortions. Other initiatives may be noncontroversial in nature, such as a simple vote to approve a bond issue.

One of the most significant propositions put forward was California's Proposition 209, also called the California Civil Rights Initiative. It originated with an official in the state university system and its goal was to eliminate all state-sponsored affirmative action programs in California. Petitions were circulated, and the required number of signatures was obtained for the proposition to appear on the ballot in 1996. Supporters of the proposition included California's Republican governor, Pete Wilson. Most Democrats opposed the ballot proposal. It became a hotly contested issue, not only in the state, but also in the presidential and Senate campaigns. Special interest groups argued that the proposition would destroy California's state university system, while other groups insisted that affirmative action programs were inherently unfair. The measure passed by over 60 percent of the vote. The governor immediately instituted new rules regarding the state's affirmative action programs.

Soon after the ballot proposal was passed, opponents of Proposition 209 filed a lawsuit in federal court. They believed that Proposition 209 was unconstitutional because it violated the equal protection clause of the Fourteenth Amendment. They also felt that the proposition violated the supremacy clause of the United States Constitution, arguing that Proposition 209 conflicted with the Civil Rights Act of 1964. Opponents also pointed out that a Supreme Court case, *University of California v Bakke*, set forth rules regarding affirmative action programs that worked well in California. The Court initially issued an injunction against California, but the appeals court reversed the ruling. The U.S. Supreme Court refused to hear the final appeal. The proposition was implemented, and all affirmative action programs in California were eliminated. As a result, minority enrollment decreased significantly in the state university system.

Evaluation of Free-Response Sample Essay 2

1. Does the essay define the initiative and referendum process?
2. Is the proposition explained through appropriate commentary and example?
3. Does the writer identify and explain a constitutional issue raised by the passage of the proposition?

1. The essay provides excellent definitions of the terms *referendum* and *initiative.* Each definition clearly highlights the differences between the referendum and the initiative. The writer also explains the processes involved with regard to both the initiative and the referendum.

2. The heart of the essay is the description of Proposition 209. The writer provides historical background, discusses how the proposition got on the ballot, describes the arguments for and against its passage, and explains the results of the vote on the ballot proposal.

3. The final part of the essay deals with the constitutionality of the proposition. The writer traces the court challenge to the proposition and discusses the constitutional arguments made. The writer also discusses the final outcome related to the court's decision.

Sample Student Response to 3

The electoral college was highly criticized after the widely disputed presidential election of 2000, when George W. Bush lost the popular vote but won the electoral vote.

The electoral college, as provided for in Article II of the Constitution and later changed by the Twelfth Amendment, establishes the procedure by which the president of the United States is elected. In the Federalist Papers, the founding fathers expressed their reservations about the direct election of a president by the public. Based on these reservations, the electoral college was established. As provided for by the Constitution, the number of electors that each state sends to the electoral college is based on its population. Thus, the larger a state's population, the more electors it can send to the electoral college. The actual number of electors that a state sends to the electoral college is equal to the number of representatives it has in the House of Representatives plus the number of members it has in the Senate. Therefore, the smallest number of electors a state can have is three. In 2000, California had 54 electors, representing its 52 House members and two Senators. Washington, D.C., on the other hand, had only three electors. The Constitution also provides the legislature of each state with the authority to decide the manner in which it selects its electors.

For a candidate to win the presidency, he must win a majority of the electoral votes cast. In the 2000 election, the number of electoral votes needed to win a majority was 270. If a candidate does not receive a majority of the electoral votes, the election is thrown into the House of Representatives, where each state receives one vote. The majority vote of each state's delegation to the House determines the winner of the state's vote. Thus, if the majority of a state's representatives is Democratic, its vote would probably go to the Democratic candidate. In instances where no candidate receives a majority of the electoral votes, the Senate determines the contest for vice president, with the winner determined by a simple majority vote.

Once electors are selected by the states, they pledge to cast their electoral vote for the winner of the states' popular vote. There have been rare instances, however, where electors have changed their minds and not cast their votes for the winner of the state's popular vote. These electors have been given the name "faithless" electors.

In the election of 2000, Vice President Al Gore won the popular vote by more than 500,000 votes, but on election night the winner of the electoral vote was still in doubt. The popular vote in Florida was so close that state law called for a mandatory recount. The votes in other states were also so close that absentee ballots had to be counted in order to confirm the winner. However, it was in Florida that the election of 2000 was determined.

Two problems that surfaced as a result of the 2000 election included the manner in which the ballots were counted in Florida and the big differences in the election machinery used throughout the country. After Florida began its recount, there was much criticism of the so-called butterfly ballots and the fact that many of them were not counted. Older machines could not read many of these ballots and the issue of hanging chads resulted in a large number of disputed ballots. These votes, if counted, could have given the election to Gore. Ultimately, the United States Supreme Court stepped in and, in *Bush v Gore,* determined that the Florida recount process was flawed. The result of this decision was that George W. Bush was awarded Florida's electoral votes, giving him an electoral majority. The second problem brought to light by the 2000 election, the lack of uniform voting equipment throughout the country, was illustrated by the fact that some states had old-fashioned voting booths while others had modern optical scanners.

One reform that has been suggested to improve the electoral college is to abolish it completely and go to a direct popular vote. This could be accomplished through a constitutional amendment. Proponents of this measure point out that the electoral college is an outdated notion and that the percentage of electoral votes that a candidate receives does not actually reflect the popular vote. They also point out that the results of the 2000 election illustrate how flawed the electoral system is because a candidate can win the popular vote but lose the electoral vote. Opponents of this reform suggest that the 2000 election was an anomaly and that the system has worked well since the Twelfth Amendment was adopted.

Evaluation of Free-Response Sample Essay 3

1. Did the essay identify and explain how the electoral college works?
2. Did the essay describe two problems brought to light as a result of the 2000 presidential election?
3. Was a proposed reform of the electoral college explained?

1. The essay did an excellent job of identifying and explaining how the electoral college works. The writer discussed its constitutional foundation, the manner in which electors are chosen and allocated, and even explained what happens when a candidate does not receive a majority of the electoral votes cast.

2. The two problems that the writer focused on related to Florida's disputed election results. Other issues that could have been discussed include the media's coverage of the election, the manner in which absentee ballots were authenticated, and the design of the butterfly ballot itself. The essay concentrated on the issue of the under and over votes involved in the Florida recount and the lack of uniformity in voting equipment nationwide.

3. An obvious reform that the writer chose to discuss was the abolition of the electoral college through a constitutional amendment. The writer explains the proposal and presents both sides of the issue. Other reforms that could have been discussed include the adoption of a system of proportional distribution of electoral votes and improving the way electors are confirmed by the states.

Sample Student Response to 4

After analyzing the table "Members of Congress—Selected Characteristics: 1981–1999," a number of dramatic features are portrayed:

- More than any other category, the increase of female representatives and senators has been dramatic.
- More representatives and senators are between 40 and 60 years old.
- More representatives have served between one and ten terms; more senators have served between one and three terms.

These statistics have a significant impact on Congress. Without a doubt, the dramatic increase in female representatives (more than double the number of representatives and triple the number of senators since 1980) was due to gender politics. In 1992 when four women were elected to the Senate and nineteen were elected to the House, it was called the year of the woman in politics. The impact that this had on the Congress was an increase in making woman-related issues part of the public agenda. Many of these issues are economic and social in nature. The response of these newly elected representatives to single mothers' concerns, to abortion rights, and to protection by the government of "safety net" issues has become a priority. Senators Carol

Moseley Braun and Dianne Feinstein have been in the forefront arguing for so-called women's issues. Even with the increase in women representatives, statistically they are still only a small percentage of the entire House and Senate. Yet with women electing Bill Clinton to a second term and a new group called soccer moms emerging, one can expect the power and influence of women in Congress to increase.

The age and seniority of representatives has a direct impact on Congress in the manner in which it develops its own rules and agenda. The 1994 congressional election was an important turning point that illustrates how age and seniority issues affect the institution. The House freshman class of 1994, though younger and more inexperienced than their counterparts, had a significant impact on the House. Realizing that this core group represented the hopes of the conservative Republican revolution, newly elected Speaker of the House Newt Gingrich pushed major reforms through the House with the support of these newly elected congressmen. The reforms included term limits for committee chairs and rules that would make it easier for less senior members to become directly involved in the legislative process. Remarkably, Gingrich also gave many of these new representatives seats on very influential House committees such as the Rules Committee, the Ways and Means Committee and the Appropriations Committee. The Republicans were able to push through a good part of their Contract With America in the first 100 days of the 104th Congress because of the support of these new representatives. Ironically, the power given to these inexperienced congressmen also contributed to the unsuccessful budget battle waged against President Clinton, which resulted in two government shutdowns. The fact that there were so many new representatives caused an ideological shift and, unlike their older more experienced colleagues, the class of 1994 thought that they were sent to Congress on a mission. The 1996 election moderated the House as the Republican majority shrunk in size.

Evaluation of Data-Based Free-Response Essay 4

1. Does the essay establish the direction the essay is taking by analyzing the data given in the table?
2. Is the foundation built using appropriate examples?
3. Does the essay reflect an application of basic principles of United States government and politics?

1. The table provides an easy vehicle for the writer to focus on the significant trends presented. Once that is done, the essay can then focus on how these trends impact on Congress as an institution. The writer does an effective job in simplifying the data to the three most significant areas—the fact that there was a tremendous increase in women representation and the fact that age and seniority both play an important role. The question asks one to analyze data, and the writer does that right from the start.

2. Once the data is analyzed, the writer is able to apply it to the central question raised by the essay—how Congress as an institution is affected by gender, age, and seniority. The gender issue gives the author the opportunity to explain that a gender gap in American politics helped contribute to the election of many of the new representatives. The essay does an effective job of explaining what the characteristics of the gender vote are and how they influence the policy agenda. The age factor became important in the 104th Congress because this Congress

featured one of the largest groups of freshmen. The essay does a nice job of explaining how these newly elected freshmen congressmen and congresswomen helped lead the Republican revolution. The issue of seniority was covered by explaining why it is such an important feature in both houses.

3. The principles of American politics and government explored in this essay were gender politics, Congress as an institution of government, age as a factor in Congress, and the role of seniority in Congress.

Glossary

Acquisitive bureaucracies—organizations that are self-perpetuating and demand funding that will result in the continued existence of the agency.

Activist court—Court that makes decisions that forge new ground such as *Roe v Wade* or *Brown v Board of Education* and establish precedent that often result in some form of legislative action.

Advise and consent—power of the Senate regarding presidential appointments.

Affirmative Action—programs for minorities supported by government as a means of providing equality under the law.

Agenda setting—policy goals typically set by political parties.

Americans with Disabilities Act (1991)—act that required employers, schools, and public buildings to reasonably accommodate the physical needs of handicapped individuals by providing such things as ramps and elevators with appropriate facilities.

Amicus curiae—"friend of the court"; briefs that may be sent to support the position of one side or the other.

Anti-Federalists—led by Thomas Jefferson, one of the first political parties urging the rejection of the Constitution. Its members were farmers and represented the interest of the common people.

Antiballistic Missile Treaty of 1972—treaty wherein America and the Soviet Union agreed to limit antiballistic missile sites and interceptor missiles.

Appropriation bill—congressional legislation that has spending as a basic characteristic. There are 13 appropriation bills that make up the federal budget.

Arms control—agreements reached by countries with the aim of reducing the proliferation of military weapons such as the Antiballistic Missile Treaty (1972), the first Strategic Arms Limitation Treaty (1972), the second Strategic Arms Limitation Treaty (1979), the Intermediate-Range Nuclear Forces Treaty (1987), the first Strategic Arms Reduction Treaty (1991), and the second Strategic Arms Reduction Treaty (1993).

Arraignment—court hearing where a person accused of a crime is formally charged.

Articles of Confederation—the first adopted written constitution of the newly independent United States. Because of its weaknesses, the period of time (1781–1789) became known as the critical period.

Baker v Carr—case that established the principle of one man, one vote. This decision created guidelines for drawing up congressional districts and guaranteed a more equitable system of representation to the citizens of each state.

Balanced budget—public policy that advocates that the federal budget spend as much money as it receives. Attempt made to pass a constitutional amendment mandating this policy failed.

Bicameral—a two-house legislature.

Bill of Rights—adopted in 1791 by the states two years after the ratification of the Constitution, it established the basis of civil liberties for Americans.

Bipartisan—refers to two political parties working together to reach a common policy goal.

Block grants—a form of fiscal federalism where federal aid is given to the states with few strings attached.

Brandeis Brief—a friend of the court opinion offered by Louis Brandeis, in the Supreme Court case *Muller v Oregon* (1908), which spoke about inherent differences between men and women in the workplace.

Brinkmanship—going close to the edge of an all out war in order to contain communism.

Bully pulpit—the ability to use the office of the presidency to promote a particular program and/or to influence Congress to accept legislative proposals.

Bureaucracies—large administrative agencies reflecting a hierarchical authority, job specialization, and rules and regulations that drive them.

Cabinet—part of the "unwritten Constitution," it was first established by George Washington and includes federal departments such as state, defense, etc.

Campaign finance reform—legislation aimed at placing limits on political candidates accepting money and gifts from individuals and special interest groups.

Cases of equity—those cases that cannot be resolved under common law precedent.

Categorical grants—include project and formula grants and aim at assisting the states in areas such as health, income security, and education.

Caucus—party regulars meeting in small groups asking questions, discussing qualifications regarding the candidate, and voting on whether to endorse a particular candidate. The Iowa caucus has taken on almost as much importance as the New Hampshire primary because of its timing.

Census—official count of the population of a district, state, or nation, which includes recording of statistics such as age, sex, occupation, and property ownership.

Checks and balances—a key aspect of the Constitution of the United States protecting the balance of power among the three branches of government. The concept was first promoted by James Madison in the Federalist Papers.

Chief executive—used to describe the president. Powers found in Article II of the Constitution.

Civil law—deals with contract issues and tort cases such as negligence and slander and defines the legal rights of individuals.

Civil liberties—those rights of the people that are protected by the Bill of Rights.

Civil Rights Act of 1964—act that prohibited the use of any registration requirement that resulted in discrimination and paved the way for the involvement of the federal government to enforce the law.

Civil rights—the application of equal protection under the law to individuals.

Civil Service Reform Act (1978)—law that replaced the Civil Service Commission with the Office of Personnel Management and the Merit Systems Protection Board. These agencies are responsible for enforcing existing civil service laws, coordinating the testing of applicants, setting up pay scales, and appointing people to federal jobs.

Clean Air Act (1970)—law that established national standards for states, strict auto emissions guidelines, and regulations, which set air pollution standards for private industry.

Clean Water Act—passed in 1987, this law established safe drinking standards and creates penalties for water polluters.

Clear and Present Danger Doctrine—established in *Schenck v United States* (1919), it gives the government the right to censor free speech if, during national emergencies such as war, it can be proven that the result of the speech will significantly hurt national security.

Cloture—the process in which it takes 60 senators to cut off a filibuster and that is aimed at protecting minority interests.

Cold war—an era of American foreign policy lasting from the end of World War II (1945) to the collapse of the Soviet Union (1991) where American policy was defined as containment of communism.

Collective security—agreement to form through treaties mutual defense arrangements, such as NATO, which guarantee that if one nation is attacked, other nations will come to its defense.

Commander-in-chief—delegated power of the president.

Commerce clause—Article I Section 8 Clause 3 of the Constitution giving Congress the authority to regulate interstate commerce and commerce with foreign countries.

Common law—based on the legal concept of stare decisis, or judicial precedent.

Competitive federalism—begun under Richard Nixon and known as the new federalism, this approach stressed the downsizing of the federal government and more reliance on revenue sharing and grants.

Concurrent power—power shared by the state and federal government, such as the power to tax.

Concurring opinion—additional opinion in a Court decision written by a member of the majority.

Confederation—approach to government that decentralizes power, giving more power to the individual states than to the central government.

Conference committee—a committee consisting of senators and representatives that meets to resolve differences in legislation.

Congressional Budget Office (CBO)—set up by the Congress, this office evaluates the cost of legislative proposals.

Congressional oversight—power used by Congress to gather information useful for the formation of legislation, review the operations and budgets of executive departments and independent regulatory agencies, conduct investigations through committee hearings, and bring to the public's attention the need for public policy.

Connecticut Compromise—offered at the Constitutional Convention at Philadelphia, it was adopted by the delegates and created a bicameral legislature, where one house is represented by population, and the other house is represented by the states.

Consent of the governed—a derivative of the doctrine of natural rights; a philosophy, later adopted by Jefferson when he drafted the Declaration of Independence, that puts the authority of the government in the people's hands.

Constituent—person living in the district of an elected official.

Constitution—provides the basic framework of government. It is the supreme law of the land.

Constitutional courts—courts that were formed to carry out the direction in the Constitution so that the Courts would exercise their judicial power.

Consumer Price Index (CPI)—a primary measure of inflation determined by the increase in the cost of products compared to a base year.

Containment—official foreign policy of the United States between 1945 and 1991 that was predicated on stopping the spread of communism.

Continuing resolution—emergency spending legislation that prevents the shutdown of any department simply because its budget has not been enacted.

Convention bump—an increase reflected in presidential preference polls immediately following a party's nominating convention.

Cooperative federalism—developed during the New Deal, it is characterized by the federal government's becoming more intrusive in what were traditionally state powers.

Council of Economic Advisors—White House staff agency created to give the president advice regarding economic and fiscal policy.

Creative federalism—developed during President Lyndon Johnson's administration, it was characterized by the Great Society programs, which placed a major responsibility on federally funded programs.

Criminal law—cases that derive from criminal laws passed by the federal and state governments.

Cruel and unusual punishment—doctrine found in the Eighth Amendment to the Constitution that prohibits the federal government from imposing excessive penalties for crimes committed.

Culture of poverty—the establishment of an income level by government that references the point at which an individual is considered to be living in poverty.

Dark horse—candidate running for office who is not well known and considered to be the underdog in the race.

De facto segregation—segregation of schools and other public facilities through circumstance with no law supporting it.

De jure segregation—segregation by law, made illegal by *Brown v Board of Education*.

Declaration of Independence—blueprint for the American Revolution containing three parts. The first part—an introduction including ideas such as natural rights as related to life, liberty and property, the consent of the governed and the concept of limited government. The second part—a list of grievances against the King of England and the third part—a declaration of independence.

Deficit spending—the government's meeting budgetary expenses by borrowing more money than it can pay back.

Democratic Party—political party that evolved from the original Democratic-Republican Party. It is one of the two major political parties.

Democratic-Republicans—led by Thomas Jefferson, they were characterized as the party of the "common man." They believed in a more limited role of the central government.

Demographics—characteristics of a population, including age, sex, and race. Demographics are often used to determine changes in the make-up of a population.

Détente—a foreign policy started by Richard Nixon and supported by Ronald Reagan that resulted in an improvement of relations with the Soviet Union during the cold war.

Devolution—political theory of returning power to the states.

Direct democracy—type of government characterized by citizens attending a town meeting and voting on issues raised, with the majority prevailing.

Direct primary—voters, including cross-over voters from other political parties, can express a preference for candidates.

Direct tax—money paid directly to the government in the form of income taxes.

Discount rates—interest levels established by the Federal Reserve that effect the ability of the consumer to borrow money. Raising and lowering rates is used as a tool to combat inflation.

Dissenting opinion—judicial opinion written that is contrary to the ruling of the full court.

Distributive policy—results in the government giving benefits directly to people, groups, farmers, and businesses. Typical policies include subsidies, research and development funds for corporations, and direct government aid for highway construction and education.

Divided government—characterized by political gridlock as the result of different political parties having control of different branches of the government.

Division of labor—skilled workers each have a specialized function, resulting in increased productivity.

Domino theory—suggestion that if one country fell to communism, others would fall like dominoes.

Double jeopardy—legal concept wherein once a verdict is handed down, you cannot be tried again for the same crime.

Dual federalism—the earliest type of relationship established between the federal government and the states where the federal government's powers were defined as delegated and the state government's powers were reserved.

Dual primary—where presidential candidates are selected and a separate slate of delegates is also voted on. New Hampshire uses this type of primary.

Eisenhower Doctrine—doctrine that stated readiness to use armed forces to aid Middle Eastern countries threatened by communist aggression.

Elastic clause—found in Article I Section 8 of the Constitution, it gives Congress the power to make "all laws necessary and proper" to carry out the other defined powers of Congress.

Electoral college—consists of presidential electors from each state. The number of electors is based on the state's population. The states with the greatest population have the most electoral votes. When the voter casts a vote for president, in reality the vote goes to one of the presidential electors designated by the candidate in that state. The number of electors for each state equals the number of senators and representatives that state has in Congress. The candidate with a majority of the electoral votes is elected to office. If no candidate receives a majority, the House of Representatives will determine the outcome of the election.

Elite and class theory—a group theory that revolves around an economic stratum of society controlling the policy agenda.

Endangered species—wildlife threatened by extinction, many protected by the Endangered Species Act.

Entitlements—those benefits guaranteed by law paid to individuals by the federal government, such as Social Security.

Enumerated powers—delegated powers of Congress, including the power to collect taxes, pay debts, provide for the common defense and general welfare, regulate commerce among the states, coin money, and declare war.

Environmental Protection Agency (EPA)—regulates air and water pollution, pesticides, radiation, solid waste, and toxic substances. It is the main environmental regulatory agency.

Establishment clause—component of the First Amendment to the Constitution that defines the right of the citizens to practice their religions without governmental interference. It also places a restriction on government creating a "wall of separation" between church and state.

Ex post facto laws—laws that take effect after the act takes place. Congress is prohibited from enacting this type of legislation.

Exclusionary rule—rule that resulted from the *Mapp v Ohio* decision determining that police may obtain only that evidence that can be had through a legitimate search warrant. Other evidence found at the scene of the crime is not admissible, or is excluded, in the trial.

Executive agreement—agreement made between the president and a leader of a foreign country that does not have to be ratified by the Senate.

Executive office of the president—created by Franklin Roosevelt in 1939; it has four major policymaking bodies today—the National Security Council, the Council of Economic Advisors, the Office of Management and Budget, and the Office of National Drug Control Policy.

Executive order—order signed by the president that has the effect of law, even though it is not passed by Congress. An example of an executive order includes President Clinton's order legalizing the abortion pill, RU486.

Executive privilege—the ability of the president to protect personal material.

Expressed power—specific power of the president as listed in Article I of the Constitution.

Faction—splinter group of a political party.

Fairness doctrine—scrapped in 1987, it provided that the media air opposing opinions of the same issue.

Family Medical Leave Act (1993)—act that gave unpaid emergency medical leave for employees with a guarantee that their job would not be taken away in the interim.

Favorable balance of trade—refers to a country exporting more than they import. The United States has had an unfavorable balance of trade since World War II.

Favorite son—the presidential candidate backed by the home state at the party's nominating convention.

Federal Election Campaign Acts (FECA)—in 1971 it set up restrictions on the amount of advertising used by a candidate, created disclosure of contributions over $100, and limited the amount of personal contributions a candidate could make on his or her own behalf. In 1974 it set up a Federal Election Commission and established a system of federal matching funds for presidential candidates.

Federal Reserve System—federal body that regulates the money supply by controlling open-market operations; buying and selling of government securities; and establishing reserve requirements, the legal limitations on money reserves that banks must keep against the amount of money they have deposited in Federal Reserve Banks and through discount rates, and the rate at which banks can borrow money from the Federal Reserve System.

Federalism—the overall division of power between the federal government and state governments; as defined in the Tenth Amendment of the Constitution. It specifically tells the states that they have reserved powers. Powers not delegated to the government by the Constitution are given to the respective states.

Federalist Papers—written using the pen name Publius; John Jay, Alexander Hamilton, and James Madison wrote a series of articles urging the adoption of the Constitution. They argued for a Constitution that would establish a government that could deal with "the tyranny of the majority" by creating three branches of government having distinctive and separate powers.

Federalist Party—headed by Alexander Hamilton, this party, made up of the country's upper class, supported a strong national government and set a policy agenda that would solve the nation's economic problems.

Fighting words doctrine—established in *Chaplinsky v New Hampshire* (1942), the decision incorporated into state law the concept that the government can limit free speech if it can be proved that the result of speech will cause physical violence.

Filibuster—tactic used in the Senate whereby a vote on legislation can be delayed through debate. The longest continuous filibuster was made by Strom Thurmond and lasted 24 hours.

Fiscal federalism—a concept of federalism where funding is appropriated by the federal government to the states with specific conditions attached. The legislation can be in the form of mandates.

Fiscal policy—policy that determines how the economy is managed as a result of government spending and borrowing and the amount of money collected from taxes.

Flat tax—an alternative to the progressive income tax where individuals pay the same percentage regardless of how much they earn.

***Fletcher v Peck* (1810)**—decision that established the precedent that the Supreme Court could rule a state law unconstitutional.

Focus group—technique used by pollsters to determine how a cross section of voters feels about a particular topic.

Food stamp program—federally funded program that gives food coupons to low-income people based on income and family size.

Franking—privilege enjoyed by members of Congress entitling them to free postage for any mailings made as part of their official duties.

Freedom of Information Act (1974)—act that incorporates sunshine laws; opened up the government's meetings of record to the public and media.

Front loading—refers to the scheduling of the early presidential primaries and its impact on the selection of the majority of presidential delegates.

Front runner—designation given to the candidate who leads in the polls.

Full faith and credit—phrase used to describe the mutual respect and legality of laws, public records, and judicial decisions made by states.

Funded mandates—those regulations passed by Congress or issued by regulatory agencies to the states with federal funds to support them.

Gender gap—a significant deviation between the way men and women vote.

General Agreement on Tariffs and Trade (GATT)—agreement wherein new trade barriers would be avoided by member nations, existing tariffs would be eliminated, and protective tariffs would be used only for emergency situations.

Gerrymandering—state legislatures, based on political affiliation, create congressional districts, many of which are oddly shaped and favor the political party in power in the state making the changes.

***Gibbon v Ogden* (1824)**—case established the principle that Congress has sole authority over interstate commerce.

***Gitlow v New York* (1925)**—landmark decision in that the Supreme Court incorporated the First Amendment to a state case for the first time.

Global interdependence—the degree of linkage among the community of nations.

Good neighbor policy—a foreign policy established by Franklin Roosevelt that aimed at improving relations with Latin America.

Government—those institutions that create public policy.

Government corporation—such as the Tennessee Valley Authority, created during the New Deal, having specific responsibilities that facilitate a specific operation of the government.

Grand Old Party—known as the GOP, another way of identifying the Republican Party.

Gridlock—describes people's perception that Congress and the president are in a state of disagreement that results in little legislation passing.

Gross Domestic Product (GDP)—currently the key economic measure that analyzes an upward or downward economic trend of the monetary value of all the goods and services produced within the nation on a quarterly basis.

Gross National Product (GNP)—the total of all goods and services produced in a year.

Habeas corpus—right that safeguards a person from illegal imprisonment. *Habeas corpus* is Latin for "you should have the body." It refers to the writ requiring that a person be brought before a court to determine whether he is being detained legally.

Hard money—federally regulated campaign contributions made to political candidates and political parties. Under current law, hard money contributions cannot exceed $1000 per individual, per election cycle.

Hatch Act (1939)—law that places restrictions on the kind of political activity a federal employee may participate in.

High-tech campaign—a major characteristic of the modern presidential campaign. The use of paid political ads, 30- and 60-second spots, paid infomercials incorporating charts and graphs, and sophisticated polling techniques have all been used in recent campaigns.

Hyperpluralism—a group theory characterized by many interest groups vying for control resulting in a government that is tied up in gridlock.

Immigration Act of 1991—act that shifted the quota of immigrants to Europe and aimed to attract immigrants who were trained workers.

Impeachment—listing of accusations against a federal official of "high crimes and misdemeanors" for the purpose of removing that official from office for such misconduct. President Clinton was the only elected president to be impeached but not removed from office.

Imperial Congress—describes a Congress that succeeds in establishing itself as dominant in legislative and foreign policy.

Imperial presidency—term developed by historian Arthur Schlesinger Jr.; refers to presidents who dominate the political and legislative agenda.

Income distribution—the portion of national income that individuals and groups earn.

Incorporation of the Fourteenth Amendment—doctrine that made the Bill of Rights apply to the states as a result of Supreme Court decisions. Even though the Fourteenth Amendment was ratified in 1868, incorporation started to take place in the 1920s. It reached a peak during the Warren Court in the late 1950s and 1960s.

Incumbents—those elected officials who are running for new terms of office.

Independent executive agency—such as the General Services Administration, which handles government purchasing and has a specific responsibility that facilitates the day-to-day operation of the government.

Independent expenditures—non-federally regulated campaign contributions made by special interest groups, labor unions, and corporations to political action committees and political parties; also called soft money.

Independent regulatory agencies—agencies that are quasi-legislative and quasi-judicial in nature and operation. Examples include the Food and Drug Administration and Environmental Protection Agency.

Indictment—a formal list of charges made by a grand jury and guaranteed in the Fifth Amendment.

Indirect tax—money paid to the government as a result of purchased goods.

Inflation—economic situation characterized by steadily rising prices and falling purchasing power. It is, in part, caused by wage rates increasing faster than productivity.

Infomercials—paid political commercials usually lasting longer than the average 30- or 60-second paid political ad.

Information superhighway—a linked conglomerate of computer-generated information also known as the Internet.

Inherent power—assumed powers of the president not specifically listed in the Constitution. Inherent powers are derived from the president's role as chief executive.

Initiative—ballot proposal put forth by the public and voted on as a result of the petition process.

Interest group—a public or private organization, affiliation, or committee that has as its goal the dissemination of its membership's viewpoint.

Intermediate Nuclear Force (INF) Treaty—agreement that called for destruction of a large part of the most dangerous nuclear warheads, the intermediate range missiles.

Intermediate Range Nuclear Forces Treaty of 1987—agreement that provided for the dismantling of all Soviet and American medium- and short-range missiles and established a site inspection procedure.

International Monetary Fund (IMF)—a clearinghouse for member nations to discuss monetary issues and develop international plans and policies to deal with monetary issues. Regulating monetary exchange rates is its primary task.

Iron triangle network—the interrelationship among bureaucracies, the government, interest groups, and the public, which also establishes a pattern of relationships among an agency in the executive branch, Congress, and one or more outside clients of that agency.

Isolationism—United States foreign policy between World War I and World War II, which resulted in the United States staying out of European affairs. Rejection of the League of Nations and Treaty of Versailles were examples of isolationist policy.

Jim Crow laws—legislation that legalized segregation even after the adoption of the Fourteenth Amendment.

Joint committee—congressional committee made up of members of both political parties from the Senate and House of Representatives.

Judicial activism—a philosophy of judicial review that results in decisions that overturn precedent.

Judicial federalism—the extension of the Bill of Rights to the citizens of the states, creating a concept of dual citizenship, wherein a citizen was under the jurisdiction of the national government as well as state governments.

Judicial restraint—a court that maintains the status quo or mirrors what the other branches of government have established as current policy.

Judicial review—derived from the *Marbury v Madison* decision, it gives the Supreme Court the power to interpret the Constitution and specifically acts of Congress, the president, and the states.

Judiciary committee—key Senate committee that is responsible for recommending presidential judicial appointments to the full Senate for approval.

Keynote address—key speech at the national nominating convention that outlines the themes of the campaign.

Laissez-faire—French term literally meaning "hands off." Used to describe an economic philosophy of nongovernment intervention in economic matters such as regulation of business or establishing tariffs.

Landslide—election where the winning candidate wins by more than 60 percent of the votes cast.

Layer cake federalism—federalism characterized by a national government exercising its power independently from state governments.

Legislative veto—provision granting Congress the right to veto regulations made by federal agencies; ruled unconstitutional by the Supreme Court.

Limited government—derived from the doctrine of natural rights, it was adopted by Jefferson and restricts the power of government especially in the area of protecting the rights of the people.

Line item veto—allows the president to veto selectively what he considers unnecessary spending items contained in legislation. It was ruled unconstitutional by the Supreme Court.

Linkage institution—the means by which individuals can express preferences regarding the development of public policy.

Literacy laws—declared unconstitutional by the Supreme Court, they were passed by southern states after the Civil War aimed at making reading a requirement for voting so that freed slaves could not vote.

Living will—a legitimate document that can be used to direct a hospital to allow an individual to direct a medical facility not to use extraordinary means such as life support to keep a patient alive. The doctrine was declared constitutional in the case of *Cruzan v Missouri Department of Health* (1990).

Lobbyists—the primary instruments of fostering a special interest group's goals to the policymakers. The term comes from people who literally wait in the lobbies of legislative bodies for senators and representatives to go to and from the floor of the legislatures.

Logrolling—a tactic used in Congress that is best illustrated by one legislator saying to another, "I'll vote for your legislation, if you vote for mine."

Loose construction—a liberal interpretation of the Constitution.

Majority opinion—Court ruling participated in by the majority of justices hearing a case.

Manifest Destiny—policy pursued in the early to late 1800s that was based upon the belief that it was God's will for the United States to expand its borders to the Pacific.

Marble cake federalism—also known as cooperative federalism, it developed during the New Deal and is characterized by the federal government's becoming more intrusive in what was traditionally states' powers.

Marshall Court—John Marshall's tenure as Chief Justice of the Supreme Court, whose leadership resulted in the landmark decisions of *Marbury v Madison*, *McCulloch v Maryland*, and *Gibbons v Ogden*. These cases shifted power to the judiciary and federal government.

Mass media—consisting of television, radio, newspapers, and magazines, they reach a large segment of the population. It is also considered one of the linkage institutions.

Matching funds—limited federal funds given to presidential candidates that match private donations raised during the campaign.

***McCulloch v Maryland* (1819)**—case that established the principle that the federal government was supreme over the state.

McGovern-Frasier Commission—commission that brought significant representation changes to the Democratic Party. It made future conventions more democratic by including more minority representation.

Medicaid—a shared program between the federal and local governments that covers hospital and nursing home costs of low-income people.

Medicare—program that covers hospital and medical costs of people 65 years of age and older as well as disabled individuals receiving Social Security.

Miranda rights—those rights directing police to inform the accused upon their arrest of their constitutional right to remain silent, that anything said could be used in court, that they have the right to consult with a lawyer at anytime during the process, that a lawyer will be provided if the accused cannot afford one, that the accused understands these rights, and that the accused has the right to refuse to answer any questions at any time and request a lawyer at any point.

Monopolistic bureaucracies—organizations where there is no competitive equal, such as the Social Security Administration, that also exists in the private sector. Thus the citizen is forced to deal with that particular government agency.

Motor Voter Act of 1993—signed into law by President Clinton, it enables people to register to vote at motor vehicle departments.

National committee—the governing body of a political party made up of state and national party leaders.

National convention—political forum in which each major political party selects its candidate for president and vice president and finalizes its respective platform.

National energy policy—public policy dealing with the consumption and protection of natural resources.

National Environmental Policy Act (NEPA)—1969 legislation that required government agencies to issue environmental impact statements with the Environmental Protection Agency whenever they proposed policies that could negatively affect the environment.

National nominating conventions—the governing authority of the political party. They give direction to the national party chairperson, the spokesperson of the party, and the person who heads the national committee, the governing body of the party. They are also the forums where presidential candidates are given the official nod by their parties.

National Security Act of 1947—act that established the National Security Council as an executive-level department. It created as its head the national security advisor.

National Security Council—chaired by the president, it is the lead advisory board in the area of national and international security. The other members of the council include the vice president, secretaries of state and defense, director of the Central Intelligence Agency, and chair of the joint chiefs of staff.

Nationalization of the Bill of Rights—a judicial doctrine of the Fourteenth Amendment that applied the Bill of Rights to the states in matters such as segregation.

Natural rights—part of Locke's philosophy; rights that are God given such as life, liberty, and property.

New Democrat—a term created by the Democratic Leadership Council in 1992, it denotes a more conservative, centrist Democrat.

New federalism—political theory first espoused by Richard Nixon and carried out by Ronald Reagan. New federalism advocates the downsizing of the federal government and the devolution of power to the states.

New Jersey Plan—offered at the Constitutional Convention at Philadelphia, it urged the delegates to create a legislature based on equal representation by the states.

New world order—President Bush's vision for world peace centering around the United States taking the lead to ensure that aggression be dealt with by a mutual agreement of the United Nations, NATO, and other countries acting in concert.

Nonpreferential primary—where voters choose delegates who are not bound to vote for the winning primary candidate.

Nonrenewable resources—those natural resources such as oil, which based on consumption, are limited.

Norris-La Guardia Act (1932)—act that prohibited employers from punishing workers who joined unions and gave labor the right to form unions.

North American Free Trade Agreement (NAFTA)—agreement that called for dramatic reductions of tariffs among the United States, Canada, and Mexico.

Nuclear Nonproliferation Treaty of 1968—agreement that stopped and monitored the spread of nuclear weapons to countries who did not have the bomb.

Nuclear Regulatory Commission—created as a part of the Energy Reorganization Act of 1974, it was given jurisdiction to license and regulate commercial use of nuclear technologies and monitor waste storage and transportation of materials arising from its use.

Nuclear Test Ban Treaty of 1963—agreement that banned atmospheric testing of nuclear weapons.

Office of Management and Budget (OMB)—its director, appointed with the consent of the Senate, is responsible for the preparation of the massive federal budget, which must be submitted to the Congress in January each year. Besides formulating the budget, the OMB oversees congressional appropriations.

Oral argument—legal argument made by each attorney in proceedings before the court in an attempt to persuade the court to decide the issue in their client's favor.

Original jurisdiction—cases heard by the Supreme Court that do not come on appeal and that "affect ambassadors, other public ministers and consuls, and those in which a State shall be a party."

Pardon—power to excuse an offense without penalty or grant release from a penalty already imposed.

Partnership for peace—President Clinton announced in 1993 a policy that allowed for the gradual admission into NATO of new member nations from the former Warsaw Pact and gave the designation of associate status in NATO to Russia.

Party caucus—also known as the party conference, it is a means for each party to develop a strategy or position on a particular issue.

Party dealignment—a shift away from the major political parties to a more neutral, independent ideological view of party identification.

Party eras—a time period characterized by national dominance by one political party. There have been four major party eras in American history—the era of good feeling, the Republican era following the Civil War, the Democratic era following the election of Franklin Roosevelt, and the Republican era following the election of Richard Nixon.

Party machine—the party organization that exists on the local level and uses patronage as the means to keep the party members in line. Boss Tweed and Tammany Hall are examples.

Party organization—formal structure of a political party on the national, state, and local levels.

Party platforms—voted on by the delegates attending the National Convention, they represent the ideological point of view of a political party.

Party realignment—the movement of voters from one political party to another resulting in a major shift in the political spectrum (characterized by the start of a party era).

Party regulars—enrolled party members who are usually active in the organization of a political party and support party positions and nominated candidates.

Pendleton Act—known as the Civil Service Act of 1883, it set up merit as the criterion for hiring, promoting, and firing federal employees.

Photo ops—photo opportunities.

Plank—any of the principles contained in a political party's platform.

***Plessy v Ferguson* (1896)**—case that ruled that states had the right to impose "separate but equal" facilities on its citizens as well as create other laws that segregated the races.

Pluralism—a group theory that involves different groups all vying for control of the policy agenda. No single group emerges, forcing the groups to compromise.

Plurality—winning number of votes received in a race containing more than two candidates but which is not more than half of the total votes cast.

Pocket veto—rejection of legislation that occurs if the president does not sign a bill within 10 days and the Congress also adjourns within the same time period.

Police power—power reserved to the states by the Tenth Amendment to the Constitution.

Policy agenda—agenda that results from the interaction of linkage institutions.

Political action committees—known as PACs, they raise money from the special interest constituents and make contributions to political campaigns on behalf of the special interest group.

Political consultant—person who specializes in running a political campaign. James Carville and Karl Rove are examples of political consultants.

Political participation—the different ways an average citizen gets involved in the political process ranging from conventional means of influencing government to more radical unconventional tools that have influenced our elected officials.

Political party—a group of people joined together by common philosophies and common approaches with the aim of getting candidates elected in order to develop and implement public policy. It is characterized by an organization that is responsible to the electorate and has a role in government.

Political socialization—the factors that determine voting behavior such as family, religion, and ethnic background.

Politics—who gets what, when, how, and why.

Poll tax—made illegal by the Twenty-Fourth Amendment to the Constitution, it was a tax instituted by mainly southern states as a condition to vote and had the effect of preventing African-Americans from voting.

Popular sovereignty—political doctrine that believes that government is created by and subject to the will of the people.

Pork barrel legislation—the practice of legislators obtaining funds through legislation that favors their home districts.

Poverty line—references the point at which an individual is considered living in what has been called a "culture of poverty."

Preamble—the introduction to the Constitution, outlining the goals of the document.

Precedent—legal concept, also known as stare decisis, by which earlier court decisions serve as models in justifying decisions in subsequent cases.

President pro tempore—temporary presiding officer of the Senate.

Presidential primary—elections held in individual states to determine the preference of the voters and to allocate the number of delegates to the party's national convention.

Press secretary—key White House staff position; the press secretary meets with the White House press corps.

Price supports—the government's price guarantees for certain farm goods. The government subsidizes farmers to not grow certain crops and also buys food directly and stores it, rather than let the oversupply in the market bring the prices down.

Privileges and immunities—the guarantees that the rights of a citizen in one state will be respected by other states. Also a clause in the Fourteenth Amendment that protects citizens from abuses by a state.

Procedural due process—a series of steps that are established by the Fifth, Sixth, and Seventh Amendments that protect the rights of the accused at every step of the investigation.

Progressive tax—a tax based upon the amount of money an individual earned, such as an income tax. Became legal as a result of the ratification of the Sixteenth Amendment to the Constitution.

Public law—includes constitutional law (involving constitutional issues) and administrative law (involving disputes over the jurisdiction of public or administrative agencies).

Public opinion polls—scientific surveys aimed at gauging public preference of candidates and issues.

Public policy—the final action(s) taken by government in promotional, regulatory, or distributive form.

Quasi-judicial—a characteristic of independent regulatory agencies that gives them judicial power to interpret regulations they create.

Quasi-legislative—a characteristic of independent regulatory agencies that gives them legislative powers to issue regulations.

Reagan Democrats—traditional Democratic middle-class voters turning to Ronald Reagan during the 1980s.

Reapportionment—the process in which a state legislature redraws congressional districts based on population increases or declines.

Reapportionment Act of 1929—act that provides for a permanent size of the House and for the number of seats, based on the census, each state should have.

Red tape—used to describe the difficulty it takes to get answers from a bureaucratic agency.

Redistributive policy—policy that results in the government taking money from one segment of the society through taxes and giving it back to groups in need. It includes such policies as welfare, Aid to Families with Dependent Children, tax credits for business expenses or business investment, and highway construction made possible through a gasoline tax.

Redistricting—process that takes place every ten years, as a result of the federal census, mandating state legislatures to redraw their congressional districts based on population gains and losses.

Referendum—practice of submitting to popular vote a measure proposed by a legislative body; also called a proposition.

REGO—better known as reinventing government, the plan introduced by President Clinton and Vice President Gore that called for reducing the federal work force by 12 percent, updating information systems, eliminating wasteful programs and procedures, and cutting red tape.

Regressive tax—a tax that is imposed on individuals regardless of how much they earn, such as a sales tax.

Regulatory policy—policy that results in government control over individuals and businesses. Examples of regulatory policy include protection of the environment and consumer protection.

Religious right—an evangelical conglomeration of ultraconservative political activists, many of whom support the Republican Party.

Renewable resources—those natural resources such as solar energy that can be used over again.

Representative democracy—form of government that relies on the consent of the people and is often called a republican government.

Republican Party—political party that evolved from the Whig Party, coming to power after Lincoln's election. It is one of the two current major political parties.

Reserved Power clause—found in the Tenth Amendment, it gives states powers not delegated to the national government.

Return to normalcy—a campaign theme of Warren Harding referring to a belief that the United States should turn inward after World War I.

Reverse discrimination—discrimination against whites or males, usually with regard to employment or education. Those who oppose affirmative action programs often claim reverse discrimination as a result of such programs. Alan Bakke is an example.

Riders—amendments to bills, often in the form of appropriations, that sometimes have nothing to do with the intent of the bill itself and many times are considered to be pork barrel legislation.

Rule of four—judicial concept employed by the Supreme Court requiring the approval of at least four justices before a case can be heard on appeal.

Rules Committee—one of the most important committees of the House of Representatives; its function is to create specific rules for every bill to be debated by the full House.

Safety net—a minimum government guarantee that ensures that individuals living in poverty will receive support in the form of social welfare programs.

Sampling error—refers to a statistical error, usually within three percentage points, inherent in the polling process.

Second Treatise of Civil Government—written by John Locke, it contains the blueprint principles found in the Declaration of Independence.

Select committees—specially created congressional committees that conduct special investigations. The Watergate Committee and Iran-Contra investigators were select Senate committees.

Senatorial courtesy—policy that gives senators the right to be notified by the president of pending judicial nominations. Once informed, the approval of the senators from the state from which the judge comes is obtained and the appointment process moves on. This courtesy does not apply to Supreme Court justice nominations.

Seneca Falls Convention—in 1848, Elizabeth Cady Stanton led the fight for political suffrage and supported a doctrine very similar in nature to the Declaration of Independence called the Declaration of Sentiments and Resolutions. It became a rallying document in the fight for women's rights.

Separate but equal—the judicial precedent established in the *Plessy v Ferguson* decision that enabled states to interpret the equal protection provision of the Fourteenth Amendment as a means of establishing segregation.

Separation of church and state—Also known as the "establishment clause," it is part of the First Amendment to the Constitution prohibiting the federal government from creating a state-supported religion.

Separation of powers—originally developed by Montesquieu in *The Spirit of Natural Laws* written during the Enlightenment and used by James Madison in Federalist No. 48. This important doctrine resulted in the establishment of three separate branches of government—the legislative, executive, and judicial branches, each having distinct and unique powers.

Shays's Rebellion—a failed attempt by Daniel Shays, a farmer who lost his property, to revolt against the state government.

Simpson-Marzzoli Act (1987)—act that resulted in more than 2 million illegal aliens who were living in this country since 1982 being allowed to apply for legal status.

Soccer mom—term coined in 1996 presidential election referring to those suburban women, some of whom are single parents, who supported President Clinton because of his articulation of their values.

Social welfare—Entitlement programs such as Social Security and programs such as Aid to Dependent Children paid for by the federal government.

Soft money—unrestricted and unregulated legal campaign contributions made to political parties and intended for party development. Significant abuses of soft money contributions were discovered during the 1996 election.

Solid South—dominance by the Democratic Party in the South following the Civil War. The Republicans made strong inroads when Ronald Reagan was elected President in 1980 and after the Republicans gained control of the Congress in 1994.

Sound bites—30- or 60-second statements by politicians aired on the evening news shows or Sunday morning talk shows.

Speaker of the House—the representative from the majority party in the House of Representatives who sets the House agenda, presides over House meetings, recognizes speakers, refers bills to committees, answers procedural questions, and declares the outcome of votes.

Special courts—courts created by Congress to deal with cases deriving from the delegated powers of Congress such as military appeals, tax appeals, and veteran appeals.

Standing committees—committees that deal with proposed bills and also act in an oversight function. They are permanent, existing from one Congress to the next, such as the House Ways and Means and Senate Appropriations.

Stare decisis—Latin for judicial precedent, this concept originated in England in the twelfth century when judges settled disputes based on custom and tradition.

State of the Union Address—constitutional requirement imposed on the president to deliver an annual report regarding the current state of the nation to Congress. Traditionally, the president delivers the State of the Union Address every January, in the form of a speech before a joint session of Congress.

Strategic Arms Limitation Talk (SALT) Treaty—agreement signed by President Nixon in 1972 that resulted in the first arms reductions since the nuclear age began.

Strategic Arms Limitation Treaty of 1972—known as SALT II, the treaty never passed the Senate as a result of Russia's invasion of Afghanistan. However, in 1986 many of the reductions were carried out by both sides.

Strategic Arms Reductions Treaty (START) of 1991—treaty between the United States and Russia that agreed to major reductions in their nuclear arsenals.

Straw vote—nonbinding vote used to determine the views of a small cross section of voters.

Strict constructionists—individuals who believe in a conservative interpretation of the Constitution.

Substantive due process—legal process that places limits related to the content of legislation and the extent government can use its power to enact unreasonable laws.

Suffrage—the right to vote guaranteed to African-Americans in the Fourteenth Amendment and women in the Nineteenth Amendment.

Super Tuesday—the Tuesday on which a number of primary votes take place, with a heavy concentration of southern states voting.

Superdelegates—Democratic Party leaders and elected party officials who automatically are selected as delegates to the National Convention.

Superfund—legislation that mandated the cleanup of abandoned toxic waste dumps and authorized premarket testing of chemical substances. It allowed the EPA to ban or regulate the manufacture, sale, or use of any chemicals that could present an "unreasonable risk of injury to health or environment," and outlawed certain chemicals such as PCBs.

Supremacy clause—clause that states that "the Constitution, and the laws of the United States . . . shall be the supreme law of the land."

Symbolic speech—form of free speech interpreted by the Supreme Court as a guarantee under the First Amendment to the Constitution, such as wearing a black armband to protest a governmental action or burning an American flag in protest for political reasons.

Taft-Hartley Act (1947)—act that outlawed the closed union shop and certain kinds of strikes, permitted employers to sue unions for violations of contracts, allowed the use of injunctions to stop union activities, and allowed states to adopt right-to-work laws, giving employers more rights regarding the establishment of union shops. Finally, the act gave the president the right to step in and prevent a strike by an entire industry, such as the steel or auto industry, if such an action would threaten the nation's health and safety.

Talking heads—politicians who use sound bites or other means to present a superficial look at a policy position rather than an in-depth approach in explaining their views.

Third political parties—political parties that can be described as ideological, single-issue oriented, economically motivated, and personality driven. Examples include the Free Soil Party, Know-Nothings, Populist, and Bull Moose Parties. In 1996 Ross Perot created a new national third party called the Reform Party.

Thirty-second spots—paid political ads 30 seconds in duration.

Three-Fifths Compromise—offered at the Constitutional Convention at Philadelphia, it was adopted by the delegates and counted every five slaves as three people for representation and tax purposes.

Ticket splitting—process by which voters choose a candidate from one political party for one elective office and another candidate from a different party for another elective office.

Tracking poll—polls conducted by media outlets to gauge the potential outcome of a political election on a periodic basis.

Trial balloons—selective leaks aimed at testing the political waters.

Truman Doctrine—policy that supported people in Greece and Turkey in resisting communism after World War II.

Twenty-Fifth Amendment—constitutional amendment outlining the criteria for presidential selection and presidential disability.

Unalienable rights—rights such as life, liberty, and the pursuit of happiness, which are derived from the doctrine of natural rights.

Unfunded mandates—those regulations passed by Congress or issued by regulatory agencies to the states without federal funds to support them.

Unitary system of government—type of government that centralizes all the powers of government into one central authority.

Universal suffrage—right of all qualified adults to vote.

Unwritten Constitution—traditions, precedent, and practice incorporated into our form of government that add to the Constitution's elasticity and its viability. Political parties, the president's cabinet, political action committees, and the federal bureaucracy are important examples.

Veto—power of the president to prevent enactment of legislation passed by Congress. A two-thirds majority vote of each house is required to override a presidential veto.

Virginia Plan—offered at the Constitutional Convention at Philadelphia, it urged the delegates to create a legislature based on the population of each state.

Voting Rights Act of 1965—act that finally made the Fifteenth Amendment a reality. As a result of this act, any state not eliminating the poll tax and literacy requirements would be directed to do so by the federal government. It also resulted in the establishment of racially gerrymandered congressional districts in the 1980s and 1990s.

Wagner Act—also called the National Labor Relations Act of 1935, it gave workers involved in interstate commerce the right to organize labor unions and engage in collective bargaining and prevented employers from discriminating against labor leaders and taking action against union leaders.

War Powers Act—1973 act that states that a president can commit the military only after a declaration of war by the Congress, by specific authorization by Congress, if there is a national emergency, or if the use of force is in the national interest of the United States.

Watergate—refers to the office complex in Washington, D.C., where members of the committee to re-elect Richard Nixon, posing as burglars, broke into the offices of the Democratic Party's national headquarters. They were caught, and the scandal ultimately lead to Nixon's resignation.

Whips—also known as assistant floor leaders, they check with party members and inform the majority leader of the status and feelings of the membership regarding issues that are going to be voted on. Whips are responsible for keeping party members in line and having an accurate count of who will be voting for or against a particular bill.

White House staff—managed by the White House Chief of Staff, who directly advises the president on a daily basis, it includes the more than 600 people who work at the White House, from the chef to the advance people who make travel arrangements. The key staff departments include the political offices of the Office of Communications, Legislative Affairs, Political Affairs, and Intergovernmental Affairs. It includes the support services of Scheduling, Personnel, and Secret Service and the policy offices of the National Security Affairs, Domestic Policy Affairs, and cabinet secretaries.

Workfare—an alternative to the traditional welfare, where an individual is trained to work instead of receiving welfare.

World Bank—called the International Bank for Reconstruction and Development, it provides monetary assistance to nations for the development of industries and aims to stimulate economic growth of third-world nations.

Writ of certiorari—Latin for "to be made more certain," the process in which the Supreme Court accepts written briefs on appeal based on the rule of four.

Index